MAKING NATIONAL NEWS

A History of Canadian Press

For almost a century, Canadian newspapers, radio and television stations, and now internet news sites have depended on the Canadian Press news agency for most of their Canadian and, through its international alliances, foreign news. This book provides the first-ever scholarly history of CP, as well as the most wide-ranging historical treatment of twentieth-century Canadian journalism published to date.

Using extensive archival research, including complete and unfettered access to CP's archives, Gene Allen traces how CP was established and evolved in the face of frequent conflicts among the powerful newspaper publishers – John Ross Robertson, Joseph Atkinson, and Roy Thomson, among others – who collectively owned it, and how the journalists who ran it understood and carried out their work. Other major themes include CP's shifting relationships with the Associated Press and Reuters; its responses to new media; its aggressive shaping of its own national role during the Second World War; and its efforts to meet the demands of French-language publishers.

Making National News makes a substantial and original contribution to our understanding of journalism as a phenomenon that shaped Canada both culturally and politically in the twentieth century.

GENE ALLEN is a professor in the School of Journalism and the Joint Graduate Program in Communication and Culture at Ryerson University. A professional journalist for 20 years at the *Globe and Mail* and the CBC, he was director of research and a senior producer for the award-winning documentary series *Canada: A People's History* and editor of its companion book.

Making National News

A History of Canadian Press

GENE ALLEN

UNIVERSITY OF TORONTO PRESS
Toronto Buffalo London

ISBN 978-1-4426-4716-9 (cloth)
ISBN 978-1-4426-1532-8 (paper)

Library and Archives Canada Cataloguing in Publication

Allan, Gene, 1952–, author
Making national news : a history of Canadian Press / Gene Allan.

Includes bibliographical references and index.
ISBN 978-1-4426-4716-9 (bound). – ISBN 978-1-4426-1532-8 (pbk.)

1. Canadian Press – History – 20th century.   2. News agencies – Canada –
History – 20th century.   3. Press – Canada – History – 20th century.
4. Journalism – Canada – History – 20th century.   I. Title.

PN4908.A45 2013   070.4'3509710904   C2013-903490-0

This book has been published with the help of a grant from the Canadian Federation
for the Humanities and Social Sciences, through the Awards to Scholarly Publications
Program, using funds provided by the Social Sciences and Humanities Research
Council of Canada.

University of Toronto Press acknowledges the financial assistance to its publishing
program of the Canada Council for the Arts and the Ontario Arts Council.

University of Toronto Press acknowledges the financial support of the Government of
Canada through the Canada Book Fund for its publishing activities.

All photographs courtesy of The Canadian Press.

For Erika

Contents

Acknowledgments

It is a pleasure to express thanks to the many people who helped bring this project to completion. Eric Morrison, who was then president of Canadian Press (CP), gave the project his unqualified support at the outset. Thanks to him, and especially to Paul Woods, who became my main contact at CP, I was given complete and unfettered access to CP's extensive archival records. Scott White, CP's editor-in-chief, has been consistently helpful and supportive. I also received valuable assistance with the CP records from Bill Becker, Sharon Hockin, Deborah McCartney, Patti Tasko, and Lee White. Several former CP journalists and executives granted interviews that greatly enriched my understanding of its history: Peter Buckley, Clark Davey, Keith Kincaid, Arch MacKenzie, Ian Munro, Jim Poling Sr., Guy Rondeau, Bill Stewart, and Mel Sufrin. Mario Cardinal, a former Radio-Canada/CBC colleague who was managing editor of *Le Devoir* in the early 1960s, provided his recollections of working with CP. Audio recordings of interviews conducted by the late Douglas Amaron in the early 1980s for a history of CP that was not written at the time have been a particularly valuable resource. No one at CP ever raised a single question about my interpretation of any point in its history, and I am as grateful for that as for all the positive assistance I have received. We would understand much more about the evolution of journalism in Canada if other major journalistic institutions made their records available to researchers in this way.

CP's extensive archival material is uncatalogued and only loosely organized, so simply determining what the collection contained was a major undertaking. Ryerson University provided funds to hire several research assistants who ploughed through reels of microfilm and boxes of documents, making detailed notes as they went. I am particularly grateful to Daphna Izenberg, June Morrow, and Jeffrey Todd, as well as to Elisabeth Collett, Martin Kuebler, and Sarah Petrescu, for their intelligent and thorough work. Charts 7A–7C were prepared using data gathered by Maurice Demers, Simon Jolivet, Tim Krywulak, Jennifer MacMillan, and Jason Satur and organized by Maurice Demers. Zoe McKnight gathered the data from the Halifax *Herald* used in Charts 7D–7J. Joe Friesen provided me with notes and photocopies from the J.F.B. Livesay fonds held at the Archives of Manitoba.

I received valuable assistance from archivists at private and public institutions in Canada, the United States, and Britain. Ian Wilson, the former National Archivist of Canada, helped me locate Canadian Press material that was donated to Library and Archives Canada (LAC) but had not yet become part of its collection, and LAC archivist Robert Fisher kindly supervised my access to it. Valerie Komor, the corporate archivist of Associated Press (AP), assisted by Sam Markham and Francesca Pitaro, helped me find CP-related material in the AP corporate archives. John Entwisle, the archivist of Thomson Reuters, similarly helped me locate CP-related material in the Reuters collection. I am especially grateful to Patricia Smart for allowing me to examine the personal papers of her father, Gillis Purcell. She and her husband, John Smart, also kindly provided accommodation and hospitality during a research trip to Ottawa in 2008. Wendy Allen was an equally gracious host during a preliminary research trip to Montreal in 2003.

I owe a special debt of thanks to Mary Vipond. On taking up a full-time academic position for the first time in my late 40s, I contacted her out of the blue to seek advice about developing a research focus. Although we had never met, she replied very helpfully, diplomatically steering me away from unpromising lines of inquiry and suggesting that it might be worth looking into Canadian Press. While this was one of several ideas in the back of my mind, Mary is at least the co-originator of this study. She also read the entire manuscript and provided me with valuable comments and suggestions. I also benefited greatly from Daniel Robinson's comments on an earlier version of chapter 3, and Marc Milner's comments on chapter 4. Two anonymous reviewers for the University of Toronto Press suggested further improvements, for which I am grateful. Michael Dupuis, an independent scholar who knows more about many aspects of CP's history than I do, kindly allowed me to read and cite his unpublished manuscript about news coverage of the Winnipeg General Strike. My editor at the

University of Toronto Press, Len Husband, has been a consistent (and patient) supporter of this book, providing me with much good advice along the way. All errors, omissions, misinterpretations, or failures of imagination in what follows are entirely my own.

The person to whom I owe the most is Erika Ritter. She has been an indefatigable supporter and wise advisor throughout this long process. Dedicating this book to her is a barely adequate acknowledgement of her contribution, and of everything else she means to me.

MAKING NATIONAL NEWS

A History of Canadian Press

Introduction

On 2 September 1917, the first organization to provide systematic, regular coverage of domestic and international news to newspapers across Canada was established. Since then, Canadian Press (CP) has been a major source (for many of its users, the main source) of news, whether in newspapers or broadcast stations (and now, on the Internet). Millions of Canadians have followed the unfolding of events great and small, domestically and around the world, through CP for more than 90 years; through CP's connections with Associated Press (AP) and Reuters, much of what people outside Canada learned of it also came from this source.

Little scholarly attention has been paid to CP; 30 years ago, it was described as possibly "one of the most overlooked institutions in Canadian life," and not much has changed since then.[1] With the exception of a volume written more than 60 years ago by one of CP's founders (who was also its ex-president), no systematic study of its history has been made.[2] CP has received some attention from students of politics and the press, in the reports of two commissions examining the news business in Canada in 1970 and 1981, and in a handful of other publications.[3]

The opportunity to study CP's history in depth comes at a time when historical work about journalism has undergone a kind of scholarly renaissance. Moving away from narrowly institutional or biographical treatments, scholars have increasingly approached journalism as "*the* sense-making practice of modernity," and have vied with each other to produce studies of greater depth and interpretive sophistication, informed particularly by the perspectives of cultural studies and the preoccupations of the "cultural turn."[4] As James Carey, a pioneer in this development, has observed, journalism is no less deserving of a searching inquiry into its social and symbolic meanings than "a Balinese cockfight, a Dickens novel, an Elizabethan drama, a student rally," because, like them, it is "a presentation of reality that gives life an overall form, order, and tone."[5] Canadian historians are now studying media as subjects of interest in themselves, not simply using them as ostensibly transparent sources for studying other, more important subjects.[6] Gerald Friesen has perhaps gone farthest along this line, presenting an ambitious reconception of Canadian history generally, in which changing modes of communication define the major epochs of the country's past.[7] Internationally, the academic literature on media history – sharing an approach that sees media not as mere reflections of social reality but as constitutive of that evolving reality itself – is vibrant and growing, and has become too extensive to provide even a cursory listing here.

The work of scholars such as Benedict Anderson, John B. Thompson, Jürgen Habermas, and Carey has been important in the reconception of journalism's past, presenting far-reaching arguments in which media, especially news media, are seen as central to the emergence of nationalism, the "public sphere" of liberal-democratic societies, and modernity itself.[8] Anderson has made the influential case that newspapers were essential to the development of the "imagined communities" of modern nationality. Not only by sharing information about the same events in their common national sphere, but especially by imagining *their fellow readers* with whom they simultaneously share each day's news, newspaper readers develop a new sense of kinship with "thousands (or millions) of others of whose existence [they are] confident, yet of whose identity [they have] not the slightest notion."[9] The knowledge they acquired was social in two senses: knowledge about the wider society, and knowledge that was known to be socially held – the sort of thing that (at least in principle) "everyone knows." (In a country like Canada, one might suggest that the work of providing the identical, simultaneous news reports at the centre of Anderson's conception was played more by the news agency, given that no individual newspaper circulated nationally before the 1980s.[10]) In a related vein, Thompson argues that one of the chief characteristics of the modern age has been the emergence of "mediated publicness," allowing very large numbers of people regularly and repeatedly to share, through media, experiences and knowledge far beyond what would be possible if they were limited to face-to-face, unmediated, encounters.

Even within the growing field of media history, though, news agencies have received relatively little attention. Several reasons are typically cited for this state of affairs. They are, in a sense, wholesalers of news and tend to operate behind the scenes. Individual newspaper or broadcast customers would rather promote their own employees' work than a product they share with other news organizations, and, for most readers, the familiar agency credit tends to fade into the background.[11] Agencies usually stress the organization and its impersonal strengths – speed, accuracy, reliability, scope of coverage – rather than the flair of the individual, heroic journalist. (One news-agency history is tellingly entitled *Reporter Anonymous*; a member of Canadian Press once described CP as "one of those faceless organizations with no soul to save and no ass to kick."[12]) But as Oliver Boyd-Barrett and Terhi Rantanen, two of the leading researchers in this area, argue, news agencies deserve scholarly attention for many reasons: "not simply because they are agents of construction of what we have come to understand as the domains of the 'national' and of the 'international' ... but more practically because there are grounds for considering what agencies do and how they do it are important for the survival of a 'public sphere' of democratic dialogue ... ."[13] In many countries, they are the only entities that regularly gather and distribute news on a nationwide basis, "so that one may say of them that they are the informational backbone, or at least a significant contributor to such a backbone, which public debate takes for granted and on which it is based."[14] Menahem Blondheim, who studied the emergence of Associated Press in the United States, concluded that "by securing for itself the position of a national news monopoly early in the second half of the nineteenth century, [AP] represented one of the most powerful centripetal forces shaping American society in the modern era."[15] Elsewhere, Boyd-Barrett and Rantanen have enumerated the various processes facilitated by news agencies:

> News contributed to processes of the construction of national identity; to imperialism and the control of colonies; it was an essential lubricant in day-to-day financial affairs, both within and between domestic markets. The collection and dissemination of this commodity was organized and rationalized ... by a small group of powerful agencies, acting globally and as a cartel. Hence the links between modernity, capitalism, news, news agencies and globalization are an outstanding but neglected feature of the last 150 years.[16]

The recent international literature on news agencies approaches them from a variety of perspectives, and an examination of this work suggests several themes to be borne in mind when considering CP's history. Much of the writing in this area has reflected, or has been a reaction to, the debate over "media imperialism." This point of view, stated perhaps most famously in a controversial 1980 UNESCO report, asserted that the large international agencies – especially Associated Press, United Press International (UPI), the British-based Reuters, and Agence France-Presse – operated in a harmful way towards the Third World, with undue emphasis on the perspectives of the wealthy North and a paltry, stereotyped, and one-dimensional picture of the countries of the South.[17] Certainly the major international agencies were, and are, extremely powerful institutions. For almost eighty years (1856–1934), the "Big Three" agencies (Reuters, the French Havas, and the German Wolff agency) operated a cartel that, like the European colonial powers, divided the world among themselves. Each was granted a monopoly in supplying news to certain parts of the world, and each agreed to exchange news from and for its exclusive territories only with the other two. This tight arrangement was brought to an end by Associated Press in 1934, but the breaking of the cartel did not mean that the international agencies (now including AP) had become significantly less powerful.

Even at the time of the NWICO (New World Information and Communication Order) debate, though, scholars noted that the relationship between international and national agencies was more complex than a simple imperialism model might suggest. The major agencies operated differently in important ways, Boyd-Barrett noted, rather than displaying "common motives and common behaviour."[18] Although there were substantial power imbalances in their relationships, international agencies also depended on national agencies in important ways, the latter being both customers (a relationship in which they could, and did, complain and resist in various ways) and suppliers of news from their countries.[19] Whether dominated or not, national agencies were "vital components in the armoury of the nation state ... institutions which new nation states came to feel they had to establish in order to be seen to be credible as nations,"[20] and thus contributed to the assertion of national identities. Moreover, British colonies of settlement, such as Canada and Australia, demonstrated patterns of involvement with (and in some cases resistance to) the big agencies that were different than one might expect to find in their relationships with Third World countries.[21]

Some recent scholarship has presented a broader challenge to the media imperialism model. Rantanen and others have called into question the underlying notion that media institutions necessarily "represent" countries in some way, and that a nation-to-nation model is the best way of understanding them and their relationships.[22] Rantanen challenges the idea that a particular nation will "reject or oppose media imperialism on the part of another country in the name of national interest," since "there is often no single national interest but separate media enterprises, which compete against each other, both nationally and globally."[23] Nations typically have more powerful and less powerful regions or groups within them, which struggle to improve or maintain their relative positions through media, as well as in other ways; here the media imperialism approach "romanticized the national, instead of seeing it as potentially as oppressive as the global."[24] In Rantanen's view, the paradigm of globalization – conceived as "a *non-linear*, dialectic process in which the global and the local exist not as cultural polarities, but as combined and mutually implicating principles"[25] – offers a better way of understanding the worldwide news system. More recently, Rantanen has suggested that the global news system is best understood in terms of the relations among and around its dominant cities rather than the nations in which they are located.[26] From a different perspective, Dwayne Winseck and Robert Pike have argued that the formation of the global media system before 1910 reflected not the expansion of and competition among different *national* interests, but a worldwide process of "capitalist imperialism."[27] Simon Potter has argued strongly that a narrow emphasis on the press as an instrument of national identity in the British dominions fails to take account of an equally important set of imperial connections.[28] Questions about the inevitability of the national frame for interpreting the global media system are useful to bear in mind, even when studying an explicitly national organization like Canadian Press. Disputes continue over just what the national interest is and who has the right to define it, in media as well as other terms, and such disputes form an important thread in CP's history. As Craig Calhoun observes, ideas of nation and nationality are essentially contested "because any particular definition of them will privilege some collectivities, interests and identities and damage the claims of others."[29]

As nationality becomes a more complex term in studying news agencies historically, other concepts come to the fore. Whether they operate globally or nationally, the question of how news agencies relate to their customers is an important thread of analysis. In France, for example, the privately run, state-subsidized Havas agency exercised tremendous power over provincial French newspapers, because it controlled not only their supply of news, but also advertising.[30] Agencies that were privately owned (such as Reuters or United Press) had a different relationship with clients than news cooperatives such as AP, Britain's Press Association (which served provincial newspapers), and CP.[31] Some agencies, such as Reuters, handled only international news; others, such as AP, operated both domestically and internationally; CP had a very small international presence; and Press Association covered national news only. In some countries, such as Australia, newspaper syndicates, often in competition with each other, organized the supply of news. Exclusivity is an important question here: some agencies (CP among them) imposed strict limits on who could take advantage of their service and how it could be used, whereas others (Reuters, for example) sold news to anyone who could pay.

This raises the question of monopoly. Critics of agencies such as AP and CP have frequently described them as monopolistic, and their regulations and efforts to thwart competing agencies at times operated in clearly monopolistic ways.[32] As Blondheim has very clearly shown in relation to AP, the economic logic of telegraphic news distribution (at least in the nineteenth and early twentieth centuries) operated in a monopolistic direction: the more subscribers there were on a single telegraphic circuit, the lower the cost of the news report was for each subscriber, the more revenue the agency had to provide a better news report, and the more difficult it became for any competitor to provide an equivalent service at the same cost.[33] Clearly, a monopoly in news distribution raises serious concerns about the potential for bias. Although news agencies are generally considered to be the foremost exponents of "objective," independent, factual journalism, it is also true that most agencies have at times (and some more frequently, even permanently) relied on governments for financial support, and those that avoided direct government involvement sometimes reflected partisan, national, or other biases.[34]

Jonathan Silberstein-Loeb has recently challenged the view that the monopolistic character of news agencies is essentially harmful. He argues that the benefits of providing a large volume of news at relatively low cost to many publications outweigh the disadvantages of monopolistic structure: "a larger amount of news content ... was *a priori* beneficial because it provided editors with more choices, and they could elect to publish, or not publish, the material provided."[35] A similar argument applies to the much-criticized cartel arrangements. Rather than emphasizing the ways in which "multinational media corporations limit freedom of expression, dull the police function of the fourth estate, and manipulate public opinion for commercial ends," Silberstein-Loeb suggests that scholars should pay more attention to "the advantages of size and market control ... the importance of economies of scale, increased managerial capabilities, or the adverse effects of competition on the information available for public consumption."[36]

In any case, the tendency towards monopoly was never unalloyed. The spread of telegraphic news also had some antimonopolistic tendencies, since newspapers in smaller towns were freed from dependence on, and were better able to compete with, their wealthier big-city counterparts.[37] Typically, agencies supplied much more news than a newspaper could print, giving each editor at least a degree of choice about what to publish.[38] News-agency practices that supported monopoly in some respects, such as giving members the right to prevent the service from being sold to local competitors, undermined it in other ways: as AP found, if enough new papers were denied the AP service, they became an ideal client base for a competing agency. Despite their best efforts, news agencies could never escape the pressures of competition.

Indeed, competition is one of the most useful general concepts for studying news-agency history.[39] Whatever structure for supplying news was adopted – cooperative or proprietary; national, international, or a combination of both – competition was a crucial factor. At the agency-to-agency level, for example, AP and United Press (or CP and UP's Canadian proxy, British United Press) competed to capture newspaper clients from each other, and to serve them faster, with more engaging news, and at a better price. Agency-versus-agency competition also operated at a strategic level, as when AP successfully pushed Reuters out of its dominant position in the mid-1930s, or when CP weighed the advantages of affiliation with AP rather than Reuters for its international news. Another type of competition that affected every news agency had to do with the interests and capacities of newspaper clients in big cities compared to those in smaller towns. Big-city papers had larger circulations, more advertising, and more revenues, and were thus better able to pay for their own independent coverage of national and even international events. At the same time, big-city markets were more competitive, so each paper had to distinguish itself from its fellows; in this situation, generic agency news – the same for every customer – played a distinctly subordinate, even if important, role for big dailies.[40] For newspapers in smaller towns, lower circulation meant less revenue and less leeway to spend money on original out-of-town coverage, and because small markets also tended to be less competitive, the use of generic agency copy did not have the same drawbacks as for larger papers. Developing a single news report that would suit the requirements of both was a difficult challenge.[41] Complicating matters further, big-city dailies often circulated in nearby smaller towns and resented any service that gave their local competitors a better supply of news. This division between large and small newspapers sometimes was explicitly recognized, as in Britain, where the provincial press was behind the formation of the cooperative Press Association; the big Fleet Street dailies, circulating nationally and ferociously competitive, gathered their own domestic news.[42] In France, Havas's greatest strength was with provincial papers, and it often faced direct competition in serving them from the big Parisian newspapers.[43] CP served both big-city and small-town clients, and the resulting tension played a central role in its history.

There were other forms of competition, too, notably with the new media of radio in the 1920s and 1930s and television in the 1950s. Newspapers and news agencies struggled with whether to adopt, reject, or try to limit radio; in this process (in North America, at least, where private ownership of radio meant that money could be made from advertising), internal divisions among news-agency members over where their best interests lay added another layer to the challenge of dealing with the new medium. (These issues are discussed at length in Chapter 3.) Given all the different levels of competition that could be in operation, it is helpful to adopt what has been described as a "media ecology" approach, in which all the participants in a particular market and all the forces acting on them – local, national, international, or medium-specific – are borne in mind.[44]

Given the persistent emphasis in news-agency histories on the relations between international and national agencies, on one hand, and on the tensions within nations (central versus peripheral regions, or big cities versus small towns) on the other, one can suggest that *scale* is a useful overall concept to bear in mind. In this conception, the national scale of organization occupies an intermediate position between the global and the local. It is a centrally important, but not a fixed, category, finding its changing historical meaning precisely through its interplay with organizations or interests that operate on larger or on smaller scales.

Another way of making this point is to draw attention to the importance of the concept of *space* and spatial organization in many news-agency studies. Blondheim, for example, adopted Harold Innis's analysis of the space-binding capacity of different media in his examination of the early years of Associated Press, and Rantanen has paid considerable attention to the development of spatial hierarchies in the evolution of the international (or global) news system.[45] By systematizing the distribution of news, agencies also contributed to important changes in the time structure of information: not only did telegraphic news reach its destination faster, it tended to reach all places at more or less the same time, reducing the advantages of cities with a favoured position in the information network. In addition, the practice of regular, daily coverage of events that agencies made possible contributed to a change in readers' experience of news: the sense that news stories were continuously unfolding in "smaller and more frequent increments" created a feeling of suspense and a wish to know how things turned out that increased readers' involvement.[46] Beyond this, the idea of the world taking shape in successive 24-hour increments – a sense of "dailiness" as a fundamental way of organizing time – was steadily more solidly entrenched.[47]

The relationship between technology and organization is an additional way of thinking about news agencies historically. Havas began its operations before the advent of the telegraph, operating mainly as a translation and forwarding bureau; only after the introduction of the telegraph did news agencies per se emerge. The underlying technology had great significance, making possible altered patterns of information transmission in relation to time and space that were among the major changes in the nineteenth-century world. Accordingly, the relationship between news agencies and the telegraph has attracted considerable attention. Blondheim has traced the often collusive relationship between Associated Press and Western Union, for example, in which AP members were expected to support Western Union against its critics and the prospect of unwanted legislation; as long as this continued, AP received preferential treatment on Western Union's lines.[48] During the early years of telegraphic news in both Britain and Canada, telegraph companies themselves controlled the supply of news, though over time there was a clear tendency for newspaper cooperatives or proprietary news agencies to take over this role.[49]

A widespread but not entirely satisfactory account of the origin of news agencies focuses mainly on the importance of sharing the costs of telegraphic news, which was much more expensive than what had gone before. The system adopted previously by most newspapers consisted mainly of clipping news from foreign or out-of-town newspapers when they arrived in the mail, a process whose cost (beyond the time of the scissor-wielding editor) was virtually zero. Cost-sharing was an important motive for the formation of news agencies, but not the only, or even necessarily the most important, reason. Blondheim correctly stresses the unprecedented *organizational* requirements imposed by the systematic use of telegraphic news.[50] With a steady flow of news reports arriving in a city like New York from all directions, someone had to assess them, establish which were more important for which clients (or regions), and organize their retransmission within the capacity limits of each telegraphic channel, and these functions had to be exercised more or less around the clock. Editing the news down to what was considered most important (and valuable) was crucial, because telegraphic news cost money for every word sent, a far cry from the "non-selective and redundant flow of news characteristic of the exchanges."[51] Thus the chief function of a news agency was the *editorial organization* of the unprecedented flow of news made possible by the telegraph. Chapter 7 illustrates how, even in the mid-twentieth century, CP's description of its own operation stressed the role of the "filing editor," the person in each main bureau who made precisely the decisions about importance, length, and priority outlined above.[52]

A final consideration involves the question of whose interests the news agency served. While some scholars stress the ways in which journalists reflect the perspectives of their news organizations' owners, the wishes of the two groups are not always aligned; even senior journalists, normally hand-picked for their roles by owners, typically want large editorial budgets, for example, whereas owners are often more concerned with cutting costs.[53] Similar tensions are also sometimes found within news agencies, especially cooperatives, where the owners (mainly newspaper owners and publishers) often want the agency to operate in ways that protect their own, local, interests (e.g., by restricting the news service's availability to potential competitors), while the manager/journalists want to have the largest possible number of clients and revenue, or are more willing to see new media as customers rather than competitors.[54] For rank-and-file journalists, news agencies are workplaces where issues of pay, working conditions, editorial control, and union recognition sometimes come to the fore, illustrating further the possible divergence between owners' and employees' wishes. In the case of Canadian Press, as discussed in Chapter 5, a bitter dispute over unionization of editorial staff in the 1950s almost led to the organization's demise.[55]

While much of the literature cited above is of general application, the present study is chiefly an account of how a durable nationwide news system was organized *in Canada*, and how this contributed to the development of an imagined community, systematically and permanently drawing Canadians more closely together in an increasingly integrated national cultural space. (As Friesen expressed this point, "[t]he economic forces of print-capitalism increasingly drew ordinary Canadians ... into a *single* community."[56]) Many aspects of CP's history relate to well-established themes in Canadian history and historical writing more broadly. These include not only the construction and nature of national identity, but also Canada's relations with Britain and the United States, regional and binational responses to the project of national integration, and the nation-building role of communication and technology in the context of capitalist economic development.[57] It must be stressed that this is not a nationalist or a triumphal account. On the contrary, the culturally nation-building project that Canadian Press undoubtedly did represent was contested for much, if not most, of its history and on several different grounds. The insistence of Winnipeg and western Canadian publishers on retaining as much autonomy as possible when CP established a properly functioning domestic news agency in 1917, an insistence that continued into the 1930s, is a clear example of western resistance to the dominance of central Canada, otherwise exemplified in such familiar contemporary developments as the Progressive movements, farmer's cooperatives, or (in part) the formation of the Co-operative Commonwealth Federation (CCF). J.M.S. Careless's ideas about metropolitanism – that Canada can productively be understood in terms of regionally powerful cities seeking to expand their respective hinterlands – also fit these aspects of CP's history very well.[58] Connecting Careless's Canadian-specific formulation with Rantanen's more recent and internationally focused notion of cosmopolitanism[59] yields the idea of a global and national hierarchy of urban places – say, from London to New York to Toronto to Winnipeg to Calgary – as a key structural feature of the international/national news system of which CP is an integral part. The theme of Canada's binational and bicultural character as a permanent counterweight to ideas of national homogeneity is also clearly present in this history, seen particularly in the challenge that Quebec publishers mounted to CP's basic methods of operation in the 1960s.

CP's experience both confirms and complicates the familiar tension between connections to Britain – political, cultural, economic, and otherwise – and to the United States in Canadian history. CP was an autonomous organization, not a branch plant or subsidiary as many twentieth-century Canadian corporations were. (News, as Mary Vipond has noted, has a degree of built-in protectionism because so much of it is local, regional, or national.[60]) But the US agency, Associated Press, had a strong directing hand in CP's creation, and was clearly the dominant partner for the whole period covered in this volume. Thus, broadly speaking, the theme of US economic dominance, especially involving cultural industries, is fundamentally borne out. CP's history presents unusual, and even paradoxical, variations on this theme, however. AP's directive role led directly to the creation, and contributed strongly to the success, of a major institution of Canadian cultural nationality. As Chapter 1 makes clear, AP forced mutually antagonistic Canadian publishers to establish a functioning national news organization when they proved unwilling to do so on their own. This was not done, at least not in any narrow sense, for profit, but for strategic reasons, especially control of subsidiary territory against potential competitors. (This also reflected the increasingly systematic codification of news into a form of property, one of the ways that CP's history illustrates larger processes of capitalist economic development.[61]) Through its close connection to AP, Canada became part of the international news system as an explicitly national unit, which was not the case in Latin America, or, after the breakdown of long-established cartel arrangements in the mid-1930s, in Europe.

The creation and maintenance of the east-to-west telegraphic network that was CP's crucial piece of infrastructure (and in many respects its greatest challenge) has obvious parallels with other nationally significant systems of transportation and communication in Canada's past, such as the rivers and railroads that supported the staple industries of furs and wheat, respectively. But in this case, the east–west national system was *fundamentally* and *essentially* connected to a north–south axis (to New York) that was, in turn, connected to the transatlantic and global telegraphic-news network. In fact, CP's experience clearly makes the case that nation-building and globalization were mutually implicating principles during the first half of the twentieth century, as Boyd-Barrett and Rantanen have powerfully argued. CP's history also presents many examples of cultural and political affinity to Britain being weighed against the largely (though not solely, as shown in Chapter 2) economic benefits of an American connection. Yet this familiar tension between British cultural and political ties and growing American economic connections, real as it was in the 1910s and 1920s, broke down for CP after 1940. This was not because of changing attitudes towards the British connection per se (though these were indeed changing[62]), but rather because the British news agency, Reuters, transformed its approach to the news business to become more like AP. In doing so, as discussed in Chapters 4 and 5, it became almost overnight an alternative to AP for the Canadians in a way that had never been the case before, but for business rather than sentimental reasons.

Both in its national and international dimensions, then, this study affirms the relevance of familiar broad themes in Canadian history but approaches them from new directions. As an examination of how the mediated nation took shape, it underscores the significance, solidity, and gravitational pull of the national framework in the era of print-capitalism. However, it also stresses the contingent and contested nature of the national framework thus established, or, to put it another way, the porousness of the boundaries between international, national, regional, and local levels of experience. At virtually every turn, CP was simultaneously national *and* international *and* local/regional.

In the chapters that follow, all the concepts outlined above are used in an effort to understand the evolution of Canadian Press. CP took shape in relation to more powerful international agencies, Associated Press and Reuters, in ways that were sometimes antagonistic and sometimes collaborative. Domestically, CP struggled to negotiate the tensions among regions (including finding ways to serve its French- and English-Canadian members equitably) and between metropolitan and smaller newspapers. It solicited and embraced government subsidies at its founding and later rejected them; in wartime, it struggled to find a balance between a supportive, patriotic stance and the journalist's tradition of an arm's length, critical approach to government. It trumpeted its status as a nonprofit cooperative, a true public service, but was also accused of monopolistic practices and waged a bitter antiunion campaign in the 1950s. CP spent 20 years trying to sort out its internal contradictions over radio, only to sweep aside all objections virtually overnight (and subsequently to find in broadcasting its biggest source of profits).

Amid all these struggles, CP journalists covered the news (deciding in the process what counted as news and how it should be treated), day in and day out. Important as the CBC has been as a cultural entity in Canada, one could argue that CP was more influential: CBC never accounted for more than a fraction of all radio stations, whereas virtually every daily newspaper (and most broadcast stations) in Canada relied on CP's service. It was the chief vehicle of "mediated publicness" in Canada for most of the twentieth century, providing a common base of information across the country (and a shared connection à la Anderson to all the others who were following the same stories). The nation as it emerged in the nineteenth century can be seen as one specific form of mediated publicness, and the news agency was a key vehicle of its consolidation in the twentieth century. It is no coincidence that CP's heyday (roughly, from the 1940s to the 1960s or 1970s) was also a high-water mark for an optimistic sense of Canadian nationality: the nation evolved in parallel with the means of its articulation.

This is, therefore, an institutional study that seeks to understand the institution in its widest possible context, as well as a study of the mediated nation that sees it as essentially contingent, changing, and contested. CP is at once a cultural, and also an economic and technologically-based organization; the aim of this study is to chart the connections between (to use Ernest Gellner's terms) culture *and* structure.

The chapters that follow do not give an exhaustive account of CP's history. Rather, while providing an overall (and generally chronological) account of how the organization evolved, each chapter focuses on one or more key themes that came to the fore during the years in question. Thus CP's relationship with Associated Press, and with the federal government, were crucial in the years leading to its founding; these are addressed particularly in Chapter 1. Chapter 2 examines the challenges of setting up a functioning organization in the 1920s and 1930s, focusing particularly on the question of subsidization, and Chapter 3 traces CP's struggle to come to terms with radio during these years. In Chapter 4, CP's close and complex relationship with the federal government and armed forces during the Second World War comes to the fore. The bitter campaign to defeat the American Newspaper Guild in the 1950s is the main focus of Chapter 5, and Chapter 6 traces new debates (and the re-emergence of old debates) in the 1960s over what it meant to be a national agency. Chapter 7 steps aside from chronology to examine the changing form and content of CP news reports, and the Conclusion assesses CP's experience in the context of journalism history, the evolution of the international news system, and the nature and significance of mediated publicness in twentieth-century Canadian life.

1 Uneasy Allies

Telegraphic news first reached British North America in January 1847.[1] Within a few years, a wealthy newspaper like the Toronto *Globe* was carrying a variety of telegraphic reports each day: on 15 March 1855, for example, this included news from the previous day's session of the provincial legislature in Quebec, an account of a fire in the nearby town of St. Catharines, a weather report from Montreal, closing prices on the New York exchange, and a substantial amount of British and European news telegraphed from New York (where steamships with the latest news from overseas docked).[2] The source of this information was not given; only the telegraph companies that transmitted it were credited, with both the Legislative Assembly and international news arriving "per Montreal telegraph line" and the Montreal weather report "via Grand Trunk line." However, it is likely that the domestic news was procured by the *Globe* itself, while the international news was provided by New York Associated Press.[3] When the Atlantic cable was completed in 1866, Canada's connections to the outside world were close and rapid to a degree that would have been unthinkable 20 years earlier. Within a few weeks of the cable's going into operation, the *Globe* was carrying London news from the day before; previously, it had taken at least 10 days, and longer still before the overland telegraph connection to New York was in place.[4] The compression of time and space through communications media is one of the key characteristics of world history since 1850,[5] and Canada was as much caught up in this transformation as any other place.

International news was provided in a systematic way to Canadian newspapers long before the same happened domestically. The world capitals of London, Paris, and Berlin were connected telegraphically to each other by 1851, and their newspapers were numerous and wealthy enough to provide a steady market for organized news services. Charles Havas in Paris and two of his former employees – Julius Reuter in London and Bernhard Wolff in Berlin – were among the first to specialize in supplying a common file of telegraphic news to multiple newspaper clients. Beginning in 1856, the three signed a series of agreements that eventually divided the world among themselves for the purposes of gathering and selling news: each claimed the exclusive right to sell international news in its assigned territories, and all agreed that they would exchange news only with each other.[6] Thus by the time the Atlantic cable was in operation, international telegraphic news was controlled by a cartel that maintained its dominance (and shaped the way Canadians received news) for the next 70 years.

Another early news agency was established in New York, a remarkably vigorous and competitive newspaper market.[7] This began in 1846 as an alliance of six publications that cooperated in running an express service for Mexican War news,[8] and subsequently expanded to include news from Baltimore, Washington, and Philadelphia – and especially Boston, which was the terminus of the Cunard steamers with their valuable cargo of European news.[9] With the expansion of the US telegraph network, the association – known as New York Associated Press – began to supply the news it received to papers in other US cities. Through the Montreal Telegraph Co., and later the Great North Western Telegraph Co., Associated Press news was also made available to newspapers in Canada.[10] In 1870, the New York agency contracted with the European cartel as a junior partner; thus it had access to the world news provided jointly by the Wolff, Havas, and Reuter agencies, offering extensive coverage of international and US news that would have been virtually impossible and prohibitively expensive for any Canadian paper to assemble on its own.

Two key developments with important implications for the development of the Canadian news system took place in the early 1890s. In 1893, a newly reorganized Associated Press signed a contract with Reuters that explicitly gave it the right to treat Canada as a subsidiary territory under the cartel's system of territorial exclusivity.[11] Soon after, AP exercised its new power, selling the exclusive right to distribute its news service (including the cartel's international news) to the telegraph department of the recently completed Canadian Pacific Railway (CPR). The CPR bought the rights to distribute AP news throughout

Canada over its own telegraph lines for the remarkably low sum of $1,500 annually.[12]

The relationship between national and international news agencies was an essential characteristic of the global news system that was taking shape around this time, and in this context AP's decision to treat Canada as a national unit rather than dealing separately with individual newspapers (as it already did in Mexico and Cuba, for example) had important consequences. Paul Starr has argued that the development of media institutions is "path dependent," in that decisions made at an earlier time both close off some possibilities and establish patterns that channel later developments in a certain direction, and this seems to be an example of that process; Canada's later creation of a national agency, Canadian Press, was in important ways a result of this decision.[13] But why did AP adopt this approach to Canada and not elsewhere? Melville Stone, AP's general manager, later explained the reason: the newly established AP was at the time in mortal combat with another news agency, United Press (UP), and with financier Jay Gould, the owner of Western Union. Gould refused to allow the new AP to use his transcontinental wires, but the CPR's cross-Canada network allowed AP to reach the US Pacific coast without having to rely on Western Union.[14] Stone's successor once complained about the unique approach taken to Canada (in private), and later boasted about it (in public), but its significance was inescapable.[15] As we shall see, AP exercised a crucial role in the formation and structure of Canadian Press in various ways.

Under the CPR contract, Canadian publishers had no direct relationship with AP. The CPR sold the service at a flat rate in which the cost of the news was bundled together with the telegraph delivery charges. The price to newspapers was relatively low. This was a sort of loss leader; the CPR hoped that by establishing a regular relationship with newspapers in this way, it would gain an advantage over its rival, the Western Union–controlled Great North Western Telegraph Co., in handling the newspapers' more lucrative "specials" business.[16] (Specials were telegraphic dispatches sent to individual newspapers.) Rates for the AP service were lowest in Ontario and Quebec, where a relatively dense network of cities and a large number of subscribing newspapers, along with proximity to the centre of AP's newsgathering and distribution operations in New York, kept costs to each individual paper low. Telegraphic transmission costs increased with distance, and so were substantially higher to western Canada. In addition, cities such as Winnipeg and Vancouver supported fewer newspapers than Toronto and Montreal, so that each western paper paid a higher proportion of the cost of delivering the service to that city. Thus a Toronto morning paper like the *Globe* paid $15 a week for 36,000 words of AP material in 1909, while the much smaller Saskatoon *Phoenix* paid more than three times as much.[17]

From the beginning, concerns were expressed that AP was not providing enough British Empire news and that American, rather than British, perspectives were being represented. The connection to Britain was central to the English-Canadian political identity that was beginning to take shape in the decades after confederation in 1867, and anti-British sentiments expressed by American politicians or appearing in American newspapers angered many Canadian readers.[18] In 1905, for example, the Toronto *Star* complained that "stories sent by American correspondents at the instance of the American editors of the Associated Press and for American consumption were often given an anti-British bias."[19] Where news from London was concerned, though, it was not usually a question of overt anti-British sentiment (since almost all AP's British and European news came via Reuters, the British-based agency) but more a matter of AP systematically playing down subjects of imperial interest in choosing which stories to transmit. The news report the CPR distributed across Canada was routed through Buffalo and was designed for the American newspapers that received it along the telegraphic circuit from New York; Melville Stone readily acknowledged that his news service "was conducted without any special regard for the needs or interests of Canadian readers."[20]

In any case, the fact that most English-Canadian newspapers expressed nationalist-cum-imperialist sentiments in one form or another[21] did not necessarily mean that they were willing to act in concert to create an effective national or imperial news system – especially when this involved real costs and obligations or might interfere with individual publishers' plans for competitive advantage. Throughout the period, as Simon Potter has shown for newspapers in the British dominions more generally, commercial motives were at least as important as patriotic ones: they "helped determine how individual press enterprises would respond to the opportunities and threats presented by plans for the creation of national and imperial news services, in turn dictating how these enterprises would appeal to different types of identity to further or foil such schemes."[22]

The first cooperative attempt by Canadian publishers to provide a better supply of British news followed Canada's participation in the

Boer War (1899–1902), an event that brought the imperial connection to the fore and generated extensive (and expensive) coverage in many Canadian newspapers.[23] Shortly after the war ended, a group of mostly big-city publishers established an organization called Canadian Associated Press (CAP), whose purpose was to supplement AP with a direct service of news of interest to Canadians from London.[24] CAP was led by the pugnacious imperialist publisher of the Toronto *Telegram*, John Ross Robertson, and its formation was the first step in a 15-year struggle for control of the Canadian news system.[25]

Simon Potter questions the frequently stated view that CAP was established mainly because Canadian publishers were unhappy with having their Boer War news come through anti-British US sources; he notes that public opinion in the United States was more supportive of Britain in this conflict than not.[26] On the contrary, he argues, CAP's formation mainly reflected the desire of leading metropolitan publishers to strengthen their position against smaller papers in nearby towns (where they competed for circulation) by controlling a commercially valuable new source of British news.[27] Potter is correct to emphasize publishers' commercial and strategic motives, but it was not an either-or proposition: CAP did represent an increase in the volume and variety of British news coming directly to Canada, which could readily be justified on imperial grounds. Thus CAP obtained an annual subsidy of $8,000 from the Canadian government to help defray the costs of cable transmission from London, stressing that its purpose was to "furnish foreign news to the Canadian public without filtering same through the American Associated Press."[28]

But CAP laboured under substantial disadvantages. It was organizationally weak, dominated by Robertson of the *Telegram*, and seen as his personal vehicle rather than a genuine news-sharing organization.[29] CAP's London representative was Robertson's half-brother, Charles, and his work was the subject of frequent complaints (it was said, for example, that he kept up with each day's British news by surreptitiously clipping the newspapers subscribed to by his London club).[30] There were problems with its content as well, which was limited to news directly involving Canadians (and sports coverage), rather than British and imperial news more broadly.[31] Because of the government subsidy, CAP was also susceptible to charges that it was politically tainted.[32]

Costs were another problem: even with the subsidy, the heavy charges for using the Atlantic cable meant that CAP typically transmitted no more than 500 words a day from London – less than one-tenth the amount sent by AP from New York for about the same cost.[33] AP received an enormous volume of international news at a low price through its arrangement with the Reuters–Havas–Wolff cartel, but CAP had to pay for its own, very limited, newsgathering operation in London. AP could also divide the cost of buying the cartel's news and transmitting it from London among more than 600 US member newspapers, while CAP's costs could only be shared among 15 or 16 subscribers.[34] Because the Canadian newspaper market was much smaller than the American market, and because Canadian publishers could only gain access to the voluminous and relatively cheap international news provided by the cartel through AP, CAP could never be anything more than a supplement, as opposed to a potential replacement.[35]

Robertson's main goal was strategic. He saw CAP as the nucleus of a larger Canadian telegraphic-news system for domestic as well as international coverage that would be controlled mainly by him and his close ally in these matters, Joseph Atkinson of the Toronto *Star*.[36] Thus despite CAP's problems, Robertson was determined to maintain control. This was underlined in 1906, when Henry Collins, a senior representative of Reuters, visited Canada to assess the possibilities of selling a Reuters news service to Canadian publishers directly. Collins found two almost insurmountable obstacles. One was the low cost of the AP/CPR service that most Canadian newspapers were already receiving; any comparable service Reuters could provide via the Atlantic cable would be considerably more expensive.[37] The other was Robertson's furious opposition to a proposal that he believed was designed to supplant CAP (and, perhaps, take over its subsidy.)[38] Collins reported that Robertson was "extremely jealous" of the Ottawa and Montreal papers, especially the Montreal *Star*, and concluded that the Toronto publishers "mean to keep the power [over CAP] entirely in their own hands." (Seven of the 16 CAP subscribers in 1906 were in Toronto, with four in Montreal, two each in Ottawa and Winnipeg, and one in London, Ontario.[39]) Even if the CAP subsidy were withdrawn, the big Toronto papers could easily afford to keep up the service, Collins reported; indeed, they might even welcome such a development, because then "the small fry would have to be content with the [AP] service from New York only," and the competitive position of the wealthy Toronto papers in smaller Ontario towns would be that much stronger. Stewart Lyon of the *Globe* told Collins that Robertson was firmly opposed to the idea of allowing numerous other newspapers, especially those in the west, to join the association "because the result would be to strengthen his contemporaries at a distance."[40] Atkinson of the *Star* confirmed both the long-term strategic goal and Toronto-centric attitude that lay behind it, telling Collins that CAP was intended to "develop ultimately into a body similar to the [Associated Press], and as such to furnish both inland [domestic] and foreign news to all the papers," and stressing "the opposition that had always been shown to the CAP by the papers in the other towns." Reuters' permanent representative in Canada, R.M. McLeod, expanded on this point later: if CAP became the nucleus of a comprehensive domestic and international news service, it could "dictate terms to any new-comer to the newspaper field, thus to a certain extent protecting the Association's present membership from the competition of new rivals. ... It is this policy of the CAP which holds the Toronto newspapers in such close fellowship, and renders it difficult for one to impress upon the others the necessity of thinking and acting for themselves in business matters irrespective of Mr. Ross Robertson's views."[41] The Toronto-based combination that Robertson hoped to create was very reminiscent of the situation in Australia, where a group of big-city newspapers effectively sidelined Reuters to assert control of the country's foreign-news supply.[42]

Collins's general approach in his discussions with editors and publishers in Ontario and Quebec was not to "put forward the 'Imperial' question because I do not think it would appeal to them to any great extent." Instead, he approached them "solely on business grounds," arguing that they "can get a better service [via Reuters] for the same or a very little more money, and on this ground alone it should commend itself to them."[43] Collins was not presenting Reuters so much as an alternative to the American AP, but to the locally controlled CAP; in this situation, there was little to be gained by an explicitly imperial argument.[44] (Atkinson underscored the importance of local control, telling Collins it was essential for the Canadians to employ their own agent in London rather than relying on Reuters; otherwise they "could do no more than complain, with possibly no more satisfaction than they are able to obtain from Mr. Stone.") When Collins travelled to western Canada, however, he found that "[i]t would be impossible to overrate the feeling of dissatisfaction that prevails everywhere, except in Toronto, with the existing regime"; here the argument that Reuters offered a better service from an imperial point of view could be freely presented, and was welcomed.[45]

While there were problems with and tensions around the supply of international, and especially British, news in Canada as of 1907, there was nothing at the time that could be called a system for covering national news. The newspaper industry was notably divided by size: wealthy metropolitan papers like the *Globe*, the Montreal *Star*, and the Winnipeg *Free Press* had little in common with the large number of smaller publications of varying profitability. The differences in scale were significant: the Montreal *Star* sold 100,000 copies a day in 1913, compared to 4,000 for the Kingston, Ontario, *British Whig*.[46] Higher circulation meant more advertising revenue, which could then be used to provide improved content – which, in highly competitive urban markets, was a necessity for higher circulation.[47]

National news from beyond each paper's immediate district was provided in a variety of ways. Newspapers that could afford to do so maintained staff reporters in news-heavy locations like Ottawa and paid to transmit their despatches by telegraph.[48] More commonly, papers made arrangements with "stringers" – often members of another newspaper's staff – in distant cities.[49] Stringers were expected to alert their out-of-town clients when newsworthy events occurred; they were usually paid by the word, on a per-occasion basis. For features and less time-sensitive stories, boilerplate services distributed ready-made pages that could be mounted directly on the press. By 1900, large papers no longer relied heavily on the exchange system, which before the widespread use of the telegraph had been the main way most newspapers received their out-of-town news (though smaller publications still did so.)[50] Under Canada's postal regulations, every newspaper in the country was entitled to send a copy of each edition to every other newspaper free of charge[51] – the receiving newspaper would simply reprint items it considered of interest, often with credit, but sometimes not, and rarely for payment. The obvious drawback was that news distributed via the exchange system was always out of date; and once the telegraph accustomed readers to a steady diet of up-to-date news, reprinting news stories days after the events described had occurred (and had been reported elsewhere) was less and less acceptable.

The only institutions that regularly provided national news to newspapers generally were Canada's telegraph companies, but this was as an afterthought to their more central involvement with the international news system. By 1909, the CPR was supplementing AP with a basic Canadian news service, but this was hardly the product of an extensive newsgathering organization. The mainstay of the CPR's Canadian news service was the material that AP's correspondent in Canada transmitted back to AP headquarters in New York; the CPR had the right to copy and distribute this to its Canadian clients as well. Beyond this, according to J.W. Camp, the chief engineer of CPR telegraphs, individual newspapers were expected to hire their own special correspondents for out-of-town Canadian news. However, western Canadian newspapers maintained that they could not afford specials "and asked us to supply them with general Canadian news clipped from papers ... [therefore] in the East, and in some places in the West, we pay a small amount to the members of the staff of some newspapers to compile reports."[52] News from western Canada was also provided to eastern newspapers at 25 cents per 100 words, though few editors were apparently aware of this service.[53] The CPR insisted that only "very rarely" did its own telegraph operators transmit news on their own behalf: "Our agent does not act as a news gatherer."[54] Camp estimated that the volume of Canadian news sent to western newspapers amounted to 1,000 words a day on average, between 10 and 20 per cent of the volume of AP material provided, although other CPR documents indicate that western subscribers got between 2,000 and 4,000 words of Canadian news a day.[55] E.H. Macklin, business manager of the Winnipeg *Free Press* (and one of the leaders of the publishers' later struggle against the CPR), described the CPR service as "always inferior, often atrocious, never acceptable," with arbitrarily high or low rates being charged to individual clients.[56] Certainly there is evidence that the railway charged different rates depending on its attitude to, or past history with, individual newspapers.[57]

The CPR's competitor, the Great North Western Telegraph Co., also provided bare-bones domestic news service, offered only to newspapers in Ontario and Quebec. The company had "agents and correspondents" at Toronto, Montreal, Ottawa, Halifax, and Winnipeg; in addition, the Great North Western telegraph operator in every locality was expected to report "all local incidents of unusual importance."[58] As described by its superintendent, George Perry, this sounded like an impressive operation, but editors like Atkinson of the *Star* printed "very, very little" of what was sent, and Perry himself acknowledged that the service was not extensively used.[59] Editors from the Maritime provinces had to make their own individual arrangements for domestic news from Toronto and Montreal (as well as cope with the vagaries of a telegraph system that regularly interrupted their news transmissions with other commercial traffic).[60] Beginning in 1909, the Toronto *Star* provided what was called a "pony" service (a limited news service sent via commercial telegraph) for smaller Ontario dailies.[61]

Although individual newspapers might carry substantial amounts of national news, Canadian publishers as a group were focused more systematically on the US and international news provided by AP. As of 1909, 48 Canadian dailies took the AP service. Most papers received about 6,000 words a day, with some taking as little as 2,000 words and others as much as 12,000.[62]

◈

In 1907, the CPR decided to greatly increase the rates it charged western Canadian newspapers for AP news, insisting that it was losing money under the existing rate structure.[63] This began a period of turmoil that lasted for 10 years. In the short term, the rate increase had two significant results. First, the two main newspapers in Winnipeg, the *Free Press* and the *Telegram*, put aside their bitter political opposition and commercial competition to arrange their own joint news service independent of the CPR (and therefore without AP). They then offered to sell this service to the 17 other western Canadian papers that would suffer under the CPR's higher rates. The new organization was called Western Associated Press (WAP). In taking this step, the Winnipeg publishers in effect replicated the basic approach that New York publishers had adopted in establishing the first incarnation of Associated Press in the 1840s, an approach also used by the *Argus–Age* combination in Australia.[64] In all these cases, relatively wealthy metropolitan newspapers organized a supply of expensive but essential telegraphic news for their own benefit, and then found a valuable market for the resale of this news in their respective hinterlands.[65]

The second key result of WAP's founding was that, in the course of its struggle with the CPR, it appealed the railway's rates for transmitting news to the national Board of Railway Commissioners. (Telegraph rates came under the newly established commission's jurisdiction.) In 1910, the commission ruled that the CPR's practice of charging a flat rate for the AP service – a single rate that included both the cost of supplying the news and the cost of telegraphic transmission – was discriminatory, in that the railway had given its news-selling business an unfair advantage over any competing news service that did not control its own telegraph lines. The flat-rate system would have to be scrapped, and the CPR would be required to offer competitors such as WAP the same rates for telegraphic transmission as it charged its own customers.[66]

This ruling had much broader consequences than anyone anticipated. Eastern Canadian publishers had not joined their western counterparts in the original appeal; they were not affected by the new western rates and were quite satisfied with the low-cost, high-volume AP service they received from the CPR.[67] But the ruling affected them as well as the westerners. Accordingly, Canadian publishers as a group began trying to work out a new arrangement with the CPR in which the cost of the news service would be distinguished from the cost of delivering it.

Depending mainly on their location, publishers had widely divergent expectations about how this should be done. Those in Toronto and Montreal wanted a new price structure that reflected their triple advantage: numerous newspapers, fairly close to New York, on a relatively compact telegraphic circuit. Thus it was argued that each of the five subscribing morning dailies in Toronto should pay one-fifth of the actual cost of transmitting AP's morning-paper report from New York to Toronto. When it was pointed out that this approach would leave the less numerous and more distant Ottawa papers paying three times as much as their Toronto counterparts, Stewart Lyon of the *Globe* replied sharply: "I have nothing to do with that. I represent the Toronto papers."[68] In western Canada, this approach would approximately double the already high cost of telegraphic news. The westerners, by contrast, proposed a system with some elements of equalization, where costs and revenues would be pooled over a larger geographical base, perhaps even on a national basis. The result would be their paying rates closer to what their counterparts in Toronto and Montreal paid.[69] But if westerners paid less, easterners would pay more; what the former urged as fairness, the latter saw as a demand for a subsidy. For the next seven years, this proved an insurmountable obstacle to the formation of a national news organization in Canada. Indeed, the question of assessments – how much each member should pay, especially in relation to what others paid – remained a volatile and often contentious issue throughout CP's history, re-emerging in the early 1920s, 1930s, and 1960s.[70]

The railway commission's ruling against the CPR created a situation in which western and eastern publishers had to work much more closely together than ever before. In February 1910, while negotiations over a new CPR rate structure for news were continuing, AP notified the CPR that it planned to cancel their contract because the railway was not preventing its Canadian subscribers (notably the Toronto *Star*) from allowing the AP report to get into the hands of the agency's US competitors.[71] Thomas Shaughnessy, the CPR's president, accepted the news with equanimity, describing the AP franchise as "a source of annoyance without any adequate return ... it will be no sacrifice of prestige or profit to let it go."[72] The publishers of Toronto and Montreal had frequently sought to take over the AP service from the railway;[73] now they would get their wish.

Even before the CPR's decision was announced, a group of Canadian papers led by the Montreal *Star* had contacted AP executives to discuss the possibility of their taking over the AP service. B.A. MacNab of the *Star* reported that the Toronto *Mail and Empire*, Ottawa *Journal*, and the Winnipeg publishers in charge of WAP were prepared to establish a holding company for AP's Canadian distribution rights. The problem was that the other Toronto publishers refused to be involved; given their proximity to the AP distribution point at Buffalo, they felt they had nothing to gain by joining a larger association. "They are all for Toronto and quite willing to let the rest of the country take care of itself."[74] (An unsigned memorandum submitted to Melville Stone at around the same time added that some papers "want the AP service to be as uninteresting as possible to Canadians because its defects make all the better background for their special services."[75]) But if Stone would "insist on dealing with the Canadian newspapers as a whole, the Toronto publishers would be compelled to fall into line."

There is no direct evidence that Stone accepted this advice. By the beginning of June, however, the Toronto publishers had made an about-face, joining a group from across the country to discuss the formation of a national association.[76] This was quickly followed up by the arrival of a delegation in New York led by Robertson, who clearly saw an opportunity to take a large step towards the creation of an overall Canadian news agency that he and his allies might dominate.[77] Stone urged the group to establish a comprehensive national association that would be "the dominant organization" in the country.

During the summer of 1910, the Canadians worked out a proposal for three regional associations – one each for the eastern provinces, Ontario and Quebec, and the west – to assume control of the AP service.[78] A contract with AP was signed in October. One important overall condition was that the new association "shall effectively provide for the protection of such [AP] news by such by-laws and regulations as may be satisfactory to the Board of Directors of The Associated Press" – in other words, AP would exercise detailed control over the Canadian group's structure and operating methods.[79] Failure to protect AP news – to ensure that it did not slip into the hands of one of its US competitors, such as UP, the New York *Sun*'s Laffan service, or Hearst's International News Service (INS) – had brought the contract with the CPR to an end earlier that year, and Stone required the new Canadian association to be much more vigilant, with the power to discipline any members who failed to follow its rules.[80] The contract also specified that "all existing Canadian newspapers" should be admitted to the new association as long as they conformed to the general membership regulations. Any newly established paper should also be allowed to join, unless the Canadian directors decided that population or local conditions in the city in question did not justify an increase in membership.

Most of these stipulations reflected concerns about competition. The cooperative news agency is an unusual institution: it requires publishers who are normally competitors to cooperate in supplying news that their competitors, as well as they, can use. To operate successfully, it requires clear rules so each participating newspaper can be sure its competitors do not receive undue advantage. One of the most stubborn problems involved the conditions under which new members could be admitted. In any given city, an existing AP subscriber would be most unwilling to see a new competitor given access to the AP service – the new paper could then compete more effectively with the established newspaper for readers and advertising. In recognition of this, AP members had a "right of protest" by which they could, in effect, prevent new memberships from being issued in their circulation area. Although this restriction may have served the interests of individual members, however, it weakened the whole association. As Stone had found out in the previous few years, new papers denied AP service were likely to sign up with one of *its* competitors.[81] The proposed contract was intended to ensure that while existing AP subscribers in Canada would, for the first time, have control over the admission of new members, newcomers could not be shut out completely.

Other contract provisions were that the new association should have at least 40 members, representing all geographic regions of Canada; that every member was required to provide its local news to the association; and that the association was similarly required to provide its Canadian news to AP exclusively (sparing AP the need, at least in theory, to pay for a Canadian newsgathering operation of its own). The contract was to run for five years at an annual rate of $6,000, the same amount the CPR had been paying. This was still a remarkably low sum; if the new association had only 40 members, the cost of AP news to each (not counting telegraphic transmission costs, which could be substantial) would be around three dollars a week! Overall, AP did everything it could to create a Canadian Press in its own image: as a nonprofit cooperative comprising the great majority of Canadian newspapers. It approached Canada not so much as a market where it could sell its service to more newspapers – it received very little revenue from this – but as a strategically important territory in its widening battle with UP, Laffan, and INS.

Stone underlined his concerns about competition once again when he visited Toronto in November 1910 to make the contract final, insisting firmly that telegraph operators of all competing news agencies should be banned from the offices of any newspaper that wished to be an AP client.[82] This elicited vigorous protests, such as from E. Norman Smith of the Ottawa *Journal*. At present, the *Journal* also took news from the British and Colonial News Association, which provided something different than AP and was thus valuable for competitive reasons; but if it wanted to keep AP, the *Journal* would have to drop the competing service.[83] (Atkinson had put the same point more strongly when told he would have to remove a UP telegraph operator from the *Star*'s newsroom as a condition of AP service: "We decline to acquiesce in what would give to the Associated Press practically a monopoly in Canada."[84]) Stone also found "a good deal of distrust of the Toronto coterie" associated with CAP, "with which there has been a great deal of dissatisfaction," and expressed concern about proposed changes to some of the organization's bylaws, which "looked very much like an attempt to establish a Toronto oligarchy." [85] Eventually, the new organization's bylaws were carefully vetted by AP's lawyer to make sure all its concerns were met.[86] In important ways, CP was created as something like an AP subsidiary.

The close relationship with AP had clear advantages. One significant aspect of the new contract gave Canadian publishers access to all AP's incoming material in New York. Under the CPR contract, the AP service was delivered at specified border points – Buffalo, Seattle, Minneapolis, and Bangor. But this was a service designed mainly for the US newspapers that received it en route from New York. As M.E. Nichols of the Winnipeg *Telegram* (and WAP) complained, the news service that arrived from Minneapolis had been previously edited down at Detroit and again at Chicago in order to meet the interests of "newspaper readers in the middle western states." In the process, "[n]ews of general public interest, and especially cable [i.e., international] news, went out of the report as state news went in."[87] The total daily file available at New York amounted in 1914 to around 100,000 words,[88] while the amount transmitted to any of the border points was no more than 12,000 words. By stationing their own editors at AP headquarters and leasing a dedicated telegraph line from there to Toronto or Montreal, the Canadian publishers could select from a much larger pool of news the material – including more British news – that they believed their readers would prefer. A more formalized relationship with the US agency gave the Canadians a chance to remedy to some extent the shortage of British news they had so frequently lamented. In this respect, closer connections with AP gave the Canadians substantially more control over the news they received.

As long as the Canadian publishers simply bought their news from the CPR by individual arrangement, there had been no need to deal with each other. That changed under the new arrangement; they had to find a way of managing the service they now jointly controlled. Provisional directors of the national association, called Canadian Press Ltd., were appointed in October 1910, representing the Montreal *Gazette*, *Star*, and *Herald*; Toronto *Globe*, *Star*, and *Telegram*; Winnipeg *Free Press* and *Telegram*; Calgary *Herald*; Halifax *Chronicle*; Saint John *Telegraph*; and Vancouver *World*.[89] AP's annual fee was to be divided among five groups: the morning and afternoon papers, respectively, of Ontario and Quebec; the western papers represented in WAP; those in British Columbia; and the papers from New Brunswick, Nova Scotia, and Prince Edward Island. These divisions reflected underlying and persistent tensions: for example, Edward Slack of the Montreal *Gazette* told Stone that his paper would refuse to join the association unless the Ontario and Quebec newspapers were allowed to operate as autonomous morning-paper and afternoon-paper sections. Otherwise, he feared, the central Canadian section would be dominated by its powerful afternoon-paper members, the Montreal *Star*, Toronto *Star*, and Toronto *Telegram*, to the *Gazette*'s detriment.[90] (Afternoon papers typically wanted news brought in to meet their deadlines, around noon, while morning papers, with deadlines of midnight or earlier, wanted a schedule that suited their needs.[91])

Another persistent problem involved the differing needs of big-city and small-town newspapers. The big dailies in Toronto (and to a lesser extent in Montreal) were not enthusiastic about forming a strong news-sharing association throughout Canada. A stronger and more efficient association meant that papers in smaller Ontario cities – Hamilton and London, Ontario, for example – would be better equipped to offer their readers complete and up-to-date coverage of international and US news. But these were places where metropolitan papers competed aggressively, counting on the more extensive coverage they could afford to supplant local publications. Because a complete and efficient AP service available to all tended to level the Ontario playing field, the big Toronto dailies were cool if not outright hostile to it.[92] J.F. MacKay, CP Ltd.'s president, said in 1914 that it was "a matter of deep regret that a section of our membership has thought their interests would be better served by opposing the development of a strong and ably-manned national organization."[93] Offsetting this, though, was the metropolitan publishers' own need for guaranteed access to AP copy, which it seemed they could now continue to receive only if they helped to establish a national association as Stone demanded. There was thus a continuing tension between cooperation and competition, in which many Toronto papers opted for the smallest degree of cooperation that would achieve their limited ends.

The relationship between western Canadian newspapers, many of them members of WAP, and those in central Canada was even more difficult. Much as WAP was dominated by the Winnipeg papers, they had established a generally cooperative and productive relationship with other western newspapers, and the long struggle against the CPR had solidified their attachment. Thus, they were not eager to see WAP subsumed in a larger national organization in which they would be a minority. When CP Ltd. was founded, WAP's president expressed optimism that it would soon offer "a domestic news service covering the whole of Canada ... under the most favourable conditions as to economy and efficiency."[94] It quickly became apparent, though, that any systematic arrangement with the central Canadians would come at an unacceptable cost – "the virtual extinction" of WAP. To avoid this, the members of WAP spelled out that the new national organization "should exist solely as a franchise holding corporation" whose authority was limited to carrying out the contract with AP.[95] The western association argued that it should name half the members of the holding company's board of directors, eventually settling for one-third of the board members to represent the west and British Columbia. For domestic newsgathering, the westerners wanted the country divided in half, with the west and British Columbia exercising complete local control.[96] For different reasons, then, many publishers in both western and central Canada were content that CP Ltd. should have strictly limited responsibilities and powers.

Even so, the central and western publishers quickly came into conflict. Almost immediately they clashed over the issuing of new memberships, with the westerners insisting that they alone should decide whether to accept or reject any new applications for membership in their region. Other CP members objected. In 1911, CP Ltd.'s secretary, Atkinson of the Toronto *Star*, told WAP that its assertion of a veto over new memberships "goes too far ... the [western] Association has not the unlimited right, under our contract with the Associated Press, to refuse franchises."[97] The western publishers urgently appealed to Melville Stone, who replied that AP would not object to western Canadian members making decisions on new members in their territory. But he once again emphasized that AP's strategic interests must be protected: "He did not want existing newspapers in Canada to maintain a monopoly of the Associated Press service, to the extent of creating conditions which would give a rival news organization a foot-hold in Canada."[98]

No sooner was one problem between east and west resolved than another took its place. As noted above, the advent of CP Ltd. brought access to a much fuller news report in New York – thus potentially mitigating the shortage of British (and international) news about which many Canadian clients of AP complained. But the western papers could only get access to this material through cooperation with the east.

To take full advantage of the direct connection with AP headquarters, the members of CP Ltd. in Ontario and Quebec agreed to pay for a leased wire connecting New York, Montreal, Ottawa, Toronto, and London, Ontario. This was a telegraphic circuit dedicated entirely to the transmission of news material, paid for at an annual flat rate per mile instead of the cost-per-word basis applied to most telegraphic messages. As long as a sufficiently large volume of material was sent to make full use of its capacity, the per-word cost of material sent over a leased wire was much lower than under the message-rate tariff. In practice, costs for individual newspapers did not usually decline under a leased-wire arrangement, but they received much more material for their money. As newspapers increasingly depended on a steady supply of news-agency copy each day,[99] a position on a leased-wire circuit was essential.

Once this key connection was in place, publishers in Nova Scotia and New Brunswick, in the territory covered by WAP, and in British Columbia arranged leased-wire contracts of their own to receive the more desirable, and more extensive, version of AP's service that CP Ltd. was intended to provide. On 1 January 1912, WAP's night leased wire between Montreal and Winnipeg went into operation, and the circuit was soon extended to Regina, Saskatoon, Edmonton, Calgary, Moose Jaw, and Nelson, British Columbia. (A day leased wire from the east, which cost twice as much per mile, was still too expensive; the afternoon-paper members of WAP made do with a shorter leased-wire connection from Minneapolis to Winnipeg.) These leased wires and their operators accounted for more than 70 per cent of WAP's budget in 1913.[100] Similarly, the Eastern Press Association leased a night wire from Montreal to Moncton, Halifax, and Sydney, and the publishers of Vancouver and Victoria leased a night wire linking up with the WAP's western circuit at Calgary.[101] The eastern, western, and British Columbia associations adopted an inflexible and unforgiving cost structure that made sense only if they were guaranteed a regular and substantial supply of news relayed by the Ontario and Quebec publishers, who controlled the connection to New York. Thus, although the separate regional associations maintained their independence and often came into conflict, the organizational, technological, and cost requirements of telegraphic news drove them into a fundamental alliance. In 1912 the president of WAP noted that the leased wire and related arrangements had "a national as well as a newspaper value" in that they brought east and west "into more intimate relations."[102] But this was at best a secondary motivation; the impetus towards wider and more systematic connections had mainly to do with all the Canadian associations' demand for a steady flow of news from AP.

But the national news pipeline established through the leased-wire network could be used for Canadian news, too. A regular service of news from western Canada was part of WAP's compensation to the morning-paper publishers of central Canada in exchange for their New York AP service.[103] For an additional $65 a month, Edward Slack of the Montreal *Gazette* (who was also manager of the morning paper section of CP Ltd. in Ontario and Quebec) provided a digest of news from eastern Canada to WAP.[104] In New Brunswick and Nova Scotia, the Eastern Press Association publishers collectively paid about $200 a month for a combined service of international and domestic news from two Montreal papers–the *Gazette* for morning papers and the Montreal *Star* for afternoon papers.[105] This pattern of dominant metropolitan news-papers recycling their own supply of news to regional clients further down the telegraphic news pipeline was more or less identical to what the three Winnipeg papers had done in 1907 when they established WAP.

One of the most immediate national implications of the leased-wire network was expanded coverage of federal politics and the federal government in Ottawa. During the 1911 federal election campaign, WAP and CP Ltd. cooperated to provide "impartial summaries of speeches by party leaders, as well as a daily record of political developments," but were unable to coordinate their coverage of election returns on voting day.[106] In 1912 the western papers took a substantial step towards cooperation in national newsgathering when Wallace Dafoe, WAP's Ottawa correspondent, systematically coordinated his efforts with the Ottawa correspondents of the *Free Press*, Winnipeg *Telegram*, and Regina *Leader* to allow more extensive coverage by avoiding duplication on routine news events.[107] By 1915, morning-paper members of WAP routinely received around 4,000 words a day of Ottawa and eastern Canadian news over the leased-wire network, and when the House of Commons was in session the volume could reach 10,000 words a day. Afternoon papers, with no leased wire to the east, received only around 700 words a day from Ottawa.[108] Eastern Canadian publishers also expanded their Ottawa coverage, sharing the cost of the *Gazette*'s Ottawa–Montreal leased wire and arranging for the Eastern Press Association's Ottawa correspondent to coordinate his efforts with the *Gazette*'s Ottawa staff as the westerners had done.[109] The Canadian imagined community that took shape in the era of telegraphic news had the national government as a key focal point (as is also borne out by the content analysis of CP's news coverage in Chapter 7).[110]

While the leased-wire network created a de facto national organization at the level of transmission, editorial decision making was another matter. WAP relied on material made available by the Ontario and Quebec members of CP Ltd., but had no control over what they provided. As long as Slack was manager of CP Ltd.'s morning paper section, all went well. But when the position was taken over by C. Langton Clarke of the Toronto *Globe*, the situation deteriorated. It was bad enough that Clarke provided nowhere near the coverage of eastern Canadian news that Slack had done. Much more worrisome was the way CP Ltd. was handling – or mishandling – the AP material to which it had access in New York. In August 1914, just after the First

World War broke out and public interest in international news was at
its height, WAP complained that CP Ltd. was deliberately using the
New York service less effectively than it could. From the 100,000 words
available in New York every night, the selection of news for Toronto –
which went from there to Winnipeg and points west – was made not by
a dedicated editor, but by an editor-telegraph operator, producing an
"attenuated and inefficient service."[111] For example, a full report of the
speech of the British foreign secretary, Sir Edward Gray, to Parliament
just before war was declared – a speech that was of the keenest interest
to English-Canadian readers – had been duly sent to AP in New York.
But the version that reached Canadian papers was "very much muti-
lated," thanks to the telegrapher's carelessness and lack of journalistic
judgment. According to E.H. Macklin, the president of WAP, this was
not an isolated incident. On the contrary, it reflected a deliberate decision by the eastern members of CP Ltd. "to place this highly efficient
and world-wide standard service of telegraphic and cable news in the
position of a supplementary, subordinate, or auxiliary news service so
far as Canadian metropolitan newspapers are concerned."[112] Because
the wealthy dailies of Toronto and Montreal could afford various special news services of their own, they were using AP as "a merely pro-
tective service" rather than as "the standard service ... for their major
cable and telegraphic requirements." The Toronto *Star*, for example,
distributed UP to other Canadian papers and thus had an interest in
the widely available AP being less rather than more comprehensive;[113]
similarly, the *Star* and other Toronto papers that circulated throughout the province could maintain more of their extra-urban circulation if
their papers, larded with special coverage, stood out as sharply as possible from the more basic AP service. (CP Ltd. was not happy with the
arrangement either, claiming it was sending WAP "a mass of war news
in exchange for a very limited service from the west."[114]) Moreover,
the Ontario and Quebec section used the leased-wire circuit to carry
its own regional news as well as the AP file, and much of the former
was of no interest to the west.[115] The AP report for western morning
papers was so meagre, WAP complained, that it had to scalp INS and
UP reports from the previous day's Montreal evening papers to fill
it out.[116]

   WAP therefore turned away from its unsatisfactory formal connec-
tion with CP Ltd. and made a separate arrangement with the Montreal
Gazette. In addition to the AP report received in the *Gazette*'s offices,
WAP was to receive a further 10,000 words of cable news nightly from

the New York *Times* service and all the *Gazette*'s eastern Canadian specials for $125 a week, thus providing a sufficient volume of high-quality news to justify WAP's heavy spending on its leased wires.[117] Whether seen in the Toronto *Telegram*'s desire to dominate the over-all supply of news in Canada, the Winnipeg publishers' organizing of a news service for the west, or the *Gazette*'s new role, the Canadian telegraphic-news system continued to give large metropolitan dailies a prominent position. This model of news distribution persisted until the 1930s in Australia,[118] and, given the hostility and conflicting interests that divided Canadian newspaper publishers, it seemed probable that Canada would follow the same course.

However, AP's desire for the Canadians to establish a national cooperative that could be a strong and reliable ally exercised an equally strong influence. The US agency's unhappiness about how CP Ltd. was handling its affairs became evident when a delegation of Canadian publishers visited New York in July 1914 to discuss renewal of their contract. Stone, flanked by AP's assistant general manager, the chief of the news department, and the superintendent of the eastern service, told the Canadians that AP was highly dissatisfied with CP Ltd. and would not renew the contract unless major changes were made. "I have been impressed that The Canadian Press lacked central force," Stone told them.

> You are divided and subdivided and cross-divided. You have an independent morning service, you have an independent evening service, and the organization itself in its nature is more a federation than a united corporation. And all of these things have led to more or less difficulty in carrying out the terms of this contract along the lines that we all have anticipated. ... [T]hrough lack of central power and directing force we have found an incapacity, an inability in a number of cases to meet what we think were our just expectations.[119]

CP Ltd.'s failings cost AP money and undermined its competitive position in the US market. A particular complaint was that newspapers from the Maritime provinces did not provide an adequate service of return news. When shipping disasters occurred, "we have been forced back to the old plan of employing our own people up there and bringing in this [news] entirely independent of The Canadian Press."[120]

Edward Slack of the Montreal *Gazette*, who was in charge of CP Ltd.'s relations with its Maritime-province members, agreed that the return service was inadequate. But he urged Stone to consider the difficulties of cooperative newsgathering in Nova Scotia:

> Whenever a disaster occurs it is the hardest thing in the world for us to get anything out of Halifax until the Halifax people have reaped the harvest. ... So long as they can get specials [i.e., orders for special coverage] elsewhere, they will not give it to The Canadian Press, although the proprietors and people in connection with those papers are very anxious to give us a return for the news we give them. But ... the men who do the work are going to look out for themselves first, and The Canadian Press, Limited, from which they derive no personal return, is an after-consideration.[121]

This situation went to the heart of AP's concerns. One of the main functions of a wire service is to exploit and control the subsidiary uses of news.[122] Before the introduction of the telegraph, most papers had received their nonlocal news through the exchange system, simply reprinting items from other newspapers when they arrived in the mail.[123] It was haphazard; it meant that nonmetropolitan papers were always late in printing the news; and, crucially, it meant that (beyond the reciprocal right to publish exchange news from other sources) the original providers of the news received no recompense for its subsidiary use. With the advent of the telegraph, smaller newspapers could receive nonlocal news as quickly as metropolitan newspapers did – and therefore compete more effectively with them for local circulation.[124] But because the timely provision of this news had to be organized by someone,[125] and because it was delivered by telegraph (where its volume was closely monitored), a cost was now assigned to it. Moreover, restrictions were placed on how and when the news could be used (typically including a prohibition on the intermediate user reselling it further down the news chain). News became, much more systematically, a kind of property.

A peculiarity of cooperative news services such as AP and Canadian Press was that all its members were required to provide return news.[126] In this system, a newspaper would first gather the news of, say, a local shipping disaster for its own use – and then was required promptly to make this news available to the other members of the cooperative. Under the terms of its contract, CP Ltd. was obliged to provide this, in turn, to AP. Again, the subsidiary use of news had been regulated to the point that it became a kind of property.[127]

The Halifax situation that Slack described was, in effect, a struggle over who would reap the benefits from the subsidiary use of news.

Reporters and editors traditionally supplemented their income by acting as stringers, forwarding news they or their papers had already gathered to other papers out of town for payment. Like the exchange system, it was a haphazard and ad hoc arrangement. But under the AP bylaws – bylaws that CP Ltd. had adopted virtually without amendment – the rights to practically all subsidiary uses of news, whether provided by the cooperative or by an individual member, belonged to the organization. Unlike the exchange system or the reliance on stringers, it was systematic and, one might say, global – every member of a national association had the same rights to use news that was provided (under clearly spelled-out restrictions) and the same obligations to provide return news back to it.

The essence of Stone's complaint was that CP Ltd. did not have sufficient authority over its members to insist that these rights and obligations were respected. "You can never make a successful organization, in my judgment," he asserted,

> until you centralize your organization and have a man in the city of Toronto, or Montreal, or wherever you choose, who is a General Manager and has the power to say to The Halifax Chronicle, "You have got to give us this news," and if they don't, call them before your board and do as we do – punish them, fine them, expel them, compel them to do their duty.[128]

Failure to enforce the rules in Canada provided an opening that AP's competitors – UP, INS, or the Laffan service operated by the New York *Sun* – could exploit. Charles Kloeber, AP's chief of the news service, complained that to maintain adequate coverage of the Maritime provinces under the present conditions, AP would have to hire correspondents at Bathurst and Chatham, New Brunswick, and at Sydney, Nova Scotia. "There is no question that it can be done, because *The Sun* and United Press have men at those places ... and *The Sun* scooped us almost daily on its splendid and intelligent service." Stone repeated the point more emphatically when it was suggested that AP might suffer if it cut its connection with CP Ltd.: "We certainly have no reason to fear when with this alliance with The Canadian Press we find that *The New York Sun*, which has no connection up there, is able to beat us day after day. ... With all the resources of The Canadian Press on our side, they are beating us."[129]

Two members of the CP delegation, Slack and J.S. MacKay of the Toronto *Globe*, generally accepted Stone's criticisms – particularly since he emphasized that he did not expect the changes to happen overnight and that they should not involve any additional costs. But Macklin, who in addition to being vice president of CP was also president of WAP and general manager of the Winnipeg *Free Press*, objected strenuously. The imposition of a strong central authority would mean the submergence of WAP, something its members had been resisting since CP Ltd. was formed. In this case at least, local self-interest was as much at stake as regional solidarity. "The *Free Press* in Winnipeg pays one-half the cost of that wire that is leased [from Toronto to Winnipeg]," Macklin told Stone. "The [Winnipeg] *Telegram* pays the other half. Should I go before my Board of Directors and suggest that the administration of that wire that we pay for should be divided through a central authority in Toronto?"[130]

But all the Canadians were sobered by Stone's ultimatum, and they agreed to consider forming a more effective national organization. The committee charged with the task quickly reached an impasse, however. The main obstacle was the costly leased wire from Winnipeg to the east. The westerners argued that in exchange for surrendering their regional autonomy, the easterners should compensate them by assuming part of this cost, which they described as an essential link in a national system of news distribution. The refusal was categorical: "the newspapers of the East would not pay one cent towards the leased-wire cost of the service in the West."[131] (This was a slight exaggeration: in fact, the publishers of Ontario and Quebec were willing to share 15 per cent of the leased wire's cost on a national basis, partly in exchange for a regular supply of news from western Canada – but no more.[132]) Slack proposed that the west and British Columbia pay almost 50 per cent of the new organization's annual budget (estimated at $350,000), while Macklin would accept no more than 40 per cent.[133] This, Slack countered, meant that the newspapers of eastern and central Canada would relieve WAP's members of substantial expenses, "which amount will have to be paid by the Eastern papers for the privilege of nationalizing the Western section."[134] Unless some way could be found to close this substantial gap, there was no chance of a national news service being established.

With the outbreak of war in August 1914, economic conditions for newspaper publishers – particularly in the west – deteriorated sharply. E.H. Macklin, the president of WAP, described the problem succinctly: "increased expenditure in news gathering accompanied by decreased newspaper revenues."[135] While advertising revenue declined, extensive coverage of war news (including the telegraphing of long casualty lists) imposed significant additional costs.[136] The result was that, by 1915,

WAP was in serious trouble. In January alone, three member papers went out of business and a fourth abandoned its expensive leased-wire service, leaving only seven papers to share the heavy fixed cost of WAP's leased-wire connection to the east.[137] Even with a wartime gift from the CPR's telegraph department (a 20 per cent reduction in rates, expected to last until the end of the war), it was reluctantly decided that WAP would have to abandon the eastern leased wire and revert to a connection with Minneapolis, despite all its drawbacks – including much less Ottawa coverage and a smaller and much less appropriate selection of US and international news.[138] But before taking this step, WAP decided to appeal to the federal government for financial assistance to keep the Canadian line in operation.[139]

The war also brought CP Ltd. into an increasingly national role in relation to the federal government's management of information. The telegraph was a technology highly susceptible to control at strategic points, and the news-agency structure, in which one story was sent to numerous newspapers, accentuated this. By the summer of 1915, Canada's chief press censor, Ernest J. Chambers (a former newspaperman himself) had determined that CP Ltd. offered a very efficient means of press censorship.[140] Thus, after consulting a group of Toronto editors, Chambers appointed C.O. Knowles (manager of the Ontario and Quebec evening-paper section) and C. Langton Clarke (manager of its morning-paper counterpart) as press censors, following this within a few months by appointing J.F.B. Livesay, the general manager of WAP, as press censor for western Canada.[141] Newspapers' cooperation in a system of "voluntary censorship" was the basis of Chambers's approach; press censors were put in place to provide rulings on which stories might raise problems under the War Measures Act, but they had no powers of enforcement.[142] Mainstream Canadian publications found this a relatively satisfactory way to proceed, and there was certainly no indication that Knowles, Clarke, or Livesay saw the censor's role as problematic; Livesay in particular was praised as "a particularly keen and capable officer."[143] These appointments also cemented CP Ltd.'s role as the dominant news organization in Canada. Papers that were not members were instructed that anything carried by CP could be presumed to be acceptable; if they had questions, guidance should be sought from CP in Winnipeg or Toronto.[144] Although the United States had not yet entered the war, and despite the near-universal view among Canadian publishers that AP presented too much of an American view of world events, Chambers did not consider CP Ltd.'s reliance on AP a problem.[145] However, the CP Ltd. censors supported the decision in November 1916 to ban Hearst's INS from Canada on grounds of pro-German bias.[146]

The appointment of war correspondents was a second area where CP Ltd.'s national role was emphasized. Early in 1915, the prime minister, Robert Borden, corresponded with CP Ltd. about the appointment of a Canadian correspondent at the front. A group of CP representatives met the prime minister and informed him that they could not afford to do this alone, suggesting that it might be possible if the government paid the correspondent's travel and cable costs.[147] The government eventually agreed to a subsidy of $400 a week, but in February 1917 the directors of CP Ltd. performed an about-face, rejecting the subsidy in some disarray and appointing Stewart Lyon of the *Globe* as the first CP Ltd. war correspondent.[148] French-English tensions over Canada's participation in the war also arose on at least one occasion, when representatives of *La Patrie* and *Le Devoir* complained that a riot by Laval University students in October 1915 was improperly characterized by CP as an antirecruitment event, and was "deliberately distorted in order to bring discredit on the French element of the province of Quebec."[149] (Knowles defended the work of CP Ltd.'s reporter on the story.)

The telegraphing of increasingly heavy casualty lists from Ottawa also brought CP Ltd. and the government into discussions. In 1916, Knowles and John W. Dafoe of the Winnipeg *Free Press* suggested to Borden that the government pay the costs of telegraphing the lists by commercial wire. (In Australia, where the telegraph network was state controlled, the lists were delivered to newspapers free.) Borden refused, and proposed that the lists be mailed by special delivery, which was eventually the solution adopted.[150] Taken together, the various contacts with CP Ltd. during the war show clearly that the Canadian government – like most governments in the British Empire[151] – was interested in having extensive coverage of the war effort, and was willing to offer subsidies in some circumstances to accomplish this. CP Ltd., for its part, was inconsistent, sometimes soliciting subsidies and sometimes rejecting them when offered.[152]

WAP's appeal for government support to maintain its Toronto–Winnipeg leased wire was the biggest subsidy request of all. The memorandum in support of the request stressed heavily the national purposes the leased wire served. Reverting to a Minneapolis connection "must be detrimental to the national interests of Canada by making Western Canada more and more dependent on United States sources of news and by seriously limiting the volume of news from Eastern Canada and diminishing the flow of Western news to the East."[153] At a time when Canada was deeply involved in the war and the United States was still neutral, arguments based on national sentiment had particular weight. The importance of providing western readers with a complete account of wartime parliamentary proceedings in Ottawa was particularly stressed – the forthcoming session would be "an occasion of the greatest importance to the public and newspapers of western Canada," but if the leased wire was abandoned, "the full and accurate parliamentary report would have to be dropped; and the people of the West would be served, as was the case some years ago, with a synopsis, much abbreviated, of parliamentary proceedings."[154] WAP maintained its own correspondent in Ottawa, and already during the war this connection "has been utilized to the advantage of the government and public – with respect to matters affecting the raising of troops, the furtherance of the patriotism and production campaign, etc."

The American character of the AP service from Minneapolis was particularly emphasized:

[T]he reports relating to international or imperial affairs were those which had been prepared, in the first instance, for the American public and were in many respects not equally acceptable, by reason of omissions or coloration, perhaps wholly unconscious, to Canadian readers. ... American news – political, commercial and industrial – bulked much larger than was necessary or desirable in a news service intended for papers published in Canada. ... [T]his must tend to the Americanization of the [ethnically] mixed population of the west and loss to the Canadian national ideal.[155]

To avoid this unfortunate result, the federal government was asked to make available, 24 hours a day, a state-owned telegraph line between Ottawa and Winnipeg for the exchange of news between eastern and western Canada. The petition did not state that this would also overcome the financial obstacle preventing the formation of a national news organization, thereby averting the threat of losing the AP service.

War pressures initially seemed to dictate delay in the question of a government subsidy. Borden; the finance minister, Sir Thomas White (the half-brother of M.E. Nichols of WAP and the Winnipeg *Telegram*); and the minister of public works (and key western political organizer), Robert Rogers, were all approached by politically well-connected western newspapermen during 1915 and 1916. The politicians showed some sympathy to the approach, but insisted that nothing could be done while an increasingly costly, bloody, and divisive war made ever-greater claims on the government's attention and revenue. Furthermore, while the petition would have a much better chance if the Ontario and Quebec publishers endorsed it as well, that seemed unlikely. "Through all these extended negotiations," Macklin told WAP members in October 1916, "the attitude of eastern publishers had not encouraged us to expect that they would support us in obtaining a Dominion subsidy on the lines of our application."[156]

Soon after this cautious assessment, though, it became apparent that the government saw the formation of a functioning national news service as a higher priority. In the fall of 1916, Livesay travelled to Ottawa in another effort to find a way of lowering the cost of transmitting casualty lists to the west and was informed that the government was now prepared to consider the leased-wire subsidy favourably.[157] WAP then decided to send Livesay personally to cover a recruiting trip across western Canada by Borden and R.B. Bennett, the director of selective service, in November and December. In an unpublished memoir written years later, Livesay recalled that "Macklin sent me on that trip with deliberate purpose and it was not long before I opened up, first through the receptive [Loring] Christie,[158] the subject of a national news service. Sir Robert was immediately interested."[159] At the end of December, Livesay reported to J.H. Woods of the Calgary *Herald* that he had received "very reassuring expression of opinion from [Borden] personally. We expect government will grant subsidy for Ottawa–Winnipeg 24-hour leased wire and that this will pave way for formation of national organization."[160] Macklin added that, based on Borden's comments to Livesay, "I think ... that this business is going through with a whoop, even if it meets with some scattered opposition from eastern publishers. But as we are sincere in expecting that the granting of this money will lead immediately to the formation of a national organization for its administration, I do not see that they can object seriously."[161]

While Borden's recruiting trip helped bring CP's claims to the fore near the end of 1916, developments in the British government's wartime propaganda efforts may also have played a role. Earlier that year, Reuters had begun sending a government-supported, semi-propagandistic news service around the world (including to Canada and the other British dominions); its main purpose was to ensure that British politicians' speeches and other official statements were widely and promptly disseminated, along with news of war efforts in the British dominions and colonies.[162] In November and early December of 1916, Reuters was reorganized under direct government control because of severe financial problems and concerns that it might fall into hands that were not favourable to the British war effort; this secret takeover lasted until 1919.[163]

As the war dragged on, the military contribution of Canada and the other British dominions and colonies took on greater importance, reflected by David Lloyd George's inclusion of dominion prime ministers in the Imperial War Cabinet.[164] Under these circumstances, an expanded inter-imperial news service was seen as an important way to maintain enthusiasm, especially for recruiting, as demands for manpower at the front became more urgent and harder to meet. The previously established "Agence Reuter" service was augmented in March 1917, with a Supplementary Imperial Service that was particularly intended to strengthen morale throughout the empire.[165] In Canada, this service, amounting to around 20,000 words a month, was delivered free of charge to the CP bureau in Ottawa, where editors distributed as much of it as they considered newsworthy. CP highly valued the service, and had no concerns about using it as long as its editors ultimately decided what to retransmit.[166]

No evidence has been found of a direct connection between the new imperial news service, the secret British government takeover of Reuters, or Lloyd George's accession to the prime minister's office, on the one hand, and the subsidy to Canadian Press on the other. But Borden must have been aware that subsidized news services were becoming an important aspect of imperial strategy, and might have wanted to make it easier to distribute the new pro-war imperial news service effectively across Canada.[167] Certainly the service was considered valuable by CP; when the Second World War broke out, one of its first concerns was to see whether it would be renewed.[168]

In any event, by late December of 1916 the question of a government subsidy for a leased wire between Winnipeg and central Canada had moved near the top of the political agenda. WAP asked for a subsidy of $32,500 a year to cover the cost of a 24-hour Winnipeg–Ottawa leased wire; the sections from Calgary to Vancouver and Montreal to Saint John were not included. Once it became clear that a subsidy was going to be granted, the Ontario and Quebec publishers realized that this offered a way out of the east–west cost impasse, and thus a way to meet AP's requirement that they form a national organization. Some expressed unease about the idea of a subsidy – Robertson was opposed, and Atkinson later resigned as CP Ltd.'s secretary-treasurer, apparently over this issue[169] – but they were a distinct minority.

As a manifestation of this newfound unity, Slack, now the president of CP Ltd., agreed to present the westerners' petition on behalf of the whole national organization, and on 16 January 1917, the publishers' delegation met a group of ministers, including Borden, Rogers, Solicitor-General Arthur Meighen, and Senator James Lougheed. (In a draft of his memoirs, Livesay gave particular credit to "the public-spirited assistance of that good Westerner," Rogers.[170]) W.A. Buchanan, a Liberal member of Parliament (MP), publisher of the Lethbridge *Herald,* and a member of the WAP delegation, emphasized "the large foreign population in the west and the national importance of assimilating them and turning them into good subjects." This, he said, could only be done by providing "a national Canadian, British and world service of news ... educating them along the lines of national solidarity." He referred to "the danger now of penetration by American news into Southern Alberta and Southern British Columbia."[171] The petition repeated the wording of a year earlier about pro-American "omissions or coloration, no doubt wholly unconscious" in AP coverage and the warning that this must lead to "the Americanization of the mixed population of the West and loss to the Canadian national ideal."

Somewhat to the petitioners' surprise, the government suggested it would be willing to pay more than was requested, enough to cover the cost of a 24-hour Winnipeg–Ottawa leased wire and the Montreal–Saint John and Calgary–Vancouver connections.[172] Rogers volunteered the opinion that the wire could hardly be considered "national" otherwise, a view supported by Lougheed and Martin Burrell, the minister of agriculture. (A forceful complaint on behalf of British Columbia publishers about being left to pay for their own telegraphic connection to Winnipeg may have had an effect, too.[173]) A Finance Ministry document outlining the reasons for the grant noted that CP Ltd. was a nonprofit cooperative representing almost all daily newspapers in Canada, and that the purpose of the subsidy was to provide leased-wire connections "over the three great natural gaps" in the Canadian telegraphic network, connections that the newspapers had initially tried to pay for themselves but "found the cost ... prohibitive," especially in the west. The alternative, in which eastern and western papers would rely on AP service delivered at Bangor, Minneapolis, and Seattle, was unacceptable:

> By this means Western and Eastern papers would secure only a small percentage of Canadian news and then it would be written from the viewpoint of the American rather than the Canadian reader. On the other hand for the purpose of maintaining unity between the east and the west and a proper understanding of national difficulties and problems it is desirable to maintain a national news service covering the country from coast to coast.[174]

The words might have been taken directly from CP Ltd.'s petition.

Clearly, the government had decided that it wanted a trans-Canada news agency and was willing to help pay for it; an annual subsidy of $50,000 was accordingly granted. This, as Macklin had predicted in December, would "overcome one great obstacle to the creation of the national news organization ... for it removes the bone of contention between east and west as to the apportioning of the cost of this long stretch of unproductive wire. ... [W]ith the above matter settled, an agreement for an equitable division of the cost among individual newspapers and districts could be quickly reached."[175] Macklin was right. With the Winnipeg leased-wire cost removed from contention, a financial basis for forming a national association was quickly agreed upon.[176]

In their appeal to the government, the publishers and senior editors expressed complicated, and somewhat contradictory, attitudes towards AP. While making the dangers of Americanized news the centrepiece of their appeal, they also went out of their way to praise AP:

> The foregoing references, of course, are not to be regarded as reflecting in the slightest measure upon the integrity, impartiality and capacity of the American Associated Press. The Canadian newspapers, by their arrangement with the Associated Press, have been given access to a service of world's news unsurpassed in scope and volume, high in character, accurate in every department and scrupulously honest in its treatment of war news. The Canadian daily newspapers and the Canadian public are unquestionably under deep obligations to this great American newsgathering organization.[177]

From CP's point of view, one of the main purposes of the government subsidy was to allow the connection with AP to continue, not to replace it.

Despite these complimentary words, CP Ltd.'s relations with its ally were deteriorating on another front. In June 1917, AP's executive committee met five leading figures of the Canadian association in New York to lodge a series of complaints. Slack insisted that the return news service from western Canada was much improved, but acknowledged that service from the east remained "very bad."[178] (AP's own internal report described it as "lamentably weak," noting that AP was now spending several hundred dollars a month on Canadian stringers to make up for CP's failings.[179]) Far more serious was AP's charge that two members of the new association – the Montreal *Star* and Toronto *Star*–were continuing their connection with UP to AP's detriment. The Montreal paper was said to be operating the Dominion News Service, which combined AP, UP, and CP copy and sent it out to other Canadian clients; worst of all, it also allowed a UP telegraph operator in its office to send AP material back into the United States.[180]

Cost issues were never far from the surface either – besides the problem of the UP operator in its newsroom, the Montreal *Star* paid much more for UP than for AP. (Stone had complained to CP's annual meeting a few days earlier that while the average AP member in the United States paid $40 a week for the service, the 86 evening papers in Canada collectively paid a total of $62.50.[181]) Internally, a senior AP journalist wondered why AP bothered to keep dealing with the Canadian association at all, instead of simply signing separate contracts with individual publications, as it did in Mexico or Cuba.[182] Charles Crandall of the Montreal *Star* denied that he was selling a combined AP–UP service elsewhere in Canada, but admitted that AP material had been regularly sent back into the United States until three months earlier. In the face of these grave concerns – failure to protect the AP report from UP had been the reason for the CPR's loss of the contract in 1910 – renewal of the contract was postponed. The Canadians objected to Stone's statement that it would continue only on a probationary basis; he withdrew the objectionable term, but everyone knew what was at stake.[183]

In this atmosphere of uncertainty, the new national organization got under way during the summer of 1917 – though not without further manifestations of the sectional tensions that had been such a prominent feature of the previous decade. The national news service over leased wires between Saint John and Vancouver was inaugurated on Sunday,

2 September, with messages from the prime minister and several provincial premiers sent across the country.[184] Borden said the service would be "the means of bringing into closer touch widely separated communities; make their people more familiar with the ideals and aims of other Provinces or districts; assist in bringing mutual understanding to all, and thus aid in the growth of a national consciousness and a truly national spirit."[185] C.O. Knowles, Robertson's right-hand man at the *Telegram*, was appointed general manager; Livesay, who had been general manager of WAP, was named assistant general manager, based in Winnipeg, (at almost the same salary).[186] A proposal to move headquarters from Montreal to Toronto was defeated, but when the Toronto-based Knowles complained that a move would be "a great financial embarrassment" it was agreed he could remain there for the time being (a decision that was never rescinded). Atkinson insisted on specifying that if the subsidy were withdrawn, the western, British Columbia, and Maritime sections would be responsible for the full cost of the leased wires in their regions.

One hundred and seventeen newspapers were listed as members, including dozens that had not previously been involved in CP Ltd. or had otherwise received a regular supply of telegraphic news. The new association had 43 editorial and administrative employees and 14 telegraph operators in eight bureaus (Halifax, Montreal, Ottawa, Toronto, New York, Winnipeg, Calgary, and Vancouver). The annual cost of the leased-wire news service ranged from $1,850 for the Brantford (Ontario) *Expositor* to $6,016 for the Vancouver *World*. About one-third of members took the much more limited (and cheaper) pony service, whose ultimate cost depended on wordage.[187] The new association brought together newspapers whose revenue and ability and willingness to pay for news varied greatly; the challenge of developing a service that met the requirements of (and could be afforded by) all was a permanent feature of its operations.

Tensions between the Toronto-based Robertson–Atkinson alliance (whose representative, Knowles, had been made general manager) and other CP members came to a head in 1919, soon after John Ross Robertson's death. Immediately after the annual meeting, the board of directors decided – for reasons having to do with "matters of internal administration" that were not otherwise spelled out – that Knowles should be placed on indefinite leave of absence and Livesay should take over as acting general manager.[188] Livesay, who had known of the possibility for a few months and had some initial misgivings about replacing his friend, Knowles, was delighted once the change was made: "The battle is over and victory won!" he told his wife a few days later.[189] "I jumped into the job with both feet." Within two weeks, a major reorganization of the news service, involving considerable new spending, was under way, including a strengthening of the editorial staff in Ottawa and New York; the incorporation of new telegraphic circuits and reorganization of existing lines between Montreal and Sydney, Nova Scotia; an improved standard of editing; a 25 per cent increase in the volume of daily copy; an end to the "chaotic" situation in Montreal where the CP night report for the eastern provinces was edited in the offices of the Montreal *Gazette* and the day report in the offices of the *Star*; the appointment of a new Halifax superintendent; and a promise to deal promptly and constructively with all complaints – all of which suggested considerable dissatisfaction with Knowles's leadership.[190]

The removal of Knowles led to a state of more or less open warfare between the Toronto *Star* and *Telegram* and almost all other CP Ltd. members.[191] Irving Robertson, who took over the *Telegram* after his father's death, did everything in his power to punish CP for its decision. For example, soon after Knowles was named general manager of CP Ltd., Robertson also put him in charge of CAP, which made it possible to merge the two operations and allowed CP Ltd. to receive the CAP subsidy for cabled material from London. Once Knowles no longer had the CP Ltd. job, however, Robertson insisted that CAP would not answer to his replacement, Livesay, leaving CP Ltd. with no control over CAP's editorial staff, finances, or decisions.[192]

On another front, John Bone of the *Star* proposed to the board in May 1920 a new cost structure that would shift $21,000 in annual costs from Ontario and Quebec papers to those in the Maritimes and the west.[193] But publishers of other big dailies in Montreal, Toronto, and Ottawa opposed the plan. Higher costs for the Maritime members would force between four and six smaller papers in the eastern section to drop their leased-wire service, Crandall of the Montreal *Star* observed, and those that remained would be unable to carry the additional burden. Stewart Lyon explained that although the *Globe* would save $1,500 a year under Bone's plan, he opposed it:

> This national association was not a cold-blooded affair of dollars and cents. It was formed to give the news of all Canada to the people of all Canada. The natural place whence the Maritime membership should get their news service was Bangor, Maine, Ontario and Quebec members

from Buffalo and Detroit, prairie members from Minneapolis, and British Columbia members from Seattle. Such were the economical sources of news supply. Why was not this done? Because this association of all the daily newspapers of Canada had stood from the first for a national, trans-Canada news connection that should aid in the building up of Canada as a nation. That was a laudable object. Mr. Lyon added, speaking on behalf of what he believed was the majority of Ontario publishers, that they were well content to pay if need be twelve thousand dollars a year to help the west carry its heavy burden of mileage and sparsely settled territory.[194]

Ottawa newspapers would also benefit under Bone's proposal, but E. Norman Smith of the *Journal* opposed it as well. The proposed rate increases for Maritime and western papers "meant the final collapse of the national organization, and when that came about control of the news service would remain in the hands of a few strong metro-politan papers. Such a plan was not in the interest of a single one of the smaller papers."[195] The national rhetoric used cannot be discounted entirely – Lyon was at least willing to pay for his convictions. Ultimately, though, the logic of his and Smith's position was that larger papers had an interest in maintaining the largest possible membership. This was a way of keeping average costs lower, thereby guaranteeing CP Ltd.'s nationwide reach and nationwide return-news coverage. The alliance against Robertson and Atkinson between the other big-city dailies and smaller papers in the east and west was decisive: Bone's proposal was roundly defeated by a vote of 72 to 13, with the minority comprising the *Star*, *Telegram*, and 11 smaller Ontario dailies.

This represented the final defeat of Robertson's hope to dominate the distribution of national and international news in Canada, dating back to 1904 and the founding of CAP. Since 1894, the question of what shape the Canadian news system would take had been contested among a range of powerful and competing interests. Big-city papers were, at some level, united against their small-town competitors (and vice versa). But their interests also diverged in important ways: morning and afternoon papers wanted different things, and even within the big-city group it often seemed as if it was a case of Toronto against everyone else. Publishers in western Canada, the Maritimes, and central provinces often aligned according to regional interest. Powerful journalistic institutions from outside Canada, notably AP and Reuters, tried (more successfully for AP than Reuters, it must be acknowledged) to shape the Canadian system in their preferred image; non-journalistic institutions such as the CPR and the Canadian government pursued their own goals as well.

Ultimately, though, publishers across Canada had one goal in common: to receive the best quality and largest quantity of telegraphic news possible at the lowest possible cost. It was this combination of volume, quality, and very low cost – already apparent in 1894 – that accounted for AP's leverage in Canada. Once the CPR was forced from the field, the organization of a steady supply of telegraphic news across Canada inexorably pushed publishers from all sections of Canada to work together. If the manner in which they did so was frequently antagonistic, that did not erase the very real core of common interest. AP, for its part, had a clear sense of what it wanted to achieve in Canada. Despite Melville Stone's gratitude to the CPR for its help in AP's battle against Western Union in the 1890s, he had more or less decided by 1901 that the publishers, not the railway, should control the news system in Canada – and that AP should maintain strong control over how that was to be done. AP's insistence that the Canadian publishers operate as a national unit was one of the most important reasons for their ending up that way.

A national government that wanted more extensive war coverage – both of events in Europe and in Canada – provided the final piece of the puzzle. Much as the Canadian publishers were driven to make serious efforts towards forming a national association by their desire to keep the AP service, they could not agree on the distribution of costs. As much as it bridged the physical gaps in the national leased-wire network, the $50,000 federal subsidy (50 per cent more than had initially been requested, it should be remembered) also bridged a stubborn gap between competing visions of how costs could fairly be allocated – of what, in the practical calculus of dollars and cents, it meant to be "national."

The weaknesses of the national news organization that was established through the intersection of these different interests were obvious. A government subsidy granted in conditions of wartime emergency was not the firmest possible foundation; besides, many publishers were opposed to subsidies on principle. The tensions between east and west, and between big cities and small towns, were more or less permanent sources of discord. CP Ltd.'s reliance on AP's voluminous and cheap supply of news left it with very little clout in dealings with the senior partner, and the modest financial circumstances of many smaller papers meant this was unlikely to change.

Yet the new organization had some notable strengths as well. The cooperative structure that was more or less imposed by AP was far from perfect, but it was certainly an improvement over control by the CPR or the Toronto cabal of Atkinson and Robertson. The newspapers now collectively controlled their association and the news it provided on a basis of one paper, one vote, and this guaranteed a degree of accountability. The inclusion of a large number of smaller papers meant a permanent bias towards penny-pinching; but through the return news policy of the cooperative, it also meant (in theory, at least) quite complete geographical coverage of the country. Also, the large number of members provided a solid basis for handling and sharing the association's continuing costs – it meant, in effect, more news for everyone, for less money – and weathering periods of economic difficulty. After years of shifting and inconsistent leadership, there was a general manager firmly in charge, supported by most (if not all) of the directors. The close alliance with AP had advantages other than cost, notably the valuable right to select news for Canada from the very large pool that arrived daily in New York, rather than accepting the choices made by AP editors there who were solely concerned with their US members. These fundamental strengths and weaknesses provided the foundation for CP's attempts at consolidation in the 1920s and 1930s.

2 Subsidies and Survival

The pursuit, acceptance, and eventual loss of government subsidies was one of the most contentious issues to face Canadian Press in its first decade of operation. A complicated mixture of often conflicting considerations was involved: questions of principle and journalistic ethics; of imperial, national, and regional identity; of commercial competition and advantage; and, to some extent, of personal antipathy. As a result, CP's position on subsidies was unstable and often unclear. In the few extant histories, the early quest for and acceptance of subsidies is seen as a short-lived anomaly, the withdrawal of the last federal subsidy in 1924 is depicted as almost a welcome relief, and CP's refusal to seek further subsidies after that date is a point of pride.[1] Yet the reliance on and uneasy pursuit of subsidies in CP's early years throws valuable light on the tensions that defined the organization, on prevailing conceptions of what it meant to be a "free press," and on how national and imperial identities were supposed to be expressed in a news system that was (CP's cooperative structure notwithstanding) characterized by the search for private profit.

One strand of the subsidy debate focused specifically on news of the British Empire. As was noted in Chapter 1, a group of larger Canadian newspapers had been receiving a subsidy to help defray the cost of transmitting news from Britain via the Atlantic cable since 1904; the amount of this grant, made to Canadian Associated Press (a separate organization controlled by John Ross Robertson of the Toronto *Telegram*) ranged from $5,000 to more than $12,000 but stabilized at $8,000 from 1916 onward.[2] The argument in favour of the subsidy had always been that, for all the value of the international news provided by CP's close ally, AP, it was intended primarily for American newspapers and readers and gave short shrift to British and imperial news from London that would be of special interest to Canadians. The subsidy was chiefly meant to offset the high charges for transatlantic cable transmission.

In 1916 and 1917, as the First World War became an increasingly difficult and costly struggle, the British government took steps to establish a subsidized, semi-propagandistic news service for the whole British Empire.[3] This was clearly a wartime measure, though, and a proposal to establish a permanent imperial news service for the postwar period was considered by the Imperial War Conference in London in July 1918.[4] The plan was developed by Lord Beaverbrook (the Canadian newspaper publisher and politician Max Aitken), British minister of information since early 1918; his chief Canadian collaborator was N.W. Rowell, the Ontario Liberal who had joined Sir Robert Borden's Unionist government only a few months earlier and was a strong supporter of closer imperial ties through enhanced news coverage.[5] Arguing that "the state of affairs by which, as at present, several of the Dominions depend largely for their news service on foreign services is a thoroughly wrong one," Beaverbrook proposed that the Ministry of Information arrange with "some agency" (clearly a reference to Reuters, whose managing director, Roderick Jones, was now acting as director of propaganda for the ministry[6]) to collect news from all British dominions and colonies at the government's expense. This would be pooled in London and made available to dominion press representatives who, with the aid of additional subsidies from their governments, would forward it to their respective countries.

Shortly before the conference, Borden informed Edward Slack, the president of Canadian Press Ltd., that the creation of a more permanent imperial news service "and the expediency of State assistance thereto" was going to be discussed, and asked for confidential suggestions on the subject.[7] In response, Slack presented familiar arguments about the importance of Canadians having an alternative to AP for coverage of British and imperial news, but his assumptions about Canadian newspapers' willingness to pay for this were revealing.

> Giving the public what it should want has never made a newspaper successful. Giving it what it wants has always been the key to success. ... until publishers find it profitable to supply a demand, whatever demand there is will go unsatisfied. ... It is not, therefore, fair to expect that the publishers of newspapers should shoulder the cost of educating public opinion as it must be educated.[8]

If the newspapers of Canada were to promote "unification of the Empire," they would have to receive government assistance to do so.

The Imperial War Conference agreed that an "adequate" news service along the lines suggested by Beaverbrook should be made available in all parts of the empire, and the British government was asked to develop a plan for consideration by all the governments involved.[9] Rowell, however, warned that Canadian publishers were not as enthusiastic about subsidies as Slack's earlier communication seemed to suggest, telling Borden that "our newspaper men" had discussed the British proposal and were "hostile to any government control or direction."[10]

This scheme did not come to fruition, and after Beaverbrook's resignation as minister in October 1918 the British government dropped the idea.[11] But in the spring of 1919, Roderick Jones – who had since resigned from the Ministry of Information in the face of allegations of conflict of interest and returned full time to Reuters – presented a comprehensive proposal "for Canadian publicity" to the Canadian Mission in London, a plan he had drawn up at the invitation of Canadian officials.[12] (When taking over as managing director of Reuters in 1916, Jones had identified expansion in Canada as one of his chief goals.[13]) Although it did not apply to the whole empire, the new proposal was similar to Beaverbrook's plan in several respects as far as Canada was concerned. It provided for 25,000 words a month of British and imperial news to be sent to Canada by cable and a return flow of Canadian news and publicity to London, to be distributed free to papers in the United Kingdom and the other dominions. A full-time Reuters representative in Ottawa would "superintend and conduct the amplification of the service of Canadian news to London. ... This correspondent will be, in effect, publicity officer for the Dominion of Canada." M.E. Nichols, who was one of CP's founders and had been appointed director of information in Ottawa, recommended the Jones proposal to the cabinet.[14] The creation of an imperial news service for Canada, he observed, would require "the close and sympathetic consideration of the Canadian newspapers who should be a party to the negotiations," while the publicity effort could be approved more simply by the government on its own initiative. Nichols made a strong case about the difficulties of relying solely on AP:

> [A]fter the United States entered the war, the great bulk of war news printed in the average Canadian newspaper told how American soldiers were waging war. The Peace Conference as reported by the American Associated Press centred largely on President Wilson, and the questions

at issue were naturally discussed from the American viewpoint. ... [These examples are] typical of its treatment of international affairs generally.

Issues such as Irish home rule, unrest in India or Egypt, and Anglo-American trade disputes expected to arise after the war "should not be presented to the Canadian people through United States spectacles. ... there was probably never more need of full and reliable presentation of British and Imperial news to the Canadian people than there is at the present time." But instead of the Canadian government paying the whole cost of an expanded imperial news service (estimated at $90,000 a year), Nichols proposed that the Colonial Office should contribute as well. As for the eventual recipients, "[i]t is highly improbable that Canadian newspapers would bear any portion of the financial burden."

In fact, CP members had more serious misgivings about the plan, focusing on Reuters' involvement and the proposed British subsidy. In August, the colonial secretary (the ardent imperialist Alfred Milner) indicated British willingness to contribute, on condition that "the selection of news to be left to Reuters' discretion, *subject to any instructions which may be given* [by the government] *in special circumstances* and subject to general condition that no sporting news, or news not of national importance may be sent on Government account."[15] CP, however, would reject "any arrangement ... unless they have the entire responsibility for the selection of news to be carried."[16] A subsidy that brought government involvement in editorial decisions was clearly not acceptable. Unwilling to let the idea die, the Colonial Office suggested that the new service might use the "machinery of Canadian Associated Press," presumably more welcome to the Canadian publishers who had long been involved with it. But since CAP had no newsgathering operation outside London, it would have to make arrangements with "such an organization as Reuters as would ensure ... Imperial character of news sent and its adequacy for purpose in view."[17]

The debate over this proposal at CP's 1919 annual meeting was marked by tortuous, but revealing, arguments about the idea of a subsidy. Some, like John Bone of the Toronto *Star*, urged simply that no further subsidies be sought or accepted; the *Star* had also opposed the 1917 subsidy for the domestic leased-wire network and was at least consistent in its views. Others, including Slack, Stewart Lyon of the Toronto *Globe*, and Charles Crandall of the Montreal *Star*, stated that they were against subsidies in principle and then explained why the principle did not apply in this case. One common argument was that large metropolitan papers might well reject subsidies, because they could afford adequate news services without them; but if smaller papers were held to the same standard, their readers would suffer from a lack of British and imperial news. Thus Slack said that "the strength of the Canadian Press was no more than that of its weakest members, that these already carried a heavy burden, and so it was impossible to inaugurate such a cable service as was proposed without Government aid."[18] J.H. Woods of the Calgary *Herald* went so far as to say that if the big-city papers rejected subsidized imperial news, they were obligated to supply their smaller counterparts with an equivalent service. Some compared the new proposal to the $50,000 subsidy that CP had already accepted, and was still receiving, to pay for leased wires across Canada. "[T]o overcome a fault in nature the Government had bridged the gap in Canada between East and West," Crandall argued, "and now for a like reason it was proposed to bridge the gap across the Atlantic." But in a further distinction between appropriate and inappropriate subsides, he urged CP to accept funds only from the Canadian, and not from the British, government – presumably because of the latter's intimate involvement with Reuters in producing wartime propaganda. It was eventually agreed that CP would contribute a maximum of $15,000 a year for an expanded cable-news service from London, doubling the amount that Canadian newspapers had been paying until now for CAP. With an additional $60,000 a year from the Canadian government or both governments jointly, 2,000 words a day of British and imperial news could be transmitted. CP would work with Reuters editors in London as it already did with AP in New York, selecting the stories for cable transmission that would be of most interest to Canadian readers. (CP already had access to all the Reuters material received in New York under its contract with AP, but had no influence on what was selected for transmission from London; as a result, items of interest to Canada were often missed or given low priority.) Having representatives at the sending end of the telegraphic news pipeline, whether New York or London, was seen as the best way for a smaller national agency to exercise meaningful control over the news received from a larger international partner.[19] In this way, Canada could be both British and independent. Melville Stone, the general manager of AP, was kept informed of the discussions, and indicated his approval: "the fact that Canada is allied to her mother country" should have no effect on "our warm feeling for you," he told Slack.[20]

In reporting CP's decision to Rowell, Slack repeated that "while several of our members objected to subsidies on principle, yet it was generally recognized that the newspapers of Canada owed it to the people to seize upon every opportunity for the betterment of the news services between Canada and the Motherland."[21] Many of those who objected to subsidies on principle were willing to forego their opposition because

> such assistance provides the only method of meeting the difficulties with which we are confronted in operating under a non-profit and co-operative basis. ... the rapid increase in the cost of doing business has, in the last few months, so materially added to the burden that our smaller newspapers have to bear, that it is quite impossible to ask them to consider the payment of anything beyond that which they are liable for under the $15,000 appropriation.

Big-city papers, then, could operate on a strictly commercial basis, while adequate coverage in smaller newspapers was presented as a kind of public service that would not be forthcoming without government support. It is striking that the very conception of the press as an independent, privately owned, and profit-seeking institution differed so substantially between large and small markets.[22]

CP's new proposal was generally acceptable to both governments, though the amount to be paid by each was reduced to $20,000 a year. In a testament to the Canadian government's eagerness to proceed, this sum was actually included in the spending estimates for 1920–21, even though the contract with CP Ltd. had not yet been signed.[23] At this point, though, a small wrinkle threatened to derail the proceedings, illustrating how fragile the CP compromise was. Through a clerical error, the government estimates stated that the subsidy was to go to Canadian Associated Press (still controlled by Irving Robertson of the Toronto *Telegram*, one of the fiercest opponents of a subsidy) rather than CP Ltd. This brought a letter of protest from Robertson to Rowell, complaining about being offered a subsidy he had not requested and did not want.[24] CP's new president, Norman Smith of the Ottawa *Journal*, assured Rowell that Robertson was only a minority voice, but this was not entirely accurate; many CP members were uncomfortable with the idea of a British subsidy in particular and others continued a rearguard action against any subsidies at all. At the 1920 annual meeting, John Dafoe of the Manitoba *Free Press* tried to mollify objectors. Since Canadian publishers had already been receiving a subsidy through CAP for the past 15 years, he argued, it was hard to see how an increase in the amount would suddenly "corrupt the press of Canada." But Crandall observed that British and Australian publishers "were just as strongly opposed to Government cash subsidies" as the Canadians, and predicted that a forthcoming conference of empire newspapermen in Ottawa would not approve any such scheme.[25] The Reuters proposal – which CP had itself presented to the government only a few months earlier, and on the strength of which $20,000 in federal funds had been committed – was then voted down. CP pronounced itself opposed to any extension of subsidies for imperial news beyond continuation of the existing $8,000 grant to CAP for one year. A motion rejecting any British government contribution was passed unanimously. CP would provide $12,600 for an improved cable service from London, but that was all. The unstable compromise on new government subsidies for imperial news had broken apart.

Surprisingly, this was not the end of the matter. Roderick Jones, who was in Canada for the Imperial Press Conference in the summer of 1920, kept the idea alive, with the result that in the autumn of 1920 CP Ltd. reapplied for the $20,000 subsidy that it had rejected a few months earlier. The British contribution was now to take the form of a reduced rate on cable transmissions of four cents a word, which many CP members considered less objectionable than a cash subsidy.[26] The climate in Ottawa was not the same as it had been in the spring, though – notably, Robert Borden, who had been a strong proponent of subsidies to the national news agency since 1916, had resigned as prime minister, succeeded by Arthur Meighen, who had a much more jaundiced view of the press, and especially of CP. But Jones, who was known for being persuasive, met the prime minister, and Meighen agreed to take the new proposal to cabinet.[27]

Once again the process was derailed by dissension within CP. The revised scheme was endorsed by 34 CP members, but 18 voted against it, including many of the largest metropolitan papers – the Montreal *Star* and Toronto *Globe, Mail & Empire, Star,* and *Telegram* – and seven French-language papers, but only one from western Canada.[28] Robertson of the *Telegram* followed this up with a blistering letter to Meighen, insisting that the new offer of British support "allow[s] them a more active control of the selection of the cabled news than was generally contemplated in this country."[29] (The British specified that no sports news or news "not of national importance" could be included, but dropped the provisions for special instructions beyond that.[30] Even this would have been a problem, however, because British sports news had been a mainstay of CAP and continued to be of considerable interest to Canadian readers.[31]) "It is for your Government to decide whether the national dignity of the Dominion will be upheld or Imperial connection strengthened by making the Canadian newspapers paid agents of the Colonial Office," Robertson wrote. CP had a monopoly on the supply of news in Canada, and there was "no competing agency to which any newspaper can turn in order to avoid whatever stigma attaches to Government subsidies."

This, finally, was the last straw. Meighen informed CP that "in view of the fact that certain newspapers comprised within the Canadian Press Limited appear to be definitely opposed to this assistance," and given the government's efforts to control spending, the request for assistance was denied. "Should it be possible for all the newspapers comprised within the Canadian Press Limited to definitely and formally agree ... you might then again bring the same to my attention," Meighen concluded, making an offer he must have been fairly certain would never be taken up.[32] Dafoe's *Free Press* replied with a scathing editorial, criticizing Meighen for repudiating "the proposition made by the preceding government, of which he was a member."[33] It noted that the chief opponents of the proposal had benefitted for 15 years from the subsidy to CAP, which they controlled, and which gave them a competitive advantage over other publications: "It was only when steps were taken to make all the Canadian daily newspapers beneficiaries of this policy of Government assistance that they were converted to the view that public subsidies are destructive to the independence of the press and against public morals." Ultimately nothing but self-interest lay behind the actions of Robertson and the other dissidents:

> To fight desperately and unscrupulously for the retention of a selfish advantage is quite characteristic of our Toronto contemporaries; still more characteristic is that they should do this fighting under the pretense that they are thereby protecting the public interest.

Satisfying as such vigorous denunciation may have been, there was no chance of the subsidy proposal being resuscitated once more. But despite all the debate and vacillation, CP members genuinely wanted a better supply of British and imperial news, and they now reached a much more limited agreement with Reuters that required no new subsidy. For $300 a month (substantially less than the monthly fee of more than $1,000 in the rejected proposal), CP's representative in London would direct Reuters editors to file 600 words a day to Canada.[34] Unlike the old CAP service, which had been geared to the afternoon papers that controlled it, this would be organized to meet the needs of morning and afternoon papers equally.[35] CP had now taken over CAP and its (apparently uncontroversial) $8,000 subsidy; beyond this, the members provided an additional $21,000 to cover the Reuters service, additional cable-transmission charges, and the operation of CP's London office. By 1922, CP's general manager, J.F.B. Livesay, reported that the London service had increased to almost 1,000 words a day, which, though the process of "skeletonizing" – compressing cable copy by dropping articles, combining words, and so on – amounted to twice as much in Canada.[36] The old CAP policy of reporting only British sports and news directly involving Canadians was dropped; now (in addition to sports) CP received Reuters and Press Association coverage of such stories as British by-elections, the Moplah agrarian riots in India, the oriental tour of the Prince of Wales, rebellion in South Africa, and labour unrest in Australia.[37] CP was thus actively fostering an expanded sense of British and imperial connection, one that (as long as the control lay in Canadian hands) fitted perfectly well with its promotion of specifically Canadian nationality and did not interfere with its close relationship with AP. These imagined communities, both imperial and national, did not arise automatically, but through conscious choice and sustained organizational efforts.

Although the $8,000 subsidy inherited from CAP continued, CP had finally reached a point where all its members were prepared to pay for (and all to benefit from) the additional British and imperial news they had long demanded. Meanwhile, the federal subsidy of $50,000 to maintain the national leased-wire network remained largely uncontroversial. With the exception of regular and somewhat ritualistic demands for its abolition by the Toronto *Star*, it seemed most unlikely that CP's members would take any steps to repudiate it.

❦

The withdrawal of this federal subsidy in 1923 was a shock to CP. The arrangement had not been without problems: newspapers that objected to CP decisions about membership or fees did not hesitate to invoke it when complaining to federal politicians and officials, suggesting that their grievances be borne in mind when the subsidy came up for renewal.[38] At one point the federal minister of labour, James Murdock, complained about CP's coverage of a strike in Cape Breton, and added: "Having in mind the fact that your organization receives from the Dominion Government a very substantial annual grant in aid of its undertakings, you will, I am sure, realize my right to lay the matter before you."[39] Years later, Livesay and others stated that the grant was withdrawn because they refused to accept political direction from the new government of W.L.M. King, though no specific instances were cited.[40]

Politics clearly played an important role in the withdrawal of the subsidy (as politics had played a role in the initial decision to award it).[41] In January 1923, King suggested to a group of Ottawa correspondents that the subsidy might be cut substantially. In response, Livesay drew up an extensive memorandum defending the subsidy and submitted it to the prime minister and all the members of his cabinet. It quoted John Dafoe's statement that the grant was "of course, a subsidy, but not a subsidy in the sense that it is a gift from the treasury to meet an outlay which otherwise the newspapers would have to meet themselves. It is a grant by the government to enable the newspapers to do a national service which otherwise they could not perform."[42] Withdrawal of the subsidy, the memorandum concluded, "will bear most heavily on the smaller newspapers of the Maritime Provinces and the West, with the result that Canadian Press Limited ... must disintegrate. This ... will not be a loss so much to Canadian newspapers as to the public of Canada." Again, the idea that national news was an ordinary commercial product for residents of big cities, but a public service that required government support for those in smaller towns and outlying regions underlay the argument. Beyond the uneasy rhetoric of a subsidy that was not really a subsidy, Livesay's memorandum expressed no overt misgivings, and the clear implication was that the government grant ought to continue indefinitely.

Within a few months, a volatile combination of issues – the question of whether CP acted as a monopoly in restricting new membership, and the political direction of news – arose to complicate matters. At the end of April 1923, Andrew Haydon, chief organizer of the Liberal party, came before CP's board of directors to seek membership for a new Ottawa paper, the *Evening Capital*, stating that "he was making application on behalf of the Prime Minister and the Liberal party."[43] The three newspapers already operating in Ottawa (the *Citizen*, the *Journal*, and *Le Droit*) all objected to the application, invoking a controversial bylaw that gave existing members the right to block the admission of new members in their areas, to be overridden only by a two-thirds majority vote of the board. The bylaw stated that new applications were to be judged "primarily in the light of conditions established by the history of newspaper publications in the district, with a view of deciding the feasibility of commercially profitable operation." There was clearly some justification in CP's giving itself the right to decide whether a new applicant had a genuine intention to put out a newspaper and a reasonable prospect of success; recently, for example, an applicant in Windsor, Ontario, had obtained a CP franchise only after threatening a lawsuit, then sold out to the other CP paper in the city shortly after it was granted.[44] But it is difficult to see how the existing Ottawa publishers' conclusion that there was no room for a new, commercially successful, competitor in their market could be interpreted as anything but self-interest. In any event, their protest was sustained with only one dissenting vote. Without CP, AP, and Reuters, the new paper would have no chance of success.

Irritation over this decision soon became apparent. A week later, during a debate on the Anti-Combines Act, a Conservative MP, H.C. Hocken, asked whether CP's rejection of the Ottawa newspaper would come under the act's provisions.[45] King replied mildly, discounting the charge of monopoly and suggesting that if Hocken thought there had been anticompetitive behaviour, he was free to bring a complaint under the act. CP was evidently concerned about these charges; E. Norman Smith, CP's president (and publisher of the Ottawa *Journal*), wrote King immediately after the debate to thank him for correcting Hocken's "misrepresentation of the facts" and to assure the prime minister that since 1911, when he first became involved with CP, he "never once saw any disposition on the part of the Board towards monopoly."[46]

The annual grants to CP were among the last items brought forward during the debate on government estimates for 1923–24; W.S. Fielding, the finance minister, apparently expected some difficulty.[47] In this he was correct: Frank Cahill, Liberal MP for the riding of Pontiac, just across the Ottawa River from the capital, began by describing the CP subsidies as "blackmail." King – who, unlike Meighen, was not overtly hostile to CP – replied that the subsidy had been in place for several years, and no objections were raised "until this year, when there was some reason to believe" that newspapers entitled to receive the news were denied it.[48] Under these circumstances, "there was considerable doubt in the minds of the Government as to the wisdom of continuing" the subsidy. But if it were cancelled immediately, "a few of the papers in the Maritime Provinces and some in western Canada would suffer a considerable cut in the news they receive." The government proposed to continue the subsidy for the current year, but after that it would be withdrawn. With that announcement, there was little left to debate, but that did not prevent Cahill, A.F. Healy (the Liberal MP for Windsor who as publisher of the short-lived Windsor *Telegram* had obtained a CP franchise the previous year and promptly sold it) and others from denouncing CP as a monopoly and questioning why newspapers, as profit-making private businesses, should receive government financial aid. After the vote, Livesay observed that the rejection of the Liberal newspaper in Ottawa "was the last straw, as I saw all along and so did the directors." [49]

Meanwhile, a second press-related subsidy that added a further sting to the withdrawal of CP's grant also came up for a vote.[50] As initially proposed by Reuters three years earlier, the government had decided to subsidize what was essentially a new effort to publicize Canada in Britain and elsewhere in the empire. For $32,000 a year, Reuters was to transmit 10,000 words a month "designed to give publicity in the United Kingdom, in other Dominions, and elsewhere abroad, to the resources of Canada and its advantages as a field for settlement and for the investment of capital."[51] Reuters was to appoint a full-time representative in Canada to write and edit the articles. In the House of Commons, J.S. Woodsworth dismissed the grant "as simply another subsidy for this particular news firm," but J.A. Robb, the trade minister, defended it as "an advertisement for Canada." The explicit involvement of a news agency in government advertising was, of course, not in keeping with conventions of journalistic independence, and Reuters evidently recognized this, warning its Ottawa representative not "to make this Service too prominent by brusquely launching it to its full extent ... it would be better for it to grow more or less gradually and so avoid raising comment."[52] But Reuters' acceptance of this subsidy was widely known, especially in journalistic circles, and this had important consequences for CP's later relationship with the British agency.[53]

Quite beyond the simultaneous and somewhat galling new grant to Reuters, the withdrawal of the $50,000 subsidy (and the $8,000 from the old CAP) presented real problems for CP. Livesay found relief in the knowledge that "at last we are free from the politicians," but worried about CP's future.[54] Smith told the board in October that "from time to time we have had had searchings of heart" about the subsidy, fearing it created "belief in the public mind that ... the Canadian Press was not as free from outside control as the best newspaper traditions would demand."[55] Thus for CP members generally, there was "a general feeling of relief ... that the Government grants are to disappear," but "from the point of view of the reading public the result is doubtful." (Here again was the view that the public-service aspect of journalism was the responsibility of government rather than publishers.) Livesay told Roy Martin, AP's general manager, that some members of King's cabinet had suggested the subsidy might be reinstated if CP requested it, but that the board voted unanimously against soliciting or accepting any further government aid.[56] But there would be serious costs. The subsidy amounted to just over 10 per cent of CP's 1923 budget – a substantial amount, though not overwhelming. CP was determined to maintain the Ottawa–Winnipeg leased wire, seen now as in 1917 as the lynchpin of the national system, but the leased wires from Montreal to Halifax and from Calgary to Vancouver would likely have to be dropped; the amount of British cable news would be reduced by 25 per cent as well. Undermining the arguments that he (among others) had regularly made in defence of the subsidy, Smith told Livesay that "the benefits even to our smaller members have been exaggerated ... between us we can find satisfactory means to carry on."[57]

The question, of course, was what these "satisfactory means" might be. The newspapers of the Maritime provinces were unable to come up with an extra $6,000 to maintain their leased-wire connection to Montreal; the best alternative was a much reduced supply of CP news via commercial telegraph. As for the newspapers of Ontario and Quebec, Smith and Livesay argued that without the Winnipeg connection they would have to pay between $10,000 and $12,000 a year in commercial telegraph tolls for a much diminished supply of western Canadian news; it thus seemed reasonable for them to contribute this amount to keep the Winnipeg line in operation. Western newspapers were to pay the rest: $20,500 for the prairie papers, and $11,300 for those in British Columbia.

This revised cost structure was accepted in the Maritimes, the prairies, and British Columbia, but there was significant opposition in Toronto – specifically, from the *Star* and *Telegram*, for whom this was the latest skirmish in a long-running battle. At a regional meeting in March 1924, John Bone of the *Star* mounted a sharp attack on the proposed cost increase for the central provinces.[58] He reminded his colleagues that when the original subsidy was approved, they had agreed that if it were ever withdrawn they would revert to a system where each geographical region paid for its own leased wires. The notion that Ontario and Quebec should contribute an extra $10,000, the amount they might have to pay in telegraph tolls for western news if the leased wire lapsed, was unfair; if the same logic were applied to the western newspapers, their commercial-wire charges for news from the east would amount to $75,000, more than the entire cost of leasing a year-round connection. Anyone who thought the Ontario and Quebec newspapers "ought to be good fellows" and accept the increased cost should realize that central Canadian newspapers were suffering as much as those anywhere else in Canada; since 1917, 16 Ontario dailies had ceased operation. The *Star's* costs for CP service had doubled since 1918, while western Canadian papers were paying less than in 1917. And for this steadily mounting cost, the *Star* was using very little of what it received: an average of 239 words a day from western Canada over the previous five months, and only 116 words a day from the Maritimes. National considerations had to be subject to commercial logic, Bone insisted.

> [H]e did not say we should not be moved on occasion by sentimental considerations, but he did say we should not be deceived by them. A 'National' wire had value only to those papers for which it produced news that their readers would read. No publisher could afford to deceive himself on that point. The theory that a coast-to-coast wire had some substantial value either tangible or intangible to a newspaper in the Ontario and Quebec Division or to the nation was not, he thought, in view of the evidence, well founded.[59]

He did not mention that the *Star* was continuing to operate a news service of its own.[60]

Norman Smith, a persistent supporter of CP's national character, fought back vigorously. Even under the 1917 formula, the Ontario and Quebec papers had agreed to pay 15 per cent of the leased wire's cost in acknowledgment of the value of return news from the west, which would already account for $7,500 of the proposed $10,000 increase. As for the *Star's* limited use of CP copy, "no doubt Mr. Bone's editors were throwing away important Canadian Press news stories and publishing instead *Star* specials at a cost many times greater than the thousand dollars extra a year the *Star* was asked to pay." For smaller papers that previously had to rely on boilerplate services, their news supply had improved immensely, for which CP was "almost entirely responsible."

CP "was not an ordinary news agency," Smith concluded. "It was doing a big work and was a real vital force for this country." If the proposed reallocation of costs was defeated, the result would be "reversion into sections," as had been the case before 1917. In effect, a slight variation on the commercial logic–public service distinction that frequently arose in discussions of the now-withdrawn subsidy was being proposed: in this case, a public service ethos justified higher charges for members in some regions than a strict numerical accounting might suggest. Bone persisted in his objections, however, proposing that a committee (including him and Robertson as members) come up with a new cost structure. Smith refused to consider this, describing it as a vote of nonconfidence in himself and CP's management. If the Ontario and Quebec papers "permitted themselves to be stampeded into a dangerous situation by two Toronto gentlemen who had given only hurried last minute consideration to the problem, he could not continue as president." In the wake of this dramatic threat, Bone's proposal was defeated by a vote of 18 to 4. The cost increase was approved – initially for six months only, and later permanently.[61] Three months after the withdrawal of the subsidy took effect, Smith reported that the crisis was over: "not only is The Canadian Press to continue as a national organization, but ... never before was the promise of its progress toward the goal set by its founders so assured."[62] The most serious loss was to newspapers in the Maritime provinces, whose leased-wire connection was not restored for a year; the heaviest cost increases, more than 20 per cent in many cases, were levied on newspapers in the west.

Coming to terms with the subsidy's withdrawal also created tension with AP. This was a complicated relationship: AP executives regularly praised CP as a valued ally, one that had adopted its own nonprofit, cooperative structure.[63] For strategic and historical reasons, AP had accepted that the revenue it received for selling its US and international news in Canada would be "nominal," but often expressed frustration when CP seemed not to appreciate how favourable this treatment was.[64]

The two agencies had been operating without a formal contract since 1917, but with an understanding that the very low differential paid by CP – representing the difference between the value of the international and US news that AP sent to CP and the Canadian news it received in return – was to increase in stages from $6,000 to $20,000.[65] In 1922, AP had agreed to defer the agreed-upon increase to $13,000, but balked when Livesay, citing the loss of the subsidy and "plead[ing] poverty," asked for a further deferral the following year.[66] Kent Cooper, the chief of AP's traffic department (and Martin's successor as general manager in 1925), pointed out that CP was still receiving the AP service at a very low rate. If the per capita formula used for US members were applied to Canada, he told Livesay, the differential would be $135,000. Cooper also complained that many CP members were continuing to use the service of AP's hated rival, United Press. Since US members of AP who did so had to pay "full card rate," it was only fair that the same should apply to Canada.[67] Frank Noyes, AP's president, agreed: "I may say that I think Mr. Livesay is extremely cavalier in his treatment of the A.P. and I think the time has come for a showdown!"[68] This did not lead to a serious or lasting breach – soon afterward a 10-year contract was signed, with a slow increase in the differential to $17,000 after five years – but it illustrated that AP's irritation over what it sometimes considered CP's ingratitude was easily provoked.

⌒⌒

Shortly after Arthur Meighen became prime minister in the summer of 1920, J.F.B. Livesay, CP's general manager, visited him to offer congratulations. As fellow Manitobans, Livesay and Meighen had known each other for years, but the courtesy visit did not go well. Livesay wrote later that he never got a chance to offer his congratulations to the prime minister,

> and left him fighting mad. For he immediately burst out: 'Livesay, you're the man I want to see. Let me tell you that if The Canadian Press does not mend its ways but continues to play up to the opposition, you will lose the Government Grant.' To which I replied ... 'Mr. Meighen, if we put out the kind of political report you would consider fair, it would so stink in the nostril of the other fellow I could not hold my job a week.'[69]

The atmosphere had obviously changed from the wartime days when Borden and Livesay played bridge together and Livesay took "charming" photos of the prime minister throwing snowballs.[70]

One of CP's proudest boasts in its early years, and in retrospect, was that it brought a new era of impartial, nonpartisan political reporting to Canada. Until now, the argument went, partisan newspapers organized their own coverage of national affairs in a way that reflected their owners' and editors' biases.[71] This is consistent with a line of argument in the academic literature that the telegraph and news agencies led to a reduction in bias (though some scholars have disputed this conclusion, noting, for example, that AP was strongly allied with the Republican

Party in the nineteenth century, and that partisan editors still retained considerable leeway in deciding which news-agency stories to print and how prominently to display them).[72] Individual newspapers in Canada continued to have clear partisan affiliations until well after the Second World War, some informal and others more explicit.[73] But the argument that news agencies in particular led to less biased coverage is a compelling one: the only way to serve newspapers of different political affiliations was to write in a neutral way that none could object to. CP made the point in its application for a new federal charter in 1923: "The Canadian Press is an absolutely non-partisan organization. ... Leanings toward any political party or any interest would be immediately detected by at least a section of the members, and the organization would collapse if there were no prompt remedy."[74] However, Meighen's consistent criticism of CP for what he considered flagrant pro-Liberal bias suggests that this view was not universally accepted.

Certainly CP's management regularly stressed the importance of nonpartisan political coverage. One of the first major stories CP covered was the December 1917 federal election; here it was considered praiseworthy that the coverage was carried out in a strictly nonpartisan way, "inherent in the very idea of co-operative news gathering, serving daily newspapers of every stripe of political opinion."[75] If the quest for impartiality led to less colourful reports, that was not too high a price. In preparation for the 1921 election, Livesay reminded CP staff and reporters from member papers who filed their stories to CP that "we do not want reports of meetings opening with the enthusiastic crowd and closing with tigers [cheers] for the chief speaker."[76] The ban lasted at least until 1935, when some directors complained that too much colour had been cut out of election stories, but Livesay continued to insist that estimates of crowd size and assessment of reactions were risky. "[W]ho is to attest these figures, appraise the enthusiasm and apportion the cheers? We must leave that to the [individual newspaper's] special correspondent."[77] When the publisher of the Vancouver *Sun* asked why CP's Ottawa coverage was much duller than its reports from London, Livesay replied that there was "more latitude handling.news from abroad and ... much less danger of speculation, but in Canada the report was watched very closely along the lines of party politics and The Canadian Press must therefore step warily."[78] In the 1925 campaign, correspondents were warned about covering "stories of [voters'] list plugging, arrests of candidates and their agents, and the like," which could easily be "political by-play staged by one party to the detriment of another." Such charges should not be covered unless they came before a court, and even then only if they would have been considered newsworthy in the absence of a campaign. "Take for instance the case of an election agent, unknown otherwise, who beats up an opponent in a brawl; obviously it is an item Canadian Press would not carry in the ordinary way and therefore will not carry it now."[79] This ultracautious approach extended to leaders' speeches: controversial statements should be quoted directly, rather than taking the risk of a paraphrase that might give grounds for complaint.[80] But partisanship was clearly still part of the fabric of Canadian journalism; in the 1926 campaign, when CP relied on local member papers for coverage of secondary political figures and meetings in western Ontario, it was taken for granted that Liberal events would be covered by the London (Ontario) *Advertiser* and Conservative events by the London *Free Press*, and into the 1930s it was accepted that many papers were party organs.[81] For some, this continuing partisanship made CP copy all the more valuable. In 1933, editors from Hamilton and Owen Sound urged CP to do a better job of filing its version of Ontario political stories in time for their deadlines; otherwise, they had to rely on scalping from nearby morning papers, whose bias was hard to eliminate.[82]

Both Liberals and Conservatives complained about CP's election and political coverage, though the Conservatives – justifiably or not – were the more aggrieved. W.L.M. King was generally on good terms with CP as an organization, the withdrawal of the subsidy notwithstanding; after King's defeat in the 1930 election, for example, Livesay wrote a personal note of consolation, describing King as "a good friend of CP" and adding: "your loss is our loss. ... it would be impossible to receive at Ottawa more kindly consideration than we have had from yourself – more generous recognition that we are trying to be fair to all."[83] Nonetheless, King complained several times in his diary about what he considered CP's Tory bias, especially when it came to election returns that misleadingly showed Conservative candidates in the lead.[84] In 1935, he reported a conversation with Livesay and the superintendent of CP's Ottawa bureau in which they acknowledged a "shading" in favour of the Conservatives and their leader, R.B. Bennett, in the previous election, but were now disposed to be "friendly" – a conversation King promptly reported to Rupert Davies, the publisher of the Kingston *Whig-Standard* (later CP's president and a Liberal senator).[85]

Overall, King had a constructive relationship with CP, regularly assisting its correspondents in arranging coverage. For example, when

King was preparing to travel to the Imperial Conference in London in 1923, Livesay informed him that George Hambleton, supervisor of CP's Ottawa bureau, would accompany him and hoped to travel on the same boat and stay in the same hotel as the prime minister: "He realises that to make a success of the work must depend on the measure of confidence he enjoys with yourself, and we shall be glad indeed to hear that you approve of his appointment, to which he will give his whole energies and attention."[86] The prime minister replied that he was "greatly pleased" to hear of Hambleton's appointment. "It is ... a pleasure to us personally, to know that he will accompany the party."[87] Meighen, however, was not impressed, observing sardonically to a Conservative editor that "[f]rom the Government standpoint Hambleton was an excellent man to be sent over by Canadian Press, and we may all rely upon it that he has put the best possible face on everything that has occurred."[88] Whether the friendly relations between King and Hambleton were, as Meighen implied, evidence of CP's pro-Liberal bias or of a journalist's concern for access to and good relations with (and subsequent deference towards) those in positions of authority – and of a politician's desire to have good relations with those covering his actions – is less clear. Even when King complained about CP coverage, Livesay recalled later, "though I don't suppose I convinced him we were fair and unbiased, his approach to these discussions was invariably courteous and reasonable."[89] Livesay also wrote that the commitment of CP's presidents to nonpartisanship waned in the 1930s. Until then, CP's presidents had been "good newspapermen all, who recognized as their successors could not and did not that the C.P. was above and beyond politics ... such loyalty could not be surpassed and, looking back, I blame myself for looking to, and expecting it from, the new regime, the untried players from the scrub."[90]

Unlike King, the combative Meighen was convinced that CP worked systematically against him and in favour of the Liberals. A 1923 letter to Arthur Ford, a committed Conservative who was editor of the London *Free Press*, gave a good indication of his attitude. "There is not the least doubt in the world" of CP's partisan bias, Meighen wrote. "Their Ottawa staff is wholly Liberal. The fact of the matter is we are practically stripped of any support in the whole press gallery."[91] A year later, his opinion had become even more definite: "Nothing can convince me now that [CP] is anything better than a Grit institution and that Livesay and his men are putting it over the Conservative papers day by day."[92] Ford's response was more measured, urging Meighen to provide examples of partisan bias that he could take up at CP's meetings, and warning that CP was "too strong an organization and the Canadian papers are too dependent upon it for the Conservative party to quarrel permanently."[93] In 1926, though, Ford complained that CP's election coverage had hurt the Conservative cause, and the Conservative solicitor-general, Lucien Cannon, charged in the House of Commons before the campaign began that CP's coverage was "directed, influenced, and controlled in a large measure" by the Liberals.[94] CP was clearly aware of these charges; in 1930, Livesay told the board of directors that he was "particularly glad" to report that R.B. Bennett, the Conservative leader, said he was well satisfied with CP's coverage of his meetings.[95]

The Meighen papers are full of angry complaints against CP; Livesay wrote in a draft of his memoirs that "no critic was more bitter nor less penetrable to reason."[96] Many of his complaints were justified, in that CP acknowledged that errors had been committed, but this did not address Meighen's belief that they were merely surface manifestations of a broader, underlying bias. Even stalwart Conservative journalists like Howard Robinson of the Saint John *Times Globe* and M.E. Nichols (then publisher of the Vancouver *Province)* tried to convince Meighen that his concerns were exaggerated.

Livesay, for his part, was aware of CP journalists who had partisan affiliations, some quite prominent. For example, Thomas Green, who worked at CP's Ottawa bureau in the 1930s, covered the Conservative party convention that chose R.B. Bennett as leader while also a delegate and member of the resolutions committee. At the convention, Green made a practice of handing resolutions to the CP telegraph operator before giving them to the convention chairman, "[s]o we could not be scooped," Livesay recalled, the lesson being that "[i]t was indeed a danger for a C.P. reporter like Green to become labelled partisan, but once in a while it was useful."[97]

Overall, it seems clear that CP in the 1920s and 1930s did bring a less partisan style of reporting to Canadian journalism (though many individual newspapers were moving in this direction, too).[98] Against Meighen's repeated assertions of Liberal bias, one should remember that many of CP's directors and presidents (including E. Norman Smith of the Ottawa *Journal*, a particularly strong supporter of Livesay in his early battles with Meighen) were Conservatives who had no reason to condone bias against their party. The very fact that complaints about biased coverage were regularly raised at directors' meetings and detailed responses had to be provided was evidence of an organizational culture that rejected overt partisan bias in news coverage. Journalists' concern for access to sources and information, together with the many advantages of incumbency, did bring deference to politicians on the government side, but there is no indication that CP was much different than other news organizations in this respect.

If CP journalists moved away from the celebratory, participant style of political journalism characteristic of the nineteenth century, they did not become (at least not right away) the dispassionate professionals assessing conflicting political claims described by Richard Kaplan in the United States, nor the Lippmann-esque experts described by Michael Schudson.[99] They were not encouraged to assess and interpret, but to describe as neutrally as possible, staying away from anything – even an estimate of a crowd's size and assessment of its reaction – that might give grounds for complaint. One can understand why Livesay might have insisted on this: in an era when (for a newspaper on the right side) every partisan crowd was rapturous and every hall filled to overflowing, here was at least one clear prescription that could be followed, one way of stopping some rote practices of partisan journalism. The price, perhaps inescapable at the time, was copy that could be dull and colourless and a cautious kind of journalism. Historians of journalism in the 1950s and 1960s tended to see these developments as inevitable, teleological progress, while more recent scholars lament what was lost and point out the shortcomings of the practices of "objectivity" that replaced overt partisanship.[100] In any case, the spread of journalism that aimed for neutrality in its treatment of the major political parties and, over time, its acceptance as the standard, correct practice marked a major shift in the way politics – and citizens' connections to politics via journalism – were conceived, a shift that clearly was one of the national news agency's chief legacies. (This did not, however, mean that CP was any more likely than the newspapers that constituted its membership to be evenhanded in dealing with marginal political parties or unpopular social groups; the "sphere of legitimate controversy," to use Daniel Hallin's term, was largely defined by the differences between mainstream political parties.[101])

⌘

Just as arranging better coverage of Britain and its empire was an important way for CP to carry out its national mandate, the question of how to handle the relations between English-language and

French-language papers was another dimension of what it meant to be "national." Throughout the late nineteenth and early twentieth centuries, telegraphic news for Canadian newspapers had come from AP in English. French-language publications had to translate, which took time (important news often missed edition deadlines for this reason) and cost additional money. (In 1924, *La Patrie* of Montreal employed 10 translators.[102]) In recognition of this, and in order to induce them to join the new organization, it was agreed when CP was established in 1917 that French-language papers would pay about 40 per cent less than their English-language counterparts.[103]

The news system in Quebec was substantially different than that in Ontario in other ways, too. There were only four cities in the province with dailies – Montreal, Quebec, Trois-Rivières, and Sherbrooke – compared to more than 20 in Ontario. This meant that the system of "return news" that member papers provided back to the cooperative was correspondingly less developed. Livesay acknowledged that CP's management had "always found it difficult to really develop the news field" in Quebec.

In the summer of 1922, it was suggested that a separate French-language circuit should be established to serve afternoon papers in Montreal, Quebec, and elsewhere in the province.[104] Livesay said the idea arose in part when he realized how little CP material was used by the French-language papers in Montreal.[105] Two bilingual editors would be hired and stationed at Montreal, where they would select the most suitable mixture of AP and CP news for the circuit – French-language papers complained that the current selection at Montreal, made by English-speaking editors for English-language papers, did not meet their requirements – and translate it into French. Oswald Mayrand of *La Presse* suggested this might be even slower than the current system, where translation was done separately in each newspaper's office, but Livesay assured him the designated editors would do a better job. Costs for each Montreal paper would increase by around $3,500, but they would no longer have to pay for translation and would have "a much improved service."[106] Once established, the wire only carried around 8,000 words a day – substantially less than the 10,000 words predicted – partly because there was no French equivalent of the elaborate "Phillips code" of abbreviations used by English-language telegraphers, and partly because the telegraphers were "rather exacting" about capitalization and the insertion of accents.[107] Hopes that the new service would induce other Quebec papers to join CP, thus reducing the average cost further, providing a better return-news service and alleviating what Livesay described as "the news gathering problem in Quebec" were not realized, however. George Macdonald, the Quebec superintendent, reported that his efforts to recruit additional French-language papers (including weeklies) in towns like Rigaud, Joliette, Nicolet, Rimouski, Rivière du Loup, and Chicoutimi were not success-ful: "a good deal of education will be required before all this can be accomplished," he concluded.[108]

Cost problems brought the French-language circuit to an end after less than a year. In the summer of 1923, *Le Nouvelliste* of Trois-Rivières announced that it could no longer afford the leased-wire connection and would revert to the cheaper and less extensive pony service, while *Le Devoir* was dropping CP entirely, making the separate circuit pro-hibitively expensive for the remaining three papers. *La Presse* and *La Patrie* said they would happily return to the English-language circuit, which provided a larger volume of news, but their provision of return news also dropped off once the circuit was discontinued.[109] *Le Devoir* was eventually convinced to stay in CP when the other Montreal papers, French and English, agreed to share an additional charge to keep its cost to $4,000 a year – if *Le Devoir* had dropped out entirely, their joint cost for leased-wire service would have increased by about twice as much. As always, the economics of a cooperative news agency were very favourable when new members joined – its fixed costs increased not at all or only slightly and could be shared among a larger number – and highly unfavourable, to the point of destabilization, when anyone left.

In 1929, the Montreal *Herald* proposed that the 1917 agreement imposing lower costs on French-language papers should be scrapped.[110] French-language publishers objected strongly, warning that breaking the agreement without their consent "will create a most serious situa-tion which might lead to a grave conflict within the Canadian Press." French-language publications still had heavy costs for translation, and "the news report as a whole was not so suited to their requirements." (The Montreal *Star* also supported them, saying their loyalty to CP "should be praised.") A reduced differential of around 20 per cent was then unanimously agreed on, which remained the basis for the (some-what attenuated) relations between CP's English-language and French-language members for the next 20 years.[111]

The fact that practically all Canadian daily newspapers were members of CP, and that each member, no matter how small or large, had one vote, meant that regional concerns, or the requirements of newspapers in small towns as well as large cities, were never lost sight of. In this geographical sense, CP operated as a quite inclusive national organization. Socially, however, things were different: the newspaper publishers who collectively owned CP were all employers of labour, as CP itself was an employer. In class terms, the labour perspective was not given the same weight as the regional perspective, and at times CP took as hard-headed an attitude to its employees as any industrialist.[112] If the promise of nationality is, as Benedict Anderson says, that of a "deep, horizontal kinship," this operated in CP's case more on a spatial than a social scale.

CP's first serious labour problems involved the Morse telegraphers who were the backbone of its news distribution system, and whose wages were one of its biggest costs. Without the sending and receiving operators in all of CP's bureaus (and in its members' newsrooms), striving to maintain a transmission speed of 60 words a minute, the flow of news across the country would come quickly to a stop. In 1918, as the wartime cost of living soared, CP was threatened with a telegraphers' strike (their contract did not expire until the following year), and only averted it by agreeing to increase wages by around 10 per cent.[113] The Winnipeg General Strike of 1919 showed how disruptive a labour stoppage could be: CP telegraphers joined the strike on May 17, making it virtually impossible to send news outside the city.[114] An offer to allow CP news to be sent out if was approved by the strike committee – "censorship," in CP's eyes – was rejected.[115] CP rerouted its national network to bypass Winnipeg, which could otherwise have stopped all exchange of news between eastern and western Canada, and a special wire was installed to St. Paul, Minnesota, on May 20;[116] using this link, CP's telegraphic superintendent filed news of the strike continuously to AP, which redistributed it across Canada via CP. CP operators in Calgary and Edmonton joined the strike as well. When some Morse operators in Regina, which replaced Winnipeg as CP's western hub, refused to transmit copy describing the strikes in Winnipeg, Calgary, and Edmonton, CP's western publishers delivered an ultimatum: all leased wires in the west would be closed unless all attempts to exercise editorial control by the telegraphers ceased. This condition was accepted, and "nearly all" the striking operators returned to their jobs after about three weeks;[117] CP's members were told that the

Winnipeg operators "expressed regret" when they returned to work. But wages continued to rise: a new contract in 1920 increased operators' wages by another 20 per cent.[118] As this contract was running out, in 1924, the telegraphers asked for further increases of around 30 per cent, while CP argued that wages had increased by almost 90 per cent (a figure disputed by the union) since 1917 and should drop in line with the decrease in the cost of living since the war ended.[119]

On 11 September 1924, CP's telegraphers went on strike, asserting that an attempt by CP to arbitrate the wage issue was contrary to their contract and rejecting a proposal by the federal labour ministry to appoint a board of conciliation. CP took the position that by rejecting arbitration, the union had broken a contract that was still in force, and refused to negotiate until the strikers returned to work.[120] Meanwhile, commercial telegraphers (members of the same union) refused to handle press material, forcing CP to fall back on a variety of expedients to maintain the flow of news, including telephone service from Toronto to its western Ontario members and between Ottawa and Montreal and the broadcasting of news to Ontario members over the Toronto *Star*'s radio station.[121] CP superintendents kept up the transmission of news over the leased-wire connection between New York, Toronto, Winnipeg, and Vancouver (but only for four hours a day), and regional managers established connections with AP at the old filing points of Bangor, Maine; St. Paul; and Seattle.[122] Expenses were high at first, but by the time the strike ended CP was saving $3,000 a week.

The strike, which lasted ten days, was a disaster for the union. Within a week, telegraphers began returning to work, and the union now proposed that a new contract be negotiated through a board of conciliation. Before allowing the strikers back to work, CP required them to sign a memorandum stating that the provisions of the existing contract no longer applied.[123] Seniority earned before the strike would no longer be recognized; those who returned to work first were now the most senior employees. Those rehired only had their jobs on a temporary basis until it was known how many employees would be required to operate the new technology CP introduced during the strike.[124] Wages would be the same as before the strike, except for a reduction of $5 a week in towns with a population less than fifty thousand, where living costs were said to be lower.[125] CP withdrew its recognition of the Commercial Telegraphers Union, and a new contract was signed with individual employees (who could, however, keep their union membership). CP realized significant cost savings; with the reduction in wages of their Morse operators to $40 a week, the Maritime province papers could afford to reestablish the leased-wire connection to Montreal that had been dropped after the loss of the federal subsidy.[126]

One of the most significant consequences of the strike was techno-logical. In the 1920s, new printer technology was being developed that allowed newspapers to receive printed text of telegraphic despatches in their offices directly, without requiring the intermediary of a Morse operator. CP had intended to move slowly in introducing this largely untried and potentially disruptive technology, but when the operators went on strike, these concerns no longer applied.[127] Three days after the strike began, a Morkum printer was installed in the Montreal bureau to receive copy from New York, and soon afterward similar machines were installed in Toronto and Ottawa. The printers never worked satisfactorily, but they "filled a gap" and were kept on the Toronto–Montreal–Ottawa circuit after the strike ended (the New York connec-tion reverting to the more familiar and reliable Morse.) The obvious attraction was cost: an unskilled man paid $120 a month could be trained to send 9,000 words in an eight-hour shift using the printer, whereas a Morse operator working at that speed was paid between $180 and $200 a month. The speed of transmission (and therefore the volume of news) increased, too; with practice, the printers could send and receive text 50 per cent faster than even the most accomplished telegraphers. Although the capital cost to install printers throughout the system was high, lower wages were expected to offset this within five years, and installing printers on CP's main circuits provided "nec-essary insurance" in case of another strike.[128] Livesay predicted that establishment of a printer wire between Toronto and New York (accom-plished in 1927) would double the volume of AP news sent to Canada and "revolutionize" service for Ontario and Quebec, just as the estab-lishment of an Ottawa–Winnipeg printer circuit had already done for western Canada.[129]

But a greater volume of news could cause problems, too. CP's Winnipeg bureau, where the heavier flow of news from New York had to be condensed for the single Morse wire to the prairies and west coast, was now overloaded with work.[130] Similarly, members in the Maritime provinces were warned that they would have to reduce the amount of routine regional news on their Montreal–Halifax wire if they wished to take advantage of the greater volume available at Montreal.[131] Just as had happened with the introduction of leased wires after 1911, the logic of the new technology created pressure to bring all parts of the system up to the new standard, as the board agreed to do in 1929.[132] Nor was it simply a matter of purchasing and installing the printers – they also brought requirements for new telegraph lines, additional supplies, technical supervision and repairs, and more editors to handle the increased flow of news.[133] With the lower cost of labour, many smaller papers that had previously been satisfied with a limited pony service could now join the leased-wire network, giving them a vastly greater supply of news – an increase from 1,000 to 20,000 words a day in some cases – while reducing the average cost of leased-wire service for everyone else.[134] Even then, some saw "printerization" as a mixed blessing. At a meeting of western members in December 1930, the editor of the Calgary *Albertan* complained that papers were receiving "far more verbiage" than they could handle; "if long, overwritten stories were properly boiled down and digested in Bureaux, it would save editorial labor all along the line."[135] Because newspapers were now publishing smaller editions, it was impossible to "print more than a fraction of this wordage." Kenvyn of the Vancouver *Province* said CP editors were simply sending reams of material to take advantage of the wire's increased capacity without worrying about quality, and similar complaints came from Ontario members, along with demands for more coverage of lighter stories, such as the scandalous embezzlement trial of Daisy DeVoe, assistant to the movie star Clara Bow, and less about politics and international affairs.[136] Others disagreed, however: Wallace of the Edmonton *Journal* wanted the printers to be kept busy, because their purpose was to provide greater diversity of news. "He did not expect The Canadian Press to edit his newspaper, and preferred to see the printer run to capacity so he could make his own selection." As always, the power of local editors to shape their own international and domestic news report depended directly on having a larger rather than a smaller amount of news to choose from. Printerization thus did for local editors something like what CP had done when it stationed its own editors at AP in New York (rather than simply receiving at border points a selection made by AP's staff), or in the offices of Reuters in London. Livesay agreed that CP's editors initially had tended to substitute quantity for quality, and urged them to keep stories shorter, livelier, and more readable.

Unfortunately for CP, the unanticipated extra costs of the printer service became apparent just as Canada was falling into economic depression in the early 1930s. Amid warnings that many papers were unable to bear additional costs, Livesay acknowledged at the 1930 annual meeting that "this task might have been entered upon with more reluctance could we have foreseen the revolution the printer was to bring in its train ... all through our cost structure is to be found the trail of the printer."[137] Additional staff was required in every bureau to handle the increased volume of news and to cover the longer hours of operation printer service made possible. Even CP's accountant needed extra staff to keep up with the printer network. To match its increased transmission capacity, CP also expanded its newsgathering efforts, relying more on reporting by its own staff. Meanwhile, it became apparent that the printers required expert mechanical supervisors to operate smoothly – which provided new jobs for many of the previously redundant (and relatively expensive) Morse operators. Livesay optimistically predicted in October 1930 that, despite the depression, CP members were still prepared to pay higher rates (a proposed increase of 3.5 per cent for the coming year) for a better service.[138]

By 1932, CP was in the grip of a full-scale financial crisis, and in this context the heavy cost of printer service drew unfavourable attention. M.E. Nichols, now publisher of the Winnipeg *Tribune*, enumerated the "impressive" cost increases that accompanied printerization, saying that despite the improvements it brought, he almost wished the device had never been invented.[139] A year later, though, after CP had gone through draconian cost reductions,[140] Livesay reported that the printer service had actually provided substantial savings. Although the capital cost of the printers ended up being more than twice the original estimate, by 1933 their cost had been amortized, and, as predicted, annual assessments began to decrease.[141] With practice, printer operators could handle two or even three circuits instead of just one, as had initially been assumed, leading to wage savings of between 25 and 60 per cent.[142]

The financial crisis that CP faced in the early 1930s threatened to put it out of business. At the 1931 annual meeting, several members criticized a proposed cost increase for the coming year while their revenue from advertising and circulation was declining; others, however, agreed with Livesay that there was no extravagance – one argued that in the face of competition from radio, this was "no time for retrenchment" – and that cuts would harm the news service.[143] That fall, it was announced that two member papers were going out of business, and a third was dropping its CP membership.[144]

Another problem was a long-term shift from morning to afternoon publication, which, under CP's cost-allocation system, meant that costs for the few remaining morning papers rose sharply.[145] In February 1932, the Vancouver *Star*, the only remaining morning paper in the city, stopped publishing.[146] With the Calgary *Albertan* seeking to move from morning to afternoon publication, this left the Victoria *Colonist* to bear the cost of the Calgary–Vancouver night wire alone; it also meant that two remaining morning papers in Saskatchewan, the Regina *Leader-Post* and Saskatoon *Star-Phoenix*, would have to pay the whole cost of the night leased wire from Winnipeg to Calgary. If they dropped out, the Winnipeg *Free Press* would then be solely responsible for the night leased wire from Ottawa. Macklin of the *Free Press* pointed out that his paper would not be the only one affected if this happened: all the afternoon papers in the west would lose access to the file of news sent to morning papers, which they used heavily, and the return-news service to eastern Canada would be severely disrupted. Nichols, now CP's president, worked out an interim arrangement with the remaining Vancouver and Victoria papers to drop their AP wire to Seattle in order to keep the night leased wire from Calgary in operation for the time being, even though they might have preferred a closer connection to US news sources.[147] Nichols praised the coast papers: they paid higher fees than their Toronto counterparts, but did so happily, feeling that CP "was not logically an economical structure so much as a national institution with the facilities for acquainting each part of Canada with every other section." Some large papers – he did not have to mention Toronto – were "spending loosely and extravagantly much more money than on The Canadian Press service, which was really their most justifiable expenditure and of more real service than anything else. The broader view was to make readily any such sacrifice in the interests of national and newspaper unity in Canada."[148]

The growing concern about CP's costs renewed old tensions between Toronto members and others. As the economic historian Stephen Shmanske has pointed out, setting a price for wire-service news is difficult because its value is not the same for different customers (to use Shmanske's example, a large metropolitan daily and a university newspaper).[149] If the agency sets a common price that is too high, small papers cannot afford it, and the agency forgoes revenue it might otherwise collect. If the common price is too low, the agency does without the extra revenue that larger and wealthier customers might be willing and able to provide. Thus, Shmanske concludes, a news agency must charge "high prices where the market will bear them and a series of lower prices elsewhere."[150] This, in effect, is what CP did – it was generally admitted that the larger members paid a greater share of CP's costs than a strict equivalency approach would dictate[151] – and the arbitrariness and (in the eyes of some members) unfairness of the price structure provided reliable fodder for complaint. Thus, in May 1932, C.O. Knowles of the Toronto *Telegram* – who had been fired as general manager 14 years earlier – complained to the board that the cost of the service was "seriously out of proportion to its value" to his paper and to the Toronto *Star*.[152] Some CP services, such as the Washington bureau and a more extensive cable service from London, "were of greater value to the smaller papers than to the larger papers, although the latter necessarily paid the lion's share of the cost." CP's cost structure was based too much on ability to pay rather than the value of the news supplied to each member. Knowles urged that CP "get back to its original idea of carrying a basic news service"; any supplementary coverage beyond that should be paid for by those papers that wished to use it. Nor were Toronto papers the only ones seeking relief – the English-language dailies of Montreal argued that in a city whose population was 60 per cent French-speaking, their fees (which, in keeping with CP's general practice, were based on the city's population) should be reduced sharply.[153] The French-language papers were unhappy, too; unless the present cost structure was changed, they were prepared to withdraw from CP "in the near future" and form their own newsgathering organization, which would meet their particular requirements better and would solve the translation problem.[154] A costs committee, with Knowles among its members, was struck to look into all aspects of the question.

In 1932, with economic conditions continuing to deteriorate, the pattern of steadily increased spending established since 1924 came to a sudden stop. At that year's general meeting, Livesay presented plans to reduce costs by $45,000 in the coming year – much of it by cutting wages across the board – but admitted that the situation had become even more serious since those figures were prepared. An additional $12,000 was then cut, including the closing of CP's Washington bureau and a reduction of $5,000 in cable costs from London.

In a situation strongly reminiscent of the 1916 crisis that led to CP's creation, the morning papers in Regina and Saskatoon announced in June that they were dropping their leased-wire service.[155] Leased-wire service to western Canada had always been CP's Achilles' heel. The combination of long distances (and thus heavy wire-rental charges, which were set by the mile), CP's policy that each region should essentially pay for its own circuits, and the relatively small number of newspapers in the west created an inherently unstable situation: the withdrawal of even a single leased-wire customer immediately threw its share of the cost on the remaining papers on that circuit and threatened to turn into a cascade of withdrawals that would end with the abandonment of the wire. The only solution was to ask someone (the federal government in 1916, or other CP members in 1923) to come up with additional funds to prevent this outcome. Thus, at an emergency meeting of western newspapers in Calgary, Nichols convinced afternoon papers throughout the west to pay extra to keep the night wire in operation; Macklin, meanwhile, said loss of the Winnipeg–Ottawa wire would be a "national calamity," and pledged that the *Free Press* would keep it in operation by itself if necessary as long as the present crisis lasted. A longer-term solution, however, depended on rate relief from CPR Telegraphs. W.D. Neil of the CPR initially offered to reduce the cost of the 24-hour leased wire from Winnipeg to Victoria to $10 a mile – a reduction of 50 per cent – for six months. CP, Neil told Nichols, was one of his company's best customers, and rate relief was not a subsidy, but "the act of a big broad-minded merchant towards a good customer of long standing in temporary difficulties." In the CPR's view, it was simply good business to help CP keep its CPR leased-wire structure in the west, "rather than risk through its abandonment the news service to Western morning papers finding other, and perhaps permanent, channels."[156]

Ultimately, CP survived the 1932–33 crisis through a combination of severe spending cuts – $136,000 from a budget of $748,000, a reduction of almost 20 per cent over two years – and a new, much more favourable five-year CPR contract based on a pattern established by AP in the United States. The CPR agreed to two major concessions: calculating distances on a direct air line rather than by railway mileage and agreeing to charge for 16 hours rather than 24 hours a day.[157] This was not, Nichols told CP members in 1933, from any motive other than "a desire to hold intact the business of a valued customer."[158] CP was, after all, the largest user of leased wires in Canada; its demand was steady from day to day and year to year; and it always paid "on the nail." Under these circumstances, it was quite understandable that the CPR felt "that this class of business is worth holding and worth the concessions that have been taken to hold it." In all, the new CPR contract brought an annual reduction in leased-wire rental of $22,800, two-thirds of it applying to the west.

The cost reductions meant that CP, never a lavish spender, operated in many ways on a shoestring. When Bernard Rickatson-Hatt, editor-in-chief of Reuters, visited Canada in 1934, he was shocked to see the state of CP's "shoddy and untidy" offices in the *Mail & Empire* building. "Even Livesay's own room is a mess," he reported to Roderick Jones.

> The walls are filthy. The paint is all off the woodwork. It is a very old-fashioned building too. The CP are far more cramped for space than we are in London. I could not even find any sign outside The Mail and Empire building indicating that it was the headquarters of the Canadian Press. Altogether it would give you a fit if you saw it.

The question of when, and on what terms, to admit new members continued to be a complicated problem for CP. Members had a right to protest against – in effect, to veto – the admission of a new paper in their city or town, and this could only be overridden by a two-thirds majority of the board of directors. The right was commonly exercised; new applications that would compete with an existing member were as likely to be turned down as to be accepted.[159] It was obviously in every existing paper's self-interest to prevent the appearance of new competitors, but CP could not admit this motive so flatly. The general membership bylaw also stressed the importance of establishing the newcomer's ability to operate successfully in terms of financial resources, newspaper experience, and so on. If the right of protest was not exercised, any new member also had to pay significant entrance fees; in 1925, the fee was three times the cost of a year's membership,[160] and in 1930 a proposal called for fees ranging from $5,000 for a paper seeking the limited pony service to $50,000 for a new paper in a city with a population of more than 100,000.[161] (If there was no existing member, the entrance fee was a more modest $500 across the board.) The higher fees were hotly debated at the annual meeting, with some urging they be increased still further to protect current members. Others, however, like J.H. Woods of the Calgary *Herald*, argued against any entrance fee at all. CP "was always on trial as to whether it was seeking to cramp free expression of views by unfair means," Woods asserted, "and therefore there should be no undue restriction against new publishers."[162] John Imrie of the Edmonton *Journal* added that "[a]ny newspaper that created a monopoly endangered itself, and suspicion of the public on that score would deprive it of [public] confidence." But Imrie was not entirely opposed to restrictions on competition; another of his arguments was that an excessively high entrance fee might make revenue-conscious board members too inclined to give new applicants the two-thirds vote to overcome a local protest.

Imrie also mentioned a relatively new consideration for CP, the prospect that a high entrance fee might drive an applicant into the arms of a competing news agency. CP had not faced such competition in its early years, but beginning in the 1920s an agency called British United Press (BUP) – an offshoot of the UP agency that was AP's great rival – had been operating in Canada. Ironically, its chief was Charles Crandall, one of the founders of CP, and until the mid-1920s one of its key members.[163] BUP operated out of the offices of the Montreal *Star* (the *Star*, under Crandall's leadership, had been distributing UP copy to other Canadian newspapers since at least 1914, often causing serious problems in the AP–CP relationship[164]). In 1930, Livesay reported to Kent Cooper, AP's general manager, that BUP was making "rather important strides" in Canada and speculated that recent demands for CP to restrain its spending may have come from "UP-minded" members.[165] Two years later, he reported being "just a bit worried as to the way the UP seems to be putting it over us in the morning papers they serve." UP's main strength was its rewrite men in New York, with their flair for turning out bright human-interest stories – which often got better play than serious news, "like it or not."[166] Around the same time, Gillis Purcell (Livesay's right-hand man and designated successor) told his chief that teleprinter copy with too many errors in it was "one of the main reasons why most editors think U.P. has a better service than we have."[167] In the mid-1930s, papers that took BUP in addition to CP included the Vancouver *Province*; Winnipeg *Free Press*; Toronto *Star*, *Telegram*, and *Mail & Empire*; Montreal *Star* and *La Presse*; Hamilton *Spectator*; and St. Catharines *Standard*.[168]

As a privately owned agency, BUP sold its news service to anyone who was willing to pay for it, and frequently accused CP of monopolistic practices. This was undoubtedly in the background when CP members discussed the problem of creating a poor public image through restrictive entrance fees. Thus CP's vulnerability "to the possible charge [it] sought to create a monopoly" was cited by Nichols in recommending a reduction in entrance fees in 1932, and his successor as president, W.B. Preston of the Brantford *Expositor*, made a similar argument in

1936.[169] Livesay defended CP's practices, insisting that for any *bona fide* publisher, the entrance fee – now as high as $150,000 for a new Toronto daily – was "relatively a bagatelle" compared to the cost of replacing CP's news service.[170] Only one Canadian daily, *L'Action catholique* of Quebec, claimed the entrance fee ($50,000 in its case) prevented it from joining CP – and in any case, the fact that *L'Action catholique* continued to publish successfully proved that CP wasn't essential. In a pamphlet intended for general public distribution, Livesay wrote (under the subheading "Not a Monopoly") that "[CP] is a monopoly only in the sense it is a natural monopoly, for so long as news must be carried over land wires, the cost of bridging the country by leased wires appears too great for Canadian newspapers to be able to support two competing national news services." For all the defensiveness, this was not an entirely spurious argument. The fragility of CP's leased-wire network had been shown many times (though the organization's resilience in overcoming these crises was also striking). If more newspapers belonged to CP, it offered a better return-news service and lower fees to everyone. If a competing news agency threatened CP directly with loss of customers – rather than simply providing a supplementary service, as was the case with almost all of BUP's existing clients in Canada – that could weaken the national agency and lead to a situation where CP offered a more basic service and wealthier papers could provide much more extensive coverage than their less wealthy counterparts. This would be something like the model that the Toronto *Telegram* and *Star* had long advocated.

The argument that preventing the emergence of new local competitors was essential to CP's health was much weaker. Even if a new competitor put an existing CP member out of business – the likelier prospect was a reduction in profit – that would still leave the same number of CP clients as before the new entrant arrived, the same revenue for CP, and the same return-news service. A requirement that new members demonstrate their ability to pay CP's fees was not unreasonable, but the main purpose of CP's restrictions on local competition was simply to protect the position and profits of its existing members. In fact, more local competition would have been, on balance, good for CP – the additional revenue from new members would more than offset the effect of reduced profits on the ability to pay CP's fees. This was one drawback of the cooperative structure: the interests of the organization were sometimes subordinated to the individual interests of its members. It was no wonder that discussions of these essentially anticompetitive policies often had a defensive tone.

❧

Livesay's relationship with CP's presidents and directors deteriorated during the 1930s. He wrote later that "the new regime, the untried players from the scrub" were "the cause of the disappointment, the sorrows of my last C.P. years."[171] Concerns that he was insufficiently vigilant about cutting costs seem to have been behind this; at a board meeting in 1931, for example, he was questioned sharply about his decision to grant salary increases to junior employees, and he later complained about CP's board to Cooper: "Some of our people are pretty small and disappointing."[172]

The board evidently had its own concerns about Livesay. In 1935, the establishment of an executive committee that could exercise more regular oversight of Livesay's decisions was proposed. Norman Smith, a former CP president and strong supporter of Livesay, objected vigorously, saying CP had been founded on the principle that member papers should not be involved in its day-to-day operations. "What was this all-powerful Committee to do? It could do nothing that would not be an interference with the day-to-day operation of the Corporation."[173] Furthermore, it would contribute to central Canadian dominance of CP, because it was unlikely that directors from the Maritimes or the west would be able to travel to Toronto for meetings at least four times a year. Directors who supported the idea went out of their way to say that the proposal did not reflect any loss of confidence in Livesay – although a future general manager might need to be supervised "more minutely." Opinion was divided on the question, though, and it was eventually decided to establish a finance committee to assist Livesay in drawing up the annual spending estimates, thus accomplishing much of what the executive committee had been intended to achieve.[174]

Livesay's retirement on grounds of ill health – he had been suffering from diabetes – was announced to the board in October 1938.[175] Livesay's plans for a potential successor had suffered a serious blow when Harold Raine, his right-hand man in Toronto, was killed in a plane crash in 1931; Raine's intended replacement, Russell Flatt, was almost killed in a car accident soon afterward and was unable to return to work. These developments, he told a colleague, "were a horrid blow to me. I felt the years galloping at my heels and the future of The

Canadian Press at stake. It seems to me vital that I bring somebody along to take my place, because I have no confidence in directors and people like that, except for one or two like Norman Smith, who himself may be dead before then."[176]

Livesay then pinned his hopes on Gillis Purcell, a young man who had joined CP in 1928 but had already impressed Livesay and others with his "ability, tireless energy and driving force."[177] Purcell was from a newspaper family in Winnipeg; his father had been editor of the Brandon *Sun* and subsequently King's Printer for Manitoba.[178] Not yet 30, Purcell was told in 1931 – after a series of postings in Winnipeg and Ottawa – that he would be appointed CP's general news editor, after which "the limitation on your career at The Canadian Press can be only of your own devising."[179]

Livesay's relationship with Purcell was paternal, demanding, and close, and he spelled out to the young man clearly and frankly his beliefs about CP and how to manage it. CP, he told Purcell, was not a job but an idea: "an idea that must prevail in Canada. ... unless you can bring the same whole-hearted devotion to the idea you will be wasting your time, and what is more important, my time, which is growing appreciably shorter."[180]

> This job needs a man of character, of absolute honesty, but with sufficient suppleness of mind to be able to deal with the quite difficult problems in any co-operative organization, such as the relation of the French and English members and the natural antagonism of morning and evening paper members. In time he must gather to himself sufficient authority to be able to meet his President and Directors on equal terms and perhaps even successfully oppose them if he thinks they are taking a course antagonistic to the interest of the Canadian Press. All this is a tall order for any young man but you will have ample time.

Purcell's toughness was one of the characteristics Livesay considered most important in a successor. "I cannot afford to waste my time working on soft and amiable people like Flatt. There must be iron in my man, he must have character, and he must be one I can work with without getting irritated or bored."[181]

For Livesay, there was little difference between his protégé's personal and professional life. When he first joined CP, Purcell was told that he should put off thoughts of marriage for the time being: he would benefit from spending at least a year in the New York bureau, and unmarried men were less expensive than married ones.[182] After Purcell was appointed assistant news editor in Toronto, Livesay warned him against taking a fellow editor as a roommate: "It strikes me that would be for you a great mistake. You have to learn to stand alone – if necessary be lonely. How can I talk you daily confidentially with the apprehension some of it may by accident slip out (as is natural) to your roommate? ... A man might as well go and live with his butler."[183]

Livesay was happy with Purcell's progress, and their correspondence shows the older man taking him more and more into his confidence on difficult management questions (along with sharp criticism of his performance when it fell short). In the spring of 1934, Livesay's health collapsed – diabetes was threatening his eyesight. The board ordered him to take a holiday in Bermuda, from where he reported back to Purcell that "with all the swimming and all, I am very fit, but the eye is still a trouble, not completely healed and shedding tears for itself. ... I wear black goggles and a helmet, not allowed to glare, nor to read and write, so all I see of the Nassau ladies is their legs. The fact is I am *not* coming home cured."[184]

On Livesay's return, Purcell was made general superintendent.[185] But soon afterward he suffered an uncharacteristic crisis of confidence, telling Livesay he had picked the wrong man for the number two job and asking to be sent back to Winnipeg. Livesay's comment that the hard-driving Purcell did not have enough sympathy for the staff had struck a nerve.

[T]he staff generally – barring a comparative few, mostly in the West who know me personally – thinks I am a hard, unsympathetic, critical Simon Legree sort of a person. I have been disturbed about this often and it was on this basis I have asked you on two or three occasions whether it would not be possible to put someone else on my job. ... I still think this is a good idea, because I much doubt whether I have the interior flexibility to permit myself to ease down when I see that things are going inefficiently or when I see that a specified system has been allowed to lapse. ...

The reason the staff feels – quite rightly – I am a Simon Legree is first, because the opposition when I came down here was such that I had to be hard to get anywhere with an eastern staff annoyed at the idea of a westerner coming in; second, because I tried to do and maybe did too much to appease howling members, howling for better service at less money; third, because the whole system, all bureaux, had lapsed into easy-going lackadasia after Harold Raines' death and especially after Russ Flatt's accident;

fourth, because even in the last six months, since I have felt we have the whole service hitting about on all eight, I haven't had the time I wanted for the so-called personal touch except possibly in Toronto bureau.[186]

In a covering note, Purcell wrote that "you shouldn't have a Mick [Roman Catholic] in this job anyway."

But Livesay had no intention of letting Purcell go. "Mick nothing," he replied."I don't think it makes the slightest bit of difference. Certainly not to me." As for the Simon Legree comparison, "There never yet was a good driving executive like yourself who was not disliked by the weaklings of the staff. ... every word you say about the reorganization of the service is true and our directors and members know it is true because I have told them repeatedly." Purcell was ordered to take a month's holiday and given a bonus – and, for good measure, criticized for not being forceful enough in his dealings with CP's directors.[187]

By the time of Livesay's retirement, it was clear that Purcell was his intended successor. It was therefore "a great disappointment" to tell Purcell in January 1939 that, "for reasons I need not enter into here," the board had rejected Livesay's recommendation.[188] J.A. McNeil, managing editor of the Montreal *Gazette* and a long-time CP director, was the unanimous choice. Reflecting the tensions between the newspapers that owned CP and the journalists who ran it, the directors had chosen one of their own rather than the still young Purcell – whose close association with Livesay may not have been an unalloyed advantage.

Reuters executives watched the developments at CP closely. Bernard Rickatson-Hatt reported the choice of McNeil in 1939 with the observation that "[f]rom the REUTER point of view, he could hardly be worse than Livesay. ... I have an idea that Macneil [sic] may not be so willing as Livesay was to subordinate the C.P to the A.P."[189] But the real puzzle was why Purcell, "easily the most brilliant man in the C.P. organization," had not been given the job in accordance with Livesay's long-established plans. His Catholic religion was the apparent reason: "Although the R.C. member papers fought hard for him, they were overruled behind the scenes by member papers from the prairie provinces and Western Canada." Reuters' New York manager added that Catholicism had also been an issue because some directors, "fearful of the influence of Quebec papers, objected to him on that score."[190] Livesay tried to make the best of things, noting that McNeil had been one of CP Ltd.'s first correspondents in 1911, "so I have always felt him one of ourselves," and that as a director and vice president, he had been "a good friend" of the staff.[191] Purcell was commended for taking the decision "in the right C.P. spirit," but the outbreak of war would show that it left a legacy of bad feelings.

⚜

Throughout the 1920s and 1930s, CP's relationship with AP and Reuters – and through them, its position in the international news system – changed decisively. In general, CP's connection to AP became ever closer, accentuated by the growing friendship between Kent Cooper, who took over as AP's general manager in 1925, and Livesay.[192] There were, however, continuing tensions over CP's concern that some AP coverage showed anti-British bias. Livesay told the board of directors in 1922 that recent events, especially coverage of the Chanak crisis, "emphasized, as never before, the unsuitable or deficient character of The Associated Press European cable service from the Canadian Standpoint. ... some of our members went so far as to suggest that the A.P. was distinctly biased in an anti-British sense."[193] In 1927, CP complained about AP's coverage of naval disarmament talks among Britain, the United States, and Japan in Geneva. Soon after the conference began, Livesay received a complaint from the Vancouver *Province* that AP's coverage had an American slant and had to be rewritten "to give the right British perspective."[194] AP rejected the criticism, however; Cooper suggested that Livesay was trying to make AP a scapegoat for his own failings, because BUP was offering special, pro-British, coverage of the conference (Cooper described it as subsidized "British propaganda") and Livesay had failed to make arrangements for his own special coverage by CP's staff in London.[195] At the board of directors meeting that autumn, Nichols questioned whether CP could continue to rely on AP, saying its coverage had lent itself to American propaganda and "utterly distorted" the British viewpoint;[196] J.H. Woods of the Calgary *Herald*, CP's president, said that in this instance AP had acted as an American, rather than an independent, news agency. But AP insisted that the coverage had been fair; any apparent pro-American bias simply reflected the fact that American delegates at the conference had been very forthcoming in stating their views, while British delegates were uncommunicative.[197] AP, in turn, objected to the publication of the allegations of bias in CP's printed minutes – Cooper describing them as "quite defamatory" – and demanded that the statements be withdrawn, which CP refused to do.[198] The main result was that CP decided to appoint a European correspondent, based in London, who could cover stories of this kind on CP's own account.[199] Heated though they were, such conflicts were the exception rather than the rule. In general, CP's connection to AP became ever closer throughout the 1920s and 1930s, accentuated by the growing friendship between Cooper and Livesay.

As the 1927 conflict illustrated, the chief limitation of the generally close and cooperative relationship with AP was CP's wish to reflect the British perspective, rather than the American, in its international coverage. That was the point of the separate arrangement with Reuters. CP's London office was in the Reuters building, and the annual fee paid to Reuters for sending stories of imperial interest to Canada that were not included in the AP file to New York had increased to $5,000 since 1921. In return, Reuters' Ottawa bureau received the Canadian news file sent to CP member newspapers in that city, as well as the Canadian news sent to AP in New York.[200] Cooper expressed surprise when he first learned of this aspect of the arrangement in the mid-1920s, reminding Livesay "in all friendliness" that CP could not supply Canadian news to anyone other than AP under the terms of their contract, and requesting further details of the Reuters agreement.[201] Livesay quickly assured Cooper that his predecessor as general manager had been kept informed, and that AP's interests were fully protected: "the vital thing is that our contract with Associated Press does and always must take precedence over everything else."[202] There was no formal contract with Reuters, and if one was reached, it would be submitted to AP for approval. In fact, Livesay turned to AP for protection after Jones asserted that the Reuters material sent to AP in New York could be withheld from Canadian newspapers unless CP made a costly separate agreement with the British agency.[203] Cooper assured Livesay that he had no grounds for worry: CP's contract with AP guaranteed its access to the full Reuters file.[204] Furthermore, AP did not object to CP's providing Canadian news to Reuters, much of which was available to Reuters through its contract with AP in any case. As long as AP's primacy was not in question, there was no objection to CP's having a supplementary relationship with Reuters "in order to correct some faults we find in the AP service from our own Canadian angle."[205]

Reuters tried repeatedly during the later 1920s and 1930s to expand its direct relationship with CP, but without success. In 1930, CP's board of directors responded critically to a Reuters suggestion that the fee for British news should be doubled, with several directors suggesting CP should drop the payment to Reuters entirely and send more of its own staff to London – finally agreeing to offer an increase to $7,500.[206]

In the early 1930s, AP's frustration over its subordinate position in the Reuters-led cartel came to a head. AP had been pushing back the limits of the cartel agreement for decades, establishing its right to sell news in Central and South America and the Soviet Union, and stationing its own correspondents in many places outside the United States.[207] The coup de grâce came in 1934 when AP made clear that it was willing to have no contract at all with Reuters rather than continue to accept restrictions on its ability to operate as it wished anywhere in the world; this put Jones in the humiliating position of telling Cooper that Reuters could not do without an AP contract and would sign one on whatever terms AP required.[208] The breaking of the cartel arrangement that had dominated the supply of international news for more than 70 years forced CP to make a definitive choice between New York and London, but it was not an easy one. When Cooper first told Livesay about the possibility of a break, Livesay was "overwhelmed" by the news:

> With all its faults [Reuters] is the news service of the British Empire and we cannot do without it. Through its affiliation with the Press Association we get from Reuters in London all sorts of essential news – sport, domestic politics and so on – you [AP] could not be expected to lay down in New York or even make available to us in London.
>
> If from the news angle it is impossible for us to do without Reuters, from the standpoint of prestige it is equally impossible, for it would lay us open at home for the old cry, the C.P. was American and not British. And it would open wide the door for our friend Charlie Crandall and his British United Press, in alliance with Reuters, to establish a real competitive service in Canada ... you will see if you have a problem we have a graver one.[209]

Livesay went to New York at the beginning of February to press his case in person – with strict instructions from CP's executive committee "that in all circumstances the Canadian Press must remain with the A.P even if this meant breaking with Reuters" – and found that Cooper was sympathetic to his concerns.[210] A few days later, Jones arrived in New York determined to salvage the AP connection on virtually any terms. As the negotiations were proceeding, Cooper reported to Livesay that he had flatly refused Jones's request for a free hand in Canada under a new Reuters–AP contract. This was a telling indication of the drastically altered power balance: While Cooper was insisting that AP should be able to deal freely with any news agency in the world without Reuters or anyone else acting as intermediary, Reuters would have no such right in Canada. When Jones insisted on the point, Cooper replied:

> "[T]hen, Sir Roderick, we're merely wasting time. I feel that The Canadian Press-Associated Press connection is indissoluble. ... you will just have to consider that for the purposes of any negotiations The Canadian Press and The Associated Press are one and the same thing." [Jones] hesitated some little time and finally said, "all right, I accept that." ... Now if this hasn't left you in a safe position there is nothing I can do to make you safe, because I truly mean that whatever good fortune might come out of this for The Associated Press, The Canadian Press shall share it fully.[211]

When the contract was ready to be signed, Jones objected to another provision relating to CP. This clause gave CP full access not only to the Reuters international-news report that AP received directly in its London office (as had already been the case for years), but also to the Press Association (PA) report of British domestic news that AP would receive from now on through a new, seperate contract with PA. (The PA, a newspaper-owned co-operative like AP and CP, was the majority owner of Reuters, and previously PA news had been available only through Reuters.) Jones argued that as a member of the British empire, CP should deal directly with Reuters, paying an additional $30,000 annual fee for access to the Reuters and PA service.[212] But (as Cooper reported to Livesay), AP's long-serving president, Frank Noyes, spoke up strongly for CP:

> "Now, my dear Roderick, The Associated Press is not going to throw The Canadian Press to the wolves, and you may just as well accept that clause as Mr. Cooper has written it." With more eloquence Mr Noyes advanced further argument and Sir Roderick capitulated.[213]

If not for the need to protect CP, Cooper stressed to Livesay on the day the new contract was signed, AP would have been happy to have no formal connection to Reuters at all.[214] "You have certainly bottled up Sir Roderick tight so far as we are concerned," Livesay replied. In particular, the new clause referring to the PA "gives us security we have not had before ... I can imagine Sir Roderick was very reluctant to agree to that but evidently you had him in a cleft stick. The whole thing must have been to him a terrific blow, but he brought it on himself by his arrogance and vanity."[215]

CP recognized that it was greatly in its interest to have the relationship with Reuters mediated by AP,[216] but this limited its freedom of action elsewhere. For example, when CP reached an agreement later that year for news exchange with Havas, the semiofficial French agency, Cooper objected on the grounds that the CP–AP contract prohibited CP from giving Canadian news to Havas (or anyone other than AP, for that matter).[217] If such an agreement had been in place before the showdown with Reuters, "we could not have presented a united front and gotten the protection to the Canadian Press that we did get." CP ended up signing a straight purchase agreement for the Havas service, with no Canadian news provided in return.[218] The AP embrace could also bring additional benefits, though, as when AP brokered an agreement between CP and TASS – intended to preclude the possibility that TASS would make an agreement with, and thereby strengthen, UP in Canada.[219]

The clear indication that Reuters wanted to remove Canada from under the AP umbrella and charge substantially more for its supply of British and imperial news was not the only reason for CP's distrust; Reuters' continuing receipt of a substantial subsidy from the Canadian government played an important part, too.[220] In 1934, Reuters' editor-in-chief, Bernard Rickatson-Hatt, visited North America on a reconnaissance mission in the wake of the disastrous conflict with AP. On the Canadian leg of the tour, he was surprised to learn that even though Reuters was not mentioned by name in the publicity contract with the Canadian government, its involvement was "very generally known to newspapermen throughout Canada. Several reporters have asked me, 'Are you here to get an increased subsidy from the Government?'" He told Jones that Reuters' former bureau chief in Ottawa was universally looked upon as "a Government official" rather than a journalist.[221] Reuters had suffered greatly from a lack of a vigorous presence in Canada, and had a "miserable and totally undeserved reputation ... in newspaper circles as a result."[222] A conversation with Livesay made it even clearer how badly the subsidy had damaged Reuters' credibility.[223] Livesay told Hatt it was widely known that Reuters lived on subsidies from the Canadian and other governments, which "meant that Reuters' news was not always trusted." For example, CP was reluctant to rely on Reuters stories about Gandhi, "because we know that the Government of India controls what you send," and Reuters' recent South African election coverage was "notoriously pro-Smuts." The Reuters service from Ottawa was "contemptible ... dull and entirely dictated by Officialdom"; unlike nonprofit agencies such as AP and CP, Reuters was mainly interested in making money "and not in collecting news." Livesay acknowledged that he had had numerous conflicts with Cooper, but insisted that AP could be trusted – a conclusion that Hatt saw only as evidence of "how completely [Livesay] is under the thumb of K.C." Nonetheless, Hatt urged Jones to improve the Reuters service from Ottawa so that Livesay and others would take it more seriously, and to assist CP men in London as much as possible: "These things will count if we are going to win over the C.P. from the A.P. and make them more dependent upon Reuters."

Some Reuters journalists also saw the subsidy as problematic. The number two man in Reuters' Ottawa bureau was Gilbert Mant, a young Australian who had been trained at Reuters in London, and had chief responsibility for the Canadian news operation. In an extended cri de coeur to Hatt in the fall of 1934, Mant enumerated the difficulties he faced. In sending cable news to London, Reuters was consistently beaten by BUP from Montreal and Central News from Toronto. If not for the need to nurture the government contract, the obvious place for Reuters' news operation would be at CP headquarters in Toronto, not a relative backwater like Ottawa, which did not even receive the full CP news report. Mant reported that he got along with Reuters' bureau chief and his assistant, who were responsible for maintaining the government contract, but that they lived in different worlds, journalistically speaking. "Their hearts are bound up in the contract and at first they were terrified lest I should wreck it by wanting to cable scandal and too much sob-stuff. ... Things are better now, but there is a singular lack of cooperation, not deliberate on their part but from forgetfulness." One source of concern was Reuters' cooperative arrangement with Hearst's INS, whose Ottawa representative had an eye for scandal: "The Contract will undoubtedly be imperilled once the Government finds out that questionable stories are being sent to the States from Reuters office." It was clear that the government contract limited Reuters' Canadian news coverage in significant ways.[224]

CP's interest in establishing an imperial cooperative news agency was a further manifestation of its distrust of Reuters. At conferences of journalists from around the empire in 1930 and 1935, CP's representatives (Livesay in 1930) repeatedly tried to get support for this idea, which amounted to a vote of nonconfidence in Reuters as the de facto imperial agency.[225] (One of Livesay's complaints to Hatt was that a Reuters story about the 1930 conference had described him as an "anachronism," and he told Cooper at the time that Reuters and CP were having a "terrific row" over the issue.[226]) At the 1935 Empire Press Union conference in South Africa, CP presented a resolution calling on members "to give early consideration to the establishment of co-operative news associations owned and controlled by the newspapers, in the belief that this will lead to an interchange of news within the Empire."[227] Despite the mild language, the anti-Reuters intent was clear; in his printed account of the conference, CP's chief delegate observed that because Reuters "receives money from various sources for commercial and other services rendered, its news services to newspapers might not be in the public mind entirely free from suspicion of propaganda." This was vigorously denied by Jones and the chairman of the Press Association (which now owned Reuters); by Jones' account, the CP delegates had been "fundamentally corrected" on this point.[228] One of CP's directors recalled later that when the idea of an imperial cooperative was first introduced, there was "some antipathy on the part of the larger papers, particularly in Australia,"[229] but the resolution was adopted, though without much discussion or apparent enthusiasm. While nothing further seems to have come of this idea – not particularly surprising, since only Canada, New Zealand, and Britain (for domestic news) had established cooperative news agencies by this time[230] – Livesay continued to believe that

> [t]he present system under which Reuters has a monopoly of the export of news is all wrong. Australians and Canadians can never understand each other until they can exchange news freely as between themselves without passing it through the tight discriminating mesh of London opinion as to what is good for us.[231]

Despite the setback represented by Reuters' 1934 contract with AP, Jones continued to press for the establishment of a separate Reuters service to Canada. In 1935, he submitted a confidential report to the newly appointed governor general, John Buchan, now Lord Tweedsmuir. Buchan and Jones were "old friends."[232] As head of the Department of Information, Buchan had been Jones's immediate superior during the First World War; he was also the first "government director" of Reuters when Jones became managing director, and continued as a Reuters director in the 1920s.[233] Jones stressed the drawbacks from an imperial point of view of CP's close relationship with AP: not only was CP modelled after AP, "[i]t is really *controlled* by the Associated Press. ... should the Associated Press decide that the Canadian Press could no longer supply their news report in Ottawa to Reuter, the Canadian Press would have to obey. ... The Associated Press management in New York have only to crack the whip and the Canadian Press comes to heel." AP's "stranglehold" over CP had an economic basis: the American agency provided "complete world coverage at comparatively trifling cost."[234] However, in Jones's view, CP could be independent only if it relied "mainly upon the only world news report that a British dominion ought to depend upon, and all the other Dominions do, namely Reuters." Jones said Livesay was "a special pal of Kent Cooper, and, like Kent Cooper, suffers from an extraordinary anti-Reuter complex. ... His fixed idea is that Reuters live on Government subsidies!!" However, the Canadian subsidy that Reuters received had no effect on its journalism: Reuters' representative in Ottawa assured Jones that the government had never asked him to send or suppress any particular story. It was important to remember that Reuters was "absolutely free and independent," since "some newspaper publishers in Canada, primed by Livesay, go about saying that Reuters live on a subsidy from the Canadian Government. This is mischievous, and it is a lie."

Jones's memorandum does not appear to have had any tangible result, however. In 1936, the subsidy for British publicity was ended, which led to the closing of Reuters' office in Ottawa.[235] The newly appointed minister of trade and commerce – co-owner of a newspaper in Kitchener, Ontario, and a CP member when the Reuters subsidy was initially granted in 1923 – quickly took the opportunity to scrap a grant that he had always opposed.[236] A year later, CP cut its remaining tie with Reuters, moving from the Reuters/PA building on Fleet Street into AP's new office in London.[237] Two additional CP editors were posted to London, and the $7,500 payment to Reuters was dropped. Livesay assured the board of directors that nothing would be lost: under the provisions of the 1934 contract, CP had access to the full Reuters and Press Association services through AP, and deciding what to send to Canada from London in close consultation with AP's editors reduced duplicate transmission of news items almost to zero.[238]

Despite all the setbacks, Reuters continued to keep an eye on developments in Canada, evidently hoping that some opportunity to make inroads would yet arise. When Livesay retired as general manager in 1938, Hatt expressed hopes that his successor, J.A. McNeil, would not be so closely tied to AP. But at CP's next annual meeting, there was no sign that anything had changed. Hatt complained that the president's address contained "nausea-provoking references" to CP's close cooperation with AP, and even the valuable service it was receiving from Havas, with "[n]ot a word anywhere about Reuters!"[239]

❦

The idea of news as a commodity is central to accounts of the evolution of the international news system.[240] While illuminating work has been done on the economic characteristics of news,[241] it is also important to remember that news is a peculiar kind of commodity, a cultural commodity. This was clearly reflected in the debates about subsidization in the 1920s and 1930s. The eventual agreement between Cooper and Livesay that subsidies were unacceptable reflected shared beliefs about acceptable standards of journalistic practice. The significance of such agreement or disagreement about journalistic practices has not often been considered in accounts of news-agency alliances.[242] Until relatively recently, many news-agency histories were written by veterans of the agencies involved, stressing their adherence to journalistic conventions of objectivity, independence, or freedom of the press.[243] Academic analysis has tended (rightly) to be sceptical about accepting such accounts uncritically, which often gloss over the economic and competitive interests involved.[244]

But journalistic unease about subsidies deserves to be taken seriously. Many Canadian, American, Australian, and British journalists (including some inside Reuters) were concerned about subsidies, often to the point of refusing them, especially when it appeared that governmental control was involved. (Subsidies that operated in an automatic or arm's length way, such as lower cable fees, were considered more acceptable.) In CP's case, there was also an overall evolution of its views. By the mid-1930s, Kent Cooper's assertion that no subsidies were acceptable under any circumstances had also become CP's settled policy.

A second cultural consideration – the desire to foster the imperial dimension of Canadian identity – often pushed CP in a different direction, though. Despite numerous setbacks and difficulties, CP never stopped wanting to get a better supply of news from Britain and the empire. Throughout the 1920s and 1930s, Reuters did everything it could to equate Britishness with a Reuters connection. The 1934 Reuters–AP contract was a decisive break – in ensuring that CP could have access to the full service of both Reuters and the Press Association through AP, without having a separate contract with Reuters, the link between Britishness and a business connection with Reuters was broken. This allowed CP to end its special payments to Reuters in 1937 without losing an imperial focus. One way of understanding the events of the 1920s and 1930s, then, is to suggest that the Canadians' growing opposition to subsidies, combined with AP's newly powerful position in the international news system, cancelled out their wishes for a closer relationship with Reuters as a way of fostering British identity. Cultural considerations augmented the dominant economic reasons for CP's "indissoluble" reliance on AP, so the connection became closer than ever. Not until Roderick Jones was forced to resign in 1941 would the shape of the three-sided relationship change once again.[245]

3 News on the Air

The emergence of radio as a news medium in the 1920s and 1930s presented Canadian Press and its members with profound challenges. It also presents the historian with a signal opportunity to examine one of the key themes in the history of communication: what is the nature and significance of technological change?[1] To what extent did a new medium like radio alter the communications landscape by itself, and to what extent was it shaped by the economic, political, and cultural context in which it emerged? How did it conflict or coexist with the older, previously dominant medium of newspapers? And what did this mean for a telegraphic news agency like CP, whose organization, until now, had been based entirely on news in print?

Certainly, many Canadian newspapers eagerly embraced the new medium of radio in its early, experimental years. As Mary Vipond has shown, they forcefully promoted this latest technological marvel in the early 1920s, bringing it to public attention.[2] Of the first 21 radio broadcasting licenses issued in Canada, eight were held by newspapers, making them the largest single group of broadcasters, and the stations they operated were "the most active and best-financed."[3]

Right from the beginning, however, the members of CP (comprising almost all daily newspapers in Canada) had great difficulty coming up with rules governing the use of the agency's news on the air that would command general support. Over the next 20 years, it proved to be one of the most divisive issues CP had to face. While some CP members, including several of the largest and most powerful newspapers in Canada, actively wanted to be involved in radio broadcasting, many (mostly smaller newspapers) did not.[4] In many situations, newspapers with radio connections were prepared to support some restrictions on the use of CP news on the air, but they were hardly died-in-the-wool opponents of broadcast news.[5] Those who wanted to ban the use of CP news on the air entirely or restrict it severely did not have sufficient collective weight within the organization to impose their wishes on the others. Even when restrictive policies were adopted, many papers ignored them with relative impunity.

Radio was controversial because it allowed news to reach more people than newspapers did, and faster than newspapers did, threatening their circulation and advertising revenue. It disrupted the way news was disseminated in time and space, and it completed the reshaping of the time structure of information that is traditionally associated with the telegraph. The telegraph allowed the virtually instantaneous dissemination of information to a great many recipients simultaneously, but it only took the revolution partway, one might say: rather than disseminating information to individual readers, the telegraph disseminated information to newspapers, which published (more or less) once every 24 hours, and, in Canada, usually no more than six days a week.[6] For readers, telegraphic news meant that they received a single, quite large block of miscellaneous, up-to-date information at about the same time once every 24 hours. Radio, in effect, completed the instantaneousness revolution, allowing news to be broadcast at any moment, as soon it was received, reaching thousands of listeners directly and immediately. In theory, every piece of news that appeared in the morning edition of *The Globe* or any other paper could have been broadcast earlier at some point in the previous 24 hours. The ability to broadcast news events live, as they actually unfolded, made radio an even more formidable competitor.[7]

Radio also changed the way information was disseminated in space. Newspapers have to be physically transported to their readers. It took at least 90 minutes to transport a newspaper published in Toronto the 60 miles to, say, Kitchener, Ontario, where it competed with the local newspaper for circulation. During that 90 minutes, its Kitchener-based competitor could continue to put later news developments into that day's edition before starting its press run, thus publishing more up-to-date news than its Toronto rival while still reaching readers at the same time. But radio was different: a Toronto station with a sufficiently strong signal could reach Kitchener and Toronto at exactly the same time, which gave the Toronto radio station a spatial reach that the newspaper did not possess, and a stronger competitive position in the distant market. The telegraph tended to strengthen the position of local newspapers against their metropolitan rivals,[8] but radio worked in the opposite direction. When radio stations were coordinated into networks, the changing spatial dynamic of information that resulted was revolutionary, allowing hundreds of thousands or millions of people in widely distant locations – all across Canada, for example, or all around the British Empire – to receive exactly the same information at exactly the same time.[9] There were, in short, clear reasons why many newspapers felt threatened by radio. The structure of time and the organization of space on which their businesses depended were radically called into question by radio's instantaneousness and its regional, national, and continental reach.

Some scholars have used the metaphor of a "press–radio war" to explain how newspapers responded to this disruptive new medium in the 1920s and 1930s.[10] A careful examination of CP's experience, however, suggests that although the "war" metaphor captures some important aspects of newspapers' role in the emergence of radio in Canada, it does not provide a good overall explanation. Rather, the conflicts between newspapers and radio are better explained by examining the evolution of the whole competitive environment in which they operated. Throughout this 20-year period, competition of different kinds and at different levels ebbed, flowed, and overlapped:

- Newspapers – virtually all of them CP members – that owned or were otherwise affiliated with radio stations competed with CP members that had no such connection.
- Radio stations affiliated with newspapers competed with those that had no newspaper ties and therefore were not bound by CP's rules.
- All news organizations (newspapers and radio stations) within cities competed with each other, providing strong defensive reasons for involvement in broadcasting.
- Metropolitan newspapers and broadcasters constantly sought to make inroads in nearby towns and cities.
- A public, nonprofit radio network competed with privately owned commercial stations after the Canadian Radio Broadcasting Commission (CRBC) was established in the 1930s.
- CP, as a provider of radio news, competed with other radio news services after 1935.
- Canadian news sources and stations competed with American services and broadcasters.

With all these different currents in operation, the overall competitive ecology[11] was highly complex and dynamic.

Although there were significant continuities throughout the first 20 years of radio broadcasting in Canada, three main phases can be identified. The years from 1922 until 1931 were characterized by tremendous disarray. CP adopted a series of ad hoc, often contradictory policies about radio, and even these were often ignored by its members. Local and regional competition was the key underlying factor. The second phase began in 1931, as radio became a more serious competitor for advertising revenue and the Canadian regulatory environment underwent radical changes with the advent of the CRBC. CP now began to approach radio much more systematically, and at a national level. The key decision came in 1933, when the formation of a strategic alliance with the CRBC saw CP as an organization become a provider of radio news for the first time. Between 1935 and 1941, US-based radio news services began expanding aggressively into Canada. This inexorably forced CP, by now committed to the radio news business for better or worse, into a series of retreats from what had previously been considered the bedrock of its approach, notably strict time limits on when radio news could be broadcast and a ban on commercial sponsorship. By 1941, these competitive pressures had effectively left CP with no choice but to become one of several commercial suppliers of radio news, imposing very few restrictions on its clients.

When the subject of radio news first came before CP's board of directors in 1922, the initial impulse was restrictive: a blanket ban on CP news being broadcast was proposed. At the annual general meeting two months later, however, the members decided to do nothing until they had a clearer idea of how they would be affected by radio. The tension between prohibition and tolerance that emerged at this early date would persist through the 1920s and 1930s.[12]

The following year, representatives of several western Canadian newspapers explained why they wanted to be involved with radio. John Imrie of the Edmonton *Journal* said radio was more important in the west than the east because of the long distances between settlements: "The obligations of a daily newspaper to subscribers reached by the paper a day or even two days later than publication involved some departures from former ideas of publication and circulation."[13] Farmers taking their grain to market needed to know the current price by early afternoon, well before that day's newspaper could reach them. F.J. Burd of the Vancouver *Province* argued that radio service to the valley settlements of British Columbia made their isolation more tolerable. For Burford Hooke of the Regina *Leader*, a mixed-media form called radiographing – sending radio reports to remote locations, where they were transcribed and posted on bulletin boards – was producing good results: "The policy of this paper was to radiograph just enough to leave the people in suspense and make them buy papers."[14] The notion that radio could "whet, but not satiate" listeners' appetite for news was one that newspaper proponents of broadcasting asserted throughout the period – against the more pessimistic view that radio news would inevitably cut into newspaper circulation because it provided the news faster. In this, as in most things concerning radio, the opinions of CP members were to remain divided.

The 1923 meeting also heard arguments about how and why radio news should be restricted. Arthur Penny of the Quebec *Chronicle* said restrictions should apply only when radio news altered the competitive balance in a particular location, but not otherwise. Stewart Lyon of the *Globe* argued that radio stations should be allowed to broadcast election returns supplied by CP only after the results had been printed in every newspaper in the city or region in question. It was accordingly agreed that CP election results could not be broadcast after 10 p.m. on an election night, guaranteeing that those eager to know the outcome would have to turn to a local newspaper the following day.

The general policy on news broadcasting that CP adopted that year was restrictive, but not an outright prohibition. Any news already published in a CP member's newspaper could be broadcast on a radio station that the newspaper owned or that it regularly supplied with news. (Several newspapers had regular supplier arrangements of this kind, which gave them on-air credit for the news broadcasts and thus had clear promotional value. The *Globe*'s arrangement with CFRB in Toronto and the *Telegram*'s alliance with CKGW were two prominent examples of this approach.) The purpose was clearly to limit the disruption caused by the unprecedented speed of radio news, making sure that newspaper readers would not hear news on the air before they had a chance to read it. The only exceptions were bulletins specifically designated by CP management for radio broadcast or news of overwhelming importance. It was generally agreed that bulletins about major accidents or natural disasters, for example, could not reasonably be withheld; these, known as extraordinary service, or EOS, bulletins, could be broadcast at any time.[15]

It is important to recognize that in imposing these time restrictions, the members of CP were not doing anything new. Cooperative news agencies such as AP and CP are in some respects very unusual organizations. Their purpose is to allow extensive and valuable cooperation in newsgathering among member newspapers that are, in many cases, direct and bitter competitors. Therefore, the rules of these organizations included very explicit and binding provisions to control competition, especially in relation to time.

The designation of every CP member as either a morning or afternoon paper was central to the time-based control of competition that was embedded in the agency's structure. Morning papers were allowed to publish only between the hours of 9:30 p.m. and 9:30 a.m., whereas afternoon papers were restricted to publishing between 9:30 a.m. and 9:30 p.m. The agency distributed its telegraphic news accordingly: a substantial news story was typically transmitted once for all papers in the 12-hour "AM" publication cycle, with an updated version being sent once during the "PM" cycle. In a city with one morning and one afternoon paper, this meant that they interfered with each other, competitively speaking, as little as possible – the morning paper could go out to its readers secure in the knowledge that the CP news it published was substantially fresher than anything that had appeared in the previous day's afternoon paper, and the afternoon paper had the same assurance. These rules were strictly enforced. A paper that published CP news outside its approved hours could be fined, and such fines were regularly levied when complaints were made.[16] Thus when the members of CP imposed time limits on radio news broadcasts to limit the competitive threat, they were simply applying rules of a kind they all accepted already. Radio was not treated as something requiring a radically new response; instead, the very real competitive pressures it represented were incorporated into a well-established structure for controlling competition among newspapers.

In any case, this restrictive approach to radio news did not last long. In 1925, CP decided that members could broadcast CP news at any time during their approved hours of publication – which left open the possibility that stories could be broadcast before they were physically printed.[17] Radio news was now controlled in relation to time in exactly the same way that printed news was controlled. This was much less restrictive than AP's approach at the time, which was close to an outright ban on the use of its news for broadcast. Institutional differences in policy between the Canadian and American news agencies, rather than the inherent characteristics of newspapers and radio as media, could lead to substantial differences in approach.[18] In 1929, the policy was amended to give J.F.B. Livesay, CP's general manager, more discretion: news eligible for broadcast must be of international or national importance, "namely of wire bulletin value, and such routine news, sports, markets, etc. as the General Manager may from time to time specify."[19]

However, CP's radio policies were widely ignored by the members and difficult to enforce. Two Toronto morning newspapers, the *Globe* and the *Mail and Empire* – both involved in broadcasting news through continuing arrangements with independent radio stations – were the prime focus of complaint. These stations were including CP news from nearby Ontario towns in their noon radio broadcasts, which was outside their approved hours of publication as morning papers. The problem, discussed at length during CP meetings in 1930, illustrated the complexity of the underlying competitive situation. To begin with, H.W. Anderson of the *Globe* disputed the charge. The news being broadcast was lifted from the noon editions of the Toronto evening papers, not taken directly from CP, he said, and the *Globe* had a right to broadcast it "because it was public property when published."[20] But if this practice were allowed to continue, it would threaten one of CP's main organizational characteristics – the requirement that all members provide the local news they gathered to the cooperative, which then disseminated it to other members. This obligation to provide "return news" was one of the great competitive strengths of cooperative agencies like CP and AP, which thereby could offer extremely broad geographical coverage without a large staff. However, problems arose when competing newspapers – often metropolitan newspapers seeking additional circulation in nearby towns and cities – used the return news supplied by a member to make inroads in its circulation area, and the spatial reach of radio made this problem more acute. Livesay pointed out to Anderson that Ontario papers outside Toronto would simply withhold their return news if they risked being scooped by Toronto-based broadcasts, and others supported this view. A.R. Alloway of the Oshawa *Times* (Oshawa was 30 miles east of Toronto) complained that when news sent to CP was broadcast before it could be published locally, it "decreased the value of that news and lowered the prestige of the newspaper."[21]

It was embarrassing to be told by people on the street that certain things had happened that morning in Oshawa, for instance. Radio listeners thought they were giving the paper a tip, whereas the paper had the story in type waiting for presses to run. The practice knocked the props from under the smaller Ontario papers, who were subjected to enough legitimate penetration by Toronto papers in their home circulation field, without radio aggravating it.[22]

To satisfy the complaining members, Anderson promised that the *Globe* would cease broadcasting CP news from Toronto noon editions, and Livesay reported that a similar agreement had been reached with the *Mail and Empire.*

Not all newspapers agreed with this solution, however. Thomas Miller of the Moose Jaw *Times-Herald* said his paper faced competition from commercial broadcasters that had no newspaper affiliation, not other newspapers that were involved with broadcasting. The unaffiliated commercial stations simply read on the air the news that appeared in the noon editions of the Winnipeg papers; since CP had no way of controlling these private broadcasters, "it hardly seemed fair to penalize newspaper broadcasting stations" that competed with them by restricting what the newspaper-affiliated stations could broadcast and when.[23] The presence of private broadcasters who could operate entirely independently of CP (and later on, the presence of private radio news services such as Transradio[24] and BUP) meant that limiting radio news on stations affiliated with CP members simply weakened their competitive position.

In any case, the Toronto newspapers did not honour the agreement. At a meeting of CP's Ontario members the following year, W.J. Motz of the Kitchener *News Record* complained that return news provided to CP was still being broadcast by Toronto stations before his newspaper had a chance to publish it. (Kitchener, 60 miles west of Toronto, was within range of its more powerful radio stations.) One day, for example, the *Mail and Empire*'s noon broadcast reported a level-crossing accident near Kitchener. This had been "the only local story worth featuring in Kitchener that day" – but by the time his paper went to press, "the news interest had gone out of the story because most people had heard it on the air."[25] It was not just a matter of the *Mail and Empire*'s actions; all four Toronto dailies were violating the regulations in various ways. Livesay concluded that the regulation restricting the hours of broadcasting had been brought into contempt by "the failure of the Toronto members to respect it in any way, shape, or form" and should therefore be rescinded. Asked why the offending Toronto papers were not compelled to follow the rules, Livesay replied that "the resolution had not behind it the authority of a sufficiently large membership opinion." He cited the experience of AP, which had started out by seeking to regulate broadcasting, "but had finally thrown up its hands in despair. Such a resolution was not enforceable unless behind it was the solid support of the membership" – support which it clearly did not have.

John Scott of the *Mail and Empire* offered a lukewarm defence of his paper's actions. "All the Toronto papers were broadcasting news in self-defence, because commercial broadcasting organizations picked up Canadian Press news and broadcast it after it was published without any interference." Once again, the competition between radio stations that were affiliated with newspapers and those that were not cut across any straightforward newspaper-versus-radio polarization. A.W.J. Buckland of the Toronto *Telegram* went further, insisting that broadcasting actually helped his paper's circulation. Arthur Ford of the London *Free Press*, which operated its own radio station, said the matter did not concern him because his paper published both morning and evening editions and could therefore broadcast CP news at any time. Livesay's testy reminder that this was not so – that only bulletin news could be broadcast in any case – seemed only to underline the organization's disarray.

In preparation for CP's 1931 annual meeting, Livesay announced a new approach.[26] From now on, members could not broadcast CP news unless it was classified "Bulletin MBB (May Be Broadcast)." This would explicitly leave all decisions about what could be broadcast to CP's management. If the new restrictions were to be effective, however, the board of directors must be prepared to "drastically deal with all breaches." Scott of the *Mail and Empire* said the Toronto papers would accept the new approach, adding that two of the four were prepared to get out of broadcasting entirely, while the other two believed this would simply leave the field open to private broadcasters. One of the latter was the *Globe*. If its noon broadcasts were dropped entirely, the *Globe*'s affiliated station, CFRB, would simply scalp the news from newspapers' noon editions, "having informed The Globe the broadcast was necessary for advertising purposes." Others continued to play down the problem; Whitaker of the Brantford *Expositor* described a radio news flash as "a teaser like a bulletin board, [which] increased reader interest," and W.A. Buchanan of Lethbridge arguing that broadcasting "merely whetted the appetite of newspaper readers who wanted a fuller story," increasing his newspaper's circulation in the process.[27] Given the different competitive environments in which different publishers operated, consensus remained elusive.

The rules under which AP made its news available to US stations also affected the competitive situation in Canada. Many American stations could be heard in Canada, and powerful stations like CFRB in Toronto and CKAC in Montreal were affiliates of American networks. Similarly, Canadian broadcasts could reach US listeners. In March 1925, AP's general manager, Kent Cooper, complained to Livesay that a Montreal station had broadcast AP news about recent tornados. These reports, which violated AP's ban on the use of its news on the air, could be heard throughout the US northeast. Cooper insisted that it was "essential for The Canadian Press, both for its welfare and ours, to put itself in line with the Associated Press attitude to broadcasting," and urged CP to seek a Canadian court ruling establishing property right in news, which had been recognized in the United States by the Supreme Court in 1918 and could therefore be used to stop the unauthorized use of AP news by US broadcasters. [28] CP was never able to obtain a Canadian court decision recognizing news as property, however; under the circumstances, all Livesay could do was to warn CP members that they were not allowed to broadcast AP news.

Soon, however, the situation was reversed. CP's initial approach to covering the federal election of 29 October 1925 was to reiterate the existing ban on the broadcasting of CP-provided election returns after 10 p.m. on voting day.[29] Four days after that policy was restated, however, Livesay essentially abandoned it. AP, facing competition of its own from US news agencies that dealt more liberally with radio, had now dropped its ban on broadcasting election results,[30] and CP quickly followed suit. A special, limited election service would be prepared for radio use only, reflecting the principle that radio news "should be designed to whet the appetite rather than satiate it." Overall national and provincial results would be reported along with summaries from the larger cities, and the election or defeat of prominent candidates, but no individual constituency results beyond that.[31] Only those broadcasters owned by or otherwise connected with a local newspaper would be allowed to use the CP service. The intention was to strengthen the competitive position of radio stations allied with CP members against stations without such a connection, not to pit newspapers against radio per se.

This sudden change of heart showed clearly that AP's decisions had to be taken into account in Canada. This was underscored again in 1930 after AP decided to allow broadcasting of major news bulletins outside the publication hours of member newspapers. CP's policy at the time was more restrictive, but as Livesay observed candidly, when Canadians could hear such bulletins on American stations (or their Canadian affiliates) but not their own, the Canadian broadcasts "became jokes."[32] CP's rules were amended accordingly and promptly. The pervasive continental dynamic of radio, as Mary Vipond has observed, was a permanent feature of the competitive ecology in which Canadian broadcasters (and the newspapers with which some of them were connected) had to operate.[33]

For almost a decade after 1922, CP's attitude towards radio was characterized by disagreement and disarray. There was a rapid succession of changing and sometimes contradictory policies, often improvised to address the most recent problem to arise. Not until April 1931 did CP address the question of radio in a comprehensive way. Eighteen months earlier, the Royal Commission on Radio Broadcasting had called for the nationalization of radio in Canada, and it was clear that the regulatory framework for broadcasting was about to undergo major and systematic changes, with important consequences for Canadian newspapers. Victor Sifton, publisher of the Regina *Leader-Post*, told CP's board of directors that the time had come for members of CP to work together with the Canadian Daily Newspapers Association (CDNA; the newspapers' industrial and lobbying organization), looking into "all angles" of the radio question. "If a joint committee decided radio was a great menace, it could decide on a programme. If all members pressed for and obtained the nationalization of radio, their troubles would be ended because broadcasting of news could be controlled and advertising probably would be cut out entirely."[34] The involvement of the CDNA signalled that radio was no longer simply a matter affecting the supply of news, which was CP's main responsibility; the whole economic basis of the industry was at stake.

The joint committee was duly set up, including many of the country's most powerful publishers. At its first meeting, M.E. Nichols (general manager of the Winnipeg *Tribune*, and one of the founders of CP in 1917) urged everyone to put aside local competitive issues, which had dominated CP's consideration of the question to date, and focus on the common interests of the newspaper industry as a whole in relation to radio. Radio broadcasting in the United States was already "a menace" to US newspapers, and "[i]f permitted to develop along similar lines in Canada, it would become a serious menace to Canadian newspapers."

The emergence of advertising as a central issue in newspapers' attitude towards radio had much to do with the development of a more united front in the early 1930s. As Mary Vipond has noted, advertising was not an established method of financing radio broadcasting until the late 1920s, so newspapers had not previously considered radio a serious competitor in this respect.[35] In 1931, though, Nichols told his colleagues that radio advertising revenue in the United States had now reached $50 million, about one-quarter of the total advertising revenue of daily newspapers.[36] The situation was not that bad in Canada yet, but could quickly become very serious if "certain broadcasting conditions are permitted to prevail." A permanent subcommittee was established whose sole purpose was to study the effect of radio advertising on newspaper revenue and to work with agencies and advertisers to find ways of limiting it.[37] In 1935, Livesay told CP's board of directors that commercial radio stations considered news the best seller for advertisers and the cheapest commodity they had to offer.[38] According to C.O. Knowles of the *Telegram*, commercial broadcasters could get three times as much for advertisements immediately before and after news broadcasts than at any other time.[39]

The sharpening focus on lost advertising revenue marked a major shift in the way CP members approached the problem of radio. For the first time, the radio medium as a whole was seen in opposition to the newspaper medium as a whole, rather than as a new but far from decisive factor overlaid on existing competitive patterns. Frederick Ker of the Hamilton *Spectator* (and an unofficial spokesman for the Southam newspapers) agreed with Nichols: American publishers were deeply concerned about radio competition for advertising. Britain's policy of full public ownership offered the "surest means for safeguarding the great potentialities of radio from exploitation for private profit instead of the welfare of the public." Public ownership would also allow CP to make arrangements with a "responsible" government body for broadcasting news, leaving newsgathering in the hands of the newspapers.[40]

Joseph Atkinson, publisher of the Toronto *Star*, had been one of the first newspapermen in Canada to operate a radio station; the *Star* still owned CFCA, though it operated at a mere 500 watts.[41] He, too, agreed that radio was a "growing menace" to newspapers, especially if Canada's two railways succeeded in their plans of establishing massively powerful 50,000-watt stations in Montreal and Toronto. Atkinson suggested approaching the subject under four general headings: (1) should broadcasting of news be limited to newspapers; (2) should newspapers broadcast at all; (3) would the interests of the newspaper industry be better guarded if radio broadcasting was nationalized; (4) invasion of radio on advertising revenues. Although many newspaper executives were in favour of nationalization, believing it would minimize, if not end, competition for advertising revenue, this view was not unanimous. Oswald Mayrand of *La Presse*, which operated one of the largest and most successful radio stations in Canada, said he believed the people of Quebec would not support nationalization, though they did favour government control of broadcasting.[42]

Unable to reach a common position on nationalization,[43] the CP–CDNA committee decided to focus on a much more limited step that almost everyone could accept: a proposal to stop, or at least limit, the publication of radio stations' broadcast schedules in newspapers. Many radio programs now included a sponsor's name as part of the title, which the publishers considered to be unpaid advertising; even if no trade name was used, publicizing sponsored programs seemed too much like helping a direct competitor for advertising revenue. As a first step, it was agreed to limit radio schedules to announcing programs of outstanding interest, eliminating all trade names. Stations that wished to list sponsored programs would have to purchase advertising space.[44]

As long as every newspaper in a particular market adopted the same approach – that is, if no one took advantage of a competitor's limitations on radio listings by resuming their publication in order to poach readers – this would have few competitive repercussions. Atkinson said the *Star* was prepared to eliminate from its news columns all reference to the *Star*'s radio station and programs, to stop publishing all radio schedules, and even to stop broadcasting news altogether – but only if all the other Toronto papers would do the same. Motz of the Kitchener *News Record* said papers in western Ontario would stop publishing radio schedules entirely as soon as the Toronto papers did, or would limit publication in accordance with whatever the Toronto papers decided. But inducing everyone to adopt the same approach was difficult. With four competing dailies in Toronto, the competitive situation was inherently unstable, as W.B. Preston of the Brantford *Expositor* observed: "While the Globe, Mail and Empire and Star were willing to reach a fair agreement [about the broadcasting of news], The Telegraph [Telegram] would not as long as The Star operated its own station."[45]

Besides limiting radio listings, CP also wanted to prevent commercial stations from simply appropriating news that appeared in local newspapers. To have any success in this area, CP would have to explore the possibility of having property rights in news legally recognized, as was the case in the United States.[46] Before anyone could see where this might lead, however, the Canadian radio landscape was radically altered by the establishment of the Canadian Radio Broadcasting Commission (CRBC) in 1932. The CRBC's plan to operate six very powerful, publicly owned stations across Canada, while allowing private stations to continue in operation under its regulations, changed the competitive radio–newspaper ecology dramatically. CP members could now focus their attention on the new national broadcaster-regulator and seek to establish working arrangements for radio news that would apply to most of Canada. The CRBC's determination not to rely on advertising meant the threat of revenue loss to newspapers was greatly reduced; its regulatory powers offered the prospect of a ban on the scalping of newspaper stories by broadcasters. But if CP was to take advantage of the possibilities of greater control over radio news offered by the creation of the CRBC, it would have to become an official and systematic news provider to the national radio service. This was a major change; previously the authorized use of CP news on radio had been limited to radio stations that were allied with individual CP members. Now, for the first time, CP as an organization was considering providing news to a nationwide radio service with which none of its member newspapers had any direct connection.

As soon as Hector Charlesworth, a prominent editor and critic, was appointed chief commissioner of the CRBC, Livesay contacted him to suggest that the commission impose a rule similar to one in effect in Australia, prohibiting the broadcasting of news without consent of the agency or newspaper that supplied it. "[T]here is quite a strong expectation on behalf of our members [that] relief in this matter of the theft of news will be secured through your Commission ... Canada is the only country in the world where this theft of news is continuing practically unchecked," Livesay wrote, adding that the CRBC's creation was "due in large part to newspaper support."[47] Charlesworth was sympathetic, but said the commission did not have the authority to make such a regulation; however, he invited CP to send a "strong delegation" to Ottawa to follow up on its request. At this meeting, in February 1933,

Charlesworth told the more than 20 CP members present that the CRBC wanted to have daily news broadcasts on its stations, especially to serve remote areas, and that he hoped arrangements to provide these could be worked out with CP.[48]

Less than two months later, an order-in-council was passed that gave Canadian newspapers much of the protection they had been demanding. Canadian radio stations were prohibited from broadcasting news taken from any newspaper or news agency unless it was a bulletin prepared by CP "for the express use of broadcasting stations," local news provided by arrangement with a local newspaper, or news gathered directly by the station or any newsgathering agency it employed. This would still allow newspaper-allied stations to broadcast news as they had been doing, but the scalping of newspaper reports by unaffiliated private stations was banned. With this explicit protection, CP's quest to establish property right in news was no longer necessary. Livesay later told CP members that the order-in-council came as "a complete surprise," adding that the commission was clearly in earnest with its plans to broadcast news to parts of the country where newspapers were unavailable, "and if CP refused to supply the bulletins the commission would have to go elsewhere."[49]

An agreement was quickly reached under which CP would provide four news bulletins a day, each of five minutes' duration (300–400 words), to be broadcast at 8 and 11 a.m. and 4 and 9 p.m. It was to be paid $6,000 annually for this service. The news broadcasts were to be sponsored by the commission, with due credit given to CP. CP news was not under any circumstances to be sold to advertisers; there could be no question of CP itself participating in the siphoning-off of advertising revenue from newspapers. All in all, the quid pro quo could not have been clearer: Charlesworth stressed that once the service began, the commission would be prepared to deal effectively with complaints from CP members about theft of their news by competing commercial broadcasters.[50]

As usual when radio was involved, the draft agreement with the CRBC provoked heated debate among CP's members. C.O. Knowles of the *Telegram* thought it was a mistake to sell news "to a rival organization, radio" and suggested nothing more was needed than effective protection against the "theft" of news.[51] Moreover, the sample newscasts that Livesay had provided were both too informative and too numerous, "exactly what shouldn't be put on the air."[52] The *Telegram's* policy was "to stimulate interest in news rather than milk the paper" (as it would if it broadcast the afternoon horse-racing results covered in the newspaper's late editions, for example). The *Telegram's* broadcasts had yielded "excellent results": interpretation (or commentary), as opposed to straight factual reporting, extended each news topic, allowing fewer items to be broadcast, and minimized the menace of wholesale broadcasting of news. (Even for a newspaper that had been consistently involved in broadcasting, this was hardly a formula to make the most of radio's potential.) Oswald Mayrand of *La Presse* expressed a similar view. Knowles also recommended against accepting any payment from the CRBC. Most members agreed with this view on the grounds that receiving a fee would compromise CP's editorial independence in the agreement. Others objected to the proposed schedule. Rupert Davies of Kingston complained that a noon broadcast would bring back the old problem of regional stories being heard on the air before provincial afternoon papers were on the street, while others said a 4 p.m. newscast would hurt the sales of evening papers, and others still said the 10 p.m. broadcast would be bad for morning papers.[53]

Supporters of the CRBC agreement generally presented it as a lesser evil of one kind or another. John McNeil of the Montreal *Gazette* said that since news broadcasts appeared inevitable, it was better if they were under CP's control. Arthur Ford of London said he was willing to see all news broadcasts eliminated – the only problem was that the public seemed to want them. John Imrie of Edmonton, while expressing some concerns that the proposed news broadcasts were too informative, said that if CP did not act, "the present indiscriminate broadcasting with increasing 'lifting' would continue, and the CRBC might make an agreement with another news provider."

Frederick Ker of the Hamilton *Spectator* urged those who opposed the deal to remember that they were "shivering in their boots" a year ago. Now, with Canadian radio under public control, Canadian publishers were the envy of their American counterparts. The agreement gave them real protection against news theft, reduced the frequency and duration of news broadcasts, and ensured that CP controlled their contents. If the agreement was rejected, Ker concluded, it was only a matter of time before Canadian broadcasters set up a rival newsgathering organization, as was already being planned in the United States.

The agreement was accordingly approved, with the provisos that no payment be accepted, that the number of daily newscasts be reduced from four to two, and that they be scheduled so as not to "prejudice unduly" daily paper publication. Eight a.m. and 6:30 p.m. were suggested as appropriate hours, but this had to be amended when Charlesworth informed the newspapermen that the CRBC was only broadcasting for three and a half hours a day, with all but 30 minutes of this in the evening. CP then settled for 6:30 p.m. and 10:30 p.m.[54] This did not completely eliminate radio's capacity to beat the printed newspaper in reaching listeners: the 6:30 bulletin was intended as a summary of news already published in the evening papers, but the 10:30 broadcast was to include developments that would be reported in the next day's morning papers.[55] The next year, the two bulletins were consolidated into one 10-minute broadcast at 10:45 p.m.[56] CP's relationship with the CRBC was a like a strategic alliance with a powerful and potentially threatening neighbour, an alliance that sought to limit (but not eliminate) the threat and to find ways of working together that were mutually beneficial. Any drawbacks could be justified on the grounds that the alternative – not having an alliance – was likely to be worse. CP, representing nearly all of Canada's newspapers, was now formally and irrevocably in the business of radio news.

Having made this fundamental change in orientation, CP soon found that new competition pushed it progressively to loosen the restrictions that initially appeared so advantageous. Less than two years after the CRBC agreement was adopted, Livesay was warning members about a new threat: "the invasion of Canada by United States radio news services."[57]

Transradio was one of several agencies established in the spring of 1934 to serve independent radio stations in the United States. This was a response to the Biltmore Agreement of December 1933, in which the main US radio networks, CBS and NBC, reached an agreement with AP, UP, and Hearst's INS to accept severe limitations on their broadcasting of news. Many independent stations remained outside the agreement, however, which meant they needed news services to supply them. Transradio was founded by Herbert Moore, a former UP writer who had been news editor for the CBS news division until it was abolished as part of the Biltmore Agreement.[58] By the summer of 1935, Transradio was serving clients in Montreal and western Canada.[59] Its promotional material stressed that it offered an alternative to "the present newspaper-controlled service," and – no doubt aware of CP's consistent attacks on BUP as essentially an American service – it promised to employ

Canadians "to insure the absolute integrity of Transradio's Canadian news."[60] Transradio also boasted that it had been eight minutes faster in reporting the death of George V than "any American newspaper press association" – a scoop made possible by its alliance with Reuters.[61] "I confess it is worrying me," Livesay told Cooper early in 1936.[62]

Transradio offered two major advantages to private broadcasters competing with the CRBC stations supplied with news by CP: the newscasts could be sold to sponsors and four news broadcasts were provided throughout the day, rather than a single broadcast late in the evening.[63] A few months after Transradio's first appearance in Canada, CP's president, W.B. Preston of the Brantford *Expositor*, recommended that the existing restrictions on radio stations allied with CP member newspapers should be scrapped. Otherwise, the stations would procure their news elsewhere. "Certainly, if CP members deem it desirable to use local stations for broadcasting, they should not be compelled to secure their news bulletins from commercial agencies."[64] As matters stood, many CP members were simply ignoring the rules. Preston confessed that he had done this himself; for a while his paper "conformed religiously" to the restrictions on using CP news for broadcasting, but finding that other newspapers' broadcasts were so much more comprehensive, he was "compelled to follow suit or get off the air."

In an effort to limit Transradio's inroads into the Canadian market, John Imrie of the Edmonton *Journal* met with the general manager of the Foothills Network, which now operated the *Journal*'s former station, along with others in Calgary and Lethbridge. Transradio was offering the Edmonton and Lethbridge stations three 15-minute broadcasts daily for $10 a week. The Calgary station was already using this service. Revenue from sponsors paid the $10 fee, plus the cost of an operator to pick up the shortwave transmission, the salary of an editor and a reporter for local news items and a reporter in Edmonton, and still left a profit. But the stations' manager also told Imrie that two 10-minute news broadcasts supplied by CP, one in the morning and one in the evening, would be preferred by Canadian listeners. If CP did not allow sponsorship, however, the service would have to be free if it was to be competitive.[65]

The board of directors was not yet willing to go that far, however: a proposal to provide a free CP service of radio news to any station that wanted it – whether affiliated with a newspaper or the CRBC, or independent of both – was turned down in November 1935.[66] But an extremely liberal policy was adopted: any member newspaper could broadcast any CP news it received at any time on a station with which it was connected. The sole limitation was that there could be no more than three broadcasts every 24 hours, with each broadcast lasting no longer than 10 minutes. As well, the board agreed that CP news bulletins – currently limited to one at 10:45 p.m. – should also be broadcast during the day, putting aside the traditional objection that this would hurt sales of afternoon papers. It was now in CP's interest to be "generous rather than parsimonious" with radio news.[67] In the summer of 1936, as the newly established CBC extended its programming into daytime hours, CP news bulletins were broadcast at 8 a.m., 12:30 p.m., and 5 p.m., as well as in the evening.[68] If CP was not prepared to compete aggressively, Transradio would spread "like German measles."[69] The attempt to control the time advantages of broadcast news lay, for the moment at least, in tatters; only the ban on selling CP's news to commercial sponsors remained. As the market for radio news grew – Livesay observed that "news on the air in one form or another has become such a marketable commodity that the radio listener is deluged with it, good, bad, and indifferent"[70] – and as new competitors entered the market, the CRBC–CBC agreement turned out not to be the panacea that many CP members had hoped for.

In the spring of 1936, with Transradio continuing to make inroads, CP revamped its approach to radio once again. Taking a more nationalistic approach than had previously been seen, CP's president told the 1936 annual meeting that it was a matter of vital national welfare for radio news to be in the hands of an organization like CP, with its devotion to the Canadian and British viewpoint, and "whose principles of accuracy and impartiality in the preparation of its news have been well established."[71] It was now recommended that CP prepare and supply four news bulletins a day to all radio stations, regardless of CRBC or newspaper affiliation. CP would not charge for the bulletins beyond a $10 weekly fee for distribution by telegraph.[72] Sponsorship was still banned, however; any station using the CP material had to give credit to CP and the local newspaper. Livesay acknowledged that this was a radical departure from past practice but defended it as the only way to meet the competition from Transradio, by now "strongly entrenched" in western Canada and northern Ontario, and making headway in Quebec and the Maritimes. This also meant that CP members were no longer allowed the complete freedom about when to broadcast news they had been granted as an emergency measure the year before; they were now limited to the four time slots specified, but this still represented an effective end of attempts to prevent time competition from radio for afternoon or morning newspapers.[73] In the long run, Livesay suggested, the new system would benefit rather than damage newspaper circulation – and if not, it could always be cancelled on three months' notice.

Once again, there was substantial dissension over the new approach. Joseph Atkinson said that much as he had tried to adopt the point of view that all news coming into Canada on the air should be patriotic and national, he could not do it. The business of newspapers was to sell their papers, not control radio news coming into the country. Reflecting the continuing importance of promotional considerations, Atkinson observed that broadcasting by newspapers created goodwill for the newspapers, but if news was given to radio stations, it created goodwill for radio stations, and this strengthened a competitor of newspapers. Although the *Star* had been involved with broadcasting since 1922 (and still was), Atkinson concluded that "news on the air took the edge off the public appetite for news. Broadcasting was not worth what it cost." While the Moose River mine collapse story was unfolding in April, the *Star* had sold 10,000 extras but would have sold 60,000 if not for radio competition. Atkinson repeated that if others stopped broadcasting news, he would do the same, and would be quite happy to see no CP news being broadcast.[74] On the other hand, Knowles of the *Telegram* described the limitation of news broadcasts to four time slots a day as "vicious"; the argument that the new policy was the only way to stop Transradio was rather like saying, "we shoot ourselves rather than let Transradio shoot us." H.P. Duchemin of the Sydney *Post* disagreed with both Torontonians. His paper, like most CP members, was not "as happily situated as the Toronto *Star* and the Toronto *Telegram* with radio stations of their own"; the new contract meant that news on the air had to be credited to CP and the local newspaper, providing valuable free publicity.

The transformation of the CRBC into the CBC in 1936 brought a larger network of stations and expanded hours of daytime broadcasting, both of which CP had seen in the past as ways of strengthening the position of its noncommercialized news against sponsored competitors. But even this did not have the hoped-for effect; if CP's noon broadcast could be heard on the new, broader network of CBC stations, many competing private stations dropped the free CP service for Transradio or another competitor, BUP.[75] (As of 1938, Transradio was serving 21 stations across Canada and BUP six, with contracts for six more.[76]) Meanwhile, there were growing strains in the CP–CBC relationship. Livesay complained as early as 1934 that the commission was not disciplining stations that broadcast CP news without permission.[77] Furthermore, not all CRBC affiliates were carrying CP's 10:45 p.m. bulletin because they used the time for sponsored programs; Livesay told Charlesworth in November 1934 that he could not receive the CP nightly bulletin at all in his home just west of Toronto.[78] There were also problems in distributing the evening broadcast to stations across Canada. Livesay was initially pleased when the CRBC agreed to take over this responsibility from CP, relieving pressure on its leased wires, but soon was complaining that the commission was not delivering it to all the stations that wanted it, including several affiliated with CP members.[79] At one point, Livesay also complained about apparent censorship of news on political grounds at the CBC's French-language service: "the order has been put out nothing must go on the air about Mr Duplessis and Mr Hepburn – presumably also Mr. Hepburn and Mr. King. ... it was fear of that sort of thing that convinced some of us it was not safe in a political ridden country like this to entrust the putting out of news on the air to any other organization but our own, which has no axe to grind and neither seeks nor receives favours from politicians."[80] However, Livesay was heartened by a CBC regulation in 1937 that required new Transradio clients to obtain the CBC's permission, which could be revoked if the service was shown to be "bad" – that is, too pro-American.[81] Gladstone Murray, the CBC's general manager, clearly shared Livesay's concerns, admitting that while he couldn't flatly prevent stations from taking Transradio, "it is always my policy to place as many obstacles as I can in the way." If anyone at CP could suggest a formula "which will enable me to suppress this invasion without giving the appearance of supporting a monopoly, I shall be more than grateful."[82]

Nonetheless, the CBC and others had many complaints about the quality of CP's radio bulletins. Herbert Sallans of the Vancouver *Sun* told Livesay that CP's Toronto-edited "eastern broadcast does not by any means give British Columbia people the selected Canadian news they want. We are not guessing when we say this. We are saying what they have told us, and they told us in decided terms too."[83] The station manager of CHAB in Moose Jaw complained that CP's newscasts were stale, with more up-to-date news coming from American stations: "This sort of thing is like giving the public moldy bread, and they react accordingly."[84] The managers of stations affiliated with the Edmonton *Journal* and Calgary *Herald* said that even without advertising revenue, they would be willing to pay three times more to receive BUP's service than the $10 a week that CP charged for telegraphic transmission, citing the limited amount of western news in the CP daytime bulletins, their inferior radio style, duplication of items in the three bulletins, and the absence of special news flashes. (Livesay acknowledged that the CP bulletin service was more limited than its competitors and that CP's editors had still not mastered radio style.[85]) As early as 1936, a senior CBC official lamented "the always unsatisfactory situation regarding the news division of our broadcasting service." The current situation, where CBC was not permitted to alter anything in the free CP news bulletin it received, had to change: "we should have ... at least an arrangement with the Canadian Press under which we would be less in a position of obligation to them and which would enable us to determine what news should be broadcast when and how, and preferably, alternative sources of supply."[86]

E.L. Bushnell, the CBC's general program superintendent, was scathing about the failings of the CP news service. The news it provided was almost always stale (most of the 10:45 p.m. broadcast was taken from 3 p.m. newspaper editions) and poorly written for radio.[87] CP people "do not know how to write material for oral delivery; they do not know to build a radio newscast giving it a shape just as a musical, or dramatic production, has a shape." Bushnell explicitly rejected CP's characterization of Transradio as "a national danger"[88]; the real concern was that whenever a big story broke Transradio sent the news immediately to its clients, who broadcast it at once. "This is really why the Canadian Press is fighting Transradio. CP is apparently not willing either to give or to sell its news to radio stations until it first has been printed." Livesay should be told that what CP was supplying simply wasn't good enough: "stale news, poorly written and oft times poorly chosen." CBC should consider alternatives such as an agreement with Reuters for foreign news coverage,[89] and use of its own staff or stringers to cover Canadian domestic news.

Meanwhile, the competitive challenge to CP from commercial news services became increasingly worrisome. BUP was using its connections with radio stations to offer an inexpensive print news service to the newspapers affiliated with them, directly challenging CP in its core business. CP was clearly not keeping up with the competition, and positions that until now had been summarily rejected, such as allowing sponsorship of CP news, or charging a realistic fee to the CBC for its CP bulletins, were increasingly put forward.[90]

A new CP–CBC agreement in 1939 went some way towards meeting the public broadcaster's concerns and CP's desire to get some revenue from radio. The CBC now had the right to specify the "timing, number, form, and length of bulletins," subject only to a commitment not to make any changes affecting the "meaning or integrity" of CP news.[91] Regional news was to make up about 25 per cent of the four daily bulletins, with distinct versions to be compiled at Halifax, Montreal, Toronto, Winnipeg, and Vancouver.[92] If the CBC wished to prepare the bulletins itself, CP's entire news service would be made available at no charge; if CP prepared the bulletins, the annual cost would be $20,000. The CBC opted to have CP continue preparing the broadcasts under its direction, but this arrangement soon had problems, too: the supervisor of news broadcasts complained to Bushnell that it was "quite impossible" to get "efficient supervision" of CP radio copy.[93]

The new, expanded bulletins were to be made available to all radio stations regardless of CBC affiliation, but could not be sold for sponsorship. The hope was that widespread availability of free, nonsponsored CP news would greatly reduce the demand for BUP and Transradio news. As Leonard Brockington, chairman of the CBC board of governors, told members of the CP board at a joint meeting in July 1939, "when the extended service of CP news bulletins had been for a while in existence, its very excellence would drive competitors out of the field."[94]

This agreement came into effect at the end of August and was followed almost immediately by the outbreak of war with Germany, which allowed CP to take much more direct aim at its troublesome competitors. In Britain, the BBC had quickly banned all non-BBC newscasts as a war measure, and CP urged the CBC to do the same in Canada, solving its competitive problems at a stroke. M.E. Nichols of the Vancouver *Province* acknowledged that this "might seem to be a broad request," but "news broadcasts lacking the accuracy and sense of responsibility of the CP news was [sic] putting the public in a serious state of nerves."[95] As a nonprofit organization, CP "did not suffer from the temptation to put news-thrillers on the air in order to get the public excited about its product. ... The CBC and the government behind it had unlimited powers which could be used in the national interest to help Canada win the war." This was a line of argument that CP relied on throughout the war: its news service was authoritative, reliable, responsible, and credible (with the clear implication that its competitors were not) and thus served the national interest.[96] (Gladstone Murray agreed, but suggested that a ban on sponsored news would have the same result, because non-CP news cost money and had to be sponsored in order to be profitable.) Later that day, Murray, Rupert Davies (CP's president), and George McCullagh (publisher of *The Globe and Mail*) formally presented the request for a ban on non-CP news to C.D. Howe, the minister of transport, who promised "full consideration and an early decision."

In December, Howe gave his answer: because some CP member newspapers objected to the proposal – presumably those connected to radio stations that profited from sponsored news broadcasts – he would not approve the request for a ban.[97] (The Canadian Association of Broadcasters, representing private radio stations, also objected strenuously.) The request was accordingly amended to a more limited ban on commercial sponsorship of news as Murray had suggested. In its revised petition to Howe, CP strongly emphasized the "foreign origin" of BUP and Transradio, asserted that sponsored news "may be colored by the interests or prejudices of its sponsors," and insisted that, since private stations could still purchase commercial news services if they wished, CP was not seeking a monopoly.[98] But 15 out of 89 CP members opposed this request, too; dissenters included the Toronto *Telegram*; the Montreal *Gazette*; *La Presse* and five other French-language newspapers in Quebec; Roy Thomson's papers in North Bay, Sudbury, and Timmins; the London *Free Press*; and the Victoria *Times*.[99] CP had been struggling with the division between its members that sought severe restrictions on radio news and those that sought to profit from it since the 1920s; an increase in the number of newspapers owning radio stations in the later 1930s (by 1939, more than one-third of Canadian private radio stations were either owned by or had affiliations with newspapers) only made the problem more acute.[100] Despite the lack of unanimity, the request for a ban on sponsorship was referred to the CBC's board of governors for a decision.

CP presented its case on 1 June 1940. Sifton complained that CP's position had been "misunderstood and misrepresented"; Nichols insisted that CP's opposition was not based on competitive considerations, but "on the belief that sponsored news was subject to improper influence, was sensationalized and was broadcast at greater length and frequency than if the profit motive was absent. Redundancy of newscasts, often exaggerated and inaccurate, was not conducive to public morale in wartime."[101] O.L. Spencer of the Calgary *Herald* added that "[a]n essential difference between radio and a newspaper was that radio was primarily an amusement enterprise and its personnel were trained in showmanship, leading them to emphasize theatrical aspects of the news." This meeting brought some significant results: Transradio was banned from operating in Canada effective July 1 because of concerns about its connection with German news sources; all other authorizations of radio news broadcasts (except CP broadcasts) were rescinded, which meant that BUP would have to reapply for permission to broadcast news.[102] But this was not enough for CP, which continued to press for abolition of sponsored news across the board. At the end of June, the board of directors declared that

> the uncontrolled radio broadcasting of news, news comment and public announcements in time of war is contradictory to the national interest, and that in a crisis such as the present, all announcements should be closely scrutinized as to source, reliability, and the consequences of their impact upon the public. ... the placing of news broadcasts in the inexperienced hands of commercial sponsors and their broadcasters entails great risks, and [the board] deplores that the CBC has not stopped the practice.[103]

CP's news service, which operated on a nonprofit basis,[104] was "the most accurate and responsible ... the best source for untainted news from a Canadian point of view."

For Transradio, the CBC decision was a severe blow. One of its European news sources was the Berlin-based Transocean News Service, the official German news-distribution agency that was considered a propaganda operation; this was the reason for the ban.[105] However, the prohibition was subsequently lifted in the face of protests from Transradio clients and others. One objector to any suggestion that the noncommercial CBC should control all radio news was C.O. Knowles, editor of the Toronto *Telegram*. The *Telegram* was willing to give up the $8,000 in annual revenue it received from commercial sponsorship of radio news, "but we will not voluntarily submit to the principle that the Dominion government, through its servile agent the C.B.C. shall edit all the news that is to go out over the air, and that no other agency may broadcast news," Knowles wrote to Conservative senator (and CP's old adversary) Arthur Meighen.[106] "Once this is recognized, it is a short step to a permanent censorship of the newspapers." Meighen agreed, complaining about "the intention of the government to take complete control of the news over all radio in Canada by permitting only Canadian Press to distribute news over the radio."[107] Although CP insisted that it received no government funds, Meighen knew that it was getting $20,000 a year for preparing news bulletins for the CBC, which he considered a subsidy: "This will be a fine organization to have sole control of all radio news in Canada, with the Government sitting at its elbow, its hand on the purse strings."[108] Transradio came under further unfavourable scrutiny in November 1940, when the US House of Representatives Committee on Un-American Activities published additional evidence about its connections with German propaganda. Asked in the House of Commons how this affected the Canadian government's position towards Transradio, Howe replied that radio stations using the service "would have a rather difficult problem in public relations, in deciding whether to continue. But as all of them violently protested the ban on the service, I think we can leave them to work out the problem themselves."[109] (Transradio denied that it acted as a conduit for German propaganda, and noted that Canadian censors had expressed no concern about any of its broadcasts.)

These events all took place against a backdrop of major developments in the European war. With the German invasion of Holland and Belgium in May 1940, and the fall of France in June, war news became "the most popular of radio programs."[110] In addition to the four daily CBC newscasts, CP provided special bulletins, sometimes on an hourly basis, and, more regularly, every two hours from morning until midnight.[111] CP's newly appointed general manager, J.A. McNeil, reported that the agency's radio news was "acclaimed in all quarters as an invaluable national service," because of its "accurate, level-headed presentation." Enthusiastic audience response was "a testimony to the responsibility we insist must be the basis of all CP news." Unfortunately, the demand for war news also benefited the less responsible providers of sponsored news, and "advertising programs of news sponsored by the butcher, the baker and the candlestick-maker are on the increase." Equally unfortunately, CP did "not seem to be receiving the fullest co-operation" from CBC in making its radio bulletins available to all stations. (The CBC was particularly reluctant to provide the CP news service to its private competitors in big-city markets.[112])

The expanded news partnership with CBC was not going smoothly in other respects either. In September 1940, the CP board recommended that the CBC should take over the preparation of news broadcasts, using material provided by CP and other organizations. If CP was to continue preparing CBC news bulletins, the CBC should cease criticizing the method of preparation, the style of announcing, and the scheduling of broadcasts. In addition, the CBC should issue a statement on the air "declaring its recognition of the value of the Canadian Press service, especially at the present time."[113]

In fact, the CBC board decided to begin its own news service on 1 January 1941, the culmination of several years of growing dissatisfaction with CP's work. The CBC was authorized to obtain the raw material for its national news service from CP, BUP, "or any other news service or agency."[114] CP's exclusive connection with the national public broadcaster, the basis of its approach to radio since 1933, had come to an end. The CBC news service would be carried on nine CBC-owned stations and 25 privately owned affiliated stations "designated as essential to maximum national coverage" with no sponsorship. In addition, all private stations would be permitted to broadcast news from "approved agencies" – not just CP – with "institutional" sponsorship. (Institutional sponsorship meant that the company name could be mentioned, but not specific products.[115]) So-called "spot" advertisements, which mentioned specific products but made no reference to the ensuing or preceding program, and thus did not constitute explicit sponsorship, could also be used immediately before or after news broadcasts. At a meeting between CBC executives and CP's directors in September 1940, the question of payment to CP for supplying its news – which CP had always refused to consider – was raised; N.L. Nathanson said the CBC assumed that CP would continue to provide its entire news service free of charge as under the existing agreement. He added that BUP was similarly willing to provide its news service to the CBC at no charge but had agreed to accept a payment of $10,000 a year "to cover certain expenses it would incur and losses it would suffer." CP was "as free to sell its service direct to [private] stations as is the BUP," and Transradio's service "would not be disturbed." CP was not happy about the new direction – the directors complained that even though the restrictions on sponsorship were a step in the right direction, the CBC had still not banned sponsored news completely – but eventually agreed to provide its news service to the CBC at no cost as long as other agencies did the same.[116] But CP clearly recognized that the ground had shifted beneath its feet and a radically new direction would have to be considered; a report on the possibility of CP selling its own news for sponsorship was to be presented to the next directors' meeting.

Rejection of sponsorship, the bedrock of CP's approach to radio news for years, was now an open question.

The subject was addressed head-on at the board meeting of 3 March 1941. Rupert Davies told his fellow directors that CP "was now faced with competition in the providing of a national news service to its member newspapers by news agencies [i.e., BUP] building up their news facilities in Canada out of profits made from the sale of news for commercial sponsorship on the air."[117] McNeil then presented a proposal for the sale of CP radio news, based in part on the practice of AP, which had abandoned its own opposition to sponsored radio news in 1939.[118] There was vigorous debate: A.J. West of the Montreal *Gazette* argued that the US parallel did not apply, because AP faced more severe competition from UP than CP did from BUP, but he was in a distinct minority. As M.E. Nichols said, "one [CP member] after another had taken UP [BUP] and made it difficult for members carrying CP only. Preservation of CP should be thought of." E. Norman Smith of the Ottawa *Journal* thought the BUP threat was being exaggerated, describing it as "a supplementary service only but no competition," but Davies replied that within five years he would change his mind. "The BUP were building up a strong radio set-up and they were out to fight The Canadian Press." Henri Gagnon of *Le Soleil* reported that newspapers owned by his employer in Sherbrooke and Trois-Rivières had been offered BUP print and radio services for less than half what they were paying CP: "If The CP did not do something it would lose two memberships there." Despite opposition, the principle of selling news for sponsorship was endorsed at the annual general meeting, and plans were made to establish a subsidiary company that would sell CP news to broadcasters.[119]

The question whether CBC should be charged for CP's news service remained unresolved; the prospect of additional revenue was offset by the realization that if CP charged for its CBC service, BUP could do the same, and would thereby be strengthened. One particularly awkward question was whether, in order to improve the revenue prospects of CP's proposed commercial news service, the CBC should be urged to ease the restrictions on sponsorship that CP had very recently insisted on. Davies acknowledged that the CBC rules were "probably interfering with sale of news for sponsorship, but it was difficult for The Canadian Press to go before the CBC and ask for the reversal of a principle for which it had been fighting for years."[120] This low-key remark, not included in the printed version of the meeting's minutes, was a tacit acknowledgment that CP's opposition to sponsorship had as much to do with profit and loss as with any principles of what constituted proper journalism, much as CP had stressed the latter in its public statements over the years. Meanwhile, McNeil reported that AP had established a subsidiary, Press Association Inc., to handle the sale of radio news.[121] CP's own radio subsidiary, Press News Ltd., began operations in July 1941.[122] In a memorandum summing up the tortuous path that had led to this point, McNeil referred to "the years of [CP's] struggle with the radio problem" – which summed up the experience in a phrase.[123] It was a surrender, but not a rout: as Rupert Davies of the Kingston *Whig-Standard* told that year's annual meeting, newspaper circulation was up in spite of radio competition and higher newsstand prices.[124]

⁓

CP's frequently changing approach to radio in the 1920s and 1930s emerged in response to a complex and dynamic competitive situation. Some kinds of competition had greater prominence in the early years of radio, and others became more important later. Before 1930, radio was mainly assimilated into structures of competition that were already well established among newspapers. These underlying local and regional tensions never disappeared, but with the establishment of the CRBC and CBC, competitive pressures also operated on a larger, national and continental, scale. Newspapers, with their territorially restricted circulation areas, had not previously had to take account of competition on this scale. Fundamental political decisions about the shape of Canadian broadcasting in the 1930s also brought new elements, notably the conflict between noncommercial and commercial broadcasters and an explicitly national framework, into the competitive mix.

Most newspapers initially became involved with radio for promotional reasons, and were not necessarily interested enough in the new medium for its own sake to commit the resources that a full-fledged involvement in broadcasting would require. Overall, it is striking how frequently newspaper publishers and editors said that they became involved with radio, or remained involved, only because of what their competitors were doing or might do. Once any newspaper in a competitive market started using radio, for whatever reason, everyone else had to take account of the changed landscape. As more newspapers became drawn into this new form of competition, and as the spatial reach of radio became more extensive, it became progressively harder for anyone to remain aloof. Over time, the impetus towards involvement with radio was cumulative. CP's decision to become a systematic provider of news to the CRBC in 1933 meant that every member of the cooperative – even those that as individual newspapers had no local involvement – was now implicated in radio.

When one looks closely at how CP responded to the emergence of radio as a news medium, it is striking that "newspapers" did not function as one entity – as one medium. They were profoundly divided by different aspects of the competitive matrix in which they were jointly enmeshed, and as a result they adopted quite different (and changing) positions towards radio. Although the actual functioning of the competitive environment changed substantially during these years, the fact of division was fundamental and long lasting.

The medium of radio that actually took shape in Canada in the 1920s and 1930s was one specific subset of a much wider range of possibilities that could have emerged out of the basic technology. Radio in Canada was shaped fundamentally by economic structures and political decisions. Would it be run entirely by private profit-seeking companies dependent on advertising, as in the United States? By a state monopoly, as in Britain? Or by a combination of the two, as in Canada? Depending on how these questions were answered, the competitive ecology was profoundly altered. In effect, the "medium" that newspapers confronted was something quite different in each of these three cases. From a comparative perspective, it is interesting to note that something much closer to a "press–radio war" did appear in Britain, where radio and newspapers were kept separate – there was not the consistent overlapping of newspapers and radio that occurred in Canada and the United States.[125] In North America, the introduction of limited public ownership and a noncommercial form of radio sent the competitive dynamic, and hence the nature of the conflict between newspapers and radio, into different directions in Canada than in the United States. In the mid-1930s, the nature of the conflict was changed yet again, not by the characteristics of radio per se, but by CP's decision to become systematically a provider of radio news and the ensuing conflict with Transradio.

The precise way in which the newspaper–radio relationship took shape in Canada – which, in large measure, was the story of CP's adaptation to radio – reflected an interplay of economic, political, institutional, technological, (and sometimes idiosyncratically personal) factors.[126] In the epilogue to her study of press–radio relations in the

United States, Gwenyth Jackaway quotes the historian of technology Carolyn Marvin: "The history of media is never more or less than a history of their uses, which always leads us away from them to the social practices and conflicts they illuminate."[127] The present account bears this out, leading away from an exclusive focus on absolute differences between media and towards an emphasis on divisions within specific media and overlapping interests among different media.

4 "A Great Responsibility": CP in Wartime

War between states is an inherently nationalizing experience. For an organization like Canadian Press, whose contribution to the construction of Canadian nationality is one of this study's major themes, the Second World War brought opportunities of several kinds. CP reorganized and expanded its news operation in order to give Canadian newspaper readers and radio listeners the most complete coverage possible of the biggest ongoing story in a generation, in the process acting as the main instrument of "mediated publicness" in an era of intense national focus. It also, and quite deliberately, cemented its own role as *the* national news provider in Canada against various competitors. To accomplish this, CP cultivated unpredecentedly close relations with Canada's military authorities – who had reasons of their own for wanting extensive coverage of the national war effort – and thereby moved some distance away from traditional notions of journalistic independence. Throughout the war, CP struggled with but mostly accepted a censorship regime whose own officials recognized that it often operated arbitrarily. CP's wartime experience left a legacy of journalistic and organizational ambition and accomplishment, along with a more explicit national and nationalizing role than it had ever played before – all held together by a significant thread of self-interest.

The outbreak of war in September 1939 brought immediate and vigorous changes to CP's news operation. September 3, when Britain's ultimatum to Germany to cease the invasion of Poland was set to expire, was a Sunday, and CP's domestic leased-wire network – normally closed between Saturday afternoon and Monday morning – was in operation beginning at 7 a.m. Halifax time. Eighteen minutes later came the report that Prime Minister Neville Chamberlain had declared war in a radio broadcast to the empire, and thereafter the wires remained open 24 hour a day, seven days a week.[1] The staff in London and New York was expanded to handle the crush of war-related news; by mid-September, an application was made to attach a CP war correspondent to British Army headquarters in France, and it was decided that a second correspondent would be appointed to cover Canadian forces once they were ready to go overseas. During the first week of September, general manager J.A. McNeil, accompanied by Victor Sifton and John Dafoe of the Winnipeg *Free Press*, travelled to Ottawa to discuss censorship arrangements with Walter Thompson, chairman of the newly created Censorship Co-ordination Committee, and Clare Moyer, clerk of the Senate and press censor.[2] It was suggested that CP should ask the federal government to declare it an essential service, exempting key employees from military service.[3]

All this, especially the staff increases and provision for heavier cable charges between London and New York, would cost additional money – more than $50,000 in the first year of the war, CP's treasurer estimated – and one of the earliest major decisions was how these extra costs would be met. There were already signs that cost increases would be resisted; for example, H.P. Duchemin of the Sydney *Morning Post* expressed little enthusiasm for sending an additional correspondent to the headquarters of the Royal Air Force, noting that "[t]he effect of any considerable increase, particularly on the smaller newspapers, might be serious, as many were already finding it extremely difficult to get along."[4] On 20 October, the finance committee agreed that the increase had to be offset by reduced spending in CP's domestic news service.[5] In war or peacetime, newspapers were businesses.

As part of the search for economies, the board of directors was determined to limit what it considered Livesay's "indiscriminate granting" of salary increases since 1935.[6] One of those caught up in the economy campaign was Gillis Purcell; less than a year after being passed over for the general manager's job, he told J.A. McNeil in October that he was "deeply disappointed" to learn that a requested pay raise had been turned down by the finance committee.[7] That decision was soon reversed, but a few months later Purcell complained that the second instalment of the $1,000 increase had been delayed.[8] McNeil appealed to CP's president, Rupert Davies of the Kingston *Whig-Standard*, to reconsider, but Davies insisted on the point. "Mr Purcell is a very valuable man," he wrote. "I do not know where we could replace him for the money." But CP had to operate under the same constraints as its hard-pressed members: "We all have to lose good men occasionally, not because we want to lose them but because we cannot afford to compete."[9] Eventually, in May 1940, the finance committee decided to go through with all the raises that had been postponed after learning that four senior employees had recently left, two of them for better pay elsewhere.[10] But the incident contributed to a strained relationship between Purcell and the board, one that soon became significantly more tense.

The dispute about Purcell's salary came at a time when he was actively considering leaving CP to join the Canadian armed forces. Other CP employees had been quick to enlist, and three days after Britain's declaration of war, Purcell wrote to E. Norman Smith of the Ottawa *Journal* asking for advice: "what would you think if I should take such a step?"[11] Smith was quick to reply that Purcell should stay where he was: "you are in my opinion carrying on a job that is of immense importance in every way to the people of Canada. ... Your services in that position are more valuable to the people of Canada and of more importance in the carrying on of the war than they could be in any military position that you might be offered." Purcell replied that he would stay where he was for at least six months, but felt that New York and London would quickly become the key locations for the CP service, and "my position here may be relegated to that of a curb-sitter watching a parade."[12] But Smith was no more impressed by that argument. "Bunk!" he scribbled on Purcell's letter before sending it back. "If London and NY don't get central direction and inspiration they'll go flooey. And so could the whole service – much to public loss."

Before the promised six months was over, Purcell had a new assignment; in November 1939, he was nominated to accompany the First Canadian Division to England as CP's war correspondent.[13] This was an exclusive arrangement: CP was the only news organization accredited.[14] Twenty-five years later, Purcell recalled that the goals of his assignment were to cover the voyage to England, provide a service of CP news for the troops, arrange for a CP war correspondent to live with the division (previously "unheard of in England"), and "arrange for a workable system of censorship that would give the folks at home day-to-day news of the troops" – all of which were accomplished by the end of January 1940.[15] But his most significant achievement was the establishment of a close working relationship with Lt.-Gen. Andrew McNaughton, commanding officer of the Canadian contingent. McNaughton's goals and Purcell's overlapped to a remarkable extent. The Canadian commander was determined that the contribution of Canadian forces to the Allied war effort should be adequately recognized, not lost sight of as part of the larger, British-led, war effort. For this, adequate news coverage was essential.[16] For his part, Purcell wanted to establish CP's priority as the main Canadian news organization, and do whatever he could to allow extensive and (as far as possible) untrammelled coverage. Within two weeks of the Canadians' arrival in Scotland, Purcell and McNaughton were speaking very frankly to each other. During a long conversation one evening, McNaughton suggested that Purcell might join his staff permanently after his present assignment ended – not as an intelligence officer, as Purcell had apparently suggested, but to "concentrate on aiding Canada through watching the handling of her war news."[17] When McNaughton added that it might be equally valuable for Purcell to remain at CP in Toronto "with a full understanding of the Canadian war effort," Purcell replied that by the same logic, McNaughton should have stayed in Ottawa. Underscoring the trust that had developed between the two men, McNaughton confessed that "if he had stayed the government would be out of office, as he could not have helped leading a revolt. He figured he was appointed GOC to get him out of the way … ."[18]

The close relationship paid obvious dividends for CP. McNaughton obtained permission from British military authorities for the CP correspondent (but no others) to be stationed at Canadian headquarters.[19] This was extremely valuable, for previously all correspondents had to be stationed at British military headquarters and seek special permission for each visit to subsidiary units.[20] The British authorities were not particularly inclined to accommodate Canadian journalists, so the new arrangement provided much greater flexibility and mobility. In a second important change, McNaughton obtained permission for journalists to identify Canadian solders below the rank of major by name (any identification of individual soldiers was otherwise banned). This made it possible for CP journalists to produce a steady stream of "name-and-hometown" articles about Canadian soldiers during the long period of training in England, which were very popular with CP publishers in Canada.[21] CP's interest in more extensive coverage and McNaughton's interest in more publicity dovetailed well. In April 1940, a meeting of western Canadian CP members in Vancouver formally acknowledged "the admirable cooperation of General McNaughton in seeking to assure for Canada the most prompt and complete news coverage."[22]

Meanwhile, Purcell had not forgotten McNaughton's invitation to join his staff. Back in Toronto, he told McNaughton at the end of May 1940 that with CP's annual meeting over he could resign soon "without being seriously detrimental to news service."[23] Military developments – the fall of France in June transformed the war and made the Canadians in England front-line defenders against a possible German invasion – and a major change in CP's approach to radio news then intervened, but by the end of August Purcell renewed his approach; he would be free to take up a new position as of 1 January 1941.[24] Within weeks, Purcell had his answer: on McNaughton's recommendation, the minister of national defence approved his appointment as public relations officer attached to the 7th Corps headquarters (McNaughton's command), effective 9 September 1940, with captain's rank.[25]

Purcell's departure presented serious problems for CP, as the directors were quick to note. Quite disingenuously, Purcell told Rupert Davies that news of the appointment was "a breathtaking surprise for me."[26] It would help CP in its relations with the army, he argued (a view supported by McNeil[27]), and "as an able-bodied young Canadian whose home and family are threatened I think I should be in England doing what little I can." Davies replied that several directors felt "that you had given very little consideration to The Canadian Press when this job came up," though he agreed provisionally to an allowance of $25 a week for one year to supplement Purcell's military salary.[28] Davies soon had second thoughts, however, telling McNeil that 17 members of the board were opposed to granting the allowance, and warning that it would be "a big mistake" to bring the matter before them. "The majority of the Directors feel very definitely that Purcell thought first of himself and secondly of The Canadian Press. I am of the same opinion."[29] Another director, M.E. Nichols, was more blunt: Purcell should have been told to keep his job or resign.[30] Eventually, however, the allowance – reduced to $20 a week – was approved for one year.[31] "It means that I am still in fact as well as heart a CP man," Purcell observed with satisfaction.[32] Ross Munro from CP's Ottawa bureau was named war correspondent with the Canadian forces in Britain.[33]

Purcell's unique position was only one manifestation of McNaughton's openness to press coverage. The clearest indication of this came in the press regulations issued in May 1941, which were based on the premise that "[t]he people of Canada have a right to be kept informed ... Military authorities fully appreciate the importance of this task."[34] Accredited press representatives were therefore to be treated "as valued colleagues with a most important mission to discharge. They will be fully trusted, treated with complete frankness and given every proper facility for their work. The sole restriction on their writings will be that they shall not contain information of value to the enemy." A correspondent for the Southam newspapers wrote in August 1941 that McNaughton (unlike some other senior Canadian officers, and especially the British War Office) "treats Canadian journalists with the greatest courtesy and gives them every facility for obtaining news about Dominion forces in this country."[35]

Both as a matter of policy and in practice, CP received preferential treatment, sometimes provoking resentment among its competitors. In the spring of 1940, for example, McNeil reported to the annual meeting that CP's hated rival, BUP – whose success in gaining radio news clients still constituted an urgent threat to CP – was making a "strenuous bid" to attach a war correspondent to Canadian headquarters with the same privileges as Munro. McNeil was instructed to "make clear to the Minister of National Defence that the privileges of the CP war correspondent attached to the 1st Division are extended to Canadian Press as covering all daily newspapers in Canada and, while CP wishes only the fullest news coverage of the Division, it is insistent that its correspondent retain priority over all others."[36] Bill Stewart, another CP war correspondent, recalled that Munro was the only correspondent covering the Canadian forces in England to be provided with a car and driver by the army.[37] Certainly the armed forces went out of their way to avoid irritating Munro; in 1942, a high-level memorandum insisted that one public relations officer should not write articles himself because "this tends to compete with activities of Munro to dissatisfaction of latter," adding that it was "[v]ery important to maintain cooperative arrangements with Canadian Press."[38] Later that year, National Defence headquarters checked with Purcell – who by this time had left McNaughton's staff and returned to CP in Toronto after losing his right leg above the knee in a serious training accident – before accrediting an AP correspondent to cover the Canadian forces. Purcell raised no objection, but repeated that he "expects Canadian Press to occupy number one position and in event that limitation has to be placed on number of correspondents accredited to or accompanying, any for Canadian Press will receive prior consideration."[39] It was no surprise that the superintendent of CP's London bureau described McNaughton as a "loyal ally," quoting the Canadian commander as saying that "Anywhere the Canadian Army goes, your correspondent will go with them. The Canadian Press has done a good job and we want them with us."[40]

While the close relationship with McNaughton worked very well for CP in its day-to-day coverage, the agency had more difficulty establishing its priority in the eyes of other authorities. Within a few days of war being declared, CP's London bureau chief asked Bernard Rickatson-Hatt, editor-in-chief of Reuters, whether texts of speeches, official communiqués, and other British government documents would be cabled free of charge to Canada as had been done in World War One by the semiofficial Agence Reuter service.[41] McNeil promptly followed up with a formal request to the British minister of information that official statements be sent to CP at government expense, which was almost immediately turned down.[42] When CP continued to press this demand, the campaign backfired: its correspondence with the information ministry somehow was made public, allowing BUP to claim that "Canadian Press was demanding that taxpayers of Great Britain pay tolls on cables" sent to Canada.[43] BUP also appealed to the prime minister, W.L.M. King, objecting to the suggestion that casualty lists would be sent directly to "a private agency" (CP) for distribution in Canada, and prompting the Department of External Affairs to ask CP what exactly it had in mind.[44] Purcell replied in an exasperated tone, complaining that it was difficult to get people in Canada "to understand that there is only one real Canadian news agency, and that is The Canadian Press." BUP was nothing more than an outlet for the American-owned United Press, he insisted. Of 95 daily newspapers in Canada, 89 were CP members, compared to 12 who took BUP, and then only as a supplementary service. It seemed strange that

> when The CP makes representations to the Ministry of Information in Great Britain for certain help in serving the Canadian people in connection with the war ... we should be interfered with by an American news agency. I am afraid that the government of Canada does not properly appreciate what The Canadian Press is doing for this country. If it did, it would not be concerned about the representations of a commercial news agency which is in the business simply for profit making.[45]

The line between CP's self-interest and the national interest was not particularly clear.

Nor was BUP the only critic. Reuters also had conflicts with CP, notably over CP's continuing reliance on AP for international news and its corresponding refusal to subscribe to Reuters' service. The Ministry of Information was unhappy about this, too; in January 1941, Reuters' general manager quoted the head of the ministry's British Empire division as saying that the ministry had practically made up their minds to leave the Canadian Press out of account. They found them impossible to deal with; they would not even issue British Official Wireless and they had just made an arrangement for taking Havas news via New York against the wishes of the British government. ... Hodgson [head of the British Empire division] said that the Canadian Press appeared to be entirely under the tutelage of the A.P., and that the A.P., on account of its consistently anti-British tendency, was the least favourably viewed of any American press association in the British Government's eyes.[46]

Told that Reuters was seeking a way to distribute its high-speed wireless service in Canada independently of CP, Hodgson replied that "nothing would please the ministry more."[47] Reuters also urged the government to stand firm in rejecting CP's request that it pay for sending casualty lists and other official statements by cable, and was gratified to learn that "there was no question of any concession" being made.[48] CP's preferential relationship with McNaughton was another sore point for Reuters, and for some Canadian diplomats in London as well; a Reuters memorandum in December 1942 reported that "a battle royal is raging between Canada House and Macnaughton [sic] who has been sold hook line and sinker to Canapress with result that anyone on Canapress can get anything at all from the Canadian military authorities here. ... an attempt is being made to break the Canapress monopoly and if this is the case, facilities will be offered to us."[49] The acting press officer at Canada House was quoted as reporting "considerable dissatisfaction in high circles in Canada House with the present arrangements [involving CP]' and the influence of the Americans on all Canadian news."[50]

    None of this weakened CP's relationship with McNaughton, however. Indeed, even after Purcell returned to CP in Canada in the wake of his catastrophic accident at the end of October 1941, the connection grew stronger. The arrangements were apparently satisfactory to McNaughton, too; early in 1942, McNeil congratulated him on a recent interview in which he reiterated the policy of taking journalists into his confidence fully: "They were told what must not be said – what we did not want the enemy to know – and the job of interpreting the Corps was left to them. This has worked out admirably ... ."[51] Purcell successfully urged McNaughton to hire another journalist, Cliff Wallace, as his replacement ("your generous and friendly attitude toward the press might be altered if you could not turn with the freest mind to your press liaison officer") and made other recommendations about communications strategy.[52] In a CBC broadcast soon after returning to Canada, Purcell praised the Canadian commander for the special censorship arrangements that made it possible to provide the names and home towns of Canadian soldiers, with the result that Canadians "hear far more about their troops overseas than is published in the English papers about British troops."[53]

CP's original news coverage during the early years of the war focused mainly on the growing number of Canadian soldiers in Britain and their training exercises. (Coverage of the fighting in Europe came from AP and Reuters.) By 1942, Ross Munro was covering four Canadian divisions, "perhaps the world's biggest routine beat, from southern England to the Scottish forests ... according to the newspaper axiom that names make news."[54] In one typical report, Munro recounted an attack drill by mortar units of a Toronto regiment, carried out "under the watchful eye" of the acting corps commander, Lt.-Gen. H.D.G. Crerar.[55] The soldiers "bracket[ed] targets with trial shots and then hit them dead-on with the bombs that would count." Not for nothing were these known as "name-and-hometown" stories:

> Lieutenant O. A. (Hoodley) Nickson of Toronto led the detachments ... . Sergeants in charge of different sections were Jack Stone, Roly Guiton and W.P. Hubbard, all of Toronto. Riflemen included Bob Catlow, Reg Barrett, Bill Ackerman, George Bolton, who drove a carrier, John Fleming, Robert Menzies, Vern Nock, Bert Connor, Joe Mochan, Ray Payton, and John Salisbury, all of Toronto. Rifleman Charlie Himmen was from Hamilton, Ont.

A second correspondent was not appointed until September 1942, a year after it was reported that Munro had "reached the physical limit of wordage for a single staffer."[56] Later, when six more correspondents were posted to London in anticipation of the invasion of Europe, CP member newspapers made it clear that they did not want articles about grand strategy, but "the same name-and-hometown job that Ross Munro was doing."[57] Even after D-Day, this emphasis continued: by 1945, stories had been written about no fewer than 78 Canadian regiments.[58]

Although arrangements for coverage of the Canadian armed forces (except the Navy) worked well, CP had a harder time getting access to British forces. London superintendent D.E. Burritt reported in April 1942 that all branches of the British military ignored representatives of the empire press, not giving them a chance to cover important stories, such as cross-Channel commando raids, or even allowing them to meet the returning invaders. Worst of all was the Admiralty, whose obsessive concern with security often made it impossible to get information about Canadian casualties. "When we seek to interview Canadian survivors, we constantly meet rebuffs, though the British press appears with voluminous stories on British survivors. The Admiralty seems to object only when Canadians or Australians are concerned."[59]

For all the relatively routine nature of much early CP war coverage, the German bombing campaign made London a dangerous posting by the fall of 1940. As far as possible, CP replaced married staffers with single men.[60] On 29 December 1940, the building that CP shared with AP on Tudor Street was destroyed by bombs, forcing both agencies to set up temporary quarters in the Reuters – Press Association building at 85 Fleet Street.[61] A few months later, it was reported that no telephone service was available in London (and virtually no taxicabs) for five days, making it necessary to collect news "from widely separated official and other news sources, with many streets obstructed or wholly blocked by the debris of bombing and fire, and delivered by hand to the cable censors."[62] A more serious loss came in May 1941: CP's recently appointed London superintendent, Sam Robertson, was among more than 100 passengers lost when the ship in which he was returning from Canada was torpedoed.[63]

The first major military engagement covered directly by CP was the Dieppe raid in August 1942.[64] As Timothy Balzer and others have clearly demonstrated, Dieppe was not only a military disaster, but a signal failure in providing accurate and timely information about Canada's war effort.[65] For CP, Dieppe left a complicated legacy. On one hand, Munro's first-person coverage of the raid was compelling and demonstrated his personal courage and resourcefulness (he rode on landing craft with the assault troops under heavy fire); it was widely admired at the time and reprinted in many US newspapers via AP and broadcast worldwide by the BBC. On the other hand, as Munro, Purcell, and others eventually realized, the initial, censored coverage had been radically incomplete at best and deceptive at worst.

Fourteen war correspondents, five of them Canadian, accompanied the raiding force to France on 19 August 1942.[66] Munro was with the first wave of landing craft as they approached the beach at dawn, but his copy, like that of all the other correspondents, was not released until he returned to London the next day; the operation's planners insisted that no correspondent's report be transmitted until all had taken part in a post-operation briefing. As well, all reports had to undergo censorship by the operation's planners in addition to the regular military censorship.[67] The first reports that reached Canadian newspapers, therefore, were based mainly on official British communiqués that emphasized the raid's accomplishments and said little about casualties. (These were of horrendous proportions; almost two-thirds of the Canadian soldiers who landed at Dieppe were killed, wounded, captured, or missing in action, but it took almost a month for this information to be made public.[68])

Munro's first-hand account of the raid, written with the aid of benzedrine to keep him awake (he had not been to bed for three days) was indeed gripping. Under the dateline "With the Canadian Raiding Force at Dieppe," he wrote:

> For eight raging hours, under intense Nazi fire from dawn into a sweltering afternoon, I watched Canadian troops fight the blazing, bloody battle of Dieppe.
>
> I saw them go through this biggest of the war's raiding operations in wild scenes that crowded helter-skelter one upon other in crazy sequence. ...
>
> While the Canadian battalions stormed through the flashing inferno of Nazi defences, belching guns of big tanks rolling into the fight, I spent the grimmest 20 minutes of my life with one unit when a rain of German machine-gun fire wounded half the men in my boat and only a miracle saved us from annihilation.[69]

The article was mainly a blow-by-blow account of Munro's own experiences from the time he boarded a ship with soldiers of the Royal Regiment in a British port the previous evening until returning to England less than 24 hours later. It strongly emphasized the fury and intensity of the German defences, and frankly reported at least some of the Canadian casualties:

> By the time our boat touched the beach the din was in crescendo. I peered out at the slope lying just in front of us and it was startling to discover that it was dotted with the fallen forms of men in battledress. The Royals ahead of us had been cut down as they stormed the slope. It came home to me only then that every one of those men had gone down under the bullets of the enemy at the top of the incline.

While preparing to disembark from their landing craft, the troops with Munro came under heavy fire. As he took shelter behind "a flimsy bit of armor plating," bullets whizzed just above Munro's head. "The fire was murderous now and the Canadians' fire-power was being reduced by casualties." With half the men in the boat wounded, a landing at the designated spot seemed impossible; somehow the landing craft managed to get away from the beach without further losses. "That attempted landing was one of the fiercest and grimmest events in the whole raid and the only spot where the landing was temporarily repulsed."

Munro's account gave little assessment of the battle as a whole, but what there was suggested strongly that it had been a success. By 10 a.m., he reported, "the Canadians ... seemed to have the town fairly well under control and to have stabilized the situation on the beaches. ... At noon the final re-embarkation was under way and the force was taken off the main beach." The raiders "left Dieppe silent and afire, its ruins and its dead under a shroud of smoke." A subsequent article gave more of an overview, referring explicitly to severe casualties ("our losses probably will not be small"); beyond that, however, readers were told only that details of Allied losses "were couched in silence." But the overall impression was that the raid had achieved its objectives. "Assault operations were successful all along the beach"; the raiders had "captured the main portions of the town" before making an orderly withdrawal "as planned, nine hours after the raid started." From this account, no one could have guessed that two-thirds of the 5,000 Canadian raiders had been killed, wounded, or captured or were missing in action.[70]

At the time, Munro's coverage of Canada's first European engagement with the enemy was seen as an unqualified triumph for CP. With its gripping first-person narrative and vivid details, the article succeeded admirably in conveying the terror and chaos of war, and at that level was a clear journalistic success. Alan Gould, head of AP's news service, sent congratulations on Munro's "thrilling and superbly-written account ... The Associated Press is proud indeed to carry this story throughout its service."[71] The story was reprinted in Britain and Australia and dramatized on radio stations. "Canada was in the newspapers and the radio networks of the world," CP boasted.[72] Munro was quickly brought back to Canada, receiving praise from the board of directors and addressing public meetings in the home cities of the seven regiments that had fought at Dieppe.[73] McNeil praised Munro's work in lavish terms: it was "an Homeric adventure by which the whole free world was thrilled, and an occasion to which [he] rose magnificently in an epic series of stories which have placed him in the front rank of war correspondents and have added incalculably to the prestige of The Canadian Press." A promotional pamphlet entitled "CP told the World ... About Canada at Dieppe" (with a cover photo of a weary-looking Munro at his typewriter just after returning to London) was quickly issued.[74]

Later, however, the limitations of the coverage became more apparent. In his master's thesis on Canada's wartime censorship operations, Purcell quoted Munro as stating that the delay in releasing accurate casualty and missing figures from Dieppe – they were not made available until 15 September – "was one of the most flagrant abuses of censorship regulations during the war."[75] In a later interview with Phillip Knightley, Munro said that he "never really felt, *except maybe on the Dieppe raid*, that I was really cheating the public at home."[76] Purcell, speaking generally of military censorship, concluded that "[m]ost Canadian war correspondents will agree that the accurate story finally came out but that for various reasons the public was not given an accurate picture of any action at the time it happened."[77] Like other correspondents, Munro had to rely on the military authorities for overall casualty figures and could not possibly have known what happened everywhere on the battlefield. It is far from certain that two levels of military censorship would have allowed a more clear-eyed assessment to be transmitted; as Balzer's research clearly demonstrates, the initial publicity planning for the raid was based on ways of portraying failure as success, and even an internal military assessment of the operation was ordered to be rewritten to stress what had been accomplished.[78] But Munro's own statement to Knightley suggests that he had a reasonably clear idea of the severity of the defeat at the time. Even after the full extent of Canadian losses was disclosed (and after he was briefed personally by Munro), Purcell advised McNaughton not to worry about "occasional newspaper criticism" of the Dieppe operation. This did reflect public opinion to some extent, but it was important to remember "that the public cannot be fully informed of such operations; is not competent to judge on many points; and tends always to be suspicious and critical except of spectacular success."[79] While Purcell's assessment in his 1946 master's thesis was more critical, his comment at the time illustrates that the notion of journalistic detachment could be easily compromised while the war was going on. (The chief concern that the minister of national defence, Col. J.L. Ralston, and McNaughton expressed about the coverage was not its overall misleading character, but the fact that the relatively small contribution of US forces had been overemphasized, and the Canadians' central role correspondingly minimized.[80] Shortly after the raid, McNaughton reported that in order to "satisfy natural desire of Canadian public I am encouraging and facilitating despatch of press accounts based on interviews with individual participants."[81])

By 1943 the tide of war was turning. In the wake of the US entry into the war in December 1941, the German defeat at Stalingrad in 1942 and subsequent retreat from Russia, and success in neutralizing the U-boat campaign in the Atlantic, an Allied invasion of Europe became increasingly likely, and CP's plans adjusted accordingly. CP in general, and Purcell in particular, continued to benefit from the close relationship with McNaughton (although others in the Canadian military establishment and among Canada's allies proved to be less accommodating). At the beginning of the year, the head of military public relations in Canada, Joseph Clark (formerly of the Toronto *Star* and brother of the war correspondent Gregory Clark) invited Purcell to join him, Cliff Wallace (Purcell's successor as public relations officer for the First Canadian Army in England) and others for a visit to McNaughton's headquarters in England in order to make plans for "an adequate press relations establishment for any major Canadian move" (i.e., the invasion).[82] The resulting three-week absence from Canada would be worthwhile, Purcell wrote, because it would "guarantee the press relations and field censorship set-ups we have asked for in event of invasion and which do not now exist." It would also help CP with its staffing decisions, and would "give us firsthand confidential information on which to base our plans." As always, the competitive situation was not far from Purcell's mind; he stressed that the purpose of his trip had to remain confidential, "lest United Press learn of our preferred position." Accordingly, at the end of January 1943 McNaughton, Clark, Wallace, Purcell, and Maj. W.G. Abel (public relations officer of Canadian military headquarters in England) discussed an ambitious plan to increase Army public relations staff to 112 from 31.[83] In a separate meeting, Purcell and McNaughton spelled out "principles governing the selection of war correspondents to accompany Canadian forces on a major operation"; the basic premise was that CP would be given "reasonable facilities" to serve Canadian newspapers.[84] It was also decided that the Canadian Army would have its own field press censors, who CP felt would handle Canadian copy more quickly and more sympathetically than British officers.[85] Purcell told McNaughton that he "went farther in your understanding of CP's problems than I could have asked."[86] Purcell played a very direct role in working out the arrangements: an aide to McNaughton forwarded to a colleague "Purcell's draft approved by General McNaughton with a few changes as indicated in pencil."[87] CP now planned to have five war correspondents with the Canadian army, one of them French-speaking,[88] and an additional correspondent covering the Royal Canadian Air Force. This would be "the greatest news story in Canada's history – the story of Canadian airmen and soldiers blasting a doorway into Europe." [89]

Military thinking about publicity and press coverage had clearly evolved tremendously since World War One, and in recommending to his superiors in Ottawa the expansion of public relations staff approved by McNaughton, Joseph Clark spelled out a clear rationale:

Public Relations is an integral part of a modern fighting force. Publicity is a weapon, just as potent in sustaining the morale of fighting men and the civilian public back of them as efficient fire power is in defeating the enemy on the field of battle.

Whether public spirit is strong or weak will be in ratio to the amount of war news made readily available to the public, and the speed with which it reaches the public, regardless of whether that news is uniformly good or intermittently bad. ... present-day instantaneous means of communication makes it imperative that every facility be provided to help speed the transmission of news to the information media.

The people depend on the news made readily available to them to guide their wartime thinking, to activate them, to stimulate patriotism, to stir war fervor, to induce them to join up or buy bonds.[90]

Purcell observed approvingly in April that most of the newly appointed public relations officers were former journalists, and that even the jeep drivers assigned to correspondents were selected for their news background.[91]

However, as Canadian soldiers began to operate outside the United Kingdom (and hence outside McNaughton's direct commend), and as McNaughton's own position in the military hierarchy was called into question (he resigned and returned to Canada at the end of 1943, ostensibly for health reason but actually as a result of losing an internal battle about the deployment of Canadian forces[92]), the agreement with Purcell about CP's priority in Canadian press arrangements could not be taken for granted. This became clear when Ross Munro accompanied Canadian forces invading Sicily in July 1943.

At first, the Sicily coverage went very well for CP. Munro's account of the Canadians' landing near Pachino on 10 July was the first direct account of the invasion to be published anywhere – another prestigious "world beat" for CP.[93] About 20 other correspondents went ashore with different invasion forces; Munro's advantage reflected a combination of resourcefulness, assistance or at least noninterference by several military personnel, and good luck. CP acknowledged in particular the assistance of Maj. Bill Gilchrist, an army public relations officer (formerly of the Saint John *Telegraph-Journal*). Munro wrote his account of the landing, which was almost unopposed, on the beach, and sent it back by landing craft to the headquarters ship where Gilchrist was stationed. From this point onward, the story was handled irregularly: Gilchrist had it censored by an intelligence officer on the ship (rather than by an authorized field press censor); the shipboard radio operator (who was not supposed to handle press material) transmitted it to Malta, from where it was forwarded urgently (and again irregularly) to London over RAF channels.[94] The Air Ministry in London then passed Munro's story to the CP bureau, although "with consternation." Probably as a result of these irregularities, the story went exclusively to CP, and was not made available to other news organizations under the pooling arrangements administered by the Ministry of Information. While the resulting beat was a matter of great pride for CP, Allied Forces Headquarters, under the command of Gen. Dwight Eisenhower, was enraged that Munro had bypassed censorship and used unauthorized and insecure transmission channels, urging that "dramatic disciplinary action" be taken. The chief of Canadian Army public relations, Lt.-Col. Cliff Wallace, had to intervene personally to convince the Allied leadership not to arrest Munro. (Munro's explanation was that having come directly from London, he was not briefed on censorship procedures for the invasion as correspondents who came with the assault force from North Africa had been.[95] Lt.-Col. R.S. Malone, who shortly afterward replaced Wallace as head of Canadian army public relations, concluded that the scoop, and its evasion of normal channels, had reflected "accident or good fortune rather than skulduggery."[96])

Objections were also raised to the arrangement between Purcell and McNaughton about CP's primacy among Canadian news organizations.

In May, McNaughton's superiors at Canadian military headquarters in London decided that the CBC and BUP should have the same status as CP.[97] This led to an apparently unsatisfactory conversation between Purcell and the chief of the general staff, Lt.-Gen. Kenneth Stuart, in Ottawa. "Any step to interfere with the adequate reporting by The Canadian Press of such a gravely-important event [invasion of Europe] is bound to have severe repercussions on the country at a most critical time," McNeil warned after Stuart's meeting with Purcell. If CP's representation were reduced to less than what it understood to be the agreed-on level of five correspondents, the first to be cut was Maurice Desjardins, "the only representative of the French-language newspapers in London. General McNaughton was specific in his understanding that provision for this man, in addition to our basic four correspondents, was an essential of minimum effective regional coverage."[98] In Sicily, meanwhile, CP was unable to get approval for a second correspondent to assist Munro until a month after the landings; he eventually collapsed from exhaustion after the invading forces reached the Italian mainland and had to be withdrawn.[99] McNeil argued forcefully with Ralston about the issue, and a supporting telegram signed by eight of Canada's major newspapers insisted that "as basic service of Canadian newspapers, Canadian Press must be given adequate staff for its job and such staff should have priority over special correspondents."[100] Ralston was adamant, however, that CBC and BUP should receive the same treatment as CP. Stuart told Canadian military headquarters in London that he had received "[s]trong representations that Canadian Press coverage far exceeds other agencies and that numerical equality not fair either to agencies or to newspapers who have accepted a junior place to the agencies."[101] One reason for increasing BUP's representation, in Ottawa's view, was that it was practically the only reliable vehicle for having Canada's part in the war covered in the British press.[102] However, a ruling by Allied headquarters that BUP was just another name for United Press – the same argument that CP habitually made about its rival – and was therefore not entitled to separate accreditation rendered the Canadian dispute about its status moot.[103] By February 1944, with the Italian campaign well advanced and the Normandy invasion imminent, Joseph Clark informed Purcell that CP would have three of the first nine correspondents (one of them bilingual) with the D-Day invasion force, compared to two for CBC (one French-speaking), two for BUP, and two independent correspondents representing individual newspapers (one from a French-language publication).[104] Any remaining positions would go to independents, who were "practically unanimous" in complaining that they were at a severe disadvantage compared to CP and CBC.[105] Purcell was able to report to the board of directors in September 1944 that "[f]acilities accorded to The Canadian Press for coverage of Canadian forces in action had met the representations made last year to the Minister of National Defense."[106] Although the heaviest fighting of the war for Canadian forces was still to come, the emphasis of CP's coverage began shifting away from "strictly military angles" in 1944 and towards postwar reconstruction, allowing some war correspondents to be redeployed to other duties in Canada.[107] As well, CP found that it could get by with fewer correspondents than originally planned once military operations moved beyond invasion and became somewhat more predictable.[108]

The combined experience of CP war correspondents and military public relations staff contributed to fast and effective coverage of the Normandy landings on 6 June 1944 – despite a potentially disastrous last-minute security lapse on the part of Purcell, who was overseeing final preparations in London.[109] Munro and Bill Stewart went ashore with Canadian troops at Bernières-sur-Mer and Courseulles, with Louis Hunter covering the RCAF and Allen Nicholson the Royal Canadian Navy.[110] "Normandy was my fifth sea-borne landing," Munro recalled later,

> and I wondered how long my luck would hold. But I got ashore at Bernières behind the leading regiment. In a slit-trench by a stone wall, I pounded out a couple of stories with my typewriter on my knees jumping like a live thing from the concussion from Canadian artillery firing in an adjacent orchard. One of my stories got back to London on a destroyer returning to England to pick up Field Marshal Montgomery. It could have been the first from the allied beaches. I was never sure.

Munro's account was the first eyewitness account from the Normandy beaches to reach newspapers around the world. His realization that the ship assigned to pick up Montgomery would not be delayed or sidetracked meant that his story of the landing reached England before anyone else's.[111] Compared to his coverage of Dieppe, it was a sober, matter-of-fact account:

> WITH CANADIAN FORCES LANDING IN FRANCE, June 6 – In two hours and 45 minutes of fighting on the beaches here, the Canadian invasion force won its beach head and shoved on inland.

At 10:45 this morning the Canadian Commander (Gen. Keller) sent this message to Gen. Crerar, G.O.C. 1st Canadian Army: 'Beach head taken. Well on way to intermediate objective.'

Bill Stewart went ashore before Munro to find that the shooting had already moved inland. "I went in at 9:30 in the morning or so," he wrote later.

But the beaches were clear then. There was no combat. I thought the beach would be shelled or mortared. And it was mined still, but not anti-personnel mines, as far as I could tell. ... there were wounded on the beach and dead, and there was a line of dead ahead of me. And, there were some wounded coming back for evacuation.[112]

In a later interview, Stewart recalled that he was equipped with a Mae West, a "typewriter waterproofed with tape and ... a trenching tool. ... And I dug myself a hole and a trench in it, and I sat down and put a little ledge in it for the typewriter and I just wrote."[113] In addition to the relay arrangements for correspondents' copy by ship, Stewart recalled that army public relations staff had also brought carrier pigeons, "but their homing instincts were confused." Within 24 hours of the landing, correspondents were permitted to file using wireless; Stewart's wireless operator had previously worked at CP's Ottawa bureau and the army field censor was a former editor at CP's Montreal bureau. It was, Stewart recalled, "[a] sort of CP invasion of Normandy."[114]

Stewart's comment reflects the generally positive working arrangements for CP journalists in particular and Canadian journalists in general that continued until the end of the war. Munro reported that Canadian journalists covering the European campaign after D-Day enjoyed "the best Army transmission set-up on the front." Senior military commanders "were all appreciative of our needs and made our problems as easy to solve as they could. Right through the Canadian Army we found officers and men who went out of their way to aid coverage."[115]

Being in the thick of the action, as Munro had been at Dieppe, was not typical of a correspondent's activities. As Stewart recalled, on an average day,

[y]ou can go to divisional headquarters and they will tell you what's going on. So you can go to wherever the action is. Or, even better still, you can go

to where, say, a battalion has come out of action and get the stories of the guys. ... [T]he important thing for people, and CP was very big on this, was the story of a battalion, what had happened in a particular action and who figured in it and where they were from. ... Sometimes ... you might be the target of mortar bombs [but] ... you weren't exposed. You were in the war area, but you weren't in combat. Correspondents didn't win the war.[116]

Six CP correspondents – Munro, Stewart, Louis Hunter, Maurice Desjardins (concentrating on French-speaking units), Alan Randal, and Douglas Amaron – followed the Canadian army through Normandy and into Germany.[117] Margaret Ecker, one of relatively few female CP journalists, arrived in Normandy during the battle for Caen and "covered hospitals and women and civilian stories"; later she went to Belgium and Holland.

CP's vigorous assertion of its central role in covering Canadian military action overseas always served two purposes. On one hand, it met the needs of member newspapers and their readers for prompt and extensive news about the war; on the other, it strengthened CP's position against BUP, which by 1940 had become a very serious competitor. In CP's dealing with the question of radio news during the war, however, self-interest and even organizational survival were by far the dominant motives.

As described in Chapter 3, CP was suffering serious losses by the end of the 1930s because of competition from BUP and a US radio-news service, Transradio.[118] It was not just a matter of radio stations across Canada preferring the service provided by Transradio and BUP to the limited free service provided by CP since 1936; the fact that CP's competitors allowed commercial sponsorship of their news broadcasts while CP did not was difficult to overcome. Beyond this, BUP was offering a cut-rate print news service to many of the CP newspapers that had radio-station affiliations, threatening its core business. In May 1942, immediately after resuming his CP position in Toronto, Purcell urged the staff to greater efforts in their "fight with United Press (we shall not call it British United Press)."[119]

CP's strategy to deal with radio competition from 1939 onward had two main thrusts. One was to expand the service it provided to the CBC, and to make this improved service available to all radio stations in Canada, thereby hoping to reduce the market for Transradio and BUP news, and possibly drive them out of business. The second – once war was declared – was to seek severe regulatory restrictions on its competitors for private radio news, up to and including an outright ban, from the CBC (which was the national broadcast regulator as well as the public broadcaster) and/or the government. But by 1941, this approach had clearly become inadequate, forcing CP to adopt a radically new approach and establish its own commercial radio-news operation.[120]

CP's radio subsidiary, Press News Ltd. (PN), began operations in July 1941.[121] By September, 15 of Canada's 74 private radio stations had contracts with PN, and 12 more were considered likely to sign up soon.[122] (Interestingly, not all stations affiliated with CP members had done so.) The service was expected to begin showing a small profit by mid-1942. In a report to the CP board, Rupert Davies acknowledged that one of PN's biggest challenges was "the prejudice of broadcasters resulting from the long opposition of The Canadian Press to commercial sponsorship of news."[123] Many owners of private stations believed that CP's only motive for entering the radio business was to establish a monopoly that could then be manipulated to the advantage of CP's newspaper members (by, for example, withholding news until it had appeared in print). Other obstacles to PN's profitable operation were the "preponderance of CBC newscasts, the curtailed form of sponsorship, easy revenue from 'spot' announcements before and after CBC newscasts and the free service of The Canadian Press to the CBC." Continuing their breathtakingly rapid reversal of previous policy, CP's directors agreed to support a request to the CBC by the Canadian Association of Broadcasters – formerly CP's bitter enemy in questions of radio-news policy – to relax restrictions on sponsorship of news broadcasts.[124] (Senior CP executives actually showed up in person before the CBC board in support of the CAB.[125]) It was recommended that advertisements should be allowed to describe specific products, and "the use of a musical theme, siren, or klaxon" should be permitted at the beginning and end of newscasts.

As questions of costs and revenue came to the fore for PN, so did the idea of requiring payment from the CBC. Previously, CP had not been paid for supplying news to CBC, although it did charge $20,000 a year to cover the direct costs of preparing radio bulletins from 1939 to 1941, when the CBC began doing this work itself.[126] In April 1942, Roy Thomson, a CP director with substantial radio interests of his own, estimated that a reasonable fee, given the number of CBC stations served, would be around $70,000 a year.[127] Rupert Davies noted that CBC-affiliated stations had sold more than $900,000 worth of advertising the previous year, yielding an operating surplus of $183,000. "There was no question that they had the money to pay for the news service." The corporation initially argued that it had no additional revenue to pay the proposed annual charge, but reluctantly agreed to consider payment beginning in 1943.[128] An annual fee of $40,000 a year for the duration of the war was eventually agreed on, on the understanding that any payment to BUP (which would certainly ask for payment once CP had done so) would be substantially less – "as damned little as possible," in the words of CBC director N.L. Nathanson.[129] (When it turned out that BUP was to be paid $25,000, however, CP reacted angrily; having pleaded poverty to obtain the $40,000 fee, the CBC's willingness to pay a substantial additional sum to BUP seemed duplicitous. CP accordingly gave notice that the CBC contract would be terminated at the end of one year unless a ratio of at least three to one was maintained between payments to CP and BUP.[130]) As was typically the case with CP's radio policy, there was substantial disagreement about the new direction. Some members who owned radio stations themselves wanted less competition from CBC stations, and some were opposed to involvement with what they considered a government agency. At the annual meeting in 1943, the proposed CBC contract was approved by a relatively narrow margin of 23 to 14.[131]

In the face of CP's threat to withdraw from the new agreement, the CBC assessed its options, noting that BUP had a specially developed service for radio (unlike CP), and in some regions the BUP newswire operated when CP's did not.[132] But it would be difficult to replace the CP service entirely. A survey of CBC newsrooms indicated that BUP's service was considered only about two-thirds as valuable as CP's; its Canadian coverage would have to be greatly expanded and its reliability improved (especially from Ottawa) to be considered more than a supplement. But neither was it desirable to rely exclusively on CP, "whose basic policy (because it is an association of newspapers) may in the long run be antagonistic to radio."[133] Another option was for CBC to establish its own newsgathering operation, but this would cost around $100,000 a year. Eventually it was recommended that if CBC (and the government) did not wish to incur the "active antagonism" of 89 Canadian newspapers, it should make the best deal possible with CP despite the likelihood that BUP would refuse to provide service for the substantially reduced fee that CP would insist on. Ultimately, the impasse was not resolved until 1945, when an additional $40,000 payment for use of CP news in CBC shortwave broadcasts produced a ratio of CP – BUP payments that CP was prepared to accept.[134] Meanwhile, PN made steady headway in signing contracts with private stations, reaching a total of 49 (compared to 50 for BUP) by the end of the war.[135]

CP was deeply involved in the organization and application of military and civilian censorship during the war. As Claude Beauregard points out, explicit censorship is fundamentally opposed to the value of free expression associated with political liberalism,[136] and its adoption, even if limited to wartime, substantially transforms the basic assumptions under which journalism is practiced. CP's involvement with censorship was less intimate than during the First World War, when CP editors also acted as press censors,[137] but as early as 1928 and again in 1936, 1938, and the spring of 1939, CP executives discussed with government officials what kind of censorship would be applied in the event of another war, acting as de facto representatives of Canadian journalists generally.[138] CP's central recommendation was that domestic censorship must be voluntary and controlled by civilian authorities, as it had been during the previous war, rather than the military. (Military censorship, which was compulsory and much more restrictive, applied to journalists covering Canadian military action outside Canada.[139]) Beauregard describes two main purposes of censorship. One, quite clear-cut, is to prevent militarily useful information from being given to the enemy; the second, much more subjective, susceptible to political manipulation, and hence highly controversial, is to avoid damage to military or civilian morale.[140] By the time war broke out in September 1939, the federal government had agreed that domestic censorship of journalism would be controlled by the secretary of state's department, not the military.[141] Walter S. Thompson, who had been director of publicity for Canadian National Railways, was named chairman of the newly established Censorship Co-ordination Committee and Clare Moyer, clerk of the Senate, was appointed press censor; both were among six nominees for these positions recommended by CP at the government's invitation. On 5 and 6 September 1939, CP's general manager, J.A. McNeil, accompanied by Victor Sifton (owner of the Winnipeg *Free Press*, Regina *Leader*, and Saskatoon *Star-Phoenix*) and John W. Dafoe of the *Free Press*, discussed with Thompson and Moyer the censorship measures that would be adopted. The details of the system had not yet been clearly worked out – in fact, press censorship was not really systematized until 1942[142] – but the general approach was to be "a self-imposed censorship, with [Thompson's] committee laying down certain broad principles, and a group of regional advisors available for consultation."[143] The terms "self-imposed" and "voluntary" meant that newspapers, radio stations, and other journalistic organizations like CP were not *required* to seek clearance of anything prior to publication. They were, however, given guidelines to follow (based on the Defence of Canada Regulations promulgated in September 1939); if journalists believed that a particular story might violate the guidelines, censors were available to provide a ruling. Even if a story was deemed to violate the guidelines, journalists still had the option of publication if they were willing to risk prosecution. However, they could not be prosecuted subsequently for publishing anything that had been approved by the censor.[144]

CP cooperated actively with the domestic censorship system throughout the war. As noted above, CP was involved in the design of the system, accepted the basic principles on which it was based, and endorsed the personnel chosen to run it. More broadly, as Wilfrid Eggleston, a journalist who became censor for the parliamentary press gallery in November 1939 (and was subsequently appointed chief press censor and eventually director of all domestic censorship) wrote in 1944, the system operated on the assumption that "every newspaper publisher is a loyal citizen, just as anxious as anyone else to win the war and defeat the enemy."[145] In keeping with this assessment, and reflecting CP's understanding of its own national role, CP's unvarying policy was to "comply implicitly" with the censors' requests.[146] This was different than the approach taken by many Canadian newspapers, and by CP's chief competitor, BUP, especially in the early years of the war. No mainstream publications were prosecuted for violating the Defence of Canada Regulations until 1942, even after being advised by censors not to publish; when it became clear there would be no serious consequences for ignoring these recommendations, newspapers increasingly either ignored them or refrained from seeking the censors' advice in the first place.[147] News organizations that did follow the censors' rulings thus faced the prospect of losing competitive ground to rivals who published stories they did not carry or beat them to publication. For CP, however, even if the delays involved in seeking and abiding by censors' rulings sometimes "placed us at a disadvantage as compared to other news agencies [i.e., BUP], it is felt there is no alternative consonant with the national interest."[148] (In a competitive situation, CP's authoritative position could be an advantage.[149]) When Eggleston retired as chief press censor at the end of 1944, he and Purcell exchanged compliments about how well the system had worked. "It has been a delight working with you through these years," Purcell wrote, "and I cannot see how censorship could have operated more efficiently or more intelligently."[150] Eggleston replied that "without the loyal and sympathetic support of the Canadian Press we should be constantly in hot water. It is almost incredible how happy our relations have been."[151]

Even when disagreements arose, the relationship was almost always cordial. McNeil reported to CP's annual meeting in May 1940 that objections to "apparently erroneous rulings" were often successful; the censors agreed that CP defended its point of view vigorously, although it ultimately complied even with objectionable rulings.[152] Virtually all those appointed as press censors were journalists or ex-journalists, who were generally seen by the military as advocates of fewer rather than more extensive restrictions.[153] "[T]he Press Censors have in many cases been able to effect a change in the military attitude when it tended to restrict the publication of news in no way affecting the national interest," McNeil wrote.[154] One noteworthy example of this came in the summer of 1941 when senior naval officers complained that a CP article about sonar, initially taken from the Toronto *Telegram* and republished in the Halifax *Herald*, disclosed military secrets. Faced with demands that the Toronto censor who had passed the original article should be fired, Eggleston prepared a detailed dossier showing that the information published had been widely available since 1920, which put an end to the military objections.[155] CP complaints were not always successful, however; the publisher of the Halifax *Herald* protested that when the destroyer *Margaree* sank on convoy duty in October 1940, the news was widely known and discussed in Halifax within a few days – but censors would not allow it to be published. Among other things, the story was being covered by American radio stations, which were not yet subject to censorship of their own, and whose signals could be clearly picked up in Halifax.[156] Vagueness in the rules or inconsistency in their application were often cause for complaint, as were concerns that local military press liaison officers too often referred questions to Ottawa, causing substantial delays.[157] These officers frequently attended meetings of CP members where they responded to criticism and tried to resolve outstanding problems, underscoring the close cooperation that existed despite the disagreements.[158] One of CP's chief concerns was that the system should work efficiently and predictably.

On several occasions during the war, however, there were more serious battles about censorship. The bitterest conflict concerned the censoring of statements by Camilien Houde, the mayor of Montreal, who called on his fellow citizens in August 1940 not to comply with compulsory registration of manpower.[159] This was an unusual situation in several respects, especially because the censors took their orders from the secretary of state and minister of justice, thus indicating political direction of the censorship regime.[160] In addition, in this instance the censors issued a preemptive blanket order to all publications not to publish Houde's statements, rather than responding to individual articles submitted for assessment, thereby moving away from the voluntary approach towards something more coercive. Newspapers were also ordered not to republish a statement that Houde had made 18 months earlier about Canadiens being "Fascists by blood, but not by name," even though this had been widely reported at the time (and even though the Toronto *Star* defied the ban with no consequences).[161] In a tacit acknowledgment that the handling of the Houde incident had been a mistake, the Defence of Canada Regulations were changed in 1942 to allow the publication of public statements considered subversive as long as they were not presented in such a way as to support, approve, or exploit the views expressed; from this point on, censors were less likely to restrict statements of opinion.[162] Purcell described the Houde incident as the censors' "worst blunder of the war," but as in other cases of disagreement, CP ultimately accepted their decision.[163] In his postwar assessment of the censorship system, Purcell endorsed Eggleston's view that newspapers should have published more often in defiance of what they considered unreasonable decisions, taking the risk of prosecution and leaving the question of whether they had actually violated the law to the courts. This, Eggleston, argued, would have given the censors greater leverage against unreasonable military demands or political direction.[164] Eggleston gave CP, along with a few Canadian newspapers, credit for "[taking] up the cudgels in behalf of free speech" during the war, and strengthening the censors' efforts to limit censorship to "essentials of military security."[165] But much as CP was ready to challenge censors' rulings, it never took the step of deliberately publishing proscribed material and, in effect, inviting a test case. Such defiance would have been difficult to reconcile with CP's basic stance of implicit compliance. CP's journalistic instinct in favour of disclosure and the inclination to question arbitrary government decisions still operated during the war, but in a way that was constrained both by law and by CP's active identification with the state that embodied the national war effort.

Censorship of military activities outside Canada operated quite differently. It was compulsory, not voluntary, and was run by soldiers rather than civilians. Prior restraint was systematically imposed. Every dispatch by a correspondent from a Canadian military zone of operation abroad had to be approved by a military censor, who had the authority to prevent or delay transmission of any information considered useful to the enemy. This typically included such things as troop movements and numbers, identification of specific units, details about casualties, the relative success or failure of particular operations, the type of equipment available or in use, type of training, or anything that might have a negative effect on military or civilian morale in Canada or Allied countries. There was no formal avenue of appeal from a military censor's decisions, (though informal protests were sometimes successful, as when Ross Munro complained to Richard Malone about being prevented from reporting that Montreal's Black Watch regiment had been virtually "wiped out" during Operation Spring in July 1944.[166]) Under this system, correspondents had little choice about compliance; the only choice was between covering Canadian military operations under heavy restrictions and not covering them at all. The serious effects of censorship on coverage of the Dieppe raid have been discussed earlier; more generally, in Purcell's assessment, censorship meant that in most cases, "the public was not given an accurate picture of any action at the time it happened"[167] (although he added that the full story usually came out eventually).

Journalists sometimes complained about censorship of reports that were embarrassing to Canadian military (or political) leaders, but not of genuine military value to the enemy. Balzer cites several examples of military censors preventing or limiting coverage that would have embarrassed the military but seemed to have no real security significance, such as the fact that McNaughton was not permitted to visit Canadian troops in Sicily while fighting was going on in the summer of 1943, or reports of Canadian soldiers being killed by friendly fire.[168] In his master's thesis, Purcell quoted Ralph Allen of *The Globe and Mail* as concluding that, even if the result was unintentional, "censorship in the field served to cover up mistakes of military commanders and save embarrassment to politicians."[169] For example, Allen observed, many war correspondents knew that Canadian units in Europe were at half-strength in the fall and winter of 1944, but military censors took the position that any discussion of the need for reinforcements – a politically charged issue in Canada – was a breach of security. Censorship also prevented critical coverage of the "highly dubious qualities of leadership" shown by some Canadian commanders between Caen and Falaise, Allen added; instead, journalists generally had to rely on official communiqués, which "almost without exception, stressed success and either underplayed, ignored or vetoed failure."[170] Balzer also argues that the ban on graphic description of such things as the effect of high explosives on human bodies effectively "sanitized the war," though it is not clear that Canadian newspapers would have provided much coverage of this kind even in the absence of formal censorship.[171]

A broader question – and one that extends well beyond CP – is to what extent Canadian journalists' attachment to the Allied cause disposed them to favourable and even heroic treatment of Canada's military efforts, regardless of the censorship regime. Charles Lynch, a Canadian who covered the European campaign for Reuters, famously concluded that "[w]e were a propaganda arm of our governments. At the start the censors enforced that, but by the end we were our own censors. We were cheerleaders."[172] Bill Stewart, however, strongly disputed that view:

> Charlie Lynch fell for this and he shouldn't have ... *that we were cheerleaders*. There was nothing very cheerful about the goddamn war. As the war broke out, Canada was a very very solemn place, because we were scarcely a generation from an appalling, a very appalling war, the First World War. Now you are getting into another. There's this madman over there that you can hear on the radio. And he is walking in here, and he is going in there, and he is kicking the hell out of the British in the desert, and he's knocking them out of Norway and he is taking over Czechoslovakia and Austria and all this. ... You see, I either wanted to go overseas as a war correspondent or go in the air force. I had three brothers in the services, and a sister, you know. So you weren't on the Germans' side, that's for sure. You wouldn't want to write anything that would help the Germans. There was a lot of heroism and you wrote about it. You were writing from one side of the issue. Were you a cheerleader, or weren't you a cheerleader? I don't think you were a cheerleader. I think you were reporting what was going on, on your side.[173]

The key phrase "on your side" is ambiguous. On one hand, it reflects the reality that correspondents physically were restricted to their own side of the battlefield. The Canadian correspondents wore military uniforms, had honorary officer's rank, and depended on the armed forces for information, food, accommodation and transportation.[174] On the other hand, it also has a clear connotation of partisanship: "our side" versus "their side." The assumption of Canada's chief censors that "every newspaper publisher is a loyal citizen, just as anxious as anyone else to win the war and defeat the enemy" applied to reporters and editors as well.[175] (There were significant differences in how this was manifested, though, with some journalists being more, and some less, critical of how the war effort was carried out.)

Because most of CP's war coverage was routed through its London bureau, British censorship was a concern as well. Here the general problems of journalism in wartime were exacerbated by the sense that, as colonials, Canadians were taken less seriously than their counterparts in the British press. After the fall of France, Britain became a battleground and censorship was tightened dramatically – so much so that overseas correspondents threatened to call a 48-hour strike at one point. On the "Black Day" of 15 August 1940, censors held up reports of German air raids on London suburbs for nine hours. In the meantime, Purcell told the CP board of directors, German propaganda multiplied the damage by a factor of 10. "Actually the raids did not take a serious toll, but because of the British censorship the North American press has nothing to contradict the German claims." This debacle led to some speeding up of decisions.[176]

In the fall of 1941, McNeil reported that the appointment of a new minister of information in Britain had brought improvements – more censors were stationed at main telegraph offices and they were instructed to give immediate rulings rather than referring back to their departments, avoiding delays.[177] Another continuing irritant was the British censor's banning transmission to Canada of commentary and opinion columns that had already been published in England – to which the Ministry of Information replied blandly that its only intention was "to prevent sending of irresponsible and distorted accounts of the Allied war effort of the kind which have aroused grave concern to our friends in many parts of the world."[178] In April 1942, the superintendent of CP's London bureau reported 60 major instances of censorship in the previous six months, with delays ranging from 38 minutes to seven hours. Nine stories were stopped completely, one for a month.[179]

Debates over CP's handling of statements from German sources about military operations shed further light on the tension between normal journalistic practices and patriotic citizenship in wartime. At a meeting of CP's western Canadian members early in 1940, Purcell reported that statements from Deutsches Nachrichtenburo, the official German news agency, were generally characterized as "claims" or "boasts," thus clearly indicating their credibility was in question.[180] If an Allied denial or admission was available, the German statement would be issued with the relevant Allied statement in brackets. Sometimes stories quoting German sources were held up "pending receipt of Allied confirmation or denial." John Dafoe argued that German claims were given too much prominence and should be played down, and Rupert Davies said carrying German propaganda claims was inconsistent with CP's reputation for accuracy: "There was no reason CP should be the vehicle for anti-British news." Others defended the practice, however: P.C. Galbraith of the Calgary *Herald* said readers were curious "about what was being fed to the German people. It was up to the individual to decide what to do with the material." McNeil agreed: if German claims were suppressed, CP would be "arbitrarily imposing a censorship and withholding from its members news that some of them desired to receive." It was better to provide the news and let people debate its value. On a show of hands, it was agreed that CP should continue to carry claims from Deutsches Nachrichtenburo and other forms of German propaganda "provided it is clearly labelled as such." Later in 1940, Charles Bruce, the superintendent of CP's New York bureau – where German reports were typically received in the first instance – said experience had shown that communiqués from the German high command were fairly accurate when dealing with the land war but inaccurate when dealing with the war at sea, and that announcements from Deutsches Nachrichtenburo were "half propaganda."[181] This effort to make distinctions between what could and could not be believed was a very journalistic reflex. In an intriguing comparison, Bruce said removing or labelling propaganda claims was similar to "expung[ing] concealed advertising in peacetime."

To use Daniel Hallin's terminology, it is clear that the operation of censorship, along with Canadian journalists' identification with the war effort, severely restricted the "sphere of legitimate controversy" during the war, especially in relation to military operations overseas.[182] But the operation of domestic censorship in particular also illustrates the complicated way that CP tried to, and did in some ways, assert the usual journalistic values even while actively playing a role as a participant in the war effort.

Even as CP's war coverage solidified its position as Canada's national news agency and enhanced its reputation internationally, the early years of the war in particular brought unusually sharp disagreements among CP publishers on partisan grounds. This mainly reflected the Conservative critique of Canada's war effort, which was seen as too hesitant and limited.[183] (It also reflected preexisting tensions within the organization – for example, when George McCullagh of *The Globe and Mail* launched his ostensibly nonpartisan Leadership League in early 1939, he denounced CP as "a creature news service" that only printed good things about the prime minister, W.L.M. King, and vowed that if he succeeded in his goal of establishing a National government, CP would be compelled to print "the truth."[184]) At CP's annual meeting in May 1940 – a few weeks after the phony war had spectacularly ended with Germany's Blitzkrieg invasion of Belgium, the Netherlands, and France – a rare public dispute with clear partisan undertones broke out when Frederick Ker of the Hamilton *Spectator* and the Southam chain complained that CP's Ottawa bureau was "negligent" in not ferreting out the real news about Canada's lack of war preparedness.[185] Canada's chief contribution to the Allied war effort to date, the British Commonwealth Air Training Scheme, was "bogged down hopelessly, and the public had not been informed because The Canadian Press was not digging up the facts." John Imrie of the Edmonton *Journal* (another Southam paper) agreed, saying CP was not carrying out its role of unifying the country because it was failing to report "the untold story of war preparations." CP's president, Rupert Davies of the Kingston *Whig-Standard* (and soon to be appointed a Liberal member of the Senate), replied that CP was a "non-political, non-partisan organization," and that the air-training scheme had become "a political football." E. Norman Smith of the Ottawa *Journal* (who, despite his newspaper's Conservative allegiance had been a consistently strong supporter of CP's management since its founding) insisted that CP had been "absolutely non-partisan" from the beginning, and that "[d]eparture from that policy would mean wrecking the organization." Clearly, a proxy battle reflecting Conservative attacks on King's war policies was being waged. Smith added that Ker's and Imrie's papers had their own correspondents in Ottawa who had done no better than CP's reporters, "because the news was not available – and for the very good reason of national security." CP should provide all the news it could obtain, "but criticism of the Government, open or implied, must be from a very responsible source. ... Every member of The Canadian Press should

be able to say that he had nothing to do with the day-to-day operations of the organization beyond laying down a clear-cut and non-
partisan policy for an able staff to pursue." Davies concluded that CP
must report faithfully on the war, but must stick to the facts – going
beyond that would threaten its whole structure. Strict adherence to
standard journalistic practices of objectivity was used to counter suggestions that CP should play a more aggressive role by investigating, drawing its own conclusions, and holding the government to
account.

Some CP members were also critical of Davies's role in relaying a
message from King to Canadian publishers on 15 June 1940, when the
fall of France appeared imminent. At King's request, Davies contacted
the 20 members of CP's board of directors by telephone. The prime minister's statement explained that the present situation was "very grave,"
with France's surrender expected within 48 hours.

> I am, therefore, asking the leading publishers of this Dominion to help
> the government at this time in maintaining a calm attitude amongst the
> people of Canada. I would like all the newspapers of Canada to help in
> steadying the country and to give us all the support they can. ... I do not
> ask for special treatment ... I do ask, however, that for the next two weeks
> the press of Canada, as a patriotic duty, refrain from criticism and recrimi-
> nations and help in every possible way to steady the country. ... without
> the steadying influence of the press, the people of Canada may become
> very much upset.[186]

C.O. Knowles of the Toronto *Telegram*, a consistent critic of CP's management, immediately sent a copy of the message to Arthur Meighen,
who from his position in the Senate was the Conservatives' strongest
critic of the government.[187] Knowles reported that he was "very disgusted" by the appeal, seeing it as "not inspired by patriotism so much
as it is by panic," and criticized CP as "a very complacent mouth-
piece for the Government."[188] Meighen, not surprisingly, agreed: "In
my judgment the Canadian Press does everything the Prime Minister
wants, whether the want is from a national or a party standpoint."[189] In
his direct correspondence with Davies, Knowles was more diplomatic,
acknowledging that Davies and the other CP directors were trying honestly to do a difficult job. But he added that CP had been "most unfair
in its news reports," an opinion shared by "prominent Conservatives
in Ottawa."[190]

Other Conservative publishers were less willing to accept Meighen's charges of systematic bias, however. M.E. Nichols of the Vancouver *Province*, one of CP's most senior directors and a former colleague of Meighen's as director of information in the Unionist government, insisted that

> there is one thing the Canadian Press does not and cannot do and that is serve the interests of any political party. ... In its membership there are Conservatives, Liberals, C.C.F.s, Social Crediters, Independents and what have you. ... a common news service prepared for 90 newspapers of all political stripes could not color its news without instant detection. In all the years I have served on the Board of Directors, I do not recall a single instance in which complaint has been made of party bias.[191]

One of Meighen's chief concerns was CP's campaign to establish a monopoly over the supply of radio news, but Nichols argued that it was better to have radio news supplied by CP than by the CBC, which he described as being under the thumb of C.D. Howe. The other suppliers of radio news were seriously compromised: BUP was "a US organization with a British label on it" and Transradio "is so much suspect that CBC only a month or so ago [June 1940] intimated that its licence would not be renewed."[192] Nichols agreed with Meighen on at least one point, however; a summary article that appeared on 1 September 1940, asserting that the first year of the war had gone well for Canada – unlike the beginning of the First World War – was "wholly foreign to all the rules and regulations of the Canadian Press as established and practiced for at least 20 years. ... The despatch was prepared by an employee who was recently transferred to the Ottawa Bureau but even so it should not have escaped the attention of the editors."[193] (Meighen's complaint was that the article painted too favourable a picture of King's government in comparison to Borden's.) More broadly, though, Nichols respectfully disputed Meighen's contention that CP's Ottawa bureau was "distinctly partisan."[194] While Meighen's complaints "at least warrant careful observation" and would be raised at the next directors' meeting, Nichols argued that CP journalists were not so much biased as deferential to authority and dependent on their sources. The average Ottawa correspondent, CP or otherwise, considered it necessary to "'stand in' with the government in order to get the news," Nichols wrote. "At times he will go out of his way to do something extra for a minister who gives him a special hand-out but this does not mean he should do less than justice to you or any other member of the opposition." But any CP editor who deliberately acted in a partisan way would put his job at risk.[195]

Imrie of the Edmonton *Journal* and other CP publishers renewed their complaints about CP's Ottawa coverage later in the fall of 1940. Imrie acknowledged that CP's Ottawa reporters must be close to whatever government was in power, but also must remain "constantly on guard to ensure that its output is not necessarily what the government would like but what the Canadian people are entitled to know."[196] CP journalists were regularly producing articles that showed the war effort in a favourable light (in contrast to the previous war, fought under a Conservative government) – coverage that "tended to develop too much complacency among the public." Meanwhile, US journalists who recently toured Canada found information that supported a more critical assessment.[197] "It was possible the Bureau staff had fallen into the habit of accepting too many handouts, without making an effort to dig out the facts." Victor Sifton agreed, describing the problem as a reflection on "the competence of the Ottawa Bureau." The visiting US journalists did not have access to any information that was not available to Canadian reporters, "but some were extraordinarily competent military observers. Some of their articles were a little cold and detached but nonetheless truthful."[198]

Competition between CP and member newspapers' Ottawa correspondents was another problem, Sifton noted. It was "regrettable that there was a definite feeling of jealousy on the part of the Press Gallery towards The CP with the result that the latter is often held off by departmental officials because they feel that if The CP gets anything exclusively they may incur displeasure from Gallery correspondents." In Sifton's view, it was "rather foolish for the individual publishers to seek to compete with The CP" on routine stories this way – "the only result was a general holdup." Davies estimated that 75 per cent of CP members (the less wealthy newspapers, clearly) were suffering because 25 per cent had their own Ottawa correspondents.[199] At the suggestion of Senator W.H. Dennis of the Halifax *Herald*, Davies asked CP publishers with their own Ottawa correspondents to help remedy the problem, but that only made the situation worse; representatives of *The Globe and Mail*, Toronto *Star*, and Montreal *Gazette* took Davies's letter as a request for CP to be given precedence and strongly objected.[200] A board resolution stating that CP should get "all official announcements, casualty lists and news of national import ... simultaneously" with any or all individual papers or agencies made it clear that CP was asking for equal, not preferential, treatment, but the underlying problem of wealthier members preferring their own exclusive coverage, sometimes to the detriment of CP's service, remained unresolved.[201]

Most complaints about CP's coverage came from Conservative publishers, but not all. In 1944 – at a time when the government was under serious pressure over the issue of conscription – Davies, now a senator, complained about unspecified bias in CP's political stories.[202] A year later, the finance committee (in effect, CP's executive committee) discussed at length "the matter of interpretation in CP news reports, particularly as related to reactions of troops overseas." (The incident in question was not specified, but may have concerned the controversial question of reinforcements and conscription.) The committee concluded that "reaction of the troops was in many instances important and significant and it was the duty of The Canadian Press to report it. However, any such dispatches should be carefully written and closely checked."[203]

Besides concerns about purported political bias and lack of enterprise in pursuing the news, financial questions absorbed a great deal of the CP board's attention during the war. As noted previously, CP (unlike other agencies) adopted a policy of strictly offsetting all cost increases for war coverage, which were substantial, by spending reductions elsewhere. In October 1939, the directors were told that the year's additional spending on war coverage would amount to almost $54,000, an increase of around 7.5 per cent.[204] McNeil confided to his counterpart at Reuters that CP's finance committee had not only ordered "stringent restrictions against any [further] new commitments, but the exploring of every possible avenue of other economies."[205] As Rupert Davies told the annual meeting in May 1940, newspapers were facing "adverse publishing conditions," making it essential to keep costs under control.[206] Frederick Ker painted a (probably exaggeratedly) bleak picture of CP's financial position during contract negotiations with CP's telegraph and printer operators the following year. His paper, the Hamilton *Spectator*, only used 20 per cent of what it received from CP, Ker insisted, but paid more for this than the remaining 80 per cent of locally produced content. "He could dispense with The Canadian Press." It was "no secret" that three of CP's largest members, which could easily afford to provide their own international and domestic news, were cool towards the agency. CP had begun as a cooperative "in the national interest," but was now "in competition with radio and other things and groups of members had threatened to drop out. How long can newspapers with diminishing returns be expected to carry on?"[207] Though Ker's confrontational remarks reflected CP's typically bare-knuckle approach to labour relations, CP's members genuinely did feel under financial pressure. For example, a proposal in September 1941 to appoint a second war correspondent was shelved in view of the $5,000 additional cost; in the summer of 1942, preparations for CP's 25th anniversary were overshadowed by a sense that "[t]he newspapers of Canada were faced with serious problems."[208] A few months later, Purcell reported to the finance committee that "any positions which might by any stretch of the imagination be considered non-essential" were being eliminated, not only to save money, but also in response to staff shortages caused by enlistment in the armed forces.[209] He also noted that while other agencies had increased their assessments by as much as 25 per cent since the war began, CP's assessments remained unchanged. In fact, it was not until the spring of 1944, after almost five years of war, that the board of directors approved an overall spending increase of 7 per cent. Arthur Ford of the London *Free Press*, CP's new president, proudly told the annual meeting that CP had been "unique among world news agencies" in holding the line for so long.[210] One reason provided for the increase was that it would be dangerous to rely too much on "non-member revenue" – that is, revenue from radio clients.[211]

The outbreak of war brought a sharp increase in the amount of foreign news that CP provided to its members, a substantial increase in Ottawa coverage, and a pronounced drop in all other Canadian news. In September 1939, the board of directors was told that "domestic news is being condensed to the limit to make space for the heaviest run of foreign news ever moved on our leased wires."[212] A year later, Purcell reported that regional news now accounted for only about 5 per cent of the 25,000 words the typical paper received daily, far below the normal amount, and even at that level it would not be allowed to hold up war news.[213] Staff correspondents in Charlottetown, Quebec City, London, Windsor, and Edmonton were dropped, and reporting staff was reduced in Toronto and Montreal.[214] At the same time, the war effort brought a great expansion in the powers of the federal government domestically, including such things as compulsory registration of manpower; rationing of food, fuel, newsprint, and other industrial products; and wage and price controls, all of which combined into "one continuous story of drastic change in a people's way of living."[215] CP's president told the 1942 annual meeting that Ottawa had become GHQ, general headquarters. In the past, he said, Ottawa was in the doldrums when Parliament was not in session, but now there was more year-round news from the departments – each of which had become a little government in itself – than from the House of Commons. Before the war there had been a total of seven foreign embassies and Commonwealth representatives in Ottawa; now there were 18. Thus the focus on the Canadian military was matched by a greater emphasis on the federal government, both of which stressed the national dimension of Canadians' experience.

The centralizing trend was further emphasized by CP's efforts to cut operating costs in the domestic news service. One way of doing this was to reduce the number of teletype and telegraph operators as much as possible. In 1943, telegraphic relay points at Winnipeg and Edmonton were eliminated and the operators laid off. Instead, CP's 23 member newspapers in western Canada were served directly on a single telegraphic circuit from Toronto. Previously, the necessity of refiling copy onto new circuits at Winnipeg and Edmonton meant that editorial decisions were made at those points about what would be of interest to those on the receiving end; now these decisions were made in Toronto. A more centralized news-transmission system reinforced the editorial focus on national subjects and themes. At the same time, the extant CP records contain no evidence that differences between French and English Canada over such issues as conscription became a subject of discussion among CP members or a particular focus of coverage.[216] References to coverage of the 1942 plebiscite on conscription were limited entirely to operational matters: how the results were gathered, and how quickly they were transmitted.[217] Other events that have subsequently become controversial, such as the forced relocation of Japanese-Canadians and seizure of their property, were apparently not so at the time; the few references to these events were low-key, simple statements of fact without colouring or commentary of any kind.[218] To borrow Hallin's terminology once more, the "sphere of legitimate controversy" did not include those perceived as domestic enemies in wartime.

By 1943, with the tide of war turning definitively in the Allies' favour, there were signs of renewed interest in domestic news. Developments such as the release of the Marsh report on social security and plans for a national health-insurance scheme signalled a growing focus on postwar Canada. Two months before D-Day, CP's general superintendent reported that member newspapers were demanding "more attention to the type of Canadian regional news that was their day-to-day bread and butter in peacetime." The board of directors identified rebuilding of the domestic news report as a top priority in September 1944, and Purcell told the 1945 annual meeting that failure to respond adequately might result in "immeasurable damage to the newspaper business." Better writing and an emphasis on research and interpretation – a more sophisticated approach to news, in effect – were promised.[219] "[A]n alert and improved Canadian news report" would be essential "in the vital post-war period when newspapers must be ready for any and all competition."[220] In the spring of 1945, with Germany's defeat drawing near but still not accomplished, the volume of war coverage was reduced by more than 25 per cent to make more room for Canadian news. Gordon Churchill of the London *Free Press* observed that during the war, member papers had lost sight of their obligation to provide their own local news coverage back to CP for redistribution regionally and across the country.

> We soon will return to peace-time standards in evaluating news. No longer will there be a glut of exciting news from abroad to make a paper worth reading regardless of the contribution you or I shall make. Unless you and I supply news, The Canadian Press cannot operate ... . it is your duty.

At a special meeting in September, members agreed to begin developing a costly new service, news photographs. In endorsing the new direction, the editor of the Owen Sound (Ontario) *Sun-Times* said he "had been lulled into a false sense of security during the war. Peacetime papers would have to be more interesting than in the past." The form of news, and the shape of the Canadian imagined community, were changing once again.

With its successful wartime experience of operating on a wider stage, CP planned to provide greatly expanded international coverage after the war. Arthur Ford of the London *Free Press*, now CP's president, told the board of directors in March 1944 that CP should "have its own men in world capitals."[221] Europe was tentatively divided up into several zones for postwar coverage; Ross Munro was to be assigned to Russia, Czechoslovakia, and the Balkans, and Bill Stewart was posted to Australia after covering the final months of the Pacific war and the surrender of Japan. CP's enhanced prestige and scope of operations, along with Canada's growing international role, reinforced each other: McNeil proudly told the board of directors in the last days of the European campaign that "[t]he Second Great War has marked the coming-of-age of The Canadian Press just as it has marked the emergence of Canada in the international field."[222] Even now, there was not unanimity: one influential director, Senator Jacob Nicol, suggested that CP's correspondent in Australia would simply duplicate what was already provided by AP and Reuters.[223] Frederick Ker offered a mild defence of the posting, observing "the world picture in its broad outlines was adequately recorded by" AP and Reuters, but "for certain details" – especially where the Canadian economy was concerned – " a Canadian microscope was sometimes required."

Staff shortages because of military enlistment and uncompetitive salaries were a persistent problem during the war. At the 1940 general meeting it was decided not to seek exemptions from possible military service for CP staff, but by 1943 – with almost 60 per cent of CP's basic editorial staff having joined the armed forces – this stance had become increasingly problematic.[224] With labour shortages everywhere, it was "virtually impossible" to find suitable replacements at any cost. In 1942, CP began hiring female editorial employees – invariably described, with either intentional irony or unconscious awkwardness, as "girl copy boys" or "girl rewrite men." By September, "girls" were replacing male editors and reporters in CP bureaus in Halifax, Ottawa, Toronto, Winnipeg, and Vancouver; McNeil reported enthusiastically that they had "taken hold with real spirit and enthusiasm, and have demonstrated their growing ability to relieve experienced men of necessary routine chores. It is not too much to hope that more than one will develop the ability to take a place under the pressure of a hard-driving filing desk."[225] But even these unheard-of expedients could not make up for the steady drain of enlistment; by early 1943, "the breakdown of competent relays at key points is imminent." Unless CP could defer enlistment indefinitely for key members of its staff, it would be impossible to maintain the service efficiently.[226] The government was prepared to give CP a high priority rating, allowing deferment for married members of staff over 25 and even some unmarried men, but the board of directors had other concerns: the proposal was rejected by a vote of 10 – 5, evidently on the grounds that it would be seen as hypocritical for publishers who supported conscription in their newspapers to accept exemptions for Canadian Press staff.[227] Once again, the board's political polarization on war issues had come to the fore, this time clearly to the detriment of the news agency's operations.

A related problem concerned CP's relatively low pay scales. Wage rates rose everywhere in response to wartime labour shortages; by 1943, new employees who replaced those enlisting in the armed forces were paid 20 to 25 per cent more than coworkers who had been at CP

since the war began, driving up overall costs and causing morale problems.[228] Early in 1945, with postwar rebuilding a key priority, Purcell
reported to the finance committee that many CP employees were paid
less than newspaper journalists doing "less exacting" work.[229] A par-.
ticular concern was that Ross Munro, whose achievements at Dieppe,
Sicily, and Normandy had brought CP great acclaim, was being offered
$50 a week more than his current salary to become European corre-
spondent for another news organization. It was quickly agreed that his
salary should be raised to $130 a week plus rent, well above the $80
that some of CP's most senior employees, the regional superintendents,
had been receiving since 1933.[230] In 1944, CP finally agreed to the first
assessment increase of the war and thus had some funds available to
increase living allowances for staff in London and New York.[231] In a pronounced change from their approach at the beginning of the war, when
the refusal to raise salaries led to several senior employees leaving for
better-paying positions elsewhere,[232] the directors declared themselves
ready to increase salaries on a competitive basis. Thus in his address to
the 1944 annual meeting, Arthur Ford complained about "higher paying services" snatching away good men, and stressed the importance of
a better-trained and better-paid staff; a year later, Jacob Nicol observed
pointedly that CP should not employ "inferior men" and that every
employee should be "top-notch in his assignment." H.P. Duchemin, in
the past a voice of frugality, stated frankly that CP employees, overall,
were underpaid and should be paid whatever rates applied generally
in the communities where they worked.[233] He added that attempts were
being made to unionize news staff across the country, and organizers
should not be able to argue that CP journalists were unfairly paid. But
long-established habits apparently died hard: in the fall of 1945, it was
reported that nine more members of the editorial staff had resigned to
take better-paying positions elsewhere.[234]

The CP-AP-Reuters relationship changed substantially during the war.
From the vantage point of 1939, it would have seemed unthinkable that
anything could disrupt the close AP-CP relationship, or that Reuters
would end up establishing close relationships with both agencies. But
after Roderick Jones was forced to resign as chairman in 1941, Reuters
moved definitively to distance itself from reliance on subsidies and
to rehabilitate its journalistic reputation.[235] The three agencies were
now broadly in agreement about what constituted proper journalistic

standards; combined with a much cooler relationship between Kent Cooper of AP and Livesay's successor at CP, this meant that economic and strategic considerations operated with fewer of the countervailing cultural and personal cross-currents that had applied earlier. Under these circumstances the inherently unstable dynamics of a three-way business relationship also came to the fore. CP was now more exposed than it had been during the period of its close alliance with AP, particularly since AP was less willing to shelter it from Reuters' demands. But CP also had more room to manoeuvre than its much smaller size and scope of operations alone might suggest. As the rehabilitated Reuters sought opportunities for expansion and revenue growth in Canada, it became apparent that an enhanced CP-Reuters relationship could offer significant advantages in bargaining with AP.

At the most basic level of explanation, personnel changes in the top management of both CP and Reuters underlay these larger developments. The executives who replaced Roderick Jones in 1941 considered it their most urgent task to reestablish Reuters' reputation in the eyes of other news agencies. This meant a definitive rejection of the reliance on subsidies that had marked Jones's tenure, and a concerted effort to convince AP and CP, among others, that Reuters had changed for good. The reestablishment of mutual confidence at the level of journalistic standards was intended to lay the foundation for the accomplishment of an equally urgent but more specific goal: revision of the "humiliating and one-sided" Reuters-AP contract that Jones's miscalculations had allowed Cooper to impose in 1934.[236]

A second personnel change, the replacement of the ailing Livesay as CP's general manager by J.A. McNeil in 1939, was equally important for the AP-CP relationship. Livesay had an extraordinarily close relationship with Cooper. When he learned of Livesay's impending retirement in 1938, Cooper told his friend that he could not imagine how a successor could be found. "It would be impossible for me to think of the Canadian Press in terms other than those that define yourself. We may always like the CP but we won't be happy in our relationship unless what the CP proposed to do is what you want it to do."[237] McNeil, a former CP director whose appointment was intended in part to reassert the board's control over the news agency's management – and thus was less resistant to their concerns about, for example, cost-cutting, than a career news-agency executive like Livesay or Purcell might have been – had a distinctly cooler relationship with Cooper. On a reconnaissance trip to Canada in the fall of 1941, William Turner of Reuters reported that McNeil was very different than Livesay, "whose hostility to Reuters has the same basis as Kent Cooper's."[238] A significant irritant arose in 1941 when Cooper, citing AP's heavy expenses for war reporting, asked CP to consider increasing its annual payment.[239] He noted that AP had recently raised basic fees for its members by $600,000 – the first general increase in 30 years – while depreciation of the Canadian dollar had effectively cut the value of CP's existing contractual payment to AP by 12 per cent. Observing pointedly that CP's charges to its own members had not increased since the war began, Cooper suggested that they were benefiting from the war coverage made possible by AP's higher spending without contributing to it.

In the past, Livesay would have responded urgently to such a request, but McNeil did not reply for more than four months. When he eventually did, Cooper concluded that because his suggestion was not "promptly and enthusiastically received, since action or even discussion of it has been delayed for one reason or another for several months, my letter can be forgotten."[240] Somewhat ominously, he suggested that it would now be best to wait to discuss CP payments to AP until the current contract expired in 1945.[241] A somewhat self-satisfied mention at CP's 1942 annual meeting that members' charges would remain unchanged for the fourth consecutive year probably added salt to the wound.[242] Other correspondence testifies to Cooper's growing exasperation with McNeil on such issues as the use of CP news on CBC international shortwave broadcasts (thus violating AP's exclusive right to all revenue from the use of CP news outside Canada) or CP's complaints when AP was beaten by UP/BUP on news coverage of the war.[243]

The distant relationship between Cooper and McNeil, combined with the rehabilitation of Reuters, soon led to difficulties for CP. One of the worst aspects of the 1934 AP contract, in Reuters' view, was a clause giving CP full access to the entire news service of Reuters and the PA in London, instead of the substantially reduced version of both that AP editors transmitted to New York.[244] Cooper had stood "shoulder to shoulder" on this issue with CP in 1934, insisting that everything AP received from Reuters must also be available to CP with no additional payment.[245] Now, however, Cooper was sympathetic to Reuters' demand that the arrangement be revised. He warned McNeil that a complete break with Reuters would hurt CP much more than AP and that it would be very costly to replace the PA service for British domestic news.[246] After several months' resistance, CP gave in to the pressure and agreed to pay Reuters £1000 a year (around $5,000) for access to the full Reuters and PA file in London.[247] (The amount doubled the following year.) Reuters recognized that the new agreement had only been made possible "through the good offices of Mr Kent Cooper and in the face of bitter protest by the CP." [248] The incident illustrated clearly that if AP was not committed to protecting CP as it had been while Livesay was general manager – the cost of which was a disposition to accept or at least consider very seriously whatever AP requested or demanded – the world could be an inhospitable place for a small agency like CP.

The relationship between the two agencies reached a low ebb during negotiations for a new contract in 1945. Near the end of 1944, an AP journalist, Harry Montgomery, was sent on a tour of Canada, ostensibly to write a series of feature articles on Canadian subjects with CP's cooperation. But part of his assignment was secretly to gather information that would "permit New York to screw C.P." in a new, tougher round of negotiations.[249] Montgomery's report, sent to the chief of AP's news service and through him to Cooper, was mainly an assessment of CP's news operation in Canada (described as "in general ... good") and an attempt to spell out whether AP could cover Canada effectively if it no longer had a contract with CP – a clear indication that such a break, which would be catastrophic for CP, was not out of the question.[250] His conclusion was that "[w]e could get along without CP – How well depending on what we did to replace it."

Montgomery's report formed the basis for a strategy memorandum by Lloyd Stratton, AP's corporate secretary, and Frank Starzel, who had taken over from Cooper the main responsibility for contract negotiations. Recently, they observed, there had been "strong indications ... that The Canadian Press was becoming less willing to understand the accrued benefits of AP's patronage," demonstrating "a financial selfishness ... with no disposition to recognize the merit of AP's position."[251] (This was clearly a reference to CP's rejection of the 1941 request for a higher wartime payment, among other irritants.) Nor had there been "material exhibits of gratitude or even great respect," but "signs from within and without of quite the other character." Stratton, who had not been directly involved with CP since the late 1930s, was struck by the change in attitude: "The thinking and clamor toward money and the expectation that AP was to give, willy-nilly, were startling." CP's handling of the dispute over CBC shortwave broadcasts had been "brash and inconsiderate ... not unusual when the parties concerned are accustomed to it and the business at hand is a rough and tumble commercial proposition. Perhaps The Canadian Press wants it that way."

The $20,000 differential that CP paid under its existing contract was based on the premise that this covered only the international news that AP supplied; AP's news from the United States and CP's news from Canada had always been assumed to be of equal value to each other. Stratton systematically rejected the arguments CP usually offered in support of this arrangement. US readers were much less interested in Canadian news than vice versa, he asserted; in addition, CP provided mainly "straight reporting of spontaneous news" and lacked "almost entirely the interpretative, background and special behind-the-news material that today and henceforth are equally vital." (He did, however, acknowledge that "the type of organization, its motive and purposes and its neighborliness," as well as "the potentially disruptive influence of foreign news agencies" should be borne in mind.) As for the value of its foreign news, AP spent around $2 million on international coverage in 1944. This worked out to about $15 for every thousand people in the US population; if CP members paid for foreign news at the same per-capita rate, the differential would be at least $80,000. The argument that Canadian newspapers could not afford higher rates was also dismissed. Twelve CP members were already paying AP a total of $50,000 for photo service, and the revenue that UP received from a single Canadian client was greater than the differential AP received for providing more than 90 papers with their basic, day-to-day supply of foreign news.

> The Canadian Press management ... has consistently pictured an inability to pay. At times the plea has been actual poverty. Yet, those Canadian newspapers supporting other services ... apparently have the money willingly to buy. ... That puts The Canadian Press in the position of paying virtually nothing for its basic service, leaving it to spend its main budget for trimmings.

The memorandum concluded with an estimate of what it would cost AP to set up its own leased-wire network to serve "leading cities in Canada" – the idea being to bypass CP and serve papers individually, as it did in other countries. This would cost about $5,100 a month, with editorial and operating staff costing as much again. AP news would be distributed on two circuits, one from Detroit to Windsor, London, Toronto, Ottawa, Montreal, and Quebec, and one from Seattle to Vancouver, Calgary, Edmonton, Regina, and Winnipeg. For each of the 12 cities served, the cost would be around $400 a month, "which is not prohibitive ... there is reason to believe that potential revenue would be sufficient to provide a satisfactory margin over distribution expenses."

As the tone and content of Stratton's memorandum suggested, negotiations for the 1945 contract were much more difficult than previous financial discussions. Walton Cole of Reuters reported to his head office that by rejecting the traditional view that CP's Canadian news was of substantial value to AP, the US agency had launched a "war of nerves."[252] Purcell, who succeeded McNeil as general manager in September 1945, reported to the board that as well as an increased differential, AP wanted the contract to cover only its basic news service; any additional features such as photos, news features, financial tables, race results, columns, and so on, could be sold separately to individual CP papers.[253] Purcell also noted that CP's failure to offer an increased wartime payment in 1941 remained a source of irritation, and proposed an additional payment of $10,000 to $12,000 as compensation.

AP's insistence on strict enforcement of its contractual right to all use of CP news outside Canada was one source of difficulty. Twenty years earlier, Cooper had reminded Livesay "in all friendliness" that CP's arrangement to provide Canadian news to Reuters violated the AP contract, but agreed to allow it as an exception. Generally, in fact, CP had previously been able to make agreements of this kind with any agency that already had a news-exchange agreement with AP, subject to AP's approval.[254] Now AP was less inclined to be accommodating, arguing that CP news in the CBC's international shortwave broadcasts, which were heard outside Canada, violated AP's exclusive right. CP, Cole wrote, was "astounded" by this demand.[255] Frederick Ker of the Hamilton *Spectator* accused AP of trying to control all international news, calling it "intolerable" that AP "could, in effect, stop the Canadian Government from broadcasting Canadian news to the world," and other directors agreed.[256] But Purcell confirmed that AP's long-established contractual right to exclusive use of CP news outside Canada was "unquestionable." He noted that AP was prepared to allow CP to exchange news with other British Empire news agencies – such as Reuters – or newspapers, but this did not satisfy Rupert Davies, who observed that the issue went beyond exchange within the empire; Canada's "voice in the world" had to be considered as well.

CP was in no position to resist, however, unless it was prepared to risk a complete break with AP. As Purcell told the board, relations with AP were "tremendously important and would have to be continued."[257] The new agreement allowing CP to exchange news with Commonwealth agencies and newspapers came at a substantial cost: a provision for cancellation of the whole AP-CP contract on three months' notice if AP decided this became "injurious" at any time. Walton Cole of Reuters reported that CP was "extremely sensitive regarding this [cancellation] clause and Purcell is ashamed of it."[258] Even the chairman of AP's board of directors, Robert McLean, suggested to Cooper that he was taking too hard a line; the looming threat of cancellation on short notice would make CP suspect that "we seek some undisclosed advantage which would keep them in thrall," and was not the way to restore the "happy relationship of mutual confidence" that had existed in the past.[259] But Cooper insisted, reminding McLean that Livesay had always acknowledged that the differential paid by CP was merely nominal, and that one of the compensations was a guarantee that CP would not sell its Canadian news to anyone else. It had come as a "shock" when McNeil suggested the differential should eventually be eliminated, rather than being raised – something that would never have happened "in days of better understanding with the Canadian Press."[260] The sale of CP news for shortwave CBC broadcasts was eventually approved in exchange for an additional payment of $10,000 for loss of exclusivity; even this, it appears, was only agreed to when CP made it clear to Cooper that the proposed restriction would cause a scandal if it were made public in Parliament.[261] AP also obtained the right to sell its basic service directly to individual Canadian newspapers, a significant breach in the agency-to-agency relationship that had existed until now, and a step towards treating Canada like every other country where AP sold its news. (As soon as the new contract was signed, AP sent two employees to negotiate direct sales to the large newspapers in Toronto and Montreal, but Purcell made sure that CP's service from New York was operating at peak efficiency, and in the event no direct AP contracts were signed.) In these negotiations, relations between CP and AP clearly displayed the pattern of a domineering international agency imposing its wishes on a smaller and weaker national agency.

In the face of this increasingly difficult relationship with AP, having another string to its bow – in the form of a separate relationship with Reuters – offered advantages for CP. In January 1944, Reuters' gregarious editor-in-chief, Walton (Tony) Cole, visited Toronto and, in a marathon round of meetings, established a close relationship with Purcell. Cole convinced Purcell (as William John Haley, a Reuters director, had previously done with Cooper) that Reuters had changed and was now a worthy partner.[262] This led to a new contract, doubling CP's fee to Reuters to £2000 a year, an amount that rose substantially in subsequent contracts but was partly offset by payments for Reuters' use of CP news.[263] Harry Montgomery of AP reported that when he visited Toronto later in 1944, Cole was there again; while CP still relied mainly on AP for international news, the new relationship meant that "CP could apparently shift the emphasis from AP to Reuters as necessary or desirable." (Cole, however, complained to Montgomery that CP's members were "skinflints," observing that a single Canadian daily paid more for the New York *Times* service than CP as a whole paid Reuters for a service that went to almost every newspaper in Canada.[264]) In the immediate postwar years, the relationship became so close as to suggest that Reuters might actually replace AP as CP's main supplier of international news and chief strategic ally.[265]

J.A. McNeil's observation in 1945 that the war marked CP's "coming of age" was well-founded in many respects. Through its war correspondents, CP had been at the centre of one of the biggest news stories of the twentieth century. Ross Munro's achievements in particular raised CP's profile in Canada and internationally; as the war approached its end, it seemed only logical that CP would keep up its new focus on original coverage of major world news stories, perhaps with resident correspondents in Europe, China, Russia, and the Pacific. Through Purcell's close relationship with McNaughton, CP expanded its opportunities for coverage and established its primacy among Canadian news organizations. This unprecedented cooperation reflected both self-interest – CP's privileged position was an important competitive advantage against BUP – and a genuine belief among CP journalists that this was a "good war" and that adopting a largely supportive stance was the right thing to do. Through its policy of implicit compliance with censorship regulations, CP successfully positioned itself as the reliable, authoritative voice of the nation at war.

Despite these successes, the war years also brought problems and stresses for CP. The directors' determination to hold the line on costs had several negative consequences, notably the loss of senior employees at a time of overall labour shortages (if not for Purcell's accident, he most likely would not have returned at least until the end of the war) and the dramatic deterioration of CP's relationship with AP. Partisan disagreement among publishers reached unusually high levels; early in the war, there was pronounced dissatisfaction with CP's Ottawa coverage, though such criticism tended to disappear after the successes of CP's war correspondents.

Over all, CP's experience during the Second World War suggests that journalism's typical assessment of its own functioning – providing "a detached, impartial, factual account of the day's most important events"[266] – did not apply, at least not in any uncomplicated way, in wartime. Instead of standing at arm's length from the authorities, reserving the right to investigate and criticize their actions, CP was a self-aware and active participant in the information side of warfare. When joining McNaughton's staff at the beginning of 1941, Purcell thanked him for "the opportunity to do a job for Canada" and expressed the hope that his efforts "may be of some aid to yourself, your staff and the objective at which we are all aiming." Even though he made these comments while leaving CP, they are good evidence of his underlying beliefs. This dovetailed nicely with the military's awareness of the importance of news coverage in terms of public opinion. The ease and frequency with which journalists moved between their own world and the military illustrates clearly that the boundary between the two became much less distinct. James Carey has famously suggested that communication – and, by extension, journalism – is essentially a ritual that asserts and reasserts shared social values, and there is much in CP's wartime activities that supports this interpretation.[267] For example, at CP's general meeting in 1942 Rupert Davies referred to Canadian newspaper editors as having "a great responsibility of guiding public opinion and stiffening public morale. ... I am confident that no matter what faces us the daily newspapers of Canada will continue to do their part gladly and hopefully in the great struggle for freedom."[268]

Modern warfare is in some essential ways a mediated experience. This is true not only for those on the home front (a term reflecting the fact that war in the twentieth century became a total social environment), but also for soldiers – even front-line fighters know only their one particular corner of the battlefield. Thus most Canadians' knowledge of the war was provided by news media and particularly by CP. In turn, the experience of war as expressed in news coverage reshaped the meaning of nationality (which, as Benedict Anderson has argued, was a largely mediated phenomenon to begin with[269]). In a recent overview of the US press's role in covering wars from 1898 to 2001, Richard Kaplan concluded that journalism is essentially "a rite of nation" – a practice inescapably caught up in the articulation and reproduction of the idea of the nation, and especially pronounced when, as in war, the nation faces a clearly identifiable external enemy.[270] CP was central to

Canadians' wartime experience in a double way, as the key vehicle for presenting the mutually reinforcing narratives of war and nationality.

Yet neither the active embrace of a participant's role nor its deeper role in asserting the very concept of nationality meant that CP put aside its normal journalistic concerns entirely or permanently. Besides feeling that he had enough of a personal stake in the outcome of the war to join the military, Purcell thought it was also "the greatest news story in Canada's history." Readers were fascinated by war news, and the extensive coverage reflected journalistic enthusiasm for the big story as well as a patriotic or ideological participation in the war effort. For CP, faster and more extensive war coverage (in addition to behind-the-scenes efforts to assure its own priority) was perhaps the most obvious way to gain ground on competitors like BUP. And even if some considered that CP's role was to guide public opinion in approved paths, there were different opinions over how this should be achieved – whether it was better to accept or critically scrutinize the government's assertions in 1940 that it was actively pursuing the war effort, for example.

Censorship was one point at which CP's national/patriotic and journalistic roles overlapped and often came into conflict. On one hand, the operation of censorship involved close cooperation and negotiation between CP and the censorship authorities. Within Canada especially, this included frequent efforts to mitigate and push back against censors' restrictions, efforts that were fairly often successful. Journalists, censors, and their military conducting officers – the latter two groups being mostly populated by former journalists – sometimes made common cause in trying to get the story out, arguing with soldiers and officials for more disclosure rather than less. On the other hand, CP's decision to "comply implicitly" even with unreasonable censorship decisions seems in retrospect to have conceded too much ground to the censors' authority. Overseas, meanwhile, the operations of military censorship meant that the "sphere of legitimate controversy" largely disappeared where Canadian forces in battle were concerned, and this extended to politically sensitive matters such as the need for reinforcements in 1944. On balance, the war brought a significant diminution of the press's traditional critical, watchdog role – although CP was far from being alone in this.

5 "No Middle Ground"

CP's postwar years unfolded quite differently than an observer in 1945 might have predicted. Hopes for a new international focus were not realized; a network of European bureaus was not set up as had been planned; and after Bill Stewart's Australian posting ended in 1947, many years passed before CP appointed another staff correspondent outside London or New York. But bolstered by a growing stream of broadcasting revenue, CP improved and expanded its domestic news operation in various ways, notably by establishing a news-photo service and French-language service.

Yet the early 1950s proved to be one of the worst, most damaging periods in CP's history. In a ferocious campaign to prevent the American Newspaper Guild from unionizing CP's editorial employees, the publishers who jointly owned CP slashed the budget, fired one in four CP journalists, closed the Washington office, threatened to close the parliamentary bureau in Ottawa, and deliberately allowed serious deterioration of the news service. It took five years after the Guild was defeated for CP's news operation to recover, and the legacy of bitterness lasted much longer.

The postwar years were also marked by increasing complexity in most aspects of CP's operations. Its dealings with the large international agencies, for example, became increasingly complicated from the mid-1940s onward. When CP was founded, it had a single channel of international news that reflected the rules and structure of the ruling cartel: Reuters sent international news to AP in New York, and AP forwarded a selection of this news (augmented with AP's own US coverage) to its exclusive Canadian client, CP. Despite Roderick Jones's efforts, Reuters never established anything more than a very limited separate relationship with CP (a state of affairs that reflected, among other things, AP's determination to make sure that such a thing did not happen, and Cooper and Livesay's shared disdain for what they considered Reuters' reliance on government subsidies and lack of independence). By the mid-1940s, however, Reuters – under new ownership and new management – established a newly constructive relationship with CP from which it derived, at long last, a reasonable amount of revenue. AP, meanwhile, had previously dealt only with CP – and not with individual newspapers, as it did in most other countries – in a relationship shaped by strategic concerns and by the affinity of their common cooperative structure rather than by ordinary commercial logic. This changed after the war, too, with AP insisting on the right to sell its services to individual CP members directly and generally adopting more of a corporation-to-corporation than a cooperative-to-cooperative approach. AP's changed attitude, in turn, made CP's relationship with Reuters more important, as a potential lifeline in the admittedly unlikely event that CP and AP had a serious falling-out.

Domestically, CP also became a more corporate operation in the 15 years after the war. Where debates at the board of directors or annual meetings over contentious issues like radio in the 1930s had been free-wheeling and were reported to the members in detail, most controversial subjects were now dealt with by the small and relatively secretive executive committee, which tersely reported its decisions but not its debates. CP continued to operate very much as a cooperative when it came to the news service; the solicitation of members' wishes and criticisms was more or less constant, and was consistently taken to heart in CP's day-to-day operations. But with a few important exceptions, such as the antiunion campaign of the early 1950s, members had less and less to do with (and less and less information about) the management of CP as a business. The trend to complexity could also be seen in the ability of members to choose from a growing list of supplementary editorial services, in the creation of a separate French-language service, and in the establishment of a new broadcasting affiliate in which private broadcasters controlled 50 per cent of the votes. At the same time, however, other developments – like the rapid spread of teletypesetting, by means of which CP news sent to member papers could be fed directly into their typesetting machines, without the intermediation of local editors – meant that CP's editorial decisions were increasingly, and by default, the decisions of its members.

As the Second World War came to an end, both AP and Reuters reevaluated their relationship with CP, although in very different spirits. A tense and difficult round of contract negotiations between CP and AP in 1945 and 1946 created an opening for Reuters in Canada. After Roderick Jones was forced out in 1941, Reuters was reconstituted as an agency owned jointly by both the provincial and metropolitan newspapers of Britain and systematically dropped almost all the subsidies and understandings with government that had disqualified it as a reliable agency in Cooper's (and Livesay's) minds.[1] The bitter 1942 dispute over CP's access to the PA service in AP's London office was in fact the first step in Reuters' rehabilitation, in that it abrogated one of the most humiliating provisions of the 1934 contract with AP. It was accomplished "through the good offices of Mr Kent Cooper" – a practical illustration of the new spirit of cooperation between the two.[2] A new CP-Reuters contract in 1944 gave CP access to the full Reuters-PA printer service in London and the Globereuter wireless service to New York for £2,000 (around $10,000); for an additional £1,230, 1,000 words a day was sent by wireless specifically on CP's behalf. CP, in turn, received £400 for Canadian news.[3] By 1961 the net differential paid to Reuters had risen to $36,000 (more than £7,000).

As always in news-agency relationships, strategic considerations were as important as immediate financial returns. Having established a friendlier but still competitive relationship with AP, Reuters sought to expand its operations in North America, and Canada played an important part in these plans. The strained AP-CP relationship meant that Reuters might one day become a more important, perhaps even the major, supplier of foreign news to CP. Thus one of Reuters' goals was simply to establish a beachhead in Canada and wait, in the expectation that the AP relationship would deteriorate further over time.[4] Walton Cole, Reuters' editor-in-chief, reported in 1947 that Reuters' presence in Canada moderated the financial and other demands that AP made, allowing CP "to play Reuters off against the AP."[5] In the early 1940s, the idea that Reuters might someday supplant AP as CP's source of foreign news would have been inconceivable; now Purcell estimated the odds of this happening as 6 to 4 against. Indeed, after news associations in Australia and New Zealand joined the British press as part owners of Reuters in 1947,[6] it was suggested that CP might join as well. However, Purcell told Cole that this was too expensive for CP, and that unlike other British dominions, Canada's interests were "in many spheres ... indivisible from those of the United States."[7] Christopher Chancellor,

Reuters' general manager, described the situation more bluntly: CP was "still very much in the position of a dependent in its dealings with the AP."[8] In April, 1947, CP's board of directors formally rejected the offer to join the Reuters ownership group, concluding that their existing relationships with AP and Reuters "are working out so well for all of us that there is at present no apparent need for altering them."[9] Still, Reuters had substantially improved its position in Canada. An additional benefit of the new understanding was a better return-news service to Britain, which "stopped up the 'leakage'" of Canadian news that competitors like BUP and the Exchange Telegraph service could offer to the British press.[10]

But Reuters' ambitions went beyond the prospect of replacing AP as a supplier of international news in Canada. Cole suggested that Canada might become Reuters' headquarters in the Americas, serving newspapers in the United States, the West Indies, Newfoundland, and Latin America, as well as Canada. These plans were not based on any particular fondness for Canada or CP, it should be noted; Reuters made a serious (but ultimately unsuccessful) attempt in 1948 to sell all its North American rights to the Chicago *Tribune*, which would bypass CP entirely.[11] In the mid-1950s, an opportunity to sell Reuters' service directly to the Montreal *Star* prompted musings about the creation of "the 'dreamboat' Reuter circuit in Canada," reaching newspapers in Montreal, Quebec, Ottawa, Toronto, and other large Ontario towns – a plan strikingly similar to part of what Lloyd Stratton of AP had proposed to Kent Cooper in 1944.[12] But in the context of a more freely competitive relationship between AP and Reuters, Canada was a place where advantage might be gained or lost, and CP could benefit from this. Nonetheless, Cole realized that CP would always need AP, if only for its US domestic news report; "[e]xtreme caution governs every move made by the CP in its relations with Reuters for fear of arousing the anger of the AP and the application of sanctions by the latter." Purcell clearly had a difficult balancing act. As he told E. Norman Smith, CP's policy should be "to retain the closest possible friendship with both AP and Reuters and not to lean to one side or other. We have the closest sentimental attachment to Reuters (and in the last three years we have put it into effective operation) but by far our most valuable possession outside from our domestic news is our AP connection. If AP and Reuters were at daggers drawn we would place us in a real dilemma."[13] Moreover, the possibility of either Reuters or AP bypassing CP to serve Canadian newspapers directly could never be forgotten. Ultimately,

Cole's view was that CP's "infinitesimal expenditure" for foreign news from AP, combined with the fact that "CP is dominated by small newspapers, its Board thinks very small in money matters, and Mr. Purcell ... has to work on a very tight budget" kept CP tightly bound to AP, and remained key obstacles that Reuters would have to overcome.[14]

⁓ ❧ ⁓

Domestically, CP's immediate focus after 1945 was rebuilding its staff and restoring the Canadian news service that had been greatly curtailed during the war. Financial restrictions continued to cause problems; Purcell reported to the board in 1946 that more than half of the CP employees who had joined the armed forces did not return after the war, lured by better pay and better hours in newspaper and non-newspaper jobs. A recent decision to match the salaries paid for the same work at member newspapers had helped somewhat, but CP had not yet established a five-day week even though many of its members had done so.[15] (The board was also warned once again that Ross Munro, CP's best-known reporter, might leave if he were not offered a better salary.[16]) Plans were also in the works to reappoint CP correspondents at locations including Calgary; London, Ontario; and Regina, and to increase the staff in Ottawa and New York. Less than a year after the war ended, the volume of domestic news had tripled; at least one "situational" story summing up emerging trends was being offered daily; and the development of a photo service was a matter of "urgency and importance."[17] Three years later, Purcell warned the executive committee that editorial staff salaries required "an immediate adjustment involving heavy expenditure over the next two years." This might cost up to $40,000 a year, "[b]ut it was well worth a five-per-cent increase in the budget to ensure a trained and competent staff, fairly paid, ready for any emergency."[18]

The restoration and improvement of the news service came rapidly to a halt early in 1950 with an attempt by the American Newspaper Guild (ANG) to organize CP's editorial employees. For the next year or more, CP's members, directors, and managers waged something like a scorched-earth campaign against the Guild. The news service was cut back drastically; more than 25 per cent of CP journalists were fired; employees who supported the Guild were transferred against their wishes, and at least one was dismissed for resisting such a transfer; and CP was attacked by labour organizations and some politicians as an antiunion employer. The campaign only ended with the defeat of the organizing drive and the eventual decertification of the ANG in 1953;[19] even then it took several years for CP to reestablish its news service at pre-1950 levels. A senior CP editor told Reuters' bureau chief in New York at one point that the directors were prepared to dissolve CP before accepting the Guild, and other evidence supports this view.[20]

It is not hard to account for the virulence of CP's response to the prospect of its editorial employees joining a union. CP had kept its staff of telegraphers nonunionized after the 1924 strike until 1938, although most in the industry were unionized. Newspapers in the Southam chain, especially the Winnipeg *Tribune* and Vancouver *Province*, had great difficulty with strikes by the US-based International Typographical Union (ITU) in 1946.[21] A union for editorial employees was an unwelcome novelty. At the beginning of 1950, only three newsrooms in Canada were represented by the Guild: the *Daily Racing Form*, the Toronto *Star*, and the Vancouver *Sun*.[22] Journalists at *La Presse* had been affiliated with the Confédération des travailleurs catholiques du Canada since 1945.[23] All other newspapers in Canada were nonunion operations on the editorial side, and their publishers wanted to keep it that way. Rupert Davies, a CP director and former president, observed in 1949 that salary and wage scales established at CP had an effect in every newspaper office across Canada; and if CP publishers disagreed about many other things, keeping wage costs down was one thing they could all endorse.[24] A confidential memorandum prepared for CP publishers in 1950 argued that the presence of the Guild in CP could "act as a pipeline across the country,"[25] allowing it to make inroads all across Canada: "if it organized the national news association, with a staff of editors only as large as that of a medium-sized newspaper, it would gain national influence by short-cut." Another major concern was that a Guild contract would surely increase CP's relatively low salaries, leading to higher assessments for all CP members. As Charles Lynch, a Canadian journalist who worked for Reuters in Ottawa, told his superior in New York: "Certainly if the union becomes established and recognized, [Purcell's] cherished bargain-basement operating budget will be knocked into a cocked hat!"[26] On top of this, a union would be a serious threat to Purcell's paternalistic and authoritarian management style; workplace control was as important to CP's managers as economic issues were to the publishers and owners. Finally, concerns were frequently expressed that the neutrality and nationality of CP's journalism would be compromised by a US-based union that was affiliated with the politically active Congress of Industrial Organizations (CIO), and that might be seen as leaning towards the CCF in Canada.

Though CP's invocation of its independence and national status often reflected its economic or competitive interests, as it did in this case, it is also true that unionization would alter established journalistic practices and lines of authority.

On 8 January 1950, about half of CP's editorial employees in Toronto met to discuss joining the Guild. Purcell immediately learned of the meeting and, after consulting the executive committee, wired a statement to all employees, with (in the words of the local ANG president, Jack Mitchell) "promises of benefits ... if the Guild were beaten and threats of staff curtailments if it wasn't." An application for union certification was submitted to the Canada Labour Relations Board soon after.[27] Seventy-eight of 130 editorial employees signed union cards. Since certification required only 50 per cent of eligible employees plus one, the ANG was clearly on track to achieve recognition.[28]

A special board meeting to plan resistance to the organizing drive was convened four days later. Besides the elected directors, George McCullagh, the notoriously antiunion publisher of *The Globe and Mail* and Toronto *Telegram* – both of which were in the process of resisting organizing drives by the Guild – was present by invitation.[29] Purcell reported that employees had few complaints about working conditions, "[b]ut the general impression of the staff was that they were not being paid as well as they should be." According to the meeting's minutes, non-economic concerns were stressed. "Most serious was the shackling of editorial employees of The Canadian Press to a union with decided political views and with headquarters in another country," the minutes stated. "The present move by the Guild in attempting to organize CP, UP, and CBC was not essentially an economic thing, but one having possible ulterior purposes. It could tie up the spinal cord of public information."[30] CP would respect the law that gave employees the right to join a union of their choice, but the federal government should consider exempting the national news agency from the law's application, considering "the possible effect on Canadian national security and the public interest." It was agreed that CP's president, Victor Sifton, and vice president, Frederick Ker, would meet the prime minister to make this case in person.

Almost immediately, and illustrating the publishers' ready access to the highest offices in the country, Sifton, Ker, and Liberal Senator Jacob Nicol, publisher of *La Tribune* of Sherbrooke, Quebec, met the prime minister, Louis St-Laurent. They made little headway, however, with their argument that federal labour law should not apply to CP journalists. St-Laurent pointed out that certification under the federal

Industrial Relations and Disputes Investigation Act could not be with-held, because CP clearly operated across provincial boundaries.[31] The publishers argued that "protection of national news from possible pro-paganda requires that actions and loyalties of editors, reporters and correspondents should not be subject in any degree to external influ-ences ... beyond the control of those responsible for the impartiality and proper conduct of the news service," but St-Laurent told them nothing in the existing legislation would allow an exemption on this basis, and there was no prospect of amendment. "They seemed to accept that view," St-Laurent's memorandum on the meeting contin-ued, "and indicated that they would refuse to accept a closed shop collective agreement even if it meant a strike and the abandonment of the co-operative newsgathering business by the CP." Following up on the suggestions of political unreliability, a Labour Ministry offi-cial made inquiries and reported that "so far as we are aware, the Guild has been carrying on its work in Canada in accordance with established laws and practices and is not controlled or dominated by Communists."[32]

Meanwhile, another board meeting and a special membership meet-ing were held on 26 January in Toronto. Ker, Roy Thomson, and Hervé Major of *La Presse* were appointed as a special committee to advise Purcell on his dealings with the ANG, with a mandate to oppose certification "by all proper means."[33] The members at large unanimously approved the board's actions to date. In a formal statement, they asserted that "[p]rotection of the integrity of national news requires that actions and loyalties of editors, reporters and correspondents should not be sub-ject in any degree to external influences" such as the US-based Guild, because "the horizons of some trade union interests and activities have extended in recent years into the fields of politics and political ideolo-gies"; this might lead to a situation where "the national news service supplied by The Canadian Press could be stopped by actions over which neither The Canadian Press management nor its editorial employees, if they are members of the Guild, would have control." Purcell explained that CP service would continue in the event of a strike and told the board that he had considered the "feasibility, advisability and legality of giving notice [of dismissal] to Press News employees and serving sta-tions by CP wire rather than with the processed PN service." However, CP's solicitor, J.J. Robinette, advised that such a step would be "illegal, unwise and dangerous" in the middle of an organizing campaign.[34]

While such draconian measures were not yet seriously considered, a systematic campaign was launched to induce employees to withdraw their support of the union. Near the end of February, Purcell told Jack Mitchell of the ANG that Guild members could no longer be employed in CP's Ottawa bureau; a week later, Purcell made the same announcement to CP's Ottawa employees, saying the bureau would be closed if necessary.[35] Mel Sufrin, who went on to hold many senior positions at CP during a long career, recalled in an interview that he had been covering the House of Commons that winter "until I signed up most of the bureau staff to Guild contracts."[36]

> And then the word came from Toronto: anybody who was a member of the Guild will not be allowed to cover political stories ... because of the danger of bias, the fear of bias was actually what it was. And so I was taken off the House of Commons ... because I refused to quit the Guild. ... I think there were only two or three of us who stayed in the Guild. ... The rest of them all quit, and therefore they were allowed to cover politics. I was put on coverage of the Bell Telephone hearings before the Transport Commission because that was not political ... . I was on it for months. Then they transferred me to Toronto. I didn't ask to go, they sent me back.

In March, Purcell visited CP bureaus across Canada, where, according to Jack Mitchell, he "harangued all employees, individually and collectively."[37] John Dauphinee, who presided over the eventual unionization of CP's editorial staff in 1976 as Purcell's successor, was Winnipeg bureau chief at the time; he recalled in a later interview with Douglas Amaron that Purcell's heavy-handedness backfired, pushing several bureau employees to support the Guild who would not otherwise have done so.[38]

On 5 April, it was announced that the Guild had won certification by a vote of 54 to 35. A week later, Purcell met union representatives for an initial bargaining session but refused to proceed as long as a representative from ANG headquarters in Washington was present. The same day, a Montreal bureau employee was fired, ostensibly because he was a Guild member, and a CP Ottawa employee, Dent Hodgson, was fired after refusing a transfer to Toronto.[39] The Guild quickly applied to the federal Labour Ministry for permission to prosecute CP for unfair labour practices.[40] But before authorizing a prosecution, the department appointed John Stitt, an Ottawa lawyer, as an industrial inquiry commissioner to look into Guild-CP situation. Stitt's mandate was to try to get the parties to bargain collectively "as required by the Act"; only if this failed would he investigate and make a recommendation about the application to prosecute.[41]

The threat of prosecution did not induce CP to begin substantive bargaining, however. On the contrary, a program of severe staff reductions and cuts in service began. On 17 April, CP's board of directors voted to close the Washington bureau and reduce the size of the London bureau, giving effect to a budget reduction of $63,000 (around 5 per cent of CP's total spending). Further staff reductions in London and New York were to be carried out "where feasible," and Purcell was authorized to close the Ottawa bureau "if a more efficient arrangement for covering the news of Parliament can be effected."[42] Member newspapers were called on to perform "duties which in recent years have been carried out by an expanding CP staff." The assertion that the layoffs were simply an effort to keep costs under control at a time when the profit margin was shrinking for most member papers was unconvincing. A confidential memorandum for members of the board – essentially providing suggested responses to complaints about CP's handling of the Guild application – more or less admitted as much: while the concern for cost-cutting arose before the Guild applied for recognition, "[i]t is not an unreasonable assumption that the advent of the Guild in CP, where it could act as a pipeline across the country, was an added factor in the publishers' uncertainty."[43] Over the previous 20 years, Canadian publishers had shown confidence in CP by doubling its staff, but "[t]hey have no confidence in the ANG. Seeing their own creation merged with it, is it not reasonable to suppose they would take steps to reduce the area of uncertainty? To cut the risk? To get down to the most economical size consistent with efficiency?" Coming in the midst of the postwar rebuilding that had been CP's chief concern since 1945, these decisions did more harm to the agency's newsgathering ability than anything that had happened since the withdrawal of the federal subsidy in 1923. On issues that might arise in bargaining, CP's position was that wages should be set individually, "based on the merit of the individual, the company to be the sole judge"; that is, there would be no standardized scale of wages for different positions. Management must retain complete control of hiring, promotion, transfers and firing. CP members were warned again that a strike might be called, and Purcell outlined how the news report would proceed in that event.

At the beginning of May, CP management agreed to begin contract negotiations with union representatives, including a staff member from ANG headquarters in Washington.[44] But this was followed almost immediately by notices of dismissal to 27 employees (12 from CP and 15 from PN), all but one of them Guild members. Eight other PN employees were warned that they might be dismissed soon. The Guild sent a furious telegram to the minister of labour, charging that CP's actions were an attempt "to defeat legitimate activities of Guild ... this constitutes illegal interference with formation and administration of a trade union."[45] In view of the fact that Stitt, the minister's nominee, was in the midst of efforts to bring the two sides together, the firings also "indicate supreme contempt for labour legislation and your department."

The firings prompted a renewed application by the Guild to prosecute CP and were added to the list of issues that Stitt was to discuss with both parties (despite the insistence of J.J. Robinette, CP's solicitor, that they simply reflected budgetary decisions on CP's part that "cannot involve any breach of labour laws"[46]). But when Purcell sat down with Stitt and Guild representatives later that month, he appeared to give ground in several areas. The statement that no employee of the Ottawa bureau could be a Guild member was simply Purcell's personal opinion, not CP policy. "Guild membership had no bearing on staff changes ... such changes were not related to this personal opinion. I recognize the right of any staff member in Ottawa to belong to the Guild."[47] CP was willing to negotiate a collective agreement covering all editorial employees in Canada. If Dent Hodgson, the Ottawa bureau employee fired for refusing a transfer to Toronto, contacted Purcell and acknowledged CP's right to transfer employees, he would be rehired, at first in Toronto on a holiday-relief basis, and would be transferred to Ottawa when the first vacancy occurred, and in any case within six months. Other employees who had been fired would get preference for rehiring if vacancies opened up; a recent budget review suggested that "except for two exceptions," further dismissals would not be necessary. In all, 12 CP employees who had been fired were put in the preferential rehiring pool, and 13 PN employees were immediately reinstated.[48] On the basis of these concessions, the Guild withdrew its application to prosecute CP.[49]

This did not mean that progress would be made towards a contract, however. In August, the Guild formally requested the appointment of a conciliator. CP was continuing to discriminate against Guild members and "has reduced its services and reorganized its operations in a manner that shows clearly it is preparing to force a strike or lockout to break the Guild if all other efforts fail." At PN, "the impression has been deliberately created that the corporation plans to close down after Sept. 1."[50] Furthermore, no headway had been made in bargaining sessions: "The Guild submits that a Management which comes to conference table empty-handed is making NO reasonable effort to conclude a collective agreement." At the most recent negotiating session, Purcell said it would be "impossible" for Guild representatives to meet the board of directors. He repeated his insistence

> that he had no authority to grant any improvement in existing conditions, [and] refused a direct request for some schedule of wages, even one which would only represent the existing conditions. When it was pointed out to him that a collective bargaining agreement which guaranteed nothing on wages and hours was unheard of, either in this union or any other, he merely smiled and remained silent.[51]

CP, however, rejected the charge of refusing to negotiate. Purcell told the Minister of Labour that CP had made some concessions from its initial proposals and denied the Guild's conclusion that "because CP has not met all their unreasonable demands it is not negotiating in good faith."[52] Stitt was duly appointed as conciliator, but quickly concluded that no progress could be made; a formal conciliation board was then convened.[53]

Meanwhile, Purcell told the executive committee that the wave of firings in the spring had led to "a definite setback in the quality of the CP news report." CP was no longer producing original features, but merely "a routine factual job." Purcell predicted that CP's coverage would "inevitably" deteriorate further; morale was poor, and further resignations were expected. One concern was that Reuters and AP might object if the Canadian news service they received from CP continued to deteriorate; in fact, this happened in 1951, when Frank Starzel of AP complained that US newspapers were using more UP stories from Canada, and that CP's recent coverage of the New Brunswick election had been "late and dull."[54] In Canada, BUP mounted a "selling spree" to radio stations, especially in Quebec, playing on fears that CP would drop its radio service as part of the cutbacks, and CP suffered "serious losses" as a result.[55] It was agreed that no further budget cuts would be imposed.[56] While some directors expressed concern about the severe reductions in the news service, Victor Sifton insisted that CP had to prepare for a strike, and the best way "to stand the siege" was to reduce the staff as far as possible; this also made it clear to the Guild "that CP was in earnest." Sifton "was not prepared to pay a nickel to appease the Guild, but was prepared to pay substantially for non-Guild service," a statement that seemed to reflect the majority, hard-line viewpoint.

The conciliation board's majority report, endorsed by the chair (Archibald Cochrane, a county court judge from Brampton, Ontario) and the union-appointed representative and issued in February 1951, was strongly critical of CP's approach to negotiations.[57] (CP's nominee issued a separate dissenting report.) It concluded that even among those who had doubts about unionization of white-collar employees, "the position taken by Canadian Press would appear to be somewhat drastic and puts the employee in the position that his only choice in many respects is to 'take it or leave it' with no recourse no matter what decision may be made concerning him by his employers."[58] CP's lawyer, Robinette, stated that no middle ground could be found between the Guild's demands and the "unyielding position of Canadian Press ... . We find it difficult to accept this attitude as evidence of bargaining in good faith as we are of the opinion that some common or middle ground can and should be found." Management could retain the right to make decisions about wages, hiring, promotion, and dismissal, while still providing "some opportunity for redress" to employees who felt they had been treated unfairly. The conciliation board could not impose such a compromise by itself, however. "In these days when collective bargaining has become the rule and not the exception and we find many employers and their unions endeavouring to find some common ground ... it was somewhat surprising to find that there are still employers who adopt the unyielding, uncompromising attitude which has been adopted by The Canadian Press ... ." The Guild was criticized as well for making "excessive" demands, but CP was clearly seen as the biggest obstacle to a settlement. Gordon Munnoch, a lawyer who was CP's representative, also blamed the Guild for making excessive demands that "may have startled" CP to the point that negotiations were prejudiced from the beginning.[59] Munnoch also referred, somewhat obliquely, to the concern that any settlement with CP would provide leverage for unionization of member newspapers: if the Guild's demands were met, "a weapon might be placed in its hand which could be dangerous to a great many of the member newspapers and might even threaten their continued existence."[60]

The majority report made several recommendations about job security, union rights, and other issues in dispute. On wages, the report did not recommend a scale, which CP absolutely refused to accept, "even though the present wages and salaries, viewed in the light of present-day living conditions, are not impressive." It suggested, modestly, that all employees paid less than $40 a week should receive an increase of $3, with those paid more than $40 getting raises of 5 per cent. CP immediately accepted this recommendation (and noted that some other recommendations reflected its current practices anyway), but there was no room for compromise on "two fundamental matters of principle": CP must retain sole discretion over hiring, promotion, and firing "in order to maintain the demonstrable integrity of the news," and "the merit system" in wages – that is, individual wage agreements with individual employees – must be maintained.[61] In the wake of the conciliation board's report, CP and the Guild held a further negotiating session that, like all its predecessors, went nowhere in view of CP's refusal to compromise on any of the main issues.[62] Robinette told the board of directors that the Guild's only remaining options were to strike or try to embarrass CP publicly: "an attempt would be made to subject CP to adverse publicity by having labor bodies put pressure on CP members. It was important that individual members be able to refute the suggestions ... that CP had not bargained in good faith."[63] Several labour organizations did indeed pass resolutions criticizing CP for its intransigence, and attempted to put pressure on local publishers.[64] The Canadian Congress of Labour, the umbrella organization to which the ANG belonged, complained to one of CP's most important clients, the CBC.[65] Among other things, CP had withdrawn its Saskatchewan correspondent and relied for coverage on Sifton's Regina *Leader-Post*, a paper with "very definite political leanings [Liberal] at complete variance with those of the present [CCF] government of Saskatchewan." A CBC news executive expressed concern that CP's uncompromising stand against the Guild put the agency "in a bad position as an impartial collector and distributor of news." If CP were found guilty of bad-faith bargaining, this would pose serious problems for the CBC as a major CP client.[66]

In September 1951, with no prospect of further negotiations and all other approaches having failed, the Labour Ministry approved the Guild's application to prosecute CP for bargaining in bad faith (despite a departmental lawyer's warning that there was not "a chance in the world of the company's being convicted on this charge, because they did comply with the procedure for collective bargaining and conciliation which is laid down in the Act."[67]) In the event, the magistrate hearing the case dismissed the charges without requiring CP to present a defence, ruling that the incidents complained of had not taken place within six months of the date when charges were laid, as specified by the Criminal Code for summary proceedings.[68] On appeal, the not-guilty verdict was upheld on more substantive grounds; Judge Sam Factor of York County Court ruled that CP had made reasonable efforts to reach a collective agreement, and that a general arbitration clause proposed by CP did provide a way to address disagreements over hiring, promotion, and dismissals, contrary to the Guild's contention.[69]

The Guild's only remaining weapon was a strike, but this would have been suicidal; CP had made it exceedingly clear that it would fight a strike tooth and nail, probably leading to the breaking of the union. The ANG, having failed to make any significant headway against CP's hard-line resistance after three years of struggle, was decertified on 18 March 1953; CP's editorial employees would not have union representation for another 20 years. CP had lost two-fifths of its editorial staff through firings and resignations, and it took another five years for the news service to be restored to 1950 levels.[70] By 1956, Frank Starzel of AP complimented Purcell on the "admitted improvement" in CP's coverage – a return to "your normal standard" that had not been met for several years "for substantial reasons" that both men understood.[71]

CP's oft-repeated concern for the quality of its news report – always constrained by considerations of costs and members' willingness or ability to pay – was mostly genuine, but the bitter fight against the Guild showed that when CP publishers' sense of their fundamental economic interests was at stake, the news report could be, and was, deliberately sacrificed. The fact that CP was a nonprofit cooperative made no difference at all where class and labour issues were concerned. In their capacity as owners of capital and employers of wage labour, the publishers who collectively owned CP could hardly have embodied the capitalist stereotype more convincingly.

The struggle over how to deal with radio that had so sorely taxed CP's ingenuity and patience in the 1930s was no longer as acute as it had been, but its legacy remained. Press News, CP's radio-news subsidiary, was serving 53 private stations (in addition to the CBC) in early 1946 compared to BUP's 38, but revenue was declining with the end of wartime special services to government departments, including the Wartime Information Board, the RCAF Public Relations Division, the Department of External Affairs, and US Office of War Information.[72] Efforts to restrict the hours when radio news could be broadcast had long been abandoned. PN now operated on a 24-hour basis, providing material for four 15-minute broadcasts a day and 12 shorter hourly summaries. Many broadcasters regarded PN's growth with alarm, stating openly that CP and its subsidiary must be prevented from threatening the Canadian operations of UP/BUP. The reason was lingering distrust, stemming from the early days of radio when CP opposed commercial sponsorship of news.[73] Many broadcasters feared that CP sought a monopoly in radio news and that, if this came about, there was no assurance "that the flow of news to radio stations would be maintained and not withheld until after publication in newspapers."[74] In 1947, with the number of PN clients rising sharply, the company's manager, Charles Edwards, urged that "the opposition [should] not be permitted to develop a panic reaction by raising the monopoly bogey."[75] He recommended that CP try to find a way (as AP had done by offering radio stations associate membership) to give its radio customers a role in PN's operation "to consolidate client gains and ensure expansion."

The radio business became an important source of profit for CP and reduced substantially the amount its members had to pay for the general news service. In 1945–46, for example, PN's revenue was $241,958, offset by expenses of $169,504. The balance, more than $72,000, was paid to CP for providing the news on which the PN reports were based. This was less than the amount that CP, somewhat arbitrarily, identified as its "service charge," so PN showed an operating deficit on paper. The fact was, though, that the revenue CP received from PN was a net gain that went directly to offset the costs paid by its member newspapers. By 1958, the sale of news to radio and television yielded almost one-fifth of CP's total revenue.[76]

The radical spending cuts imposed in the anti-Guild campaign of 1950 and 1951 affected PN as well. CP considered closing down PN entirely, but rejected the idea; with a reduced staff, "[t]he service was carried on with difficulty but its development was severely retarded."[77] A committee on relations with broadcasters, intended to find ways of easing the distrust that private broadcasters felt towards CP and PN and stopping the competitive losses, was set up in April 1951; it recommended that a new company be established, in which broadcasters would hold four seats on a nine-person board of directors.[78] (It also warned that "a sudden shift of practically all private stations to U.P." was a distinct possibility.[79]) Roy Thomson, a committee member who owned newspapers as well as radio stations, endorsed the reorganization, saying it would help CP reach its goal of having radio pay a fixed proportion of its annual costs; with seats on the board, broadcasting clients could see for themselves "the bargain they are getting." Frederick Ker stressed the continuing strategic importance of radio. Going into broadcasting in the first place had been an exercise in self-preservation, and "[a]ny financial advantage had been subsidiary to CP's regaining an unchallenged position as the national news-gathering agency." Now, in the face of a new threat, "the idea was to rearrange the setup to meet it." The new company, called Broadcast News (BN), began operations on 1 January 1954.[80] Thomson, then CP's president, was also the first president of BN. PN continued to provide news to CBC separately; the private broadcasters distrusted CBC (which was their regulator as well as their competitor) almost as much as they did CP.[81]

While BUP continued to be a troublesome competitor during the 1940s and much of the 1950s, the establishment of BN eventually gave CP a decisive advantage. In 1942, BUP had been on the verge of signing a lucrative 10-year agreement with Imperial Oil to produce a regular national newscast to be called The Esso Reporter, a Canadian version of a program already offered in the United States and South America; only the active intervention of two CP directors, M.E. Nichols and Howard Robinson, prevented the agreement from going ahead. (Imperial Oil was told that the plan would "unbalance" the news situation in Canada and threaten to turn every Canadian station into a BUP client.[82]) When Harry Montgomery of AP made his assessment of the Canadian news scene in 1944, he observed that most papers taking BUP did so for its US and foreign news. Its Canadian news operation, including the Ottawa bureau, was weak (and the Ottawa bureau chief was a "notorious" Conservative partisan).[83] This weakness in Canadian coverage was an important reason for the progress that PN made in taking radio clients away from BUP.[84] In general, BUP copy was considered to be written in a livelier style, and was sometimes faster than CP-AP, but was often inaccurate.[85]

By 1957, BN had about twice as many radio clients as BUP, which was said to be losing $100,000 a year on its Canadian operations.[86] BUP had recently abandoned its Quebec radio wire and was now proposing that private broadcasters take over BUP as their own news service in order to prevent a CP-BN monopoly. By 1960, BN had 223 of Canada's 237 private radio stations as clients. Total revenue was $741,000, and the profit of $156,000 went directly to lower the assessments that CP's member newspapers paid.[87] The CBC paid $311,000 more for use of CP news on radio and television.[88] Letting broadcasters join the management of BN had proven to be a key strategic move, allowing CP to overcome BUP as a broadcasting competitor once and for all. The steady and growing flow of additional income to CP made it possible to offer enhanced service with no increase in assessments. According to Charles Edwards, CP's president, R.J. Rankin, commented in the mid-1950s: "I just never believed we could do this well."[89]

Given the long history of difficulties between CP and radio, it was somewhat surprising that the advent of another new medium, television, caused relatively few disruptions. It did, however, add momentum to the general trend towards more interpretive and feature articles as a way of providing newspapers with distinctive material.[90] It was also suggested that the arrival of television contributed to radio's growing interest in news (and hence its growing reliance on CP) as entertainment programming, previously dominant, largely migrated to TV.[91] As previously noted, some CP members objected strenuously to CP's contracts with the CBC, and this applied to television as well as radio. But this had to do with the CBC as an institution, not the medium in which it operated. In fact, with a few exceptions, television fit quite easily into the structures that had previously been set up to deal with radio. Among the few owners of private television stations in the 1950s, most were already involved in radio, and thus connected to CP through BN; at the CBC, radio and television were under the same management. Through BN for the private operators and PN for the CBC, CP simply made its news available for television on the same basis as it already did with radio; in practical terms, the only issue to be negotiated was the level of payment, rather than the tangled issues of timing, sponsorship and credit that had been so difficult with radio.[92] Roy Thomson, who was CP's president in 1954 and one of those on the board who encouraged CP to move beyond its newspaper orientation, told the annual meeting that year that there was no need to fear competition from television:

> Some people are worried – television is pressing in, times are tightening up, anything may happen. In my opinion, newspapers needn't worry if they do their job. Not so long ago, radio was considered to be a threat. What did it do? It actually helped to build circulation and widened the field of newspaper advertising. What will TV do? It will create a need for more advertising and I predict that once again the newspaper advertising field will be enlarged. There is no indication that circulation will be adversely affected. Television cannot do a complete job of news reporting – not even as complete as radio. The newspaper remains the one place where you can get the news when you want it.[93]

CP briefly investigated the idea of trying to provide a newsfilm service for television (as UP did in the United States), but did not follow through; the UP service, meanwhile, made few inroads in Canada because of the heavy tariffs imposed on film crossing the border.[94] Television's role as the predominant news medium of the later twentieth century was not established until well after 1960. One sign of what was to come emerged during the visit of Princess Margaret to Canada in July 1958; when she toured HMCS *Crescent* in Victoria, BC, press photographers (including CP's) were restricted to a few posed photos, while CBC television cameras were allowed to film continuously.[95] CP took the opportunity to reassert its claim to first priority if restrictions were to be imposed on coverage – a principle established during the Second World War[96] – and was reassured that television would not be given priority over newspapers during the forthcoming Royal visit. But this was an early indication that television might eventually prove as disruptive as radio had been. For the time being, radio and television journalists were still considered second-class citizens in the journalistic world; for example, they were only admitted as members of the parliamentary press gallery in Ottawa in 1959.[97]

Despite severe staff and service reductions during the Guild organizing drive, CP expanded in several ways in the early 1950s. Service in French was inaugurated in October 1951, using funds that had previously been given to French-language newspapers to translate the CP report individually; the initiative arose in part in response to BUP's proposal to set up a similar service.[98] As in the 1920s, the CP report was translated in a central bureau and transmitted in French. Ten members took the service at first, receiving 25,000 words a day, including 4,000 words of Quebec regional news.[99] An outside observer concluded in 1954 that it had succeeded in bringing French-language publishers into a closer connection with CP.[100] There was still relatively little material produced originally in French, however; not until 1959 was a French-speaking reporter assigned permanently to Ottawa.[101]

The development of CP's picture service was more controversial. As was often the case, the requirements for news photographs and ability to pay for them varied greatly among CP's members. The largest papers, such as the Montreal *Star* and Toronto *Star*, sold their photographs to other newspapers and resisted the advent of a CP photo service as they would resist any competitor; indeed, the Toronto *Star*'s purchase of Canadian rights to photographs from Reuters and the Press Association in 1951 without CP's being given an opportunity to bid caused a serious (if temporary) breach in the otherwise cordial relationship between CP and Reuters.[102] Beyond this, larger papers had their own photo-engraving facilities and were willing to pay for transmission using relatively costly wirephoto equipment, whereas smaller papers were willing to settle for photographic "mats" (stereo-typed mats that could be fitted directly onto the press) sent by mail.[103] Since 1945, AP had been providing a photographic-print service of US and world photos to CP members wealthy enough to make their own engravings or mats, but there was no Canadian photographic exchange. CP began an experimental photo-exchange service in 1948, which was made permanent a year later.[104] By 1950, 23 papers took CP's photo-graphic print service and 40 were using mats. One result was that member papers ran more Canadian photos and fewer "minor United States shots, especially Hollywood 'cheesecake.'" [105] It was decided in 1952 that photographs should be a general part of the news service avail-able to all members, instead of a paid extra service. There were numer-ous difficulties, including concerns that if members were required to make all their photos available to CP as they did with return news, it would interfere with the larger papers' independent photo services; this objection was met with the assurance that only 50 photos a week would be involved, all others remaining the property of the originat-ing paper.[106] Distribution continued by air mail, but it was hoped that creation of the national service might speed up the adoption of wire-photo distribution.[107] By 1954, 16 member newspapers had wirephoto service, which sped up the distribution of pictures to everyone.[108]

Adoption of the picture service on a permanent basis in 1955 was the occasion of a rare revolt of the members against the board of directors. This was one of several occasions when Roy Thomson acted as cham-pion of CP's smaller members, who typically wanted a more extensive service than their big-city counterparts – the Thomson chain was com-posed exclusively of small-town papers, and Thomson's prominence on the board and eventually as CP's president gave him a platform that he was not hesitant to use.[109] Thus when a board committee recommended that the photo service be established on a full cost-recovery basis, drop-ping the subsidy from general revenue that had so far kept costs rela-tively low, Thomson objected to this "retrograde step," predicting that higher costs would force many smaller papers to drop the service.[110] Richard Malone of the Winnipeg *Free Press* replied that many members wanted only the basics from CP, and that the picture service should be paid for by its users.[111] The board was deeply divided; the cost-recovery plan passed by a vote of 8 to 7, but was rejected at the annual meeting, where higher charges were accepted but the continuation of a subsidy from general revenue was also affirmed for the time being.[112] (The subsidy was eliminated the following year over Thomson's renewed protests.[113])

In addition to the picture service, Thomson developed and essentially imposed on CP a plan in 1951 to send CP copy by teletypesetter to the newspapers he owned, mostly in northern Ontario. The cost per mile of telegraphic transmission by leased wire had generally been declining over time; for example, CP's 10-year contract with the CPR that took effect in 1947 brought a 17 per cent reduction in annual charges.[114] This allowed CP to expand its services, particularly in central Canada, where a "triple-trunk" wire provided papers in Windsor, London, Hamilton, Toronto, Ottawa, and Montreal with up to 65,000 words of news a day; papers in eastern and western Canada, and at other points in Ontario and Quebec, received around 25,000 words a day over a single wire.[115] The use of the teletypesetter – which sent CP copy in the form of per- forated tape that could be fed directly into typesetting machines in the receiving newspaper office – promised even greater savings. It greatly reduced the need for linotype operators, with substantial reductions in wage costs.[116] It also meant that editors in the receiving newspapers did not have to handle the copy unless they wished to do so (and were willing to incur the cost of having any changes typeset). This proposal came in the midst of the dispute with the Guild, and CP was apparently concerned about the possibility of objections by the ITU, which repre- sented typesetters in many CP member newspapers. Thomson told the executive committee that ITU rules required copy to be set either by ITU members or by members of the Commercial Telegraphers Union (CTU) working for a news agency; because CP had a contract with the CTU, no difficulty was expected.[117] "If his punching were handled by CP his operation would be perfectly legitimate under I.T.U. rules." However, the experiment was not carried out at CP's head office, but at the Toronto offices of Thomson newspapers, where the editorial selection was done by Thomson staff.[118] According to one of Thomson's biographers, he threatened to quit CP and take his business to UP when the proposal was initially resisted.[119]

The experiment was clearly a success; by 1956, 75 per cent of CP members were using teletypesetter copy, paying an extra charge of $30 a week.[120] In effect, all but the very largest papers, which were less likely to use CP copy as is on a wholesale basis, were operating this way.[121] CP's president, R.J. Rankin of the Halifax *Mail-Star*, encouraged members to ensure that "this convenience does not lead to indifference on our part – to taking the news file too much for granted." But avoiding expenses both for typesetting and editing was a substantial attraction. In 1957, Purcell noted that since teletypesetting was introduced, most members had adopted Canadian Press style – the complex set of rules governing such things as when titles were to be capitalized, how and when abbreviations were to be used, how foreign place names were spelled, and so on. CP's Style Book, first published in 1940, accordingly became a fixture in most Canadian newsrooms. More substantially, although smaller papers had likely not done substantial editing of CP copy in any case – a luxury reserved for those that employed larger editing staffs – reliance on teletypesetting meant that the local editor's function was limited to deciding where articles were to be displayed, and at what length, rather than querying or altering their content. As Purcell described it, teletypesetting "in effect sat our filing editors down at members' news desks and in their composing rooms. ... copy-in-type tends to get into papers as laid down." In this way, the editing done at CP's bureaus and head office (which accounted for more than half of the journalistic work that CP performed[122]) became correspondingly important, and the picture of Canadian and international events that appeared in newspapers across the country relatively more uniform. At the same time, demands on CP editors to avoid errors and cut stories to usable length increased.[123]

By the end of the Second World War, CP had become much more like a corporation, and less like a cooperative. The finance committee had been established in 1937, a compromise between those who were happy with the status quo (which gave the general manager, consulting the president and vice presidents when necessary, great discretion over both day-to-day operations and budgeting) and those who wanted an executive body that would provide more direction for (and tighter control of) the general manager between the semi-annual board meetings. Purcell's departure to join McNaughton's staff at the end of 1940 – a decision that J.A. McNeil had approved on his own despite the objections of most of the directors – brought further demands for an executive committee that would do more than simply help him draw up spending estimates.[124] In September, 1944 – at the same meeting where the directors were told of Livesay's death – it was agreed to transform the finance committee into an executive committee with extensive powers to "decide ... such matters as they may deem necessary to be provided for" in the interval between directors' meetings.[125] Rupert Davies of the Kingston *Whig-Standard*, who had been CP's president when Purcell joined the army, complained specifically that McNeil had made major staff appointments without consulting the president, though others defended him against this charge.

A second change in CP's practices accentuated the concentration of authority in the executive committee's hands. Since Western Associated Press was first established in 1907, through the creation of Canadian Press Ltd. in 1911, the cooperative ethos had meant that debates and discussions at annual general meetings and board meetings had been extensively reported to the members. Differing views were recorded at length, important items of correspondence and memoranda were reprinted, and a remarkable degree of frankness was generally evident. By 1940, though, the growing competition with BUP led to stricter limits on how much of the discussion at annual meetings and directors' meetings was printed in CP's annual reports – which also meant less knowledge of the pros and con of various decisions on the part of members and less effective oversight of directors' and executive committee decisions. In the fall of 1940, Kent Cooper of AP asked McNeil to make sure that letters Cooper sent "as a blood brother in this effort" not be printed in CP's minutes, which "are received promptly by our chief competitor."[126] McNeil replied that CP already excluded any discussion of confidential matters from its minutes; in addition, CP's printed minutes were now accompanied with a notice stating that they were confidential documents, and that "care should be observed lest they fall into unauthorized hands," because disclosure to outsiders had "on several recent occasions, worked to the serious disadvantage of The Canadian Press and its members."[127] Throughout the 1950s, only the sketchiest accounts of executive committee decisions – with virtually no information about any debate or discussion behind them – were communicated to the board and to CP members generally.[128] The annual meeting also became a much more tightly scripted event, with relatively few comments and questions from the floor; in 1953, the president, Roy Thomson, responding to complaints about the meeting being "dull and formal, too cut-and-dried" introduced a period for an "open-forum discussion of anything any member has on his mind."[129] But this was a pale affair compared to, say, the vigorous debates about radio during the 1930s; it ended up as an opportunity for members to bring up disjointed questions, complaints, and suggestions, with no sustained debate and little discussion.[130] I. Norman Smith, who was CP's president in the late 1960s, told interviewer Douglas Amaron that he tried to combat the trend of formulaic meetings:

> I had noticed over the years that some of the CP presidents, or vice-presidents or board members – maybe I was guilty myself sometimes, sometimes the management, Gil [Purcell] or John [Dauphinee] or maybe [Doug] Amaron – in a cocktail party after a meeting would say, gee, that was great, we had hardly any questions and we're all through by 3:30. Gee, this is fine. Now I didn't think that was a good measurement. It seems to me that the measurement should be how many of the members went back to home offices ... and realized that perhaps they hadn't opened their mouth. Or that they had really not understood why a particular decision was made ...[131]

One area where CP maintained, and perhaps even strengthened, its cooperative traditions was in the operation of the news service. Senior management constantly reinforced the importance of member papers bringing their requirements and complaints about the day-to-day operation of the news report promptly to the attention of CP staff. For example, from 1953 on, CP members on the Ontario wire (mainly those outside Toronto) took part in an annual Criticism Day where they rated CP's performance in various areas and suggested improvements.[132] In 1959, 59 newspapers responded to a detailed survey on their requirements for news features.[133] But this customer-service ethos was quite different than the cooperative ethos that had prevailed previously, with the result that on larger corporate questions affecting CP, individual members played a diminishing role.

CP carried out relatively little of its own international reporting in the 1950s, especially in view of the ambitious plans of 1944 and 1945.[134] Bill Boss, who had been a CP war correspondent in the last years of the Second World War, was sent to Korea with the Canadian contingent in December 1950 and continued to cover the conflict until 1953.[135] Boss was then sent to Moscow on an experimental basis in November 1953. Charles Peters of the Montreal *Gazette* – characteristically, a representative of a larger paper – questioned the assignment, saying he was not sure that it was "the sort of thing CP should do," though another director said "CP had to move outside Canada to give this country independent information on world situations."[136]

Conditions for reporting in the Soviet Union were extremely difficult. Boss recalled in an interview with Douglas Amaron that he was not "trying to penetrate the Iron Curtain in any intellectual or whatever way. It was simply a question of doing feature stories. But the Russians couldn't see this. They couldn't understand that a reporter would be there for other than devious purposes."[137] Even for feature stories on relatively uncontroversial subjects like education or health care, it was very difficult to find Soviet citizens who were willing to talk to a Western journalist. Boss obtained his best material during a long train trip:

> Compartments usually accommodated six people ... Once the blinds were drawn and the berths were set, things changed dramatically, if you spoke Russian. And I spoke Russian. ... Night after night I sat up talking with Russians, who were delighted to have the opportunity to talk with a foreigner, and exchange ideas. And who every day, the next morning, when we arrived at whatever station or platform it was, when the curtains went up would be perfectly proper and correct and they've never seen me before in their lives.

Filing stories from Moscow was also extraordinarily difficult. Compared to the Allied military censorship he had worked under for several years, Boss found the Soviet system almost impossible to understand. For one thing, while reporters dealt with military censors in person and could discuss "tricky points," the Soviet censors were always anonymous. The reporter's copy was passed through a wicket in the post office and no interaction was permitted.

> The copy is pencilled, returned, and must be rewritten, repeatedly if necessary, until it will pass. ... Pencilled copy means another submission, another whack at getting the same facts passed, another way. Sometimes the second submission works. If not, you try again. When in the end it becomes clear that the facts in question will not go, the story is retyped without them and passed.

Eighty-five of CP's 91 members used at least part of Boss's 12-part series on Russia that appeared in the summer of 1954.[138] Most of the articles were written in a room in the Royal York Hotel after Boss returned to Canada to avoid the application of censorship.[139]

With the exception of Boss's Moscow posting and several shorter-term international assignments, CP did very little coverage of news outside Canada in the 1950s. This led to some high-profile criticism in 1956, when historian Arthur Lower complained to a royal commission examining Canada's broadcasting system that the CBC was doing a better job of covering international news from a Canadian perspective than CP.[140] Rupert Davies thought Lower's criticism had some merit: reporters "were bound to be influenced by their personal and national background," and some of CP's foreign news "might reflect American policy." In general, "CP must look ahead to a broadening of its independent coverage of foreign affairs."[141] But R.W. Southam of the Ottawa *Citizen* argued that the "importation and resultant influence of American copy was almost inevitable," and that "CP was doing well with what was available." Charles Peters of the *Gazette* said that "he regarded news as *news* and felt that, in general, a competent reporter's story would stand up in any country" – although there would always be some situations where a reporter's nationality, Canadian or not, would show up in copy. Purcell, meanwhile, explained how CP editors in London and New York assessed the suitability for Canadian audiences of material received from Reuters and AP, adding that Reuters' service for North America was largely handled by Canadians (some of them former CP employees) in London. The adequacy of CP's international coverage was to receive more attention in the coming years.

While the 1950s were the height of the Cold War, the corporate records contain few explicit references to it. One telling illustration of CP's underlying assumptions, however, appeared in 1951 when Purcell brushed off a complaint by Libbie Park of the Toronto Peace Council about CP's designation of the group as "Communist": "The term should have been properly applied to your affiliate, the Canadian Peace Congress," Purcell replied.[142] (A senior CBC editor forwarded the complaint to his superior, seeking guidance on how to refer to organizations "that, according to common knowledge, are communistic," and noting that while neither CP nor BUP had a fixed practice, CP usually described the Canadian Peace Congress as communist.[143])

Concerns about monopoly and competition in the operation of the general news service arose regularly in the postwar years. CP still had the ability to refuse service to new applicants or impose heavy entrance fees in cities or towns where a CP member already published. In 1948, the board of directors turned down the membership application of a new cooperatively owned paper in Winnipeg, the *Citizen*, on the grounds that its financial viability had not been demonstrated; even if this were established, the entrance fee would be more than $116,000, while the annual cost of CP service would be only $11,250.[144] (The application was complicated by the opinion, expressed by A.J. West of the Montreal *Star*, that the paper "would die sooner or later and was permeated with Communists.") But some expressed concern about the decision: Rupert Davies of the *Whig-Standard* noted that AP's decision to deny the Chicago *Sun* membership had recently led to a US Supreme Court decision that struck down AP's restrictive membership rules. M.J. Coldwell, the leader of the national CCF, complained publicly that the *Citizen* had been unable to get either CP or BUP service because of "the vested interests of the other two Winnipeg dailies," making "a mockery" of press freedom in Canada.[145]

The necessity for and legitimacy of high entrance fees were frequently debated. In 1949, Thomson tried to convince the board of directors that applicants outside the boundaries of cities served by existing CP members but within a 10-mile radius should pay the low entrance fee of $500 for publishing in a "vacant field" rather than the much higher competitive fee.[146] He noted that the application of the *British Columbian* in New Westminster, BC – eight miles outside Vancouver's city limits – had been blocked by the Vancouver members, a situation he described as unfair. (The competitive entrance fee for Vancouver at the time was $176,391.[147]) Others vigorously opposed Thomson's proposal, however, on the grounds that it would eliminate protection for existing members in their "normal circulation fields," and it was defeated by a vote of 9 to 2. But Victor Sifton, the president at the time, noted that some revision of the membership fee rules was necessary, because "CP had been under attack as monopolistic."

Undeterred, Thomson raised his proposal again at the annual meeting. According to I. Norman Smith of the Ottawa *Journal*, he was

pretty viciously treated by some of the old guard who did not confine their arguments to the obvious weaknesses and dangers of the Thomson resolution but wandered afield to sing that the C.P. membership situation was honest, above-board and above reproach and that anything Coldwell and others had to say was quite unfounded ... . I didn't like this atmosphere. I know from talks with Gil Purcell and others that our by-laws are in some places not very fair. And I know that some of the members feel that some of the entrance fees are so high as to be in fact monopolistic.[148]

At the end of the meeting, Smith suggested that an inquiry be conducted into CP's membership regulations – "I have a hunch that their operation is not so good," he wrote a few days later – but was "attacked" by Frederick Ker of the Hamilton *Spectator*, a key member of the executive committee. A few months later, Smith wrote to Purcell that even if the membership rules were said to be fair in principle, "they are operated rather artfully."[149]

Sometimes the restrictions on new members clearly worked against CP's interests. In 1945, the executive committee was informed that *L'Évangéline*, a weekly published in Moncton, was thinking of moving to daily publication, giving CP an opportunity to enlist a new member. The entrance fee quoted was $15,000, but with the agreement of the existing members from New Brunswick, this was reduced to $12,000.[150] The publisher replied that his paper had already signed a contract with BUP, noting specifically that the absence of an entrance fee had been an important consideration in the decision. In 1953, when the BUP contract was about to expire, *L'Évangéline* approached CP, saying it was attracted by the recently established service in French and wished to take up the earlier offer. But the other New Brunswick papers were no longer willing to offer any remission of the entrance fee, now set at $25,000. To get around this application of CP's own bylaws, the executive committee – declaring it to be "in the long-term interests of CP" – proposed that *L'Évangéline* be served on a contract basis rather than becoming a member (meaning that no entrance fee need be paid).[151] Several directors supported the idea, saying that CP had to be able to provide its service on a competitive basis, and that there was room for a French-language paper in New Brunswick. Others, however, argued that this was an attempt to circumvent CP's bylaws (which it clearly was) and that contract service should not be provided over the objections of local CP members. Illustrating the arbitrary power that CP's bylaws gave existing members, T.F. Drummie of the Saint John *Telegraph-Journal* first complained that *L'Évangéline* competed for local advertising, then said the approach to CP was simply a bargaining ploy to get a better deal from BUP, and finally admitted that he had "no real objection" to its getting the CP service. The executive committee's recommendation to offer a contract was at first rejected, but six months later it was agreed that as the only French-language paper in New Brunswick, *L'Évangéline* qualified for the $500 entrance fee for a newspaper in a "vacant field."[152] In this case, the high entrance fee and opposition of local newspapers to a new competitor – even one that operated in a different language – had delayed the arrival of a new CP member by eight years. Similarly, by consent of the other Vancouver papers, the New Westminster *British Columbian* was admitted as a CP member in 1952 with no entrance fee, but this was three years after the issue had first arisen. CP's restrictions on new members clearly operated in anticompetitive and arbitrary ways, and many members wanted to change the situation. In 1953, entrance fees were reduced substantially, to twice the annual fee for a newspaper in the city in question, with a stipulation that it was "not aimed at preventing the entry of new members."[153]

The trend towards consolidation of newspaper ownership in the later 1950s reinforced concerns about CP's restrictive membership practices. In 1957, for example, the independently owned Vancouver *Sun* and Southam-owned *Province* entered a joint-operating agreement under the umbrella of Pacific Press. This merger was referred to the Combines Investigation Branch of the Department of Justice, and a question was asked in the House of Commons about "the possibility of monopolies being fostered" by CP's membership rules.[154] The justice minister, E. Davie Fulton, specifically stated that CP would be investigated if it were determined that its practices promoted monopolies. The formation of FP Publications in 1958, merging the Winnipeg *Free Press*, Victoria *Times* and *Colonist*, Calgary *Albertan*, and Lethbridge *Herald*, and taking over the Ottawa *Journal* in 1959, did not immediately raise any further concerns about CP's membership rules. A steady increase in consolidation during the 1960s, however, meant that this issue – along with several others involving the way newspapers carried out their work – attracted more, often unfavourable, public attention. Although CP was a nonprofit cooperative, its structure and rules clearly reflected the interests of its privately owned, profit-seeking members; as a result, it could not avoid being caught up in debates about whether private ownership of the press was consistent with a genuine public-service mandate for journalism.

6 Being National in the 1960s

The question of what it meant to be a "national" agency had been central to CP since its founding, but several dimensions of this question came together in the 1960s in an unprecedented way. CP faced growing demands to expand its international coverage and provide a Canadian perspective on world events; the adequacy of its French-language service was heavily criticized in Quebec, by CP's own French-language members, among others; and the financial compromise between big-city and small-town newspapers that made all its news coverage possible reached a level of crisis more acute than had been seen since the early 1920s. In all these ways, CP was forced to readdress long-standing challenges in a new and more demanding context. The question of nationality, it seemed, was never permanently solved; old issues kept requiring new, and in some ways more complex, solutions.

The question of how much independent international reporting CP should do, "in view of the excellent service provided by AP and Reuters" was thoroughly debated by the board of directors in May 1960.[1] As always, questions of cost were weighed against the desirability of providing a Canadian version (whatever that might be) of events elsewhere. CP had permanent bureaus in Washington, London, and New York, though the latter was chiefly focused on channelling the flood of Reuters and AP copy that arrived there to Toronto rather than reporting, and much of London's work was similar. D.B. Rogers of the Regina *Leader-Post* argued that CP should do more of its own foreign reporting, but "would get best value" by leaving most major stories to AP and Reuters and sending CP reporters to cover "Canadian-angle stories" on an occasional basis as required. Rupert Davies of the Kingston *Whig-Standard* agreed: "CP should not duplicate the other services but hit hard matters of Canadian interest not covered by AP and Reuters." St. Clair McCabe, the chief representative of the Thomson chain, observed that CP's reputation was at stake, too: notwithstanding the quality of AP and Reuters' coverage, "to avoid criticism Canadian newspapers needed something independent to sweeten the flood of non-Canadian reporting of world events." (This concern about public and governmental criticism of how CP, and the press generally, carried out its job was to become increasingly prominent as the decade progressed.) Purcell summed up the current practice: CP regularly covered foreign stories with "a strong Canadian angle," such as Prime Minister John Diefenbaker's recent visit to Mexico or NATO meetings in Europe, while "some marginal stories were skipped." More international coverage could be provided if members wanted it, though. Charles Bruce, the number two news executive, spelled out CP's cautious approach more explicitly in his annual report: "CP assigns staffers to certain international news events when the time and expense involved appear likely to be justified by the flavour of direct Canadian reporting this adds to the report."[2] The chief of CP's New York bureau stressed the close and cooperative working relations that CP enjoyed with the two larger agencies, with AP displaying "constant readiness to fill a request or search out a story" of Canadian interest.[3] CP had access to AP bureaus all around the world.

But when international coverage was discussed at the annual meeting a few days later – with AP's general manager, Frank Starzel, in attendance – some members argued against the notion that CP should limit itself strictly to Canadian-angle stories, implicitly raising the question of potential pro-American or pro-British bias by AP and Reuters. John Lecky of the Vancouver *Sun* reported that his publisher wanted more CP coverage of "the big spot events," such as anti-apartheid protests in South Africa. Canadian reporters might have "a more objective outlook on world affairs than those of some other countries," and Canadian readers preferred their work.[4] R.L. Curran of the Sault Ste. Marie *Star* agreed: "Other agencies reflected the point of view of their own countries rather than the general or Canadian point of view." Others urged caution, however: Beland Honderich of the Toronto *Star* insisted that "CP papers could never provide their own full news service. The present system of assigning staffers to international assignments from

London, New York, or domestic bureaus seemed far less costly than permanent assignments."[5] (The fact that the *Star* was currently in a dispute with CP about the growing assessment it paid, and that it, unlike most other CP papers, could afford much of its own international coverage, no doubt underlay the warning.[6]) Richard Malone of the Winnipeg *Free Press* suggested that CP might use local freelancers more often on international stories "rather than get into too much full-time staffing." Despite a preponderance of comments in favour of more staff reporting abroad, Peters summed up the discussion by saying only that Purcell should be given "more leeway" to assign staff to international stories.

Starzel addressed the underlying issue of whether AP represented an acceptably neutral or unacceptably pro-American point of view at the 1962 annual meeting, telling Rogers of the *Leader-Post* that his assertion of State Department influence over AP coverage was "nonsense."[7] "AP was writing for a world audience. It frequently was criticized for *not* promoting the US viewpoint, and its reply was that the best patriotism is to report honestly to the world." Walton Cole of Reuters said news agencies had to give "the facts," but acknowledged that correspondents sometimes had to deal with "psychological censorship." "Even where direct censorship is not applied, in some countries the correspondent knew that he faced expulsion if his stories were regarded as derogatory."[8] This did not address the question of potential bias, however.

For the time being, the policy of sending a reporter to cover international stories if there was a major Canadian angle continued. In August 1960, a CP reporter was sent to Congo, where Canadian troops were part of a UN peacekeeping force, at a cost of $1,350 a month; the assignment ended after 11 months, "when it became apparent that general interest in the story had fallen off."[9] In 1963, T.E. Nichols of the Hamilton *Spectator* commended a recent CP series from the Soviet Union, repeating that CP should expand its international operations despite the cost; 44 CP members used all nine parts of the series and 32 others printed parts of it.[10] Other CP staffers covered stories in Mexico, Cuba, Israel, and Cyprus (again accompanying Canadian peacekeepers), and new assignments were planned in the Caribbean and South America.[11]

In 1964, CP sent Jack Best, a reporter from the Ottawa bureau who had done well on previous international assignments, to Moscow.[12] Although Best was described as a "resident correspondent," the executive committee did not see this as a long-term commitment – it was initially supposed to end by May 1965, then extended to until May 1966.

After 18 months, it was decided to keep the bureau open indefinitely.[13] The cost of keeping Best in Moscow was the main element in a $40,000 increase for international coverage in the 1966 budget.[14]

Peter Buckley, a young reporter from CP's London bureau, was sent to replace Best in 1967.[15] In an interview more than 35 years later, Buckley recalled the complications and limitations of the assignment, undertaken in the midst of the Cold War. To begin with, the Soviet authorities did not allow CP to use AP's leased wire to New York via Helsinki, which meant that CP had to pay onerous cable fees for anything filed by telegraph.[16] This dictated an emphasis on features, which could be sent by mail, rather than daily news. Buckley eventually came to see this as an advantage, allowing him to travel and write about different aspects of life in the USSR, while his AP counterparts were typically tied to the news of the day and rarely left Moscow. "I wrote features about things that interested me" – such as the state of the Soviet school system – "rather than things that screamed news value," he recalled. Buckley's features were made available to AP clients through the AP-CP news-sharing arrangement and sometimes were picked up by US newspapers, making the AP reporters "a little envious."

Buckley recalled that permission to travel outside Moscow was sometimes granted and sometimes denied – "it depended on whether you were in their bad or good books at the time." He was always accompanied by an interpreter, provided by an agency that was a branch of the KGB, the Soviet secret police. In general, the official view of North American reporters was that "all these journalists were spies" whose activities had to be carefully controlled. Although Buckley arrived with an inclination to be sympathetic, or at least not overtly hostile, the authorities "created situations which they must have known would turn you against them."

Buckley (who later became CP's chief news editor during the expansionist years of the 1980s) strongly defended the value of having a correspondent who concentrated on features rather than news. "It may make sense in terms of prestige to have your own employee's name on the big story of the day, [but] it didn't necessarily provide you with more important or more interesting coverage." AP had five or six reporters in Moscow, and Reuters had almost as many, making it practically impossible for a one-person bureau to compete in daily news coverage. Buckley's view, shared by CP's senior executives and most of its members, was that it made little practical difference if the top story of the day from Moscow carried an AP reporter's byline instead of one from CP; he could spend his time doing other, possibly more interesting, things, and CP's members thus benefitted from a broader range of coverage than if he had tried to duplicate what the other agencies were doing. That was always the tradeoff involved: how much was it worth to provide CP coverage of the day's top story that would sometimes be different from that of AP or Reuters, perhaps more "Canadian," but might also more or less duplicate it much of the time? And when it was a question of five or six reporters versus one, CP-specific coverage might also be slower or less thorough.

The more an international story directly involved American interests, the greater was the interest in having CP's own coverage. Latin America was one particular area of concern. In 1964, R.A. Graybiel of the Windsor *Star* urged CP to appoint a full-time staff reporter in Latin America "to help balance a deluge of the U.S. viewpoint from across the border" and James Lamb of the Orillia *Packet and Times* complained that much of the news from Latin America "seems written from the American viewpoint."[17] Walton Cole of Reuters – who had plans of his own for expanding the CP-Reuters relationship – acknowledged that he, too, felt his agency's Latin American coverage was inadequate, but had appointed four new staff correspondents there recently and "was anxious to help meet CP's requirements for objective South American news."[18] By 1969, despite earlier reservations about CP international staffing, the Toronto *Star* supported the idea of a CP staff correspondent in Latin America; Beland Honderich criticized CP's "dependence on American news service" for Latin American coverage and observed that in view of the *Star*'s experience "an individual paper cannot justify the cost of assigning a staffer to Latin America ... perhaps CP should consider assigning a man there."[19] In the fall of 1965, the board of directors heard that the lack of CP coverage of the US involvement in Vietnam – "a Canadian view" – had been criticized at regional editors' meetings.[20] But the policy was still that AP and Reuters could be relied on – "CP staffers are normally sent only when direct Canadian interests are involved." For example, a CP man might be sent to Vietnam "if the Chinese move into North Viet Nam as they did into Korea, if there is a major Commonwealth involvement in the fighting or if Canada becomes directly involved thru assignment of troops, aircraft or other military support." A year later, as the war continued to escalate and became an issue of growing importance in US domestic politics, CP did send a staff reporter.[21]

CP's spending on international reporting increased steadily during the 1960s, though not by huge amounts. In 1961, the executive committee cut Purcell's proposed budget by $21,000, but specified that the extra $17,000 allocated for foreign coverage (on top of the cost of the London, Washington, and New York bureaus) should be spared.[22] In 1963, Purcell was asked to explain why the international reporting budget had been underspent; he reasserted CP's commitment to international coverage, noting that the underspending "was not a reflection of Toronto members' attitude toward CP international coverage."[23] Eight months' staff coverage of Canadian peacekeepers in Cyprus had cost $15,000, while the Moscow bureau was estimated to cost $18,000 a year (it ended up being closer to $25,000).[24] The extra $40,000 allocated for international coverage in 1966 meant the average member's assessment would go up by 9.3 per cent rather than the previously projected 7.2 per cent.[25] By way of comparison, CP paid AP $88,800 for its full international news service in the mid-1960s and paid Reuters $60,000.[26] Within a few years, CP's approach to covering foreign news became a prominent public issue as one of the central questions considered by the Senate Committee on Mass Media in 1969–70.[27]

⚜

The question of what it meant to be a national news agency in an international system was never far beneath the surface of CP's foreign-coverage decisions. Domestically, the agency's awareness of its national mandate in the 1960s came through especially clearly in debates about the *Service français*. These were the years of the Quiet Revolution in Quebec; debates about Quebec's place in Confederation and the status of the French language became dominant national issues. Under these circumstances, the adequacy of CP's service to French-language newspapers came under close and often critical scrutiny.

The French service that CP established in the 1950s was an advance over what had existed before, but it was still very limited.[28] CP was an English-language institution, headquartered in Toronto, that operated almost entirely in English. There was no original reporting in French; the *Service français* was essentially an improved translation service.

An important development came in 1959, when Guy Rondeau, who had previously worked for CP covering the Quebec National Assembly, was sent to Ottawa "to report on federal affairs, in French, from the point of view of French Canada."[29] (Rondeau was later appointed chief of CP's Montreal bureau, in charge of both English- and French-speaking staff, and eventually became one of CP's vice presidents.) The cost was shared among all CP members, not just French-language publications; John Bassett, publisher of the Toronto *Telegram*, argued that "Canada was a bilingual country, and CP as a national organization should be bilingual at the capital."[30] In a later interview, Rondeau recalled that this was a time when very little business in Ottawa was conducted in French – there was no simultaneous translation in the House of Commons, for example. The atmosphere for a French-speaking reporter "wasn't hostile, but you weren't considered important."[31] CP's Ottawa bureau chief, Fraser McDougall, let Rondeau make most of his own decisions about what to cover. Rondeau's main focus was the French-speaking ministers in the Diefenbaker government: "I attached myself to them, and covered questions of interest to Quebec. That was the point of the exercise." The new approach was evidently a success; the executive committee was told in October 1960 that Rondeau's copy "was getting first-class play."[32] A second French-language reporter was sent to Ottawa in 1966, and a third in 1968.[33] From the early 1960s onward, two CP reporters in the Quebec City bureau reported on provincial politics in French as well.[34]

According to Bill Stewart, the anglophone but fluently bilingual chief of CP's Montreal bureau (and therefore head of the French service), many French-speaking journalists distrusted CP. He reported to Purcell in 1960 that francophone journalists were "sore about" CP because they believed publishers used the French service "as a defence against ... progress as the journalists see it" – that is, the establishment of a separate French-language news agency "they would run themselves and by which they would propagandize new people and movements."[35] Their preferred approach to journalism was almost exactly opposite to CP's: "They feel the thing to guard against is 'neutral' reporting – that what is needed is 'opinion journalism' going a lot further than interpretative reporting." Publishers, however, were uneasy about the prospect of more opinionated journalism. With the exception of *Le Devoir* and *La Presse*, "[t]he journalists feel or suspect that CP works hand-in-glove with French-language newspaper managements that have not trained them to tell about what is going on in the province or won't let them tell about it because there is no confidence in their views." One senior Quebec journalist, Gérard Pelletier, the editor of *La Presse* from 1961 to 1964, spoke dismissively in his memoirs of "the wretched Canadian Press, whose proprietors (the newspapers of Canada organized cooperatively) were notoriously stingy."[36] In the spring of 1963, Purcell reported (somewhat cryptically) to the board of directors that the French service "had recently been criticized by some persons not well-informed on its operation – criticism that was not necessarily malicious but widely circulated and hence of concern."[37] He was referring to the actions of the Société St-Jean-Baptiste, which had called for the establishment of a separate French-language news agency.[38]

Criticism of this kind from Quebec nationalists, while not welcome, was not by itself a great shock to CP. But in June 1963 a group of CP's senior managers – including Purcell, Stuart Keate of the Vancouver *Sun* (then CP's president), Bill Stewart, and Douglas Amaron (CP's general executive) – were shocked when several of CP's own French-language members raised the idea of a separate French service during a regional meeting in Quebec City. (A decision to appoint a full-time staff writer to cover Quebec culture who did not speak or understand French may have contributed to their dissatisfaction.[39]) Amaron, who interviewed several CP veterans in the late 1970s for a history that he was unable to complete before his death, recalled in an interview with Keate that the meeting "shook everybody ... it was quite a shattering experience."[40] The French-language newspapers asked for a report on CP's finances in order to estimate the cost of an independent service. Amaron recalled with some amusement that the English executives were at a loss about how to respond: "My recollection of it, when they asked for this report on CP's finances, in particular aid for the French service, you [Keate] looked at Bill Stewart and looked at Gil to figure out which one was going to answer."

CP's senior managers took the situation seriously, adopting a strategy of openness and engagement, all with the goal of blunting demands for an independent French-language service. A few months after the Quebec City meeting, a committee of French-language editors (including the head of the *Service français*, Bertrand Thibault, and representatives of *Le Soleil*, *L'Action* [formerly *L'Action catholique*], *Le Nouvelliste* [Trois-Rivières], *Le Devoir*, *La Presse*, and *Le Droit*) was set up with a mandate to consider improvements to the service and to determine whether "it could be improved in order to accomplish what would be expected of an autonomous agency."[41] One specific task was to estimate the cost of establishing and operating a separate French-language news service. Endorsing the committee's establishment, Aurèle Gratton of *Le Droit* told the board of directors that Quebec nationalists like those in the Société St-Jean-Baptiste "never considered operating cost. Where could the French newspapers go with the money now spent for CP and BN services?"[42] The committee should be given access to detailed financial information "to show these people that their suggestion is not feasible." Paul Desruisseau of Sherbrooke *La Tribune* agreed: there was currently "some feeling among French-language journalists that there should be a French news service regardless of cost" and that this was a good time "to put the right picture before them."[43] The executive committee, which controlled access to CP's financial information closely (the board of directors, for example, was typically only shown financial summaries), agreed that "all possible information" should be made available.[44] Clearly, it was important to CP that its French-language members be convinced of the benefits of affiliation rather than independence.

Purcell and Bill Stewart attended the committee's meetings, and Purcell's sympathy for the requirements of the French-language papers was universally acknowledged.[45] (A study caried out for the Royal Commission on Bilingualism and Biculturalism also noted, however, that "one of CP's main problems is the existence of a paternalistic system in the relations between managers and employees, a system that seems to exist equally in the relations between Mr. Purcell and *Service français*."[46]) At the committee's request, Purcell provided cost estimates for two different types of French news service, one partly integrated into CP and the other entirely autonomous. The current annual cost of the French service supplied to 10 member newspapers (and to 55 radio stations through Broadcast News) was $527,086. A partly integrated service would cost $626,088, Purcell estimated (a cost increase of almost 20 per cent), while an autonomous service would cost $721,994 (an increase of 37 per cent). The committee considered these estimates to be, if anything, too conservative, suggesting that the actual cost of a separate service would be 50 per cent more than they were currently paying. It concluded that "establishment of a completely autonomous French service is financially impossible ... and in fact would not provide a better service than now provided by CP."[47] The idea of a possible government subsidy to offset the increased costs was rejected out of hand; it would compromise CP's independence. (At the 1963 general meeting, A-F. Mercier of *Le Soleil*, CP's president, noted that no Quebec newspapers had taken advantage of provincial legislation that would have protected them from increases in the price of newsprint because there were "a few strings" attached: "They preferred to pay more for their newsprint rather than permit government interference in their business."[48])

Along with the stick (the prospect of higher costs) went the carrot (promises of improved service). In September 1964, responding to one of the committee's early recommendations, CP reached an agreement to obtain the international news service of Agence France-Presse (annual cost $8,000), which was much in demand by its French-language members; one of the great advantages of AFP was that its copy arrived in French, obviating the delays normally caused by translation.[49] This was hailed in the committee's final report as a major improvement. Its other recommendations were significant, though not radical. Stories from Quebec City should be written originally in French because most events there took place in French; in Montreal, stories should be written either in English or in French depending on the original language of the event, and no story about a French activity should be written in English and translated into French. At least two French-language reporters were needed in Ottawa, and again, any Ottawa event that took place in French should be reported in French. Double translation (where an event that took place in one language was initially reported in the other, then translated back) was to be avoided at all costs; the effect of this on direct quotations was particularly egregious. At the same time, French-language newspapers in Quebec were called on to do a better job of providing local news to CP. As the staff of the Royal Commission on Bilingualism and Biculturalism had noted, CP's French-language members were noteworthy for their refusal to collaborate in this respect.[50] (The efforts of La Presse to expand its circulation outside Montreal in the late 1950s and early 1960s, thus competing directly with other provincial papers, probably contributed to this mutual distrust.[51])

Despite the committee's positive report, some aspects of its underlying analysis were less favourable to the CP connection. Michel Roy, news editor of Le Devoir and a former CP employee in the French service,[52] wrote in a supplementary report that despite the financial impossibility of a separate agency, many French-Canadians were dissatisfied with the status quo. Some of these may have been misinformed or politically motivated, but "it remains no less true that real dissatisfaction is apparent with regard to the French service of Canadian Press, and that this dissatisfaction is shared by French-speaking journalists. It will not be countered simply by stating that it is only a question of the effects of the wave of indépendantisme."[53] It should be possible to have a French service within CP that responded better to the new needs and legitimate demands of the French-speaking population. An English news cooperative with a French service that is "completely subject to a management whose methods, spirit, language and preoccupations – are foreign to French Canada" couldn't be considered a "truly Canadian" news agency. CP should be a bicultural institution, not just bilingual, "structured so that the two [linguistic] communities are equally integrated in it." It followed from this that the French and English services of CP should be of equal quality, equally complete, and equally fast. Eventually, Roy suggested, the French service might report directly to the board of directors rather than through the Montreal bureau chief or even the general manager. Most of these observations were not included in the committee's more diplomatic final report, but it was clear that the demands for equality associated with the Quiet Revolution were being applied to CP as well. In an interview with Soucy Gagné, a researcher for the Royal Commission on Bilingualism and Biculturalism who conducted an extensive study of CP, Roy repeated that in general he thought highly of CP's service and recognized that a separate French service would be financially ruinous. (*Le Devoir*, which regularly depended on subsidies from the other Quebec newspapers to pay its CP fees, would have been as well aware of this as anyone.[54]) But more original journalism in French was required, especially in Ottawa, and the French service needed more autonomy. Roy also recognized that Purcell had a challenging task in convincing the majority of CP members from English-language newspapers that they should assume a share of the costs of an improved French service, which would cost more than the revenue brought in by the French-language members.[55]

The committee's recommendations were favourably received. In 1965, CP's president, Stuart Keate, told members that "we continue to hear the views, expressed in Quebec, that that an independent French-language news agency is required to give expression to the aspirations of the French-speaking people." He concluded that if CP were divided into two separate agencies, "each would be weaker financially and each would be more exposed to the pressures of interests who regard themselves as better judges of news values than newspaper men." He applauded the report of the study committee, adding that it was up to CP's French-language members "to keep us informed about any real need for an arrangement basically different than the present in CP as regards the two Canadian communities."[56]

The report of the French service committee also played an important part in CP's response to the Royal Commission on Bilingualism and Biculturalism. Established in 1963, the commission took a particular interest in CP, and especially in the adequacy or otherwise of its French service. (One of the commissioners, Jean-Louis Gagnon, was a former editor of *La Presse*.) The commission carried out an extensive survey of

CP members in 1964, focusing on the adequacy of the French service but going beyond it as well. Of the French-language newspapers surveyed, three described themselves as generally satisfied with the French service, three were moderately satisfied, and none were dissatisfied.[57] But six out of eight were unhappy with the quality of translation, and five described the service as too slow, whether due to the time taken for translation, or to problems caused by insufficient news-sharing cooperation.[58] While six were satisfied with the way CP operated as a cooperative with French and English members, two were moderately satisfied, and none dissatisfied, all said they considered CP an English institution.[59] In fact, Gagné reported, some people refused to refer to CP by its French name, La Presse canadienne, and insisted on calling it "Canadian Press."[60] Ultimately, however, "they all stated, without exception, that the advantages of the formula outweighed the disadvantages." The service was provided at a reasonable price, and every member was free to monitor, criticize, and suggest improvements. When asked explicitly if they would prefer one organization or two, two members said they wanted a separate French agency, while five others supported the idea of a single organization, though with various qualifications (such as an autonomous French service within CP or two parallel, partly autonomous sections under one general management).[61] The parallels with broader discussions about Quebec's place in Canada's federal structure were plain to see.

While Gagné put more emphasis on the French service's status within CP, her conclusions broadly echoed those of the news study committee. One major problem was the lack of French-speaking staff in Ottawa and other major cities to "capture the living *canadienne* reality and better inform French-language readers."[62] She also lamented the French-language newspapers' "almost total dependence ... on an information infrastructure that escapes them administratively," which was "clearly resented " by the French publishers. "The institution that represents the information infrastructure *par excellence* is not seen by the francophones who work there as a properly Canadian – that is to say, 'bicultural' – institution."[63] These problems notwithstanding, the French newspapers "seem for the most part in agreement in recognizing CP's efforts to improve its French service, and they are ready to support it with their money if it continues in this vein."[64]

Gagné also surveyed CP's English members, and their views were revealing, both where they were similar to those of the French papers and where they differed. Six of the 18 English newspapers surveyed said they were dissatisfied with CP's coverage of French Canada, as opposed to six who were satisfied and five who were moderately satisfied.[65] More generally, about half of those surveyed mentioned various disadvantages of the CP service, primarily uniformity, dullness of coverage, "grey news," or failure to capture the significance of events.[66] One member said CP's news coverage was too shallow and superficial – efforts to make it palatable to a large number of members "enforce severe limitations on really good writing."[67] (The growing emphasis on newsfeatures and more analytical coverage during the 1960s were attempts to respond to such criticisms.[68]) A variety of improvements was called for: more international coverage; more staff reporters to develop national coverage, especially on major stories; more bilingual staff; and better coverage of French Canada.[69]

On the positive side, CP's English members agreed with their French-language counterparts about the value of the news service they received. One explained the advantages as follows: "CP provides news exchange on nationwide basis and international basis, cost of which would be prohibitive to smaller newspapers particularly without a cooperative."[70] Twelve of the 18 surveyed mentioned affordability as a key advantage. More broadly, several cited the benefits of exchanging news across Canada, which contributed to "better national understanding." Objective and balanced coverage of topics such as national politics was seen as another advantage.[71] The cooperative structure (even if the large chains exercised more and more influence) was appreciated, too: as one BN subscriber observed, "[i]t places ownership of the wire service out of the grasp of any one individual or company, which is definitely desirable."[72] Having many masters may have caused some problems for CP, but it had advantages, too.

The news study committee's conclusion that it would be financially impossible to set up an independent French-language news service, and that in any case it could not provide better service than CP currently offered, was the centrepiece of CP's formal presentation to the Bilingualism and Biculturalism Commission on 15 December 1965.[73] The brief was presented by a recent past president of CP, A.-F. Mercier, of Quebec *Le Soleil*. Purcell, Stewart, and Bertrand Thibault, head of the *Service français*, were also present to answer questions. The questioning was relatively mild, though Stewart recalled later that Jean-Louis Gagnon insisted on questioning him in English, although it was widely known that Stewart was fluently bilingual. (He replied in French.[74]) Overall, though, CP executives felt their presentation went well: Mercier had given "detailed explanation of the reasons an independent French-language news agency is unnecessary and unfeasible," and the commissioners' questions "gave no indication they felt any dissatisfaction" with CP.[75] Ultimately, the commission never published its promised report on mass media, so CP's performance was not systematically assessed.[76] This did not mean, however, that the issue disappeared from public debate.

One continuing embarrassment was that three French-language dailies in Montreal – Montreal Matin (controlled by the Union nationale), Le Journal de Montreal, and Metro-Express – were not CP members, suggesting a distinct lack of interest in CP's service along linguistic lines.[77] Purcell acknowledged in the fall of 1965 that the situation "was a reflection on CP, especially in view of its expressed aim to provide the best possible service for French-language papers."[78] (It was also a source of strength for United Press International,[79] CP's long-time rival, which supplied Montreal Matin with news.) Walter O'Hearn of the Montreal Star described Montreal Matin's success as a nonmember of CP as "a heavy weapon in the armory of CP critics among French-language journalists"; if it could be persuaded to join CP, "it would be an important victory in saving CP's French-language service for the foreseeable future." Thus the board of directors considered the unusual step of offering Montreal Matin membership without the normal entry fee, which would have been more than $100,000, though Purcell warned that "[e]ven on this basis, it would be a selling job." Several directors objected strongly to this proposal, wondering how it could be explained to papers that had been required to pay heavy entrance fees (e.g., the Quebec City Catholic daily L'Action had recently paid $40,000 to join CP). Though Purcell had numerous discussions with Montreal Matin and Le Journal de Montreal over the next several years (with the board of directors receiving regular updates on what was obviously seen as a significant problem), no agreement was ever reached.[80]

CP's existing French-language members also continued to criticize the French service, especially Claude Ryan of Le Devoir. CP's reporting on Charles de Gaulle's controversial visit to Canada in 1967, including his "Vive le Quebec libre" remarks in Montreal, was the occasion for some unusually frank soul-searching. Commenting on criticism in the French-language press of how English papers had covered the visit, Ryan complained that "it often seemed CP did not grasp the real meaning of events."[81] For example, CP's coverage of a speech Ryan gave recently "was not false but the gist of what he said was missed."

This was why Quebec French-language newspaper men turn to CP coverage as a last resort. It was not so much a matter of biculturalism as of professional competence. Service in French has insufficient staff to catch the spirit of everything going on in a nation in turmoil or keep abreast of all the lively developments in Quebec.[82]

Maurice Dagenais of *La Presse* said CP's coverage of de Gaulle's speech was accurate, "but the atmosphere ... did not come through." He complained that CP repeated the "Vive le Quebec libre" comment and described it as a separatist slogan in subsequent stories, but failed to add that de Gaulle had also said "Vive le Canada" four times: "This was unbalanced coverage." (T.E. Nichols of the Hamilton *Spectator*, among others, disagreed, saying that CP had done "an extraordinarily good, cool job" of covering de Gaulle.) Gabriel Gilbert of *Le Soleil* raised a larger question, urging his colleagues to make "a real effort ... to learn why CP is not considered by French-language reporters in Quebec to be a reliable source of information. ... Political figures in French Canada had no respect for CP and this created strong feeling for a separate French service." Bill Stewart urged the editors and publishers of CP papers to "work hard to improve the attitude toward CP of their own staffs," suggesting that CP was unfairly blamed for depriving them of good assignments. He also noted "a feeling among journalists that CP is English-dominated." One reason why Quebec politicians had a cool attitude towards CP "was that they know they can impose no control of its treatment of the news."[83] In 1966, the board of directors was informed that the new Union nationale government in Quebec was planning its own news service, distributing handouts to newspapers and broadcasters by teletype.[84]

As a result of this discussion, a small group of publishers and senior editors (Gilbert, O'Hearn, Ryan, and Aurèle Gratton of *Le Droit*) was asked to assess the French service once again. After several months of study, the committee concluded that "serious discrepancies" continued to exist between the service available to English-language and French-language members.[85] "[I]n spite of management's efforts" this discrepancy would not disappear soon, especially since only nine of CP's 100 members were French-language papers and of these only two had circulation greater than 100,000. Recalling the conclusions of the 1964 study committee, the group also acknowledged that the cost of a fully developed French service would be "obviously nearly prohibitive" and made several specific, relatively limited, recommendations: that a third

French-speaking reporter (already approved by the executive committee) be sent to Ottawa;[86] that more news in French be provided from provincial legislatures elsewhere in Canada; that a roving French-language reporter be available "to cover any newsworthy event anywhere in the country"; that French-language members should be pressed harder "to help Service in French to reach its potential"; and that CP should be free to recruit reporters from its members' newsrooms. There was considerable truth to Bill Stewart's observation that "the English-speaking publishers and the French-speaking publishers got along better with each other than they would get along with anybody else."

Continued access to the international news provided by Agence France-Presse (AFP) was another important issue for CP's French-language members. Beyond the clear benefit of avoiding translation, some French-Canadian journalists (among others) favoured AFP as an alternative to the perspectives represented by Reuters and AP.[87] The original 1965 contract with AFP expired after three years when the two agencies could not agree on terms of an extension.[88] The problem from CP's point of view was that AFP was of very little use for English-language papers; its sole value was to avoid the necessity of translating the AP or Reuters service.[89] But as Walter O'Hearn warned, "CP would gain nothing if it decided to explain itself to French-language journalists and at the same time cancelled AFP"; Ryan added that its French-language members "would be badly placed to defend CP" if it became known in French-speaking circles that the English-speaking side felt AFP was needed only to reduce translation. Eventually the contract was renewed until 1971.[90]

❧

Tensions between small-town and big-city newspapers had been a constant feature of CP's operation since the beginning, but in the early 1960s matters came to a head in a more acute way than they had in 40 years. In a rare moment of solidarity, the three Toronto newspapers – the *Globe and Mail*, *Star*, and *Telegram* – sent a letter to Purcell in January 1962 complaining about the assessment increase of 6.3 per cent that took effect at the beginning of the year, and threatening to withdraw from membership if their fees were not reduced.[91] The publishers argued that with the continuing expansion of their own newsgathering operations, they were using CP copy "less than ever before," but costs continued to rise. In 1962, their combined assessment was $216,273, around one-eighth of all member contributions. One area where reductions could be made immediately, they argued, was CP's Newsfeatures service. For many CP members, this was an important expansion of CP's coverage beyond the bare-facts type of daily news that had long been its stock in trade. Newsfeatures provided interpretive and background articles that complemented the daily news – an important way for newspapers to compete with television[92] – but the Toronto papers supplied their own features, this being an area where having one's own distinctive coverage was seen as a competitive advantage. (For smaller papers, which typically faced less local competition, this was not a problem.) The Toronto publishers wanted Newsfeatures (which cost $86,000 a year) to be considered an extra service that would be paid for separately by those who used it, rather than a part of the general service that everyone paid for. In addition, they urged that the fees paid by CP's radio clients (through BN) should be raised, thus reducing the overall amount to be paid by newspapers. In determining assessments, the large contribution that the Toronto papers made to CP's pool of domestic news by virtue of their extensive local coverage – which they estimated cost more than $1 million annually – should be taken into account as well.

Summing up the letter at a special meeting of the board of directors, John Bassett of the *Telegram* made it clear that withdrawal was being seriously considered.

> Toronto members paid for a great deal of CP news they did not require, while paying extra for – as special services – a great deal of news they did require. The papers were getting close to the point where they felt that for less than their CP assessment they could get or create a news service more explicitly tailored to their needs. ... It was doubtful that the Toronto papers would continue to pay present rates – plus providing a return news service – for what they were getting now.

W.T. Munns, editor of the *Globe and Mail*, said each Toronto paper was paying $7,000 a month for CP, $1,000 of which was for extra services (such as the financial and race results). "Not much of what was received for the other $6,000 was used." J.D. MacFarlane of the *Telegram* reported that during the previous week, his paper had printed only 83 CP items (not including material from AP and Reuters). Beland Honderich of the *Star* reported that a spot check conducted on 25 January showed that his newspaper used 7.5 columns of CP material (again excluding

AP and Reuters) that day, filling 4.5 per cent of its news space, while smaller newspapers used much more (ranging from 36 columns in the St. Catharines *Standard* to 10 columns in the Guelph *Mercury*.) "It was obvious the Star was paying too much for what it was able to use."

Honderich also urged CP to seek more revenue from its radio and TV clients. Toronto radio stations paid $270 a week for the full CP report, which supplied between 14 and 72 newscasts a day. Others, however, replied that broadcasters were already making a substantial contribution; Charles Edwards, the manager of BN, noted that projected broadcasting revenue for 1962 was $544,792 (an increase of more than $75,000 from 1961), reducing the amount paid by newspapers for the overall news service by more than 30 per cent. R.A. Graybiel of the Windsor *Star* observed that revenue from broadcasting had almost quadrupled in four years. "It might be almost time to look at whether it was not reaching a danger point. CP could lose the Toronto members with less financial damage than it could lose broadcasting revenue." Charles Peters of the Montreal *Gazette* suggested that "it would take very little for private radio and CBC to set up independent news networks." If CP tried to double charges to radio, "this would be the end of CP's dealings with radio, and a step toward the end of the co-operative system among newspapers in Canada."

Besides Newsfeatures, the Toronto group objected to substantial spending on foreign coverage. Honderich said he found it "impossible to justify a four-man CP staff in London when half were working on features that might be obtained cheaper otherwise." The *Star* felt that CP international staff could be limited to one person in Washington, one at the UN, one or two in London, and occasional staffing for Canadian angles of European news. Again, this raised objections, such as from Walter Blackburn of the London *Free Press*: the Toronto papers couldn't expect "other members who want some international coverage written by Canadians to give up the advantage of co-operative cost-sharing through CP. Many papers could not afford their own coverage. ... He did not think members outside Toronto would want to restrict their foreign coverage to that provided by AP and Reuters." Munns replied that concentrating on domestic news "did not rule out staffers judiciously placed [abroad] – though not in extravagant numbers. ... there was a difference between staffers sent on specific assignments and staffers on full-time assignment abroad." W.B.C. Burgoyne of the St. Catharines *Standard* saw the dispute as "a basic difference of interest in what CP should do. Many newspapers wanted the co-operative saving of having CP do the basic coverage job."

Purcell, who was known as a tough negotiator, did not appear fazed by the threat of withdrawal, even when the extent of CP's reliance on the Toronto papers' local coverage was pointed out. He noted that CP already covered the Ontario legislature and many Toronto sports events with its own staff; "[w]ith an efficient scalping job, plus addition of some men, a good coverage job [in Toronto] could be done for $40,000 or $50,000 a year" without help from the *Star*, *Globe*, or *Telegram*. (An unpublished portrait of Purcell, written by a long-time CP employee, R.J. "Barney" Anderson, also claimed that Purcell had taken the preventive step of renewing CP's contracts with Reuters and AP before they expired to prevent the Toronto publishers from making separate agreements for their foreign news.[93])

Other CP members observed that they, too, had to pay higher fees. St. Clair McCabe, chairman of the Assessment Committee and representative of Thomson newspapers – the largest group in CP – noted that the increase for his newspapers was even higher than that imposed on Toronto.[94] D.B. Rogers of the Regina *Leader-Post* commented that not much Toronto news was used in the west, "but it had never occurred to him to complain." He described Newsfeatures as "an integral part of the service, a means of reporting in depth," which was "the newspapers' best defence against broadcasting." The Toronto papers could afford their own experts, but smaller papers couldn't: "If all took this selfish attitude CP was finished."

Several members resisted what they saw as a move towards making CP an à la carte rather than a comprehensive service. McCabe saw "a danger in chopping up the CP service into bits and pieces. As far as he was concerned, for instance, he could do without Reuters." Graybiel said the board was being asked to decide "whether CP dues should be based on consumption by individual papers. If so, that criterion would have to apply to all. It was a shaking principle for any co-operative even to consider."

More generally, McCabe warned against responding to the Toronto publishers' demands on an ad hoc basis. "It would be a mistake to jump too quickly, to change the population basis of assessment, to destroy the present formula. There could be great dissatisfaction at the annual meeting if the board subsidized some members at the expense of others." Peters (representing a Southam paper) concurred: whatever concessions were offered to Toronto would be demanded by everyone else. "The solution must be found in equity to all, not just to answer the Toronto problem." Munns, however, repeated that "the Toronto papers need something now to keep them in the membership." If their 1 January assessment increase was cancelled, that would be taken as "a suitable token gesture"; a longer-term solution could wait until the annual meeting at the end of April.

After the three Toronto representatives left the meeting, it became clear that their demands would not be met, at least not fully. McCabe complained about being presented with an ultimatum: "If such small groups of members could demand adjustments, CP would not amount to anything. Might it not be smart politics in the long run to let the Toronto papers leave CP and look for economies to overcome the lost revenue?" Walter Blackburn of the London *Free Press* said he initially felt some concession was required "but had almost reached the conclusion that no concession should be made because of problems that would arise elsewhere." If the Toronto papers withdrew, "CP would be damaged severely but could be held together and rebuilt." It was decided that the assessment increases for 1962 would be put into a suspension account pending a full report by a special committee (the executive committee, plus McCabe) on how CP's payment structure could be reformed, including spending reductions. But there was clearly little support for the idea of removing Newsfeatures from the general service; the discussion ended with comments that it was essential to preserve the CP service "in its present improved form" and that "nothing must be done to downgrade the news service." This was confirmed at a regular board meeting three months later where directors voted 13 to 1 to indicate "their personal opinion" that Newsfeatures was an integral part of the CP service.[95]

The special assessment committee accordingly stayed away from Newsfeatures in its consideration of possible cost reductions. On the contrary, the committee went out of its way to defend the service, describing it as "an integral part of the CP service, in fact one of its greatest improvements in recent years ... it provides the interpretative and background type of news required to keep newspapers competitive with radio, magazines, and television; it is invaluable to small and medium-size newspapers and has been of prime importance in the improvement these papers have shown over the last 10 years." Only modest cost reductions were proposed. The small honoraria paid to staff of member papers to act as CP's local liaison should be discontinued, for annual savings of just over $15,000 a year. CP's Newsmaps service, which provided maps to indicate the location and geographical context of news events, would be made an extra service, saving another $9,000. But that was all. The idea of cutting the $18,000 paid annually for off-hours coverage (i.e., coverage during the period when, say, a morning newspaper would not normally have reporters at work) would be considered, but the likelihood of this happening was indicated by Purcell's warning that such a step would cause "definite damage" to the news report. The fee structure for broadcasters was also "working well and should not be disturbed." [96]

By the time the issue came up again in September 1962, the assessment figures had been revised to take account of population statistics from the 1961 census, with the result that the charge to each Toronto paper was reduced by $5,000.[97] But this was not enough: Honderich continued to insist that the board acknowledge "that there is something basically wrong in the present CP assessment structure," and give "some indication that something might be done" about Newsfeatures and the off-hours coverage payments. "Then perhaps he would be prepared to wait." The only concession was a vague agreement to continue studying these questions. There was no guarantee that anything would change, Purcell told members, but there was "definite assurance of careful study ... perhaps something could be done."[98]

Ultimately, the solution was not found in cost-cutting. CP's assessments continued to increase through the decade: 5 per cent in 1965, 9 per cent in 1966, and 10 per cent in 1967.[99] The size of the editorial staff and the extent of services such as Newsfeatures steadily increased.[100] But the charges were distributed differently, with a move away from a system based on the population of each city (which had been the basis of assessment since CP was created) to one based more on the actual circulation of each newspaper, weighted so that the rate per thousand dropped as circulation increased. (Otherwise the formula would have led to "exorbitant charges" for large-circulation papers in Toronto and Montreal and unjustifiably low rates for the smallest papers.[101]) As Clark Davey, who was a member of the committee that devised the new assessment formula (and went on to become CP's president in the 1980s), explained in an interview, "everybody was happy" under the new system, which took effect in 1964. "The small papers paid less than they should have, the medium-sized papers paid more than they should have and the really big papers didn't pay as much as they should have."[102] The new approach was explicitly approved by Munns, presumably with the agreement of the other two Toronto newspapers;

in any case, there was no further talk of withdrawal.[103] If the Toronto publishers' attempts to limit CP's increasing costs and expanded service had been largely unsuccessful, their underlying concern about how much they paid had nonetheless been addressed.

In March 1961, Purcell told the executive committee that CP's five-year contracts with AP and Reuters were going to expire at the end of the year, and warned that Reuters was expected to "insist on a heavy increase."[104] In the event, the new Reuters contract rate was more than 40 per cent higher.[105] AP, now overseen by the "dour and tough" Wes Gallagher, increased its rate by a relatively modest 7.6 per cent in the new contract but by 20 per cent in the 1966–71 contract.[106] Reuters was increasingly interested in selling its full service (more extensive than the standard service provided via CP) directly to the CBC and large Canadian newspapers. By the end of the decade, even though the rates it was allowed to charge under its CP contract yielded virtually no profit, Glen Renfrew, Reuters' North American manager, reported that the arrangement "has worked to our advantage by getting us solid and consistent play in the leading newspapers and on the news services of the CBC." Indeed, Renfrew's CBC counterparts had recently told him "that Reuters was their leading source of international news, including news from the United States."[107] One difficulty arose when Reuters also arranged to sell its French-language service to newspapers that were nonmembers of CP, the elusive *Montréal Matin* and *Journal de Montréal*. CP was "strenuously opposed" to this arrangement, which would give up some of the leverage it had to induce the two French-language papers to join, "and would also object if it was indicated through Reuters that CP was responsible for the service being withheld from non-members."[108] The experiment was discontinued in light of CP's strong protests.[109]

The major change in the Reuters-AP-CP relationship came in 1967, when Reuters decided to begin its own newsgathering operation in the United States without relying on AP (or Dow Jones, which until then had been the British agency's main source of economic news).[110] This development came at the same time as Reuters began to focus on providing business information, now considered at least as important as general news.[111]

The early 1960s was, in many respects, a favourable time for Canadian newspapers. Aggregate circulation increased by 200,000 in the two years after 1958, and continued to increase, though somewhat more slowly, throughout the 1960s.[112] But this went along with increased scrutiny and criticism of the press. As CP's president, John Motz of the Kitchener-Waterloo (Ontario) *Record*, told the annual meeting in 1962, CP members had to face "general sniping at something called 'the press' – particularly generalizations such as that monopoly is a bad thing, that publishers are money-grubbers, that newspaper salaries are too low, that most of the news in newspapers" is provided by public-relations firms.[113] In part, this was the Canadian manifestation of a trend that had seen major government inquiries since the end of the Second World War into how well the press did its job in Britain and the United States.[114] The fact that a relatively healthy economic climate for newspapers went along with increasing consolidation and chain ownership was another concern.

One high-profile event that drew public attention to consolidation was the decision of the family-owned Vancouver *Sun* and Southam-owned *Province* to enter a joint operating agreement – essentially sharing production costs and advertising revenue, but maintaining separate newsrooms – under the umbrella of Pacific Press in 1957.[115] This was retroactively approved by the Restrictive Trade Practices Commission on grounds of economic necessity, but with a stipulation that the arrangement not be changed in a way that reduced either newspaper's independence.[116] In 1963, Max Bell bought the *Sun* for FP Publications, which meant that two of Canada's largest chains now shared the Vancouver market, bringing a call from T.C. Douglas of the New Democratic Party for a royal commission on press ownership.[117] Another major consolidation agreement came in 1965, when *The Globe and Mail* joined FP, making it the largest Canadian chain by circulation.[118] Between 1958 and 1970, the circulation of chain-owned newspapers increased from 25 per cent of the Canadian total to 47 per cent, and by the mid-1960s there was genuine competition between dailies in only eight Canadian cities.[119]

In the spring of 1964, a sharp decline in competition for election to the board of directors led to a wide-ranging debate about the influence of newspaper chains within CP. Almost half of CP's 103 members were now owned by chains. The Thomson chain owned 28 mostly small-town publications at the time;[120] the Southam chain owned nine newspapers (most in larger cities) and had a substantial interest in three others; and the FP chain owned by Max Bell and the Sifton family had six larger newspapers (seven after FP's purchase of *The Globe and Mail*). Fred Auger of the Southam-owned Vancouver *Province* suggested to the board of directors that chain ownership was partly responsible for the growing number of positions on the board filled by acclamation: "voting by the membership tended to support group [chain] candidates and this might keep down the number of nominations accepted by representatives of independent papers."[121] There was disagreement, however, about whether the growing representation of chains on the board was a necessarily bad thing. On one hand, Beland Honderich of the Toronto *Star* suggested that "it might be wise for groups to limit their board representation." They already accounted for nine out of 19 directors; that was "not a majority and not necessarily too big a share, but CP's image could be harmed if too many group men were elected."[122] Clifford Sifton of the Saskatoon *Star-Phoenix* made a similar point: "the public or the government might use it to CP's disadvantage if the news service as well as the newspaper industry became dominated by groups."[123] R.S. Malone said that FP Publications, which he represented, "had never voted as a group," but agreed that having a majority of directors from chains should be avoided.[124] Charles Peters of the Montreal *Gazette* agreed that "CP had been deprived of the services of some good men who did not feel they could be elected."

On the other hand, W.T. Munns of the *Globe and Mail* played down concerns about too many positions going to chain representatives: "it had been his experience ... that group men invariably placed the over-all interest of CP far ahead of the interest of their own groups."[125] R.H. Sutherland of the New Glasgow (Nova Scotia) *News*, a Thomson paper, denied that any chain could dominate CP, because candidates for the board had to get the general support of the membership to be elected. In any case, the prominence of chains meant that smaller Canadian papers – which accounted for almost all the Thomson newspapers – were "better represented on the CP board than ever." I.H. MacDonald of the Cornwall (Ontario) *Standard-Freeholder* (another Thomson paper) rejected a suggestion that chain representatives should be active publishers rather than head-office representatives; "he could not see how a publisher of a small paper might contribute as much, for example, as Mr. McCabe." (McCabe was in charge of Roy Thomson's newspaper operations in North America after Thomson moved to Britain in 1954.[126])

It was suggested that the problem might be resolved by having a nominating committee select a slate of candidates for the board who would be broadly representative. Kenneth Thomson, Roy Thomson's son and publisher of the Kirkland Lake (Ontario) *Northern News*, expressed misgivings about the idea, but was prepared to go along with it because it would "remove apprehension from the minds of Thomson Newspapers representatives. ...Whatever happened in today's voting for the three Ontario directorships, his group would be suspect." But Walter Blackburn of the London *Free Press* said voting was as much of a problem as nomination: "Sometimes members of groups voted for selected candidates. He had seen one group representative vote a fistful of proxies last year."[127] Eventually it was decided that no formal measures needed to be adopted, but that members should be made aware of their obligation to run for board positions.

A related problem, that very little spontaneous discussion took place at annual meetings, was noted in 1965 (the issue had also come up more than 10 years earlier[128]). Somewhat ironically, the problem was noted by the members of the executive committee, whose tight control of CP's strategy and operations meant there was not much role for ordinary members to play. One suggestion was that specific subjects might be put forward for discussion at meetings of the board and general membership rather than waiting for questions to arise spontaneously.[129] While this idea was never adopted, it reflected a growing sense that individual members, even though each still had one vote, had less and less to do with CP's overall direction as an organization. Another aspect of this was that as CP's operations became more complex, it was increasingly difficult for publishers, whose involvement with CP was necessarily on a part-time basis, to exercise executive functions in a meaningful way. In the spring of 1954, for example, Purcell visited Roy Thomson at his home outside Toronto, bearing "the speech he had written for Thomson's last presidential address."[130] (A previous president, Victor Sifton of the Winnipeg *Free Press*, was reported once to have said that his address was "as brief as Mr. Purcell has been able to make it."[131]) John Dauphinee, who replaced Purcell as general manager in 1969, told Douglas Amaron it was "inevitable" that the board of directors, the executive committee, and the president took their direction from CP's full-time managers, and especially the general manager. "I don't think that a board that meets twice a year is equipped to determine policy without guidance, and the only place that guidance can come from is management. CP is not like Imperial Oil that has directors that are fully employed all year round and go to meetings once a week or once a month."[132]

The establishment of a Press Council in Britain in 1953 – another manifestation of increased public scrutiny of the press – led to debate over whether a similar step should be taken in Canada. A striking aspect of the discussion was the widespread view that public confidence in journalism was fading. T.E. Nichols of the Hamilton *Spectator* warned the board of directors in the fall of 1968 about "a mounting hostility to the press – a feeling that the press is glib and irresponsible, stressing activist groups and giving a false picture of situations and events."[133] Beland Honderich of the Toronto *Star* said that he supported the idea of a press council, which would address three problems currently facing the news media: "a growing gap between what the communications industry does and what the public thinks; a lack of confidence in the press among business leaders who control advertising funds, raising a question whether sufficient advertising revenues will continue to be available; and the absence of a forum where people who feel they have been harmed by the press can take their cases." St. Clair Balfour of Southam agreed that "a proper press council would be a safety valve to release the pressure of public criticism and restore public confidence." Pressure for a press watchdog of some kind was particularly evident in Quebec, and journalists warned that if they did not establish some such forum themselves, a council would be forced upon them. Walter O'Hearn of the Montreal *Star* noted that Quebec newspapers had already been working towards the establishment of a provincial press council for two years. "He hoped it would not become a tool of government or a voice of unions only, but some sort of Quebec council was inevitable; a national press council would not satisfy Quebec." Maurice Dagenais of *La Presse* said Quebec journalists had been considering the idea for at least 10 years; "now all but one newspaper and most broadcasters were going along with the idea. There had been some fear that the Quebec government might use a provincial council to impose a form of censorship, but there was no possibility of this with a council set up along British lines" (i.e., a voluntary, industry-run organization). Dagenais argued that the press had to accept its responsibilities if it wished to preserve its freedom, specifically by recognizing "the right of reply by anyone disagreeing with its viewpoints." Gabriel Gilbert of *Le Soleil* added that unless a press council were established soon, "pressure from labor and political parties in Quebec will force legislation to control the press."

On the other hand, R.S. Malone of FP Publications said newspapers should look at their weaknesses, but considered formation of a press council premature. The British council had been established "because of extreme irresponsibility on the part of some newspapers there," but any abuses in Canada were less severe. St. Clair McCabe of the Thomson chain, with its mostly small-town publications, also urged caution. "Perhaps the council idea should be tried first in the big cities; he felt there was less problem in smaller centres where newspapers could be closer to their public." J.D. MacFarlane of the Toronto *Telegram* was virtually alone in rejecting the idea entirely. "Newspapers were not in a popularity contest," he argued. "A press doing its job would irritate people for various reasons." Setting up a council would simply give credence to the notion that the press was "sinful," and would provide governments with a means to "exert pressure on the press in times of emergency." The discussion did not lead to any decision, but it was clear that almost everyone recognized the emergence of a more critical climate and the need for some positive response. In any case, the creation of a press council in Quebec was generally seen as inevitable. (This happened in 1973; the Ontario Press Council was established in 1972.)

CP's policy on entrance fees – which in the past had operated to protect existing members from new competitors – changed substantially during the 1960s. In part, there was a growing realization that a restrictive policy was difficult to justify. But underlying this was the fact that with consolidation and chain ownership, the news business had become much less favourable to new competitors, so restrictive measures were less necessary. Until 1965, however, any new member was required to pay two years' subscription fees in advance. In large cities, this amounted to a substantial sum; when the short-lived Vancouver *Times* joined CP in 1964, the entrance fee was $105,382.[134] Beland Honderich of the Toronto *Star* told the board in April 1965 that he considered the present system of entrance fees "a deterrent intended to keep out competition"; a few months later, Walter Blackburn of the London *Free Press* said some other way should be found to establish the bona fides of an applicant for membership because the fee as it existed "might well be in restraint of trade."[135] While Honderich thought the entrance fee should simply be abolished, he expressed support for a less radical proposal that would reduce the amount and provide a rebate of 50 per cent after one year's membership. Others suggested a $100,000 ceiling on the entrance fee.

The notion that current CP members had had built up a share in the organization's equity and that newcomers should be expected to make an equivalent contribution was frequently cited by those who supported entrance fees. A-F Mercier of *Le Soleil*, T.E. Nichols of the Southam-owned Hamilton *Spectator*, and R.A. Graybiel of the Windsor *Star* were jointly quoted as asserting that existing CP members had "built up a valuable equity in their co-operative and there should be no bargain-counter sale of the right of membership."[136] Aurèle Gratton of *Le Droit* and Kenneth Thomson also insisted that new members should be required to make some payment. R.S. Malone argued that the fee should be "much smaller, based carefully on actual equity and at a level that could be justified to anyone." CP's desire to attract *Montréal Matin* into the membership by waiving the entrance fee played into the debate: as Fred Auger of the Vancouver *Province* observed, "it would be awkward to have any Vancouver investor who lost money in the *Times* ask him to explain why no fee was collected from papers entering membership in Montreal."[137]

A proposal to reduce the entrance fee by 50 per cent (making it one year's assessment rather than two) and collect it over five years was eventually approved in April 1966. When this was discussed at the general meeting, Nichols of the *Spectator* observed that "nowadays most newspapers are in strong monopoly positions," making protection against new competitors unnecessary.[138] Still, the proposal led to heated debate. St. Clair McCabe argued that CP was "selling the farm too cheap" and wanted the proposal sent back for further study. Others, however, stressed that the appearance of restricting competition was damaging to CP. St. Clair Balfour of Southam said that "politically, present fees look too high, particularly in major centres like Montreal and Vancouver." Ralph Costello, speaking for the committee that developed the proposal, said the entire group "had come to the strong view that the present level of entrance fees looked like a deterrent to competition." The reduction was then approved, with some suggestion that further reductions might follow. It was also agreed that the board could reduce the entrance fee for a new member without consulting existing members within a 50-mile radius, "thus eliminating any possible implication that these members have a veto power."[139] These were substantial changes, but the fee charged in cities or towns where a CP newspaper was already in operation was still twice as high as in places with no competition.

In 1967, the entrance fee was scrapped and replaced by a system of discounts for continuous membership, increasing from 5 per cent after one year to 25 per cent after five years. This still had the effect of requiring new members to pay considerably more than established competitors, but it was also easier to defend. Two years later, it was proposed that a new member should pay an entrance fee equal to one year's assessment, with the entire amount to be returned in three annual installments after the first year.[140] Some members of the board argued that no further change was needed, because the continuity discount "had gone a long way toward eliminating the old criticism of entrance fees."[141] But with CP's appearance before the Senate Committee on Mass Media only a few months away, others stressed that the discount system still imposed an extra charge on new members, which "might be hard to justify to a public inquiry." With the decision in 1970 to return the entire entrance fee over three years, CP finally did away with a restrictive, anticompetitive approach to new members that had lasted for more than 50 years.

The key development in CP's often tense relationship with broadcasters during the 1960s was a substantial increase in revenue, which reduced the amount that newspapers had to contribute to the operation of the news service. In 1954, when BN was established to manage CP's service to private broadcasters, the net payment to CP was a mere $12,756.[142] By 1961, CP's revenue from private broadcasters and the CBC was more than $400,000, 25 per cent of its total revenue;[143] by 1965, the amount was $680,000, about one-third of total revenue.[144]

There were two main reasons for this rapid increase. First, the number of BN's clients rose steadily, from 112 in 1954 to 235 in 1961.[145] The establishment of BN, which had equal representation from broadcasters and CP-member newspapers on its board, had gone a long way towards easing broadcasters' concerns about CP's attitude towards radio and television. BN's success essentially chased UP, which previously (as BUP) had been such a formidable competitor, out of the general-news market for Canadian broadcasters. In 1964, the executive committee was told that UPI (the successor to United Press) would no longer offer a separate radio news wire, which meant that its value to broadcasters "would be primarily as a supplementary service."[146] While the number of BN's television clients increased substantially, radio subscribers did, too; one of the consequences of television's emergence was that radio broadcasters focused more on news. "For many radio stations, the future appeared to lie in developing information broadcasting," BN's brief to the Davey Committee on Mass Media concluded; news was "vital for the continued existence of many radio stations."[147]

The second source of increased broadcasting revenue was the CBC. The public broadcaster's payments to PN rose even faster than BN's other sources of revenue.[148] In 1942, when the CBC began paying CP for its news service, the rate was $40,000 a year; by 1961, the annual rate had soared to $311,400, reaching $475,000 by the early 1970s.[149] William Hogg, a former CP employee who now handled CBC's relations with the news agency, reported somewhat glumly to his superior in 1961 that CBC had "never been in a good bargaining position" because "we are so dependent on CP." A survey of CBC newsrooms across Canada showed that more than 60 per cent of CBC's radio news and 40 per cent of its television news came directly from CP. "Editors advise that CP indispensable," Hogg concluded. Three years later, in an interview done for the Royal Commission on Bilingualism and Biculturalism, Hogg reported that CBC was less dependent on CP than in the past (especially for local television news), and considered CP's service expensive. CBC was sometimes tempted to end the CP contract and establish its own national newsgathering operation, but "independence is simply not practical. The cost would be unjustifiably great."[150] In view of its substantial payment, the CBC "inquired informally" in the early 1960s whether it might have a representative on CP's board of directors, but this was rejected on the grounds that directors received too much confidential information. It was suggested in return that the PN board meet annually with a CBC delegation, and this was adopted.[151] CP executives considered the meetings a success, paving the way for closer cooperation with CBC news staff generally, though the CBC's impressions were not quite as favourable; in 1966, Eugene Hallman, the vice president of programming, reported that CP had informed them about plans to improve the speed of its service to newspapers, but didn't mention broadcasting: "CP's thinking is still almost wholly print-oriented."[152] Hallman looked forward to a time when CP's value to CBC would be mainly supplementary, providing tips about stories "which our own reporters or correspondents can follow up." Clark Davey, who was a CP director in the 1960s and later CP president, recalled that the CBC contract was "a sweetheart arrangement" for CP. "My sense was that the CBC didn't make a lot of demands on CP, that it was quite happy to take this overwhelming flood of national Canadian copy ... this was a guarantee that the CBC wasn't going to miss something that was happening in Canada. And CBC paid through the nose for it, over the years."[153] Over all, Davey observed, selling news to broadcasters worked out very favourably for CP:

> We'd already collected the news and we traded it with each other; we now had a chance, with very little manipulation, to sell it to a third party. And even though the third party was a "competitor," the money that was gene-rated through this recycling operation, which is basically what it was in those days, was fantastic. ... And it was one of the kind of unspoken secrets of Canadian Press: don't let anybody find out how much money we were making from those guys.

Despite the fact that public and private broadcasters paid for a sub-stantial and growing share of CP's overall operations during the 1960s, many CP members continued to express concerns about competition (especially from radio); others argued that broadcasters' fees were too low. In 1961, the executive committee heard familiar complaints that CP news provided to BN was broadcast before the newspaper that did the original reporting could appear in print.[154] The board of directors discussed whether it would be possible to embargo local news on the BN wire to prevent this. St. Clair McCabe said this was a particular problem in small communities, such as British Columbia's Okanagan Valley. He recognized that BN couldn't be expected to do without local news entirely, but it was "reasonable to require a radio station not to broadcast news supplied by the paper until it was on the street."[155] R.P. McLean of the Kelowna *Courier* complained that in his city, "much of the radio station's regional news came via BN from the *Courier*'s newsroom. He did not object to competition but resented supplying it with all his sales material." J.R.H. Sutherland of the New Glasgow (Nova Scotia) *News* said many smaller newspapers simply held back their local news from CP "to keep it off the air," adding that the situa-tion would be improved if "broadcasters could be sold on the idea of not using newspaper stories until a newspaper is published." But Walter Blackburn of the London *Free Press* warned that "[i]f radio were denied the newspapers' local news, stations would be forced to improve their own coverage and might be led to form their own news co-operative. Radio would not understand a local-news cutoff." Charles Edwards, BN's manager, said radio stations "increasingly understand newspaper

problems and want to be fair." Radio stations might be willing to withhold local stories if it could be guaranteed that their broadcasting competitors would do the same, "but this seemed impractical in view of the
wide coverage area of local stations." He agreed that any suggestion of
an embargo on local news "would be dangerous to BN's competitive
situation."

Instead of wanting to impose tougher conditions on BN clients,
Edwards argued that they deserved better treatment from CP. In the
early 1960s, he consistently urged that BN fees should level off rather
than being increased, in view of broadcasting's "substantial" contribution to CP revenues.[156] Others disagreed, including some CP members
who were also involved in broadcasting. For example, John Bassett –
who was publisher of the Toronto *Telegram* as well as controlling share-
holder of CFTO-TV[157] –told the executive committee that he paid more
for UPI's picture service than for BN even though he considered BN
more valuable. "He wanted to be sure that BN was getting enough
for the news." This was tied directly to the overall cost concerns of
the three big Toronto dailies: "Toronto newspapers were concerned
about the increasing cost of CP and felt they were paying more than
their share." The clear implication was that more revenue from
broadcasting was one solution.[158] Beland Honderich of the Toronto *Star*
was adamant that the value of local news that broadcasters received
from CP – which he estimated to be a minimum of $2.5 million – was
not fairly reflected in the fees they paid.[159] (As Edwards recalled later in
an interview with Douglas Amaron, Honderich regularly complained
that his newspaper "had, whatever, 200 reporters, 250 or something,
and covering all the suburban areas. And when the Toronto *Star* came
off the press with each edition, there were taxis from each station lined
up in the alley, to pick up the paper and rush it out to their stations."[160])
At the 1967 annual meeting, Honderich (supported by Cleo Mowers
of the Lethbridge *Herald*) again complained that private broadcasters
paid too little for the news they received.[161] However, Edwards warned
that broadcasters were "actively considering the possibility of setting
up their own news service" and that "any move by CP to increase its
charges drastically would certainly precipitate such a move." A study
was conducted, which showed that, after steadily increasing for many
years, the percentage contribution of broadcasting to CP's budget might
decline in the future.[162] But while the subject continued to be raised at
various CP meetings, notably by Honderich,[163] no substantial changes
were made by 1970. This might have been because CP's top managers

had little enthusiasm for the idea; as Purcell told I. Norman Smith of the Ottawa *Journal* in 1969, this was "perhaps our most important problem, except that it isn't a problem and really only affects about three CP members."[164] By 1969, broadcasting revenue offset CP members' assessments by 37 per cent.[165]

It was striking that CP's continuing uneasiness over its relationship with broadcasting had more to do with radio than the newer medium, television. But this was understandable. Unlike radio, television stations did not have hourly newscasts that could report local news items before they appeared in print; and in terms of revenue, radio stations outnumbered television stations as BN clients by a ratio of around five to one. Discussions of television as a competitor focused more abstractly on the need for newspapers to provide more analytical and background coverage (reflected in the steady growth of CP Newsfeatures). In a speech to the Commonwealth Press Union in 1965, Purcell argued that television had almost killed radio, but radio survived by changing its focus from entertainment programs to news – "news as often as possible."[166] Meanwhile, television made the most of its advantages in news coverage, notably "fabulous" speed and "unrivalled production on set-piece stories like sport, space shots and elections." What kept newspapers from being eclipsed was "the cherished advantage of the printed page in preserving a tangible, extensive and detailed record," along with their ability to provide "meaning and the background" to what people had already heard about on TV or radio. Newspapers' role had shifted "from the purely factual to the explanatory." In fact, newspapers had an opportunity "to capitalize on the increased news-interest among the millions who watch the set-piece sports events, space shots and elections" by answering "the myriad questions that TV spot spectaculars leave unanswered." Thus they could "fill a reader demand that TV has created." Handled properly, a new medium did not necessarily supplant an older one, but could provide new opportunities.

In March 1969, the Senate of Canada voted to establish a special committee to examine the mass media in Canada.[167] In view of the increased public and governmental scrutiny of the press in other western countries since the end of the Second World War, Canada was probably overdue for a systematic examination. But for CP, as for other Canadian news organizations, the idea of having to defend itself in public was not especially welcome. A few months after the committee was established, but before its hearings began, J.R.H. Sutherland, publisher of the New Glasgow (Nova Scotia) *News* and CP's president, told Purcell that he had taken a trip to Halifax to hear "the boss senator" (Davey) give a speech about the committee to weekly newspaper editors. Sutherland reported that he "did [his] best ... to keep from grinding my teeth. I was mindful of words from [Norman Smith] that we must pretend to welcome this inquiry."[168]

Smith, publisher of the Ottawa *Journal* and one of CP's longest-serving directors, collaborated closely with Purcell in writing CP's brief for the committee. Their approach was mostly defensive: to produce a neutral, low-key document that would not provoke aggressive questions or sarcastic comments from the committee members.[169] Smith expected that the committee would probably subject individual newspapers or chains to harsh scrutiny; in this situation CP's best strategy was to keep a low profile. Not everyone agreed with this approach, however. St. Clair Balfour, president of Southam, complained that the brief didn't do CP justice but was "coldly formal," painting CP as "nothing more than an efficient organization without a soul." On the contrary, CP was "a great national institution whose service to the country should be played up, not down."[170] But Smith was adamant: "We may be sure they're loaded for bear if we claim too much."

CP's coverage of international news was one area where criticism was anticipated (quite accurately, as it turned out). Purcell forwarded to Smith a question that Beland Honderich had posed to the executive committee when considering a draft of the brief: "Why do we not get a Canadian view on foreign affairs."[171] (Or as Purcell expressed the point: "If one paper like The New York Times can do it why can't 100 Canadian papers do it?"[172]) A suggested response was provided, too: "The cost would be prohibitive – foreign staff of 50 or 60 or 70 would be just beyond our means." Sutherland, CP's president, raised the same issue a few days later: "[T]he strongest criticism I ever hear is that CP doesn't staff the world AP style – or CBC. I've had to explain it as a matter of dollars and cents and that we don't tap the taxpayer nor want to. I further point out that a report from a New Zealander working for AP in Spain ... is as objective as if he were from Saskatoon."[173]

Detailed information about CP's foreign-news supply was provided in a background memorandum prepared by John Dauphinee (who took over from the retiring Purcell at the end of November, 1969) and Charles Edwards of BN.[174] During the week of 19–25 October 1969, 743 items of foreign news (not including sports or routine financial reports) arrived at CP headquarters from its New York bureau, totalling 177,000 words. Of these, AP accounted for 426 items (57 per cent of the total) totalling 100,000 words (56 per cent); Reuters had 224 items (30 per cent), accounting for 40,000 words (22 per cent); CP had 93 items (12.5 per cent), amounting to 37,000 words (21 per cent). With an average length of almost 400 words, CP's stories were more likely to be features than the shorter, news-focused items provided by AP (average length of 234 words) and Reuters (178 words). For CP's French service, 75 per cent of foreign news came from AFP, with about 13 per cent from CP and the rest from AP and Reuters.

"World news agencies have no over-riding national bias," Dauphinee and Edwards wrote. "Most of their news from any country comes from the national news agency and the newspapers of that country." Most reporters for international agencies were nationals of whatever country they were located in, and because AP and Reuters sold their news all around the world, they could not afford a slant, which would reduce their sales. The decision to withdraw CP's correspondent from Moscow earlier that year was made "because the news value of the assigned [sic] proved negligible – our allies were doing a solid, balanced job." CP did not consider it necessary or economically feasible to have journalists in all the major news centres of the world, but would "assign its own staff reporter or reporters anywhere when there are specific newsworthy Canadian angles that night not be covered adequately by our allied agencies."

The CP delegation appeared before the committee on 10 December, the second day of hearings. In his opening remarks, Sutherland noted that CP's written brief was "just supposed to be a businesslike and factual document trying to give some idea of how CP works," and acknowledged that some people had wanted something more inspiring. As publisher of the New Glasgow *News*, a newspaper with a circulation of 10,000, Sutherland was well placed to make one of the strongest arguments in CP's arsenal:

> Because of CP – and only because of CP – the New Glasgow *News* can have the same news report as is provided to the much larger papers in Sydney and Halifax and Saint John and Moncton.
>
> If I do my job as publisher, the people of my community will be as well informed as any Canadians.

Amid allegations of monopolistic practices, inadequate foreign report-ing, and paternalistic labour relations, among other shortcomings, this was an argument that would carry weight with the most sceptical observer.

Questioning of CP's representatives was pointed but far from hostile. The first question to Dauphinee, now general manager, concerned CP's system of entrance fees, reflecting the view that CP imposed onerous conditions on new entrants to discourage competition. (The written brief quoted CP bylaws which stated that membership was open "to the widest extent compatible" with the expectation that a new member can become a "self-sustaining business enterprise.") Dauphinee explained the recently established continuity discount, under which a new member's fees were reduced by 5 per cent annually for the first five years (which meant that the newcomer initially paid 25 per cent more than an established member).[175] He also noted that a proposal to require a new member to pay its entire first year's fee in advance, with no other entrance requirement, was being considered.[176] (This was adopted in 1970.) Asked directly whether CP's existing members could prevent a new entrant from coming in, Sutherland insisted that no one had been turned down in this way since the mid-1930s.[177] (This, as we have seen, was a questionable assertion.[178]) This was the point that *The Globe and Mail* stressed in its coverage of CP's appearance before the committee, in an article headlined "CP head denies discrimination against admitting new members."[179]

The adequacy of CP's French service was another potentially controversial subject. CP noted in its presentation that the French service now had 21 French-speaking reporters and editors, compared to six when it began in 1951. It provided almost 35,000 words a day of international and general domestic news in French; about half was original reporting by CP staff or "return news" from member papers. "Thus it is inaccurate to say that CP's Service in French is simply a translation service." Gabriel Gilbert of *Le Soleil* was asked why the number of French-language members of CP had been six in 1917 and had only increased to seven by 1969, when there were 11 French-language newspapers in Quebec.[180] This was clearly not an occasion for the kind of frank discussion that CP had held internally; Gilbert replied simply that for non-subscribing papers, "it must be mainly a matter of budget,"[181] adding that CP had been trying for several years to induce *Montreal Matin* to join, but without success. When committee counsel Yves Fortier asked Gilbert directly whether he "receive[s] adequate service from Canadian Press as a French-Canadian newspaper publisher in Quebec," the reply was simple: "Definitely."[182] But Claude Ryan of *Le Devoir*, who testified later that day, gave a more negative assessment: "French-language newspapers are seriously handicapped as compared with their English-speaking colleagues."[183] Most English-language papers in Ontario and Quebec received twice as much news as their French-language counterparts.[184] In Ottawa, CP had only three French-speaking journalists as opposed to 10 who worked in English. CP's copy often arrived too late for *Le Devoir*'s deadlines, and in many cases the newspaper had to translate it into French. CP's brief acknowledged that French-language papers received less news, adding that "they realize that this is dictated by financial factors and the directors of CP are constantly working to improve the situation." Still, Ryan's public criticism carried considerable weight.

As expected, the question of CP's foreign news coverage came up as well. The brief adopted an almost combative stance on this issue:

The suggestion is sometimes made that CP should gather all its own foreign news to assure freedom from 'foreign bias.' (Paradoxically, the suggestion seeks to have Canadians read foreign news written from a 'Canadian viewpoint.')

To have CP men in all 75 or so important countries would be gratifying but it is not economically feasible. Nor is it necessary.

CP does not rely on any one foreign news service or on any service with a "foreign bias." The Associated Press, Reuters and Agence France-Presse all must be objective news services because they serve many hundreds of newspapers in scores of countries. The nationality and character of these papers box the compasses of geography, creed and politics. ...

[A]t New York, London, Washington, Paris – and at head office in Toronto – senior editors are continuously vigilant against any suggestion of non-objectivity in news stories not clearly attributed to the source.

Fortier asked Sutherland whether "ideally" CP should not have its own staff in foreign countries "rather than having to rely on foreign news services."[185] Sutherland acknowledged that cost was a limiting factor: but even if CP had staff wherever AP, Reuters or AFP did, "in many instances it would be a duplication. The actual story would remain the same."[186] Dauphinee was quick to say that the main issue was not cost, but "providing top-notch news service without waste." The experience of operating a Moscow bureau for four years had provided important lessons: "the high cost of maintaining that Moscow office was not justified by the relatively small amount of material that we obtained that we did not already have access to" through AP or Reuters. In the past year, CP's policy of assigning reporters to international stories "when

there is a specific Canadian interest" had led to CP coverage of sto-
ries in Iceland, the Netherlands, Belgium, the United Kingdom, France,
Czechoslovakia, Hungary, Yugoslavia, the Middle East, Nigeria, and
Central America.

Following up on the cost question, and addressing CP's reputation
as obsessively frugal, Fortier asked Dauphinee whether the budget was
"tight or loose." Dauphinee replied that it was "flexible" – a response
that evoked "a chortle in the back of the room."[187] Dauphinee said later
in an interview with Douglas Amaron that some listeners considered it
"a smart-alec remark," but that was not his intention.

> What I said was that it was flexible to the extent that if I had a program
> that I felt needed to be carried out, anything that I needed money for, if I
> presented it right to the board, I would get the money. This was [about]
> whether we had enough money for foreign coverage, which I think was
> really the key. ... If as general manager I said that it was absolutely essen-
> tial that we have an extra $100,000 to put four people in the Congo or four
> people in India, if I sold it right, the money would have been provided.

Dauphinee added that CP's budget had doubled in the past 11 years,
and the staff had increased by one-third. Fortier pressed his cross-
examination, however: "Is it your statement that you are not prevented from doing any work of a special nature on account of financial
resources?"[188] Dauphinee replied that if CP decided a story was worth
covering, "then there is no problem of budget." Asked whether, for
example, CP could expand its arts coverage with the existing budget,
Dauphinee said he could not do so immediately, but could do so within
six months "if the need is there, and if the problem could be solved at
the Board of Directors."

Overall, the CP executives felt their appearance before the committee had gone well. "We had a very good day," Dauphinee recalled in
his interview with Amaron. "We went out to Norman [Smith]'s house
afterwards. Everybody was very happy."[189]

However, other witnesses before the committee were much more
critical of CP. The Canadian Labour Congress criticized CP's foreign
news coverage, describing it as "little more than a collecting and editing
agency." It suggested that CP's weakness in this area reflected Canadian
publishers' unwillingness to spend money for a good news service. The
CLC brief also proposed that trade unions or cooperatives might get

involved in publishing newspapers to counter a lack of competition, but warned that these would have to be able to compete fairly: "There should be no arbitrary exclusion from access to wire services."[190] The ITU made the same point in its presentation.[191]

The testimony of Pierre Péladeau, publisher of *Le Journal de Montréal*, was particularly damning. CP operated like a "private club that discriminates in selection of new members," he charged. Péladeau recalled that when *Le Journal* began publishing in 1964 during a strike at *La Presse* that prevented the newspaper from publishing, CP spelled out "impossible conditions" for becoming a member, including an entrance fee of $136,000.[192] "We thought it a very clear manner of indicating to us that the administrators of this agency did not want to supply us with their services." *Le Journal* ended up signing a contract with UPI for less than half of what CP was proposing to charge. CP's approach was not to refuse new applicants explicitly, but to "render admission so inaccessible that, without appearing to do so, they discriminate in their selection." (He added that since CP had now dropped its entrance fees, *Le Journal* would probably join CP.) All in all, anyone following press coverage of the committee's hearings would have been left with the image of CP as, in effect, a cartel that excluded new competitors as a matter of course.[193]

Sutherland replied to CP's critics in his presidential address at the 1970 general meeting. The complaints about entrance fees (such as Péladeau's) referred to policies that were no longer in force, he insisted, and even the continuity discount was about to be abolished. As for charges that CP operated like a private club to keep out new members, he asserted that no member had the right to veto a new applicant, either in its own city or elsewhere.[194] CP had also been criticized as a monopoly, to which Sutherland replied that while almost all Canadian newspapers and broadcasting stations did indeed rely on CP, it was "not a monopoly in the ordinary unfavourable connotation of that word."

> There are monopolies granted by a state or ruler. That doesn't apply to us. There are monopolies created by the acquisition of competitors. That doesn't apply to us either . ... Quality of service – not anything sinister or contrary to public interest – is the reason. Why should anyone object to that?

Like many defences of CP's structure and activities, this might have gratified its members but would not necessarily convince outside critics.

Although restraint of competition had clearly been the main thread of criticism, the Senate committee's final report did not emphasize this aspect of CP's operations. Indeed, the committee's general assessment was extremely positive: over all, "we hold a pretty high opinion of Canadian Press." CP did the job of exchanging news among its members "supremely well .... it supplies a daily news report that is fast, comprehensible, reliable, tough, and more colourful than it is often given credit for." Demands and complaints from members kept the organization "on its toes." CP's operation in two languages was praised: "In this, and in its basic job of information exchange between the regions, CP is a strong force for national unity."[195] As for complaints that CP kept new members out "either by black-balling or making the cost of entry prohibitively high," the committee reported that it "could find no evidence that this is the case, though it may have been close to the truth in former years," and noted approvingly that the continuity discount system had recently been dropped.[196] CP's decision to provide service to the short-lined Vancouver *Times* in 1964–65, despite its belief that the newspaper could not survive for long, was evidence that new competitors were not excluded.

The complaints of French-language newspapers were considered more serious; endorsing Claude Ryan's comments, the report asserted that French-language CP subscribers "can fairly claim that they receive a service that is inferior to all the rest."[197] French-language members were left with an unpalatable choice: "either (i) be satisfied with the synthetic fare provided daily in French by the CP; or (ii) make their own translations and adaptations of the Canadian coverage that comes to them in English ... which is generally fresher and more complete than that available in French."[198] There was, however, "no quick solution." Costs had to be taken into account; the committee quoted Ryan's observation that the French service was already "subsidized to an abnormal extent in relation to the contributions of the French-language members alone." Over all, then, CP was commended for "its determined effort to give adequate service to its French-language members." Little had changed since the conclusions of the 1964 study committee: French-language subscribers believed that CP "is doing everything it can to meet their needs. So do we."

The committee's main criticism concerned CP's reliance on AP, Reuters, and AFP for international news. CP should do more of this coverage itself, "reporting the world scene *as Canadians speaking to*

Canadians."[199] CP's assertion that this was unnecessary was noted, but if so, why have Canadians in Washington, London, Paris, and at the United Nations at all? Associated Press is

> a fine service, but it is an American service, and no amount of tinkering with AP copy in CP's New York office will give it a Canadian character. An American reporter, writing for an American audience, writes in the American idiom, which is not yet the Canadian idiom. He writes from a background of American experience and American national interest, which are not the Canadian experience and the Canadian interest. He uses American illustrations which are not Canadian illustrations, and he draws on a literature, a history, and a political tradition which are his and not ours.
>
> To an importer of widgets, the nationality and allegiance of his supplier are not particularly important. To an importer of news they are crucial.
>
> Every reporter has a bias. We think it is immensely important that the reporters who give us our picture of the world should reflect the kind of bias that Canadians tend to share, rather than the bias that Americans or Frenchmen or Englishmen tend to share.[200]

The echoes of CP's original application to the Canadian government for a subsidy in 1916[201] were deafening, if apparently unplanned.

In more practical terms, the committee suggested that an expanded foreign-news staff should concentrate on analytical and situational writing – the kind of thing that was becoming increasingly popular in CP's Newsfeatures service – and leave daily spot-news coverage to the other agencies. CP's decision to withdraw its Moscow correspondent because he was restricted to writing "specials" and could not compete with AP and Reuters on spot news was exactly the wrong approach – "those 'specials' may have told readers a lot more about Russia and eastern Europe than reports of diplomatic comings and goings, or the managed news announcements rewritten from TASS."[202] CP gave the same reason for not posting a correspondent in China, "where Canada and China have succeeded in establishing diplomatic relations" (and the United States had not yet done so).[203] If CP hired six foreign correspondents at an annual cost of $40,000 each, that would add $10,000 a year to the assessment of the big Toronto dailies, $3,800 to that of a paper with a circulation of 50,000, and about $1,200 for a paper with 10,000 circulation. In this way, the smallest papers would get "six writers of international stature, explaining for its readers the trend of affairs in the world's news centres" for around $100 a month, about 25 per cent of what a local reporter would be paid: "A bargain." If six correspondents were considered too many, CP could start with three. "Only begin."[204]

Persuasive as it may have seemed, this recommendation had little chance of being adopted. The revolt of the Toronto papers in 1962 had made it quite clear that they would not put up with paying higher fees for an expanded foreign-news service, especially one that so closely duplicated the situational writing that their own correspondents provided. The policy of covering international stories with significant Canadian angles on a per-occasion basis was a typical CP compromise between the interests of large, wealthy papers and smaller, less wealthy ones, and was very unlikely to change.

For CP, the Senate committee report was seen as very good news. Selectively ignoring the strong recommendation about expanded foreign coverage, Smith congratulated Dauphinee on the "enthusiastic tribute" to CP in the report. This was "doubly gratifying because that committee looked into all the criticisms and found them wanting."[205] Ten years later, another federal commission of inquiry would scrutinize CP with a more jaundiced eye; in retrospect, the almost sunny tone of the Davey committee's comments on CP seemed to mark the end of an era.

～◦⁀◦～

The end of a decade does not necessarily correspond with the close of a historical era, but one development in 1969 marked an important change in how CP operated: Gillis Purcell retired after 41 years at CP, 24 of them as general manager. CP employees' assessments of his personality and approach are largely in agreement, describing him as "tough and rugged ... frugal with praise and devastating with criticism"; "a son of a bitch in a lot of ways, but he also was a man of some depth"; "a hugely dominant personality ... very, very demanding."[206] According to Mel Sufrin, "the guy really was brilliant, no question. He was a bit of a martinet, could be really nasty with people, but they really put out for him. And the result was a quality news report."[207] Ian Munro, who worked at CP from 1928 to 1978 and ended his career as head of the traffic department, said Purcell "would take on anybody. He would take on the chairman of the board just as well as he'd take on the office boy, you know. And he was a tough bugger but he also had a kindness to him that was different, you know."[208] Charles Bruce, who worked closely with Purcell for many years, said that to outsiders, "CP staffers seemed more a cult than an organization, with Purcell as the resident guru."[209]

Clark Davey recalled his first encounter with Purcell at a CP regional meeting of Ontario editors in the 1960s:

[T]he meeting was in St. Thomas, in the old hotel in St. Thomas. There was this great wide staircase going up to the second floor and ... Purcell was standing at the head of the staircase, sort of greeting everybody and saying hello to them and drinking his favourite Mount Gay rum. ... I noticed that when Purcell's drink ran out, he put his hand out, empty like that, and one of the CP minions made haste to fill that empty hand with a glass with the right mixture in it! I thought, man, that's power.

A lot of CP staffers had a kind of a residual fear of GP but they all had a tremendous respect for him. He really, really knew what he was doing. He knew how to make that organization hum, he really did. And he worked very, very hard.

John Dauphinee, who succeeded Purcell as general manager and was a much less combative figure, recalled in an interview with Douglas Amaron that Purcell's approach had been shaped in some respects by his early years with CP.

Gil had been there for a quarter of a century, and he worked on the tradition that somehow you cut corners, you saved money, you made special deals. CP never paid its way with AP or Reuters, or with the telegraph companies.

There was always a deal. Everything was a personal challenge, a victory. He took us to the brink of war with AP on one contract renewal and he ended up paying exactly what Wes Gallagher had asked for in the first place. But we were at the point when there was talk at meetings of whether we'd have the AP service and this sort of thing.[210]

Amaron, who had also worked closely with Purcell for many years, asked Dauphinee about the views he had heard from some CP members that Purcell "ran a one-man show and pretty well bulldozed the Executive Committee and the board. ... Charlie Peters [of the Montreal *Gazette*] felt that the members were frightened of him; that management was running CP under Gil's domination far more than the members were running CP."

Dauphinee said that description was "probably true to the extent that Gil had been there for 25 years and everybody felt he knew so much about CP and what it was supposed to be that there was some question whether it was safe to raise a serious question because you were going to get slapped down by someone who was accepted as God by a great number of people at whatever meeting you're talking about."[211]

By every account, then, Purcell was a dominating, and domineering, figure. His close attention to every detail of CP's operations, and the certainty that anyone who failed to meet his standards would be sharply criticized, had much to do with the ethos of the organization. CP was an enormously complex operation, collecting news from scores of sources in Canada and around the world, conducting original reporting in its eight Canadian and three foreign bureaus, collating and editing everything that was collected, and setting priorities on the fly for transmitting 300,000 words a day to some 400 clients (including radio and television clients of BN). All this took place while facing a "deadline every minute" – the pressure of time was constant and unrelenting. Smooth operation, the avoidance of errors and miscues, demanded a near-obsessive attention to how the system worked, awareness of success and quick, unfailing and sometimes ruthless correction of failure. The drawbacks of Purcell's outsize personality were clear: for example, it was hard to imagine his paternalistic and personalized management style ever accommodating an editorial union at CP (which was eventually established in 1976). But Purcell had led important developments in CP's editorial operations, such as the creation and expansion of the French service, and had overseen a continuous process of technological and editorial modernization. Between 1958 and 1969, CP's budget more than doubled, to almost $3.7 million.[212] The bill for news staff salaries had increased at an even faster rate; after the desert years of the anti-Guild campaign, the 1945 promises of a stronger and larger staff were finally being realized. Members' assessments had only risen by 77 per cent, though, thanks to the strong flow of revenue from broadcasting. Although tensions remained and continued, CP's embrace of broadcasting turned out in retrospect to be one of the best decisions the organization had ever made.

7 Covering the News, 1920–1970

The previous chapters focused mainly on Canadian Press as an organization, one that is of particular interest because of its dedication to
the production and distribution of news. News-agency histories, especially those produced by insiders, typically focus on the major stories
that their organizations handled. Reflecting the importance of journalistic competition, they point with special pride to occasions when the
agency sent out the news before its rivals.[1] To commemorate the 75th
anniversary of its founding, CP produced its own version of such a
volume in 1997, with accounts of how it covered the 1917 Halifax explo-
sion, the Persons Case of 1929, the beginnings of the Great Depression,
the birth of the Dionne quintuplets, and so on.[2] More recently, Michael
Dupuis has examined how CP covered the Winnipeg General Strike
and the sinking of the *Titanic* in 1912.[3] Focusing on major stories is not
the only, or perhaps the best way to understand CP as a news organization, however. Rather, CP's ordinary, daily, regular coverage – the
material described, somewhat oxymoronically, as "routine news"[4] –
may deserve more attention than it often receives. Big stories have an
undeniable impact on their readers, but the overall picture of a local
community, a nation, and the larger world is built up more slowly
and incrementally. (This interpretation reflects Michael Billig's notion
of "banal nationalism" – the idea that national identity is regularly
reinforced in myriad small, almost invisible, ways rather than mainly
through moments of crisis or high drama.[5]) The dailiness of news, its
insistent regularity, is of fundamental importance. John Sommerville
has argued that the emergence of daily publication schedules in
seventeenth-century England was of signal importance in the history
of journalism, and Benedict Anderson's linking of newspapers to the

emergence of modern nationalism depends substantially on their regular, predictable, and ubiquitous appearance.[6] Menahem Blondheim opened his valuable study of the origins of Associated Press by quoting Edmund Burke as saying "Let a man only tell you his story every morning and evening, and at the end of a twelvemonth he will have become your master," which expresses the point well.[7]

The sheer volume of material produced by CP makes assessing it a challenge. Depending on the period being considered and the newspapers involved, CP members received anywhere from 10,000 to 175,000 words of news a day – millions of words annually, over a period of almost 60 years covered by this study – and no cumulative repository of this material exists. However, by combining elements of a database created for a research project on national news in Canada before 1930[8] with a detailed examination of CP news printed in one fairly typical member newspaper (the Halifax *Chronicle-Herald*) between 1940 and 1970, a useful portrait of CP's typical news coverage emerges. This, in turn, will guide a more detailed textual analysis of selected articles, throwing light on such questions as the evolution of practices of objectivity and the relationship between news and structures of authority. This statistical and textual analysis will be complemented by an account of how CP's news operation functioned and evolved, including the elaboration of its own explicitly stated rules for news coverage.

A representative sample of CP articles that appeared in 17 Canadian newspapers from coast to coast in 1920 and 1930 is analysed in Charts 7A, 7B, and 7C.[9] The dominance of Ottawa coverage is clear (Chart 7A). CP in this sense was a strongly nationalizing institution, though it should be noted that Canadian newspapers also focused heavily on Ottawa coverage before CP was established.[10]

Toronto was the next most important news location (though much less prominent than Ottawa), reflecting both Toronto's importance as a news centre and its position as CP headquarters. Interestingly, more CP articles from Winnipeg were identified in 1920 and 1930 than from Montreal. In part, this reflects the continuing influence of WAP, the Winnipeg-based news service established in 1907 and absorbed into CP (with considerable reluctance) in 1917.[11] As well, there was a general tendency among Canadian newspapers to pay relatively less attention to news from Quebec and more to news from the western provinces

Figure 7A: Canadian Press articles by location (city), 1920 and 1930

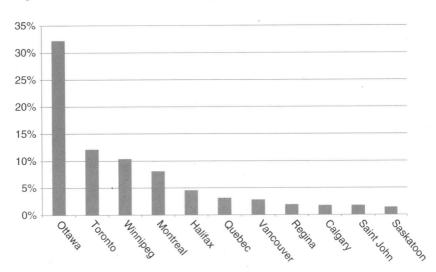

(N = 568) Source: See Appendix at end of chapter

after 1910.[12] Besides Ottawa, Toronto, Winnipeg, and Montreal, no other Canadian city accounted for more than 5 per cent of CP news articles.

Looking at the total from the provincial rather than urban point of view provides a somewhat different picture. As Chart 7B shows, Ontario locations (not including Ottawa) accounted for about twice as much CP news as any other province. The crucial factor here was that Ontario had many more daily newspapers than other provinces, comprising at least 40 per cent (and sometimes more than 50 per cent) of CP's total membership; because CP's domestic coverage depended heavily on redistributing "return news" provided by its members, the weight of numbers was reflected in volume of coverage.[13] Taken together, Ottawa- and Ontario-based news accounted for more than half of all CP domestic coverage in 1920 and 1930, clearly dominating the national news agenda. Quebec and Manitoba were of about equal, but clearly secondary, importance.

In terms of news subjects, the strong emphasis on federal politics and government, accounting for more than one-sixth of all articles, mirrors the geographical focus on Ottawa (Chart 7C). Beyond this, a cluster of economic subjects (general economy and business; agriculture; transportation and communication; and labour) accounted for

Figure 7B: Canadian Press articles, by location (Province), 1920 and 1930

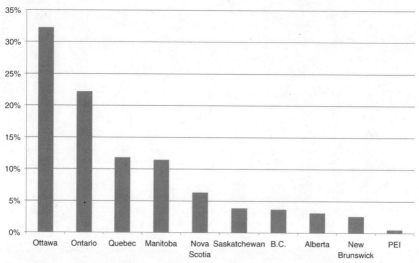

(N = 568) Source: See Appendix at end of chapter

Figure 7C: Canadian Press articles, by subject, 1920 and 1930

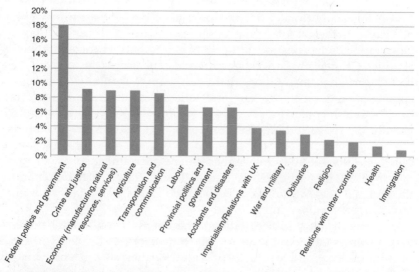

(N = 568) Source: See Appendix at end of chapter

Figure 7D: Halifax *Chronicle-Herald*, Canadian news location, 1940 to 1970

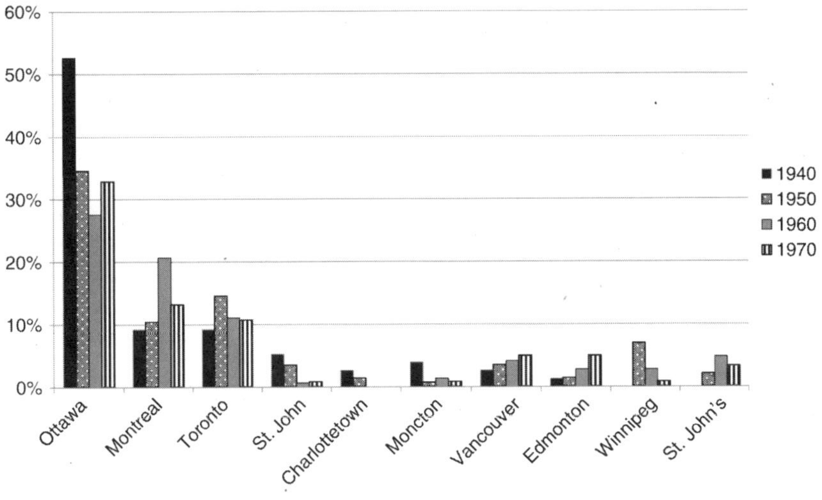

Source: See Appendix at end of chapter

around one-third of the total. The staples of more sensationalistic news coverage (crime and accidents and disasters) were also fairly well represented, but it is noteworthy that CP focused most heavily on serious topics overall. However individual newspapers may have handled their local coverage, the foundation of their collective national-news report until 1930 was serious to the point of sobriety.

A different approach was adopted to discern the patterns of CP news coverage for the period from 1940 to 1970: CP news printed in one representative newspaper, the Halifax *Chronicle-Herald*, was analysed. Besides general Canadian news, as covered in the 1920–30 figures, the 1940–70 data include specialized departmental news (especially sports and routine business-section coverage) and foreign news.

Chart 7D shows Ottawa's continuing dominance in the geographical origin of general national news from CP. This was especially pronounced in the war year of 1940, but Ottawa accounted for at least one-quarter and usually closer to one-third of all national news at other times. Montreal and Toronto were next most important – fairly evenly matched, with Montreal having a slight edge. No other Canadian city accounted for more than 5 per cent of CP national news in the *Chronicle-Herald*. Although the result is based on a small number of articles, the

Figure 7E: Halifax *Chronicle-Herald*, Canadian news subjects, 1940 to 1970

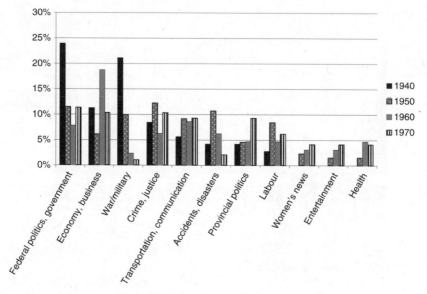

Source: See Appendix at end of chapter

decline in news from Winnipeg seems noteworthy, along with modest increases in the proportion from Edmonton, St. John's, and Vancouver.

The pattern of CP stories on domestic news subjects in the *Chronicle-Herald* between 1940 and 1970 (Chart 7E) is consistent with the 1920 and 1930 results in some respects, but also shows some significant differences. Most striking is the relative decline in coverage of federal politics and government after 1940, being narrowly outweighed in 1950 by coverage of crime, and surpassed by coverage of business and economic news in 1960. The rapid decline of military-related coverage is entirely understandable, with no major Canadian military involvements in 1960 or 1970 to replace the intense focus on the Second World War in 1940 and the Korean War in 1950. The economy/transportation/ labour constellation still accounted for a substantial proportion of the total, around 20 per cent in 1940 and 1950, and more than 25 per cent in 1960 and 1970. Over the whole period, the proportion of CP news in the *Chronicle-Herald* devoted to crime was about the same as for Canada

Figure 7F: Halifax *Chronicle-Herald*, all news locations, 1940 to 1970

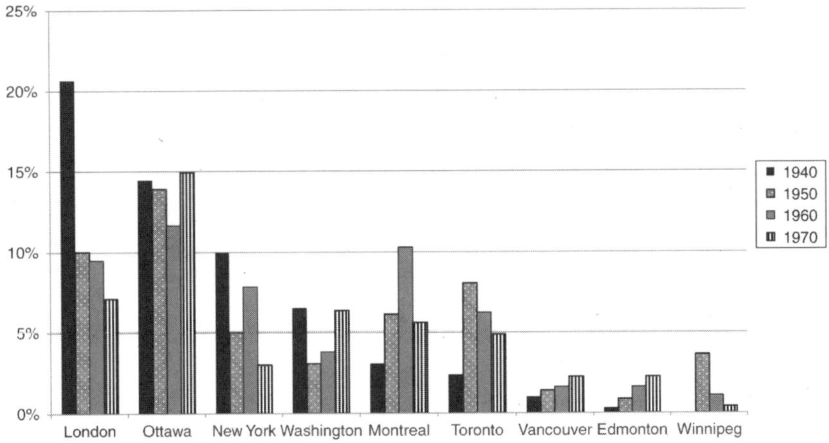

Source: See Appendix at end of chapter

as a whole in 1920 and 1930. Though based on very few examples, the increases in coverage of women's news, health, and entertainment in 1960 and 1970 are consistent with the diversification of CP's service beyond traditional hard news during these years.

For a paper like the *Chronicle-Herald*, CP provided almost all of its foreign news, through its arrangements with AP and Reuters, as well as out-of-province Canadian coverage. Chart 7F shows that London and New York (and, to a lesser extent, Washington) had significant weight. This was especially so in 1940; by 1970, coverage from both London and New York declined significantly from its wartime level. Washington, however, grew in relative importance again after 1950, so that by 1970 it accounted for a slightly larger proportion of all CP news in the *Chronicle-Herald* than Montreal or Toronto. CP news established and maintained a clear hierarchy of places, nationally and internationally, with news-agency head offices in places like London, New York, and Toronto having particular importance.[14]

The overall pattern of CP coverage, including specialized departmental news (such as sports and routine business) and foreign news, is shown in Chart 7G. One striking point is the growing importance of sports coverage, increasing from around 10 per cent of the total in 1940

Figure 7G: Halifax *Chronicle-Herald*, news sources, 1940–1970

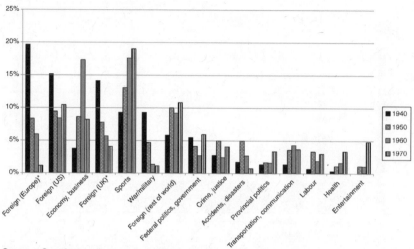

Source: See Appendix at end of chapter
*In 1940, most of the articles classified as "Foreign (Europe)" and "Foreign (UK)" concerned the European theatre of the Second World War and Britain's military effort. The "War/military" category specifically concerned Canada's war effort.

Figure 7H (i): Halifax *Chronicle-Herald*, foreign news sources, 1940

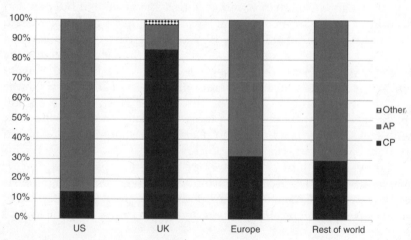

Source: See Appendix at end of chapter

to almost 20 per cent in 1970. News coverage from outside Canada consistently represented a substantial proportion of the total: 55 per cent in 1940 (again reflecting the overwhelming importance of war news), 35 per cent in 1950, 30 per cent in 1960, and just over 25 per cent in 1970. Within this category, there were some sharp differences, with marked declines over time in coverage of Britain and the rest of Europe, a fairly consistent emphasis on the United States, and a growing focus on areas beyond North America and Europe. In this comprehensive context, news about federal politics and government in Canada was of distinctly secondary importance; in the six editions examined in 1970, it had little more weight than entertainment coverage.

As noted in Chapter 6, the extent of CP's original foreign-news coverage (as opposed to that provided by AP and Reuters) was frequently discussed and debated during the 1960s. The four versions of Chart 7H show that 1940 was the high-water mark for CP's own foreign coverage, reflecting the large additions to CP's London staff and the bureau's position as the hub of CP's war coverage. More than 80 per cent of all London-datelined news in the *Chronicle-Herald* carried a CP credit in 1940, as did 30 per cent of European news (most of which concerned the progress of the ground war) and 30 per cent of news from outside Europe and North America. Once the war was over (see Charts 7H [ii], 7H [iii] and 7H [iv]), CP's original foreign coverage followed a pattern that remained relatively stable for the next 20 years: a respectable proportion of British news (25 per cent in 1950 and 35 per cent in 1960, but only 10 per cent in 1970); relatively little from the United States (ranging from less than 5 per cent in 1950 to almost 15 per cent in 1970); very little original European coverage from 1950 to 1970 (the proportional increase in Chart 7H(iv) gives a misleading impression, being based on only four articles); and between 15 and 20 per cent of foreign coverage coming from outside Britain, Europe, and the United States. In terms of CP's reliance on other agencies, none of CP's foreign-news coverage was credited to Reuters in 1940 (the nadir of the CP–Reuters relationship[15]) but it became increasingly important from 1950 onward, not just in Britain but also in Europe and elsewhere in the world. By 1970, Reuters even provided almost 20 per cent of the US news printed in the *Chronicle-Herald*, reflecting its more competitive relationship with AP. The *Chronicle-Herald* also relied on United Press/BUP for some of its foreign news, though this declined over time (again, the apparent increase for European news in 1970 is based on BUP providing one of four articles in this category). Despite all the discussion and debate – or

Figure 7H (ii): Halifax *Chronicle-Herald*, foreign news sources, 1950

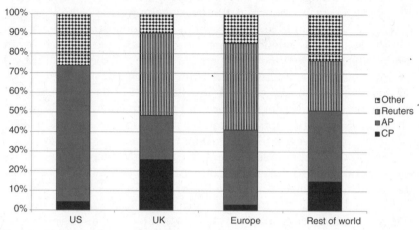

Source: See Appendix at end of chapter

Figure 7H (iii): Halifax *Chronicle-Herald*, foreign news sources, 1960

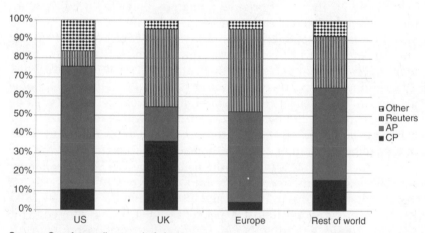

Source: See Appendix at end of chapter

Figure 7H (iv): Halifax *Chronicle-Herald*, foreign news sources, 1970

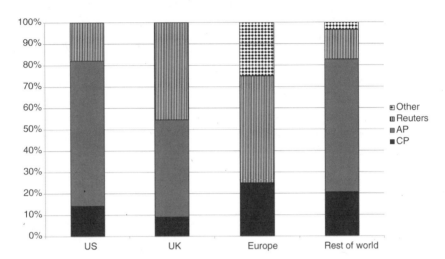

perhaps because of it, considering the wealthy Toronto papers' insistence on limiting the expansion of CP's international news coverage – only one out of every six articles from outside Canada carried a CP credit in 1970. This was an something of increase from the level in 1950, but not enough to overcome the criticisms recorded in the report of the Davey committee, for example. CP still relied overwhelmingly on outside agencies for its foreign news.

Over the past 25 years, scholars have paid considerable attention to news language and news form.[16] This work, based on the premises that news language can never be neutral and is often highly tendentious, and that the assumptions underlying linguistic and structural choices must be brought to the surface and analysed along with the explicit text, provides a useful framework for an examination of CP's news content. Explanations of changing news form have variously favoured technological causes (especially the telegraph, as cited by James Carey in particular[17]), or political, cultural, and economic reasons. Recently there has been a welcome tendency to see journalistic practices as evolving according to their own logic, rather than interpreting them mainly as effects of other, more fundamental, causes.[18] But relatively little attention has been paid to the language and form of news-agency articles specifically, a surprising omission considering that agencies supply a substantial amount of the news that appears in individual publications or news broadcasts and that standards adopted by news agencies often influence their clients or members.[19] The lack of attention to agency news in a historical context is particularly striking. An examination of how the form and content of CP news changed over the 50 years covered in this study yields interesting conclusions about the nature and evolution of news form generally.

By the time CP was established in 1917, Canadian newspapers had mostly moved away from the conventions of Victorian journalism, which might be summarized as a "compiler's" approach to nonlocal news characterized by reprinting short, discrete (and sometimes contradictory) items received from other sources. By contrast, twentieth-century newspapers adopted an "editor's" approach, bringing together and reworking separate pieces of information into the form of coherent, self-contained "stories."[20] The key feature of the twentieth-century news-story form was the introductory paragraph, or lead. This, in essence, stated the outcome or salient result of the event in question and was supposed to answer most of the basic questions about what happened, who was involved, where and when the event took place, and how and why it happened. Chronologically, the account was discontinuous, in effect beginning at the end (outcome) and moving forward and backward through time as required to provide further detail about points mentioned in the lead, relevant background information and context, and assessments of an event's causes, significance, and/ or consequences.[21] Unlike virtually every other form of narrative, the news story did not have an ending, but was written with what was considered the least important information in the bottom paragraphs so they could be cut if necessary. This was accompanied by suppression (rhetorically at least) of the individual journalist's subjectivity. A sharp distinction (less sharp in practice) was supposed to be observed between factual and evaluative statements, with the latter being clearly and invariably attributed to sources recognized as credible or authoritative. As generations of critics (and journalists) have observed, the fact that the journalist must choose among many possible alternatives at every stage – what to stress in the lead, which details to include and which to omit, whom to recognize as credible sources, what sort of background or contextual information to include – makes it impossible for any such account to be seen as "objective," if that is taken to mean a neutral and transparent recounting of a reality that is independent of the observer's account of it. Yet the *attempt* to be objective in this sense – to take account impartially of conflicting perspectives, for example, and to stress verifiable factual information over personal evaluation – is strongly established in journalistic practice, and describes accurately how most journalists do in fact carry out their work.[22]

The specific characteristics of news-agency journalism are often explained in relation to the telegraph. Agencies such as Havas in France (usually known as "correspondence bureaus") predated the telegraph, but the expansion of news agencies in the nineteenth and twentieth centuries was strongly associated with telegraphic networks. (Julius Reuter's motto for expanding his agency's operations around the world was "Follow the cable."[23]) James Carey has made several related claims about how the telegraph affected news form. At the broadest level, Carey argues, the telegraph "reworked the nature of written language and finally the nature of awareness itself."[24] One specific point mentioned by Carey is that telegraph-dependent news agencies ended the tradition of partisan journalism because the news they provided had to be suitable for all comers, an argument that CP's defenders often advanced.[25] While it does seem clear that CP adopted and promoted a much less partisan approach to journalism in Canada, one should not be too quick to banish partisanship from the history of journalism. Richard Kaplan, for example, makes the convincing point that in competitive markets, partisanship continued to be an effective approach to market differentiation long after the advent of the telegraph and agency news, and points out that even if they received the same news reports from an agency, individual newspapers could still choose which stories to display prominently on Page 1 and which to bury deep on an inside page or ignore entirely.[26]

At a more basic level, news agencies that relied on the telegraph are said to have demanded a spare, stripped-down, generic language (in part because of cost concerns) – in Carey's words,

> something closer to a 'scientific' language, one of strict denotation where the connotative features of utterance were under control, one of fact. If a story were to be understood in the same way from Maine to California, language had to be flattened out and standardized. The telegraph, therefore, led to the disappearance of forms of speech and styles of journalism and

storytelling – the tall tale, the hoax, much humor, irony and satire – that depended on a more traditional use of language. The origins of objectivity, therefore, lie in the necessity of stretching language in space over the long lines of Western Union.[27]

Telegraphic news supplanted the correspondent, "who provided letters that announced an event, described it in detail, and analyzed its substance," with the stringer, "who supplied the bare facts."[28] This "divorced the announcement of news from its analysis and required the reader to maintain constant vigilance to the news if he was to understand anything."[29]

Along with these pronounced changes in the quality of telegraphic / agency news, Carey argues, changes in quantity were significant too. The telegraph "brought an overwhelming crush of ... prose to the newsroom." This, in turn, required that

news judgment had to be routinized and the organization of the newsroom made factorylike. ... The spareness of the prose and its sheer volume allowed news, indeed forced news, to be treated as a commodity: something that could be transported, measured, reduced, and timed. News became subject to all the procedures developed for handling agricultural commodities.[30]

The structure of CP's news operation is important to bear in mind when assessing the evolution of its typical news forms. With the important exception of Ottawa coverage, most Canadian domestic news was not produced originally by CP journalists, but by journalists working for its member papers. An individual news item was then filed to the local CP bureau as part of the member paper's obligation to provide "return news" from its coverage area; it was then assessed by a CP editor. If the item was considered worth sending to other CP members, it was typically edited and/or rewritten, and in most cases shortened. Depending on its significance, the rewritten article might be sent to newspapers in the immediate region, or to CP's Toronto headquarters, from where it could be distributed to the national membership generally, and possibly to AP in New York. In this aspect of its operation, CP was more an organization of editors than of reporters, though bureau staff also undertook reporting assignments.[31] The chief exception to this pattern was CP's Ottawa bureau, which provided a great deal of original coverage by staff reporters, and where reporters outnumbered editors. CP staff correspondents in London and Washington also provided original coverage, although most British and US news that reached CP members in Canada was selected by CP editors in London and New York from the flood of material provided by AP and Reuters.

As a result, CP's Ottawa coverage, which the organization controlled more directly, might be a better reflection of its news values than much other Canadian news, where CP typically exercised editing control only. A sample of CP Ottawa stories from 1920 and 1930 shows two main types: straightforward accounts of government announcements or parliamentary debates and "insider" stories that clearly relied on the reporters' political contacts. Thus in early February 1920, the following article was among those produced by CP's Ottawa bureau:

> The Research Council has appointed an Air Research Commission with a membership of four, with a large association throughout the Dominion, to advise and co-operate with the Air Board of the Dominion on the lines of research to develop aeronautics in Canada. This commission will report on the possibilities for this work which may be found at various centres in the Dominion, and it will undertake investigations independently also.[32]

Another Ottawa article that day reported on statistics released by the Department of Agriculture: Canada had exported 141,655 horses, 1,081,756 cattle, 459,809 sheep, and 302,437 swine in the previous five years.[33] This straightforwardly factual, nonevaluative reporting of official statements was in some ways the basis of Ottawa coverage, and it reminds us that for many news stories the objectivity convention of getting all sides of the story did not apply – there was no "other side" to report. The key editorial decision was acknowledgment of the Research Council or the Department of Agriculture as a credible authority. What seems most significant about articles of this type is precisely the common-sense representation and hence reinforcement of governmental authority.

The political-debate form can be seen in an article from September 1930:

> Ottawa, Sept. 17 – Vigourous condemnation of the Government's proposals launched by Rt. Hon. W. L. Mackenzie King, leader of the opposition, and a spirited defence of them by Hon. H. H. Stephens, Minister of Trade and Commerce, led off the tariff debate in the House of Commons today.[34]

This is practically a template for the "objective" form of news story, with directly opposing views presented in relation to each other and complete reliance on statements attributed to clearly identified, author-itative speakers. It is noteworthy that identical versions of this article appeared in newspapers of sharply opposed political affiliation, such as the Liberal *Chronicle* and Conservative *Herald* in Halifax. (In 1915, by contrast, before CP's domestic news service was established, the *Herald* and *Chronicle* regularly carried articles about political events that were clearly biased in favour of one party or the other; here the advent of a national news agency serving newspapers with different affiliations did clearly lead to more even-handed coverage.[35]) This was a dura-ble form, appearing relatively unchanged decades later.[36] The article occupies the journalistic zone that Daniel Hallin has described as the "sphere of legitimate controversy," where opposing views are routinely given approximately equal weight. In Hallin's conception, the sphere of legitimate controversy is quintessentially defined by debates between mainstream political parties, as opposed to the spheres of consensus or deviance, where opposing views are ignored or discounted.[37]

The extraordinary length of this article – approximately 2,300 words in the Halifax *Chronicle*, devoted entirely to recounting in great detail the parliamentary speeches made by King, Stephens, and other MPs – is also noteworthy. While this was a significant debate on a new gov-ernment's major economic policy, the extent of the coverage illustrates that parliamentary debate was seen (and reinforced) as a central part of the political process, and this evaluation continued until well after the Second World War. Arch MacKenzie, who was posted to CP's Ottawa bureau in the late 1950s, recalled in an interview that standing orders at the time required at least one paragraph for every speaker in a parlia-mentary debate.[38] This penchant for serious, detailed coverage was evi-dent in political stories from outside Ottawa as well. For example, when Hugh Guthrie, the federal minister of justice, returned to Canada from an Imperial Conference in November 1930, a CP journalist reported at length on a shipboard interview, including extensive discussion of such questions as how various British statutes (the Colonial Laws Validity Act, the Merchant Shipping Act, and the Naturalization of Aliens Act) would be amended in view of the 1926 Balfour Report declaring the dominions to have equal status with Britain. Granted, this was an issue of major political importance at the time, but overall, the seriousness and detail of CP's coverage are striking. The assertion that commercialized journalism after 1900 largely replaced serious discussion of matters of public interest with frivolous, entertainment-based news is not borne out by an examination of CP's news coverage.[39] By the 1960s, stories based on a specific statement, debate or event were augmented by a more interpretive type of coverage that sought to capture emerging trends even if there was no immediate news development.[40]

A second type of Ottawa article, based on inside sources rather than public statements, also strongly reinforced authority, though in an implicit rather than explicit way. Consider the following two Ottawa items from 1920:

Ottawa, Nov. 19 – Transfer of natural resources to the western provinces is likely to be again soon to the forefront. Again and again within recent years the question has been discussed but no solution has been found for the difficulties encountered.

The view taken by the Dominion government, it is stated in well informed circles, is that the question is entirely for settlement between eastern and western provinces ...

Reports of possible legal action to enforce transfer of the resources have aroused much interest here but it is not thought likely that such steps will meet with success.[41]

Ottawa, April 6 – The parliament buildings will resume its [sic] sessional appearance today, following the Easter recess, when both the house of commons and senate will take up their activities. It seems likely that the week will be a busy one as the franchise bill, one of the most contentious measures to come before parliament this session must be put through the committee stages. Several of the less contentious clauses have already been disposed of but the real fight in committee is yet to come ... .

Department estimates are yet to be disposed of, and those of the railway department are likely to cause much controversy. The opposition seems in no mood to let any of the estimates by without considerable discussion ... .

It seems unlikely that the budget speech will be delivered this week, but when it does come there probably will be much criticism from both opposition and cross-benches. There is, as yet, no indication what the tariff proposals of the government will be, but they will certainly not meet with the approval of the widely differing factions in the house.[42]

An article written 50 years later, on a proposed increase in MPs' salaries, followed much the same form.[43] In these cases, the reporter is relying not on official statements or parliamentary speeches, but on informal conversations with political sources in the government and (in the case of the second article) opposition parties. Although specific attribution of statements to clearly identified sources is often considered one of the hallmarks of "objective" journalism, attribution in these articles is vague to the point of disappearance. Passive constructions such as "it is stated in well informed circles" and "it is not thought likely" are effective means of masking the identity of specific sources. In the second article, constructions such as "it seems likely" (or "unlikely") have a similar effect. Authority is real and present in these articles, but disembodied and apparently all-pervasive, which in a sense makes it more powerful: politics becomes something like the weather, a manifestation of impersonal forces rather than a reflection of the choices made by individual politicians and their parties.

John Dauphinee, who became CP's general manager in 1969, was news editor in the Ottawa bureau during the 1940s. In an interview with Douglas Amaron, he recalled how news of this kind was gathered by the long-serving bureau chief, Andrew Carnegie:

> Once we'd heard a rumour there was a story in one of the government departments. McCook had worked on it, and Flaherty and Blackburn, and they got nowhere. About 11:45 Randall or I would go into Carnegie and say, "We hear that so and so ... and can't raise it."
>
> "Leave it with me, leave it with me, John," he would say.
>
> So we'd leave it with Andy, and at two o'clock Andy would come back from the Rideau Club, having had lunch with half the cabinet, and say, "John, I'll write the story." And he would.[44]

A section devoted to "News from Unnamed Sources" in the 1968 edition of CP's style guide testified to the regularity and importance of news of this kind. It took pains to indicate that the practice was essential:

> (M)any important stories are obtained from people who cannot be publicly named. For instance ... no reporter is present at cabinet council, or the meetings of defence committees, or the inner conclaves of labor unions, to name merely a few possibilities.
>
> Matters may develop at such places that are of great public interest, and yet would never be made public if it were not for some newspaper or news agency reporter and the relationship that exists between him and someone closely connected with the meeting or situation in question; someone whose name cannot be made public without jeopardizing his position.[45]

Reporters were urged to distinguish between matters of fact as opposed to expressions of opinion in such stories, and to make sure that the latter would be seen as fair by "readers who do not hold the same belief or opinion." In addition, the source for any important or controversial story should be identified to head office.[46] As always, the story should be written so that "no unsourced beliefs or opinions are ... to be attributed to CP."

The reliance on inside contacts, in many cases built up over the course of long association, was something of a double-edged sword. On one hand, contacts made it possible to get stories that were otherwise unobtainable, and certainly not through ordinary channels. On the other hand, the journalist's discretion in not publicly identifying sources gave politicians a way to put their views forward without being held accountable. Whether they like it or not, journalists can never be completely independent observers of the political process: the mere fact of their reporting politicians' statements (or not) is an action with political consequences. But with "insider" reporting of the kind seen above, journalists risk being drawn further into their sources' political calculations (as when an unattributed or loosely attributed trial balloon is launched, for example, or when one party to an internal partisan or bureaucratic dispute surreptitiously leaks information that reflects badly on its opponents). In any case, insider political coverage was a common story form throughout CP's history, and it assigned great authority to those sources defined as credible. It also deviated substantially from what many scholars have identified as one of the main conventions of objectivity.

CP's Ottawa coverage was important because it was the main source of national political news for many Canadian newspaper readers. In the 1950s, besides the Ottawa dailies, only five Canadian newspapers had more than one Ottawa correspondent, and most had none.[47] Under these circumstances, it is surprising that students of political communication in Canada have paid relatively little attention to CP (noteworthy exceptions are the studies done for the Senate Committee on Mass Media in 1969 and the Royal Commission on Newspapers in 1980 and a study by Arthur Siegel.[48]) References to CP's Ottawa bureau in Patrick Brennan's study of parliamentary reporting from the 1930s to the 1950s are few and dismissive: in the late 1940s, Brennan wrote, the Department of External Affairs held Canadian Press "in the lowest regard of all [news organizations] because of its excessive reliance on American wire-service reports which invariably downplayed Canada's significance in any international story. Understandably, gaffs like the assignment of a sports reporter to cover the Paris Peace Conference did not enhance the news agency's reputation in the East Block."[49] Brennan also concluded that "Liberal insiders all seemed to agree that The Canadian Press ... was a nest of Tories," although this would have come as a surprise to Arthur Meighen.[50] Yet there was concern in the immediate postwar years that CP's Ottawa bureau was not sufficiently sophisticated to keep up with the growing complexity of federal government policy and operations. In 1950, CP president Victor Sifton told the executive committee about complaints from senior public servants "that there was no one in the Press Gallery capable of interviewing them intelligently or reporting them capably."[51] By the 1960s, though, specialized beat reporters in such areas as defence and transportation had been assigned to Ottawa. Soon after Arch MacKenzie joined the Ottawa bureau in 1957, he was assigned to specialize in northern issues (including the construction of the Mid-Canada Line of air-defence stations in keeping with the "northern vision" that John Diefenbaker enunciated as prime minister). Clark Davey, who was managing editor of *The Globe and Mail* in the 1960s, recalled that CP reporter John LeBlanc "covered the railway rate hearings because he understood them and he was the only reporter in Ottawa who did. And the rest of us were more than happy to rely on his coverage." David McIntosh was "probably the only person who was covering defence in Canada, as such, and really working at his beat. ... one of the great things about Canadian Press was, by and large, particularly their staff-originated coverage was the kind of thing you could take to the bank."[52] By 1970, the trend towards beat reporters in Ottawa had led to the appointment of specialists in science and health and welfare, with the suggestion that further appointments would be made soon to improve coverage of labour, broadcasting, and the arts.[53]

CP's coverage of Canadian news from outside Ottawa was more varied, but many of the same journalistic conventions applied. Serious treatment of significant issues predominated, as the four CP reports that appeared on the front page of the Calgary *Herald* edition of Feb. 10, 1930 suggest: "No Reason for Panic on Wheat Situation Says Finance Chief"; "No Canadian Wheat Boycott in Britain Many Officials Say"; "Proposes Parley with Sask. on Resources Terms" (about W.L.M. King's latest suggestion concerning the transfer of control over natural resources to the prairie provinces); "Conference Opens at Toronto Today on (Stock) Exchange Laws."[54] The focus on official and institutional news of national importance is typical, and there is correspondingly little coverage of news that did not emerge from or have to do with established institutions. Here again, Hallin's notion of the sphere of legitimate controversy as a place where divisions can be expressed between mainstream political parties and institutions or within government or corporate bureaucracies is helpful; so, too, is the observation that journalists' reliance on reporting statements from sources tends to favour accounts provided by officials and established institutions, around which newsgathering routines can be organized.[55] A report about the sentencing of leaders of the Winnipeg General Strike in 1920 is an interesting example of where the boundaries of legitimate controversy lay: as the record of a court proceeding, the CP article is based on the proceedings of an established institution of authority, but within this framework, ideas that might normally slide into the sphere of deviance could be raised straightforwardly. Thus a statement by one of the strike leaders that "the class struggle had been clearly shown in the trial when well dressed women had been given reserved seats in the court to gloat over the suffering of himself and comrades" was reported directly (although it came after the judge in the case denounced such comments as constituting contempt of court). A second defendant, R.J. Johns, spoke even more bluntly: "The crown ... had contended that there was [sic] no classes in Canada. There were two classes, a working class and a capitalistic class – who opposed each other. Social ownership, he claimed, was inevitable in time, to support human life."[56] But the reporting of such opinions was unusual (not just for CP); acceptable boundaries were normally maintained. In a similar way, an appeal in 1930 for wider access to birth control for women was reported straightforwardly as a resolution duly passed by the Labor Women's Social and Economic Conference.[57] The key development in this case was the initial identification of the women's conference as a newsworthy event.

Not all CP articles were equally serious, however.

NEW YORK, June 22 [1920] – United States immigration authorities at Ellis Island today face the problem of straightening out a 'love triangle' born of moonlit nights on the swelling Atlantic, in which Captain R. Kitchen, of Sydney, C.B., late of the Canadian Field Artillery, is portraying the role of rejected suitor.[58]

Another colourful article prefigured the more recent obsession with news of celebrities:

MONTREAL, Nov. 19 [1920] – Deaf ears unstopped, mute tongues loosened, palsied and atrophied limbs restored to their normal functions, so that crippled and palsied persons walked off a platform and a deaf mute spoke and gave evidence of ability to hear, were witnessed Thursday night in Old St. Andrew's church before a crowded congregation when Mrs. Aimee Semple McPherson, the woman evangelist, exercised her healing ministry.[59]

Most surprising in this case was the apparent lack of journalistic skepticism.

Particularly in its first decades, CP's news coverage was not typically "telegraphic" in the sense of being terse and lean. There is no doubt that wire capacity limited the volume of news that could be delivered – with a maximum transmission speed of around 3,000 words an hour for much of the period under study,[60] there was clear incentive not to be prolix. Yet the system of leased wires that CP relied upon meant that there was no direct cost implication for sending more rather than fewer words. As long as the leased wire's daily transmission capacity was not exceeded, the fact that one story was longer simply meant that another had to be shorter – or, depending on the discretion of a filing editor, it might not be sent at all.[61]

To a present-day observer, many CP stories from before the Second World War are positively verbose. Consider, for example, the lead paragraph of a CP article that appeared in the Halifax *Chronicle* in 1930:

OTTAWA, Mar. 31 – Whether the province of Saskatchewan is entitled to the reimbursement of the sum of $206,834,960 from the Dominion Government in return for the alienation of 61,326,982 acres of land which, since 1870, the Federal administration has distributed to settlers, railway companies, and other agencies which had western lands parcelled among them, is a question which is still unsettled, according to the correspondence tabled in the House of Commons today.[62]

Many similar examples can be found among CP articles from 1920, 1930, and afterward, but there was a clear tendency towards greater economy of expression from 1940 onward. For example, this was the brisk lead paragraph of CP's article about the appointment of Lord Beaverbrook to Winston Churchill's cabinet:

LONDON, May 14 – Prime Minister Churchill today placed Lord Beaverbook in charge of aircraft production and ordered him to increase production in a hurry.[63]

Edward Slack of the Montreal *Gazette* was president of Canadian Press Ltd. when it became a functioning national news organization in 1917.

E. Norman Smith, editor of the Ottawa *Journal*, was one of CP's strongest supporters in its early years. He was president in 1923, when CP lost its $50,000 government subsidy.

CP's board of directors held its fall 1923 meeting in Winnipeg. Among those attending were (first row from left to right), the general manager, J.F.B. Livesay; C.O. Knowles of the Toronto *Telegram*; E.H. Macklin of the Manitoba *Free Press*; E. Norman Smith of the Ottawa *Journal*, CP's president; and M.E. Nichols of the Winnipeg *Tribune*.

M.E. Nichols, one of the founders of Western Associated Press and of Canadian Press, was CP's president from 1931 to 1933. As director of information for Sir Robert Borden's Union government in the early postwar period, Nichols promoted the idea of an imperial news service.

In the 1930s, CP's newsroom was located in the *Mail and Empire* building in Toronto. "The walls are filthy," Bernard Rickatson-Hatt of Reuters told his chief, Sir Roderick Jones, after a 1934 visit. "The paint is all off the woodwork. It is a very old-fashioned building too. ... Altogether it would give you a fit if you saw it."

J.F.B. Livesay, CP's general manager, in the 1930s.

CP war correspondent Ross Munro, staying awake with the aid of benzedrine, writes his account of the disastrous Dieppe raid in August 1942.

Four CP war correspondents in England, 1942: from left, Maurice Desjardins, Louis Hunter, Bill Stewart, and Foster Barclay.

John Dauphinee (left) and Gillis Purcell, 1942. Dauphinee succeeded Purcell as CP's general manager in 1969.

J.A. McNeil, left, was CP's general manager from 1939 to 1945. Here he is seen with Russ Wheatley, centre, and Charles Bruce.

CP's Toronto newsroom in the 1950s. CP moved into its own building on University Avenue in 1948.

CP had a close but often complicated relationship with Associated Press and Reuters. In 1957, guests at CP's annual meeting included (left to right) Sir Christopher Chancellor, general manager of Reuters; D.B. Rogers, CP's president; Frank Starzel, AP's general manager; and Walton (Tony) Cole, editor-in-chief of Reuters.

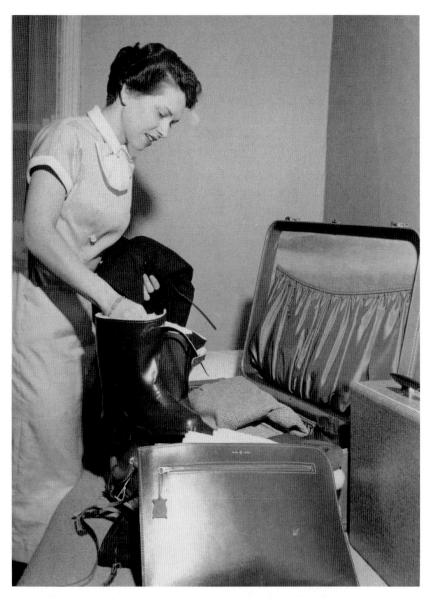

Female journalists were a rarity at CP before the 1970s. CP's caption for this 1957 photo described Carolyn Willett as "the woman reporter on the Ottawa bureau staff," who "specializes in news of interest to women but covers anything that comes along."

R.K. Carnegie, CP's long-serving Ottawa superintendent. John Dauphinee recalled that when no one else could track down a story, Carnegie would say "'Leave it with me, leave it with me, John.' ... at two o'clock Andy would come back from the Rideau Club, having had lunch with half the cabinet, and say, 'John, I'll write the story.' And he would."

Guy Rondeau was assigned to CP's Ottawa bureau in 1959, with a mandate "to report on federal affairs, in French, from the point of view of French Canada."

(Above and Opposite.) Three CP Moscow correspondents: Bill Boss, Jack Best (1964), and Peter Buckley (1967).

Arch MacKenzie, CP's Washington correspondent, in 1966.

In the late 1960s, computers began making inroads into CP's operations. In 1967, general traffic chief M.W. Bradbury (left) and traffic supervisor Ian Munro demonstrate a computer that automatically set CP copy for standard-width newspaper columns.

J.R.H. Sutherland (standing, centre), CP's president in 1969, delivered CP's presentation to the Special Senate Committee on Mass Media. Senator Keith Davey stands at right, and newly appointed general manager John Dauphinee is seated at left.

A technological explanation – that the telegraph required terse forms of expression, which became the hallmark of news-agency prose – cannot possibly explain the timing of this change, which came some 95 years after the telegraph was first introduced in North America, and after a long period of more loosely written telegraphic news. The real explanation involves changing journalistic practices – something that emerged within journalism rather than from outside it. Ian Munro, who began working for CP in 1928 and was in charge of all its transmission facilities when he retired 50 years later, recalled in an interview that CP's long-serving general manager, Gillis Purcell, played a major role in making CP's style more consistent:

> Purcell was the guy that really organized CP. Livesay did his part, but when Purcell came in, he started to set down the regulations, the rules and regulations for things. [Previously], well, hell, any spelling, your own spelling at times. ... And then we got into proper day leads and stuff like that, you know. The story broke and the facts had better be in the first paragraph.[64]

Purcell's acknowledgment to Livesay in 1934 that he did not have "the interior flexibility to permit myself to ease down when I see that things are going inefficiently or when I see that a specified system has been allowed to lapse" reinforces Munro's assessment.[65]

Livesay had issued a sheet of general instructions for CP correspondents on member newspapers as early as 1927. CP's seriousness of purpose was stressed: in addition to spot news about sudden deaths, fires, accidents, and crimes, "the Canadian Press aims to present day by day a complete news picture of Canada. ... constructive news, covering such things as the development of the basic industries of agriculture, mining and fisheries; departmental activities of the Federal and Provincial Governments; the progress of manufacture; and the social and economic life of the Country." Brevity was crucial: "Good wire style demands short words, short sentences, short paragraphs, short stories" (though as we have seen, this injunction was not always observed). Any material filed to CP must be impartial:

> The Canadian Press is a non-partisan organization, serving daily newspapers of every political stripe, and in politics wants records of fact without comment. Endeavor to keep all color and prejudice out of despatches. We do not want the editorial opinion of member newspapers, notwithstanding that such often has real news value.[66]

It is telling that newspapers were still considered to have a distinct "political stripe."

CP's first comprehensive style guide, written by Purcell and published in 1940, was a clear manifestation of CP's growing concern with consistency and clarity in style, along with systematization of the news operation.[67] It is a revealing document, because it spells out many preferred journalistic practices explicitly, whereas journalistic norms are often transmitted informally. For example, under the heading "Accuracy," "strict adherence to the following practices" was ordered:

> *Full investigation* before transmitting any story or identifying any individual in a story where there is the slightest reason for doubt.
>
> *Citation of competent authorities and sources* as the origins of any information open to question.
>
> *Impartiality* in consideration of all news affecting parties or matters in controversy, with equal representation in the report to the sides at issue.
>
> *Limitation of subject matter to facts*, without editorial opinion or comment and with proof available for publication in event of denial.[68]

The guide went on to specify that "where information is disputable and proof not available for publication in event of denial," the name of the source must precede the assertion, which "precludes giving an editorial impression and contributes to clarity of expression." Concern about being able to support any statements that might be challenged, either by referring to a "competent authority" as the source, or by providing other proof of factual accuracy, comes through strongly. At one level, these injunctions are similar to the academic practice of providing citations to support factual assertions. But the almost complete effacement of the reporter's subjectivity is striking, too; the journalist is presented as a transparent vehicle for the presentation of facts and the views of others who have been judged to be credible (without an account of the criteria by which such judgments, not themselves self-evident, are made). The question of what does or does not count as a fact was elaborated on to some extent: under the heading "Facts – Not Comment," the guide stated that "[d]esignations employed by any person or organization, such as 'Reds,' 'Canada's young defenders,' or 'noble experiment' are editorial [i.e., opinionated] expressions unless attributed to those who use them."[69] The intention to avoid explicitly evaluative language is clear, but the complexity of deciding what constitutes a fact more generally is not addressed: there is a significant difference between stating that the Montreal Canadiens won the Stanley Cup in 1944 (a specific event) and stating that the Great Depression (itself an abstraction) began with the stock-exchange crash of 29 October 1929 (assertion of a causal link). News articles are typically as full of these more complicated, essentially disputable, kinds of facts as of the more simple ones.

The journalistic meaning of impartiality was also spelled out in some detail.

> Parties in controversy, whether in politics or law or otherwise, receive equal consideration. Statements issued by conflicting interests receive equal prominence, whether combined in one dispatch or used at separate times. ...
>
> When the question at issue is of major importance, or as adherence to impartiality demands, efforts are made to obtain for simultaneous publication both sides of the matter in controversy. Partisan statements are solicited only with this aim in view.[70]

The stipulation that partisan reaction could be sought only in limited circumstances is striking, perhaps a compensatory reaction to past practices of making sure that anything controversial was presented through the approved partisan lens. Reinforcing this point (and reflecting an earlier prohibition against estimating the size of partisan political rallies as inherently subject to manipulation), the guide banned estimates of crowd size at conventions or other public gatherings "*in figures* except [as] an official estimate attributable to the source." (In a fine example of editorial hair-splitting, however, it was acceptable for a CP reporter to say that a building or arena with a known capacity was half- or three-quarters full.[71])

CP reporters and editors were also cautioned against drawing inferences from the statements and facts they reported. "No conclusions or inferences are drawn in any matter," the guide stated.

> Developments which might seem cumulative should not be treated as such without studied examination. An event which has no bearing upon another similar event should not be *unjustifiably* coupled with it in reporting the later one.[72]

No one could object to a warning against drawing spurious connections between unrelated events, or against reaching conclusions without careful thought. But this is also further evidence of how the journalist's subjectivity was suppressed; it was safest to stay away from doing anything other than reporting statements and facts without very strong grounds for doing so. Taken together, these injunctions comprise a clear, programmatic statement of the journalistic practice of objectivity, with its strengths (full investigation, impartiality, reliance on clearly identified supporting evidence, and factual accuracy) and limitations (an unwillingness to explore institutional and social values that condition which voices are, or are not, heard and which statements about the world are recognized as facts and considered relevant).

CP's members sometimes criticized this cautious approach. For example, Purcell noted at regional meetings of CP members in 1942 that he had received requests for "more speculation, particularly out of Ottawa."[73] Opinion was clearly divided; some said that "factual reporting was CP's job" and that speculative articles should be left to individual newspapers' special correspondents. Newspapers, according to Rupert Davies, were inherently political, "and if speculation were carried there would be complaints that CP was being used by government or opposition." Frederick Ker went so far as to say that CP's function "was a mechanical one, of picking up news from its member newspapers and relaying it to others." But Gordon Churchill of the London *Free Press* argued that CP "was a little timid at times ... . Speculation should be carried labeled as speculation." He also noted that AP "took more chances in this regard." Arthur Ford, CP's newly elected president, said there were many opportunities to provide more evaluative coverage out of Ottawa – "interpretation of the various orders-in-council and regulations" – without "going into political speculation." At a later meeting of Maritime province members, Ford said one of the main problems with CP's Ottawa bureau "was the tendency to sit back and wait for the government to make an announcement. The public wanted more interpretative stories." This discussion clearly mirrored debates among members of the board of directors about the Ottawa bureau's adequacy at the time.[74] That fall, McNeil reported to the board that "without venturing into the treacherous field of political speculation," the Ottawa staff was doing a better job of informing Canadians about "the background of significant situations and ... possible future developments."[75] But extreme caution in going beyond the facts was clearly still the watchword.

The assumption that credibility and factuality were self-evident reflects an important operational characteristic of news agencies: hundreds of quick decisions about what should be covered and how had to be made in the course of a day. It is difficult to imagine discussions about the nature of facts or searching examinations of the potential bias that might arise from, say, systematic reliance on official sources taking place on a regular basis in a busy newsroom. The efficiency of established news routines has been noted by many observers; it is much more time consuming and otherwise difficult to provide an account of an arrest by tracking down witnesses than by relying on the police desk sergeant, with whom the reporter regularly checks for new developments. Official sources such as these have obvious limitations, most notably a tendency towards self-justification and suppression of information that reflects badly on them, but they are also likely to provide authoritative information in most cases and can be held to account if the information proves inaccurate.

The need to work quickly and efficiently is particularly pronounced for news agencies. "Quick action on spot news around the clock is essential because with five time zones, editions are almost invariably going to press at some points, regardless of the hour," the style guide stated on its opening page. ("But being reliable is more important than being fast.") The need to ensure that CP's eight Canadian bureaus and three foreign bureaus (London, New York, and Washington) worked in a coordinated way as parts of a single news system operating within the constraints of a telegraphic leased-wire network dictated a strongly hierarchical organization. The style guide was itself an important instrument of editorial hierarchy, furnishing an increasingly detailed set of rules in successive editions for handling everything from questions of the broadest principles to minor points of spelling or word use (avoidance of "hospitalize," for example, or the correct spelling of "autogyro"). More directly, early editions of the guide contained instructions to seek guidance from head office on a wide range of sensitive issues: for example, editorials from member newspapers were not to be transmitted "except in extraordinary circumstances as sanctioned by the General Manager"; all corrections must be reported to head office "for decision on treatment"; head office should be consulted when deciding whether to cover speakers who were not parliamentarians or candidates during election campaigns, or whether to report election-campaign rumours or charges that might be libellous, or whenever legal issues arose. In one case, editors were warned that the CP adage "When in Doubt Cut it Out" could be "distorted by twisted thinking," leading to promising news angles being dropped: "The safe rule: 'Never Ditch a Good Angle without Tipping Head Office.'"[76] The style guide was taken seriously: it was known as the Red Bible, and Arch MacKenzie, who spent 35 years at CP and held a variety of senior positions, recalled that "[t]he style book was everything. ... you went by the style book, and it ruled your life in a way. Accuracy was all-important, and to be non-editorial, that was the thing."[77] The fact that the domineering Purcell, who was known for his harsh criticism, was the author and enforcer of these standards doubtless gave them additional weight; as Ian Munro recalled, if anyone made a mistake in transmitting Canadian casualty lists during the Second World War, for example, "Purcell not only sat on your ass, he kicked the hell out of you."[78] (Even until the 1950s, CP staffers were expected to inform Purcell when they got married – though they no longer were expected to ask permission first, as had happened before the war.[79]) This authoritarian style of leadership, reflecting partly the structural imperatives of the news agency's organization and partly Purcell's particular personality, was in some ways the mirror image of CP's unvarying reliance on "credible authorities" in its newsgathering.

By 1968, the style guide was in its sixth, expanded edition, but much of the original text remained. A section on situational stories – a move away from the traditional hard-news approach, these sought to "outline the emotional, social or economic situation on which a given set of facts is imposed" – that first appeared in 1947 seemed to give reporters more leeway in assessing the significance of what they wrote about: in addition to the previous warning against overemphasis ("A shortage is not a famine, a forecast is not a fact, a strike-vote is not a strike"), they were also urged to avoid underemphasis ("Concealment in advance increases the impact of a disagreeable fact").[80] The gradual move away from complete reliance on a hard-news approach was also indicated by the substantial section devoted to CP Newsfeatures, now a highly popular service. Newsfeatures could run as long as 3,000 words, but most were around 500 words long: they included profiles of people in the news, Cross-Canada Surveys "rounding up a situation on national basis," flashbacks of important past events, and rewritten features from member newspapers that could run at any time.[81]

The ban on reporters drawing their own conclusions or making inferences remained in force, however; impartiality was still a cardinal virtue, and practices of attribution remained strict. Under the same "Facts – Not Comment" heading that first appeared in 1940, the list of evaluative descriptions to avoid had been updated to include "separatist," to be used only if "backed up by stated facts or attributed."

Discretion was advised in characterizing the Viet Cong (not "National Liberation Front," it is worth noting) as "Communist troops or simply the Communists," and references to "the enemy" in Vietnam should be attributed clearly.[82] In one respect, the insistence on tight attribution of statements to sources was loosened slightly – in stories about official reports, the substance of the news could now appear before the name and title of the source, "but not too far ahead."[83]

There was also more tolerance for using lesser-known, unofficial organizations as sources, but in these cases the names of everyone involved, "and their positions in life," were to be provided "as a guide to readers in assessing [the group's] importance and probably influence."[84] Here is a trace, at least, of the changing social terrain of the 1960s. But skepticism remained the watchword:

> Some organizations are fly-by-night groups set up for a specific and temporary purpose. Sometimes the only news in their existence is *why* they have been organized, and *by whom*.
>
> In any case, it is necessary for the writer himself to *know*. Organizations with high-sounding names sometimes turn out to consist of nine disgruntled individuals from lower Main Street.[85]

The injunction to find out who stands behind an organizational name is always journalistically appropriate, but it is noteworthy that only unofficial groups faced such scrutiny. Respectability – a socially loaded concept, the more powerful for being defined only implicitly, as in the "lower Main Street" example – was evidently a key criterion for recognition. One sign of a somewhat more skeptical approach to official sources was the recommendation that if police or other civilian agencies withheld names of accident victims until next of kin could be notified, "[a]ny legitimate reporting means may be used to circumvent such civilian delays."[86] But the disposition to rely on official sources, even in controversial matters, could readily be found in practice as late as 1970, when a CP article in which provincial agriculture ministers defended the safety of pesticides did not include any comment from environmental groups, for example.[87]

The 1968 version of the "Politics" section seemed to reflect Cold War values.

> The unlimited freedom of speech that this country enjoys, and the fact that the press of Canada is careful to give everyone his say, offer an opportunity

for certain elements to seek overthrow of such freedoms. When the individuals and what they say are news, report them. But place their utterances in perspective by naming the organizations they are affiliated with, their record, what has been said or done about them by the government.

Remember that many of these are experts in hanging yards of old familiar propaganda on small hooks of new material.[88]

CP's 1950s-era practice of referring to the Canadian Peace Congress as a communist organization, for example, was evidently a manifestation of this policy.[89] The guide went on to say that "[i]t is dangerous and unfair to label an individual or small group Communist unless that can be *proved* from public statement or privileged record"; such labelling was fine as long as it was done accurately.[90] "Red China" or "Communist China" might sometimes be required for clarity, "but generally China stands all right alone for the Communist mainland."[91]

Changes in specific points of style illustrated how CP navigated through a period of social turmoil, sometimes accepting and sometimes rejecting new ways of speaking. There was no sign of feminist concerns, for example: a married woman addressed as Mrs. was "*always* ... referred to by her husband's Christian name, never by hers."[92] Oddly, a divorced woman was still to be referred to as Mrs. with the husband's surname, "but may use either her own Christian name (Mrs. Mary Smith) or her own surname in lieu of a Christian name (Mrs. Johnston Smith)."[93] Feminine forms of words were to be avoided except actress, fiancée, hostess, laundress, postmistress, and saleswoman – chairwoman, mistress of ceremonies and poetess, among others, were specifically proscribed.[94] In other small acknowledgments of changing times, the list of CP-preferred spellings now included such entries as "à gogo"; names of currently popular dances (frug, watusi, twist, monkey) were not to be capitalized. [95]

One general stylistic injunction was to "[a]void Americanisms and the writing style of *Time*."[96] CP editors in New York were specifically warned to "lop out" such Americanisms as "railroad" (instead of the Canadian "railway"); Canadian Indians lived on "reserves" rather than "reservations"; defendants in court cases testified from the "witness box," not the "witness stand," and were represented by lawyers or barristers, not attorneys.[97] In these respects CP enunciated a Canadian identity that was not supplanted by its close relationship with AP. CP did, however, adopt the American "-or" suffix for words like labour and colour; the long-standing justification was that dropping the extra letter saved wire space.

Besides explaining how the news was to be covered, the style guide paid special attention to the job of CP's filing editors. This is a key journalistic position that only exists in news agencies; as Menahem Blondheim has argued, "continuous coordination of a large and widely dispersed network interacting with a central headquarters through a system of complex communication machines" was the underlying cause for the formation of AP in 1846,[98] and such coordination was essentially the filing editor's job. Each filing editor served the newspapers on one telegraphic circuit (for example, the Ontario afternoon dailies outside Toronto, excluding northwestern Ontario), and the editor's job was to organize the ever-changing flow of news in accordance with the member papers' requirements, the capacity of the wire, and the relative imminence of deadlines. The first page of the style guide stated that "The answer to the question of what is news lies in the judgment of the filing editor, aided by the check of other editors on the circuit and the views of deskmen on member newspapers."[99] In a speech commemorating the agency's 50th anniversary in 1967, Purcell described filing editors as "already a sort of computer even before they were thought of," and insisted that no new technology could ever replace them.[100]

The fact that only one story could be sent at a time constituted the main technological constraint that filing editors faced. The basic challenge of the position was described as follows:

News is predominantly spontaneous. The order of its receipt seldom remains the order of its importance for relay. The filing editor is continually reshuffling his copy in the order of its importance.

In addition, he gauges the capacity of the wire as a measure of what can and should go.

Slashing of copy to enable moving more stories requires judgment, not routine dropping of paragraphs from the end up. Every story can be cut and remain complete. Skilful editing in this task is the talent by which a filing editor justifies his key position.[101]

In a 1943 article for *Canadian Printer and Publisher,* Purcell provided an amusing profile of the current Ontario day filing editor, Ab Fulford.[102]

Fulford directed the daily news report to 23 afternoon dailies between Cornwall, Sarnia, and Timmins, and the article reproduced the job memo he relied on to refresh his memory:

> Soo [Sault Ste. Marie] wants steel and wolves in full ... Kingston gets all drama and Welsh ... Orange [Order] celebrations and cheese in full for Woodstock ... cheese for Belleville ... obits for Galt ... odd stories for Peterborough ... Brantford likes postwar plans but hates misplaced 'todays'; items with morgue-picture possibilities for Welland ... rubber for Sarnia.[103]

The Ontario day wire ran from 6:30 a.m. until 3 p.m., and during that time the filing editor cut between 60,000 and 80,000 words of material to a maximum of 20,000. The editor was supposed to follow a clear schedule, beginning at 6:30 a.m. with overnight bulletins (i.e., major news not covered in that day's morning papers), the day's news budget (listing all the major stories written or expected), and a note detailing which stories could be picked up from that day's morning papers "so that only fresh news need go on the teletype," then proceeding through early sports (6:45), early front page news (7:15), night report briefs (7:45), sports cleanup (8:00) day leads from parliament (8:20), provincial spotlight (8:45), remaining front page stories (9:00), war news (10:00), and general news (10:15), followed by last-minute additions and advances for the next day if time permitted (1:15).

CP's New York bureau was, in essence, staffed entirely by filing editors. This was where the flood of international news from AP and Reuters and US news from AP arrived, to be selected, edited and in some cases rewritten for transmission to Toronto based on Canadian news priorities. Around 200,000 words of copy arrived each day, on nine separate wires. Of this total, some 75,000 words was relayed to Toronto.[104] Not everyone found work in the New York bureau, often a rite of passage towards higher CP positions, congenial. In 1967, a young CP journalist who had spent "happy years" in the Montreal bureau complained bitterly to Bill Stewart that his recent move to New York had not turned out as expected. Instead of covering the United Nations, he spent most of his time doing

> what we call 'pig-editing' in the bureau here, i.e., editing stock-market and commodity tables, doing Central Hockey League roundups and chasing AP and Reuters for a thousand and one stories of one-point interest in

Canada. This makes no sense. I am no genius but I am too bright to be spending my life doing this kind of work. ... By and large, we are simply the strainer through which the AP and Reuters tea is poured into the Canadian cup.[105]

The letter probably did not greatly impress Stewart; two years later he made his own complaint about a research report for the Davey committee that characterized news-desk work for CP's French service as tedious and unsatisfying. "The same outside view might be taken of a great deal of work in CP or any other news service," Stewart wrote. "It has not the glamor of byline reporting and the travel often associated with it. However, putting together a news service in any language is painstaking and often tedious work that has its own satisfactions."[106] In the early 1970s, the New York bureau was closed: with the expansion of transmission facilities[107] everything previously received there could now be sent directly to Toronto.

Scott Young, a former CP journalist, described CP's postwar news operation in the December 1948 edition of *Maclean's Magazine*. He noted that CP employees were typically paid between one-quarter and one-third less than journalists on big-city dailies, and worked harder: "They work to every deadline on every newspaper they serve and the pressure is intense every minute."[108] Of CP's 93 daily-newspaper members at the time (with a combined readership of around 10 million people), 70 received all their nonlocal news, features, and photos from CP. Young concluded that there was "much truth" to the complaint that CP depended too much on "bloodless reportage which doesn't sell newspapers, doesn't give the reader the interpretative background he sometimes needs to grasp the significance of what he's reading." But CP executives "feel it is not too high a price to pay for simplicity and impartiality." Thanks to the efforts of filing editors ("the most important men in the rank-and-file of CP") to customize the news report in accordance with the interests of the newspapers on their respective circuits, "the Canadian Press news report in any day is really five or six reports, depending on which part of the country gets it." Young also noted a tradition of camaraderie marked by late-night backroom poker games when the shift was over, lubricated by alcohol – "CP has no rules against drinking, as long as the job is done well." Purcell was credited with setting the standard of "hard, rapid work at lower-than-average pay and also ... of loyalty to CP which is part of every long-term employee's character."

❧

An abiding concern for accuracy and impartiality, seriousness of purpose, reinforcement of authority (with a corresponding lack of room for CP journalists to assess or interpret events), and what might be called epistemological and social conservatism – these were some key characteristics of the CP news report in its first 50 years. In a postmodern era, when the boundaries between professional journalism and personal opinion are becoming increasingly blurred, it is easy to underestimate the significance of these standards. With the advent of teletypesetter service in the 1950s, CP copy was set directly in type for most Canadian newspapers with minimal local editorial intervention. This represented an extraordinary collective and continuing vote of confidence in CP's journalism. Through rigorous adherence to conventions of objectivity and neutrality (with all their limitations), CP copy genuinely tried to be a transparent reflection of reality. Events might be controversial, but CP's coverage should not be; the repeated injunctions in the style guide that solid evidence must be available to support every assertion and strict policies about attribution were meant to guarantee that CP's coverage could always be defended. In retrospect, it is remarkable that CP copy was so pervasive, yet practically invisible. But the low profile of CP news, its modest, taken-for-granted character, was also a measure of its credibility, of its widespread acceptance by publishers, editors and readers.

Scholarly analyses of journalism sometimes fail to appreciate how difficult it is to maintain standards of factual accuracy, for example, in a large, physically dispersed institution with a "deadline every minute." A news agency that did not make accuracy a priority, that drew attention to itself by numerous errors, could hardly expect to enjoy the kind of confidence that was signified by being taken for granted. As far as possible, CP produced news that was consistent in form and quality – a commodity, to be sure, but one that was valued particularly because of these characteristics. Similarly, CP's system of newsgathering and distribution was characterized by complex flows – from local newspaper to local CP bureau, to CP regional bureau and head office (and perhaps on to AP in New York or Reuters in London), then back again through regional circuits to local newspaper clients. At every one of these relay points, every story faced the possibility of delay or inadequate exercise of journalistic judgment. A detailed set of rules, unwavering attention to how they were carried out and relentless correction of shortcomings were the only way to ensure that news moved through the different channels and subchannels of this articulated system as quickly, smoothly and (in journalistic terms) appropriately as it did. As was the case with other news agencies, perhaps the most significant aspect of CP's operation was its hard-won and doggedly maintained mastery of these flows. If much of the work involved was not especially glamorous (as both Bill Stewart and his disappointed young colleague agreed), it underlay the pervasiveness of CP news, both in terms of space (reaching practically every community in Canada) and time (being distributed not only every day, but every hour).

The nation, in Craig Calhoun's phrase, is essentially a "discursive formation ... a way of speaking that shapes our consciousness."[109] That is to say, nations are constituted by culture. Over the 50 years covered by this study, the regular, reliable flow of CP news constantly asserted and reasserted the reality and relevance of Canada to newspaper readers (and eventually radio and television audiences). In the aggregate, the steady stream of incidents, places and people that CP wrote about defined "[t]he dimensions and boundaries of [readers'] imaginations"[110] about what Canada was, making clear which were its important places and which were its backwaters. In wartime, CP both promoted and benefited from a heightened focus on the nation. The "sphere of legitimate controversy" of political life was largely populated by CP news coverage, especially for readers in smaller cities and towns. It does not make sense to speak of CP as essential to Canadian nationality in the twentieth century – one can easily imagine Canada existing without CP or an agency like it. But it was the organization through which much of the cultural construction of nationality in Canada actually *did* take place. This cultural result, moreover, was largely accomplished by cultural means: a set of journalistic practices that, much as they reflected the constraints and possibilities of the telegraph, arose mainly from deliberate and systematically applied ideas about what journalism ought to be.

Appendix

The results for 1920 and 1930 are based on a subset of material gathered for a larger study of national-news coverage in 17 Canadian daily newspapers between 1890 and 1930.[111] A "constructed week" sampling method was used, in which, say, a Monday from February, a Tuesday from April, a Wednesday from June (and so on) were examined. The specific dates examined are listed below. For an account of the constructed-week method, see Daniel Riffe, Stephen Lacy, and Fred Fico, *Analyzing Media Messages: Using Quantitative Content Analysis in Research* (Mahwah, NJ, and London: Lawrence Erlbaum Associates, 1998), 97–8. The newspapers examined were the Halifax *Herald*, Halifax *Chronicle*, Saint John *Globe*, Quebec *Le Soleil*, Montreal *Gazette*, Montreal *La Patrie*, Montreal *La Presse*, Montreal *Star*, Kingston *Whig*, Toronto *Globe*, Toronto *Daily Star*, London *Free Press*, Winnipeg *Free Press*, Winnipeg *Tribune*, Calgary *Herald*, Vancouver *World* (succeeded by Vancouver *Sun*), and Victoria *Times*. Microfilm editions of the Saint John *Globe* for 1930 could not be obtained, so only 16 newspapers were studied in 1930. These cities and newspapers were chosen mainly to provide broad regional representation.

For the purposes of this study, "national news" was defined very broadly. It included all general Canadian news from outside each newspaper's province of publication. Editorials, opinion columns, and routine coverage of sports and business (reports of out-of-town hockey games, for example, or stock market results) were not classified as national news unless they appeared on the front page or other general news pages (rather than on pages dedicated to sports or business). In each edition, all national-news items up to a maximum of 20 were recorded. These included all items on the front page and the most prominent news items on inside pages. Newspapers were examined on the following dates: (1920) 9 February, 6 April, 23 June, 16 September, 19 November; (1930) 10 February, 1 April, 25 June, 18 September, 21 November.

Explicit crediting of articles to Canadian Press was inconsistent in 1920 – some national-news articles were credited to CP, but many others were not. The 1920 results are based on the assumption that all national-news articles appearing in more than one newspaper, whether explicitly credited or not, were produced by Canadian Press. (There was no other organization producing identical national-news articles for Canadian daily newspapers at the time; CP's competitor, British United Press, did not begin operations until after 1920.) The headline and/or first sentence of every article was recorded, making it possible to identify those that were identical and to eliminate duplicates from the sample. By 1930, crediting practices were much more consistent. From the 165 newspaper editions examined in 1920 and 1930, a total of 568 unique items were identified as having been produced by CP.

The figures for 1940, 1950, 1960, and 1970 are based on a constructed-week sample of editions from the Halifax *Chronicle* (later the *Chronicle-Herald*). Unlike the 1920 and 1930 figures, the *Chronicle* results not only include general national news credited to CP, but also CP-credited foreign news, sports, business, entertainment, and so on – all sections of the newspaper. Except for tabular material (such as hockey standings and stock-market tables), all articles credited to CP in these editions were counted. These figures cannot be directly compared to the 1920–30 figures, but they provide additional useful information about the different types of CP material that this reasonably typical newspaper used and how this changed over time. Editions examined: (1940) 22 January, 5 March, 15 May, 4 July, 27 September, 23 November; (1950) 23 January, 7 March, 17 May, 6 July, 29 September, 25 November; (1960) 18 January, 1 March, 11 May, 30 June, 23 September, 19 November; (1970) 19 January, 3 March, 13 May, 2 July, 25 September, 21 November.

Conclusion

Shortly before retiring as general manager in 1969, Gillis Purcell published an article about Canadian Press in the *International Communication Gazette*.[1] Essentially a description of CP's structure and operations, the article made clear that, more than 50 years after its founding (almost 60 years if Canadian Press Ltd. is included), CP continued to operate as a *telegraphic* news agency. Today, at a time of rapid change in news media, this long period of relative stability seems unusual and noteworthy. What were the main characteristics of this long-lasting telegraphic news system in Canada? What was the significance of Canadian Press's operating in much the same way for so many decades?

CP's telegraphic news system was, above all, strongly nationalizing. As we have seen, this was not the result of nationalist sentiment on the part of Canadian publishers collectively, certainly not in the first instance.[2] AP's sale of the franchise to distribute its service to the Canadian Pacific Railway on a Canada-wide basis in 1894, rather than dealing with individual newspapers separately (as it did in the Caribbean and Latin America), was a crucial first step in this evolution. Once the right to distribute AP's service throughout Canada belonged to the CPR, the national frame was further reinforced and shaped by the Canadian regulatory structure; it was a ruling by the federal Board of Railway Commissioners in 1910 that forced the CPR to give up the AP franchise, paving the way for Canadian publishers to take it over collectively. When it became apparent that Canadian Press Ltd. was not strong enough to insist that its members provide Canadian news to AP in a prompt and systematic way, AP demanded that CP establish a national organization with enough authority to enforce AP's rights to Canadian news.[3] In this instance, the constitutive role of international influences in the formation of nationality is particularly clear. CP's exclusive possession of the AP franchise for Canada has remained an important asset up to the present day.

CP was monopolistic as well as nationalizing, and the two characteristics reinforced one another. Once CP established a national system of leased wires, it was almost impossible for anyone else to do the same. It would have been extraordinarily difficult for any competitor to replicate the complex and often confrontational negotiations about cost-sharing that underlay CP's operations, especially when newspaper closings or other unforeseen revenue losses threatened the fragile consensus over allocation of fixed costs. The result was that CP occupied the entire Canadian news territory both for newsgathering and distribution. It operated *essentially* at a national level, which was another great competitive strength, because no competitor could offer coverage that was as geographically complete. Having almost all Canadian dailies as members was another strong advantage that tended to monopoly. The more customers CP (or any news agency) had, the more widely its costs could be shared, and the lower the cost to any individual subscriber. In addition, the cooperative form of ownership shared by CP and AP was, as Stephen Shmanske has demonstrated, particularly effective in keeping competitors at bay.[4] The economic and institutional organization of the news agency was as important as the underlying technology in the development of CP's monopolistic advantage. The "right of protest" that limited the emergence of new competitors in local newspaper markets (an approach that, as practiced by AP, was condemned as anticompetitive by the US Supreme Court in 1945[5]) and the exorbitant entry fees that remained in place until almost 1970 had nothing to do with the telegraph specifically, but powerfully reinforced its monopolistic possibilities.

CP's national character was also advantageous from a sales, marketing, and political point of view. This was especially so at times of increased news focus on the nation, such as wartime; in Britain, the BBC's national character was similarly advantageous.[6] CP was also prepared to invoke its national status directly against competitors in the political/regulatory environment, as when it argued at the outbreak of World War Two that the Canadian government should ban competing providers of radio news from the airwaves.[7] Being the national agency in these different respects strengthened CP's monopolistic advantages, which, in turn, reinforced its position as the preeminent national agency.

CP's supporters usually responded to concerns about monopoly by denying that this was the case, or by arguing that the national news agency was a "natural monopoly" like the long-distance telephone network or the distribution of electricity.[8] Recently, Jonathan Silberstein-Loeb has made the case that the results of news-agency monopoly or cartel arrangements were positive over all; these kept the cost of international and domestic news for newspapers relatively low, provided a larger quantity of news, and made it available to more people. Furthermore, he argues that anticompetitive structures were always subject to "gales of creative destruction" unleashed by new technologies, so the development of mass media was not held back.[9] Oliver Boyd-Barrett has observed that "the business model for a successful national news agency often seem[s] to require effective monopoly status ... . A national agency needs to be seen to offer a credibly comprehensive and authoritative 'national' service and there is generally room in the market for only one such provider."[10]

In any case, CP was not entirely immune from competition. British United Press was never a practical alternative to CP as an agency that could serve virtually all Canadian newspapers (as Purcell observed in 1941, only 12 of 95 daily newspapers used BUP[11]), but it did compete in daily news coverage. If BUP had a story that CP did not have, or had it sooner, or presented it in a more appealing way, CP managers took notice, and CP journalists were called to account. Competition of this kind was part of the day-to-day business of newspaper journalism, and was never a matter of life and death. Radio, however, presented a much more serious challenge. (Silberstein-Loeb's point about the "creative destruction" caused by new technologies applies here powerfully.) It was not so much a particular agency that presented the threat in this instance, because both Transradio and BUP were involved, but a radically different approach to radio news that took advantage ruthlessly of CP's inability to resolve its internal contradictions. The key point was that both Transradio and BUP treated radio as something to be exploited to the fullest possible extent, without worrying about its effect on newspapers. Transradio's and BUP's major advantages – selling news for commercial sponsorship and allowing multiple newscasts at any time of day – stemmed from this basic orientation. The fact that both mastered radio style more effectively than CP was a corollary, another result of their willingness to put radio first and make the most of its possibilities. For CP, this was a competitive threat that really did challenge its dominant position. Eventually, CP publishers and managers saw clearly what was at stake, threw aside all the limitations on when and how radio news could be used, and beat back the challenge (although broadcasters' suspicion of CP as a news provider lasted for years afterward and never entirely disappeared). It is one of the ironies of this history that broadcasting revenue became a major support of CP's newsgathering operation, providing its newspaper members with much more news for less money than would have been possible otherwise.

CP news also had a significant nationalizing effect in cultural terms. Anderson has identified the mass-produced newspaper as a key element in the creation of the "imagined community" of nationality, but (at least in a country like Canada) a stronger claim can be made for the news agency's nationalizing role. Through CP, almost every newspaper across the country received the same basic daily budget of stories, with a strong common focus on the federal government and politics in Ottawa, and a secondary focus on news from Ontario.[12] M.E. Nichols made the point effectively in his 1933 presidential address:

> The Canadian Press through the daily newspapers it serves keeps the people of Canada in daily touch with each other. It makes known to the whole country simultaneously the goings on in every part of the Dominion. ... In whatever part of the country the event occurs it is made immediately available to every daily newspaper in Canada and through the newspaper it is made known to its readers. If that is not a great national service; if keeping the people of Canada informed every day of occurrences and the trend of thought in every one of the nine provinces – does not promote national unity, national consciousness and national understanding, I confess to a warped judgment of the factors and forces that promote the building of a nation.[13]

During critical periods, CP's news was very strongly nationalizing – as it was during the Second World War, with detailed, systematic and affecting coverage of Canadians' military activities, combined with a greater focus than ever on "general headquarters" in Ottawa. It is noteworthy that the war, when CP carried out the most extensive international newsgathering operations in its history, and when the accomplishments of Ross Munro and other CP correspondents were celebrated in Canada and abroad, is generally considered the agency's golden age. But CP's role in shaping and reinforcing ideas of Canadian nationality was at least as great in ordinary times and quieter circumstances. Michael Billig's notion of "banal nationalism" – what might more neutrally be called "everyday nationalism" – is highly relevant to the study of journalism in general and news agencies in particular.[14] The regular, unexceptional assertion of shared geography and common citizenship and the enumeration of shared points of reference inherent in CP's domestic news coverage operated in the barely conscious realm of the self-evident and taken-for-granted conditions of life. Sometimes explicitly but mostly implicitly, CP's news coverage systematically and regularly underscored the idea of a "here" that is Canada and a "we" who are Canadian. Anderson has identified the era of "print-capitalism" beginning in the mid-nineteenth century as the period when print media, including journalism, promoted the growth of nationalism as an idea. In assessing the half-century of CP's operation as a telegraphic news agency, one might conclude that the news-agency era is one of the major periods in which twentieth-century ideas of nationality were asserted and consolidated.

Anderson observes that the *idea* of nationalism is based on the promise of "deep, horizontal comradeship" among fellow citizens, but in practice, the organizationally and culturally national framework that CP helped establish was not necessarily equal.[15] As long as CP remained reliant on the telegraph, differential access to news on the basis of location and cost was a central aspect of its operation, with implications for how and where power over news selection was exercised. The leased-wire network had three main components at the end of the 1960s: a circuit linking New York with Toronto, Montreal, Ottawa, Hamilton, London, and Windsor; two additional circuits for domestic Canadian news connecting the same six cities; and single-wire regional circuits serving eastern and western Canada and smaller cities in Ontario. (See Map 1.) Every newspaper in the six larger central Canadian cities received around 80,000 words of news a day, six days a week. International news arrived directly from New York, and the remainder came from or through CP's head office in Toronto.

The great majority of CP's member newspapers, however – 89 out of 100 in 1968[16] – operated in a much more constrained environment. These papers received a combined service of international, domestic, and regional news, transmitted on a single wire that carried only about 40 per cent of what the more favourably located newspapers received.

Two factors, location and size, determined whether a newspaper was on the high-capacity central circuit or a lower-capacity single wire. In terms of location, every newspaper east of Montreal and west of Ontario was on a single wire. This was the result both of distance (more leased-wire mileage meant higher costs) and of relatively low population density (there were fewer newspapers to divide the costs among themselves). The disadvantages of location were often reinforced by a

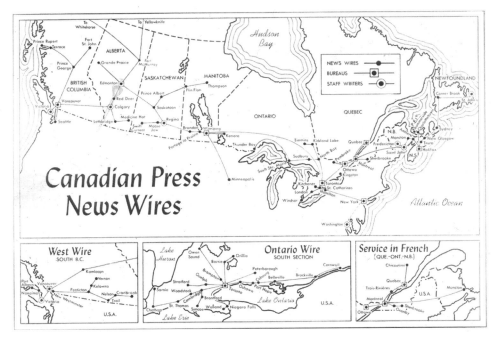

Map 1 . Canadian Press News Wires circa 1969
Source: Gillis Purcell, "The Canadian Press (CP)," International
Communication Gazette 15 (1969), 151–8.

newspaper's size (circulation) and ability to pay, but these could also
operate independently. Within Ontario, for example, around 25 smaller
newspapers were relatively close to the central circuit, but were unable
or unwilling to pay their share of its cost. So they, too, received single-
wire service.

At one level, CP tended to equalize access to news across Canada,
putting readers in big cities and smaller towns on a similar footing.
But the structure of the telegraphic-news system also asserted a cultural and organizational hierarchy of places. New York was the focal
point for the distribution of international and US news; Toronto and
Montreal were key points for distributing news to western and eastern
Canada, respectively; and Ottawa was the main focus of CP's Canadian
newsgathering operation. Toronto, where most decisions about news
selection were made – which items would be transmitted, and in which
order of priority – had significant editorial authority, and thus significant power, over places on the receiving end of such decisions, and

differential access to news through the leased-wire network reinforced Toronto's editorial authority. If the newspaper in a medium-sized city like London, Ontario, received 80,000 rather than 35,000 words a day, its editors could exercise much more control locally over what was eventually printed. (This also required hiring a large enough staff to make such decisions, something not all small newspapers were prepared to do.[17]) This unequal distribution of editorial autonomy was not simply the result of the telegraph, but of its institutionalized cost structure (based on the rate charged per mile of leased wire by CPR Telegraphs) in relation to the ability or willingness of different CP members to pay more for greater capacity. The frequent crises over financial arrangements throughout CP's history reflected (among other things) the fact that regional interests often came into conflict about what was a fair division of costs. The rate schedule was fundamentally the product of a *political* agreement within CP. Cutting across regional divisions, the tension between big-city newspapers (which typically were in competitive markets, could afford other news sources and therefore were satisfied with a relatively bare-bones CP service) and small-town newspapers (which could not afford and did not require other services and wanted CP to meet almost all their requirements) was more or less permanent.

CP was not only a domestic news agency, however; international connections were a major aspect of its structure, and these were another element of what it meant to be "national." As Boyd-Barrett and Terhi Rantanen have observed about the international news system more generally, telegraphic news in Canada was simultaneously nationalizing *and* globalizing.[18] CP clearly had subordinate status in its relationship with AP and relied on it heavily for international news. As shown in its complicated and shifting relationship with Reuters, CP often had to weigh the desire for membership in an imperial imagined community against the more practical benefits of a primary relationship with AP – which is to say that the international communication system offered different kinds of supranational connection. The stationing of CP editors in New York and London gave the Canadians more control over the supply of international news than they would otherwise have had, but they did not control news generation (and hence did not determine what was covered and how in the first place), only selection.

The manner in which international news was provided to Canadian newspapers was not a simple question of cultural imperialism, although there were significant imbalances of power. During the 1930s,

CP's relationship with AP was so close as to be practically suffocating, but this also brought clear advantages. The Livesay–Cooper connection not only guaranteed a reliable, voluminous, and still inexpensive supply of US and other international news, but also provided a powerful bulwark against Roderick Jones's plans to make Canada a larger source of revenue for Reuters. At the same time, the alliance made it impossible for CP to pursue other connections without AP's approval. Each international agency appealed to a different kind of cultural affinity: the imperial and British connection in Reuters' case, and the journalistic model of a politically independent, nonprofit cooperative that rejected the idea of government subsidies in AP's case. After Livesay's successor (perhaps unintentionally) offended Cooper by not responding promptly and enthusiastically to his pointed suggestion that CP voluntarily make an extra wartime payment, the relationship changed to "a rough and tumble commercial proposition" in which CP's relatively weak negotiating position became painfully clear. Paradoxically, a cooler relationship with AP led to the option at least of a closer connection with Reuters, though in a system with only three parties it was the *prospect* of a change in alliance that gave CP a somewhat better bargaining position; if CP ever actually switched to Reuters as its main supplier of international news, whatever leverage it had with AP would likely be lost for good.

CP also struggled with the question whether AP's control of its foreign news supply was problematic from the point of view of Canadian nationality. Sometimes, as was the case when CP was founded during the First World War and wanted a federal government subsidy, it was useful to play up the disadvantages of relying on AP. Fifty years later, CP insisted to the Senate Committee on Mass Media that coverage by AP journalists was generally no different than what Canadian journalists in the same situation would provide – unless there was a particular Canadian interest involved, in which case a CP reporter could be assigned on an ad hoc basis. (AP also often provided special coverage of Canadian-interest news on request.[19]) To the extent that AP was the dominant partner, it was mostly with the consent of CP's owners and managers. A willingness to pay substantially more for foreign news would have bought CP more freedom to manoeuvre, but this was a price the agency was never prepared to accept.[20]

The maintenance of national and international news as a *wholesale* commodity was another important consequence of CP's long reliance on the telegraph, with implications for the structure of the whole journalistic ecosystem. Several basic characteristics of the telegraphic news system limited its users to other relatively large institutions (newspapers) rather than, say, individual consumers. First, telegraphic news required specialized encoding and decoding devices and specialized staff. Initially, these comprised Morse equipment and trained telegraphers (press operators were considered the elite of their profession) to send and receive messages. Beginning in the 1920s, telegraphic printers were installed in newsrooms, eliminating the need for most receiving operators; and from the 1950s onward, "punchers" in CP offices produced perforated tape that could be fed directly into typesetting machines at the receiving end. (As previously noted, this tended to reduce the editorial autonomy of smaller newspapers, because a local editor's intervention was no longer necessary before CP copy was typeset.[21]) In all these cases, the cost of specialized equipment and knowledge required to operate it helped to keep telegraphic news a wholesale commodity.

It is also significant that the telegraphic news-distribution network was not switched as a telephone network is; one was either physically connected to a specific telegraphic circuit and hence received everything it carried, or not. With leased wires requiring a continuing financial commitment (and mandatory membership in the publisher-owned cooperative), a newspaper's position on the news-distribution circuit was permanent and continuous, not occasional or discretionary. The delivery of national and international news to readers was therefore a two-step process: (1) telegraphic distribution to the local newspaper though its leased-wire CP connection and (2) the processing and assembly of this news into the day's newspaper, a physical commodity that was physically delivered to readers (whose consumption *was* discretionary.) Much has properly been made of the fact that the telegraph separated communication from transportation, a key characteristic of all subsequent electrical or electronic forms of information transmission;[22] but the local newspaper that contained this telegraphic news still had to be transported physically to each of its readers, just as international news before the Atlantic cable was inseparable from the letters or printed London newspapers that contained it. A modal shift took place in each local newspaper office, in which a series of electrical impulses was transformed into printed words on paper. (The relationship among the news agencies, newspapers, and readers is shown in Figure 1.)

Given the institutional and financial commitment that a position in the telegraphic news network required, the necessity for specialized expertise and equipment for encoding and decoding, and the impossibility

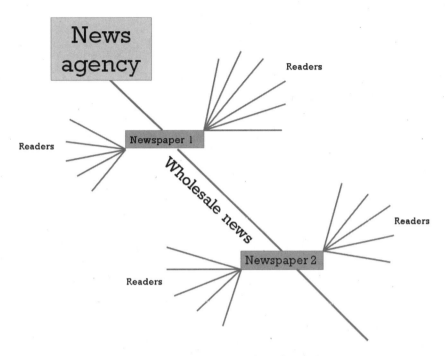

Figure 1   The news agency–newspaper–reader relationship

of switching that might allow some degree of individual choice, individual readers had no access to the wholesale flow of news, only to the version that appeared in the local newspaper. In light of the present-day situation in which readers increasingly do have such choices, with serious consequences for the local-newspaper publication model, the long-lasting stability of the wholesale–retail structure that underlay CP's telegraphic news system seems noteworthy.

The journalistic practices of filing editors were another crucial element in the mature system of telegraphic news. Their job was, in effect, to manage the limits of wire capacity from an editorial point of view. Menahem Blondheim identified the need for "continuous coordination of a large and widely dispersed network interacting with a central headquarters through a system of complex communication machines" as the underlying cause for the formation of Associated Press in 1846[23]; more than 120 years later, the filing editor was still a crucial cog in what was essentially the same machinery. The ability to balance conflicting demands and shuffle priorities on the fly in response to unexpected news developments, making sure that each paper got the kind of news it required in time to meet its deadlines, was the filing editor's key attribute. The collective knowledge and experience-based skill that CP's corps of filing editors possessed was a crucial repository of intellectual capital – a kind of software, one might say – adapted specifically to the differential access to telegraphic capacity that was embedded in CP's structure. CP's telegraphic news network was never merely a set of physical devices with connecting wires, but an articulated, multifaceted system whose parts included the basic technology; the institutional, legal, and regulatory structures that shaped it; the international and national contexts within which it operated (and which it helped to reinforce); and considerations of cost and benefit at every level (with important implications for the hierarchy of places). The journalistic practices embodied by filing editors were another key component of this system, an entirely cultural element that was based on tacit knowledge or explicit decisions about which items of news were of most value to which customers, and when.

CP's status as a nonprofit cooperative also had important implications for the way it did its job, though these were not as unambiguously positive as its members liked to assert. The cooperative structure did make CP strongly responsive to its members' requirements, however. Having many demanding masters may have made life difficult for CP journalists, but the resulting culture of accountability for any shortcomings in the speed, accuracy, or quality of coverage was a major asset for any journalistic organization. CP's cooperative ownership structure also reinforced its policy of strict editorial impartiality, especially where partisan politics was concerned. Even at times of heightened political conflict among members with opposing party affiliations (as happened during the Second World War, for example) it was generally recognized that CP could not stay in operation if the news it produced was not acceptable to all members. (However, CP's desire to avoid giving any of its owners grounds for complaint could produce coverage that tended to be cautious and, by default, was oriented to the status quo.) The likeliest alternative to a cooperative like CP would have been a syndicate organized around one or more of the largest newspapers in Toronto or Montreal, with much more opportunity for an individual publisher's likes and dislikes to affect the news coverage that was distributed nationally. As Daniel Hallin and Paolo Mancini have observed, "[a]n orientation toward the center [sic] and toward the political 'mainstream' is still a political orientation,"[24] but CP's news was notable for its consistent factual basis and, with rare exceptions, independence of any partisan point of view. Furthermore, though some CP publishers' denunciation of radio news for its reliance on advertising was transparently hypocritical – their newspapers relied heavily on advertising revenue even if CP as an institution did not (at least not directly) – there is virtually no evidence in the historical record that CP's news coverage was watered down, made more frivolous or entertaining, in response to commercial pressures. Considering that Hallin and Mancini, among others, identify pressure to create "market-friendly news" as a significant weakness of commercialized journalism,[25] it is worth noting that CP's cooperative structure appears to have largely insulated it from this pressure. Of all the complaints made about CP, no one ever criticized its news report as too sensational or too oriented to celebrity. The issues and events that CP considered central to Canadian political, economic, and social life were treated in a serious, even-handed way.

The cooperative structure mitigated to some extent the hierarchy of newsworthiness and power over news generation and selection described earlier. At the board and membership level, regional concerns about relative costs and the adequacy of the news service were regularly discussed, and discussed seriously. Perhaps the most striking example of this was the systematic review and expansion of CP's French-language service in the 1960s in response to complaints by French-language publishers. Granted, the political turmoil in Quebec in the early 1960s of which this was a manifestation was much more than a typical example of persistent Canadian regional tensions, and Purcell's personal determination to make improvements in this particular area was widely recognized. Still, Bill Stewart's comment that "the English-speaking publishers and the French-speaking publishers got along better with each other than they would get along with anybody else" also applies more broadly. CP was, at one level, a club of fellow publishers from across the country who understood each other's business and developed lasting relationships and often friendships through their joint involvement with the agency. (As Nichols frankly observed in his 1933 presidential address, besides promoting "the interests of the nation," CP's other main purpose was "to further our own interests."[26]) Shortcomings of the news service and possible solutions were regularly discussed at regional meetings between CP journalists (usually including senior representatives from the head office) and editors and publishers of member newspapers, and local publishers' views were systematically heard at meetings of the board of directors and at the annual general meeting. The result was a national organization that – within the limits of the leased-wire cost structure discussed previously – genuinely tried to operate on a basis of geographical equality (or at least mutual respect), and in many ways succeeded.

But if CP as a publishers' cooperative adopted an ethos of geographical (horizontal) equality, the same could not be said in social or class terms (vertical equality). As the relentless and in some ways brutal campaign to stop the American Newspaper Guild's organizing drive in 1950–51 made abundantly clear, CP was an organization of owners and employers of wage labour that had no qualms about confrontation with its employees.

Daniel Hallin's idea of the three zones of journalistic coverage – the spheres of consensus, legitimate controversy, and deviance – has been frequently cited in this study. It is a valuable schema because it recognizes that many important social, economic, and political issues (those within the sphere of legitimate controversy) are regularly addressed in North American journalism, and insofar as this is so, journalism does establish a genuine and meaningful public sphere. At the same time, it also recognizes that many significant issues – class conflict being one prominent example – are *not* systematically addressed in North American journalism, or are addressed in a limited or prejudicial way. The reference above to "the issues and events that CP considered central to Canadian political, economic, and social life" is meant to take account of this distinction; issues that CP did not consider central were not covered in the same serious and even-handed way (and perhaps not covered at all).

Hallin's analysis of journalistic professionalism, which takes account of both its strengths and limitations, similarly applies well to CP. Journalistic professionalism, Hallin states, is based on "a value system and standards of practice of its own, rooted in an ideology of public service, and with significant autonomy."[27] It emerged through an evolution in which "owners increasingly (withdrew) from the day-to-day management of newspapers, turning that task over to professional journalists." News organizations of this type "are characterized by extensive editorial hierarchies with many 'checks and balances' on the work of individual journalists ..." All these observations apply strongly to CP, where the board of directors had virtually no day-to-day involvement in CP's news operation and where the professional journalistic hierarchy was sharply articulated, consistently maintained and highly valued. (Purcell's paeans to filing editors, the largely anonymous but crucial organizers of CP's daily news flow, illustrate this point well.) But the professional ethos had contradictory elements as well. "It constrains owners and often has served to increase journalistic autonomy ... But it also constrains journalists, who are expected to renounce any ambition of using their position as a platform for expressing their own editorial views, and to submit to the discipline of professional routines and editorial hierarchies." Indeed, Hallin concludes, "professional routines can lead to subservience of the news media not to the particular political commitments of individual owners, but to a broader dominant view among political elites"; the idea of neutral professionalism depends on "a large ground of shared values and assumptions whose inclusion in the news is not seen as politically partial." Professionalism thus plays an important role in asserting and reinforcing social and political consensus, including, broadly speaking, the legitimacy of the existing political, social, and economic order. This is particularly so in relation to coverage of politics and government, where there is a "strongly institutionalized relationship ... between journalists and government officials ... . Mutual dependence between state and media institutions means that the structure of each reflects its relation with the other: news organizations are structured to a large extent around the 'beat' system that connects reporters to their sources in the state ..." Formal independence from political parties notwithstanding, "news content is powerfully shaped by information, agendas and interpretive frameworks originating within the institutions of the state."[28]

Discussions of journalism often have a strong normative thrust, dealing with such questions as whether journalism does its job properly (depending, of course, on how "properly" is defined). These are important questions to consider, but the present study mainly seeks to understand the job that journalism actually did. This approach reflects John Hartley's observation that journalism is "*the* sense-making practice of modernity" and is "caught up in all the institutions, struggles and practices of modernity; contemporary politics is unthinkable without it, as is contemporary consumer society, to such an extent that in the end it is difficult to decide whether journalism is a product of modernity, or modernity a product of journalism."[29] It is equally difficult to imagine how contemporary ideas of the nation and nationality would have developed in the absence of journalism. In more than 50 years of operation as a telegraphic news organization, Canadian Press provided a powerful and durable cultural underpinning for the idea of Canadian nationality and the basic institutional arrangements that went along with it. This was the period when ideas of English-Canadian nationality were consolidated and awareness of "Canadian" as a primary aspect of identity grew.[30] The nation thus evolved in parallel with the means of its articulation.

In a recent discussion of the "liberal order framework" as a way of thinking about Canadian history generally from the mid-nineteenth to mid-twentieth century, Ian McKay notes that "a (national and transnational) network of communications media" played an important part in its elaboration, and cites Antonio Gramsci's observation that the everyday objects of popular culture, including "newspaper articles, television advertisements and web pages," are part of the apparatus by which hegemony is exercised.[31] Making a similar point to Hallin's notion of the different spheres of journalistic discourse, McKay argues that the Canadian "public sphere" was based on "agreement on certain fundamentals (property, morality, respectability, progress, order) [as] the entry-ticket for debates over their implications (tariff policy, temperance, policing, workers' rights, diplomacy)," and that while these debates "are not of minor significance ... they do not call into question the fundamental institutions and patterns ..."[32] Exactly how this cultural work was accomplished, however, has not received a great deal of detailed attention to date; a more detailed examination of the content of Canadian Press news coverage than has been undertaken here might provide fertile ground for further exploration of these questions.

The relatively stable structure of telegraphic news distribution in Canada described above lasted for more than 50 years. I have consistently argued that it was not simply the product of a particular technology, but of an articulated technologically-based system that included political-economic, regulatory, institutional, and cultural elements. It is also true, however, that the underlying technology occupied a lynchpin role in this system. Thus when CP replaced the telegraph with much higher-capacity multiplexed telephone lines for data transmission in the early 1970s, the news-distribution system changed in important ways. Notably, all CP members could now have access to the same volume of news, thereby weakening the Toronto-focused spatial hierarchy of the mature telegraphic system.[33] This meant that major dailies in Vancouver and Winnipeg, for example, could finally receive the same amount of copy as those in Toronto or Montreal, shifting a significant editorial decision-making role away from CP's head office and into the hands of local editors. With much greater transmission capacity (transmission speed increased exponentially, to around 1,000 words per minute[34]), CP members could and did demand not only a greater volume, but different kinds of news: more interpretive writing and feature articles, more coverage of social trends in addition to event-based news, more business, sports and lifestyle coverage, and so on.[35]

New technology in the 1970s did not displace everything that went before, however. The practices of filing editors that had grown up in relation to the telegraph also survived its demise. With high-speed, high-capacity circuits available to all CP members after the early 1970s, the management of scarce transmission capacity was no longer important; now the challenge was to manage an abundant, potentially overwhelming, flow of information. The filing editor's role therefore remained central. While the "filing editor" title is no longer used, the current (online) edition of the Canadian Press *Stylebook* includes a lengthy section on "The News Report," setting out requirements for organizing and monitoring the flow of news that are different in detail but similar in spirit and overall thrust to those in the first CP style guide, published in 1940.[36] Looking back at Blondheim's emphasis on organization of the flow of news as the key to the formation of Associated Press in 1846, one could conclude that these journalistic practices are the most enduring element of all in the electrical/electronic distribution of news.

Canadian Press continued to evolve after the end of the telegraphic era. In addition to major technological changes, the further consolidation of Canadian newspapers throughout the 1980s and 1990s had important consequences for CP's operation. In 1996, a threat by the Southam chain (no longer under family ownership) to withdraw from CP precipitated a crisis that ended with a proposal for the agency to go out of business. This challenge was ultimately overcome, but in 2007 the former Southam papers and the *National Post* (then owned by the CanWest organization) did withdraw from membership, followed in 2010 by the Quebecor chain, with 40 daily newspapers. At the same time (as happened to many Canadian companies in the aftermath of the 2008 stock-market crash), a shortfall in the financing of CP's corporate pension plan became increasingly serious, a situation that could have led to bankruptcy. On top of this, the Canadian newspaper industry as a whole began to suffer significant losses in advertising revenue to the Internet and entered a period of contraction that continues at the time of writing.

With CP requiring a considerable infusion of capital to shore up its pension plan, its membership declining, the remaining members unwilling or unable to provide additional funds, and the crisis in the newspaper industry dictating a sustained search for new sources of revenue, the agency ceased to be a nonprofit cooperative in November, 2010. It was jointly purchased by three of its largest members, Torstar Corp. (parent company of the *Toronto Star*), The *Globe and Mail*, and the parent company of La Presse.[37] Although the new owners have stated firmly that they intend to run CP as a profitable business and stress the possibilities of new sources of revenue (from corporations, for example), the continuing challenges faced by the Canadian newspaper industry also present grounds for some concern about the agency's future. (New Zealand's national news agency folded in 2011, for example.[38])

CP remains the backbone of the Canadian domestic-news system. Scores of newspapers, hundreds of radio and television stations, corporations and government departments, numerous websites and mobile services – and thus millions of Canadians – rely on CP news. It is an honest, independent organization with strong traditions: seriousness of purpose, accuracy, timeliness, and accountability. In recent years it has been a leader in journalistic innovation, integrating print, broadcast, and online media effectively. Anyone with an interest in the health of the Canadian public sphere can only hope it continues to thrive for many years to come.

Chronology

1846 New York Associated Press established.

1847 Telegraph lines from New York reach Toronto and Montreal.

1849 Nova Scotia and New Brunswick connected to North American telegraph system.

1856 Havas, Wolff, and Reuters news agencies sign the first of a series of cartel agreements.

1866 Transatlantic cable connects Europe and North America.

1894 Canadian Pacific Railway purchases exclusive Canadian rights to Associated Press news service.

1904 Canadian Associated Press established, led by Toronto *Telegram* publisher John Ross Robertson.

1907 CPR announces significant cost increases for newspapers in western Canada.

Winnipeg *Free Press* and *Tribune* establish Western Associated Press as an alternative to CPR–AP service.

1910 (January) Board of Railway Commissioners rules that CPR's flat-rate system of news distribution must be scrapped.

(February) AP notifies CPR that contract will not be renewed.

(October) Canadian publishers establish Canadian Press Limited to take over AP rights in Canada.

1911 Ontario and Quebec members of CP Ltd. establish leased-wire connection between Toronto and New York.

1912 WAP establishes night leased wire from Montreal to Winnipeg and other western points.

1914 AP warns that contract with CP Ltd. will not be renewed unless CP establishes a stronger national organization.

1915 Facing financial pressure, WAP decides to abandon Montreal-Winnipeg leased wire.

1917   (January) Federal government provides $50,000 subsidy for national leased-wire system in response to petition from western and eastern Canadian publishers.

(January) Publishers agree to transform CP Ltd. into a unified national news agency.

(September) National news service of Canadian Press begins.

1919   (April) C.O. Knowles replaced as general manager by J.F.B. (Fred) Livesay.

(May) Winnipeg strike forces temporary reorganization of national news circuits.

1921   CP pays $300 a month for limited Reuters service from London.

1922   (March) Board of directors recommends banning use of CP news on radio; annual meeting of members disagrees.

CP establishes French-language circuit in Quebec (discontinued the following year).

1923   Federal subsidy for CP withdrawn (effective 1924).

Federal government agrees to pay Reuters $32,000 a year for Canadian publicity and news service from Ottawa (ended in 1936).

1924   Unsuccessful strike by CP telegraphers.

1932   Canadian Radio Broadcasting Commission established.

1932
–33   CP imposes severe spending cuts.

1933   CP agrees to provide radio news bulletins to CRBC stations.

1934   AP contract with Reuters effectively breaks long-standing cartel arrangements; CP sides with AP.

1938   Livesay resigns as general manager.

1939   (January) J.A. McNeil appointed general manager.

(September) Canada declares war against Germany.

1940   Gillis Purcell leaves CP to join Gen. Andrew McNaughton's staff; returns to CP in 1941 after being severely injured in a training accident.

1941   (January) CBC establishes its own news operation, ends exclusive arrangement with CP.

(March) CP decides to allow its radio news to be sold for sponsorship.

(July) CP's radio subsidiary, Press News Ltd., established.

Reuters reorganized after Roderick Jones resigns as managing director.

1942   Ross Munro's coverage of Dieppe raid distributed internationally.

1944   CP contract with Reuters provides full access to Press Association news service.

1945   Purcell appointed general manager.

1947   CP decides not to join Australian and New Zealand press associations as part-owners of Reuters.

1950   American Newspaper Guild attempts to organize CP editorial
           employees.
1951   Teletypsetter service established.
           (October) Service in French established.
           (November) ANG charges against CP of bad-faith bargaining dis-
           missed in court.
1953   ANG decertified as bargaining agent for CP journalists after defeat of
           organizing effort.
1954   Broadcast News established; private broadcasters represented on board
           of directors.
1956   CP criticized for inadequate international reporting.
1957   Vancouver *Sun* and *Province* establish joint operating agreement.
1958   Sale of news to broadcasters provides nearly 20 per cent of CP's total
           revenue.
           FP Publications established.
1959   Guy Rondeau appointed as first French-language member of CP's Ot-
           tawa bureau.
1962   Toronto *Globe and Mail, Star,* and *Telegram* threaten to withdraw from
           CP over assessment increases.
1963   French-language publishers in Quebec explore idea of an independent
           French-language news service.
1964   Reporter Jack Best posted to Moscow as "resident correspondent";
           bureau closed in 1969.
           CP acquires international service of Agence France-Presse.
1965   CP executives testify at hearings of Royal Commission on Bilingualism
           and Biculturalism.
           FP Publications acquires *Globe and Mail.*
           Sale of news to broadcasters accounts for nearly one-third of CP's total
           revenue.
1967   Entrance fees replaced by discount for continuous membership.
1969   (November) John Dauphinee appointed general manager.
           (December) CP executives testify at hearings of Senate Committee on
           Mass Media.
1970   Entrance fees effectively abolished.

Names of Organizations and Abbreviations

Agence France-Presse (AFP)–France's national news agency (successor to Havas), established 1944.

American Newspaper Guild (ANG) – CIO-affiliated union representing newspaper editorial employees; led unsuccessful attempt to unionize CP journalists, 1950–51.

Associated Press (AP) – Cooperatively owned US news agency, first established 1846 and reorganized in 1893 and 1901.

British United Press (BUP) – Montreal-based affiliate/subsidiary of United Press; sold UP news to Canadian and British newspapers and radio stations.

Broadcast News (BN) – New company to provide CP news to private broadcasters, established 1954; successor to Press News.

Canadian Associated Press (CAP) – Established 1904 to provide supplementary service of cable news from Britain for Canada; effectively absorbed by Canadian Press in 1920.

Canadian Broadcasting Corporation (CBC) – Successor to the CRBC (see below), established 1936.

Canadian Daily Newspapers Association (CDNA) – Industry association of Canadian newspapers.

Canadian Pacific Railway (CPR) – The CPR's Telegraph department held exclusive rights to distribute the US and international news of Associated Press in Canada from 1894 to 1910.

Canadian Press (CP) – Canada's national news agency, established 1917, providing a full domestic news service as well as international news to its members. It retained the official name "Canadian Press Limited" until the early 1920s, but for purposes of clarity is referred to simply as "Canadian Press" or "CP" after September 1917.

Canadian Press Limited (CP Ltd.) – Took over the rights to AP service in Canada in 1910; a loose federation of regional press organizations, with no significant Canadian news service or integrated management.

Canadian Radio Broadcasting Commission (CRBC) – Canadian public broadcaster/regulator, established 1932; succeeded by CBC, 1936.

International News Service (INS) – US news agency owned by Hearst interests.

Press Association (PA) – Britain's domestic news agency, a newspaper-owned cooperative like AP and CP; became majority owner of Reuters news agency in 1926.

Press News (PN) – CP subsidiary established 1941 to sell radio news to broadcasters. After Broadcast News was established, PN continued to handle CP's relationship with the CBC.

United Press (UP) – Privately owned US news agency, the nemesis of AP and (through its affiliate BUP) of CP.

United Press International (UPI) – US news agency formed after merger of UP and INS in 1958.

Western Associated Press (WAP) – Western Canadian news agency established 1907 by Winnipeg *Free Press* and *Tribune* as alternative to CPR/AP news service. Incorporated into Canadian Press in 1917.

Notes

Introduction

1 Carman Cumming, "The Canadian Press: A Force for Consensus?" in *Journalism Communication and the Law*, ed. G. Stuart Adam (Scarborough, ON: Prentice-Hall of Canada, 1976), 86.

2 M.E. Nichols, *(CP): The Story of the Canadian Press* (Toronto: Ryerson Press, 1948).

3 Arthur Siegel, *Politics and the Media in Canada*, 2nd ed. (Toronto: McGraw-Hill Ryerson, 1996), especially Chapter 8, "Canadian Press and the Parliamentary Press Gallery," 186–214; *Report of the Special Senate Committee on Mass Media*, Vol. 1, *The Uncertain Mirror* (Ottawa: Information Canada, 1970), 229–35; Carman Cumming, Mario Cardinal, and Peter Johansen, *Canadian News Services*, Vol. 6. of *Research Studies on the Newspaper Industry* (Ottawa: Royal Commission on Newspapers, 1981); Peter Buckley, *The National Link* (Toronto: Canadian Press, 1997); Carlton McNaught, *Canada Gets the News* (Toronto: Ryerson Press, 1940), especially Chapters. 4 and 5; Patrick White, "News Agencies in Canada: At the Crossroads," in *News Agencies in the Turbulent Era of the Internet*, ed. Oliver Boyd-Barrett (Barcelona: Government of Catalonia, Presidential Department, 2010), especially 107–13.

4 The phrase is taken from John Hartley, *Popular Reality: Journalism, Modernity, Popular Culture* (London: Arnold, 1996), 34. For an excellent overview of these developments, see David Paul Nord, "The Practice of Historical Research," in *Mass Communication Research and Theory*, eds. Guido H. Stempel III, David Weaver, and G. Cleveland Wilhoit (Boston and New York: Allyn and Bacon, 2003), 362–85. See also James Carey, "The Problem of Journalism History," in *James Carey: A Critical*

Reader, eds. Eve Stryker Munson and Catherine A. Warren (Minneapolis: University of Minnesota Press, 1997), 86–94; Michael Schudson, "Toward a Troubleshooting Manual for Journalism History," *Journalism and Mass Communication Quarterly* 74, no. 3 (Autumn 1997), 463–76. The most recent overview of Canadian literature dealing with the history of journalism is William J. Buxton and Catherine McKercher, "Newspapers, Magazines and Journalism in Canada: Towards a Critical Historiography," *Acadiensis* 28, no. 1 (Autumn 1998), 103–26; see also Russell Johnston, "Value Added: Recent Books in the History of Communications and Culture," *Acadiensis,* 32, no. 1 (Autumn 2002), 129–39.

5 James Carey, "A Cultural Approach to Communication," in *Communication as Culture: Essays on Media and Society,* ed. James Carey (New York: Routledge, 1992, first pub. 1989), 21.

6 Mary Vipond, "The Mass Media in Canadian History: The Empire Day Broadcast in 1939," *Journal of the Canadian Historical Association* 14, no. 1 (2003), 1–21. See also the essays in Gene Allen and Daniel Robinson, eds., *Communicating in Canada's Past: Essays in Media History* (Toronto: University of Toronto Press, 2009); Jeffrey L. McNairn, "Towards Deliberative Democracy: Parliamentary Intelligence and the Public Sphere" *Journal of Canadian Studies* 33, no. 1 (Spring 1998), 39–60; Minko Sotiron, *From Politics to Profit: The Commercialization of Canadian Daily Newspapers, 1890–1920* (Montreal and Kingston: McGill-Queen's University Press, 1997); Marjory Lang, *Women Who Made the News: Female Journalists in Canada, 1880–1945* (Montreal & Kingston: McGill-Queen's University Press, 1999); Barbara Freeman, *The Satellite Sex: The Media and Women's Issues in English Canada, 1966–1971* (Waterloo, ON: Wilfrid Laurier University Press, 2001); and *Beyond Bylines: Media Workers and Women's Rights in Canada* (Waterloo, ON: Wilfrid Laurier University Press, 2011); Jeff A. Webb, "Canada's Moose River Mine Disaster (1936): Radio–Newspaper Competition in the Business of News," *Historical Journal of Film, Radio, & Television* 16, no. 3 (August 1996) and *The Voice of Newfoundland: A Social History of the Broadcasting Corporation of Newfoundland, 1939–1949* (Toronto: University of Toronto Press, 2008). Until recently, the main works on media history in English Canada were those by Paul Rutherford, especially *A Victorian Authority: The Daily Press in Late Nineteenth-century Canada* (Toronto: University of Toronto Press, 1982); *When Television Was Young: Primetime Canada, 1952–1967* (Toronto: University of Toronto Press, 1990).

7 Gerald Friesen, *Citizens and Nation: An Essay on History, Communication and Canada* (Toronto: University of Toronto Press, 2000).

8 Benedict Anderson, *Imagined Communities: Reflections on the Origin and Spread of Nationalism*, rev. ed. (London: Verso, 1991); Jürgen Habermas, *The Structural Transformation of the Public Sphere: An Inquiry into a Category of Bourgeois Society*, trans. by Thomas Burger (Cambridge, MA: MIT Press, 1989); John B. Thompson, *The Media and Modernity: A Social Theory of the Media* (Stanford, CA: Stanford University Press, 1995); Carey, "A Cultural Approach to Communication," 13–36.

9 Anderson, *Imagined Communities*, 35.

10 The situation is different in countries such as England or France, where for reasons of geography, urban structure, and especially the combined roles of political, cultural, and economic capital played by London and Paris, the dominant newspapers were distributed widely from the mid-nineteenth century onward.

11 Cumming, "The Canadian Press: A Force for Consensus?" 86.

12 George Scott, *Reporter Anonymous: The Story of the Press Association* (London: Hutchinson & Co., 1968); Jack Brayley, *The Brayley Years* (unpublished manuscript), N 50.

13 Oliver Boyd-Barrett and Terhi Rantanen, "News Agencies as News Sources: A Re-evaluation" in *International News in the Twenty-first Century*, eds. Chris Paterson and Annabelle Sreberny (University of Luton Press, 2004), 42.

14 Ibid., 42–3.

15 Menahem Blondheim, *News over the Wires: The Telegraph and the Flow of Public Information in America, 1844–1897* (Cambridge, MA, and London: Harvard University Press, 1994), 7.

16 Oliver Boyd-Barrett and Terhi Rantanen, "The Globalization of News," in *The Globalization of News*, eds. Oliver Boyd-Barrett and Terhi Rantanen (London: Sage Publications, 1998), 1–2. See also Terhi Rantanen, "The Globalization of Electronic News in the 19th Century," *Media, Culture, & Society* 19 (1997), 605–20.

17 *Many Voices, One World: Towards a New, More Just and More Efficient World Information and Communication Order* (Paris: UNESCO, 1980), 37, 145–6. For a useful overview of the "cultural imperialism" thesis (though focusing mainly on television), see Thompson, *The Media and Modernity*, 164–73.

18 Oliver Boyd-Barrett, *The International News Agencies* (London: Constable and Co., 1980), 28.

19 Ibid., 58, 195, 201, 204, 206, 209.

20 Boyd-Barrett and Rantanen, "The Globalization of News," 5.

21 For Canada, see Gene Allen, "News Across the Border: Associated Press in Canada, 1894–1917," *Journalism History* 31, no. 4 (2006); for Australia, see

Peter Putnis, "Reuters in Australia: The Supply and Exchange of News, 1859–1877," *Media History* 10, no. 2 (2004), 67–88; "How the International News Agency Business Model Failed: Reuters in Australia, 1877–1895," *Media History* 12, no. 1 (2006), 1–17.

22 Terhi Rantanen, *The Media and Globalization* (London: SAGE, 2005).

23 Ibid., 79

24 Ibid., 80

25 Ibid., 29

26 Terhi Rantanen, "The Cosmopolitanization of News," *Journalism Studies* 8, no. 6 (2007), 843–61. Rantanen concludes that "the nationalization of news was an outcome of [news agencies'] development rather than a reason for it ... " (858).

27 Dwayne Winseck and Robert Pike, *Communication and Empire: Media, Markets, and Globalization, 1860–1930* (Durham, NC: Duke University Press, 2007).

28 Simon Potter, *News and the British World: The Emergence of an Imperial Press System* (Oxford: Clarendon Press, 2003), 13–16, 215.

29 Craig Calhoun, *Nationalism* (Buckingham, England: Open University Press, 1997), 98.

30 Michael B. Palmer, *Des Petits Journaux Aux Grandes Agences: Naissance Du Journalisme Moderne* (Paris: Éditions Aubier Montaigne, 1983), 44–5, 52–6.

31 For the history of Reuters, see Donald Read, *The Power of News: The History of Reuters* (Oxford: Oxford University Press, 1992); for UP, see Richard Schwarzlose, *The Nation's Newsbrokers*, Vol. 2, *The Rush to Institution: From 1865 to 1920* (Evanston, IL: Northwestern University Press, 1990) and Joe Alex Morris, *Deadline Every Minute: The Story of the United Press* (New York: Greenwood Press, 1968); for the Press Association, Scott, *Reporter Anonymous*, and Oliver Boyd-Barrett, "Market Control and Wholesale News: The Case of Reuters" in *Newspaper History from the Seventeenth Century to the Present Day*, eds. George Boyce, James Curran and Pauline Winngate (London: Constable and Co., 1978), 192–204; for Associated Press, Schwarzlose, *The Nation's Newsbrokers*, and Blondheim, *News over the Wires*.

32 In 1945, the US Supreme Court ruled that AP, as then constituted, was a combination in restraint of trade, though not a complete monopoly; US Supreme Court, *Associated Press v. United States,* 326 U.S. 1 (1945).

33 Blondheim, *News over the Wires*, 1–4, 7, 43, 99–100, 109, 151.

34 Palmer, *Des Petits Journaux Aux Grandes Agences*, 42, 104, 106–7, 260; Read, *The Power of News*, 63–6, 86–9, 122–30, 148–9, 186–8, 190–3; Blondheim, *News over the Wires,*131–7, 176–84.

35 Jonathan Silberstein-Loeb, "Business, Politics, Technology and the International Supply of News, 1845–1950" (University of Cambridge PhD dissertation, 2009), 14.

36 Ibid., 157

37 Ibid., 4, 46; Gene Allen, "Monopolies of News: Harold Innis, the Telegraph, and Wire Services," in *The Toronto School of Communication Theory: Interpretations, Extensions, Applications,* eds. Rita Watson and Menahem Blondheim (Toronto and Jerusalem: University of Toronto Press/Magnes Press, 2008), 170–98.

38 See Boyd-Barrett, *The International News Agencies,* 20.

39 Potter notes that competition often trumped appeals to imperial solidarity; *News and the British World,* 97–8.

40 See Putnis, "How the International News Agency Business Model Failed." Speaking of the London dailies, Boyd-Barrett notes that "[t]he wealthier a newspaper, the more likely it was to resent the role of Reuters, since the agency functioned to minimise the advantage of substantial independent reportorial strength overseas for any given newspapers." Boyd-Barrett, "Market Control and Wholesale News," 195.

41 Putnis, "Reuters in Australia," notes the difficulties of finding agreement among morning and afternoon dailies in Australia on their supply of international news; see also Putnis, "How the International News Agency Business Model Failed."

42 Boyd-Barrett, "Market Control and Wholesale News."

43 Palmer, *Des Petits Journaux Aux Grandes Agences,* 52–4, 56, 234, 247, 251–2, 261.

44 This "ecological approach" borrows from John Nerone's analysis of the antebellum Cincinnati press. Nerone suggests that a medium should be considered not so much a thing in itself as "exactly what the word suggests: something in between other things. ... a set of relationships within a social and cultural ecology." The proper unit of study "is not the individual medium, but the whole set of media within a particular ecology." John C. Nerone, "A Local History of the U.S. Press: Cincinnati, 1793–1858," in *Ruthless Criticism: New Perspectives in U.S. Communication History,* eds. William S. Solomon and Robert W. McChesney (Minneapolis and London: University of Minnesota Press, 1993), 39.

45 Blondheim, *News over the Wires,* 2–4; Terhi Rantanen, "The New Sense of Place in Nineteenth-century News," *Media, Culture, & Society* 25, no. 4 (2003), 435–9.

46 Blondheim, *News over the Wires,* 38.

47 For the importance of periodicity in news generally, see John Sommerville, *The News Revolution in England: Cultural Dynamics of Daily Information* (New York and Oxford: Oxford University Press, 1996).

48 Blondheim, *News over the Wires*, 151.

49 Boyd-Barrett, "Market Control and Wholesale News," 3. For Canada, see p. 39.

50 Blondheim, *News over the Wires*, 56–9.

51 Ibid., 56.

52 See Chapter 7 for an extended discussion of the role of CP filing editors. See also Stephen Ford (a pseudonym for CP's general manager, Gillis Purcell), "The Canadian Press (CP)" (n.p., 1967). At the time, most of CP's editorial staff, which numbered more than 300, was "filing editors (who cut incoming copy to the capacity of their outgoing circuits and keep the best news constantly ahead) and rewrite men (who boil down the copy received from CP member newspapers."

53 For example, note the actions of the publisher of the *Los Angeles Times* and editor of the *Chicago Tribune*, who resigned in July 2008 rather than carrying out the demands for severe staff cuts by the newspaper's new owner, Sam Zell. (Richard Pena, "Two Leaders Stepping Down at Big Tribune Newspapers," *New York Times*, July 15, 2008, C2.) The firing of *Ottawa Citizen* editor Russell Mills in 2004 for criticizing the CanWest chain's policy on national editorials is a high-profile Canadian example.

54 See Oliver Boyd-Barrett and Tehri Rantanen, "Global and National News Agencies: Threats and Opportunities in the Age of Convergence," in *Global Journalism: Topical Issues and Media Systems*, eds. Arnold de Beer and John C. Merrill (Boston: Allyn & Bacon, 2008), 33–47.

55 See Chapter 5 below. See also Hanno Hardt, "Without the Rank and File: Journalism History, Media Workers, and Problems of Representation," in *Newsworkers: Toward a History of the Rank and File,* eds. Hanno Hardt and Bonnie Brennen (Minneapolis: University of Minnesota Press, 1995), 1–29. For a present-day approach to these issues, see Catherine McKercher and Vincent Mosco, eds., *Knowledge Workers in the Information Society* (Lanham: Lexington Books, 2007).

56 Friesen, *Citizens and Nation*, 162.

57 For a useful and succinct account of the significance of communication for Canadian history generally and the broad historical context within which communication media developed, see Mary Vipond, *The Mass Media in Canada*, 4th ed. (Toronto: James Lorimer & Co., 2011), 9–21.

58 J.M.S. Careless, "Frontierism, Metropolitanism, and Canadian History," *Canadian Historical Review* 35, no. 1 (March 1954), 1–21 and "Metropolis

and Region: The Interplay of City and Region in Canadian History before
1914," *Urban History Review* 3 (Feb. 1979), 99–119.
59 Rantanen, "The Cosmopolitanization of News."
60 Vipond, *Mass Media in Canada*, 17.
61 As Friesen observes in his useful summary of the main currents of social
history in Canada, the increasingly strict codification of property rights of
all kinds – "the right to use and to prohibit others from using land or tools
or capital" – was a crucial element in the increasing dominance and integration of markets in twentieth-century Canada; *Citizens and Nation*, 124.
62 José Igartua, *The Other Quiet Revolution: National Identities in English
Canada, 1945–71* (Vancouver: UBC Press, 2006).

Chapter 1

1 Ernest Green, "Canada's First Electric Telegraph," *Ontario Historical Society
Papers & Records* 24 (1927): 369–70. The telegraph line from Montreal to
Toronto was completed in August 1847, and a line from the American
border across New Brunswick to Nova Scotia went into operation on
1 January 1849; John Murray, *A Story of the Telegraph* (Montreal: John Lovell
& Co., 1905), 114 (CIHM No. 73328).
2 *Globe*, 15 March 1855.
3 Library and Archives Canada, Ottawa (hereafter LAC), Board of Railway
Commissioners for Canada (Railway Commission), testimony of James
Camp, 21 March 1910 (RG 46, vol. 43, p. 1587). Jonathan Silberstein-Loeb's
doctoral dissertation refers to a "Canadian association" of newspapers
that received AP news in the 1870s, but I have found no other references
to such an association during this period. See Silberstein-Loeb, "Business,
Politics, Technology and the International Supply of News, 1845–1950,"
(University of Cambridge PhD dissertation, 2009), 46–7, citing Orton to
E. Brooks, 27 March 1877, Smithsonian Institution, Western Union,
201B-19, 98.
4 *Globe*, 1 Sept. 1866.
5 See, for example, David Harvey, *The Condition of Postmodernity: An Enquiry
into the Origins of Cultural Change* (Cambridge, MA: Blackwell, 1989).
6 Terhi Rantanen, "The Struggle for Control of Domestic News Markets (1)"
in *The Globalization of News*, eds. Oliver Boyd-Barrett and Terhi Rantanen
(London: Sage Publications, 1998), 35; Donald Read, *The Power of News:
The History of Reuters* (Oxford: Oxford University Press, 1992), 9, 53–8;
Silberstein-Loeb, "Business, Politics, Technology and the International
Supply of News, 1845–1950," 196.

7 Isabelle Lehuu, *Carnival on the Page: Popular Print Media in Antebellum America* (Chapel Hill and London: University of North Carolina Press, 2000); Michael Schudson, *Discovering the News: A Social History of American Newspapers* (New York: Basic Books, 1978).

8 Menahem Blondheim, *News over the Wires: The Telegraph and the Flow of Public Information in America, 1844–1897* (Cambridge, MA, and London: Harvard University Press, 1994), 49–50.

9 With the completion of the telegraph line from New York to Halifax in 1849, Halifax (where the Cunard ships called before reaching Boston) became the North American terminus for telegraphic news from Europe. The extension of the telegraphic network to St. John's, Newfoundland, in 1855 meant that news from Europe was first received there.

10 Blondheim, *News over the Wires,* 98–9. For the involvement of the Montreal Telegraph Co. with NYAP circa 1852, see *Globe,* 13 Aug. 1902, p. 4, letter of Robert F. Easson. For the role of the Great North Western Telegraph Co., see Easson, "The Beginnings of the Telegraph," in J.E. Middleton, *The Municipality of Toronto, A History,* vol. 2 (Toronto: Dominion Publishing Co., 1923), 767–69.

11 Read, *The Power of News,* 33, 58, 81.

12 LAC, Railway Commission, testimony of Camp, 15 Nov. 1909 (RG 46, vol. 40, p. 12491), and 21 March 1910 (RG 46, vol. 43, p. 1587). See also Canadian Pacific Archives (Montreal), Charles Hosmer (manager of CPR Telegraphs) to William Van Horne, 4 Jan. 1894; and contract between Associated Press and CPR, 2 Jan. 1894, O.D. 2167, president's office correspondence no. 67164. Before 1894, the CPR had no news service in eastern Canada and provided material from UP (AP's competitor) to western Canada. When the CPR acquired the AP service, the Great North Western Telegraph Co. assumed the rights for UP in the east. (Railway Commission, 21 March 1910 [RG 46, vol. 43, p. 1587]).

13 Paul Starr, *The Creation of the Media: Political Origins of Modern Communications* (New York: Basic Books, 2004), 1–3.

14 Canadian Press documents (hereafter CP documents), Minutes of the annual general meeting of the members of the Canadian Press, Toronto, 28 April 1925.

15 For the complaints, see Associated Press Corporate Archives (APCA), AP 02A.4 Special Member files series I. Canadian Press, 1913–28 (box 1), folder 1, 1913–19, Kent Cooper to Stone, 8 June 1917. In his later book *Barriers Down: The Story of the News Agency Epoch* (New York: Farrar and Rinehart, 1942), Cooper, then AP's general manager, held up the arrangement with CP as a model for AP's dealings with the rest of the world's press.

16 CP Archives, Hosmer to Van Horne, 4 Jan. 1894.

17 LAC, Railway Commission transcripts of hearings, 15 Nov. 1909 (RG 46, vol. 40, p. 12482) and 21 March 1910 (RG 46, vol. 43, p. 1507). See also Gene Allen, "Monopolies of News: Harold Innis, the Telegraph and Wire Services," in *The Toronto School of Communication Theory: Interpretations, Extensions, Applications*, eds. Rita Watson and Menahem Blondheim (Toronto and Jerusalem: University of Toronto Press/Magnes Press, 2008).

18 Phillip Buckner, ed. *Canada and the British Empire* (Oxford and Toronto: Oxford University Press, 2008); José Igartua, *The Other Quiet Revolution: National Identities in English Canada, 1945–71.* (Vancouver: UBC Press, 2006); Carl Berger, *The Sense of Power: Studies in the Ideas of Canadian Imperialism, 1867–1914* (Toronto: University of Toronto Press, 1970); Simon Potter, *News and the British World: The Emergence of an Imperial Press System* (Oxford: Clarendon Press, 2003), 33–4.

19 "Whole World Pays Tribute to the Requirements of the Telegraph Editor of a Modern Daily," Toronto *Star*, 26 Aug. 1905.

20 The Reuters Archive, Thomson Reuters (RA), Jones Papers, section 1, box 1, Henry Collins to de Reuter, New York, 4 Nov. 1906. Collins was a Reuters emissary sent to Canada in 1906; see pp. 22–3.

21 Carman Miller points out that not all Canadian newspapers were equally enthusiastic supporters of Canadian participation in the Boer War; Liberal papers tended to support Laurier in wanting to proceed cautiously, whereas Conservative papers such as the Montreal *Star* and Toronto *Telegram* were vigorous proponents of Canadian involvement. Miller, *Painting the Map Red: Canada and the South African War, 1899–1902* (Montreal & Kingston: Canadian War Museum/McGill-Queen's University Press, 1993), 25–6, 37–8.

22 Potter, *News and the British World,* 9.

23 Ibid., 48–53; Miller, op. cit.

24 Potter, *News and the British World,* 92–9. For CAP's structure, see LAC, Canadian Associated Press, draft form of letters patent, 16 Jan. 1904 (RG 95, vol. 1221); Thomas L. Walkom, "The Daily Newspaper Industry in Ontario's Developing Capitalistic Economy: Toronto and Ottawa, 1871–1911" (PhD diss., University of Toronto, 1983), 51.

25 For a journalistic biography of Robertson, see Ron Poulton, *The Paper Tyrant: John Ross Robertson of the Toronto Telegram* (Toronto and Vancouver: Clarke, Irwin & Co., 1971).

26 Potter, *News and the British World,* 50. Arthur Ford, who was editor of the London (Ontario) *Free Press* for many years and was active in Canadian journalism in the early 1900s, cited dissatisfaction with AP's coverage of the British election of 1904 as the reason for the *Free Press*'s decision to

subscribe to CAP; Arthur Ford, "Early Days in Gathering News" London *Free Press*, 13 July 1955.

27 Potter, *News and the British World*, 54–5.

28 LAC, Canadian Associated Press (RG 95, vol. 1221), Malone, Malone, and Holden to secretary of state, 8 Jan. 1904. Department of Finance – Canadian Press, memorandum, "Canadian Press Limited," n.d. (RG 19, vol. 98, file 101-29-32). The subsidy to CAP varied in amount, from a high of $12,284 in 1911–12 to a low of $5,000 in 1915–16, stabilizing at $8,000 from 1916 to 1922.

29 See, for example, Sir Thomas Shaughnessy to Robertson, 16 June 1906. CP Archives, president's office correspondence, no. 81273. See also Potter, *News and the British World*, 96–9. Arthur Ford stated that CAP correspondents in London "receive their instructions" from Robertson; "Early Days in Gathering News" London *Free Press*, 13 July 1955.

30 CP Archives, president's office correspondence, Archer Baker (European Manager) to Shaughnessy, private and confidential, 27 June 1906.

31 See, for example, LAC, Department of the Secretary of State, chief press censor, 1915–20 (RG 6 E, vol. 617, file 314) – "Desire for an Imperial News Organization," newspaper clipping, n.d. [30 Oct. 1916] quoting comments of E.H. Slack, president of CP Ltd., to the Royal Commission on the Dominions. The city editor of the *Globe* told Henry Collins that the CAP service was "to a very large extent useless, that trashy items of a personal character are sent ... while important news is altogether omitted." RA, Jones Papers, section 1, box 1, Henry Collins to Baron Herbert de Reuter, 28 Nov. 1906.

32 RA, Collins to de Reuter, 16 Nov. 1906. Hugh Graham, publisher of the Montreal *Star* and a member of CAP, told Collins that CAP was "constructed solely with the object of serving the political aims of the government." However, Sir Wilfrid Laurier, the prime minister, was not impressed with CAP's service: see LAC, Laurier fonds, p. 153118 (microfilm reel C-874), Laurier to Northcliffe, 8 March 1909.

33 RA. Confidential. Extracts from report of the president submitted to the annual meeting of the Canadian Associated Press, 1 June 1906; "Whole World Pays Tribute to the Requirements of the Telegraph Editor of a Modern Daily," Toronto *Star*, 26 Aug. 1905.

34 AP had 622 subscribing US members in 1900 and 1,027 in 1918. See Richard A. Schwarzlose, *The Nation's Newsbrokers: Vol. 2, The Rush to Institution* (Evanston, IL: Northwestern University Press, 1990), 248–9. By 1920, when CAP was taken over by the newly established Canadian Press, it had only seven remaining subscribers; LAC, RG 95, vol. 522, E. Norman Smith to acting secretary of state, 1921 July 14.

35 Potter, *News and the British World,* 34–5. The economics of news agencies and the strong monopolistic tendencies that result are well explained in Blondheim, *News over the Wires,* especially 99–100. As Potter has also noted (96–7), keeping the CAP service relatively expensive served the interests of the larger and wealthier papers that were its main subscribers; if CAP was too expensive for the small-town newspapers in whose territory the big-city dailies circulated, this gave the larger papers a competitive advantage.

36 RA, Collins to de Reuter, 28 Nov. 1906: "Mr. Robertson was not going to permit his control over the CAP to be in any way lessened ... The Toronto journals are ... very wealthy; it is here that the members of the CAP Executive reside, and they mean to keep the power entirely in their own hands."

37 RA, Collins to de Reuter, 4 Nov. 1906. Collins decried "the supineness, want of enterprise, and lack of self respect on the part of Canadian newspapers who preferred to place themselves in a state of subordination to a powerful organization rather than pay adequately and so gain their independence." See also Collins to de Reuter, 18 Nov. 1906. Despite their usual claims of poverty, the largest Canadian papers appeared very prosperous. The *Telegram,* among others, was "magnificently equipped, the counters of polished marble ... everything is done on a lavish scale, and we have nothing in Australia to compare with the premises of the *Telegram,* the *Globe,* and one or two of the other Toronto journals."

38 RA, Collins to de Reuter, 28 Nov. 1906.

39 RA. Confidential. Extracts from Report of the President submitted to the annual meeting of the Canadian Associated Press, 1 June 1906.

40 RA, Collins to de Reuter, 28 Nov. 1906. Stewart Lyon added that he too shared this view: the *Globe* did not want to strengthen the papers in nearby Hamilton, where it competed vigorously for circulation.

41 RA, R.M. McLeod to de Reuter, 4 May 1907.

42 Peter Putnis, "How the International News Agency Business Model Failed – Reuters in Australia, 1877–1895," *Media History* 12, no. 1 (2006): 1–17. See also Putnis, "Reuters in Australia: The Supply and Exchange of News, 1859–1877," *Media History* 10, no. 2 (2004): 67–88.

43 RA, Collins to de Reuter, 21 Nov. 1906.

44 In fact, Collins's first stop had been to visit Melville Stone, the general manager of AP, in New York. Stone said he had no misgivings about Reuters' plans for Canada, which he recognized as a supplementary service not intended to displace AP. RA, Collins to de Reuter, 4 Nov. 1906. Collins repeated that he did not intend to attempt to replace AP in a conversation with Hugh Graham of the Montreal *Star.* RA, Collins to de Reuter, 16 Nov. 1906.

45 RA, Collins to de Reuter, Vancouver, 2 Jan. 1907.
46 Minko Sotiron, *From Politics to Profit: The Commercialization of Canadian Daily Newspapers, 1890–1920* (Montreal and Kingston: McGill-Queen's University Press, 1997), 76.
47 Walkom, "The Daily Newspaper Industry," 83–4.
48 "Whole World Pays Tribute to the Requirements of the Telegraph Editor of a Modern Daily," Toronto *Star*, 26 Aug. 1905.
49 Ross Harkness, *J.E. Atkinson of the Star* (Toronto: University of Toronto Press, 1963), 64.
50 As Peter Goheen has shown, metropolitan papers in particular were quick to abandon the exchange system when telegraphic news first became available; Goheen, "The Impact of the Telegraph on the Newspaper in Mid-Nineteenth Century British North America," *Urban Geography* 11 (1990): 107–29.
51 31 Vic. cap. X, An Act for the Regulation of the Postal Service (1867), s. 22
52 LAC, Board of Railway Commissioners for Canada RG 46, vol. 40, transcripts of hearings, Winnipeg, 15 Nov. 1909, 12509, 12510.
53 Ibid., transcripts of hearings, Ottawa, 8 June 1910, 8185–7.
54 Ibid., transcripts of hearings, Winnipeg, 15 Nov. 1909, 12510–11.
55 Ibid., 12513, 12481. See also file no. 84868, n.d. [1907].
56 CP documents, Western Associated Press (hereafter, WAP) annual meeting, Oct. 1917, 13.
57 CP Archives, RG 1, Roblin to Shaughnessy, private, 28 July 1906. When the AP contract was signed in 1894, the head of the CPR telegraph department said he could "hardly over-estimate the value of having control of such a service ... and also a more or less direct control over every correspondent that gathers news for them throughout the entire country," with revenue a distinctly secondary consideration. CP Archives, Hosmer to Van Horne, 8 Jan. 1894, president's office correspondence, no. 76164.
58 Robert F. Easson, "The Beginnings of the Telegraph," in J.E. Middleton, *The Municipality of Toronto, A History*, vol. 2 (Toronto: Dominion Publishing Co., 1923), 768.
59 LAC, Railway Commission RG 46, vol. 43, transcripts of hearings, Ottawa, 21 March 1910, 1564–5, 1568, 1581.
60 Ibid., 1528–9, 1544.
61 CP documents, John Tibbs, news service report for meeting of members and editors of Ontario pony service papers, 28 April 1925. For another overview of Canadian newspapers' domestic-news arrangements before the establishment of CP Ltd., see J.F.B. Livesay, "The Canadian Press – Its Birth and Development" reprint from Quebec *Chronicle-Telegraph*, 21 June 1939.

62 LAC, Railway Commission RG 46, vol. 40, transcripts of hearings, Winnipeg, 12491. The number of AP clients had presumably been larger before 1907, when most of the 13 members of WAP were still taking the CPR service.

63 For example, the Winnipeg *Free Press* was told that the $300 a month it was paying (for both the day and night report) would be increased right away to $500, and eventually to as much as $1,200 (CP documents, WAP annual meeting, 1917, remarks of E.H. Macklin). These events are described in considerable detail in M.E. Nichols, *(CP): The Story of the Canadian Press* (Toronto: Ryerson Press, 1948), 20–69. Nichols was a direct participant in these events, and although the book has much value as a source, his partiality to the point of view of the Winnipeg publishers must be kept in mind.

64 For the formation of the first Associated Press, see Schwarzlose, *The Nation's Newsbrokers, Vol. 1: The Formative Years: From Pretelegraph to 1865* (Evanston, IL: Northwestern University Press, 1989), 89 ff and 105–6; and Blondheim, *News over the Wires*, 46, 55.

65 Although WAP was a proprietary organization dominated by the two big Winnipeg papers, it somewhat misleadingly described itself as a cooperative. It only adopted a truly cooperative structure in 1915 after wartime financial pressure made it impossible for the Winnipeg papers to continue operating it as a proprietary association. See, for example, CP documents, WAP, minutes of directors' meeting, 29 Nov. 1911, J.H. Woods (Calgary *Herald*) to Nichols.

66 LAC, Railway Commission RG 46, vol. 47, order no. 9226, 8 Jan. 1910.

67 Ibid. (RG 46, vol. 43, p. 1506), comments of George Henderson (lawyer for eastern publishers), 21 March 1910.

68 Ibid., 1645.

69 Ibid., comments of M.E. Nichols, 1724.

70 For the assessment dispute in the early 1920s, see pp. 66–8 for the 1930s, Chapter 2, pp. 81–4; for the 1960s, Chapter 6, pp. 226–232.

71 APCA, AP 01 correspondence, (file) Correspondence re Canadian Press association/contracts, minutes, correspondence, 1910, Diehl to Kent, 24 Feb. 1910. Melville Stone, AP's general manager, had expressed concerns about AP's service to Canada being provided by a railway company since at least 1901; see Stone to James Kent, general manager, CPR Telegraph Department, 30 May 1901; APCA, AP 01, Correspondence re Canadian Press Association, correspondence and contract, Canadian Pacific Railway, 1894, 1901. See also RA, Collins to de Reuter, 4 Nov. 1906, and Associated Press, minutes of annual meeting, 1910, 95.

328 Notes to pages 28–9

72 CP Archives, Shaughnessy to Kent, 22 Feb. 1910, LB. 96, p. 874. The rail-way's decision to get out of the news business was not made public until after a second round of railway commission hearings in June.

73 LAC, Railway Commission RG 46, vol. 43, 21 March 1910, 1578, comments of Stewart Lyon and George Henderson.

74 APCA, AP 01, Correspondence re Canadian Press Association, 1910, MacNab to Diehl, 12 April 1910.

75 Ibid., "Memo re AP," n.d.

76 Ibid., Crandall to Stone, personal and confidential, 8 June 1910.

77 Ibid., "News Service to Proposed Canadian Publishers' Ass'n," New York, 15 June 1910. Delegates from Winnipeg, Regina, Calgary, and Vancouver were said to be representing WAP, and two men from the Toronto *Telegram* went on behalf of CAP. The Montreal *Star* was also represented. (Somewhat misleadingly, Robertson told Stone that the association of publishers also was affiliated with CAP, "an organization controlling eighteen or twenty papers.") CP documents, letter of John Ross Robertson, 15 June 1910. Soon afterward, a group of publishers and editors from New Brunswick and Nova Scotia established the Eastern Press Association, appointing their own delegate "to co-operate in the formation of a general Canadian news association." CP documents, Eastern Press Association, minutes of meeting, 28 June 1910.

78 APCA, AP 01, correspondence re Canadian Press Association, 1910, Crandall to Stone, Halifax, 12 Aug. 1910.

79 Ibid., contract, 6 Oct. 1910, between AP and undersigned Canadian news-paper publishers.

80 For AP's concern over competition from UP and INS, see Schwarzlose, *The Nation's Newsbrokers*, Vol. 2, 215, 221, 229, 233. In economist's terminology, Stephen Shmanske stresses the importance for news agencies of excluding so-called "free riders" who use its news without paying; see Shmanske, "News as a Public Good: Cooperative Ownership, Price Commitments, and the Success of the Associated Press," *Business History Review* 60, no. 1 (1986): 57–8.

81 APCA, AP 01, correspondence re Canadian Press Association, 1910, Stone to Atkinson, Lyon and Crandall, 26 Sept. 1910. John W. Dafoe of the Winnipeg *Free Press* reported that Stone insisted that new franchises not be restricted unduly: "The Associated Press was suffering from undue restrictions which had contributed to the establishment of rival news agen-cies. It was this situation that Mr. Stone hoped to prevent in the Canadian field, at present only in its earliest development, and he made this verbally a condition of the arrangement." (CP documents, minutes of the special

general meeting of the shareholders of the Port Arthur and Prairie Division
of the Canadian Press Limited, 16 March 1914, p. 9.) As Thomas Walkom
notes, the formation of CP Ltd. gave Canadian publishers for the first
time the ability to limit new competitors' access to AP, which they had not
been able to do under the CPR regime; Walkom, "The Daily Newspaper
Industry," 102.

82 CP documents, minutes of directors' meeting, 7 Nov. 1910.
83 APCA, AP 01, Correspondence re Canadian Press Association, 1910,
Atkinson to Stone, 27 Oct. 1910, enclosing E.N. Smith to Lyon.
84 Ibid., Atkinson to Kent, 18 Jan. 1910, enclosed in Kent to Diehl,
21 Jan. 1910.
85 Ibid., Stone to Noyes, 8 Nov. 1910.
86 Ibid., F.B. Jennings to Stone, 26 Oct. 1910.
87 Nichols, *(CP): The Story of The Canadian Press,* 27, 28.
88 CP documents, WAP, meeting of board of directors, 13 Aug. 1914, remarks
of E.H. Macklin.
89 CP documents, meeting of the newspaper publishers of Ontario and
Quebec, 3 Oct. 1910; CP documents, meeting of provisional directors,
Canadian Press, 8 Nov. 1910.
90 APCA, AP 01, correspondence re Canadian Press Association, 1910, Slack
to Stone, 27 Oct. 1910. Slack later thanked Stone for the news AP provided
of the British elections, which was faster and better than that supplied by
CAP; this was "an awful blow" to Robertson, who was "as limp as a linen
collar in the dog days," and had greatly helped Slack convince the other
morning papers to throw in their lot with AP. Ibid., Slack to Stone,
6 Dec. 1910.
91 CP documents, minutes of meeting of newspaper publishers of Ontario
and Quebec, 3 Oct. 1910, Stone to Atkinson, Lyon and Crandall, 25 Sept.
1910.
92 For the Toronto papers' aggressive interest in the Ontario market, see
Walkom, "The Daily Newspaper Industry," 49, 123. E.H. Slack of the
Montreal *Gazette* observed later that one of the chief obstacles to the establishment of a national news service had been "the feeling that a general
news service tended to strengthen the weaker newspapers at the expense
of the stronger." LAC, Department of the Secretary of State, chief press
censor, 1915–20, RG 6 E, vol. 617, file 314 – Desire for an Imperial news
organization; newspaper clipping, n.d. [1916].
93 CP documents, meeting of shareholders of Canadian Press Ltd., July 1914.
94 CP documents, meeting of Western Canadian publishers, 2 Nov. 1910,
p. 36.

95 CP documents, minutes of WAP meeting, Calgary, 2 Nov. 1910.
96 Ibid.
97 CP documents, Canadian Press Ltd., minutes of directors' meeting, 17 Feb. 1911.
98 CP documents, memorandum submitted by M.E. Nichols to members of WAP about interview with Melville Stone, 20 Nov. 1911.
99 Allen, "Monopolies of News."
100 CP documents, WAP, expenditures for year ended 31 August 1913; WAP, minutes of meeting held at Calgary, 28 Feb. 1912.
101 CP documents, Eastern Press Association, minutes of shareholders' meeting, 2 Feb. 1914.
102 CP documents, WAP annual general meeting, 7 Oct. 1912, presidential address (Nichols).
103 The western papers were also responsible for one-quarter of the $6,000 annual AP franchise fee.
104 CP, WAP, minutes of directors' meeting, 2 Oct. 1912.
105 CP documents, Eastern Press Association, Slack to Pearson, 15 Jan. 1914 and 26 Jan. 1914; Pearson to Crandall, 15 Feb. 1914. See also report of James Hickey (manager of the EPA's leased wire) to Pearson, 2 Feb. 1914.
106 CP documents, WAP annual meeting, 2 Oct. 1911.
107 CP documents, WAP annual meeting, 6 Oct. 1913; J.F.B. Livesay, report of the delegation representing shareholders of the prairie section of the Canadian Press, Ltd., Dec. 1912. The Vancouver *Sun* later joined the Ottawa arrangement.
108 CP documents, WAP, meeting of morning paper publishers at Calgary, 21 Jan. 1915.
109 CP documents, Slack to Pearson, 15 Jan. 1914.
110 See Chapter 7, pp. 256–261. For further development of this point, see Gene Allen, "News and Nationality in Canada, 1890–1930," *Journal of Canadian Studies* 43, no. 3 (Fall 2009): 30–68.
111 CP documents, WAP, minutes of directors' meeting, 13 Aug. 1914.
112 Ibid.
113 LAC, Department of the Secretary of State, chief press censor, 1915–20, RG 6 E, vol. 645, file 195. John W. Tibbs, Star News and Picture Service, to Chambers, 6 Sept. 1915.
114 CP documents, C. Langton Clarke to J.F.B. Livesay, 10 Dec. 1914.
115 CP documents, E.H. Macklin to E.F. Slack, 4 Oct. 1914.
116 CP documents, Livesay to Macklin, Aug. 1915.
117 CP documents, WAP, minutes of directors' meeting, 13 Aug. 1914.

118 Putnis, "How the International News Agency Business Model Failed";
Potter, *News and the British World*, 30–31, 89–91; Rantanen, "The Struggle
for Control of Domestic News Markets (1)," 35–48.

119 CP documents, minutes of a conference held between representatives of
The Associated Press and a committee of The Canadian Press, Limited,
held at the offices of The Associated Press, New York, July 3, 1914, p. 1.

120 Ibid., 4.

121 Ibid.

122 This point is made strongly by Rantanen, who argues that the concept of
exclusivity in the use of news is crucial to an understanding of the relationship between international and national news agencies; see Rantanen,
"The Struggle for Control of Domestic News Markets (1)," 36–7. See also
Shmanske, "News as a Public Good."

123 Richard B. Kielbowicz, *News in the Mail: The Press, Post Office, and Public
Information, 1700–1860s* (New York: Greenwood Press, 1989), 147–51. The
exchange system operated similarly in Canada.

124 For a broader discussion of the centralizing and the decentralizing
aspects of telegraphic news, see Allen, "Monopolies of News."

125 On this point, see Blondheim, *News over the Wires*, 59.

126 Proprietary agencies such as United Press sometimes made agreements
that imposed return-news obligations, but this was not applied universally. See, for example, CP documents, minutes of the board of directors'
meeting, 9 Aug. 1917.

127 Rantanen describes this process as "the transformation of news from
a public to an exclusive good"; Rantanen, "The Struggle for Control
of Domestic News Markets (1)," 36. This analysis fits the relationship
between AP and CP very well.

128 CP documents, minutes of a conference held between representatives of
The Associated Press and a committee of The Canadian Press, Limited,
held at the offices of The Associated Press, New York, 3 July 1914, p. 4.

129 Ibid., 9, 14.

130 Ibid., 10.

131 CP documents, minutes of special committee meeting, 4 Aug. 1914.

132 CP documents, WAP and Canadian Press Ltd., proposed nationalization
of news services in the Dominion of Canada. App. A, approximate statement of annual expense of a national 24-hour leased-wire press service,
p. 8.

133 Ibid., App. B, Plan of Mr. Slack, p. 12.

134 Ibid., App. A, approximate statement of annual expense of a national
24-hour leased wire press service, p. 8.

135 CP documents, WAP, annual meeting, 1 Nov. 1915.
136 CP documents, Cates to Macklin, 10 Nov., 1915; annual meeting of Canadian Press Ltd. Evening Paper Section, Ontario and Quebec Division, 15 Nov. 1916, report of the manager.
137 CP documents, WAP, minutes of directors' meeting, 11 Feb. 1915.
138 CP documents, meeting of morning paper publishers at Calgary, 21 Jan. 1915.
139 CP documents, WAP, minutes of directors' meeting, 11 Feb. 1915.
140 Jeffrey A. Keshen, *Propaganda and Censorship During Canada's Great War* (Edmonton: University of Alberta Press, 1996), 70–1.
141 LAC, Department of the Secretary of State, chief press censor, 1915–20, RG 6 E, vol. 645, file 195, Chambers to Livesay, 4 Oct. 1915.
142 Keshen, *Propaganda and Censorship During Canada's Great War.*
143 LAC, Department of the Secretary of State, chief press censor, 1915–20, RG 6 E, vol. 589, file 267 – Associated Press articles, Chambers to Malcolm A. Reid, 29 Oct. 1916 (file 267). The only problem appeared to be a complaint by the Toronto *Star* editor in charge of its United Press service to several other Ontario newspapers; it was hardly fair, John Tibbs observed, that when UP had a scoop, it had to be approved by "the managers of an 'opposition' syndicate." Ibid. (vol. 645, file 195), John W. Tibbs, [Toronto] Star News and Picture Service, to Chambers, 6 Sept. 1915.
144 CP documents, circular no. C.P.C. 38, confidential circular for Canadian editors from Ernest J. Chambers, chief press censor for Canada, Department of the Secretary of State, 16 Nov. 1916.
145 LAC, Department of the Secretary of State, Chief Press Censor, 1915–20, RG 6, E vol. 589, file 267 – Associated Press articles, E.J. Chambers to R.M. Coulter, 23 Feb. 1916: "The Associated Press of New York is kept thoroughly posted by the managers of the Canadian Press, Limited, who act as Press Censors at Toronto, as to the character of the matter which is objected to ... Mr. Stone, the manager of the New York Associated Press, who is strongly pro-British in sympathy, has expressed his desire to co-operate with us to the fullest possible extent."
146 Keshen, *Propaganda and Censorship During Canada's Great War,* 81. See also LAC, MG 26-H, Sir Robert Borden fonds, 48262-3, excerpt of letter from C.O. Knowles, 11 Dec. 1917: "In reference to the embargo on the I.N.S., I find that there is still a pretty strong feeling that the Hearst people are not to be trusted. I discussed this matter with several of our prominent publishers and fail to find any sentiment favourable." See also excerpt of letter from Livesay, 8 Dec. 1917: the readmission of INS and Hearst papers to Canada would be "a first class disaster to our cause. I believe this view

is shared by nearly every responsible newspaper editor and publisher in Canada, except of course such as are lined up on the side of Germany."

147 CP documents, Canadian Press Ltd., annual report of evening paper section, Ontario and Quebec division, November 17, 1915, manager's report. In response, Borden quite reasonably asked whether CP Ltd. had access to the $8,000 subsidy paid to CAP, which was intended to offset the cost of telegraphing news via cable from London; Knowles replied, somewhat disingenuously, that there was no connection between CAP and CP Ltd. CP documents, annual report of the Manager, 1916, Canadian Press Ltd. Evening Paper Section, Ontario and Quebec Division.

148 CP documents, minutes of the special meeting of the evening paper section, Ontario and Quebec Division, Canadian Press Ltd., 19 Feb. 1917.

149 CP documents, annual meeting of the Canadian Press Ltd. evening paper section, Ontario and Quebec division, 15 Nov. 1916, pp. 1–3, 15.

150 CP documents, annual meeting of the Canadian Press Ltd. evening paper section, Ontario and Quebec division, 15 Nov. 1916, report of the manager.

151 Potter, *News and the British World,* 190, notes that during the war, governments across the board increased their direct involvement with the press via censorship, propaganda, and direct government involvement in news services.

152 In 1918, after the $50,000 leased-wire subsidy had been offered and accepted, the board was told that the federal government wanted a CP correspondent to accompany the Siberian expedition, offering to pay the correspondent's expenses and cable tolls, and this time the offer was accepted (CP documents, special meeting of the board of directors, 30 Aug. 1918). But a subsequent government request that CP provide special coverage of the peace conference in Paris (with no subsidy attached) was turned down on cost grounds (CP documents, board of directors meeting, 19 Dec. 1918). Eventually, the cable costs of John W. Dafoe's reports from Paris were paid by the government (report of the annual meeting, 26 Nov. 1919, report of the management, 18).

153 CP documents, memorandum in support of the petition of the daily newspapers of Western Canada and British Columbia that the Dominion Government shall assume cost of a 24-hour leased wire between Ottawa and Winnipeg to be operated for the benefit of the newspapers of Canada.

154 Ibid., 3.

155 Ibid., 6–7.

156 CP documents, WAP, report of annual meeting, 2 Oct. 1916.

157 CP documents, WAP, circular letter of Macklin to WAP members, 23 Dec. 1916.

158 Loring Christie was a senior adviser to Borden. In January 1916, Christie had written that "a policy of *east and west news* is as vitally important to the national welfare and spirit of the Dominion as the policy of 'east and west trade'; and a similar principle would hold for the whole British Commonwealth" (Potter, *News and the British World*, 198, citing Borden fonds 86606-7).

159 Excerpt from "Newspapermen I Knew," draft of memoir by J.F.B. Livesay, Archives of Manitoba, MG 9 A100, file 9.

160 CP documents, Livesay to Woods, 28 Dec. 1916.

161 CP documents, Macklin to Woods, 29 Dec. 1916.

162 Read, *The Power of News*, 127; Peter Putnis, "Share 999: British Government Control of Reuters during World War One," *Media History* 14, no. 2 (2008): 154; Potter, *News and the British World*, 195.

163 Putnis, "Share 999."

164 Potter, *News and the British World*, 186–210. Lloyd George replaced Herbert Asquith as British Prime Minister in December of 1916, vowing to use the press much more aggressively to support the war effort; M.L. Sanders and Philip M. Taylor, *British Propaganda during the First World War, 1914–18* (London and Basingstoke: The Macmillan Press, 1982), 11–12. Both the existing Canadian government subsidy and the proposed imperial subsidy bring to mind the observation of Boyd-Barrett and Rantanen that "the state has strong interests in news transmission ... and these become especially visible in times of national or international crisis which are a threat to the state itself." Oliver Boyd-Barrett and Terhi Rantanen, "Introduction: News Agencies in the Furnace of Political Transition," in *The Globalization of News*, 104.

165 Peter Putnis and Kerry McCallum, "Reuters and the Australian Press during World War I," paper presented to the International Communication Association Conference, Singapore, June 2010.

166 APCA, AP 02A.4, Special Member files series I. Canadian Press, 1913–28, box 1, folder 1 (1913–19), Edward Slack to Melville Stone, 24 Nov. 1919; National Archives (United Kingdom) (hereafter NA) INF 4/1B, Printed for the War Cabinet, September 1917. Secret. John Buchan to Sir Edward Carson, scheme of working for the Department of Information; LAC Borden fonds, secretary of state for the colonies to governor-general, confidential, 13 Aug. 1919, pp. 50832–3. Potter states that the service was provided free of charge "so as to avoid miring Reuters in negotiations with the agencies [presumably including CAP] that served the Canadian press"; Potter, *News and the British World*, 194–95.

167 In addition, British military intelligence began secretly funnelling pro-British articles to the Dominion press through the Royal Colonial Institute in January 1917; NA INF 4/1B, Secret. Military Press Control. A History of the Work of MI7 1914–1919, p. 18; NA INF 4/4B, War Office to Treasury, April 1916.

168 See Chapter 4, p. 139.

169 Harkness, *J.E. Atkinson of the Star,* 99. The official reason given for Atkinson's resignation was "pressure of work"; CP Ltd., minutes of meeting of the board of directors, 5 Nov. 1917. Atkinson was replaced on the board by John Bone, the *Star*'s managing editor.

170 Livesay, "Newspapermen I Knew." Both Rogers and Lougheed had been involved in publishing Conservative newspapers in the West; Charles Bruce, *News and the Southams* (Toronto: Macmillan of Canada, 1968), 138.

171 CP documents, minutes of meeting of members of WAP at Chateau Laurier in Ottawa, 15 Jan. 1917.

172 Ibid.; "Delegation Waits on the Government," 16 Jan. 1917.

173 LAC, RG 19, vol. 98, file 101-29-32 Department of Finance – Canadian Press, J.S. Matson to Sir Thomas White, n.d. [16 Jan. 1917]. Burrell had previously been editor of a weekly newspaper; Arthur Ford, *As the World Wags On* (Toronto: Ryerson Press, 1950), 138.

174 LAC, RG 19, vol. 98, file 101-29-32, Department of Finance – Canadian Press, "Item 321 – Canadian Press Limited," n.d. [ca 1917].

175 CP documents, circular letter, Macklin to WAP members, 23 Dec. 1916.

176 CP documents, minutes of meeting of members of WAP at Chateau Laurier, 15 Jan. 1917.

177 CP documents, WAP petition, 28 Dec. 1916, p. 6. The Canadians probably also wanted to depict AP as a "loyal" news organization, unlike Hearst's INS, which had just been banned in Canada and other British territories because of its pro-German bias.

178 APCA, AP 02A.4 Special Member files series I. Canadian Press, 1913–28 (box 1), folder 1, 1913–19, "Canadian Press contract" – minutes of meeting between AP executive committee and a committee of CP Ltd., 27 June 1917.

179 Ibid., CEK, "Character of Canadian Press Service," 11 June 1917.

180 The need to prevent competing agencies from using AP news was a growing concern for AP at the time; see Associated Press, annual report, 1917, 4–5. AP was still angry over CP's failure to provide adequate coverage of the sinking of the *Empress of Ireland* in the St. Lawrence in May 1914, a disaster that had claimed more than 1,000 lives. AP had ended up covering the story itself and then sending coverage from New

York to its delinquent Canadian clients; adding insult to injury, the UP operator in the Montreal *Star* office had sent this back to UP clients south of the border.

181 CP documents, minutes of the annual general meeting, 13 June 1917. A few months later, AP observed that it received less revenue from the 72 members of CP than from the three newspapers it served in Havana, Cuba. AP 02A.4, Special Member files series I. Canadian Press, 1913–28 (box 1), folder 1, 1913–19, F.R. M[artin], "Canadian Press, Limited," 24 Sept. 1918.

182 Ibid., Kent Cooper to Stone, 8 June 1917.

183 Crandall reported to Kent Cooper, AP's traffic chief, in August that the UP operator had been moved out of the *Star*'s newsroom and into an adjacent building, thus complying with the bylaws; AP 02A.4, Special Member files series I. Canadian Press, 1913–28 (box 1), folder 1, 1913–19, Crandall to Cooper, 24 Aug 1917. The Montreal *Star*–UP connection was the beginning of British United Press, CP's most bothersome competitor; see Chapter 2 below.

184 CP documents, minutes of the board of directors' meeting, 5 Nov. 1917, 17.

185 "Premier of Canada Congratulates the Press on its New National Service," *The Globe*, 3 Sept. 1917, p. 1.

186 CP documents, meeting of the board of directors of Canadian Press Ltd., 13 June 1917.

187 CP documents, plan for the National News Association, App. B.

188 CP documents, report of the annual meeting, 1919, 33. The idea had apparently been under consideration for at least a few months by this point; see LAC I. Norman Smith Papers (MG 31, D 94, vol. 13), box 12, file 1, The Canadian Press, 1919–41, correspondence to J.F.B. Livesay and E. Norman Smith, Livesay to J.H. Woods, confidential, 12 April 1919.

189 J.F.B. Livesay, *The Making of a Canadian* (Toronto: Ryerson Press, 1947), 3

190 Ibid., 34–37. See also CP documents, annual general meeting, 19 May 1920, 29.

191 CP documents, copy of resolutions passed at a meeting of Ontario newspaper publishers, 19 Feb. 1920, enclosure in T.H. Preston to Livesay, 24 Feb. 1920.

192 CP documents, Canadian Press Ltd., meeting of the board of directors, 18 May 1920, 11.

193 Ibid., 3–8.

194 CP documents, special general meeting, 19 May 1920, 17.

195 Ibid., 19.

Chapter 2

1 M.E. Nichols, *(CP): The Story of The Canadian Press* (Toronto: Ryerson Press, 1948), 182–3.

2 Library and Archives Canada (hereafter LAC) RG 19, vol. 98, file 101-29-32 Department of Finance – Canadian Press. Memorandum, "Canadian Press Limited," n.d.

3 See Chapter 1, p. 45.

4 See also Simon Potter's account of these negotiations: *News and the British World: The Emergence of an Imperial Press System* (Oxford: Clarendon Press, 2003), 196–9, 202–4.

5 House of Lords Record Office, Beaverbrook Papers, BBK E/3/8, memorandum from the minister of information to the Imperial War Cabinet on the subject of a British Imperial News wireless service (draft, n.d., circa June 1918); memorandum to war cabinet re creation of "Inter-Imperial News Service," 18 June 1918; National Archives, United Kingdom (NA) T/1/12227, 44657/1918 Confidential. Imperial War Conference, 1918. Imperial News Service. Memorandum by the minister of information, 18 June 1918. For Rowell, see Robert Craig Brown, *Robert Laird Borden, A Biography: Vol. 2, 1914–1937* (Toronto: Macmillan of Canada, 1980), 110; Margaret Prang, *N.W. Rowell: Ontario Nationalist* (Toronto: University of Toronto Press, 1975).

6 Peter Putnis, "Share 999: British Government Control of Reuters during World War One," *Media History* 14, no. 2 (2008), 141–65; Donald Read, *The Power of News: The History of Reuters* (Oxford: Oxford University Press, 1992), 129.

7 LAC, MG 26-H, Sir Robert Borden fonds, 75290, Borden to Slack, secret & confidential, 3 May 1918.

8 LAC, Borden fonds, 50799–50806, n.d. (circa June 1918), Edward Slack, "Memorandum regarding the establishment of a subsidized Empire cable service," enclosure in Slack to Rowell, 22 Sept. 1919, Borden fonds 50797-8.

9 NA T/1/12227, 44657/1918, Beaverbrook to Walter Long (colonial secretary), 11 Sept. 1918; 44657/1918 confidential. Henry Lambert (CO) to Treasury, 18 July 1918.

10 LAC, Borden fonds, 86266, N.W. Rowell to Borden, re: Imperial News Service, n.d. [July 1918]. The Empire Press Union also expressed its opposition to subsidies; Potter, *News and the British World*, 198–9.

11 Potter, *News and the British World*, 199, 204–5.

12 LAC, Borden fonds, 131687d, Sir Roderick Jones to Sydney Walton (Publicity Department, Canadian Mission in London), 23 May

1919, enclosing proposal "for Canadian publicity" dated May 22 (131687e–131687i); Walton to Lloyd Harris, n.d., 131687b, encl. in Henry B. Thomson (food controller, Ottawa) to Walton, 27 May 1919, 131687c.

13 Putnis, "Share 999," 153. North America accounted for only 0.3 per cent of Reuters' revenue in 1918 and 1938; Oliver Boyd-Barrett, "'Global' News Agencies," in *The Globalization of News*, eds. Oliver Boyd-Barrett and Terhi Rantanen (London: SAGE, 1998), 31.

14 LAC, Borden fonds, 131688–131688e, M.E. Nichols, memorandum for Sir Robert Borden re British–Canadian News Service, 30 June 1919; Borden memorandum, 3 July 1919, 134691.

15 LAC, RG 25, series 1, vol. 173, file C13/33, cable from Milner to Devonshire, 13 Aug. 1919. These were very similar to the conditions under which Reuters had operated while under government control during the war; see Putnis, "Share 999," and Read, *The Power of News*, 124–31.

16 LAC, RG 25, series 1, vol. 173, file C13/33, Devonshire to Milner, 5 Sept 1919; Milner to Devonshire, 2 June 1920.

17 LAC, Borden fonds, 50834, Milner to Devonshire, copy of telegram, 1 Oct. 1919, confidential.

18 CP documents, minutes of the annual general meeting, 26 Nov. 1919, comments of Edward Slack.

19 See Chapter 1, pp. 30–1. The Australian press made a similar arrangement with Reuters in 1926; Read, *The Power of News*, 165.

20 Associated Press Corporate Archives (APCA), AP 02A.4, Special Member files series I. Canadian Press, 1913–28, box 1, folder 1 (1913–19). Slack to Stone, 24 Nov. 1919, and Stone to Slack, 26 Nov. 1919.

21 Borden fonds, 50826–7, Slack to Rowell, confidential, 4 Dec. 1919.

22 Government subsidies to news agencies in other countries were not unusual, though often problematic. For example, the Havas agency became increasingly subservient to the French government in the 1930s as it received more direct financial support; Jonathan Fenby, *The International News Services: A Twentieth Century Fund Report* (New York: Schocken Books, 1986), 52–3. Extremely low postal rates for US newspapers were another form of subsidy; Paul Starr, *The Creation of the Media: Political Origins of Modern Communications* (New York: Basic Books, 2004).

23 LAC, RG 19, vol. 98, file 101-29-32, telegram from administrator, Ottawa, to secretary of state for the colonies, March 15 1920; CP documents, board of directors meeting, 18 May 1920.

24 Ibid.

25 On the opposition of Australian journalists to subsidies, see Peter Putnis and Kerry McCallum, "Reuters and the Australian Press during World

War I," paper presented to the International Communication Association Conference, Singapore, June 2010. The war years "left a legacy of secrecy about aspects of Reuters' operations and obfuscation in public announcements about its relations with the British government. These were accompanied by lingering suspicion amongst the press, particularly outside Britain, about Reuters' credibility as a truly independent news agency. ... A meeting of the Australian Press Association in March 1924 criticized Reuters' service as 'largely propaganda, especially from India' and expressed doubts as to Reuters' independence." Putnis, "Share 999," 159.

26 LAC, MG 26-I, Arthur Meighen fonds, 23789–91, Livesay to E. Norman Smith, 11 Oct. 1920. The standard press rate at the time was seven cents a word, with 10 cents for rush material. The Imperial Press Conference in 1920 had stressed lower cable rates as an acceptable form of government subsidy; Potter, *News and the British World*, 205–6.

27 LAC, Meighen fonds 23788, Meighen to Nichols, 6 Oct. 1920.

28 CP documents, minutes of special general meeting, Montreal, 24 Nov. 1920. See also LAC, Meighen fonds, 23810–11, Bone to Meighen, 6 Jan. 1921.

29 LAC, Meighen fonds, Irving Robertson to Meighen, 3 Dec. 1920, 23802–3.

30 LAC, Meighen fonds, copy of telegram from secretary of state for the colonies (Milner) to governor general of Canada, 12 Oct. 1920, 23798.

31 The Reuters Archive, Thomson Reuters (RA), box LN 795, file 1/974753, Livesay to Jones, confidential, 6 Jan. 1921.

32 LAC, Meighen fonds, 23805, Meighen to E.N. Smith, 11 Dec. 1920.

33 Manitoba *Free Press*, "The Canadian Press and a Cable Subsidy" 25 Jan. 1921, encl. in LAC, Meighen fonds 23816, *Free Press* to Meighen, 3 Feb. 1921.

34 RA, box LN 795, file 1/974753, Livesay to Jones, 18 May 1921.

35 Livesay to Jones, 18 May 1921, encl. in Livesay to Cooper, 14 Sept.1925, AP 02A.4 Special Member files series I. Canadian Press, 1913–28 (box 1), file 5, 1925–26.

36 CP documents, minutes of the annual general meeting, Toronto, 2 May 1922.

37 CP documents, board of directors meeting, 21 Oct. 1921, news report of the management.

38 See, for example, A.E. Arsenault (premier of Prince Edward Island) to H. Boiville (deputy minister of Finance), 30 Jan. 1918, LAC, RG 19, vol. 98, file 101-29-32 Department of Finance – Canadian Press: "It seems manifestly unjust that this Province should be paying its share of the subsidy granted to the Canadian Press, Limited, for improved telegraph service

and as a result to have an inferior service than formerly." See also R.P. Allen, *Daily Mail*, Fredericton, to W. S. Fielding, 30 March 1932, ibid.; W.M. Davidson, *Morning Albertan*, Calgary to W.L.M. King, 9 May 1923, LAC, MG 26-J, William Lyon Mackenzie King fonds, 72221–2.

39 Quoted in Nichols, *(CP)*, 176.

40 See, for example, Nichols to Meighen, private & confidential, 21 Aug. 1940, LAC, Meighen fonds 110079–81: the subsidy was given up "for no other reason that the fact that your successors in office demanded preferred treatment which the Canadian Press refused to grant." See also RA, Jones Papers, Section 1 Reuters, iv, Reuters General, 1926–33 (b), box 35, extracts of letter from Bernard Rickatson Hatt, Montreal, to Jones, 21 March 1934. According to Livesay, the subsidy "was stopped by Mackenzie King, when Livesay refused to carry a service out of Ottawa 'agreeable' to the Liberal government of the day."

41 See Chapter 1.

42 CP documents, E. Norman Smith and J.F.B. Livesay, memorandum for the Right Honourable the Prime Minister, n.d. [January 1923], in minutes of the annual general meeting, 1 May 1923.

43 CP documents, board of directors meeting, 30 April 1923.

44 CP documents, board of directors meeting, 25 Oct. 1922.

45 Nichols, *(CP)*, 176–7. Associated Press, which had a similar provision in its bylaws, was found guilty of violating the Sherman Anti-Trust Act in 1945; *Associated Press et al v United States,* No. 57, Supreme Court of the US, 326 U.S. 1; 65 S. Ct 1416; 1945 U.S. LEXIS 2663; 89 L. Ed. 2013; 1945 Trade Cas. (CCH) P57, 384; 1 Media L. Rep. 2269.

46 LAC King fonds, E. Norman Smith, Canadian Press Ltd., to W.L.M. King, May 8, 1923, 80492–3.

47 Nichols, *(CP)*, 178.

48 House of Commons *Debates*, 29 June 1923.

49 Livesay to Smith, n.d., quoted in Nichols, *(CP)*, 182.

50 AP 02A.4, Special Member files series I. Canadian Press, 1913–28 (box 1), file 2, 1920–23, Roy Martin (general manager, Associated Press) to Frank Noyes (AP president), 14 Nov. 1923.

51 RA, LN 943, 1/013232, red file, Canada. R.M. MacLeod to Grange, Ottawa, 1 June 1923. There was already a long tradition of Canada and other dominions paying for such publicity efforts; see Potter, *News and the British World*, 74–81, 187–8.

52 RA, LN 943, 1/013232, red file, Canada. S. Carey Clements, manager, London, to MacLeod, confidential, 11 July 1923.

53 See pp. 96–8.

54 Livesay to Smith, n.d., quoted in Nichols, *(CP)*, 182.
55 CP documents, board of directors meeting, 8 Oct. 1923.
56 AP 02A.4, special member files series I, Canadian Press, 1913–28 (box 1), file 2, 1920–23, Martin to Noyes, 14 Nov. 1923.
57 CP documents, Smith to Livesay, 30 June 1923, cited in cost report of the management, 21 Sept. 1923.
58 While Nichols' account of CP's history is useful and largely accurate, this is one of several places where it is not: his conclusion that "harmony had entered the door when the subsidy flew out the window" (185) is distinctly misleading.
59 CP documents, meeting of the Ontario and Quebec division, 17 March 1924.
60 CP documents, meeting of the Ontario division, 26 Sept. 1927.
61 CP documents, meeting of the Ontario and Quebec division, 5 May 1924.
62 CP documents, annual general meeting, 4 June 1924.
63 See, for example, AP 02A.4, Special Member files series I. Canadian Press, 1913–28 (box 1), file 6 – 1927–28, Kent Cooper to Paul Block, confidential, 26 Oct. 1927: CP "is practically a child of the Associated Press. It has developed along cooperative lines to be a really remarkable success and we are proud of our ally." Cooper added that because of CP's "efficiency" and alliance with AP, United Press had "never been able to make any kind of a dent" in the Canadian market.
64 In a memorandum of a conversation with Livesay in 1923, Roderick Jones quoted Livesay as saying that Canadian newspapers "from the beginning had been spoilt by the cheap news dumped in Canada from the United States. This dumping had got even the best Canadian newspapers into the way of thinking that they should pay next to nothing for their telegraphic news services." Confidential. Note on conferences between Sir Roderick Jones and Mr. J.F.B. Livesay at Ottawa on 4 Sept. 1923. RA, box LN 795, file 1/974753. See also CP documents, board of directors meeting, 26 Nov. 1919, remarks of Roy Martin: "It was true that the sum now paid was nominal ... Canadian papers were paying but relatively small sums for their basic news service as compared with Associated Press members."
65 AP 02A.4, Special Member files series I. Canadian Press, 1913–28 (box 1), file 2, 1920–23 Livesay, The Canadian Press – memorandum on relations with the Associated Press, 16 April 1924.
66 Ibid. and Martin to Livesay, 19 Oct. 1922.
67 Ibid., Cooper to Noyes, 22 Aug. 1923; Cooper to Livesay, 22 Aug. 1923.
68 Ibid., Noyes to Cooper, 16 Sept. 1923.

69 "Newspapermen I Knew," draft of memoir by J.F.B. Livesay, Archives of Manitoba, MG 9 A100, file 9.

70 LAC, Borden fonds, Borden to Livesay, 26 Dec. 1916, 35061. See also Borden to Livesay, 2 Jan. 1917, 35084: "My dear Mr. Livesay – I appreciate very greatly your kindness in sending me photographs which I have just received. They are very good indeed and reflect the greatest credit on your artistic skill. I shall treasure them as a souvenir of our tour in aid of the National Service." The photograph, according to Livesay, was a "a charming shot of him throwing snowballs with precision at a telephone pole during a stop in the Rockies."

71 The memoir of Arthur Ford, for many years editor of the London *Free Press*, and a committed Conservative, contains many amusing examples of this tendency, as when an editor at the Conservative-affiliated Winnipeg *Telegram* wrote a headline about Laurier being cheered by his followers, only to be told that "no Grit is ever cheered in the *Telegram*." Arthur Ford, *As the World Wags On* (Toronto: Ryerson Press, 1950), 5–6.

72 The most frequently cited study is Donald L. Shaw, "News Bias and the Telegraph: A Study of Historical change," *Journalism Quarterly* 44: 1. For criticism of this view (or at least of Shaw's study), see Richard Kaplan, *Politics and the American Press: The Rise of Objectivity, 1865–1920* (Cambridge: Cambridge University Press, 2002), 173–4; Michael Schudson, *Discovering the News A Social History of American Newspapers* (New York: Basic Books, 1978); Menahem Blondheim, *News over the Wires: The Telegraph and the Flow of Public Information in America, 1844–1897* (Cambridge, MA and London: Harvard University Press, 1994), 174–88.

73 The Quebec city newspaper *Le Soleil* carried the motto "Organe du parti libéral" on its front page until the 1950s.

74 LAC, RG 13, vol. 272, file 1956–22, memorandum by E. Norman Smith.

75 CP documents, annual meeting, 12 June 1918, report of the management.

76 CP documents, dominion elections 1921, circular no. 1, 15 Sept. 1921.

77 CP documents, board of directors meeting, 4–5 November 1935.

78 CP documents, board of directors meeting, 21 Oct. 1929. For an account of the operations of CP's Ottawa bureau and an analysis of typical forms of coverage, see Chapter 7, pp. 268–74.

79 CP documents, dominion election, 1925, circular no. 7(b), 13 Oct. 1925.

80 CP documents, dominion election, 1925, circular no. 1, 8 Sept. 1925.

81 CP documents, report of the management on dominion election, 1926; Gillis Purcell Papers, Livesay to Purcell, Charlottetown, 11 Sept. 1932.

82 CP documents, meeting of Ontario members and news editors, 25 Sept. 1933.

83 LAC, King fonds, 150424, Livesay to W.L.M. King, personal, 28 July 1930.
84 LAC, King fonds, diary, 4 Oct. 1932, 278: "Canadian Press always under-states the Liberal returns and overstates the Tory returns."; 17 April 1934, 107, refers to "the Canadian Press usually tory sources." See also 14 Oct. 1935 and 14 Sept. 1926, 257.
85 LAC, King fonds, diary, 26 Jan. 1935.
86 LAC, King fonds, 75613–4, Livesay to W.L.M. King, 19 June 1923.
87 LAC, King fonds, 75615, King to Livesay, 22 June 1923.
88 LAC, Meighen fonds, 54616–9, Meighen to C.A.C. Jennings (editor-in-chief, *Mail and Empire*), 9 Nov. 1923.
89 Livesay, "Newspapermen I Knew" (passage crossed out).
90 Livesay, "Newspapermen I Knew." He did not name any of the "untried players from the scrub," but presumably they included Rupert Davies of the Kingston *Whig-Standard*, a prominent Liberal and future senator who became CP's president in 1939.
91 LAC, Meighen fonds, 51118, Meighen to Ford, 12 March 1923.
92 LAC, Meighen fonds, 63847–8, Meighen to Ford, 14 Jan. 1924.
93 LAC, Meighen fonds, 51119, Ford to Meighen, 8 March 1923, confidential.
94 CP documents, report of the management on dominion elections, 1926.
95 CP documents, board of directors meeting, 6 Oct. 1930.
96 See, for example, LAC, Meighen fonds, 62481–3, Meighen to Livesay, 14 Jan. 1924 ("Anything further in the way of contention of the neutral-ity of the Canadian Press, under its present management, need not be addressed to me"); 68329, Livesay to E.N. Smith, 10 Nov. 1925; 63862–3, Livesay to Tolmie, 18 Jan. 1924; 98003, Meighen to R.B. Hanson. 18 July 1940; 98030–1, Hanson to Meighen, private and confidential, 27 Aug. 1940; 98039–41, Hanson to Howard Robinson (Saint John), 9 Sept. 1940; Livesay, "Newspapermen I Knew." Referring to their disagreement in 1920, Livesay wrote that he and Meighen "had many other clashes of the like kind," but that "the President and the board invariably supported me."
97 Livesay, "Newspapermen I Knew." Unlike Meighen, Bennett "extended his hostility to the entire press. ... including with fine impartiality men of the Press Gallery whose papers supported him through thick and thin."
98 CP was not the only organization moving in this direction. M.E. Nichols notes in his history of CP that John Willison, editor of the *Globe*, began moving away from partisan political reporting in the years after 1900, as did Sam Kydd of the Montreal *Gazette* (194–5). Clifford Sifton made the following comment about changes in news practices in the 1920s: "the old-time custom of large newspapers taking a violent stand on

every question that comes up in a community, and trying to bludgeon
their views into their readers, is a thing of the past. It rarely does any
good and sometimes does a great deal of harm. In questions where the
community is violently divided the general attitude of the newspaper
is to give the news and articles on both sides, as they are presented."
Quoted in D.J. Hall, *Clifford Sifton, Volume 2: A Lonely Eminence, 1901–1929*
(Vancouver: UBC Press, 1985), 321.

 99 Kaplan, *Politics and the American Press*; Schudson, *Discovering the News*.
100 W.H. Kesterton, *A History of Journalism in Canada* (Toronto: McClelland
    and Stewart, 1967); Minko Sotiron, *From Politics to Profit: The
    Commercialization of Canadian Daily Newspapers, 1890–1920* (Montreal and
    Kingston: McGill-Queen's University Press, 1997).
101 Daniel Hallin, *The 'Uncensored' War: The Media and Vietnam* (New York:
    University of California Press, 1989; first published 1986), 116–8. See also
    Chapter 7, pp. 269–70.
102 CP documents, meeting of the members of the Ontario and Quebec divi-
    sion, 5 May 1924, remarks of L.J. Tarte.
103 CP documents, report of the annual meeting, 26 Nov. 1919, distribution of
    cost; board of directors meeting, 30 April 1929.
104 CP documents, meeting of the Quebec members, 27 June 1922.
105 CP documents, meeting of Quebec members, 24 Oct. 1922.
106 CP documents, report of the management, meeting of the Quebec mem-
    bers, 27 June 1922.
107 CP documents, report of the eastern superintendent, 9 June 1923.
108 Ibid.
109 CP documents, meeting of the Quebec members, 25 July 1925.
110 CP documents, board of directors meeting, 30 April 1929.
111 CP documents, annual general meeting, 1 May 1929. For the inauguration
    of CP's French-language service in 1951, see Chapter 5 p. 200.
112 Some scholars have argued that the absence of a class/labour perspec-
    tive is a general characteristic of journalism history; see Hanno Hardt,
    "Without the Rank and File: Journalism History, Media Workers, and
    Problems of Representation," in *Newsworkers: Toward a History of the Rank
    and File*, eds. Hanno Hardt and Bonnie Brennen (Minneapolis: University
    of Minnesota Press, 1995), 1–29.
113 CP documents, board of directors meeting, 18 Dec. 1918.
114 CP documents, annual general meeting, 26 Nov. 1919, "Strike of telegraph
    operators in Western Division." The three Winnipeg dailies also ceased
    publication on May 17 when unionized press operators and stereotyp-
    ers joined the strike, but all resumed publishing by May 24; see Michael

Dupuis, "A Cloak for Something Far Deeper: The Press Coverage of the Winnipeg General Strike" (unpublished manuscript, 2008), 21, 71. Dupuis also provides a detailed account of the CP Winnipeg bureau's operations during the strike, 167–87. See also Nichols, (*CP*), 205–6.

115 CP documents, submission of J.F.B. Livesay to board of conciliation, n.d. (1924).

116 Dupuis, "A Cloak for Something Far Deeper," 189.

117 Nichols, (*CP*), 206; ibid., 237.

118 CP documents, board of directors meeting, 4 June 1924, financial report of the management.

119 CP documents, circular no. 17, 21 Aug. 1924; Livesay to J. Clark, general chairman Canadian Press division, Commercial Telegraphers Union of America, n.d., encl. in circular no. 17. According to the union's figures, wages had increased between 40 and 50 per cent since 1917, while the cost of living was 65 per cent higher; Clark to Livesay, 12 Aug. 1924.

120 The union disputed this, saying that arbitration was not intended to apply to wages and citing a clause that allowed the contact to be cancelled on 60 days' notice; CP documents, Clark to Livesay, 12 Aug. 1924.

121 CP documents, circular no. 17C, private and confidential, 10 Sept. 1924.

122 CP documents, board of directors meeting, 10 Oct. 1924, report of the management on the strike and its costs.

123 CP documents, report of the management re: Board of Conciliation, Livesay to E. Norman Smith, 5 Oct. 1924.

124 CP documents, memorandum to Morse operators for reemployment.

125 CP documents, agreement between the Canadian Press and the Morse Telegraphers in its employ, 28 Oct. 1924.

126 CP documents, minutes of the meeting of the Maritime division, 13 Jan. 1925.

127 CP documents, board of directors meeting, 10 Oct. 1924, report of the management on automatic printer equipment; Livesay to Smith, 5 Oct. 1924.

128 CP documents, board of directors meeting, 21 Oct. 1929.

129 CP documents, meeting of members of the Quebec division, 30 Aug. 1926.

130 CP documents, board of directors meeting, 7 Oct. 1926.

131 CP documents, meeting of the members of the Maritime division, 13 Sept. 1927.

132 CP documents, board of directors meeting, 21 Oct. 1929.

133 CP documents, annual general meeting, 30 April 1930.

134 CP documents, circular dated 3 March 1930 to Ontario members.

135 CP documents, meeting of western members, 1 Dec. 1930, remarks of Leighton.
136 CP documents, meeting of Ontario members, 28 Jan. 1931. Livesay replied that in his opinion, an international story, the Indian Round Table Conference, had been "the biggest and most dramatic story since 1921," adding that "it was part of the function of editors to educate readers to the importance of stories and attract their interest."
137 Ibid.
138 CP documents, board of directors meeting, 6 Oct. 1930.
139 CP documents, board of directors meeting, 10 Oct. 1932.
140 See p. 84.
141 CP documents, board of directors meeting, 10 Oct. 1932.
142 CP documents, board of directors meeting, Nov. 1933, management report.
143 CP documents, annual general meeting, 29 April 1931.
144 CP documents, board of directors meeting, 6 Oct. 1931.
145 Ibid., memorandum by the general manager, 24 June 1931.
146 CP documents, board of directors meeting, 2 May 1932.
147 Ibid., management report; meeting of western (Prairie and BC) members, 13 July 1932.
148 CP documents, board of directors meeting, 2 May 1932.
149 Stephen Shmanske, "News as a Public Good: Cooperative Ownership, Price Commitments, and the Success of the Associated Press," *Business History Review* 60, no. 1 (Spring 1986): 58.
150 Ibid., 58.
151 See, for example, Livesay, "The Canadian Press – Its Birth and Development" reprint from Quebec *Chronicle-Telegraph*, 21 June 1939: "These smaller newspapers willingly concede that this accomplishment is due largely to the unselfish cooperation of their fellow members in the larger centres, who have contributed the major share of the necessary cost."
152 CP documents, board of directors meeting, 2 May 1932.
153 CP documents, meeting of eastern members of cost committee, 22 Aug. 1932.
154 CP documents, memorandum submitted by Montreal members, 4 Oct. 1932, to cost committee.
155 CP documents, circular from Livesay, 1 July 1932, to members of western division.
156 CP documents, meeting of western (Prairie and BC) members, 13 July 1932.

157 CP documents, memorandum, 7 May 1933, re: proposed new leased-wire contract.

158 CP documents, annual general meeting, 7 June 1933.

159 See, for example, CP documents, board of directors meeting, 28 April 1930, discussion of proposed membership for Sudbury *Citizen*.

160 Showing concern about possible charges of monopolistic practices, Livesay later defended this decision as designed to prevent situations where "new publishing ventures, supporting one or other political parties, might make their appearance and with perhaps shoe-string resources bedevil the field"; Livesay, "The Canadian Press – Its Birth and Development" reprint from Quebec *Chronicle-Telegraph*, 21 June 1939.

161 CP documents, board of directors meeting, 27 April 1925; circular, 28 March 1930.

162 CP documents, annual general meeting, 30 April 1930.

163 CP documents, board of directors meeting, 13 April 1964, obituary notice for Crandall.

164 See p. 48. BUP also developed a radio news service in the mid-1930s that caused serious problems for CP; see Chapter 3, pp. 86–7, 123–4.

165 APCA, AP 02A.4, Special Member files series I. Canadian Press, 1913–28 (box 1), folder 11, 1929–30, Livesay to Cooper, personal, 12 May 1930.

166 Ibid., folder 15 – 1932, Livesay to Cooper, personal, 23 March 1932; Livesay to Cooper, personal, 28 March 1932.

167 Gillis Purcell Papers, Purcell to Livesay, 13 Sept. 1932. See also Purcell to Livesay, Vancouver, 18 July 1933 and same to same, 5 Sept. 1933.

168 RA, Jones Papers, Section 1 Reuters, iv, Reuters General, 1926–33 (b), box 35, Rickatson Hatt to Jones, private and confidential, Montreal, 21 March 1934. See also the CP obituary of Crandall, 10 March 1958 (Canadian Press Library, Toronto). BUP was taken over explicitly by United Press in 1941.

169 CP documents, annual general meeting, 5 May 1932; annual general meeting, 29 April 1936.

170 Livesay, "The Canadian Press – Its Birth and Development."

171 Livesay, "Newspapermen I Knew."

172 CP documents, board of directors meeting, 27 April 1931; APCA, AP 02A.4, Special Member files series I. Canadian Press, 1913–28 (box 1), file 16, 1933, Livesay to Cooper, personal, 14 Dec. 1933.

173 CP documents, board of directors meeting, 5 Nov. 1935.

174 CP documents, board of directors meeting, 2 Nov. 1936.

175 CP documents, board of directors meeting, 3 Oct. 1938.

176 Gillis Purcell Papers, Livesay to Eddie Johnston (New York superintendent), 23 Nov. 1931.

177 Purcell Papers, Turner (Winnipeg superintendent) to Livesay, 21 Oct. 1931.
178 Purcell Papers, Purcell to Livesay, 25 Oct. 1928.
179 Purcell Papers, Livesay to Purcell, 7 Nov. 1931, personal.
180 Ibid.
181 Purcell Papers, Livesay to Eddie Johnston, 23 Nov. 1931.
182 Purcell Papers, Livesay to Purcell, 30 Oct. 1928.
183 Purcell Papers, Livesay to Purcell, 20 Dec. 1931.
184 Purcell Papers, Livesay to Purcell, Nassau Beach, n.d. (ca. March 1934).
185 Purcell Papers, Livesay, memo to staff, 16 May 1934.
186 Purcell Papers, Purcell to Livesay, personal, 9 July 1934
187 Purcell Papers, Livesay to Purcell, 6 Aug. 1934.
188 Purcell Papers, Livesay to Purcell, personal, 18 Jan. 1939.
189 RA, BRH (Rickatson Hatt) to Jones, private, 24 Jan. 1939, microfilm reel 0201.
190 RA, William Moloney to Jones, private, 1 Feb. 1939, microfilm reel 0201.
191 Purcell Papers, Livesay to Purcell, personal, 18 Jan. 1939.
192 See, for example, Cooper's heartfelt tribute to Livesay in 1937: "Had it not been for you or someone like you ... it is my candid opinion that practically every newspaper in Canada would now be a member of the Associated Press. ... It was a happy day when you took hold of the Canadian Press. Otherwise it might not now be in existence and I don't mean maybe. It was your work that established a Canadian news service." APCA, AP 02A.4, Special Member files series I. Canadian Press, box 3, 1934–39, folder 20, (1937), Cooper to Livesay, 13 May 1937.
193 CP documents, board of directors meeting, 25 Oct. 1922, cable report of the management. During the Chanak crisis, the Canadian government resisted British government suggestions that it should provide troops for possible military action in Turkey. See C.P. Stacey, *Canada and the Age of Conflict, Vol. 2: 1921–1948, the Mackenzie King Era* (Toronto: University of Toronto Press, 1981), 17–31; Potter, *News and the British World*, 208–10.
194 APCA, AP 02A.4, Special Member files series I. Canadian Press, 1913–28 (box 1), folder 7, Livesay to Harold Raine, New York superintendent, 27 June 1927, enc. in Cooper to Noyes, 30 Dec. 1927.
195 Ibid., Cooper to Noyes, 30 Dec. 1927.
196 CP documents, board of directors meeting, 24 Oct. 1927.
197 Ibid., cable service report of the management.
198 APCA, AP 02A.4, Special Member files series I. Canadian Press, 1913–28 (box 1), file 7, Cooper to Noyes, 24 Feb. 1928; Noyes to J.H. Woods

(CP president), 25 Feb. 1928; minutes of board of directors, 30 April 1928, enc. in Wood to Noyes, 28 May 1928.

199 CP documents, board of directors meeting, 15 Oct. 1928.

200 APCA, AP 02A.4, Special Member files series I. Canadian Press, box 1, folder 5 (1925–26), Livesay to Cooper, 14 Sept. 1925.

201 Ibid., Cooper to Livesay, 11 Sept. 1925.

202 Ibid., Livesay to Cooper, 14 Sept. 1925.

203 Jones suggested in 1923 that the Reuters service CP received was actually worth $50,000 a year, reporting that Livesay "physically jumped" when he made this comment. RA, box LN 795, file 1/974753. Confidential. Note on conferences between Sir Roderick Jones and Mr. J.F.B. Livesay at Ottawa on 4 Sept. 1923.

204 APCA, AP 02A.4, Special Member files series I. Canadian Press, box 1, folder 5 (1925–26), Cooper to Livesay, 16 Sept. 1925.

205 Ibid., Livesay to Cooper, 14 Sept. 1925.

206 CP documents, board of directors meeting, 6 Oct. 1930 and 27–28 April 1931.

207 Terhi Rantanen, *Howard Interviews Stalin: How the AP, UP, and TASS Smashed the International News Cartel*, no. 3, Roy W. Howard Monographs in Journalism and Mass Communication Research (Bloomington, IN: Indiana University School of Journalism, 1994), 10–12, 19–23. See also Read, *The Power of News*, 172–6; Jonathan Silberstein-Loeb, "Business, Politics, Technology and the International Supply of News, 1845–1950," (University of Cambridge PhD dissertation, 2009), 203, 208–9.

208 Cooper's own view of these developments is in his book, *Barriers Down: The Story of the News Agency Epoch* (New York: Farrar & Rinehart Inc., 1942).

209 Indiana University, Lilly Library (hereafter LL) Cooper mss. 1934, 13–28 Jan. Livesay to Cooper, confidential, 25 Jan. 1934.

210 RA, Jones Papers, Section 1 Reuters, iv, Reuters General, 1926–33 (b), box 35, extracts of letter from Hatt to Jones, 21 March 1934; LL, Cooper mss. 1934, 1–5 Feb., Cooper to Noyes, 4 Feb. 1934.

211 LL, Cooper mss. 1934. 12–28 Feb., Cooper to Livesay, personal and confidential, 10 Feb. 1934.

212 APCA, AP 02A.4, Special Member files series I. Canadian Press, box 4, 1940–43, folder 24 (1940) Cooper to J.A. McNeil, 9 Oct. 1940.

213 LL, Cooper mss. 1934. 12–28 Feb., Cooper to Livesay, confidential, 13 Feb. 1934. See also Cooper's published account of CP's role in the Reuters negotiations in *Barriers Down*, 262–3.

214 LL, Cooper mss. 1934, 12–28 Feb., Cooper to Livesay, confidential, 14 Feb. 1934.
215 Ibid., Livesay to Cooper, personal, 14 Feb. 1934.
216 APCA, AP 02A.4, Special Member files series I. Canadian Press, box 2, folder 16, Livesay to J.S. Elliott [assistant general manager], personal, 28 Sept. 1933; box 3, folder 19, Livesay to Cooper, personal, 5 March 1936.
217 APCA, AP 02A.4, Special Member files series I. Canadian Press, box 3, folder 17 (1934), Cooper to Livesay, 8 Oct. 1934.
218 APCA, AP 02A.4, Special Member files series I. Canadian Press, box 3, folder 17 (1934), Livesay to Camille Lemercier [general manager of Havas], 9 Oct. 1934.
219 APCA, AP 02A.4, Special Member files series I. Canadian Press, box 3, folder 17 (1934), Cooper to Livesay, 17 Oct. 1934.
220 Reuters' supporters understood clearly that Livesay's continuing anger over the subsidy coloured his attitude to the British agency; RA, microfilm reel 0202, W.L. Murray [European general manager of Reuters] to Jones, 6 April 1936. Reliance on subsidies was a general feature of Reuters' operating practice under Jones's leadership; Putnis, "Share 999," 158.
221 RA, Jones Papers, Section 1 Reuters, iv, Reuters General, 1926–33 (b), box 35, Hatt to Jones, private and confidential, 6 April 1934.
222 Ibid.
223 RA, Jones Papers, Section 1 Reuters, iv, Reuters General, 1926–33 (b), box 35, Hatt to Jones, 21 March 1934.
224 RA, LN 1011, 1/014384 Gilbert Mant to BRH (Hatt), 10 Sept. 1934.
225 CP documents, board of directors meeting, 6 Oct. 1930; annual general meeting, 12 June 1935, "Fifth Imperial Press Conference. Report of the Honorary President."
226 APCA, AP 02A.4, Special Member files series I. Canadian Press, box 2 (1929–33), folder 11, 1930, Livesay to Cooper, 24 June 1930.
227 CP documents, annual general meeting, 12 June 1935, "Fifth Imperial Press Conference. Report of the Honorary President," 32–5.
228 RA, Jones 16, 1/974255, 1935 correspondence. Strictly confidential. Memorandum on the press in Canada for Lord Tweedsmuir.
229 CP documents, annual general meeting, 1935, remarks of Rupert Davies.
230 Smith concluded: "We got the very distinct impression that the initiative in the development of Empire news services must continue to come from the Dominions rather than from the motherland publishers." CP documents, annual general meeting, 12 June 1935, "Fifth Imperial Press Conference. Report of the Honorary President."

231 Purcell Papers, Livesay to C.A. Hayden, Vernon, B.C., 21 Nov. 1936.

232 Roderick Jones, *A Life in Reuters* (Garden City: Doubleday & Co., 1952), 170.

233 Putnis, "Share 999," 152; Read, *The Power of News*, 163.

234 RA, Jones 16, 1/974255, 1935 correspondence. Strictly confidential. Memorandum on the press in Canada for Lord Tweedsmuir.

235 RA, microfilm reel 0202, McDougall to Jones, private and confidential, 30 April 1936; overseas general manager (Turner) to Jones, 17 Dec. 1936.

236 RA, microfilm reel 0202, McDougall to Jones, 14 March 1936. A few weeks after the vote in Ottawa, Reuters' European general manager, W.L. Murray, had lunch in London with the official in charge of publicity for the Canadian High Commission. Both agreed that Livesay, who "apparently couldn't forget" the subsidy issue, was "our enemy who is stirring up matters." RA, microfilm reel 0202, note by W.L. Murray for Jones, 6 April 1936.

237 APCA, AP 02A.4, Special Member files series I. Canadian Press, box 3, folder 19 (1936), printed notice, London, 4 Jan. 1937.

238 CP documents, board of directors meeting, 2 Nov. 1936.

239 RA, microfilm reel 0201, Hatt memorandum, 12 May 1939.

240 See, for example, Oliver Boyd-Barrett and Terhi Rantanen, "The Globalization of News," in *The Globalization of News*, eds. Boyd-Barrett and Rantanen (London: SAGE, 1998), 1–14.

241 Shmanske, "News as a Public Good"; Gerben Bakker, "Trading Facts: Arrow's Fundamental Paradox and the Emergence of Global News Networks." In *International Communication and Global News Networks: Historical Perspectives*, ed. Peter Putnis, Chandrika Kaul, and Jürgen Wilke (New York : Hampton Press, 2011), 9–54.

242 Exceptions are Read, *The Power of News*; Michael Palmer, "What Makes News," in *The Globalization of News*, eds. Boyd-Barrett and Rantanen, 177–90; Xin Xin, "Structural Change and Journalism Practice: Xinhua News Agency in the Early 2000s," *Journalism Practice* 2, no. 1 (2008): 46–63. Terhi Rantanen's *After Five O'Clock Friends: Kent Cooper and Roy W. Howard*, no. 4, Roy W. Howard Monographs in Journalism and Mass Communication Research (Bloomington, IN: School of Journalism, Indiana University, 1998) is unusual in stressing the importance of the personal relationships between news-agency executives.

243 For examples of agency histories written by journalists or ex-journalists, see Oliver Gramling, *AP: The Story of News* (New York and Toronto: Farrar and Rinehart, 1940), which manages to say nothing at all about the AP–Reuters breach in the 1930s; Morris, *Deadline Every Minute*; and Nichols, *(CP): The Story of The Canadian Press*. Memoirs by news agency

executives such as Roderick Jones (*A Life in Reuters*) and Kent Cooper (*Barriers Down*) are more obviously partisan.

244 The need for critical assessment of journalism's claims to serve the public interest, especially in view of its structures of ownership and reliance on advertising, is a common theme in media-studies literature. See, for example, Robert McChesney, *Rich Media, Poor Democracy: Communication Politics in Dubious Times* (Urbana and Chicago: University of Illinois Press, 1998).

245 See Chapter 4, pp. 173–5, 178–9.

Chapter 3

1 See, for example, Lisa Gitelman, *Always Already New: Media, History, and the Data of Culture* (Cambridge, MA: MIT Press, 2006); John Nerone, "Approaches to Media History," in *A Companion to Media Studies,* ed. Angharad N. Valdivia (Malden, MA: Blackwell Publishing, 2005); James Curran, "Rival Narratives of Media History," in *Media and Power* (London: Routledge, 2002); Rudolph Stöber, "What Media Evolution Is: A Theoretical Approach to the History of New Media," *European Journal of Communication* 19, no. 4 (2004).

2 Mary Vipond, *Listening In: The First Decade of Canadian Broadcasting, 1922–1932* (Montreal and Kingston: McGill-Queen's University Press, 1992), 18, 22.

3 Ibid., 20, 21, 44. By the end of 1922, 14 newspapers operated radio stations; ibid., 44–5.

4 In the 1920s, newspapers with radio connections included *La Presse* of Montreal; the Toronto *Star, Globe, Mail and Empire,* and *Telegram*; the Vancouver *Sun* and *Province*; the Calgary *Herald* and Edmonton *Journal*; the Halifax *Herald*; and the London *Free Press.* Many smaller papers, such as the Lethbridge *Herald* (or Roy Thomson's northern Ontario newspapers in the 1930s), also were involved with radio.

5 There were similar divisions among newspapers in the United States; see Gwenyth L. Jackaway, *Media at War: Radio's Challenge to the Newspapers, 1924–1939* (Westport, CT: Praeger, 1995), 11, 15, 19. While Jackaway recognizes that conflict within the newspaper industry about how to respond to radio was widespread before 1933, she interprets this as a first, intra-industry, stage in a broader press–radio war.

6 In large cities particularly, newspapers published multiple editions and often published extras outside their usual edition times for big stories. There was thus some modification of the 24-hour cycle, but this remained the basic form.

7 See, for example, Jeff Webb, "Canada's Moose River Mine Disaster (1936): Radio – Newspaper Competition in the Business of News," *Historical Journal of Film, Radio & Television* 16, no. 3 (August 1996): 365–77.

8 Gene Allen, "Monopolies of News: Harold Innis, the Telegraph and Wire Services," in *The Toronto School of Communication Theory: Interpretations, Extensions, Applications,* eds. Rita Watson and Menahem Blondheim (Toronto and Jerusalem: University of Toronto Press/Magnes Press, 2008).

9 As Webb has suggested with reference to the Moose River mine disaster of 1936 and Mary Vipond has done with the Empire Day broadcast of 1939, this experience of simultaneity across long distances had a powerful effect on listeners' sense of being connected to a larger social reality. Radio thus created even stronger "imagined communities" than print. See Webb, "Canada's Moose River Mine Disaster," and Mary Vipond, "The Mass Media in Canadian History: The Empire Day Broadcast in 1939," *Journal of the Canadian Historical Association,* New series vol. 14 (2003). The widely used term "imagined communities" was coined by Benedict Anderson – see Anderson, *Imagined Communities: Reflections on the origin and spread of nationalism* (New York and London: Verso; rev. ed., 1991).

10 For recent examples of this argument, see Jackaway, *Media at War*; Michael Emery et al. *The Press and America: An Interpretive History of the Mass Media* (Needham Heights, MA: Allyn and Bacon, 2000), 320–1; Sian Nicholas, "All the News That's Fit to Broadcast: The Popular Press versus the BBC, 1922–45," in *Northcliffe's Legacy: Aspects of the British Popular Press, 1896–1996,* eds. Peter Catterall, Colin Seymour-Ure, and Adrian Smith (Houndmills, Basingstoke, Hampshire, and London: Macmillan Press Ltd., 2000), 121–48. The Canadian literature is more nuanced on this point; see Mary Vipond, "The Continental Marketplace: Authority, Advertisers and Audiences in Canadian News Broadcasting, 1932–1936," *Journal of Radio Studies* 6, no. 1 (1999): 169–84. One US scholar has explicitly questioned the press–radio war interpretation; see Alf Pratte, "Going Along for the Ride on the Prosperity Bandwagon: Peaceful Annexation, Not War, Between the Editors and Radio, 1923–1941," *Journal of Radio Studies* 2: 123–39.

11 For the notion of "competitive ecology," see John C. Nerone, "A Local History of the U.S. Press: Cincinnati, 1793–1858," in *Ruthless Criticism: New Perspectives in U.S. Communication History,* eds. William S. Solomon and Robert W. McChesney (Minneapolis and London: University of Minnesota Press, 1993), 39. Similar approaches, though not using the same terminology, have been used by Richard Kaplan for Detroit between 1865 and 1920 and by Thomas Walkom, who looked at the whole Toronto newspaper industry between 1871 and 1911. See Richard L. Kaplan, *Politics and the American Press: The Rise of Objectivity, 1865–1920* (Cambridge: Cambridge

University Press, 2002); Thomas L. Walkom, "The Daily Newspaper Industry in Ontario's Developing Capitalistic Economy: Toronto and Ottawa, 1871–1911" (University of Toronto PhD diss., 1983).

12 CP documents, circular no. 4, J.F.B. Livesay to all members of Canadian Press Limited, 22 March 1922; annual general meeting, 2 May 1922.

13 CP documents, annual general meeting, 1 May 1923.

14 Ibid.

15 The assassination of a political leader or a major disaster is an example of EOS news – events of such great news value that the normal time restrictions on publication did not apply. Member newspapers were also permitted to publish extras containing EOS news outside their regular publication hours.

16 For a more detailed account of CP's structure and its relation to competition, see Chapter 1, pp. 28–30.

17 CP documents, board of directors meeting, 29–30 April 1925.

18 AP was a cooperative like CP, but its position was further complicated by the fact that there were two competing, commercially based news agencies in the United States (UP and Hearst's INS), which were entirely willing to sell their news to radio stations; Jackaway, *Media at War*, 16–18.

19 CP documents, annual general meeting, 1 May 1929.

20 CP documents, board of directors meeting, 28 April 1930. This observation underscored a key legal difference between the competitive situation in Canada as opposed to the United States; a US Supreme Court ruling in 1918 recognized news as property that could be protected legally, but this legal protection was never granted in Canada. See also pp. 111, 115–6.

21 CP documents, board of directors meeting, 28 April 1930.

22 CP documents, board of directors meeting, 27–28 April 1931.

23 CP documents, board of directors meeting, 28 April 1930.

24 See pp. 118–21.

25 CP documents, meeting of Ontario members, 28 Jan. 1931.

26 CP documents, board of directors meeting, 27–28 April 1931.

27 CP documents, board of directors meeting, 27–28 April 1931, and annual general meeting, 29 April 1931.

28 Associated Press Corporate Archives (APCA) AP 02A.4, Special Member files series I. Canadian Press, 1913–28 (box 1) Cooper to Livesay, 27 March 1925; CP documents, annual general meeting, 28 April 1925, report of the management on radio broadcasts.

29 CP documents, dominion elections, 1925, circular no. 6, from J.F.B. Livesay, general manager, to all members and staff of the Canadian Press, 12 Oct. 1925.

30 Jackaway, *Media at War*, 18.
31 CP documents, dominion elections, 1925, circular no. 8, from J.F.B. Livesay, general manager, to all members of the Canadian Press, 16 Oct. 1925.
32 CP documents, board of directors meeting, 28 April 1930.
33 Vipond, "The Continental Marketplace."
34 CP documents, board of directors meeting, 27–28 April 1931.
35 Vipond, *Listening In*, 63.
36 According to figures provided by Gwenyth Jackaway, Nichols was exaggerating somewhat: in the United States, she notes, newspaper advertising revenue dropped from around $800 million in 1929 to $450 million in 1933, while radio advertising revenue rose during the same period from $40 million to $80 million, for a ratio that rose from around 5 per cent to 18 per cent. Jackaway, *Media at War*, 20.
37 CP documents, meeting of joint radio committee, 1 June 1931, confidential.
38 CP documents, board of directors meeting, 4–5 Nov. 1935, "News on the Air."
39 CP documents, meeting of the radio committee, 19 May 1936.
40 CP documents, meeting of joint radio committee, 1 June 1931.
41 Mary Vipond has noted that, like the *Star*, many newspapers were unwilling to make the heavy investment required to operate a high-powered station; *Listening In*, 45. It cost $1,000 to put the Hamilton *Spectator*'s station, CHCS, on the air in 1922; Charles Bruce, *News and the Southams* (Toronto: Macmillan of Canada, 1968), 394.
42 CP documents, meeting of the joint radio committee, 1 June 1931, confidential.
43 Ibid. Many newspapers, especially the *Star* and the Southam and Sifton chains, strongly supported nationalization, whereas the *Telegram* and *La Presse* were strongly opposed. Other opponents included the *Financial Post*, the *Globe*, London *Free Press*, and Calgary *Albertan*. A survey of newspaper opinion circa 1930 showed 34 in favour of nationalization, 16 against, and 14 noncommittal. Vipond, *Listening In*, 232, 239.
44 The two dailies in Winnipeg, the *Free Press* and *Tribune*, took matters further, jointly agreeing in September 1930 to drop radio listings entirely and maintaining this policy until December 1931, when it was abandoned in the face of a threatened boycott of the *Free Press* by a coalition of advertisers representing broadcast stations, radio-equipment manufacturers, and related businesses. CP documents, Nichols to Livesay, 29 Dec. 1931; memorandum, "The Winnipeg Newspapers and Radio Programmes," 16 Dec. 1931, enclosures in Livesay to joint radio committee, 2 Jan. 1932.

45 CP documents, board of directors meeting, 6 Oct. 1931. The *Telegram* was particularly upset because the *Star* station, CFCA, had been given its own frequency, while CKGW, the *Telegram's* affiliate, had to share its frequency with another station, allowing it to broadcast only half-time. The *Telegram* asserted that Atkinson's connections with the Liberal government explained the different treatment. See Vipond, *Listening In*, 177–8, 203–4.

46 CP documents, board of directors meeting, 2 May 1932.

47 Library and Archives Canada (LAC), RG 41, vol. 172, file 11-17-3 (pt. 1), Livesay to Charlesworth, 30 Dec. 1932.

48 CP documents, meeting of radio subcommittee, 13 June 1933, enclosing memorandum from Livesay about proposed agreement with the Canadian Radio Broadcasting Commission, 3 June 1933. The relationship that took shape between CP and the CRBC has been previously, and clearly, described by Vipond; see "The Continental Marketplace," 171–4.

49 CP documents, board of directors meeting, 5 June 1933.

50 CP documents, meeting of radio subcommittee, 13 June 1933, enclosing memorandum from Livesay about proposed agreement with the Canadian Radio Broadcasting Commission, 3 June 1933.

51 CP documents, board of directors meeting, 5 June 1933.

52 Here are several items from a "Specimen" broadcast script, 29 May 1933 (CP documents, 1933):

"Wilbur Glen Voliva of Chicago, who contends that the earth is flat, is himself in that condition financially and receivers were today designated for his religious colony.

"Sixteen Canadians tonight are anxiously awaiting the result of the English Derby, for they hold tickets in the Irish Hospital Sweepstake. The winning ticket is worth $120.000.

"Neville Chamberlain, chancellor of the British Exchequer, today announced he had agreed to an immediate Australian bond issue not exceeding five years maturity for the purpose of refunding certain Australian loans bearing interest at 6-1/2 per cent.

"Unless last minute changes occur, Premier Bennett, Hon. E.N. Rhodes, minister of finance; Dr. W.C. Clark, deputy minister; L.D. Wilgress, director of commercial intelligence service of the trade and commerce department; N. A. Robertson of the external affairs department; and R.K. Finlayson, Mr. Bennett's chief secretary, form the Canadian delegation to the economic conference.

"And here's some cheerful news. In the first four months of 1933, Canada has more than doubled her supply of apples in the United Kingdom and has taken first place from the United States, according to an Ottawa despatch."

53 CP documents, board of directors meeting, 5 June 1933.

54 CP documents, meeting of radio subcommittee, 13 June 1933.

55 CP documents, board of directors meeting, 13 Nov. 1933, management report. The Press–Radio Bureau in the United States, established after the Biltmore Agreement of December 1933, ended up adopting a pattern that was similar in many respects to the CP–CRBC agreement. See Jackaway, *Media at War*, 27–9.

56 CP documents, board of directors meeting, 4–5 Nov. 1935, "News on the Air."

57 CP documents, annual general meeting, 12 June 1935.

58 Jackaway, *Media at War*, 29.

59 CP documents, board of directors meeting, 4–5 Nov. 1935, "News on the Air."

60 Livesay's view was that "pretty much every American news broadcast is at times anti-British in character"; see Livesay to Charlesworth, 12 March 1935. LAC, RG 41, vol. 173, file 11-17-3 (pt. 5).

61 APCA AP 02A.4, Special Member files series I. Canadian Press, box 3, 1934–39, folder 19, 1936, Transradio Press Service, circular letter, 29 Jan. 1936, enc. in Livesay to Cooper, personal, 8 Feb. 1936. Livesay and Cooper both hoped to convince Reuters to break its connection with Transradio; Cooper to Noyes, 24 Feb. 1936 and Livesay to Cooper, personal, 5 March 1936. Reuters ended the association in January 1937; ibid., folder 20, 1937, Livesay to W. McCurdy, Winnipeg *Tribune*, 23 June 1937.

62 APCA AP 02A.4, Special Member files series I. Canadian Press, box 3, 1934–39, folder 19, 1936, Livesay to Cooper, personal, 8 Feb. 1936.

63 Ernie Bushnell of the CBC listed two reasons for Transradio's success succinctly: "a) The news supplied by this agency can be sold. b) It is better news." LAC, RG 41, vol. 173, file 11-17-3 (pt. 8), Bushnell to Murray, 4 June 1938.

64 CP documents, board of directors meeting, 4–5 Nov. 1935.

65 Ibid.

66 CP documents, report of radio committee, 3 Nov. 1935; board of directors meeting, 4–5 Nov. 1935.

67 CP documents, board of directors meeting, 4–5 Nov. 1935, "News on the Air."

68 Livesay to Charlesworth, 24 June 1936, LAC, RG 41, vol. 173, file 11-17-3 (pt. 6).

69 The phrase was Livesay's: CP documents, board of directors meeting, 2 Nov. 1936.

70 CP documents, board of directors meeting, 4–5 Nov. 1935, "News on the Air."

71 CP documents, annual general meeting, 29 April 1936.

72 Ibid.

73 CP documents, meeting of the radio committee, 19 May 1936; board of directors meeting, 30 April 1936.

74 CP documents, meeting of the radio committee, 19 May 1936. For the impact of radio coverage of Moose River, see Webb, "Canada's Moose River Mine Disaster."

75 CP documents, board of directors meeting, 11–12 Oct. 1937. BUP, an off-shoot of United Press in the United States, was intended to provide UP with an entry into the Canadian and British markets. For the origins of BUP, see Chapter 2, p. 86.

76 CP documents, board of directors meeting, 3 Oct. 1938.

77 LAC, RG 41, vol. 173, file 11-17-3 (pt. 4), Livesay memorandum, "Agreement with Radio Commission," n.d., enc. in. Livesay to Charlesworth, 15 Nov. 1934.

78 LAC, RG 41, vol. 173, file 11-17-3 (pt. 4), Livesay to Charlesworth, 15 Nov. 1934. CP's British Columbia superintendent speculated that the CRBC was quite willing to let the CP broadcasts "go by" in some areas of the country in order to earn more advertising revenue. J. Richardson, Pacific superintendent, to Livesay, 22 Nov. 1934; LAC, RG 41, vol. 173, file 11-17-3 (pt. 4).

79 LAC, RG 41, vol. 173, file 11-17-3 (pt. 4), Livesay to Charlesworth, 17 Sept. 1934; Livesay memorandum, "Consolidation of Radio News broadcasts," n.d., enc. in Livesay to Charlesworth, 10 Oct. 1934.

80 LAC, RG 41, vol. 173, file 11-17-3 (pt. 8), Livesay to Murray, 23 Dec. 1938.

81 LAC, RG 41, vol. 173, file 11-17-3 (pt. 8), Livesay to Murray, 1 March 1938; Livesay to Murray, 23 Dec. 1937. Livesay told Murray (with what seemed to be a touch of disappointment) that a close examination of three days' worth of Transradio broadcasts had shown nothing specifically anti-British "but it was loaded up with American news, including much crime, and there was practically not a word of Canadian or British news."

82 LAC, RG 41, vol. 173, file 11-17-3 (pt. 8), Murray to Livesay, confidential, 25 March 1938.

83 LAC, RG 41, vol. 173, file 11-17-3 (pt. 4), Herbert Sallans to Livesay, 22 Nov. 1934, copy.

84 LAC, RG 41, vol. 173, file 11-17-3 (pt. 7), Carson Buchanan H.N. Stovin, supervisor of station relations, CBC, 14 July 1938.

85 CP documents, board of directors meeting, 11 Oct. 1937.

86 LAC, RG 41, vol 173, file 11-17-3 (pt. 7), E.C. Buchanan, director of public relations, to Murray, memorandum, 12 Dec. 1936.

87 LAC, RG 41, vol. 173, file 11-17-3 (pt. 8), Bushnell memorandum to Murray, 30 Dec. 1938.

88 So described in Livesay, memorandum on relations of the Canadian Broadcasting Corporation and The Canadian Press, n.d., enc. in Livesay to Leonard Brockington, 14 June 1937. LAC, RG 41, vol. 173, file 11-17-3 (pt. 7).

89 In fact, Bushnell had already met with a Reuters representative to inquire about the possibility; The Reuters Archive, Thomson Reuters (RA), microfilm 0467, Globereuter – Canapress, 1938–1945, report by Moloney for Roderick Jones, 3 Nov. 1938.

90 CP documents, board of directors meeting, 11 Oct. 1937 and 3 Oct. 1938; management report, 27 April 1938; annual general meeting, April 1938.

91 LAC, RG 41, vol. 172, file 11-7-3-3 (pt. 2), private and confidential, memorandum of proposed agreement between the Canadian Broadcasting Corp. and the Canadian Press for a Comprehensive news service, 2 May 1939; CP documents, 23 Oct. 1939, general superintendent's memo re: "News on the Air" (no. 5), agreement between the Canadian Broadcasting Corporation and The Canadian Press.

92 CP documents, strictly confidential, memorandum on facsimile (for minister of transport), 11 July 1939; board of directors meeting, 23 Oct. 1939, report of general manager. The new service required six full-time and five part-time staff.

93 LAC, RG 41, vol. 172, file 11-7-3-3 (pt. 2), D'Arcy Marsh, supervisor of news broadcasts, to E.L. Bushnell, 18 Aug. 1939.

94 CP documents, board of directors meeting, 23 Oct. 1939, Gillis Purcell, "News on the Air" (no. 5); The Canadian Press, confidential. Memorandum: Conference of Canadian Press Radio Committee with Board of Governors of the Canadian Broadcasting Corporation, Ottawa, 6 July 1939.

95 CP documents, meeting of the radio committee, 24 Oct. 1939 and 25 May 1940.

96 As Rupert Davies expressed it: "Public anxiety and tension were being aroused by the news broadcasts of other services and this condition would be intensified when the Canadian troops were overseas." CP documents, meeting of the radio committee, 24 Oct. 1939.

97 CP documents, report of the radio committee, 13 Dec. 1939.

98 CP documents, "News on the Air," memorandum by the general manager (no. 6), 25 May 1940.

99 CP documents, meeting of the radio committee, 25 May 1940.

100 Frank W. Peers, *The Politics of Canadian Broadcasting, 1920–1951* (Toronto: University of Toronto Press, 1969), 286. By this time, Peers concluded, most newspapers "began to see possibilities for sizeable financial returns from their broadcasting activities," marking a change from the widespread earlier belief that radio should mainly be a public service and should not compete for advertising revenue. This also happened in the United States. Between 1934 and 1938, the number of US radio stations owned by or affiliated with newspapers increased from around 100 to 211, accounting for about 30 per cent of the total; Jackaway, *Media at War*, 32.

101 CP documents, meeting of the communications committee, 1 June 1940.

102 CP documents, meeting of the communications committee, 25 June 1940; *Editor & Publisher*, 8 June 1940; Halifax *Chronicle-Herald*, 23 Nov. 1940, p. 3, "To consider Transradio situation."

103 CP documents, special meeting of the board of directors, 25 June 1940.

104 Of course, although CP itself operated on a nonprofit basis, the newspapers that collectively owned it and relied on its news service did not.

105 In the summer of 1939, Rupert Davies visited several European countries in his capacity as CP's president. While in Berlin, he met the directors of Transocean, who proposed to sell their news service to CP. Davies responded that it was no more than propaganda, to which his interlocutor replied: "No more so than Havas." Davies later received a sample of the Transocean news service and dismissed it as "largely propaganda." CP documents, board of directors meeting, 23 Oct. 1939.

106 LAC, MG 26-I, Arthur Meighen fonds, 109950, Knowles to Meighen, 9 July 1940. Knowles added that that he had "just had a serious clash" about this issue with CP's president (and soon-to-be Liberal senator) Rupert Davies.

107 LAC, Meighen fonds 98003, Meighen to R.B. Hanson, 18 July 1940. Meighen noted that this would shut out the *Telegram* and Toronto *Star*, which currently were affiliated with private broadcasting stations that sold news commercially, but suggested that the *Star* at least might be satisfied to take its news from CP, "which is in my judgment as good as Grit through and through."

108 CP consistently (and convincingly) argued that the $20,000 was neither a subsidy nor a fee for providing its news service to the CBC, but was

simply to cover out-of-pocket costs for the additional staff required to prepare the CBC bulletins.

109 "News Problem Up to Stations," *Globe and Mail*, 23 Nov. 1940, p. 2.
110 CP documents, board of directors meeting, 29 May 1940, memorandum, "News on the Air," no. 6.
111 CP documents, board of directors meeting, 29 May 1940, "Domestic News."
112 CP documents, board of Directors meeting, 23 Oct. 1939, "News on the Air," no. 5.
113 CP documents, board of directors meeting, Ottawa, 9 Sept. 1940.
114 Ibid., resolution of CBC board of governors, 20 Aug. 1940.
115 The approved form was "Through the courtesy of (Name and business of Sponsor), Station OLB presents XYZ news (i.e., CP or BUP) as a service to its listeners." Resolution of CBC board of governors, 20 Aug. 1940, reprinted in CP documents, board of directors meeting, Ottawa, 9 Sept. 1940. See also board of directors meeting, 15 Sept. 1941, Report of the President to the Board of Directors of The Canadian Press on the Organization and Progress of Press News Ltd.
116 CP documents, board of directors meeting, 10 Sept. 1940.
117 CP documents, board of directors meeting, 3 March 1941.
118 For AP's decision, see Jackaway, *Media at War*, 33.
119 CP documents, annual general meeting, 5 March 1941; special meeting of the board of directors, 19 May 1941.
120 CP documents, special meeting of the board of directors, 19 May 1941.
121 CP documents, special meeting of the board of directors, 19 May 1941, report of the general manager.
122 CP documents, board of directors meeting, 15 Sept. 1941, Report of the President to the Board of Directors of The Canadian Press on the Organization and Progress of Press News Ltd.
123 CP documents, board of directors meeting, 3 March 1941, memorandum from J.A. McNeil on "Conditional Plan for Sale of CP News for Radio Broadcasting."
124 CP documents, annual general meeting, 5 March 1941.
125 See Nicholas, "All the News That's Fit to Broadcast."
126 For example, it is noteworthy that newspapers in structurally very similar competitive positions, such as the *Star* and *Telegram* in Toronto, had different ideas about how best to compete, which led to their adopting quite different approaches to radio – one opposing, and one supporting, the idea of nationalization.

127 Jackaway, *Media at War*, 153, quoting Carolyn Marvin, *When Old Technologies Were New: Thinking about Electric Communication in the Late Nineteenth Century* (New York: Oxford University Press, 1988).

Chapter 4

1 Canadian Press documents, board of directors meeting, Ottawa, 23 Oct. 1939, report of the general manager.
2 CP had been involved in censorship planning since 1936 – see p. 155.
3 The suggestion was ultimately rejected; see p. 171.
4 CP documents, board of directors meeting, 23 Oct. 1939, report of the general manager.
5 CP documents, circular no 23., from J.A. McNeil, general manager, Toronto, 8 Dec. 1939. See also McNeil to William Moloney (Reuters), 21 Oct. 1939: "our Finance Committee has been in session for the past few days, and the facts laid before it as to existing and anticipated increases in our expenditures due to war conditions, have impelled them to lay down not only stringent restrictions against any new commitments, but the exploring of every possible avenue of other economies." The Reuters Archive, Thomson Reuters (RA), microfilm reel 0467.
6 CP documents, finance committee meeting, 22 May 1940, comments of Victor Sifton.
7 Gillis Purcell Papers, Purcell to McNeil, 22 Oct. 1939.
8 Gillis Purcell Papers, Purcell to McNeil, 13 Feb. 1940.
9 Gillis Purcell Papers, Davies to McNeil, 25 March 1940.
10 CP documents, finance committee meeting, 22 May 1940; Gillis Purcell Papers, McNeil to Davies, 25 March 1940.
11 Gillis Purcell Papers, Purcell to E. Norman Smith, 6 Sept. 1939.
12 Gillis Purcell Papers, Purcell to E. Norman Smith, personal, 16 Sept. 1939.
13 Gillis Purcell Papers, Norman Rogers to McNeil, 28 Nov. 1939.
14 CP documents, board of directors meeting, 29 May 1940, report of the general manager.
15 Gillis Purcell, "Assignment: WAR – 25 Years Ago Today," Toronto *Star*, 17 Dec. 1964 (clipping in Gillis Purcell Papers).
16 The Army had already decided that it would rely mainly on "regular journalists" rather than official news coverage (as Max Aitken had provided during the First World War). See Timothy J. Balzer, "The Information Front: The Canadian Army, Public Relations, and War News during the Second World War" (PhD dissertation, University of Victoria, 2009), 34.
17 Gillis Purcell Papers, diary, 8 Jan. 1940, very confidential.

18 Ibid.
19 CP documents, board of directors meeting, 9 Sept. 1940; Balzer, "The Information Front," 45.
20 CP documents, board of directors, 25 June 1940, report of the general manager.
21 Library and Archives Canada (LAC), Andrew George Latta McNaughton collection, MG30-E133, McNaughton for VCGS, 27 Aug. 1942, secret; vol 198, file PA 6-9-C-5; McNeil to Cliff Wallace, 28 Dec. 1942. For an example of these articles, see p. 141.
22 CP documents, meeting of western division members, Vancouver, 12 April 1940.
23 Gillis Purcell Papers, quoted in Purcell to McNaughton, personal, 25 Aug. 1940.
24 Gillis Purcell Papers, Purcell to McNaughton, personal, 25 Aug. 1940.
25 Gillis Purcell Papers, Purcell memorandum, 18 Sept. 1940.
26 Gillis Purcell Papers, Purcell to Rupert Davies, confidential, 19 Sept. 1940. Although the specific position may have been a surprise, Purcell had been discussing the possibility of some such appointment with McNaughton on and off since January.
27 Gillis Purcell Papers, McNeil to Davies, 14 Dec. 1940.
28 Gillis Purcell Papers, Davies to Purcell, 18 Nov. 1940; CP documents, board of directors, 15 Nov. 1940.
29 CP documents, J.A. McNeil memorandum, 24 Oct. 1940; LAC, McNaughton Collection, vol. 198, file PA 6-9-C-5, Purcell to McNaughton, 31 Dec. 1940; Gillis Purcell Papers, Davies to McNeil, 20 Jan. 1941.
30 Gillis Purcell Papers, Nichols to McNeil, 12 Feb. 1941. See also McNeil to Henri Gagnon (*La Presse*) and all other directors, 1 Feb. 1941, and J.M. Dennis (Halifax *Herald*) to McNeil, 19 Feb. 1941; and CP documents, board of directors meeting, 3 March 1941.
31 CP documents, board of directors meeting, 3 March 1941.
32 Gillis Purcell Papers, Purcell to Davies, 14 Dec. 1940.
33 CP documents, McNeil memorandum, 24 Oct. 1940.
34 LAC, McNaughton Collection, vol. 145, file PA 3-7, vol. 3, "Regulations for Press Representatives with the Canadian Army in the United Kingdom," 24 May 1941.
35 LAC, McNaughton Collection, vol. 145, file PA 3-7, vol. 1, Purcell to McNaughton, 14 Aug. 1941.
36 CP documents, annual general meeting, May 1940.
37 "And you can just imagine the time-saving that was. He didn't have to line up for transportation. ... his driver would get gas." Author interview with

Bill Stewart, 2 Nov. 2002. For an overview of Stewart's work as a CP war correspondent, see Stephen Thorne, "CWCA's 'Quiet, Unflappable' Warco Bill Stewart Dies at Age 90," *Canadian War Correspondents' Association Newsletter* [n.d., n.p.].

38 LAC, McNaughton Collection, vol. 145, file PA 3-7, vol. 1, to Defensor from Canmilitary, 11 Feb. 1942 (for Stuart from Crerar).

39 LAC, McNaughton Collection, vol 145, file PA 3-7, vol. 1, to Canmilitary from Defensor, 26 June 1942.

40 CP documents, report of general manager, 12 Sept. 1942. McNaughton was grateful for the accolades, telling McNeil that "[i]t gives me the greatest satisfaction to know that our Press policy continues to work out in such a way as to meet the needs of the Canadian Press." McNaughton to McNeil, 24 Oct 1942.

41 RA, microfilm reel 0201, memo of Bernard Rickatson Hatt, 9 Sept. 1939. For the operations of Agence Reuter, see p. 45.

42 CP documents, special meeting of the board of directors, 25 June 1940.

43 CP documents, annual general meeting, 5 March 1941, report of the general manager.

44 LAC, RG 25, vol. 2863, file 1786-40, R.W. Keyserlingk (general manager, BUP) to Robertson, 22 Feb. 1941, enclosing letter to W.L.M. King; Robertson to Rupert Davies, 1 March 1941.

45 LAC, RG 25, vol. 2863, file 1786-40, Purcell to Norman Robertson, 15 March 1941.

46 RA, microfilm reel 0201, Christopher Chancellor, report for Sir Roderick Jones, 15 Jan. 1941. For British Official Wireless, see Read, *The Power of News*, 148, 256.

47 RA, microfilm reel 0201, Christopher Chancellor, report for Sir Roderick Jones, 15 Jan. 1941. For the development of Reuters' wireless service, see Read, *The Power of News*, 157–8.

48 RA, microfilm reel 0201, CJC (Chancellor) memorandum re: Canadian Press, 4 March 1941.

49 RA, microfilm reel 201, memorandum to J.T. (Turner) from W.A.C. (Walton Cole), 3 Dec. 1942. Canada House was the office of the Canadian High Commission in London, and "Canapress" was Reuters' abbreviation for Canadian Press.

50 RA, microfilm reel 201, memorandum, Canapress and British News, 18 Dec. 1942.

51 LAC, McNaughton Collection, vol. 198, file PA 6-9-C-5, McNeil to McNaughton, 11 Feb. 1942.

52 LAC, McNaughton Collection, vol. 198, file PA 6-9-C-5, McNeil to McNaughton, 10 March 1942, quoting Purcell to McNaughton, 15 Jan. 1942; Purcell to McNaughton, 3 June 1942.

53 LAC, McNaughton Collection, vol. 198, file PA 6-9-C-5, text of Purcell CBC broadcast, 11 Jan. 1942.

54 CP documents, report of the general manager, 8 April 1942.

55 Ross Munro, "Q.O.R. Mortars Fast, Accurate," Toronto Globe and Mail, 16 March 1942, p. 7. The same report appeared in that day's Toronto Star: "Stage Attack Drill Overseas," p. 33.

56 CP documents, report of the general manager, 10 Sept. 1941.

57 CP documents, annual general meeting, 14 April 1943.

58 LAC, MG 28 I 134, vol. 8, file Canada at War, (Unit Stories – France) – 27B. This file also included a list of every active Canadian regiment and its corresponding hometown.

59 CP documents, report of the general manager, 8 April 1942.

60 CP documents, board of directors meeting, 9 Sept. 1940.

61 CP documents, report of the general manager, 25 Feb. 1941.

62 CP documents, report of the general manager, 10 Sept. 1941.

63 CP documents, special meeting of the board of directors, 19 May 1941. It was reported that Robertson was missing at sea and presumed dead. See also Toronto Star, 7 May 1941, "Relatives of 122 Missing Clinging to Slight Hopes."

64 Munro had previously covered the joint British–Canadian–Norwegian raid on Spitzbergen, which was unopposed; CP documents, report of general manager, 10 Sept. 1941. Ross Munro, "Canadians Hold Spitzbergen," Globe and Mail, 9 Sept. 1941, p. 1. CP was the only news organization to cover the operation. (General manager's report, board of directors meeting, 15 Sept. 1941.)

65 Timothy Balzer, " 'In Case the Raid Is Unsuccessful...': Selling Dieppe to Canadians," Canadian Historical Review 87, no. 3 (September 2006): 409–30. See also Phillip Knightley, The First Casualty (New York and London: Harcourt Brace Jovanovich, 1975); 317–20.

66 Timothy Balzer, The Information Front: The Canadian Army and News Management during the Second World War (Vancouver and Toronto: UBC Press, 2011), 97. The other Canadians included Fred Griffin of the Toronto Star, Wallace Reyburn of the Montreal Standard, and Bob Bowman of the CBC. Different figures are given in Knightley, The First Casualty, 318.

67 For a general account of wartime censorship and how it affected CP, see pp. 155–162 below.

68 Balzer dissertation, 420–1.
69 "Munro's First Cable After Dieppe," in Canadian Press, "CP Told the World ... About Canada at Dieppe" (Toronto, 1942).
70 Balzer, *Information Front*, 89.
71 Quoted in "CP Told the World ... About Canada at Dieppe."
72 "CP Told the World ... About Canada at Dieppe."
73 CP documents, board of directors, 14 Sept. 1942, report of general manager, 12 Sept. 1942.
74 LAC, McNaughton Collection, vol. 135, file PA 1-8-1 (Dieppe), Purcell to McNaughton, 28 Sept. 1942. By the time the pamphlet was issued, the casualty lists had been published, leading to a more equivocal assessment of the raid: "History will tell whether the raid was a success or a failure."
75 Gillis Purcell, "Wartime Press Censorship in Canada" (MA thesis, University of Toronto, 1946), 131. Balzer (dissertation, 285–92) provides a thorough account of the delay, which was more due to British than Canadian concerns.
76 Knightley, 319, italics added.
77 Purcell, "Wartime Press Censorship," 131.
78 Balzer, *Information Front*, 91–5, 106.
79 Gillis Purcell Papers, Purcell to McNaughton, 28 Sept. 1942.
80 LAC, McNaughton Collection, vol. 135, file PA 1-8-1 (Dieppe), Ralston to McNaughton, 27 Aug. 1942; McNaughton to Ralston, 1 Sept. 1942. To correct this, Ralston's office arranged to have CP send its Dieppe coverage to Washington, where copies were handed out by the press attaché at the Canadian legation.
81 LAC, McNaughton Collection, McNaughton for VCGS, 27 Aug. 1942, secret.
82 Gillis Purcell Papers, Purcell to McNeil, personal and confidential, 2 Jan. 1943. See also Balzer, *Information Front*, 30.
83 LAC, McNaughton Collection, file PA 3-7, vol 2. Memorandum, 3 Feb. 1943 of conversation among McNaughton, Clark, Purcell, Wallace, 28 Jan. 1943, secret. See also Maj. W.G. Abel (public relations officer), report for week ending 6 Feb. 1943 and Balzer dissertation, 49.
84 LAC, McNaughton Collection, memorandum, 8 Feb. 1943, secret, Lt.-Col. D.C. Spry (PA to McNaughton), re: meeting between McNaughton and Purcell, 6 Feb. 1943. Disagreements arose later over what this formula meant in practice; see pp. 148–50.
85 Balzer dissertation, 54.
86 Gillis Purcell Papers, Purcell to McNaughton, 7 Feb. 1943.

87 LAC, McNaughton Collection, vol. 198, file PA 6-9-C-5, Lt.-Col. D.C. Spry (PA to McNaughton) to DDPR, First Cdn Army, n.d.

88 CP's nine French-language members agreed in 1942 to jointly assume the cost of the francophone war correspondent, Maurice Desjardins. CP documents, report of general manager, 12 Sept. 1942.

89 CP documents, annual general meeting, 14 April 1943; report of general manager, 6 April 1943.

90 LAC, MG27 IIIB11 James Layton Ralston fonds, vol. 76, file "Public Relations Organization 1943." J.W.G. Clark, chief of information, armed forces, to Lt.-Col G.S. Currie, deputy minister of defence, 23 March 1943.

91 CP documents, report of the general manager, 6 April 1943.

92 John Swettenham, *McNaughton*, vol. 2, 1939–1943 (Toronto: Ryerson Press, 1969), 327–8, 349.

93 Canadian Press, "Red Patch in Sicily," (Toronto: Canadian Press, 1943), 2; "Munro Story on Sicily Scores 7-Hour Scoop," *Globe and Mail*, 12 July 1943, p. 7; Balzer, *Information Front*, 117.

94 CP documents, report of general manager, n.d., for board of directors meeting, 13 Sept. 1943. Bill Stewart had a more critical view of Gilchrist; see "Army Public Relations in WWII Had Rough Start," *Canadian War Correspondents' Association Newsletter* (n.d., n.p.).

95 Balzer, *Information Front*, 118. See also McNaughton Collection, vol. 135, file PA 1-8-1. P.J. Montague, Senior Officer, Canadian Military HQ, to Senior Combatant Officer, Canadian Army in UK, confidential, n.d. but received 11 Nov. 1943, noting "resentment directed at CMHQ since the incident of Ross Munro getting the first story out of Sicily."

96 R.S. Malone, *A World in Flames: A Portrait of War*, Part 2 (Toronto: Collins, 1984), 22.

97 LAC, McNaughton Collection, vol. 145, file PA 3-7, vol. 3, McNeil to Minister, 10 Aug. 1943. This would not have been the first conflict over press relations between the First Canadian Army and CMHQ; see Balzer dissertation, 26, 47, 216 ff; Balzer, *Information Front,* 135 ff.

98 LAC, McNaughton Collection, vol. 178, PA 5-0-45, McNeil to Lt-Gen Kenneth Stuart, CGS, 11 June 1943. The threat to remove Desjardins would have been quite potent in view of Ralston's insistence on more coverage of French-Canadian soldiers; Balzer dissertation, 51–2. Canadian military authorities saw the threat to cut Desjardins as a "mere pretext to obtain an additional CP place." LAC, RG 24, vol. 12376, 4/press/28/2, Abel, "Memorandum: Canadian Press, Priority of War Correspondents," 7 Aug. 1943, quoted in Balzer dissertation, 139. Balzer, 135–6, notes that the five-correspondent standard was CP's interpretation of the February

1943 agreement with McNaughton, but that this was not spelled out explicitly.

99 CP documents, board of directors, 13 Sept. 1943; LAC, McNaughton Collection, vol. 145, file PA 3-7, vol. 3. McNeil to minister, 16 Sept. 1943. Balzer, *Information Front*, 36. See also LAC, RG 41, file 11-17-3-4, Purcell to Ralston, 16 Sept. 1943, copy enc. in Purcell to Dan McArthur, 16 Sept. 1943.

100 LAC, McNaughton Collection, vol. 145, file PA 3-7, vol. 3. McNeil to Ralston, 10 Aug. 1943; LAC, RG 24, vol. 60, file 650-92-98. Telegram to CMHQ, London, 3 Aug. 1943, signed by George McCullagh, A.W.J. Buckland (*Telegram*), James Kingsbury (Toronto *Star*), G.H. Carpenter (Montreal *Gazette*), A.J. West (Montreal *Star*), M.E. Nichols (Southam), G.V. Ferguson (Sifton), and W.H. Vaughan (Windsor *Star*). For a detailed account of the frustrations faced by independent correspondents who remained in Africa, see Balzer, *Information Front*, 210–16.

101 LAC, McNaughton Collection, vol. 145, file PA 3-7, vol. 3, Ralston to McNeil, 19 Aug. 1943; to Canmilitary from Defensor, 2 Sept. 1943, most secret, for Montague from Stuart.

102 LAC, McNaughton Collection, vol. 145, file PA 3-7, vol. 3, Defensor to Canmilitary, 21 Oct. 1943. See also Keyserlingk (BUP) to Purcell, 2 Sept. 1943, LAC, RG 41, file 11-17-3-4.

103 LAC, RG 24, vol. 60, file 650-92-98, Canmilitary to Defensor, 1 Oct. 1943. The unfavourable decision about accrediting BUP correspondents was the result of a complaint by AP; Balzer, *Information Front*, 39.

104 Two CP correspondents, Munro and Bill Stewart, eventually landed with the Canadian invasion force on June 6. CP documents, Canadian Press Book Research Material (Douglas Amaron), memorandum by Ross Munro, 4 June 1984. Other CP correspondents were attached to the Royal Canadian Air Force and Royal Canadian Navy.

105 LAC, RG 36-31, vol. 14, Wartime Information Board, file 8-18, "Canadian Press," J.W.G. Clark to Purcell, 20 Feb. 1944.

106 CP documents, board of directors meeting, 23 Sept. 1944.

107 CP documents, board of directors meeting, 28 March 1944.

108 CP documents, general manager's report, 1944, 13. See also Balzer dissertation, 80: "In January 1944, Abel raged against the CP that had insisted at the onset of the campaign on a requirement of three correspondents to cover Italy because overwork in Sicily had led to a collapse in Munro's health. Abel mused to Joe Clark, 'perhaps we did not kill Ross Munro after all.' Clark, with Abel's permission, showed the DDPR's complaints to

Purcell who 'blew a gasket,' protesting it as 'unfair' because it 'misrepresents the effective effort to straddle two theatres simultaneously.'"

109 CP documents, Douglas Amaron, Canadian Press Book Research Material, "How the GM of CP nearly blew the Normandy landing and wound up in the Tower." by Ross Munro, 4 June 1984. Munro had given Purcell a list detailing his estimate of the Allied order of battle for the landing: "The list was eerily accurate and enemy agents would have been delighted to have it." Purcell put the list in his briefcase, which he then left in a milk bar on the Strand during a blackout. The proprietor sent the briefcase to a local police station, from where it was successively forwarded to Scotland Yard and to Canadian Military Headquarters, where Purcell and Munro eventually reclaimed it. "Gil and I were paraded before the Canadian senior general there and given utter hell for breach of security," Munro wrote. "He then gave Gil back his brief case." Munro feared that he might lose his correspondent's credentials over the incident, but "the Brits concluded that the memo had not been seen by anyone who would imperil the operation."

110 CP documents, Douglas Amaron, Canadian Press Book Research Material, Description of CP D-Day coverage by Ross Munro.

111 Balzer, *Information Front*, 57, quoting Munro in *Gauntlet to Overlord*, 66

112 CP documents, Douglas Amaron, Canadian Press Book Research Material, Description of CP D-Day coverage by Bill Stewart.

113 Author interview with Bill Stewart.

114 CP documents, Douglas Amaron, Canadian Press Book Research Material, Description of CP D-Day coverage by Bill Stewart. See also "War Correspondents," report of Ross Munro in report of the general manager, CP annual report, 1945, 30.

115 CP documents, board of directors meeting, 10 April 1945, "War Correspondents," Ross Munro. See also LAC, RG 24, vol. 60, file 650-92-99, vol. 1, Charles Bruce (London superintendent) to Col. Abel (deputy director PR), 22 Aug. 1944.

116 Author interview with Bill Stewart

117 CP documents, "War Correspondents," report of Ross Munro in report of the general manager, CP annual report, 1945, 30.

118 The question whether BUP was an American or British news service was disputed. CP considered it a simple offshoot of the US-based United Press, and UP provided most (but not all) of BUP's news service. BUP's supporters pointed out that its legal headquarters were in Canada and emphasized its original Canadian and British coverage. See Chapter 2, pp. 86–7.

119 CP documents, Purcell memorandum to CP editorial staff, personal, 2 May 1942. Purcell noted that the entry of the United States into the war had "removed some of the objections to US-handled world copy," making it easier for BUP to sell its "US-built" news service to Canadian newspapers and radio stations.

120 These developments are covered in Chapter 3, p. 129.

121 CP documents, board of directors, 15 Sept. 1941, report of the president to the board of directors of the Canadian Press on the organization and progress of Press News Ltd.

122 CP documents, board of directors, 15 Sept. 1941, report of Press News board of directors.

123 CP documents, board of directors, 15 Sept. 1941, report of the president to the board of directors of the Canadian Press on the organization and progress of Press News Ltd.

124 For CP's previous disagreements with the CAB, see, for example, CP documents, memorandum submitted to the chairman and board of governors of the Canadian Broadcasting Corporation, 8 May 1940 (a response to the CAB brief of 16 Nov. 1939).

125 CP documents, board of directors, 13 April 1942.

126 CP documents, executive committee meeting, 27 Jan. 1947.

127 CP documents, board of directors meeting, 13 April 1942, confidential.

128 CP documents, special committee meeting, re: CBC contract, Montreal, 20 June 1942.

129 CP documents, meeting of the special CP committee and the CBC committee, re: new CBC contract, Toronto, 25 July 1942; meeting of the special committee, re: CBC contract, Quebec, 12 Sept. 1942; LAC, RG 41, vol. 172, file 11-17-3 (pt. 9), memo, unsigned, n.d., "Various Arrangements with The Canadian Press"; special committee meeting, re: CBC contract, Montreal, 20 June 1942.

130 CP documents, annual general meeting, 14 April 1943; meeting of the radio committee, 29 March 1943.

131 CP documents, executive committee minutes, 27 Jan. 1947. When the agreement came up for renewal a few years later, John Bassett Sr. complained that by working with the CBC, "Canadian publishers had reared a gargantuan competitor in radio. They were in effect subsidizing a government agency against themselves," and several others, including George McCullagh of the Globe and Mail, supported this view.

132 LAC, RG 41, vol. 172, file 11-17-3 (pt. 9). Confidential, comment on Mr. McNeil's letter, n.d. (1943).

133 It was also noted that "there is a great deal of active, as well as latent, antagonism to the CBC among member papers of the Canadian Press."

·134 LAC, RG 41, vol. 172, file 11-17-3 (pt. 9), memorandum, unsigned, n.d., "Various Arrangements with the Canadian Press"; CP documents, board of directors meeting, 9 April 1945.

135 CP documents, board of directors meeting, 25 Sept. 1945; LAC, RG 36/31, vol. 13, Wartime Information Board, File 8-6, British United Press, R.W. Keyserlingk to A.D. Dunton, general manager, Wartime Information Board, 2 Jan. 1945.

136 Claude Beauregard, *Guerre et Censure au Canada, 1939–1945* (Quebec: Septentrion, 1998), 11–12. There are also implicit, nonlegal, forms of "censorship" that have more to do with social consensus about what is or is not proper to discuss; ibid., 15–16. For a recent account of the censorship system during the war, see Mark Bourrie, *The Fog of War: Censorship of Canada's Media in World War Two* (Vancouver: Douglas & McIntyre, 2011).

137 See Chapter 1, pp. 41–2.

138 Beauregard, *Guerre et Censure au Canada, 1939–1945*, 27–28, 29; CP documents, meeting of the press censorship committee, Ottawa, 4 May 1936; board of directors meeting, 23 Oct. 1939, report of the general manager.

139 Beauregard, *Guerre et Censure au Canada, 1939–1945*, 126–7. See pp. 159–62 below for an explanation of how military censorship operated.

140 Ibid., 14, 42.

141 Responsibility for all censorship was centralized under the Minister of National War Services in 1942; ibid., 38.

142 Purcell, "Wartime Press Censorship in Canada," 10, 13. Richard Malone, who was appointed staff secretary to the minister of national defence, Col. J. L. Ralston, in 1939, recalled later that at beginning of war "press censorship and censorship regulations constituted a complete mare's nest. ... no one, either press or armed services, knew where real authority lay or what constituted a war secret. Every general and admiral, of course, together with every deputy and directorate, wished to censor anything that reflected adversely on his department. All the fat-headed blunders must be covered up, and reporters who tried to expose stupidity and waste were obviously traitors." Richard S. Malone, *A Portrait of War, 1939–1943* (Toronto: Collins, 1983), 87. See also Wilfred Kesterton, *History of Journalism in Canada* (Toronto: McClelland and Stewart, 1967), 247–8.

143 CP documents, board of directors meeting, 23 Oct. 1939, report of the general manager.

144 Wilfrid Eggleston, *While I Still Remember* (Toronto: The Ryerson Press, 1968), 259.

145 LAC, RG 36/31, vol. 7, file 2-6-1, W. Eggleston and Fulgence Charpentier, background memorandum on voluntary press censorship, 11 Dec. 1944, quoted in Daniel German, "Press Censorship and the Terrace Mutiny: A Case Study in Second World War Information Management," *Journal of Canadian Studies* 31, no. 4 (Winter 1996): 124–42.

146 CP documents, board of directors meeting, 29 May 1940, report of the general manager.

147 The system did not work well at the beginning of the war. In July 1940, the censors asked for additional powers to act against newspapers that were ignoring regulations or disregarding censors' instructions, and in December they warned that censorship was ineffective because their recommendations for prosecution were not followed. The overall level of compliance did not improve until 1942, with Canadian forces in active operations, the US entry into the war, and the first prosecutions of newspapers for violations. (The first newspaper to be prosecuted was the Vancouver *Sun*, in March 1942, followed by *Le Devoir* in April.) Throughout the entire war, however, there were only five prosecutions of daily newspapers (Beauregard, *Guerre et Censure au Canada, 1939–1945*, 62–5, 68). Eleven publications were suppressed outright, some for opposition to the war effort in general, some for pro-Communist politics, and some for pro-Nazi politics. See "Final Report on Censorship of Publications, Appendix 1" in Paul-André Comeau, Claude Beauregard, Edwidge Munn, *La Democratie en veilleuse: Rapport des censeurs 1939–1945* (Montreal: Editions Quebec/Amerique, 1995), 108–9.

148 CP documents, board of directors meeting, 29 May 1940, report of the general manager.

149 For the BBC, positioning itself as an authoritative news source during the war – in the sense of being endorsed by those in authority – proved to be enormously successful in establishing its legitimacy and strengthening its position against the newspapers. See Sian Nicholas, "All the News That's Fit to Broadcast: The Popular Press versus the BBC, 1922–45" in *Northcliffe's Legacy: Aspects of the British Popular Press, 1896–1996*, eds. Peter Catterall, Colin Seymour-Ure, and Adrian Smith (Houndmills, Basingstoke, Hampshire and London: Macmillan Press Ltd., 2000), 121–48.

150 Eggleston, *While I Still Remember*, 278.

151 LAC, Wilfred Eggleston fonds, MG 30, D 282, vol. 13, file "Directorate of Censorship – Correspondence and Memoranda 1944–1945," Wilfred

Eggleston to Gil Purcell, 21 Dec. 1944. Quoted in German, "Press Censorship and the Terrace Mutiny."

152 Canadian Press documents, annual general meeting, 29 May 1940; "Final Report on the Censorship of Publications," reprinted (in French translation) in Comeau, Beauregard, and Munn, *La Democratie en veilleuse*, 63.

153 Beauregard, *Guerre et Censure au Canada, 1939–1945*, 69. In their postwar narrative of censorship operations, Eggleston and his deputy, Fulgence Charpentier, concluded that the armed forces eventually ended up considering the censors allies of a journalistic fraternity that was determined to compromise the success of military operations ("Final Report on the Censorship of Publications," in Comeau, Beauregard, and Munn, *La Democratie en veilleuse*, 69). Eggleston noted that military officers found it difficult to distinguish between issuing information officially and preventing newspapers from publishing information they already possessed. In 1941, the armed forces also began appointing journalists as military press officers. In the opinion of Richard Malone, assigned by Ralston to reorganize the military's public relations operation, journalists were much better suited for this kind of work than "regular army types, who, in most cases, considered reporters the scum of the earth." (Malone, *World in Flames* 91–2).

154 CP documents, annual general meeting, 29 May 1940, report of the general manager.

155 "Final Report on the Censorship of Publications," 68–9; Beauregard, *Guerre et Censure au Canada, 1939–1945*, 69–71.

156 CP documents, board of directors, 15 Nov. 1940.

157 In October 1940, R.J. Rankin of the Halifax *Mail* complained that one military liaison officer prohibited pictures of the arrival of German prisoners of war from being published, while another allowed it. (CP documents, meeting of Maritime members, Moncton, 25 Oct. 1940.) The problem in 1939 was that the regulations for the defence of Canada were extremely sweeping, and questions of where the line should be drawn were nowhere answered clearly, leaving censors to find a way of working that respected "les besoins légitime d'une presse d'information." (Beauregard, *Guerre et Censure au Canada, 1939–1945*, 58). See also CP documents, board of directors, 15 Nov. 1940.

158 CP documents, meeting of Maritime members, 12 June 1942; 29 Sept. 1943; 14 April 1944; 20 April 1945.

159 The incident is described in detail in Purcell, "Wartime Press Censorship," 51–64.

160 "Final Report on the Censorship of Publications," 64.

161 Purcell, "Wartime Press Censorship," 71, 74

162 Ibid., 55–6, 66–7.

163 Ibid., 65.

164 Ibid., 145–6, 150. Another controversial incident involved the army's efforts to impose military-style prior censorship domestically when conscripts at Terrace, British Columbia, mutinied in late 1944 on hearing reports that they were about to be sent to fight in Europe. This was eventually prevented by Eggleston, who threatened to resign over the issue. See Daniel German, "Press Censorship and the Terrace Mutiny: A Case Study in Second World War Information Management," *Journal of Canadian Studies* 31, no. 4 (Winter 1996): 124–42; Eggleston, *While I Still Remember*, 265. See also Balzer, *Information Front*, 83–5.

165 LAC, Wilfred Eggleston fonds, MG 30, D 282, vol. 13, file "Directorate of Censorship Correspondence and Memoranda, 1945–1950, 1978," W. Eggleston to Gillis Purcell, 11 April 1946, cited in German, "Press Censorship and the Terrace Mutiny."

166 R.S. Malone reported that after severe Canadian losses in Operation Spring (25 July 1944), Munro came to see him, complaining that his story had been delayed by censors, who refused to allow his comment that the Black Watch regiment had been virtually "wiped out." Malone found that the order had been given by Crerar, the overall commander, who was concerned about the effect of such a report on civilians in Montreal. Malone argued that since the story would come out eventually anyway, delay would only make things worse, and Crerar relented. (Malone, *Portrait of War*, 57).

167 Purcell, "Wartime Press Censorship," 131.

168 Balzer, *Information Front*, 127–8, 161–6.

169 Purcell, "Wartime Press Censorship," 133.

170 Ibid., 134.

171 Newspapers typically did not provide graphic descriptions of the injuries of people killed in traffic accidents, for example. Balzer also acknowledges this point; *Information Front*, 174.

172 Quoted in Phillip Knightley, *The First Casualty* (New York and London: Harcourt Brace Jovanovich, 1975), 333.

173 Author interview with Bill Stewart. Stewart also questioned whether correspondents were in a position to assess military strategy: "A correspondent couldn't possibly know whether an operation was well thought out or not. How the hell would they tell? You are in a killing ground." See also Balzer, *Information Front*, 98.

174 Balzer stresses the fact that Canadian war correspondents wore military uniforms and had the honorary rank of captain: "Under military discipline, uniformed and with officer status, correspondents were in effect part of the military, much more so than the recent 'embedded journalists.'" (57) Though Balzer cites the official military regulations governing war correspondents in support of this interpretation, his account is contradicted by that of Richard Malone, who was in charge of the Canadian military public-relations operation for the last years of the war: "While [correspondents] had to obey army orders in the field, they were not subject to normal military discipline, nor governed by the Manual of Military Law. They could come and go as they wished and could write whatever they liked, subject only to operational security. I had no power to charge them, court martial them or discipline them in any way, though for any serious breach of conduct I could cancel their accreditation and order them from the field." (*World in Flames*, 98)

175 See also Balzer dissertation, 304: "The war correspondent was no neutral observer, dispassionately viewing the war from both sides, but shared the goal of defeating the Axis powers." Balzer goes on to conclude that these "blurred boundaries limited the news media from performing one of most important roles attributed to it in a liberal democracy, that of holding the government and institutions accountable for their actions. For the war was not only sanitized of much of its horrors but also of elements that could have led to public questioning of the decisions of commanders and government and military policy." (Balzer, 329)

176 CP documents, board of directors meeting, 9 Sept. 1940 (continued 10 Sept.).

177 CP documents, report of the general manager, 10 Sept. 1941.

178 CP documents, report of the general manager, Toronto, 8 April 1942.

179 CP documents, report of the general manager, 8 April 1942.

180 CP documents, meeting of western division, Vancouver, 12 April 1940.

181 CP documents, board of directors meeting, 9 Sept. 1940 (continued 10 Sept.).

182 The term is Daniel Hallin's; see Hallin, *The "Uncensored War": The Media and Vietnam* (New York and Oxford: Oxford University Press, 1986; paperback ed., 1989), 116–18.

183 See, for example, J.L. Granatstein, *Canada's War: The Politics of the Mackenzie King Government, 1939–1945* (Toronto: University of Toronto Press, 1990 [first published 1975]), 94, 129–30, 204–6.

184 Ross Harkness, *J.E. Atkinson of* The Star, 329. Maggie Siggins, *Bassett* (Toronto: James Lorimer & Co., 1979), notes that in one of McCullagh's

Leadership League radio broadcasts in 1939, he said CP was in the pocket of "poor, bumbling Mackenzie King" and should be made to print the truth (42).

185 CP documents, annual general meeting, 29 May 1940.

186 LAC, Meighen fonds, 109885, message from Rupert Davies, 15 June 1940.

187 LAC, Meighen fonds, 109884, Knowles to Meighen, confidential, June 1940; Larry A. Glassford, "Arthur Meighen," *Dictionary of Canadian Biography Online*, accessed 14 Dec. 2010.

188 LAC, Meighen fonds, 109898, Knowles to Meighen, 21 June 1940. This was at odds with Davies's later public account; he told CP members in March 1941 that "in every instance I was given the most complete cooperation." CP documents, annual general meeting, 5 March 1941.

189 LAC, Meighen fonds, 109895, Meighen to Knowles, confidential, 20 June 1940. Meighen also described Davies as a "Grit sycophant"; Meighen to Hanson, 29 Aug. 1940, 98032-3.

190 LAC, Meighen fonds, 109952-4, Knowles to Davies, 9 July 1940. Knowles contrasted the "honest" efforts of Davies et al. with those of the previous regime: "I got so disgusted with the Norman Smith – Livesay steam roller that went ruthlessly over everybody that didn't subscribe to the family compact, that I withdrew to conserve my nervous energy and save what few shreds of my personal popularity might be left among the newspaper men of the country. The Toronto Daily Star adopted the same attitude for much the same reasons." Knowles, of course, had been replaced by Livesay as CP's general manager in 1919; see Chapter 1, pp. 49–50.

191 LAC, Meighen fonds, 109962-4, M.E. Nichols to Meighen, 15 July 1940.

192 LAC, Meighen fonds, 98003, Meighen to R.B. Hanson, 18 July 1940; Nichols to Meighen, 15 July 1940.

193 LAC, Meighen fonds, 110114, Nichols to Meighen, private and confidential, 2 Oct. 1940.

194 LAC, Meighen fonds, 110081, Meighen to Nichols, confidential, 28 Aug. 1940.

195 LAC, Meighen fonds, 110097, Nichols to Meighen, personal, 6 Sept. 1940.

196 CP documents, western division meeting, Saskatoon, 31 Oct. 1940.

197 See, for example, "War Effort's Peak in Canada Year Off," New York *Times*, 1 Oct. 1940, p. 10.

198 Others made similar complaints. P.C. Galbraith of the Calgary *Herald* said Chicago *Daily News* correspondent Leland Stowe had done a better job than CP in covering the German invasion of Norway and the Low countries: "There must be more realism and more effort to look behind the scenes."

199 CP documents, board of directors meeting, 15 Nov. 1940.

200 CP documents, board of directors meeting, 3 March 1941.

201 Ibid. The fact that BUP had scooped CP with news of the death of Sir Frederick Banting was of particular concern.

202 CP documents, finance committee, 24 Jan. 1944.

203 CP documents, finance committee, 25 Jan. 1945.

204 CP documents, board of directors meeting, 23 Oct. 1939.

205 RA, McNeil to Moloney, 21 Oct. 1939, microfilm 0467.

206 CP documents, annual general meeting, 29 May 1940.

207 CP documents, meeting of board of directors with committee of operating staff, 16 1941

208 CP documents, board of directors meeting, Sept. 15, 1941; meeting of special committee on CP's anniversary celebration, 25 July 1942.

209 CP documents, finance committee, 8 Sept. 1942.

210 CP documents, board of directors meeting, 27 March 1944.

211 CP documents, annual general meeting, 29 March 1944.

212 CP documents, board of directors meeting, 23 Oct. 1939, report of general manager.

213 CP documents, meeting of western division, Saskatoon, 31 Oct. 1940.

214 CP documents, board of directors meeting, 24 Sept. 1945.

215 CP documents, report of general manager, 8 April 1942.

216 See, for example, CP documents, meeting of Quebec members, Montreal, 10 June 1942, at which there was apparently no mention of the plebiscite or CP's coverage of it.

217 CP documents, report of the general superintendent on the Dominion plebiscite, 19 May 1942.

218 CP documents, report of general manager, 8 April 1942 and 12 Sept. 1942.

219 CP documents, board of directors meeting, 9 April 1945 and 26 March 1945.

220 CP documents, annual general meeting, April 1945.

221 CP documents, board of directors meeting, 27 March 1944.

222 CP documents, board of directors meeting, 10 April 1945, report of the general manager.

223 CP documents, board of directors meeting, 9 April 1945.

224 CP documents, memorandum on staff problems for general manager, 25 Jan. 1943.

225 CP documents, report of general manager, 12 Sept. 1942. For a description of the job of a CP filing editor, see Chapter 7, pp. 285–7. An anecdote in a 1948 memorandum found in the Canadian Press clipping library gives

a good idea of the prevailing attitudes toward female employees: "Many a hard-pressed editor was forced to summon up all his battered ideas of chivalry to prevent use of harsh words when repeated calls for a copy 'boy' found her powdering her nose. Some of the gals just had no sense of urgency!" HR memorandum, March 1948, "The Canadian Press" clipping file, Canadian Press library, Toronto.

226 CP documents, memorandum on staff problems for general manager, 25 Jan. 1943.

227 CP documents, board of directors meeting, 12 April 1943.

228 CP documents, memorandum on staff problems for general manager, 25 Jan. 1943.

229 CP documents, finance committee, 25 Jan. 1945.

230 CP documents, memorandum on editorial and superintendents' salaries, 13 Sept. 1945.

231 CP documents, board of directors meeting, 27 March 1944.

232 Gillis Purcell Papers, McNeil to Davies, 25 March 1940; CP documents, finance committee, 22 May 1940.

233 CP documents, annual general meeting, 29 March 1944; board of directors meeting, 9 April 1945 and 26 March 1945.

234 CP documents, memorandum on editorial and superintendents' salaries, 13 Sept. 1945.

235 Read, *The Power of News*, 214, 234, 236, 249–50.

236 RA. Confidential – note for the Reuter board of directors from the general manager – "The United States and Canada," 5 Jan. 1948.

237 APCA AP 01.7 Board President Robert McLean Papers, folder 661, Canadian Press, correspondence, 1937–1941, Cooper to Livesay, 3 Oct. 1938. When Livesay died in 1944, Cooper told his wife, Florence, that "I have lost a wonderfully true and great friend ... all of us here who knew him loved him." AP 02A.4, Special Member files series I. Canadian Press, box 5 – 1944, folder 31 – Jan.–June 1944. Telegram from Cooper to Florence Livesay, 15 June 1944.

238 RA, "Canadian Diary" [Turner, 1941].

239 APCA AP 01.7 McLean Papers, Cooper to McNeil, 23 July 1941. See also CP documents, board of directors meeting, 16 Sept. 1941.

240 APCA AP 01.7 McLean Papers, Cooper to Charles Bruce, 12 Dec. 1941. He added pointedly that "for the record, I say that you are of course aware that the members of The Canadian Press who take the United Press have, for a year or two, been paying an additional war assessment ... and paying it without question."

241 APCA AP 01.7 McLean Papers, Cooper to McNeil, 5 Dec. 1941.

242 CP documents, annual general meeting, 15 April 1942.

243 APCA AP 01.7 McLean Papers, Cooper to McNeil, 18 Sept. 1940; Cooper to McNeil, 29 April 1941.

244 RA. Confidential – note for the Reuter board of directors from the general manager – "The United States and Canada," 5 Jan. 1948.

245 APCA AP 02A.4, Special Member files series I. Canadian Press, box 4, 1940–43, folder 24, 1940. Cooper to J.A. McNeil, 9 Oct. 1940.

246 APCA AP 02A.4, Special Member files series I. Canadian Press, box 4, 1940–43, Cooper to McNeil, 25 May 1942.

247 CP documents, board of directors meeting, 12 April 1943 (Reuters news agreement for 1945–48).

248 RA. Confidential – note for the Reuter board of directors from the general manager – "The United States and Canada," 5 Jan. 1948.

249 RA, microfilm reel 0164, "Canada" (unsigned, undated memorandum by Walton Cole about his visit to Toronto, April 1947).

250 APCA AP 02A.4, Special Member files series I. Canadian Press, box 5 – 1944, folder 32, 1944 July–Dec. Memorandum, Harry T. Montgomery to AJG (Alan Gould), 18 Dec. 1944.

251 APCA AP 02A.4, Special Member files series I. Canadian Press, box 5 – 1944, folder 32, 1944 July–Dec. Memorandum, Lloyd Stratton to Kent Cooper, 29 Dec. 1944.

252 RA, microfilm reel 0164, "Canadian Press – partnership, March 1945 to March 1949"; "Canada" (unsigned, undated memorandum by Walton Cole, 1947).

253 CP documents, board of directors meeting, 1 April 1946.

254 APCA AP 01.7 McLean Papers, Cooper to McLean, 29 Oct. 1945.

255 RA, microfilm reel 0164, "Canadian Press – Partnership, March 1945 to March 1949"; "Canada" (unsigned, undated memorandum by Walton Cole, 1947). AP had more general concerns about involvement with the CBC, considering it "a government institution, which used the Canadian Press report (including AP) for the purpose of Canadian propaganda," but these could be borne as long as AP did not deal with the broadcaster directly, but only through the intermediary of CP. (APCA, AP 01.7 McLean Papers. File Associated Press – Canadian Press 3-2 #1, memorandum on contract negotiation meeting, 22 March 1945.)

256 CP documents, board of directors meeting, 1 April 1946.

257 Ibid.

258 RA, microfilm reel 0164, "Canadian Press – Partnership, March 1945 to March 1949"; "Canada" (unsigned, undated memorandum by Walton Cole, 1947).

259 APCA AP 01.7 McLean Papers. File AP – Canadian Press 3-2 #2. McLean to Cooper, 23 Jan. 1946.

260 APCA AP 01.7 McLean Papers. File AP – Canadian Press 3-2 #2. Cooper to McLean, 11 Jan. 1946.

261 CP documents, board of directors meeting, 1 Oct. 1946; RA, microfilm reel 0164, "Canadian Press – Partnership, March 1945 to March 1949"; "Canada" (unsigned, undated memorandum by Walton Cole, 1947).

262 RA, microfilm reel 0201, Cole to Purcell, personal, 11 March 1944; Chancellor to Norman Smith, personal, 7 March 1944: "Reuters has a bad history in Canada, and it is an enormous relief to feel that those years of misunderstanding are now behind us and that we shall be able to build up a dignified and close relationship with the CP."

263 RA, microfilm reel 0201, Cole to Purcell, personal, 11 March 1944; McNeil to Chancellor, 6 April 1944.

264 APCA AP 02A.4, Special Member files series I. Canadian Press, box 5 – 1944, folder 32, 1944 July–Dec. Memorandum, Harry T. Montgomery to AJG (Alan Gould), 18 Dec. 1944.

265 See Chapter 5, pp. 178–9.

266 Richard L. Kaplan, "American Journalism Goes to War, 1898–2001: A Manifesto on Media and Empire," *Media History* 9, no. 3 (2003): 210.

267 James Carey, "A Cultural Approach to Communication," in *Communication as Culture: Essays on media and society,* ed. James Carey (New York: Routledge, 1992, first pub. 1989), 13–36.

268 CP documents, annual general meeting, 1942.

269 Benedict Anderson, *Imagined Communities: Reflections on the Origin and Spread of Nationalism* (New York and London: Verso; rev. ed., 1991).

270 Kaplan, "American Journalism Goes to War, 1898–2001." Kaplan's observation that "While the press may create the nation, so, too, is the nation intrinsic to the press as the subject of its reports, as the underlying value that guides its judgments and plots, and as the collectivity that implicitly defines its audience" is also relevant to CP's wartime experience.

Chapter 5

1 Donald Read, *The Power of News: The History of Reuters, 1849–1989* (Oxford: Oxford University Press, 1992), 234–50.

2 The Reuters Archive, Thomson Reuters (RA), microfilm reel 0201, confidential – note for the Reuter board from the general manager – "The

United States and Canada," 5 Jan. 1948. For the 1942 dispute and its resolution, see Chapter 4, pp. 174–5.

3 RA, microfilm reel 0201, Cole to Purcell, personal, 11 March 1944; McNeil to Chancellor, 6 April 1944.

4 RA, microfilm reel 0164, Canadian Press – partnership, March 1945 to March 1949, "Canada" (unsigned, undated memorandum by Walton Cole, ca. April 1947).

5 RA, microfilm reel 0164, Cole to Rogers, confidential, 2 Nov. 1948.

6 Read, *The Power of News*, 258–9.

7 RA, microfilm reel 0164, Canadian Press – partnership, March 1945 to March 1949, "Canada" (unsigned, undated memorandum by Walton Cole, ca. April 1947). .

8 RA, microfilm reel 0164, C.J. Chancellor to R.A.G. Henderson (Sydney *Morning Herald*), 18 March 1947, personal.

9 RA, microfilm reel 0164, Purcell to Chancellor, 29 April 1947.

10 RA, microfilm reel 0164, Cole to Chancellor, 19 July 1945.

11 RA, microfilm reel 0164, Cole to Rogers (NY), confidential, 2 Nov. 1948.

12 RA, microfilm reel 0164, Cole to Rogers, 29 Nov. 1956.

13 Library and Archives Canada (LAC), MG 31 D 94, I.N. Smith Papers, box 12, file 3, Canadian Press correspondence, 1939–1949, Purcell to E. Norman Smith, confidential, 1 Dec. 1947.

14 RA, microfilm reel 0164, Canadian Press – partnership, March 1945 to March 1949, "Canada" (unsigned, undated memorandum by Walton Cole, ca. April 1947); confidential – note for the Reuter board from the General Manager – "The United States and Canada" –5 Jan. 1948.

15 CP documents, board of directors meeting, 1 Oct. 1946; executive committee, 27 Jan. 1947. For an account of working conditions in the CP newsroom circa 1948, see Chapter 7, p. 287.

16 CP documents, board of directors meeting, 7 Oct. 1947.

17 CP documents, annual general meeting, 3 April 1946.

18 CP documents, executive committee, 16 Feb. 1949; 30 April 1949.

19 CP documents, executive committee, 11 April 1953.

20 RA, microfilm reel 0201, Rogers to Chancellor, confidential, 2 May 1950. At a board meeting in April, 1950, Frederick Ker specified that CP's contracts with AP, Reuters, CBC, CPR, and other organizations should provide "for their fulfillment if necessary by successors and assigns"; that is, by a new organization that might come into being if CP were shut down. CP documents, board of directors meeting, 17 April 1950. See also board of directors meeting, 11 Sept. 1950; if any new employees were hired for specific

purposes, they should be employed "by a subsidiary company and not by CP proper."

21 Charles Bruce, *News and the Southams* (Toronto: Macmillan of Canada, 1968), 327–32.

22 Ross Harkness, *J.E. Atkinson of The Star* (Toronto: University of Toronto Press, 1963), 374; Bruce, *News and the Southams,* 353. The ANG signed a contract covering editorial employees of the Ottawa *Citizen* in April 1950; "Guild Pact Signed by Ottawa Citizen," Toronto *Star,* 8 April 1950.

23 Pierre Godin, *L'information-opium: Une histoire politique du journal La Presse* (Montréal: Éditions Parti Pris, 1972), 118.

24 See also Frederick Ker's comment about negotiations with CP's operating staff a few years earlier: "an effort had been made to keep out of the contract anything that would set precedents in individual newspaper offices." CP documents, board of directors meeting, 1 April 1946.

25 LAC, RG 27, vol. 1807, file 760:69:50 (1950), mimeographed document from CP, n.d. [1950]. See also LAC, MG 31, D 94, I.N. Smith Papers, box 12, file 3, Canadian Press, Smith to C.P directors, 7 July 1950.

26 RA, microfilm reel 0201, Rogers (NY) to Chancellor, 16 Jan. 1950.

27 LAC, RG 27, vol. 1807, file 760:69:50, Jack Mitchell and Stephen Ripley, American Newspaper Guild, to minister of labour (Humphrey Mitchell), 4 Aug. 1950.

28 CP documents, special meeting of the board of directors, 14 Jan. 1950.

29 "Guild Asks Bargain Rights for Globe, Mail Circulation, " Toronto *Star,* 7 June 1950; "Charges Witness Intimidated by Editor," *Globe and Mail,* 27 April 1950.

30 A set of talking points later distributed to CP members stressed that soon after joining the CIO, the ANG union central had stated that farmers and labour must be prepared to pursue independent political action and issued a statement of support for the Loyalist side in the Spanish Civil War; in 1947, the ANG called on local units for "full voluntary participation" in the CIO's political action campaign. LAC, RG 27, vol. 1807, file 760:69:50 (1950), mimeographed document from CP, n.d. [1950].

31 LAC, MG 26L, vol. 139, Louis St Laurent fonds, file P-40-2, Press-Cdn Press 1950-51-52-53. Confidential, memorandum for minister of labour, Ottawa, 19 Jan. 1950.

32 LAC, MG 26L, vol. 139, Louis St Laurent fonds, file P-40-2, Press-Cdn Press 1950-51-52-53. A. MacNamara to J.W. Pickersgill (special assistant to prime minister), confidential, 30 Jan. 1950.

33 CP documents, board of directors meeting, 27 Jan. 1950.

34 CP documents, Canadian Press Book Research Material (Douglas Amaron), interview with Charles Edward. Edwards, the general manager of PN, recalled in this interview that the executive committee had actually voted to dismiss all PN employees, but reconsidered after Edwards pointed out that this would drive most radio stations into the hands of BUP.

35 LAC, RG 27, vol. 1892, file 764:4:50, application for consent to prosecute, 13 April 1950.

36 Author interview with Mel Sufrin, 10 June 2009.

37 LAC, RG 27, vol. 1807, file 760:69:50, Jack Mitchell and Stephen Ripley, American Newspaper Guild, to minister of labour (Humphrey Mitchell), 4 Aug. 1950.

38 CP documents, Canadian Press Book Research Material (Douglas Amaron), interview with John Dauphinee: "there were all sorts of things done that seemed to me at least unfair, maybe even improper."

39 LAC, RG 27, vol. 1892, file 764:4:50, American Newspaper Guild, press release, 26 June 1950.

40 LAC, RG 27, vol. 1892, file 764:4:50, application for consent to prosecute, 13 April 1950; John Osler to Hon. Humphrey Mitchell, 13 April 1950.

41 LAC, RG 27, vol. 1892, file 764:4:50, Department of Labour news release, 27 April 1950.

42 CP documents, board of directors meeting, 17 April 1950.

43 LAC, MG 31, D 94, I.N. Smith Papers, box 12, file 3, Canadian Press correspondence, 1939–1949, handwritten memorandum to CP directors, 7 July 1950.

44 LAC, RG 27, vol. 1807, file 760:69:50, Stephen Ripley, international representative, ANG, to M.M. Maclean (director of industrial relations, Ministry of Labour), 15 Aug. 1950. This was the result of Stitt's efforts; LAC, RG 27, vol. 1807, file 760:69:50, Jack Mitchell and Stephen Ripley to minister of labour (Humphrey Mitchell), 4 Aug.1950.

45 LAC, RG 27, vol. 1892, file 764:4:50, Jack Mitchell, president Canadian Press Unit, ANG, to Hon. Humphrey Mitchell, 5 May 1950.

46 LAC, RG 27, vol. 1892, file 764:4:50, draft statement for minister of labour re Canadian Press situation, 8 May 1950; telegram, J.J. Robinette to Mitchell, 9 May 1950.

47 LAC, RG 27, vol. 1892, file 764:5:50, memorandum detailing results of discussion before J.H. Stitt, Esquire, industrial inquiry commissioner, held at Toronto on May 25th and 26th, 1950.

48 LAC, RG 27, vol. 1892, file 764:4:50, American Newspaper Guild, press release, 26 June 1950.

49 LAC, RG 27, vol. 1892, file 764:4:50, James H. Stitt to Hon. Humphrey Mitchell, 30 June 1950.

50 LAC, RG 27, vol. 1807, file 760:69:50, Jack Mitchell and Stephen Ripley, ANG, to minister of labour (Humphrey Mitchell), 4 Aug. 1950.

51 LAC, RG 27, vol. 1807, file 760:69:50, Stephen Ripley to M.M. Maclean, 15 Aug. 1950.

52 LAC, RG 27, vol. 1807, file 760:69:50, Gillis Purcell to Milton Gregg, 9 Aug., 1950.

53 LAC, RG 27, vol. 1807, file 760:69:50, Stitt to Hon. Milton Gregg, minister of labour, 8 Sept. 1950.

54 CP documents, board of directors meeting, 30 Sept. 1952.

55 CP documents, memorandum, no signature, 10 April 1953, "Reasons for Separate Company"; board of directors meeting, 8 Oct. 1951.

56 CP documents, board of directors meeting, Banff, 11 Sept. 1950. Editorial staff had been reduced from 134 to 104.

57 LAC, RG 27, vol. 1860, file 761:25:50, majority report, "In the Matter of the Industrial Relations and Disputes Investigation Act and a dispute between The Canadian Press (Employer) and American Newspaper Guild (Bargaining Agent)," signed A. Cochrane and Herbert Orliffe, 8 Feb. 1951.

58 Ibid.

59 LAC, RG 27, vol. 1860, file 761:25:50, minority report by Gordon R. Munnoch, 8 Feb. 1951.

60 Munnoch went on to state that editorial employees in CP "are undoubtedly engaged in an intellectual pursuit. It is common knowledge that those engaged in intellectual pursuits do not receive rewards which are equivalent to those received in industrial activities," so the CP–Guild negotiations should not be approached on the basis of what goes on in industry, especially where wage levels were concerned. "[A]nyone who chooses to earn his living by his mind must be prepared to accept the scale of reward provided by competition for his services," Munnoch concluded.

61 LAC, RG 27, vol. 1860, file 761:25:50, Robinette to Maclean, 22 Feb. 1951; "Federal Board Reports in CP, Guild Dispute," Globe and Mail, 16 Feb. 1951.

62 CP documents, board of directors meeting, 16 April 1951.

63 Ibid.

64 LAC, RG 27, vol. 1892, file 764-10-51, Canadian Congress of Labour, circular letter, no. 260, 6 June 1951, P. Conroy, secretary-treasurer. The CCL asked local unions, labour councils, and federations of labour to "make known to the newspaper publisher in your community that your members do not approve of the anti-labour attitude of the Canadian Press, and that the Canadian labour movement is seriously alarmed." For examples of

these efforts, see "Set Up Delegation to Ask Intervention," Toronto *Star*, 6 April 1951; "Canadian Press Criticized by Labor Over Union Case," 10 April 1951; "Agreed to Part of Report Labor 'Misinformed' – 'C.P.'," 28 April 1951.

65 LAC, RG 41, vol. 172, file 11-17-3 (pt. 9). Jack Williams, Canadian Congress of Labour, to D.C. McArthur, 18 Oct. 1951.

66 LAC, RG 41, vol. 172, file 11-17-3 (pt. 9). Dick (Elson?) to "Dear Dan" (MacArthur), 25 Oct. 1951.

67 LAC, RG 27, vol. 1892, file 764-10-51, A.H. Brown (Labour Ministry), memorandum to A. MacNamara, 10 Aug. 1951; M.M. Maclean memorandum to A.H. Brown, 7 June 1951; certificate of consent to prosecute, 7 Sept. 1951.

68 "Court Dismisses 5 Guild Charges Against CP," *Globe and Mail*, 10 Nov. 1951.

69 "Upholds Decision by Lower Court in Favor of CP," *Globe and Mail*, 21 June 1952.

70 CP documents, executive committee, 29 Sept. 1952; board of directors meeting, 5 Oct. 1955.

71 Associated Press Corporate Archives (APCA), AP 01.7, Board President Robert McLean Papers, File AP – Canadian Press 3-2 #2, Starzel to Purcell, personal and confidential, 13 Jan. 1956.

72 CP documents, executive committee, 21 Jan. 1946; progress report by the manager of Press News Ltd., 26 Jan. 1946; progress report by the manager of Press News Limited, C.B. Edwards, Toronto, 15 Sept. 1944.

73 CP documents, executive committee, "Reasons for Separate Company," memorandum, n.d. [1953].

74 CP documents, report of the president to the board of directors of the Canadian Press on the organization and progress of Press News Limited (1941); progress report by the manager of Press News Ltd., 6 Oct. 1947.

75 Ibid.

76 CP documents, annual general meeting, 1958, 14.

77 CP documents, "Reasons for Separate Company"; Douglas Amaron interview with Charles Edwards.

78 CP documents, annual general meeting, 30 April 1952, report of the radio relations committee.

79 CP documents, executive committee, 18 Feb. 1952; report of the radio relations committee to the executive committee, 2 Jan. 1952. Charles Edwards, the general manager of PN, recalled in an interview with Douglas Amaron that private broadcasters, including many owned by CP members, were positively hostile to PN. "They were really bitter ... so much so, that when I first started across the country, I had people who

refused to talk to me. I would write them that I was coming to see them
... and I'd get there, and they'd say, 'I don't want to talk to you. I don't like
the Canadian Press.'" At the annual dinner of the Canadian Association of
Broadcasters, representatives of BUP – but not PN – were invited to sit at
the head table. Canadian Press Book Research Material (Douglas Amaron),
interview with Charles Edwards.

80 CP documents, executive committee, 28 Sept. 1953.

81 As Charles Edwards explained in an interview years later, "[i]f the CBC
got in [to Broadcast News] they'd want it dominated. They had the
Government, the national corporation behind them and a great deal of
money. They would want to have things done for their own reasons." CP
documents, Canadian Press Book Research Material (Douglas Amaron),
interview with Charles Edwards.

82 CP documents, memorandum to CP board re: special broadcasts, 9 April
1945; progress report by the manager of Press News, 16 Sept. 1945.

83 Even the Montreal *Star*, which was effectively the Canadian headquar-
ters of BUP – A.J. West, the managing editor, referred to BUP reporters
as "our boys" even while holding the title of vice president of Canadian
Press – gave its staff standing orders not to use stories from the BUP
Ottawa bureau. APCA AP 02A.4, Special Member files series I. Canadian
Press, box 5 – 1944, folder 32, 1944 July–Dec., memorandum, Harry T.
Montgomery to A.J.G. (Alan Gould), 18 Dec. 1944.

84 Ibid.

85 See, for example, LAC, RG 41, vol. 172 file 11-17-3 (pt. 9), McArthur to
director general of programs [E.L. Bushnell], urgent and confidential,
14 May 1947; Hogg to McArthur, 15 April 1946.

86 RA, microfilm reel 0201, Rogers to Cole, 17 Feb. 1957, enclosing report of
Charles Lynch.

87 CP documents, confidential memorandum, 1972, "CP–BN Relationship –
Historical Background."

88 LAC, RG 41, vol. 564, file 22, Canadian Press – contract. Purcell to Donald
Macdonald, chief news editor, CBC, 6 Oct. 1966.

89 CP documents, Canadian Press Book Research Material (Douglas
Amaron), interview with Charles Edwards.

90 CP documents, annual general meeting, 28 April, 1954.

91 This point was stressed in BN's presentation to the Special Senate
Committee on Mass Media in 1969; see Chapter 6, p. 240.

92 See, for example, the CP–CBC correspondence in LAC, RG 41, vol. 598, file
334, Canadian Press.

93 CP documents, annual general meeting, 28 April 1954.

94 CP documents, board of directors meeting, April 19, 1955

95 CP documents, annual general meeting, 1959, report of the general manager.

96 See Chapter 4, pp. 136, 138–9.

97 CP documents, annual general meeting, 1959, 11.

98 For the historical background, see CP documents, report of the general manager re Canadian Press service in French, J.A. McNeil, 8 Nov. 1944; executive committee, 14 April 1951, 3 (b) service in the French language. Press News had begun serving radio stations in French in 1945; board of directors meeting, 9 April 1945 and 25 Sept. 1945.

99 CP documents, annual general meeting, 30 April 1952; Bill Stewart memorandum, "CP Service in French," 12-04-78, file "History of CP Service in French."

100 RA, microfilm reel 0201, Rogers, report for the general manager, 3 May 1954.

101 CP documents, board of directors meeting, Sept. 30, 1959

102 CP documents, board of directors meeting, 16 April 1951; RA microfilm reel 0201, Cole to Rogers, confidential, 27 Feb. 1951; Purcell to Cole, 25 May 1951. The *Star* was paying $130 a week for the Reuters–PA photo service, far more than CP could afford. A.J. West of the Montreal *Star* observed that a general CP picture service would "have distinct disadvantages to larger papers; existing independent arrangements would be affected." CP documents, board of directors meeting, 28 April 1952.

103 CP documents, memorandum for the board re Canadian Press Picture Service, 3 Sept. 1945. CP's first wirephoto network was established in 1954, with 14 members in eight cities, all in southern Ontario or Montreal. Board of directors meeting, 5 Oct. 1955.

104 CP documents, board of directors meeting, 5 Oct. 1948; annual general meeting, 4 May 1949.

105 CP documents, board of directors meeting, 11 Sept. 1950; annual general meeting, 18 April 1951; executive committee, 26 April 1952, picture service integration.

106 CP documents, board of directors meeting, 28 April 1952.

107 CP documents, annual general meeting, 30 April 1952.

108 CP documents, board of directors meeting, 29 Sept. 1954.

109 Thomson was appointed to the executive committee in 1947. His biographer, Russell Braddon, observed that the availability of "Canadian Press's wire service, at a price reasonably related to cash flow," was a key part of the successful Thomson formula; Russell Braddon, *Roy Thomson of Fleet Street* (London and Toronto: Collins, 1965), 150.

110 CP documents, board of directors meeting, 19 April 1955.
111 In a similar vein, John Bassett of the Toronto *Telegram* complained in
    1958 that his paper was paying much more for CP than the service
    was worth: "Its chief value was for insurance and he certainly would
    expect to pay for that protection," but the service was mainly designed
    to meet the requirements of the more numerous small papers. Bassett
    suggested the time had come to move away from the one-member-one-
    vote system, under which smaller papers had considerable weight, and
    replace it with a weighted voting system that depended on how much
    each member paid. CP documents, executive committee, 24 Feb. 1958.
112 CP documents, annual general meeting, 20 April 1955.
113 CP documents, board of directors meeting, 30 April 1957.
114 CP documents, executive committee, 25 April 1947.
115 CP documents, board of directors meeting, 28 April 1947.
116 See John Dauphinee, "Revolution in Sending News," *Saturday Night*,
    2 Aug. 1952: "[O]ne operator working in a central office can set type
    simultaneously in 10, 20, 50 or 100 other offices."
117 CP documents, executive committee, 17 April 1951.
118 CP documents, executive committee, 6 Oct. 1951, teletypesetter operation.
119 Braddon, *Roy Thomson of Fleet Street*, 166.
120 CP documents, annual general meeting, 18 April 1956, 17.
121 CP documents, executive committee, 29 Sept. 1952, model 20 operation.
122 CP documents, annual general meeting, 18 April 1956, 12.
123 CP documents, executive committee, 29 Sept. 1952, model 20 operation.
124 CP documents, board of directors meeting, 3 March 1941.
125 CP documents, board of directors meeting, 23 Sept. 1944.
126 APCA AP 02A.4, Special Member files, box 4, 1940-43, folder 24, 1940,
    Cooper to McNeil, personal, 25 Sept. 1940.
127 Ibid., McNeil to Cooper, 27 Sept. 1940; CP documents, annual general
    meeting, 1942.
128 See, for example, CP documents, annual general meeting, 1954, 1–2.
129 CP documents, annual general meeting, 15 April 1953, 14.
130 See, for example, CP documents, annual general meeting, 15 April 1953,
    18–19.
131 CP documents, Canadian Press Book Research Material (Douglas
    Amaron), interview with I. Norman Smith.
132 CP documents, annual general meeting, 1956, Canadian News/Ontario,
    22–3; annual general meeting, 1959, reports of bureau chiefs/Ontario, 32.
133 CP documents, annual general meeting, 1959, report of the general
    manager, 21.

134 See Chapter 4, pp. 170–1.

135 CP documents, annual general meeting, 18 April 1951, report of the general manager; Canadian Press Book Research Material (Douglas Amaron), interview with Bill Boss.

136 CP documents, board of directors meeting, 27 April 1954.

137 CP documents, Canadian Press Book Research Material (Douglas Amaron), interview with Bill Boss.

138 CP documents, board of directors meeting, 27 April 1954 and 29 Sept. 1954.

139 CP documents, Canadian Press Book Research Material (Douglas Amaron), interview with Bill Boss. For examples of Boss's series, see "Mud Hut with Dirt Floor No Bath, Is Worker's Home in Russian Central Asia," Toronto *Star*, 28 April 1954; "Old Revolutionaries Going, Technicians Running Russia – Boss," 29 April 1954; "Security Too Tight to Get Full Story of Life in Russia," 30 April 1954.

140 "Claims CBC Best in Presenting Canadian Angle," *Globe and Mail*, 18 Sept. 1956.

141 CP documents, board of directors meeting, 26 Sept. 1956.

142 LAC, RG 41, vol. 172, file 11-17-3 (pt. 9), Purcell to Libbie Park, Toronto Peace Council, copy, 13 Aug. 1951.

143 LAC, RG 41, vol. 172, file 11-17-3 (pt. 9), memorandum, confidential. Hogg to McArthur, 1 Aug. 1951.

144 CP documents, board of directors meeting, 5 Oct. 1948.

145 Canadian Press Library, "New Papers Prevented by Monopoly – Coldwell," 21 April 1949. Purcell denied that service had been explicitly refused to the *Citizen*, arguing that its first request had been withdrawn, and a second request was pending when the paper went out of business; CP Library, "Canadian Press Chief Denies Service Refused," 22 April 1949.

146 CP documents, board of directors meeting, 2 May 1949.

147 CP documents, executive committee, 18 Feb. 1952. The *British Columbian* was eventually given service on a contract basis, without entrance fee; executive committee, 26 April 1952.

148 LAC, MG 31, D 94, I.N. Smith Papers, box 12, file 3, Canadian Press correspondence, 1939–1949, INS, memorandum, 5 May 1949.

149 LAC, MG 31, D 94, I.N. Smith Papers, box 12, file 3, Canadian Press correspondence, 1939–1949, Smith to Purcell, 31 Aug. 1949.

150 CP documents, executive committee, memorandum on *L'Évangéline*, 17 Sept. 1945.

151 CP documents, board of directors meeting, 13 April 1953.

152 CP documents, board of directors meeting, 29 Sept. 1953.
153 CP documents, annual general meeting, 1954, interim report of committee on assessments, 8.
154 "Press Monopoly Questions Asked in Parliament," *Globe and Mail*, Aug. 8, 1958. The *Province*'s move to morning publication, an essential element of the Pacific Press restructuring, was approved by CP's board in October 1957. CP documents, board of directors meeting, 2 Oct. 1957.

Chapter 6

1 CP documents, board of directors meeting, 3 May 1960, remarks of Charles Peters. For an account of CP's foreign news coverage as it appeared in one representative Canadian newspaper between 1940 and 1970, see Chapter 7, pp. 259–65.
2 CP documents, annual report, 1960, "The News Report."
3 Ibid., "The Cable Desk." Keith Kincaid, who joined CP in the 1950s and became president in the 1980s, recalled in an interview that "[w]e could ask for coverage of some obscure Canadian delegation in Saigon or something, and [AP] would bust their ass to get it to us." Author interview with Keith Kincaid, 18 July 2006.
4 CP documents, annual general meeting, 4 May 1960.
5 Ibid.
6 See pp. 226–32.
7 CP documents, annual general meeting, 1 May 1962.
8 Ibid.
9 CP documents, board of directors meeting, 5 Oct. 1960; executive committee, 1 Dec. 1960 and 11 Sept. 1961.
10 CP documents, board of directors meeting, 17 Sept. 1963; special meeting of members, 18 Sept. 1963.
11 CP documents, annual report, 1964, report of the general manager, 32
12 CP documents, annual report, 1965, "The News Report," 29.
13 CP documents, executive committee, 4 Dec. 1964, 20 Sept. 1965, 16 Nov. 1965, 19 Sept. 1966.
14 CP documents, executive committee, 16 Nov. 1965.
15 CP documents, executive committee, 27 Feb. 1967.
16 Author interview with Peter Buckley, 18 April 2003.
17 CP documents, board of directors meeting, 13 April 1964; annual general meeting, 14 April 1964.
18 Ibid. For Reuters' interest in expanding its relationship with CP, see Chapter 5, pp. 184–6.

19 CP documents, annual general meeting, 15 April 1969.
20 CP documents, board of directors meeting, confidential, 22 Sept. 1965.
21 CP documents, board of directors meeting, confidential, 21 Sept. 1966.
22 CP documents, executive committee, 6 Dec. 1961.
23 CP documents, executive committee, 25 Feb. 1963. For the Toronto papers' resistance to CP's spending plans, see pp. 226–32.
24 CP documents, executive committee, 4 Dec. 1964.
25 CP documents, executive committee, 16 Nov. 1965.
26 Associated Press Corporate Archives (APCA), memorandum of Frank J. Starzel (AP general manager), 12 Dec. 1961; The Reuters Archive, Thomson Reuters (RA), LN 233, 87/3518, agreement between The Canadian Press and Reuters Limited, effective from 1 April 1962.
27 See pp. 244–5, 247–8, 250–2.
28 See Chapter 5, p. 200.
29 CP documents, executive committee, 2 May 1960; Davey Committee file, William Stewart, "Service in French Development," 4 Dec. 1969.
30 CP documents, executive committee, 2 May 1960.
31 Author interview with Guy Rondeau, 19 Nov. 2008.
32 CP documents, executive committee, 3 Oct. 1960.
33 CP documents, executive committee, 28 Feb. 1966 and 5 Dec., 1968.
34 CP documents, annual general meeting, 30 April 1963.
35 Concordia University Archives, Bill Stewart Fonds, Stewart to Purcell, personal, 23 Nov. 1960 (Gillis Purcell and Family file in correspondence).
36 Gérard Pelletier, *Years of Choice, 1960–1968* (Methuen: Toronto and New York, 1987), 142.
37 CP documents, board of directors meeting, 29 April 1963.
38 CP documents, Bill Stewart memorandum, "CP Service in French," n.d., 12-04-78, file "History of CP Service in French."
39 CP documents, Canadian Press Book Research Material (Douglas Amaron), interview with Stuart Keate, comments of Amaron.
40 Ibid.
41 CP documents, annual report, 1965, report of committee on service in French, 24–5.
42 CP documents, board of directors meeting, 23 Sept. 1964.
43 Ibid.
44 CP documents, executive committee, 4 Dec. 1964.
45 See, for example, author interview with Guy Rondeau; Royal Commission on Bilingualism and Biculturalism. Presented by The Canadian Press to Royal Commission on Bilingualism and Biculturalism – 1965. La Presse Canadienne – Addenda – Considérations générales:"la situation du service

français s'est amelioré depuis quelques années grâce à un éveil chez les journaux de langue française et à la sympathie de M. Gillis Purcell."

46 Ibid., author's translation.

47 CP documents, annual report, 1965, 24.

48 CP documents, annual general meeting, 30 April 1963.

49 CP documents, executive committee, 21 Sept. 1964; author interview with Mario Cardinal, 19 Nov. 2008.

50 Guy Rondeau made a similar point; author interview with Rondeau.

51 Pierre Godin, *L'information-opium: Une histoire politique du journal La Presse* (Montréal: Éditions Parti Pris, 1972), 125–6.

52 Author interview with Bill Stewart, 2 Nov. 2002.

53 Royal Commission on Bilingualism and Biculturalism. Michel Roy, *Le Devoir*, Project de recommandation, 2 April 1965.

54 See, for example, CP documents, executive committee, 6 Dec. 1961 and 1 Feb. 1962.

55 Royal Commission on Bilingualism and Biculturalism. Soucy Gagné, Interview préliminaire – Rencontre avec M. Michel Roy, chef de l'information du *Devoir*, le 25 fevrier, 1965. Another former CP French-service employee, Richard Daigneault, later wrote a much more damning account of CP's service to French-language papers for the *Confédération des syndicats nationaux*, stating that the "triage" of foreign news destined for Canada is carried out "par des journalistes canadiens-anglais postés à Londres et à New-York par l'agence Canadian Press. ... Les dépêches sont acheminées en premier lieu aux journaux d'expression anglaise puis traduits et redistribuées aux journaux francophones qui doivent s'en accommoder bon gré, mal gré. ... les journaux du Québec paient leur part des frais occasionnés par cette sélection (du fait de leur appartenance à la Canadian Press) mais n'y participent pas. Il est évidemment plus économique pour l'agence de sélectionner l'information pour une seule des deux communautés culturelles et de relayer l'autre au rôle de traductrice." Quoted in Godin, *L'information-opium: Une histoire politique du journal La Presse*, 344.

56 CP documents, annual general meeting, 27 April 1965.

57 Royal Commission on Bilingualism and Biculturalism. Soucy D. Gagné, "Sondage sur la Presse Canadienne," Projet interne de recherche de la Commission royale d'enquête sur le bilinguisme et le biculturalisme, Dec. 1966, 12.

58 Ibid., 13, 19.

59 Ibid., 15, 17.

60 Ibid., 80.

61 Ibid., 17.

62 Ibid., 23.

63 Ibid.

64 Ibid., 22.

65 Ibid., 29.

66 Ibid., 35.

67 Ibid.

68 See pp. 227, 282.

69 Gagné, "Sondage sur la Presse Canadienne," 36–7.

70 Ibid., 33.

71 Ibid., 34.

72 Ibid., 65.

73 "Il est financièrement impossible de former une agence indépendante de nouvelles de langue française (Mercier)," *L'Action*, 16 Dec. 1965, 12. The story was written by CP's reporter, Guy Rondeau. A copy of CP's brief to the commission can be found in Library and Archives Canada, RG 41, vol. 907, PG 10–13 (pt. 1), 1957–69.

74 Author interview with Bill Stewart.

75 CP documents, executive committee, 28 Feb. 1966.

76 The commission decided in the fall of 1970 not to go ahead with the proposed Vol. VII of its report, which was to have dealt with media and arts and letters; Léon Dion, *La révolution déroutée, 1960–1976* (Boréal, 1998), 269. Dion, one of the commission's research directors, had concluded in the summer that the manuscript produced by the research group working in this area was "un brouillon irréparable" and recommended that it be rejected, which was done. See also Jean-Louis Gagnon, *Les apostasies, tome 3: Les palais de glace* (Montreal: Les éditions La Presse, 1990), 171–2.

77 *Le Journal de Montréal* and Metro Express were established during the strike at *La Presse* in 1964, while *Montréal Matin* had been publishing since 1930. See Joseph Bourdon, *Montréal Matin: Son histoire, ses histoires* (Montreal: Les Éditions La Presse Ltée, 1978), 3. Among them, the three papers had a combined circulation of 200,000; CP documents, board of directors meeting, confidential, 22 Sept. 1965.

78 Ibid.

79 United Press International was the product of a merger between United Press and the International News Service in 1958.

80 CP documents, board of directors, confidential, 21 Sept. 1966; executive committee, 5 Dec. 1969. *Metro Express* ceased publication in September 1966.

81 CP documents, board of directors meeting, confidential, 20 Sept. 1967.

82 Senate of Canada. Proceedings of the Special Senate Committee on Mass Media, no. 2, 10 Dec. 1969, 2: 72.

83 In a later interview with the author, Guy Rondeau recalled that CP did not have close relations with Quebec politicians, possibly "because it was above all an anglophone institution. ... it was a time of very strong Quebec nationalism." Mario Cardinal, a senior editor for *Le Devoir* and *Le Soleil* in the 1960s, recalled in an interview with the author that one of the main problems with CP's coverage from Quebec was its reliance on copy from the Montreal *Star* and *Gazette,* which in his view did not provide an accurate view of Quebec society.

84 CP documents, board of directors meeting, confidential, 21 Sept. 1966.

85 CP documents, annual report, 1968, report of committee on service in French, 20 April 1968, 21–22.

86 The committee had met in Ottawa with Auguste Choquette, a Liberal MP who presented a petition signed by 50 other MPs, urging CP to appoint a third French-language reporter.

87 Author interview with Mario Cardinal. See also, for example, Jacques Poisson, "Le Québec colonial et l'information," *L'Action nationale,* 563–6; Pierre Godin, *L'information-opium: Une histoire politique du journal La Presse,* 335: "des informations relatives au Québec, préparées par des journalistes canadiens-anglais, reviennent au consommateur québécois traduites en français et sont publiées comme si elles avaient été écrites au Québec par des journalistes francophones. Voilà à n'en pas douter une forme d'aberration que seul un peuple en voie d'assimilation culturelle peut tolérer."

88 CP documents, annual report, 1965, report of the general manager, 26; board of directors meeting, 29 April 1968, report of executive committee, 12–13.

89 CP documents, executive committee, 20 Sept. 1965; board of directors meeting, confidential, 20 Sept. 1967.

90 Ibid.

91 CP documents, special meeting of the board of directors, 2 Feb. 1962, J.S. Atkinson, John Bassett, and Oakley Dalgleish to Purcell, 16 Jan. 1962. The *Telegram* had been complaining about CP costs for at least five years by this point; see executive committee, 29 April 1957, where John Bassett stated that "the larger newspapers ... increasingly regard CP as a large expenditure without corresponding return." A year later, he said CP was designed to meet the needs of small newspapers, not large ones, and recommended that the voting system (where each member had one vote) should be replaced by a system where each member's vote was weighted according to the amount paid; executive committee, 24 Feb. 1958.

92 See Chapter 5, p. 199.

93 Gillis Purcell Papers, R.J. A[nderson], "The Jeep," copy of typescript.

94 Clark Davey, who represented *The Globe and Mail* on CP's board of directors later in the decade, went on to become publisher of the Ottawa *Citizen*, Vancouver *Sun*, and Montreal *Gazette*, and served as CP's president in the 1980s, observed in an interview that the large number of Thomson papers belonging to CP gave McCabe considerable clout. "Thomson had all the votes. Thomson had the votes to run Canadian Press any which way he wanted. And McCabe was very conscious of that, and was very concerned that it not be seen to happen, even if it did." Author interview with Clark Davey, 19 July 2004.

95 CP documents, board of directors meeting, 30 April 1962.

96 CP documents, report of special assessment committee, 5 April 1962 and 17 April 1962.

97 CP documents, board of directors meeting, 25 Sept. 1962.

98 CP documents, special meeting of members, 26 Sept. 1962.

99 CP documents, executive committee, 20 Sept. 1965, 16 Nov. 1965, 19 Sept. 1966, and 6 Dec. 1966.

100 In 1966, CP was providing 5,500 words a day of Newsfeatures; CP documents, executive committee, 28 Feb. 1966.

101 CP documents, Davey Committee file, Gillis Purcell, "Notes on CP Assessment Formula," 29 Nov. 1969.

102 Author interview with Clark Davey. The new approach also resolved a long-standing complaint of Montreal newspapers about being assessed on the basis of the total population of the Montreal region when a substantial proportion read only French or only English.

103 CP documents, board of directors meeting, 17 Sept. 1963.

104 CP documents, executive committee, 8 March 1961.

105 RA, LN 233, 87/3518, Agreement between The Canadian Press and Reuters Limited, effective from April 1, 1962; compare to LN 236, 8713810, Agreement ... June 1956.

106 APCA, memorandum of Frank J. Starzel, 12 Dec. 1961; CP documents, board of directors meeting, confidential, 21 Sept. 1966. The description of Gallagher was by Gerald Long, who succeeded Walton Cole as Reuters' general manager in 1963; Donald Read, *The Power of News: The History of Reuters* (Oxford: Oxford University Press, 1992), 315.

107 RA, LN 937, 1/103508, report on Canadian Press by G. Renfrew, 28 Oct. 1971.

108 CP documents, executive committee, 23 Sept. 1968.

109 CP documents, executive committee, 5 Dec. 1968.

110 Read, *The Power of News*, 314–16.

111 Ibid., 283–311.

112 *Canadian Printer & Publisher*, May 1961, 5; Feb. 1968. Jean de Bonville has
noted that the increase in circulation of Montreal newspapers between
1951 and 1971 did not keep up with population growth; *Les quotidiens
montréalais de 1945 à 1985: Morphologie et contenu* (Québec: Institut québécois de recherche sur la culture, 1995), 39–40, 41, fig. 1.3.

113 CP documents, annual general meeting, 1962, 23.

114 The U.S. Hutchins Commission (Commission on Freedom of the Press)
reported in 1947; Britain's Royal Commission on the Press delivered
its report in 1949, and a second Royal Commission on the same subject
reported in 1962.

115 Charles Bruce, *News and the Southams* (Toronto: Macmillan of Canada,
1968), 366.

116 Marc Edge, *Pacific Press: The Unauthorized Story of Vancouver's Newspaper
Monopoly* (Vancouver: New Star Books, 2001), 62; Bruce, *News and the
Southams*, 368.

117 Bruce, *News and the Southams*, 369; Edge, *Pacific Press*, 94.

118 Bruce, *News and the Southams*, 377; Edge, *Pacific Press*, 70; R.S. Malone,
"Development of F.P. Publications: Historical Outline" (Toronto, 1966:
typescript held in Ryerson University Library), 29.

119 Edge, *Pacific Press*, 64–5. See also CP documents, annual report 1965,
report of the assessment committee, 9.

120 *Canadian Printer & Publisher*, August 1961, "How to Buy Newspapers and
Run Them at a Profit."

121 CP documents, board of directors meeting, 13 April 1964.

122 Ibid.

123 CP documents, annual general meeting, 14 April 1964.

124 Ibid. Stuart Keate, who was publisher of an FP paper, the Victoria *Times*,
and later publisher of the Pacific Press (hence FP-Southam)-owned
Vancouver *Sun*, recalled in an interview with Douglas Amaron that
Malone once told him how to vote at a CP meeting. Keate said that
he was "madder than hell," but did not specify whether he took the
advice or not. Keate added that others sometimes watched how Malone
voted and followed his lead. CP documents, Canadian Press
Book Research Material (Douglas Amaron), interview with Stuart
Keate.

125 CP documents, annual general meeting, 14 April 1964.

126 Susan Goldenberg, *The Thomson Empire: The First Fifty Years* (Methuen:
Toronto and New York, 1984), 32.

127 CP documents, annual general meeting, 14 April 1964.

128 See Chapter 5, pp. 204–5.
129 CP documents, annual report, 1965, 13; executive committee, 4 Dec. 1964.
130 Cited in Braddon, *Roy Thomson of Fleet Street*, 208.
131 Ibid.
132 CP documents, Canadian Press Book Research Material (Douglas Amaron), interview with John Dauphinee.
133 CP documents, board of directors meeting, 25 Sept. 1968.
134 CP documents, executive committee, 21 Sept. 1964.
135 CP documents, board of directors meeting, 26 April 1965, 22 Sept. 1965.
136 CP documents, board of directors meeting, 26 April 1965.
137 CP documents, board of directors meeting, 18 April 1966.
138 CP documents, annual general meeting, 19 April 1966.
139 CP documents, executive committee, 20 Sept. 1965.
140 CP documents, executive committee, 15 Sept. 1969.
141 CP documents, board of directors meeting, 17 Sept. 1969.
142 CP documents, Broadcast News: charges for service: possible general reduction, 3 March 1961.
143 CP documents, board of directors meeting, 13 Sept. 1961.
144 CP documents, executive committee, 4 Dec. 1964.
145 CP documents, Broadcast News: charges for service: possible general reduction, 3 March 1961.
146 CP documents, executive committee, 21 Sept. 1964.
147 CP documents, Broadcast News, brief for Davey Committee.
148 LAC, RG 41, vol. 564, file 11-17-3-4, Hogg to chief news editor, 1 Aug. 1961, confidential. Renewal of Canadian Press contract – 1962–66.
149 LAC, RG 41, vol. 564, file 11-17-3-4, confidential. Hogg to executive assistant to acting general manager, network broadcasting, English, 3 Nov. 1966; CP documents, confidential. CP–BN relationship – historical background (8 Sept. 1972).
150 Royal Commission on Bilingualism and Biculturalism. CBC News and the Canadian Press, report of an interview with William Hogg, director of news and public affairs, English networks.
151 CP documents, executive committee, 1 Feb. 1962; executive committee, 23 Sept. 1962.
152 LAC, RG 41, vol. 907, PG10-13 (pt. 1), 1957–69, memorandum, 13 Dec. 1966 – E.S. Hallman to CBC president.
153 Author interview with Davey.
154 CP documents, executive committee, 11 Sept. 1961.
155 CP documents, board of directors meeting, 13 Sept. 1961.

156 CP documents, executive committee, 1 Dec. 1960; executive committee, 6 Dec. 1961.

157 Michael Nolan, *CTV: The Network That Means Business* (Edmonton: University of Alberta Press, 2001), 22.

158 CP documents, executive committee, 17 April 1961.

159 CP documents, annual general meeting, 15 April 1969.

160 CP documents, Canadian Press Book Research Material (Douglas Amaron), interview with Charles Edwards.

161 CP documents, annual general meeting, 2 May 1967.

162 CP documents, board of directors meeting, 25 Sept. 1968.

163 Ibid.

164 CP documents, broadcasting – BN general, 1958–1969, Purcell to Smith, 10 March 1969.

165 CP documents, annual general meeting, 14 April 1970, 20.

166 *Canadian Printer & Publisher*, February 1966, 39.

167 *Globe and Mail*, 28 March 1969, "Davey Is Chosen to Head Probe of Mass Media."

168 LAC, MG 31, D 94, I. Norman Smith Papers, box 12, file 16, executive committee, 1969, Sutherland to Purcell, 13 Aug. 1969.

169 LAC, MG 31, D 94, I. Norman Smith Papers, box 12, file 11, CP brief to Senate on CP, Smith to John (Dauphinee), 13 May 1969; Smith to St. Clair Balfour, 17 Nov. 1969.

170 Ibid., St Clair Balfour to Purcell, 14 Nov. 1969.

171 Ibid., Purcell to Smith, 1 July 1969.

172 Ibid., Purcell memo to "Dear Bee" (Honderich), 11 July 1969.

173 Ibid., Sutherland to Purcell, 16 July 1969.

174 CP documents, rough comment by JD-CBE on questions in Davey Committee Guidelines, 28 Nov. 1969.

175 Senate of Canada. Proceedings of the Special Senate Committee on Mass Media, no. 2, 10 Dec. 1969 (2:14).

176 Ibid. (2:15).

177 Ibid. (2:36).

178 See, for example, Chapter 5, pp. 208–10.

179 *Globe and Mail*, 11 Dec. 1969. The Toronto *Star* used CP's own story about the testimony, which stated the matter more positively: "The Canadian Press accepts into membership any applicant who has serious intent and the necessary finances." But the headline was also presented as a denial: "News agency says it has no blacklist," Toronto *Star*, 12 Dec. 1969.

180 Senate of Canada. Proceedings of the Special Senate Committee on Mass Media, no. 2, 10 Dec. 1969 (2:24–5).

181 Ibid. (2:25).

182 Ibid. (2:26).

183 Ibid. (2:72).

184 A background document prepared by Bill Stewart stated that the average volume of news sent to a French-language subscriber was 45 columns a day, comprising 16,500 words of international news, 7,500 words of Canadian news, and 9,500 words of Quebec news. CP documents, William Stewart, "Service in French Development," 4 Dec. 1969.

185 Senate of Canada. Proceedings of the Special Senate Committee on Mass Media, no. 2, 10 Dec. 1969 (2:34).

186 Ibid. (2:35).

187 Ibid. (2:35); CP documents, Canadian Press Book Research Material (Douglas Amaron), interview with John Dauphinee.

188 Senate of Canada. Proceedings of the Special Senate Committee on Mass Media, no. 2, 10 Dec. 1969 (36–7).

189 CP documents, Canadian Press Book Research Material (Douglas Amaron), interview with John Dauphinee.

190 *Globe and Mail*, 23 Jan. 1970, p. 27, "CLC Calls for End to One-paper Situations."

191 Toronto *Star*, 18 Feb. 1970, p. 10, "News Service Limits May Curb New Papers, Printers Say."

192 *Globe and Mail*, 25 Feb. 1970, 8, "Publishing Firm Says Canadian Press Like a Select Private Club"; "News Service Entry Fee Too High for Paper, Publisher Tells Probe."

193 In February 1970, when publication of the Vancouver *Sun* and *Province* was stopped by a strike, a new union-backed newspaper, the *Express,* applied for interim CP service. A researcher hired by the committee reported that CP's bylaws would require the consent of all CP members within a 50-mile radius. (*Globe and Mail*, 20 March 1970, p. 3, "Senators Watch to See if *Express* Obtains Interim Service from CP"). Committee members said they wanted to keep abreast of the situation, evidently to see whether CP acted in an anticompetitive way in this situation. In April, CP's executive committee was told that the *Express* had inquired on two occasions about receiving CP's service, and had been told what the bylaws specified; there had been no further contact since March 10. CP documents, annual report 1970, 15; executive committee, 12 April 1970. The strike ended in May, so the *Express*'s application was never formally considered.

194 CP documents, annual general meeting, 14 April 1970.

195 Senate of Canada. Proceedings of the Special Senate Committee on Mass Media, no. 2, 10 Dec. 1969 (2:30).
196 Ibid. (2:31).
197 Ibid. (2:32).
198 Ibid. (2:32).
199 Ibid. (2:33, original italics).
200 Ibid. (2:33–4).
201 See Chapter 1, pp. 43, 46.
202 This was also the argument made by Peter Buckley; see pp. 214–5.
203 Ibid., 235.
204 Ibid.
205 Gillis Purcell Papers, I. N. Smith to John Dauphinee, 9 Dec. 1970.
206 These assessments are taken, respectively, from Jack Brayley, *The Brayley Years* (unpublished manuscript), n.5, n-8; author interview with Arch MacKenzie; author interview with Clark Davey.
207 Author interview with Mel Sufrin.
208 Author interview with Ian Munro.
209 Bruce, *News and the Southams*, 154.
210 CP documents, Canadian Press Book Research Material (Douglas Amaron) interview with John Dauphinee.
211 Ibid. See also Stephen Franklin. "The Man Behind the News," *Weekend Magazine*, 31 Jan. 1970. The article quotes Sydney Gruson, a former CP employee who was then assistant to the publisher of the New York *Times*: "I think it was psychologically necessary for him to establish his dominance over everybody around him. ... He did not create a good atmosphere at CP. No one had room to breathe and one always felt that Big Brother's eye was on you. Yet he was incredibly successful, mainly, I think, because despite everything else he was a wonderful newspaperman who could get to the guts of a story as fast as anybody I knew and who could chuck off the incidental trivia that hamstring so many newspaper executives and editors. And he could get people to work and want to please him."

See also the reminiscence by I. Norman Smith (who had worked for CP in the 1930s before succeeding his father as publisher of the Ottawa *Journal*): "Then there was a man who was called various things but whose name I think was Purcell. Having a bit of a boss eye he could browbeat two deskmen at the same time and each would think he was the one who was about to lose two vital articles. ...When Purcell outbreaks were at their awesome best Harvey Eccles would crash in from the cable room ... that quite stilled Purcell's act for his keen-honed skill at dissecting

demanded operating room silence." Even when Smith left Toronto, Purcell kept an eye on him: "Absence only made his heart grow fonder of sending me weeks later the original copy I had wired or cabled, outraging its clean lissome prose with deletions, queries, exclamation marks, and just short of obscene exclamations. A trick of his would be to circle an entire ten line paragraph of mine of perhaps two tortuous sentences, and run his circled line down the margin to where he had written ... three short sentences of four lines altogether, with the query: 'Is this what you meant?' The trouble about Gillis Purcell was that once you got over your wounded pride and bloody rage ... you realized he was almost invariably right!" LAC, I. Norman Smith Papers, MG 31, D 94, box 12, file 1, The Canadian Press, correspondence and memoranda, 1916–1946, Smith to "Dear Barney" [Anderson] n.d.
212 CP documents, Purcell to executive committee, 20 Jan. 1969. If the two broadcasting subsidiaries were included, the total budget was more than $6 million. CP documents, annual general meeting, 1970, report of general manager, 26.

Chapter 7

1 See, for example, Joe Alex Morris, *Deadline Every Minute: The Story of the United Press* (New York: Greenwood Press, 1958, first published 1957); Reporters of the Associated Press, *Breaking News: How The Associated Press has Covered War, Peace and Everything Else*, with a Foreword by David Halberstam (New York: Princeton Architectural Press, 2007). Michael Schudson has noted that the "beats" so frequently celebrated may not be of much significance for readers, though; "When: Deadlines, Datelines and History," in *Reading the News*, eds. Robert Karl Manoff and Michael Schudson (New York: Pantheon Books, 1987), 79–108.
2 Peter Buckley, *The National Link* (Toronto: The Canadian Press, 1997).
3 Michael Dupuis, *A Cloak for Something Far Deeper: The Press Coverage of the Winnipeg General Strike* (unpublished manuscript, 2008); "Canadian Journalists in New York," in Paul Heyer, *Titanic Century: Media, Myth, and the Making of a Cultural Icon* (Santa Barbara, CA: Praeger Publishers, 2012).
4 "Routine news is that class of news that comes without any special effort through customary and organized channels. It is common property to all current newspapers within its scope, and if it provides a 'scoop' for one of these it is due to negligence or inefficiency of the news agency, the

correspondent or the local reporter serving competing papers, or, less often, to accident.

"No news item is too big to be routine, provided it develops through regular channels. The loss of the Titanic was routine news because the story broke simultaneously to all news agencies through a single wireless message.

"Special news, on the contrary, is that class of news that is discovered, created or developed by individual initiative or effort. ... Anything that comes to the reporter on his daily round is routine news; but if he stops and 'digs' on his own or at his city editor's behest, the treasure he gathers is special news." CP documents, meeting of the Ontario and Quebec division, evening paper section, 14 Jan. 1920, report of the management.

5 Michael Billig, *Banal Nationalism* (London: SAGE Publications, 1995).
6 John Sommerville, *The News Revolution in England: Cultural Dynamics of Daily Information* (New York and Oxford: Oxford University Press, 1996); Benedict Anderson, *Imagined Communities: Reflections on the Origin and Spread of Nationalism* (New York and London: Verso; rev. ed., 1991). Anderson's influence is clear when Sommerville observes that the crucial thing about periodical publications is not the information they contain, "but the sense that regular customers have of being current with developments. Newspapers maintained contact with their audience, binding it together and giving it direction. Readers could be sure that hundreds of other people were reading exactly the same thing at exactly the same time." They were thus exposed to a common diet of facts "that will be the basis for discussion and generate what we know as public opinion. And this public opinion, rather than traditional wisdom or learned philosophy, is the basis for a new kind of society." Sommerville, 20.
7 Quoted in Menaham Blondheim, *News over the Wires: The Telegraph and the Flow of Public Information in America, 1844–1897* (Cambridge, MA, and London: Harvard University Press, 1994), 1.
8 See Gene Allen, "News and Nationality in Canada," *Journal of Canadian Studies* 43, no. 3 (Fall 2009): 30–68.
9 See the appendix for an explanation of how all figures in this chapter were derived.
10 See Allen, "News and Nationality in Canada." Without venturing too far into the thickets of counterfactual history, it is fair to suggest that newspapers would have found ways of obtaining coverage of national politics even in the absence of a national agency – as they did until 1930 in Australia, for example. The point is not that CP established

something entirely new, but that it was the institution through which the overwhelming majority of Canadian newspaper readers, and ultimately radio and television audiences, actually *did* receive their impressions of national politics, as well as of most other events that happened in Canada, from 1917 onward. James Carey's description of communication as "a symbolic process whereby reality is produced, maintained, repaired, and transformed" is relevant here – the maintaining, repairing, and continuing legitimation of what already exists being as significant as the creation of entirely new ideas. James Carey, "A Cultural Approach to Communication," in *Communication as Culture: Essays on Media and Society,* ed. James Carey (New York: Routledge, 1992, first pub. 1989), 23.

11 For WAP and Winnipeg's role in it, see Chapter 1, p. 26, 32.

12 Allen, "News and Nationality," 44.

13 Ibid., 43–5.

14 Terhi Rantanen argues that it makes better sense to think of the international news system as being organized around dominant cities rather than nations; Rantanen, "The Cosmopolitanism of News," *Journalism Studies* 8, no. 6 (2007): 843–61.

15 See pp. 99–100, 139–40.

16 See, for example, the essays in Robert Karl Manoff and Michael Schudson, eds. *Reading the News* (New York: Pantheon Books, 1987); Donald Matheson, "The Birth of News Discourse: Changes in News Language in British Newspapers, 1880–1930," *Media Culture & Society* 22, no. 5 (2000), 557–73; Roger Fowler, *Language in the News: Discourse and Ideology in the Press* (London and New York: Routledge, 1991); Colleen Cotter, *News Talk: Investigating the Language of Journalism* (Cambridge, UK: Cambridge University Press, 2010); Martin Conboy, *The Language of Newspapers: Socio-Historical Perspectives* (London and New York: Continuum International Publishing Group, 2010); Deborah Cameron, "Style Policy and Style Politics: A Neglected Aspect of the Language of the News," *Media Culture & Society* 18, no. 2 (1996): 315–33; Horst Pöttker, "News and Its Communicative Quality: The Inverted Pyramid – When and Why Did It Appear?" *Journalism Studies* 4, no. 4 (2003), 501–11; Marcus Errico et al., "The Evolution of the Summary News Lead," *Media History Monographs* 1, no. 1 (1997–98); Allan Bell, *The Language of News Media* (Oxford and Cambridge, MA: Blackwell, 1991); Kevin G. Barnhurst and John Nerone, *The Form of News: A History* (New York: The Guilford Press, 2001).

17 James Carey, "Technology and Ideology: The Case of the Telegraph," in *Communication as Culture: Essays on media and society,* 201–30.

18 As Horst Pöttker concludes, "There must be a general recognition that the standardised form of news did not emerge as a function of technical, political, or cultural developments, but because of its communicative quality that coincides with the journalistic task of creating publicness and public discourse and also with the financial interests of the publishers." Pöttker, "News and Its Communicative Quality," 510. See also Cameron, "Style Policy and Style Politics," 316.

19 Colleen Cotter emphasizes the influence of "language mavens" or "language bosses" on standardization of news language, a point that applies strongly to news agencies; see pp. 277–84. Cotter, *News Talk: Investigating the Language of Journalism*, 189.

20 See Matheson, "The Birth of News Discourse," and Gene Allen, "Telegraphic News as a Way of Knowing: Canada, 1870–1930," paper presented to the Conference on Media History in Canada, Brock University, St. Catharines, Ontario, November 2008.

21 Bell is especially good on the time structure of news stories: see *The Language of News Media*, 147–156.

22 For a recent and influential statement of this approach, see Bill Kovach and Tom Rosenstiel, *The Elements of Journalism: What Newspeople Should Know and the Public Should Expect*, 1st rev. ed. (New York: Three Rivers Press, 2007).

23 Read, *The Power of News*, 48, notes that Julius Reuter did more than merely following the cable, often arranging for construction of new lines himself.

24 James Carey, "Why and How? The Dark Continent of American Journalism," in *Reading the News*, eds. Robert Karl Manoff and Michael Schudson, 164.

25 See, for example, Chapter 6, p. 247 and discussion of partisanship in Chapter 2.

26 Richard Kaplan, *Politics and the American Press: The Rise of Objectivity, 1865–1920* (Cambridge: Cambridge University Press, 2002). Donald Shaw's 1967 article ("News Bias and the Telegraph: A Study of Historical Change," *Journalism Quarterly* 44: 3–12) has been the source of many claims about the ostensible neutralizing effect of the telegraph on news, especially provided by news agencies, but this argument has been criticized by Michael Schudson, among others; see Schudson, "The Objectivity Norm in American Journalism," *Journalism* 2, no. 2 (August 2001): 158–60.

27 Carey, "Why and How? The Dark Continent of American Journalism," 164–5.

28 Ibid., 165.

29 Ibid., 166.

30 Ibid., 165.
31 About half of CP's editorial employees were editors; CP documents, annual general meeting, 1956, 12.
32 "Air Research Body Is Named," Victoria *Daily Times*, 9 Feb. 1920, p. 1.
33 "Canada's Livestock in Fine Condition," Victoria *Daily Times*, 9 Feb. 1920, p. 1.
34 "Condemns Proposals of Bennett," Halifax *Chronicle*, 18 Sept. 1930, p. 1; "Leaders Join in Debate," Halifax *Herald*, 18 Sept. 1930, p. 1.
35 See, for example, "Let Full Light be Turned on That Deal with Liberals," Halifax *Herald*, 23 June 1915; "Rogers' Fine Hand Seen in Latest Manitoba Move," Halifax *Chronicle*, 23 June 1915.
36 "Raps 'State Health' Plan," Halifax *Chronicle-Herald*, 1 March 1960, p. 1.
37 Daniel C. Hallin, *The "Uncensored War": The Media and Vietnam* (New York: University of California Press, 1989; first published 1986), 116–18.
38 Author interview with Arch MacKenzie, 26 May 2009. He recalled that CP reporters were expected to cover Senate debates as well, and that Senator Rupert Davies, publisher of the Kingston *Whig-Standard* and a CP director, "would watch the gallery in the Senate. And the only people in the gallery of the Senate, ever, were CP. And if CP wasn't there, he would phone Purcell, and Purcell sent a rocket down to the bureau to get somebody into the Senate. ... what we used to do was put a tie on the office boy and send him in ... he'd just sit there."
39 See Minko Sotiron, *From Politics to Profit: The Commercialization of Canadian Daily Newspapers, 1890–1920* (Montreal and Kingston: McGill-Queen's University Press, 1997). For a broader discussion of commercial versus political journalism, see Gene Allen, "Business, Culture and the History of News: A Case Study of the 'Political–Commercial' Dichotomy," in *Essays in Honour of Michael Bliss: Figuring the Social,* eds. Elsbeth Heaman, Alison Li and Shelley McKellar (Toronto: University of Toronto Press, 2008).
40 See, for example, the article on Canada's growing involvement in Law of the Seas negotiations: "Canadians Show Way in Planning Sea Law," Halifax *Chronicle-Herald*, 18 Jan. 1960, p. 1.
41 "Natural Resources Question Again to Forefront in Capital," Winnipeg *Tribune*, 19 Nov. 1920, p. 1.
42 "Parliament to Have Busy Week," Winnipeg *Evening Tribune*, 6 April 1920, p. 10.
43 "Commission to Study MP Salaries Question," Halifax *Chronicle-Herald*, 19 Jan. 1970, p. 1.

44 CP documents, Canadian Press Book Research Material (Douglas Amaron), interview with John Dauphinee.

45 *CP Style Book* (Toronto: The Canadian Press, 1968), 62.

46 Ibid., 63

47 Patrick Brennan, *Reporting the Nation's Business: Press-Government Relations during the Liberal Years, 1935–1957* (Toronto: University of Toronto Press, 1994), 154.

48 Soucy D. Gagné, "Sondage sur la Presse Canadienne," Projet interne de recherche de la Commission royale d'enquête sur le bilinguisme et le biculturalisme, Dec. 1966; Canada. Royal Commission on Newspapers. Research Studies on the Newspaper Industry, Vol. 6. Carman Cumming, Mario Cardinal and Peter Johansen, "Canadian News Services" (Ottawa, 1981); Arthur Siegel, "Canadian Press and the Parliamentary Press Gallery," in Siegel, *Politics and the Media in Canada,* 2nd ed. (Toronto: McGraw-Hill Ryerson Ltd., 1996), 186–214.

49 Brennan, *Reporting the Nation's Business*, 131–2.

50 Ibid., 155. For Meighen's view that CP was systematically biased in favour of the Liberals, see Chapter 2, pp. 69–73, and Chapter 4, pp. 164–6.

51 CP documents, executive committee, 20 Feb. 1950. However, because CP was considering closing its Ottawa bureau at the time in response to the American Newspaper Guild's application for union certification, it was agreed that no action would be taken for the time being. For the proposed closing, see Chapter 5, pp. 190–1.

52 Author interview with Clark Davey, July 19, 2004.

53 CP documents, annual general meeting, 14 April 1970, address of the president, 20.

54 All from Calgary *Herald,* 10 Feb. 1930, p. 1.

55 See, for example, Leon V. Sigal, "Who? Sources Make the News," in Manoff and Schudson, *Reading the News;* Edward S. Herman and Noam Chomsky, *Manufacturing Consent: The Political Economy of the Mass Media* (New York: Pantheon Books, 1988), 18–25.

56 "Labor Leaders Sentenced to Year in Jail," Vancouver *Daily World,* 6 April 1920.

57 "Women Advocate Birth Control," Vancouver *Sun,* 1 April 1930, p. 1.

58 "Miss Butler Pleads for Freedom," Halifax *Chronicle,* 23 June 1920, p. 1.

59 "Faith Healer 'Cures' Dumb, Maimed, Blind," Winnipeg *Tribune,* 19 Nov. 1920, p. 1.

60 The maximum hourly rate increased to around 4,500 words by the late 1960s.

61 For the role of the filing editor, see pp. 285–7. There was distinct pressure to be "telegraphic," however, when it came to the very limited capacity

and high cost of transmission via the transatlantic cable. Cable transmissions also relied on "skeletonizing," a rough and ready system of combining and omitting words to reduce cable charges; for a description of this practice, see Richard M. Harnett, *Wirespeak: Codes and Jargon of the News Business* (San Mateo, CA: Shorebird Press, 1997). I am grateful to Paul Woods for bringing this source to my attention.

62 "Likely to Put Claim Up to Supreme Court," Halifax *Chronicle*, 1 April 1930, p. 1.

63 "Beaverbrook in Cabinet," Halifax *Herald*, 15 May, 1940. The emphasis on brevity continued to evolve over time; where CP's style guide recommended in 1940 that paragraphs should be no longer than 50 or 60 words, the limit was reduced to 30 or 40 in the 1968 edition.

64 Author interview with Ian Munro, 12 Dec. 2002. A "day lead" is a version of a story that had previously appeared in morning newspapers, rewritten for use in that day's afternoon newspapers.

65 Gillis Purcell Papers, Purcell to Livesay, personal, 9 July 1934.

66 CP documents, J.F.B. Livesay, "Instructions for Correspondents," circular no. 34, 1927 (26 Nov. 1927).

67 *(CP): A Guide for Writers and Filing Editors* (Toronto: Canadian Press, 1940).

68 Ibid., 11.

69 Ibid., 14

70 Ibid.

71 Ibid., 15. For the earlier ban on estimates of crowd size at political rallies, see Chapter 2, p. 70.

72 Ibid., 16.

73 CP documents, Ontario members meeting, 9 June 1942. By "speculation," Purcell probably meant what is currently described as "interpretation" or "analysis."

74 See Chapter 4, pp. 163–6.

75 CP documents, report of the general manager, 12 Sept. 1942.

76 *(CP): A Guide for Writers and Filing Editors* (Toronto: Canadian Press, 1940), 14; *CP Style Book: A Guide for Writers and Filing Editors* rev. and extended (Toronto: Canadian Press, 1947), 16, 40, 41–2, 47, 10.

77 Author interview with Arch MacKenzie. The Red Bible reference is from Scott Young, "The Men Behind the Front Page," *Maclean's Magazine*, 15 Dec. 1949.

78 Munro subsequently developed a method of double-checking the details that were transmitted to CP bureaus "because I didn't want to get skinned alive." Author interview with Ian Munro, 12 Dec. 2002.

79 Author interview with Mel Sufrin, 10 June 2009.

80 *CP Style Book* (Toronto: The Canadian Press, 1968), 3–4.

81 Ibid., 6.

82 Ibid., 21.

83 Ibid., 19.

84 Ibid., 21.

85 Ibid., 22.

86 Ibid., 9.

87 "Agriculture's View – Pesticides Needed," Halifax *Chronicle-Herald*, 2 July 1970, p. 2.

88 *CP Style Book* (Toronto: The Canadian Press, 1968), 59.

89 See Chapter 5, p. 207.

90 *CP Style Book* (Toronto: The Canadian Press, 1968), 60.

91 Ibid., 102.

92 Ibid., 95.

93 Ibid., 96.

94 Ibid., 37

95 Ibid., 43, 119.

96 Ibid., 38.

97 Ibid., 38, 73.

98 Blondheim, *News over the Wires,* 59.

99 *CP Style Book* (Toronto: The Canadian Press, 1968), 1.

100 CP documents, FYI (Canadian Press internal newsletter), 3 May 1967.

101 *CP Style Book* (Toronto: The Canadian Press, 1968), 3.

102 Stephen Ford, "Minute Man," *Canadian Printer and Publisher*, December 1943. Stephen Ford was Purcell's favoured pseudonym.

103 Ibid. The "drama and Welsh" for Kingston reflected the national and artistic interests of the *Whig-Standard*'s publisher, Senator Rupert Davies.

104 Royal Commission on Bilingualism and Biculturalism. Soucy Gagné, Interview préliminaire – Rencontre avec M. Michel Roy, chef de l'information du Devoir, le 25 fevrier, 1965, "Canadian Press – The New York Office."

105 Concordia University Archives, Stewart fonds, unsigned letter to Stewart from CP New York, 10 Jan. 1967.

106 CP documents, Davey committee file, Stewart to Dauphinee, 3 Dec. 1969.

107 See Conclusion, p. 306–7.

108 Young, "The Men Behind the Front Page." CP began to narrow the gap in wages and working conditions in the 1960s.

109 Craig Calhoun, *Nationalism* (Buckingham, England: Open University Press, 1997), 3.

110 Gerald Friesen, *Citizens and Nation: An Essay on History, Communication, and Canada* (Toronto: University of Toronto Press, 2000), 147–8.

111 Allen, "News and Nationality in Canada, 1890–1930."

Conclusion

1 Gillis Purcell, "The Canadian Press (CP)," *International Communication Gazette* 15 (1969): 151–8.
2 See Chapter 1, pp. 20, 31–3.
3 Chapter 1, pp. 37–40.
4 S. Shmanske, "News as a Public Good: Cooperative Ownership, Price Commitments, and the Success of the Associated Press," *Business History Review*, 60, no. 1 (1986), 64–9.
5 *Associated Press et al v United States*. No. 57, Supreme Court of the US, 326 U.S. 1; 65 S. Ct 1416; 1945 U.S. LEXIS 2663; 89 L. Ed. 2013; 1945 Trade Cas. (CCH) P57, 384; 1 Media L. Rep. 2269. Dec. 5, 6. 1944, Argued 5–6 Dec. 1944, Decided 18 June 1945.
6 Sian Nicholas, "All the News that's Fit to Broadcast: the Popular Press versus the BBC, 1922–45" in *Northcliffe's Legacy: Aspects of the British Popular Press, 1896–1996*, eds. Peter Catterall, Colin Seymour-Ure, and Adrian Smith (Houndmills, Basingstoke, Hampshire and London: Macmillan Press Ltd., 2000), 121–48.
7 Chapter 4, pp. 124–7; CP documents, minutes of the radio committee, 24 Oct. 1939, Ottawa.
8 J.F.B. Livesay, "The Canadian Press – Its Birth and Development," reprint from Quebec *Chronicle-Telegraph*, 21 June 1939.
9 Jonathan Silberstein-Loeb, "Business, Politics, Technology and the International Supply of News, 1845–1950," (University of Cambridge PhD dissertation, 2009), 13.
10 Oliver Boyd-Barrett, "National News Agencies in the Turbulent Era of the Internet," in *News Agencies in the Turbulent Era of the Internet*, ed. Oliver Boyd-Barrett (Barcelona: Government of Catalonia, Presidential Department, 2010), 9.
11 See Chapter 4, p. 139.
12 Chapter 7, pp. 256–7.
13 CP documents, M.E. Nichols, presidential address, annual general meeting, 7 June 1933.
14 Michael Billig, *Banal Nationalism* (London: SAGE Publications, 1995).
15 Benedict Anderson, *Imagined Communities: Reflections on the Origin and Spread of Nationalism* (New York: Verso; rev. ed., 1991), 7. For a critical view of the assumption that nations are the natural, obvious, and virtuous counterparts of the global in thinking about media, see Terhi Rantanen, *The*

Media and Globalization (London: SAGE Publications, 2005), 75: "[T]he idea that national media can be just as homogenizing as global media opens up a new way of thinking about homogenization and heterogenization. In the cultural imperialism paradigm the national was celebrated as something worth protecting, without taking into account that it could be as oppressive to many people as the global."

16 CP documents, traffic report, annual general meeting, 30 April 1968.

17 Keith Kincaid, who was in charge of CP's main news desk in the early 1960s (and later became the agency's general manager/president), described the situation for smaller newspapers at the time this way: "It meant that they weren't making the selection. CP was making the selection for them. CP was packaging it for them in nice tidy little packages. Here are the business briefs, and here's the business feature for today – no, you can't have that one, we're sending you this one." Author interview with Keith Kincaid, 18 July 2006. Silberstein-Loeb also stresses this point: "a larger amount of news content, especially given the restrictions under which news associations and agencies operated, was a priori beneficial because it provided editors with more choices, and they could elect to publish, or not publish, the material provided." "Business, Politics, Technology and the International Supply of News, 1845–1950," 14.

18 Oliver Boyd-Barrett and Terhi Rantanen, "The Globalization of News," in *The Globalization of News*, eds. Boyd-Barrett and Rantanen (London: SAGE Publications, 1998), 5.

19 Author interview with Keith Kincaid. "We could ask for coverage of some obscure Canadian delegation in Saigon or something, and they would bust their ass to get it to us."

20 It is noteworthy that the largest and wealthiest CP members, with their own alternative sources of foreign news, were the strongest opponents of expanded international coverage in the 1960s. Under CP's one-member-one-vote governance structure, the large number of smaller papers with limited circulation and budgets did introduce a permanent bias toward penny-pinching. (As late as the early 1960s, CP journalists had to request permission to make long-distance telephone calls. Author interview with Keith Kincaid.) But as noted above, it was generally the smaller papers, relying almost entirely on CP for all their extra-local content, that were willing to pay more for a wider range of services.

21 See pp. 207, 288.

22 James Carey, "Technology and Ideology: The Case of the Telegraph," in *Communication as Culture: Essays on Media and Society*, ed. James Carey (New York: Routledge, 1992, first pub. 1989), 203.

23 Menahem Blondheim, *News over the Wires: The Telegraph and the Flow of Public Information in America, 1844–1897* (Cambridge, MA, and London: Harvard University Press, 1994), 59.
24 Daniel Hallin and Paolo Mancini, *Comparing Media Systems: Three Models of Media and Politics* (Cambridge: Cambridge University Press, 2004), 210.
25 Ibid., 227.
26 CP documents, M.E. Nichols, presidential address, annual general meeting, 7 June 1933.
27 Hallin and Mancini, "Comparing Media Systems," 217.
28 Ibid., 219, 225, 226, 239, 233, 234.
29 John Hartley, *Popular Reality: Journalism, Modernity, Popular Culture* (London: Arnold, 1996), 34.
30 See José Igartua, *The Other Quiet Revolution: National Identities in English Canada, 1945–71* (Vancouver: UBC Press, 2006).
31 Ian McKay, "Canada as a Long Liberal Revolution: On Writing the History of Actually Existing Canadian Liberalisms, 1840s–1940s," in *Liberalism and Hegemony: Debating the Canadian Liberal Revolution*, eds. Jean-François Constant and Michel Ducharme (Toronto: University of Toronto Press, 2009), 360, 431 n. 58.
32 Ibid., 372.
33 On this point, see also Carman Cumming, "CP: A Force for Consensus?" in *Journalism Communication and the Law*, ed. G. Stuart Adam (Scarborough, Ont.: Prentice-Hall of Canada, 1976), 93–4.
34 Interview with Keith Kincaid, 18 July 2006. "We thought it was lightning speed – a thousand and forty words a minute. That's slow now, but compared to the TTS wires which were something like 75 words a minute. So when the story broke we could get it out pretty damn quick." Kincaid was CP's general manager from 1978 until 1996, and oversaw the introduction of new production and transmission technology in the early 1970s. See also CP documents, "Assessments – Presidents' Letters: Capital Expenditures 1968 to 1976."
35 Author interviews with Peter Buckley and Keith Kincaid.
36 Canadian Press stylebooks online, accessed 17 Feb. 2012, http://stylebooks.thecanadianpress.com/online/?do=chapter&pub=style.
37 "Major Publishers Invest in CP; Torstar among 3 Owners that Will Turn the Co-op into For-profit Business," Toronto *Star*, 27 Nov. 2010.
38 "NZPA to close after 130 years," *The Dominion Post* (Wellington, New Zealand), 7 April 2011.

Bibliography

Archival Collections, Manuscripts, and Interviews

Archives of Manitoba (Winnipeg)
    MG 9 A100, John Frederick Bligh Livesay fonds.
Associated Press Corporate Archives (New York)
    AP 01, Correspondence re Canadian Press association/contracts.
    AP 01.7 Board President Robert McLean Papers.
    AP 02A.4, Special Member files series I. Canadian Press.
Author Interviews
    Peter Buckley, 18 April 2003.
    Mario Cardinal, 19 November 2008.
    Clark Davey, 19 July 2004.
    Keith Kincaid, 18 July 2006.
    Arch MacKenzie, 26 May 2009.
    Ian Munro, 12 December 2002.
    Guy Rondeau, 19 November 2008.
    Bill Stewart, 2 November 2002.
    Mel Sufrin, 10 June 2009.
Canadian Pacific Archives (Montreal).
Canadian Press documents (Toronto)
    Canadian Press Book Research Material (Douglas Amaron). Interviews
        with Bill Boss, John Dauphinee, Charles Edwards, Stuart Keate; memo-
        randum by Ross Munro, "How the GM of CP nearly blew the Normandy
        landing and wound up in the Tower…," 4 June 1984; Descriptions of CP
        D-Day coverage by Ross Munro and Bill Stewart.
    Uncatalogued. Includes records of Eastern Press Association, Western
        Associated Press, Canadian Press Ltd.; minutes of annual general

meetings and special general meetings, board of directors meetings, executive committee meetings, finance committee meetings; internal and external correspondence; memoranda; circulars, and so on.

Concordia University Archives (Montreal)
P 195, Bill Stewart Fonds.

House of Lords Record Office, United Kingdom (London)
BBK E/3/1 (1917–1918), The Beaverbrook Papers.

Library and Archives Canada (Ottawa)
MG26-G, Sir Wilfrid Laurier fonds.
MG26-H, Sir Robert Borden fonds.
MG26-J, William Lyon Mackenzie King fonds.
MG26-L, Louis St Laurent fonds.
MG27-IIIB11, James Layton Ralston fonds.
MG28-I134, Canadian Press fonds.
MG30-E133, Andrew George Latta McNaughton collection.
MG31-D94, Irving Norman Smith fonds.
MG31-D106, Ernest Norman Smith fonds.
RG 6 Series E, Secretary of State, Chief press censor, 1915–20.
RG 13, Justice, vol. 272.
RG 19, Finance, vol. 98.
RG 24, National Defence, vol. 60.
RG 25, External Affairs, vol. 2863.
RG 27, Labour, vols. 1807, 1860, 1892.
RG 30 vol. 10485, Minute Book, Montreal Telegraph Co.
RG 36 Series 31, Wartime Information Board.
RG 41, Canadian Broadcasting Corporation.
RG 46, Canadian Transport Commission (Board of Railway Commissioners for Canada).
RG 95, Corporations branch, vol. 1221 (Canadian Associated Press).

Lilly Library, Indiana University
Kent Cooper mss., correspondence, 1921–34.

The National Archives, United Kingdom (London)
CO 537, Colonial Office and predecessors: Confidential General and Confidential Original Correspondence.
INF 4/1B, War of 1914 to 1918 Information Services.
T/1/12227, Colonial Office. Provision of an imperial news service: recommendations of the Imperial War Conference, July 1918; erection of wireless stations.

Gillis Purcell Papers (privately held).

The Reuters Archive, Thomson Reuters (London)

Jones Papers.
Boxes LN 233, 236, 795, 937, 943, 1011.
Microfilm reels 0164, 0201, 0202, 0467.

Secondary Sources and Printed Documents

Allen, Gene. "Business, Culture and the History of News: A Case Study of the 'Political-Commercial' Dichotomy." In *Essays in Honour of Michael Bliss: Figuring the Social*, ed. Elsbeth Heaman, Alison Li, and Shelley McKellar, 146–73. Toronto: University of Toronto Press, 2008.
– "Monopolies of News: Harold Innis, the Telegraph and Wire Services." In *The Toronto School of Communication Theory: Interpretations, Extensions, Applications*, ed. Rita Watson and Menahem Blondheim, 170–98. Toronto: University of Toronto Press, 2008.
– "News Across the Border: Associated Press in Canada, 1894–1917." *Journalism History* 31, no. 4 (2006): 210–16.
– "News and Nationality in Canada, 1890–1930." *Journal of Canadian Studies. Revue d'Etudes Canadiennes* 43, no. 3 (2009): 30–68.
– "Telegraphic News as a Way of Knowing: Canada, 1870–1930." Paper presented to the Conference on Media History in Canada, Brock University, St. Catharines, Ontario, Canada, November 2008.
Allen, Gene, and Daniel Robinson, eds. *Communicating in Canada's Past: Essays in Media History*. Toronto: University of Toronto Press, 2009.
Anderson, Benedict. *Imagined Communities: Reflections on the Origin and Spread of Nationalism*. New York: Verso, 1991.
Associated Press. Annual Report, 1917.
Associated Press et al v United States. No. 57, Supreme Court of the US, 326 U.S. 1; 65 S. Ct 1416; 1945 U.S. LEXIS 2663; 89 L. Ed. 2013; 1945 Trade Cas. (CCH) P57, 384; 1 Media L. Rep. 2269. Dec. 5, 6. 1944, Argued June 18, 1945, Decided.
Bakker, Gerben. "Trading Facts: Arrow's Fundamental Paradox and the Emergence of Global News Networks." In *International Communication and Global News Networks: Historical Perspectives*, ed. Peter Putnis, Chandrika Kaul, and Jürgen Wilke, 9–54. New York: Hampton Press, 2011.
Balzer, Timothy. "'In Case the Raid is Unsuccessful … ': Selling Dieppe to Canadians." *Canadian Historical Review* 87, no. 3 (2006): 409–30.
– *The Information Front: The Canadian Army and News Management during the Second World War*. Vancouver: UBC Press, 2011.

- "The Information Front: The Canadian Army, Public Relations, and War News during the Second World War." PhD dissertation, University of Victoria, British Columbia 2009.

Barnhurst, Kevin G., and John Nerone. *The Form of News: A History*. New York: The Guilford Press, 2001.

Beauregard, Claude. *Guerre et Censure au Canada, 1939–1945*. Quebec: Septentrion, 1998.

Bell, Allan. *The Language of News Media*. Oxford: Blackwell, 1991.

Berger, Carl. *The Sense of Power: Studies in the Ideas of Canadian Imperialism, 1867–1914*. Toronto: University of Toronto Press, 1970.

Billig, Michael. *Banal Nationalism*. London: Sage, 1995.

Blondheim, Menahem. *News over the Wires: The Telegraph and the Flow of Public Information in America, 1844–1897*. Cambridge, MA: Harvard University Press, 1994.

Bonville, Jean de. *Les quotidiens montréalais de 1945 À 1985: Morphologie et contenu*. Québec: Institut québécois de recherche sur la culture, 1995.

Bourdon, Joseph. *Montréal Matin: Son Histoire, Ses Histoires*. Montreal: Les Éditions La Presse Ltée, 1978.

Bourrie, Mark. *The Fog of War: Censorship of Canada's Media in World War Two*. Vancouver: Douglas & McIntyre, 2011.

Boyd-Barrett, Oliver. "'Global' News Agencies." In *The Globalization of News*, ed. Oliver Boyd-Barrett and Terhi Rantanen, 19–34. London: Sage, 1998. http://dx.doi.org/10.4135/9781446250266.n2

- "Market Control and Wholesale News: The Case of Reuters." In *Newspaper History from the Seventeenth Century to the Present Day*, ed. George Boyce, James Curran, and Pauline Winngate, 192–204. London: Constable and Co, 1978.

- "National News Agencies in the Turbulent Era of the Internet." In *News Agencies in the Turbulent Era of the Internet*, ed. Oliver Boyd-Barrett, 16–44. Barcelona: Government of Catalonia, Presidential Department, 2010.

- *The International News Agencies*. London: Constable and Co, 1980.

Boyd-Barrett, Oliver, and Terhi Rantanen "Global and National News Agencies: Threats and Opportunities in the Age of Convergence." In *Global Journalism: Topical Issues and Media Systems*, ed. Arnold de Beer and John C. Merrill 33–47. Boston: Allyn & Bacon, 2008.

- "Introduction to Part II: News Agencies in the Furnace of Political Transition." In *The Globalization of News*, ed. Oliver Boyd-Barrett and Terhi Rantanen, 104–7. London: Sage, 1998.

- "News Agencies as News Sources: A Re-evaluation." In *International News in the Twenty-First Century*, ed. Chris Paterson and Annabelle Sreberny. London: John Libbey Publishing, 2004.
- "The Globalization of News." In *The Globalization of News*, ed. Oliver Boyd-Barrett and Terhi Rantanen, 1–14. London: Sage, 1998. http://dx.doi.org/10.4135/9781446250266.n1

Braddon, Russell. *Roy Thomson of Fleet Street*. London: Collins, 1965.

Brayley, Jack. *The Brayley Years*. Unpublished manuscript (nd, circa 1977).

Brennan, Patrick. *Reporting the Nation's Business: Press-Government Relations during the Liberal Years, 1935–1957*. Toronto: University of Toronto Press, 1994.

Brown, Robert Craig. *Robert Laird Borden, A Biography: Vol. 2, 1914–1937*. Toronto: Macmillan of Canada, 1980.

Bruce, Charles. *News and the Southams*. Toronto: Macmillan of Canada, 1968.

Buckley, Peter. *The National Link*. Toronto: The Canadian Press, 1997.

Buckner, Phillip, ed. *Canada and the British Empire*. Oxford: Oxford University Press, 2008.

Buxton, William J., and Catherine McKercher. "Newspapers, Magazines and Journalism in Canada: Towards a Critical Historiography." *Acadiensis* 28, no. 1 (1998): 103–26.

Calhoun, Craig. *Nationalism*. Buckingham, England: Open University Press, 1997.

Cameron, Deborah. "Style Policy and Style Politics: A Neglected Aspect of the Language of the News." *Media Culture & Society* 18, no. 2 (1996): 315–33. http://dx.doi.org/10.1177/016344396018002008.

Canada. Parliament. House of Commons *Debates*, 29 June 1923.

Canada. Parliament. Senate. *Proceedings of the Special Senate Committee on Mass Media*, No. 2, 10 December 1969.

Canada. Parliament. Senate. Special Senate Committee on Mass Media. *Report of the Special Senate Committee on Mass Media, Vol. 1: The Uncertain Mirror*. Ottawa: Information Canada, 1970.

Canada. Royal Commission on Newspapers. Research studies on the newspaper industry, Vol. 6. Carman Cumming, Mario Cardinal and Peter Johansen, "Canadian News Services" (Ottawa, 1981).

Canadian Press. "CP Told the World … About Canada at Dieppe." Toronto: Canadian Press, 1942.
- "Online Guide for Writing and Editing." http://stylebooks.thecanadianpress.com/online/?do=chapter&pub=style. Accessed 17 February 2012.
- "Red Patch in Sicily." Toronto: Canadian Press, 1943.

Careless, J.M.S. "Frontierism, Metropolitanism and Canadian History."
    Canadian Historical Review 35, no. 1 (1954): 1–21. http://dx.doi.org/10.3138/
    CHR-035-01-01.
– "Metropolis and Region: The Interplay of City and Region in Canadian
    History before 1914." *Urban History Review. Revue d'Histoire Urbaine* 3 (1979):
    99–119.
Carey, James. "A Cultural Approach to Communication." In *Communication
    as Culture: Essays on Media and Society,* ed. James Carey, 13–36. New York:
    Routledge, 1992.
– "Technology and Ideology: The Case of the Telegraph." In *Communication
    as Culture: Essays on Media and Society,* ed. James Carey, 201–30. New York:
    Routledge, 1992.
– "The Problem of Journalism History." In *James Carey: A Critical Reader,*
    ed. Eve Stryker Munson and Catherine A. Warren, 86–94. Minneapolis:
    University of Minnesota Press, 1997.
– "Why and How? The Dark Continent of American Journalism." 149–196. In
    Reading the News, ed. Robert Karl Manoff and Michael Schudson New York:
    Pantheon Books, 1987.
Comeau, Paul-André, Claude Beauregard, and Edwidge Munn. *La Democratie
    en veilleuse: Rapport des censeurs 1939–1945.* Montreal: Editions Quebec/
    Amerique, 1995.
Conboy, Martin. *The Language of Newspapers: Socio-Historical Perspectives.*
    London: Continuum, 2010.
Cooper, Kent. *Barriers Down: The Story of the News Agency Epoch.* New York:
    Farrar & Rinehart, 1942.
Cotter, Colleen. *News Talk: Investigating the Language of Journalism.*
    Cambridge: Cambridge University Press, 2010. http://dx.doi.org/10.1017/
    CBO9780511811975
(CP): A Guide for Writers and Filing Editors. Toronto: Canadian Press, 1940.
CP Style Book. Toronto: The Canadian Press, 1968.
CP Style Book: A Guide for Writers and Filing Editors, rev. and extended. Toronto:
    Canadian Press, 1947.
Cumming, Carman. "The Canadian Press: A Force for Consensus?"
    In *Journalism Communication and the Law,* ed. G. Stuart Adam, 86–103.
    Scarborough, ON: Prentice-Hall of Canada, 1976.
Curran, James. *Media and Power.* "Rival Narratives of Media History." 3–54.
    London: Routledge, 2002.
Dion, Léon. *La révolution déroutée, 1960–1976.* Montréal: Les Editions du
    Boréal, 1998.
Dupuis, Michael. "A Cloak for Something Far Deeper: The Press Coverage of
    the Winnipeg General Strike." Unpublished manuscript, 2008.

– "Canadian Journalists in New York." In *Titanic Century: Media, Myth, and the Making of a Cultural Icon*, ed. Paul Heyer, 91–100. Santa Barbara, CA: Praeger, 2012.

Easson, Robert F. "The Beginnings of the Telegraph." In *The Municipality of Toronto, A History*. vol. 2. ed. J.E. Middleton, 767–9. Toronto: Dominion Publishing, 1923.

Edge, Marc. *Pacific Press: The Unauthorized Story of Vancouver's Newspaper Monopoly*. Vancouver: New Star Books, 2001.

Eggleston, Wilfrid. *While I Still Remember*. Toronto: The Ryerson Press, 1968.

Emery, Michael, Edwin Emery and Nancy L. Roberts. *The Press and America: An Interpretive History of the Mass Media*. Needham Heights, MA: Allyn and Bacon, 2000.

Errico, Marcus, with John April, Andrew Asch, Lynnette Khalfani, Miriam A. Smith, and Xochiti R. Ybarra. "The Evolution of the Summary News Lead." *Media History Monographs* 1, no. 1 (1997–98). http://www.scripps.ohiou.edu/mediahistory/mhmjour1-1.htm (Accessed June 9, 2013).

Fenby, Jonathan. *The International News Services: A Twentieth Century Fund Report*. New York: Schocken Books, 1986.

Ford, Arthur. *As the World Wags On*. Toronto: Ryerson Press, 1950.

Ford, Stephen [Gillis Purcell]. "The Canadian Press (CP)." N.p., 1967.

Fowler, Roger. *Language in the News: Discourse and Ideology in the Press*. London: Routledge, 1991.

Freeman, Barbara. *Beyond Bylines: Media Workers and Women's Rights in Canada*. Waterloo, ON: Wilfrid Laurier University Press, 2011.

– *The Satellite Sex: The Media and Women's Issues in English Canada, 1966–1971*. Waterloo, ON: Wilfrid Laurier University Press, 2001.

Friesen, Gerald. *Citizens and Nation: An Essay on History, Communication and Canada*. Toronto: University of Toronto Press, 2000.

Gagnon, Jean-Louis. *Les apostasies, tome 3: Les palais de glace*. Montreal: Les éditions La Presse, 1990.

German, Daniel. "Press Censorship and the Terrace Mutiny: A Case Study in Second World War Information Management." *Journal of Canadian Studies. Revue d'Etudes Canadiennes* 31, no. 4 (1996): 124–42.

Gitelman, Lisa. *Always Already New: Media, History and the Data of Culture*. Cambridge, MA: MIT Press, 2006.

Glassford, Larry A. "Arthur Meighen." In *Dictionary of Canadian Biography Online*. http://www.biographi.ca/en/bio/meighen_arthur_18E.html (accessed June 9, 2013).

Godin, Pierre. *L'information-opium: Une histoire politique du journal La Presse*. Montréal: Éditions Parti Pris, 1972.

Goheen, Peter. "The Impact of the Telegraph on the Newspaper in mid-Nineteenth Century British North America." *Urban Geography* 11, no. 2 (1990): 107–29. http://dx.doi.org/10.2747/0272-3638.11.2.107.

Goldenberg, Susan. *The Thomson Empire, The First Fifty Years*. Toronto: Methuen, 1984.

Gramling, Oliver. *AP: The Story of News*. New York: Farrar and Rinehart, 1940.

Granatstein, J.L. *Canada's War: The Politics of the Mackenzie King Government, 1939–1945*. Toronto: University of Toronto Press, 1990.

Green, Ernest. "Canada's First Electric Telegraph." *Ontario Historical Society Papers & Records* 24 (1927): 369–70.

Habermas, Jürgen. *The Structural Transformation of the Public Sphere: An Inquiry into Category of Bourgeois Society*. Trans. Thomas Burger. Cambridge, MA: MIT Press, 1989.

Hall, D.J. *Clifford Sifton, Volume 2: A Lonely Eminence, 1901–1929*. Vancouver: UBC Press, 1985.

Hallin, Daniel. *The "Uncensored War": The Media and Vietnam*. New York: University of California Press, 1989.

Hallin, Daniel, and Paolo Mancini. *Comparing Media Systems: Three Models of Media and Politics*. Cambridge: Cambridge University Press, 2004. http://dx.doi.org/10.1017/CBO9780511790867

Hardt, Hanno. "Without the Rank and File: Journalism History, Media Workers, and Problems of Representation." In *Newsworkers: Toward a History of the Rank and File*, ed. Hanno Hardt and Bonnie Brennen, 1–29. Minneapolis: University of Minnesota Press, 1995.

Harkness, Ross. *J.E. Atkinson of The Star*. Toronto: University of Toronto Press, 1963.

Harnett, Richard M. *Wirespeak: Codes and Jargon of the News Business*. San Mateo, CA: Shorebird Press, 1997.

Hartley, John. *Popular Reality: Journalism, Modernity, Popular Culture*. London: Arnold, 1996.

Harvey, David. *The Condition of Postmodernity: An Enquiry into the Origins of Cultural Change*. Cambridge, MA: Blackwell, 1989.

Herman, Edward S., and Noam Chomsky. *Manufacturing Consent: The Political Economy of the Mass Media*. New York: Pantheon Books, 1988.

Igartua, José. *The Other Quiet Revolution: National Identities in English Canada, 1945–71*. Vancouver: UBC Press, 2006.

International Commission for the Study of Communication Problems. *Many Voices, One World: Towards a New, More Just and More Efficient World Information and Communication Order*. Paris: UNESCO, 1980.

Jackaway, Gwenyth L. *Media at War: Radio's Challenge to the Newspapers, 1924–1939*. Westport, CT: Praeger, 1995.

Johnston, Russell. "Value Added: Recent Books in the History of Communications and Culture." *Acadiensis* 32 (2002): 129–39.

Jones, Roderick. *A Life in Reuters. Garden City.* Doubleday, 1952.

Kaplan, Richard L. "American Journalism Goes to War, 1898–2001: A Manifesto on Media and Empire." *Media History* 9, no. 3 (2003): 209–19. http://dx.doi.org/10.1080/1368880032000145533.

– *Politics and the American Press: The Rise of Objectivity, 1865–1920*. Cambridge: Cambridge University Press, 2002.

Keshen, Jeffrey A. *Propaganda and Censorship During Canada's Great War*. Edmonton: University of Alberta Press, 1996.

Kesterton, W.H. *A History of Journalism in Canada*. Toronto: McClelland and Stewart, 1967.

Kielbowicz, Richard B. *News in the Mail: The Press, Post Office, and Public Information, 1700–1860s*. New York: Greenwood Press, 1989.

Knightley, Phillip. *The First Casualty*. New York: Harcourt Brace Jovanovich, 1975.

Kovach, Bill, and Tom Rosenstiel. *The Elements of Journalism: What Newspeople Should Know and the Public Should Expect*. New York: Three Rivers Press, 2007.

Lang, Marjory. *Women who Made the News: Female Journalists in Canada, 1880–1945*. Montreal: McGill-Queen's University Press, 1999.

Lehuu, Isabelle. *Carnival on the Page: Popular Print Media in Antebellum America*. Chapel Hill: University of North Carolina Press, 2000.

Livesay, J.F.B. "The Canadian Press: Its Birth and Development." Reprint from Quebec *Chronicle-Telegraph*, 21 June 1939.

– *The Making of a Canadian*. Toronto: Ryerson Press, 1947.

Malone, Richard S. "Development of F.P. Publications: Historical Outline." Typescript held in Ryerson University Library. Toronto, 1966.

– *A Portrait of War, 1939–1943*. Toronto: Collins, 1983.

– *A World in Flames: A Portrait of War, Part 2*. Toronto: Collins, 1984.

Matheson, Donald. "The Birth of News Discourse: Changes in News Language in British Newspapers, 1880–1930." *Media Culture & Society* 22, no. 5 (2000): 557–73. http://dx.doi.org/10.1177/016344300022005002.

McChesney, Robert. *Rich Media, Poor Democracy: Communication Politics in Dubious Times*. Urbana: University of Illinois Press, 1998.

McKay, Ian. "Canada as a Long Liberal Revolution: On Writing the History of Actually Existing Canadian Liberalisms, 1840s–1940s." In *Liberalism and Hegemony: Debating the Canadian Liberal Revolution*, ed. Jean-François

Constant and Michel Ducharme, 347–452. Toronto: University of Toronto Press, 2009.

McKercher, Catherine, and Vincent Mosco, eds. *Knowledge Workers in the Information Society*. Lanham: Lexington Books, 2007.

McNairn, Jeffrey L. "Towards Deliberative Democracy: Parliamentary Intelligence and the Public Sphere." *Journal of Canadian Studies. Revue d'Etudes Canadiennes* 33, no. 1 (1998): 39–60.

McNaught, Carlton. *Canada Gets the News*. Toronto: Ryerson Press, 1940.

Miller, Carman. *Painting the Map Red: Canada and the South African War, 1899–1902*. Montreal: Canadian War Museum/McGill-Queen's University Press, 1993.

Morris, Joe Alex. *Deadline Every Minute: The Story of the United Press*. New York: Greenwood Press, 1968.

Murray, John. *A Story of the Telegraph*. Montreal: John Lovell & Co, 1905.

Nerone, John C. "A Local History of the U.S. Press: Cincinnati, 1793–1858." In *Ruthless Criticism: New Perspectives in U.S. Communication History*, ed. William S. Solomon and Robert W. McChesney, 38–65. Minneapolis: University of Minnesota Press, 1993.

– "Approaches to Media History." In *A Companion to Media Studies*, ed. Angharad N. Valdivia, 93–114. Malden, MA: Blackwell, 2005.

Nicholas, Sian. "All the News that's Fit to Broadcast: the Popular Press versus the BBC, 1922–45." In *Northcliffe's Legacy: Aspects of the British Popular Press, 1896–1996*, ed. Peter Catterall, Colin Seymour-Ure, and Adrian Smith, 121–48. Houndmills: Macmillan Press, 2000.

Nichols, M.E. *(CP): The Story of The Canadian Press*. Toronto: Ryerson Press, 1948.

Nolan, Michael. *CTV: The Network that Means Business*. Edmonton: University of Alberta Press, 2001.

Nord, David Paul. "The Practice of Historical Research." In *Mass Communication Research and Theory*, ed. Guido H. Stempel, III, David Weaver, and G. Cleveland Wilhoit, 362–85. Boston: Allyn and Bacon, 2003.

Palmer, Michael B. *Des petits journaux aux grandes agences: Naissance du journalisme moderne*. Paris: Éditions Aubier Montaigne, 1983.

– "What Makes News." In *The Globalization of News*, ed. Oliver Boyd-Barrett and Terhi Rantanen, 177–90. London: Sage, 1998. http://dx.doi.org/10.4135/9781446250266.n11

Peers, Frank W. *The Politics of Canadian Broadcasting, 1920–1951*. Toronto: University of Toronto Press, 1969.

Pelletier, Gérard. *Years of Choice, 1960–1968*. Toronto: Methuen, 1987.

Potter, Simon. *News and the British World: The Emergence of an Imperial Press System*. Oxford: Clarendon Press, 2003. http://dx.doi.org/10.1093/acprof:oso/9780199265121.001.0001

Pöttker, Horst. "News and Its Communicative Quality: The Inverted Pyramid — When and Why Did It Appear?" *Journalism Studies* 4, no. 4 (2003): 501–11. http://dx.doi.org/10.1080/1461670032000136596.

Poulton, Ron. *The Paper Tyrant: John Ross Robertson of the Toronto Telegram*. Toronto: Clarke, Irwin & Co, 1971.

Prang, Margaret. *N.W. Rowell: Ontario Nationalist*. Toronto: University of Toronto Press, 1975.

Pratte, Alf. "Going Along for the Ride on the Prosperity Bandwagon: Peaceful Annexation, not War, Between the Editors and Radio, 1923–1941." *Journal of Radio Studies* 2, no. 1 (1993–94): 123–39. http://dx.doi.org/10.1080/19376529309384512.

Purcell, Gillis. "The Canadian Press (CP)." *International Communication Gazette* 15, no. 2 (1969): 151–8. http://dx.doi.org/10.1177/001654926901500207.

– "Wartime Press Censorship in Canada." MA thesis, University of Toronto, 1946.

Putnis, Peter. "How the International News Agency Business Model Failed: Reuters in Australia, 1877–1895." *Media History* 12, no. 1 (2006): 1–17. http://dx.doi.org/10.1080/13688800600597103.

– "Reuters in Australia: The Supply and Exchange of News, 1859–1877." *Media History* 10, no. 2 (2004): 67–88. http://dx.doi.org/10.1080/1368880042000254810.

– "Share 999: British Government Control of Reuters during World War One." *Media History* 14, no. 2 (2008): 141–65. http://dx.doi.org/10.1080/13688800802176771.

Purcell, Gillis, and Kerry McCallum. "Reuters and the Australian Press during World War I." Paper presented to the International Communication Association Conference, Singapore, June 2010.

Rantanen, Terhi. *After Five O'Clock Friends: Kent Cooper and Roy W. Howard*. Roy W. Howard Monographs in Journalism and Mass Communication Research, No. 4. Bloomington: School of Journalism, Indiana University, 1998.

– *Howard Interviews Stalin: How the AP, UP, and TASS Smashed the International News Cartel*. Roy W. Howard Monographs in Journalism and Mass Communication Research, No. 3. Bloomington: School of Journalism, Indiana University, 1994.

– "The Cosmopolitanization of News." *Journalism Studies* 8, no. 6 (2007): 843–61. http://dx.doi.org/10.1080/14616700701556765.

- "The Globalization of Electronic News in the 19th Century." *Media Culture & Society* 19, no. 4 (1997): 605–20. http://dx.doi. org/10.1177/016344397019004006.
- *The Media and Globalization*. London: Sage, 2005.
- "The New Sense of Place in 19th Century News." *Media Culture & Society* 25, no. 4 (2003): 435–49. http://dx.doi.org/10.1177/ 01634437030254001.
- "The Struggle for Control of Domestic News Markets (1)." In *The Globalization of News*, ed. Oliver Boyd-Barrett and Terhi Rantanen, 35–48. London: Sage, 1998. http://dx.doi.org/10.4135/9781446250266.n3

Read, Donald. *The Power of News: The History of Reuters*. Oxford: Oxford University Press, 1992.

Reporters of the Associated Press. *Breaking News: How The Associated Press Has Covered War, Peace and Everything Else*, with a Foreward by David Halberstam. New York: Princeton Architectural Press, 2007.

Royal Commission on Bilingualism and Biculturalism. CBC News and the Canadian Press. Report of an interview with William Hogg, director of news and public affairs, English networks.

- Presented by The Canadian Press to Royal Commission on Bilingualism and Biculturalism. La Presse Canadienne – Addenda – Considérations générales, 1965.

Royal Commission on Bilingualism and Biculturalism and Soucy Gagné. Interview préliminaire – Rencontre avec M. Michel Roy, chef de l'information du *Devoir*, le 25 fevrier 1965.

Royal Commission on Bilingualism and Biculturalism and Soucy D. Gagné. "Sondage sur la Presse Canadienne." Projet interne de recherche de la Commission royale d'enquête sur le bilinguisme et le biculturalisme.

Royal Commission on Bilingualism and Biculturalism and Michel Roy, *Le Devoir*. Project de recommendation, 2 April 1965.

Rutherford, Paul. *A Victorian Authority: The Daily Press in Late Nineteenth-Century Canada*. Toronto: University of Toronto Press, 1982.

- *When Television was Young: Primetime Canada, 1952–1967*. Toronto: University of Toronto Press, 1990.

Sanders, M.L., and Philip M. Taylor. *British Propaganda during the First World War, 1914–18*. London: The Macmillan Press, 1982.

Schudson, Michael. *Discovering the News: A Social History of American Newspapers*. New York: Basic Books, 1978.

- "The Objectivity Norm in American Journalism." *Journalism* 2, no. 2 (2001): 149–70. http://dx.doi.org/10.1177/146488490100200201.

- "Toward a Troubleshooting Manual for Journalism History." *Journalism & Mass Communication Quarterly* 74, no. 3 (1997): 463–76. http://dx.doi.org/10.1177/107769909707400302.
- "When: Deadlines, Datelines and History." In *Reading the News*, ed. Robert Karl Manoff and Michael Schudson, 79–108. New York: Pantheon Books, 1987.

Schwarzlose, Richard. *The Nation's Newsbrokers, Vol. 2. The Rush to Institution: from 1865 to 1920.* Evanston, IL: Northwestern University Press, 1990.

Scott, George. *Reporter Anonymous: The Story of the Press Association.* London: Hutchinson & Co, 1968.

Shaw, Donald. "News Bias and the Telegraph: A Study of Historical Change." *Journalism Quarterly* 44, no. 1 (1967): 3–12, 31. http://dx.doi.org/10.1177/107769906704400101.

Shmanske, Stephen. "News as a Public Good: Cooperative Ownership, Price Commitments, and the Success of the Associated Press." *Business History Review* 60, no. 1 (1986): 55–80. http://dx.doi.org/10.2307/3115923.

Siegel, Arthur. *Politics and the Media in Canada.* 2nd ed., 186–214. Toronto: McGraw-Hill Ryerson, 1996.

Sigal, Leon V. "Who? Sources Make the News." In *Reading the News*, ed. Robert Karl Manoff and Michael Schudson, 9–37. New York: Pantheon Books, 1987.

Siggins, Maggie. *Bassett.* Toronto: James Lorimer & Co, 1979.

Silberstein-Loeb, Jonathan. "Business, Politics, Technology and the International Supply of News, 1845–1950." PhD dissertation, University of Cambridge, 2009.

Sommerville, John. *The News Revolution in England: Cultural Dynamics of Daily Information.* New York: Oxford University Press, 1996.

Sotiron, Minko. *From Politics to Profit: The Commercialization of Canadian Daily Newspapers, 1890–1920.* Montreal: McGill-Queen's University Press, 1997.

Stacey, C.P. *Canada and the Age of Conflict, Vol 2: 1921–1948, the Mackenzie King Era.* Toronto: University of Toronto Press, 1981.

Starr, Paul. *The Creation of the Media: Political Origins of Modern Communications.* New York: Basic Books, 2004.

Stöber, Rudolph. "What Media Evolution Is: A Theoretical Approach to the History of New Media." *European Journal of Communication* 19, no. 4 (2004): 483–505. http://dx.doi.org/10.1177/0267323104049461.

Swettenham, John. *McNaughton Vol. 2, 1939–1943.* Toronto: Ryerson Press, 1969.

Thompson, John B. *The Media and Modernity: A Social Theory of the Media.* Stanford, CA: Stanford University Press, 1995.

Vipond, Mary. *"Listening In": The First Decade of Canadian Broadcasting, 1922–1932*. Montreal: McGill-Queen's University Press, 1992.
– "The Continental Marketplace: Authority, Advertisers and Audiences in Canadian News Broadcasting, 1932–1936." *Journal of Radio Studies* 6, no. 1 (1999): 169–84. http://dx.doi.org/10.1080/19376529909391716.
– *The Mass Media in Canada*. 4th ed. Toronto: James Lorimer & Co, 2011.
– "The 2003 Presidential Address of the CHA : The Mass Media in Canadian History: The Empire Day Broadcast of 1939." *Journal of the Canadian Historical Association* (2003): 1–22. http://dx.doi.org/10.7202/010317ar.
Walkom, Thomas L. "The Daily Newspaper Industry in Ontario's Developing Capitalistic Economy: Toronto and Ottawa, 1871–1911." PhD dissertation, University of Toronto, 1983.
Webb, Jeff A. "Canada's Moose River Mine Disaster (1936): Radio-Newspaper Competition in the Business of News." *Historical Journal of Film, Radio & Television* 16, no. 3 (1996): 365–76. http://dx.doi.org/10.1080/01439689600260351.
– *The Voice of Newfoundland: A Social History of the Broadcasting Corporation of Newfoundland, 1939–1949*. Toronto: University of Toronto Press, 2008.
White, Patrick. "News Agencies in Canada: At the Crossroads." In *News Agencies in the Turbulent Era of the Internet*, ed. Oliver Boyd-Barrett, 125–38. Barcelona: Government of Catalonia, Presidential Department, 2010.
Winseck, Dwayne, and Robert Pike. *Communication and Empire: Media, Markets, and Globalization, 1860–1930*. Durham, NC: Duke University Press, 2007.
Xin, Xin. "Structural Change and Journalism Practice: Xinhua News Agency in the Early 2000s." *Journalism Practice* 2, no. 1 (2008): 46–63. http://dx.doi.org/10.1080/17512780701768501.

Newspaper and Magazine Articles

"Agreed to Part of Report Labor 'Misinformed' – 'C.P.'." *Star* (Toronto), 28 April 1951.
"Agriculture's View – Pesticides Needed." *Chronicle-Herald* (Halifax), 2 July 1970.
"Air Research Body is Named." *Daily Times* (Victoria), 9 February 1920.
"Beaverbrook in Cabinet." *Herald* (Halifax), 15 May 1940.
Boss, Bill. "Mud Hut With Dirt Floor No Bath, Is Worker's Home in Russian Central Asia." *Star* (Toronto), 28 April 1954.
– "Old Revolutionaries Going, Technicians Running Russia – Boss." *Star* (Toronto), 29 April 1954.

- "Security Too Tight to Get Full Story of Life in Russia." *Star* (Toronto), 30 April 1954.
"Canada's Livestock in Fine Condition." *Daily Times* (Victoria), 9 February 1920.
"Canadian Press Chief Denies Service Refused." Canadian Press Library, 22 April 1949.
"Canadian Press Criticized by Labor Over Union Case." *Star* (Toronto), 10 April 1951.
"Canadians Show Way in Planning Sea Law." *Chronicle-Herald* (Halifax), 18 January 1960.
"Charges Witness Intimidated by Editor." *Globe and Mail*, 27 April 1950.
"Claims CBC Best in Presenting Canadian Angle." *Globe and Mail*, 18 September 1956.
"CLC Calls for End to One-paper Situations." *Globe and Mail*, 23 January 1970.
"Commission to Study MP Salaries Question." *Chronicle-Herald* (Halifax), 19 January 1970.
"Condemns Proposals of Bennett." *Chronicle* (Halifax), 18 September 1930.
"Court Dismisses 5 Guild Charges Against CP." *Globe and Mail*, 10 November 1951.
Dauphinee, John. "Revolution in Sending News." *Saturday Night*, 2 August 1952.
"Davey Is Chosen to Head Probe of Mass Media." *Globe and Mail*, 28 March 1969.
"Faith Healer 'Cures' Dumb, Maimed, Blind." *Tribune* (Winnipeg), 19 November 1920.
"Federal Board Reports in CP, Guild Dispute." *Globe and Mail*, 16 February 1951.
Ford, Arthur. "Early Days in Gathering News." *Free Press* (London), 13 July 1955.
Ford, Stephen [Gillis Purcell]. "Minute Man." *Canadian Printer and Publisher*, December 1943.
Franklin, Stephen. "The Man Behind the News." *Weekend Magazine*, 31 January 1970.
"Guild Asks Bargain Rights for Globe, Mail Circulation." *Star* (Toronto), 7 June 1950.
"Guild Pact Signed by Ottawa Citizen." *Star* (Toronto), 8 April 1950.
"How to Buy Newspapers and Run Them at a Profit." *Canadian Printer & Publisher*, August 1961.
"Il est financièrement impossible de former une agence indépendante de nouvelles de langue française (Mercier)." *L'Action*, 16 December 1965.

"Labor Leaders Sentenced to Year in Jail." *Daily World* (Vancouver), 6 April 1920.

"Leaders Join in Debate." *Herald* (Halifax), 18 September 1930.

"Let Full Light be Turned on That Deal with Liberals." *Herald* (Halifax), 23 June 1915.

"Likely to Put Claim Up to Supreme Court." *Chronicle* (Halifax), 1 April 1930.

"Major Publishers Invest in CP; Torstar among 3 Owners That Will Turn the Co-op into For-profit Business." *Star* (Toronto), 27 November 2010.

"Miss Butler Pleads for Freedom." *Chronicle* (Halifax), 23 June 1920.

Munro, Ross. "Canadians Hold Spitzbergen." *Globe and Mail*, 9 September 1941.

– "Q.O.R. Mortars Fast, Accurate." *Globe and Mail*, 16 March 1942.

"Munro Story on Sicily Scores 7-Hour Scoop." *Globe and Mail*, 12 July 1943.

"Natural Resources Question Again to Forefront in Capital." *Tribune* (Winnipeg), 19 November 1920.

"New Papers Prevented by Monopoly – Coldwell." Canadian Press Library, 21 April 1949.

"News Agency Says it Has No Blacklist." *Star* (Toronto), 12 December 1969.

"News Problem Up to Stations." *Globe and Mail*, 23 November 1940.

"News Service Limits May Curb New Papers, Printers Say." *Star* (Toronto), 18 February 1970.

"NZPA to Close after 130 Years." *The Dominion Post* (Wellington, New Zealand), 7 April 2011.

"Parliament to Have Busy Week." *Evening Tribune* (Winnipeg), 6 April 1920.

Pena, Richard. "Two Leaders Stepping Down at Big Tribune Newspapers." *New York Times*, 15 July 2008.

Poisson, Jacques. "Le Québec colonial et l'information." *L'Action nationale*, 563–66.

"Premier of Canada Congratulates the Press on its New National Service." *The Globe*, 3 September 1917.

"Press Monopoly Questions Asked in Parliament." *Globe and Mail*, 8 August 1958.

"Publishing Firm Says Canadian Press Like a Select Private Club." *Globe and Mail*, 25 February 1970.

"Raps 'State Health' Plan." *Chronicle-Herald* (Halifax), 1 March 1960.

"Relatives of 122 Missing Clinging to Slight Hopes." *Star* (Toronto), 7 May 1941.

"Rogers' Fine Hand Seen in Latest Manitoba Move." *Chronicle* (Halifax), 23 June 1915.

"Senators Watch to See if Express Obtains Interim Service from CP." *Globe and Mail*, 20 March 1970.

"Set Up Delegation to Ask Intervention." *Star* (Toronto), 6 April 1951.

Thorne, Stephen. "CWCA's 'Quiet, Unflappable' Warco Bill Stewart Dies at Age 90." *Canadian War Correspondents' Association Newsletter* [nd, np].

"To Consider Transradio Situation." *Chronicle-Herald* (Halifax), 23 November 1940.

"Upholds Decision by Lower Court in Favor of CP." *Globe and Mail*, 21 June 1952.

"War Effort's Peak in Canada Year Off." *New York Times*, 1 October 1940.

"Whole World Pays Tribute to the Requirements of the Telegraph Editor of a Modern Daily." *Star* (Toronto), 26 August 1905.

"Women Advocate Birth Control." *Sun* (Vancouver), 1 April 1930.

Young, Scott. "The Men Behind the Front Page." *Maclean's Magazine*, 15 December 1949.

Index

Wallace, Cliff, 35, 80, 140, 146, 148
war correspondents, 25, 35, 42,
      134–8, 141–3, 145–7, 149–51, 159,
      168, 171–2, 179–80, 205, 295
War Measures Act, 41
Wartime Information Board, 196
Washington, 18, 83, 182, 190, 191,
      247, 251, 261, 268
West, A. J., 25, 40, 43, 46, 58, 63, 90,
      129, 151, 185, 208
Western Associated Press, 26–8,
      30–6, 40–1, 43–6, 49, 204, 256
western Canada, 13, 14, 19, 22,
      23, 25, 26, 27, 28, 32, 33, 34, 36,
      37, 40, 41, 43, 44, 46, 47, 48, 50, 51,
      52, 60, 64, 66, 67, 68, 77, 79, 82, 83,
      84, 88, 91, 105, 120, 136, 161, 169,
      202, 296
Western Union, 11, 19, 52, 268
White, Sir Thomas, 44
Wilson, Woodrow, 56

Windsor (ON), 64, 65, 168, 176, 202,
      238, 296
Windsor (ON) *Star*, 215, 228
Windsor (ON) *Telegram*, 65
Winnipeg, 13, 20, 22, 25, 26, 28, 31,
      32, 34, 35, 36, 37, 40, 41, 43–7, 49,
      66, 77, 78, 79, 82, 84, 109, 124,
      169, 171, 176, 208, 255, 256, 257,
      260, 306
Winnipeg *Citizen*, 208
Winnipeg *Free Press*, 24, 25, 26, 31,
      35, 40, 42, 59, 61, 82, 84, 86, 134,
      155, 201, 210, 213, 235, 290
Winnipeg *Telegram*, 26, 31, 35, 40, 44
Winnipeg *Tribune*, 81, 112, 187, 290
Winseck, Dwayne, 7
Wolff news agency, 6, 18, 22
Woods, J. H., 44, 58, 85, 92
Woodsworth, J. S., 65

Young, Scott, 287